THE OFFICIAL ENCYCLOPAEDIA
OF
TOTTENHAM HOTSPUR
FOOTBALL CLUB

AUDERE-EST-FACERE

Compiled by Tony Matthews

A
britespot
PUBLICATION

ACKNOWLEDGEMENTS

So many people have contributed in some small way to make this Encyclopaedia the definitive history of the club resulting in a terrific publication. But I must say a special big 'thank you' to Spurs club official historian & statistician, Andy Porter, who has done a wonderful job by supplying me with, and allowing me to reproduce, some very interesting articles. He has also clarified many facts and figures, listings, club and player records and general information.

I would also like to thank Jim Cadman (Football Heroes), Jim Duggan, Les Gold, Bob Goodwin, Mike Green, Bryan Horsnell, Trevor Jones, Bryan Lyons, Nick Manning, Chris Oakley, Alan Rosenthal, John Russell, Tom Roe, John Russell and Robin Thornton and Daniel Wynne with special thanks to Neville Evans.

I also acknowledge the assistance afforded to me by the Commercial Department of Tottenham Hotspur Football Club, especially Viv King and Paul Torre who kindly gave me and Britespot access to the club's picture library and, indeed, for agreeing to endorse the book itself and publicise it through the various channels within the club.

I have also referred to scores of club histories, Who's Who books, player guides, biographies, autobiographies, yearbooks, handbooks, weekly and monthly soccer magazines, AFS bulletins etc etc....far too many to list here without boring you! Each and every publication I have picked up has produced something of interest which has been inserted in this encyclopaedia, however small.

I say 'thank you' - and 'sorry' for the inconvenience caused - to my loving wife Margaret, who once again has had to put up with being without me for hours upon end whilst I've been sat at the computer, tip-tapping away on the keyboard, thumbing through the various pages of scores of reference books, matchday programmes and soccer magazines, checking and re-checking the thousands of statistics and stories.

Last but by no means least I must give a sincere thank you to everyone who has worked on the book at Britespot Publishing, especially to Roger Marshall, Paul Burns and Chris Sweet.

The majority of the pictures used in this book have come from serious collectors of football memorabilia, mainly Spurs fanatics. They have come out of old scrapbooks, photograph albums and programmes, all owned by avid supporters. We must also thank Action Images for there permission to reproduce a number of images within this publication. However, there are some photographs for which we have been unable to establish clear copyright. The publishers would therefore be pleased to hear from anyone whose copyright has been unintentionally infringed so that we may include the appropriate acknowledgement in any subsequent edition.

The Official Encyclopaedia of Tottenham Hotspur Football Club
A Britespot Publication

First Published in Great Britain by
Britespot Publishing Solutions Limited, Chester Road, Cradley Heath, West Midlands B64 6AB

October 2001

© Tony Matthews 2001

ISBN 0 9539 2881 0

Printed and bound in Great Britain by
Cradley Print Limited, Chester Road, Cradley Heath, West Midlands B64 6AB

Design and layout © Paul Burns, Britespot Publishing Solutions Limited

INTRODUCTION

I have attempted to make this Encyclopaedia of Tottenham Hotspur Football Club as comprehensive as possible, utilising all the statistical information available which I have obtained from various sources over the past three years.

The end product is a bumper 300 plus page, 250,000-word book covering, in detail, the history of one of the biggest football clubs in Europe (if not the world).

- There is an extensive Who's Who of virtually every player who has represented the club down the years.
- Spurs' complete playing record at senior level is covered in depth with details of their Premiership/Football League, FA Cup and League Cup statistics given against each club they have opposed.
- Also Spurs' European record is featured fully. Short but precise match reports are included on all the Cup Finals.
- There is an international section listing the honours won by Spurs players down the years.
- Details are given of the club's top appearance-makers and champion goalscorers in all competitions.
- There are categories appertaining to abandoned games, admission prices, age, attendances (home and away), benefit and testimonial matches, club chairmen and directors, friendly matches (including tours made by the club), overseas/foreign players, grounds (with a thorough survey of White Hart Lane), the biggest and heaviest in wins, draws and defeats, a check of sendings-off, plus reserve, youth and wartime football.
  There are biographies of all the club's managers; a section on substitutes, all the big-money and record-breaking transfers; players' nicknames - and much, much more.

You will see that I have tried to cover everything there is to cover on Tottenham Hotspur Football Club.

Over the past year or so, I have chatted with soccer statisticians and archivists, supporters and ex-players about Spurs. I have gathered in sheet after sheet of information regarding the team and the club itself.

As a result literally hundreds of facts and figures (some interesting, some not so interesting) have been entered into the computer, along with scores of fond memories, many points of view, some sobering thoughts and a great deal of general news appertaining to Spurs. Whether supplied verbally, by letter, by fax or e-mail, it has all been fed into the system and as a result I feel I have put together a bumper book, perhaps one of the best ever produced (statistically) on a major football club, certainly in the U.K.

As you can see, I have tried to cram as much into the book as I possibly could. I just hope I haven't missed too much, but if I have, I would dearly love to hear from you, so that my records can be updated and/or amended in readiness for the next 'big book' on Tottenham Hotspur FC, which hopefully will be an up-dated version of this 'A-Z Encyclopaedia'.

With so many facts and figures, statistics, listings and features condensed in this publication, I feel sure there will be a discrepancy, a small error, a spelling mistake, even a missing player or even a word somewhere down the line. I am only human, like every one else, and even the great writers of the past made the odd mistake here and there, or missed out something which should have been included, got a year or a date wrong. Please accept my apologies if something is amiss. I have, with the assistance of several willing helpers, tried to ensure that everything in this book is factual, up-to-date and precise in every detail.

As said earlier, Tottenham Hotspur is a big, big club...but the team has not yet won the Premiership. That will surely come later. The diehard supporters last cheered on a League Championship winning side some 40 years ago - way back in 1961 when, of course, the double was also achieved. That success was quickly followed by victories in the FA Cup Finals of 1962 and 1967 and the European Cup-winners Cup Final of 1963. Since then there has been three more FA Cup triumphs, plus glory in both the League Cup and UEFA Cup competitions.

White Hart Lane is now one of the country's finest all-seater stadiums and when Spurs are winning, the support they can generate is tremendous with an average turnout of 35,000 plus guaranteed at every home game. Slowly but surely the ground capacity will be increased and who knows, one day White Hart Lane may once again be able to accommodate 50,000 or more spectators - most of them cheering on their favourites in white shirts!

There is plenty in this book to keep you occupied during the winter months and certainly enough information contained within the pages to enable you to get your friends and colleagues talking continuously about Spurs down the pubs and clubs, in the stands, on the streets, anywhere in fact, where football - and Spurs - is the major subject!

Best wishes

Tony Matthews

AUDERE-EST-FACERE

A
BANDONED MATCHES

Details of games involving Spurs that have been abandoned:

Snow saw the end to this game!

Date	Opponents	Venue	Score	Time	Reason
FOOTBALL LEAGUE					
23.10.1909	Preston North End	(a)	0-0	50 mins	Heavy rain
28.01.1911	Oldham Athletic	(h)	1-1	45 mins	Fog
06.01.1912	West Brom Albion	(a)	0-0	52 mins	Fog
12.10.1912	Notts County	(h)	1-3	80 mins	Fog
27.11.1948	Nottingham Forest	(h)	0-0	17 mins	Fog
17.12.1969	Everton	(h)	0-0	29 mins	Floodlight failure
FA CUP					
20.02.1904	Aston Villa	(h)	0-1	20 mins	Crowd overspill
17.01.1907	Hull City	(a)	0-0*	110 mins	Poor light
19.02.1996	Nottingham Forest	(a)	0-0	15 mins	Snow

* Score allowed to stand but replay ordered.

FOOTBALL LEAGUE SOUTH					
23.12.1939	Southend United	(h)	3-4	60 mins	Fog
07.09.1940	West Ham United	(a)	4-1	80 mins	Air raid warning
12.10.1940	Arsenal	(h)	2-3	47 mins	Air Raid warning
23.11.1940	Luton Town	(h)	2-1	60 mins	Air raid warning
SOUTHERN LEAGUE					
21.10.1899	Bristol Rovers	(h)	1-0	55 mins	Fog
UNITED LEAGUE					
15.03.1897	Kettering Town	(a)	1-1	25 mins	Injury to player
SOUTHERN DISTRICT COMBINATION					
24.04.1900	Woolwich Arsenal	(a)	1-2	75 mins	Bad language

LONDON COMBINATION					
16.12.1916	Portsmouth	(n)	1-0	15 mins	Fog
LONDON PROFESSIONAL FOOTBALL CHARITY FUND					
03.11.1924	Clapton Orient	(a)	1-2	110 mins	Poor light
FRIENDLIES					
10.11.1883	Brownlow Rovers	(a)	1-0	55 mins	Ball burst
19.11.1887	Royal Arsenal	(a)	2-1	75 mins	Poor light
12.12.1891	Forest Swifts	(h)	1-1	60 mins	Poor light
24.09.1896	Luton Town	(h)	0-0	75 mins	Heavy rain
29.11.1954	Accrington Stanley	(a)	0-0	52 mins	Heavy rain
FA YOUTH CUP					
14.12.1965	West Ham United	(h*)	2-1	75 mins	Fog

* Game played at Cheshunt

Talk Back

The last abandoned game involving Spurs was in February 1996. It was a 5th round FA Cup encounter against Nottingham Forest at the City Ground, which was being covered live by Sky TV Sport. The action was halted in the 15th minute due to a severe snow blizzard. The scoreline was blank at the time.

In February 1904, Aston Villa were leading Tottenham Hotspur 1-0 in a Second Round FA Cup-tie at White Hart Lane when hundreds of 'home' supporters behind one of the goals spilled onto the pitch, forcing the game to be abandoned in the 20th minute. As a result the FA ordered the replay to take place at Villa Park and on this occasion Spurs won 1-0.

Spurs had 10 scheduled games postponed during the harsh winter of 1947 when only three matches were played in the month of January and just two in February. During the arctic winter of 1962-63 Spurs did not play a single League game between 20 January and 22 February and in fact fulfilled just two First Division fixtures over an eight-week period between 27 Dec and 1 March. Not one game was abandoned once it had started during these two harsh winters.

ABERDEEN

Spurs' playing record v. The Dons:

Comp	P	W	D	L	F	A
UEFA Cup	2	1	1	0	5	2

The Dons were Spurs' victims in a second round UEFA Cup-tie in October/November 1973. There were 30,000 fans present at Pittodrie to witness the first leg that ended level at 1-1. Ralph Coates was the Spurs goalscorer. And for the return clash at White Hart Lane, 21,785 spectators attended to see Spurs ease home 4-1 to take the contest 5-2 on aggregate. Martin Peters, Jimmy Neighbour and Chris McGrath (2) netted for Spurs in the second match.

Players with both clubs include: Steve Archibald, Tom Atherton, Ted Ditchburn (Dons WW2 guest), Arthur King, Willie McNair, Bobby Mimms, Joe Moffatt, Charlie O'Hagan, Tommy Pearson (Spurs WW2 guest), Willie Young.

Also associated: Keith Burkinshaw (Spurs coach & manager, Dons' Director of Football).

ACCRINGTON/ACCRINGTON STANLEY

Spurs have never met these two former Football League clubs at competitive level, although they have played them both in friendly matches. The one against Stanley at Peel Park in 1954 was called off due to torrential rain early in the second-half (see also under abandoned matches) whilst the fixture against Accrington was played on Boxing Day 1895 which Spurs won 3-0 (at home).

Players with both clubs include: Stan Alexander and Bill Almond (Accrington); John Ryden (Stanley)
Wartime guests (with either Stanley or both clubs): Reg Edwards, Harry Jackson (WW2) and Joey Walters (Spurs WW1).

ADAMS, CHRISTOPER JAMES
Essex-born forward Chris Adams scored once in six League outings for Spurs before joining Norwich City in 1953. He also assisted Watford and retired with a knee injury.

ADAMS, WILLIAM H
Full-back Billy Adams played all his 12 games for Spurs between 1939 and 1946. He guested for Bradford City, Middlesbrough, Millwall and Reading among others during the War and left White Hart Lane for Carlisle. He was born in Cumberland.

ADMISSION PRICES
When Spurs gained entry into the Football League in 1908, the charge for admission to the 'ground' (the terraces) for a home game (depending on the context of the fixture) varied from 1d (1/2p) to 6d (3p).
That 6d charge was the minimum entrance fee until after World War One (1919) when it was increased to one shilling (5p).
For the next 23 years that ('bob'/shilling) admission price remained in force, but for the 1942-43 Wartime season it went up to 1s 3d (7p) and in 1946 it was raised to 1s 6d (8p).
Thereafter it was steadily increased: 1952-53 up to 1s 9d (9p); 1955-56 up to 2s (10p); 1959-60 up to 2s 6d (13p); 1960-61 up to 3s (15p); 1962-63 up to 4s (20p); 1966-67 up to 5s (25p); 1969-70 up to 6s (30p); 1970-71 up to 7s 6d (38p) and then upwards from 40p to 50p and on to a £1 by 1978-79, rising after that to £1.30, £1.50, £2.00, £3.00, £5.00 and then £6.00 before all-seater stadia came into force.
The dearest and cheapest admission prices to White Hart Lane over the last ten years have risen slowly, from £5-£10, up to £6 - £12, £8-£14 and £10-£20.
For the 1995-96 season the cheapest seat was priced at £14, the dearest at £32. In 1996-97 the prices were £15 and £33 respectively; in 1997-98 they were £18 and £35 and for the 2001-02 season the dearest matchday seat at White Hart Lane sets the supporter back some £55 (the cheapest being £11 for a child).

Season Tickets
Season tickets were first issued by Tottenham Hotspur Football Club during the 1890s, and were only available for seats in the main (west) stand.
Season tickets for the club's first season in the Football League (1908-09) cost 20s or 15s if the purchaser was either a shareholder or a lady (or both). These were not for a designated seat, within the central blocks either side of the directors' box.
For the 1909-10 campaign (the first in Division One) the price of a similar season ticket rose to 25s (£1 for shareholders), whilst for the first time the club also offered numbered and reserved seat season tickets, costing 42s (£2.10) or 31s 6d (£1.58) for shareholders. The next known price rise came in 1918-19 when a main stand season ticket cost the buyer £3.10s

(£3.50), by now all seats being numbered and reserved. This price remained extant until the 1938-9 campaign.
After the Second World War (for season 1946-7) the cost had risen to five guineas (£5.25). In 1950-51 (following promotion from Division Two) a season ticket cost six guineas £6.30) and in 1951-52 (after winning the First Division championship) the price had been upped to seven guineas (£7.35).
There was another price increase for the following season (1952-53) up to eight guineas (£8.40) and likewise in 1959-60 up by over a £1 to nine guineas (£9.45).
As reigning 'double winners' Spurs fans had to pay 10 guineas (£10.50) for a season ticket in 1961-62. The price rose to 11 guineas (£11.55) in 1964-65 and the following year it went up to 13 guineas (£13.65).
The 'guinea' was dropped for the 1966-67 season when a season ticket went up to £16.5s (£16.25) and in 1969-70 a 'reserved seat' was priced at £17.16s (£17.80). Twelve months later the supporter was charged £20, in 1974-75 it was £25.60 and in 1979-80 the price had risen quite alarmingly to £57.85.

Price-rise of a season ticket at White Hart Lane since 1984:

Season	Seats	Cheapest Ground
1984-85	£125-£250	£60
1985-87	£130-£260	£63
1986-88	£156-£264	£72
1988-90	£138-£276	£69
1990-91	£161-£299	£92
1991-92	£218-£314	£108
1992-95	£390-£442	£117
1996-97	£500 plus*	-
1999-01	£795	-
2001-02	£850-£215	-

*Various prices with concessions.

NB In late 1960s Spurs became one of first clubs to offer Cup-tie tickets within their season ticket price; they still do so today.

Complimentary Tickets
For Football League matches, the visiting club can normally claim in the region of 40 complimentary tickets - 25 for use by the players, manager and coach - and 12 for the Directors.
However, there is no set limit on how many complimentary tickets the home club can issue.

AGE
Oldest
Jimmy Cantrell (born 7 May 1882) was 40 years, 349 days old when he played his last competitive game for Spurs at home to Birmingham on 21 April 1923....and he starred in a 2-0 victory.

Youngest
Ally Dick is the youngest player to appear for Spurs in a League game.
He was 16 years, 301 days old when he made his debut at home to Manchester City on 20 February 1982. The youngest player to star for Spurs in the Premiership has been Andy Turner who was 17 years, 145 days old when he made his debut in the competition at Southampton on 15 August 1992.
Frank Saul is Spurs' youngest-ever League goalscorer (aged 17 years, 18 days) when he found the net against Arsenal in Division One on 10 September 1960.

Age Concern

Future Spurs player Jason Dozzell was the youngest League player for Ipswich Town when he made his debut against Coventry City in a First Division match on 4 February 1984 at the age of 16 years, 56 days. He also became the First Division's youngest goalscorer when he netted in that same match.

Ian 'Chico' Hamilton made his Football League debut for Chelsea against Tottenham Hotspur on 18 March 1967 at the age of 16 years, 138 days, the Stamford Bridge club's youngest-ever footballer.

Andy Sinton is the youngest player to appear in a senior game for Cambridge United; he was 16 years, 228 days old when he made his Football League debut v. Wolves on 2 November 1982.

Neil McNab - at the age of 16 years and 10 months versus Chelsea in April 1974 - was the youngest Spurs' player to appear in a League game before he lost the 'title' to Ally Dick in 1982.

Matt Etherington was only 15 years, 262 days old when he became Peterborough United's youngest-ever debutant v. Brentford on 3 May 1997.

Ronnie Dix holds the record for being the Football League's youngest scorer - aged 15 years, 180 days for Bristol Rovers v. Norwich City (Division 3 S) on 3 March 1928. He was to join Spurs in 1939.

Stanley Matthews played his last game at White Hart Lane on 14 December 1963 - for Stoke City in a 2-1 defeat by Spurs. The former Blackpool and England right-winger was approaching his 49th birthday at the time.

AGGREGATE SCORE

The biggest aggregate victory so far recorded by Spurs (in a two-legged game) is 15-1 over the Icelandic side, Keflavik in the first round of the UEFA Cup in September 1971. After winning 6-1 away, Spurs rounded things off with an impressive 9-0 triumph at White Hart Lane.

AJAX AMSTERDAM

Spurs' playing record against Ajax

Comp	P	W	D	L	F	A
EC-winners Cup	2	2	0	0	6	1

Spurs started their 1981-82 European Cup-winners Cup exploits with a 1st round victory over Ajax, winning 6-1 on aggregate.

There were 35,000 spectators present to see goals by Ricky Villa and Mark Falco (2) give Spurs a 3-1 victory in Amsterdam on 16 September. Then 13 days later, 34,606 fans turned up for the return leg to see Ossie Ardiles, Tony Galvin and Mark Falco find the net in a comprehensive 3-0 win.

Associated with both clubs: Vic Buckingham (Spurs player, Ajax coach), Ray Clarke & Ally Dick (players), Jack Rowley (Spurs WW2 guest, Ajax manager).

ALDERSHOT

Spurs' record v. The Shots:

Comp	P	W	D	L	F	A
Wartime	13	10	1	2	39	13

Spurs have not played the 'Shots at competitive level:

Players with both clubs include: Bill Bann, Ken Flint, Alan Gilzean, Georgio Mazzon, Ron Reynolds, John Sainty (Spurs reserve), Fred Sargent, Teddy Sheringham, Bert Sproston, Les Stevens, Sonny Walters, Ralph Wetton.

Wartime guests (with either or both clubs): Wally Alsford, Frank Boulton, Bobby Browne, Stan Clayton, John Davie, George Dorling, Harry Dukes, Alf Fitzgerald, Doug Hunt, Jakey Jackson, Jimmy Jinks, Phil Joslin, Tom Kiernan, Colin Lyman, Ernie Marshall, Jackie Martin, Les Medley, John Oakes, Taffy O'Callaghan, Jack Pattison, Bob Pryde, Jack Rowley, Albert Sibley, Sid Tickridge, Joe Wilson, Vic Woodley.

Also associated: Harry Evans (Aldershot player & secretary-manager, Spurs assistant-manager).

ALEKSIC, MILIJA ANTONY

Born in Newcastle-under-Lyme, Staffordshire on 14 April 1951 (of a Yugoslavian father) goalkeeper Milija Aleksic, nicknamed 'Elastic' by the fans, had played for Luton Town on loan for Oxford United and Ipswich Town before joining Spurs for £100,000 from Plymouth Argyle in December 1978 at the age of 27. An FA Cup winner in 1981, he made 32 League and Cup appearances (over 50 first team outings in all) during his three-and-a-half years at White Hart Lane, when he also assisted Sheffield United and Luton (again) both on loan.

Released by Port Vale manager Sir Stanley Matthews as a teenager, the former England winger saying that he 'wouldn't make the grade', Aleksic went on to appear in some 150 first-class games before joining the rebel South African tour in 1982.

ALEXANDER, STANLEY

Northumberland-born forward who scored once in nine League games for Spurs during his two seasons with the club: 1936-38. Alexander also played for Hull City, Millwall, Bradford City and Accrington Stanley.

ALLEN, CLIVE DARREN

Striker Clive Allen had a fine career, averaging a goal every two games, including 230 in 467 League and Cup appearances with his English clubs.

Born in East London on 20 May 1961, two weeks after Spurs had completed the double, he signed professional forms with Queen's Park Rangers in 1978. There followed three big-money transfers, to Arsenal, Crystal Palace (without having played for the Gunners) and back to Queen's Park Rangers, for £1.25 million, £1.25 million and £700,000 respectively, before he switched to White Hart Lane in August 1984, also for £700,000.

He scored 85 goals for Spurs in 141 competitive games (112 in 175 matches at first team level) including a club record 49 in 1986-87 appearing and scoring in the 1987 FA Cup Final defeat by Coventry City.

In May 1988 he was sold to Bordeaux for £1 million but returned to England and Manchester City twelve months later, this time for a fee of £1.1 million.

A further move to Chelsea for £250,000 materialised in Dec 1991 and after a brief spell with relegated West Ham United (from March 1992, signed for £250,000) he embarked on a new career in American football, playing briefly for the London Monarchs.

Clive Allen presented with the PFA Award 1987 by Sir Stanley Matthews

ALLEN, JIMMY

Versatile Londoner Jimmy Allen netted once in 12 first-class games for Spurs before leaving the club to join Mansfield Town in in 1898.

ALLEN, JOSEPH

Signed from Mansfield Town in 1932, inside-forward Joe Allen scored in his only League game for Spurs v. Bradford City. He also played for QPR, Racing Club De Roubaix (France) and Clapton Orient.

ALLEN, LESLIE WILLIAM

Les Allen was a fine marksman who scored over 60 goals in less than 150 competitive games for Spurs in his six years with the club. Born in Dagenham, Essex on 4 September 1937, he was signed from Chelsea in December 1959 for £20,000 in a deal that took Johnny Brooks to Stamford Bridge. On leaving White Hart

Goal! But not this time. Les Allen being disallowed against Bolton.

Lane in July 1965, he chose to stay in London to play for QPR with whom he gained a League Cup winners medal in 1967, having earlier won a First Division and two FA Cup winners medals with Spurs. He later managed QPR (1968-71), was player-manager of Woodford Town, took charge of Swindon Town and also managed a team in Greece. Capped by England at Under-23 level, he teamed up well with Terry Dyson and Bobby Smith in 1960-61 when his 27 goals helped Spurs clinch the League and Cup double. He lost his place following the arrival of Jimmy Greaves. On retiring from football Allen worked in the car industry. His son, Clive, also played for Spurs as well as Arsenal, QPR and Crystal Palace, among others.

ALLEN, PAUL KEVIN

Member of the famous Allen family, midfielder Paul became the youngest player ever to appear in an FA Cup final at Wembley when, at the age of 17 years and 256 days, he helped West Ham United beat Arsenal 1-0 in the 1980 Wembley showdown. Born in Aveley, Essex on 28 August 1962, he represented Essex Schools and played for England's Youth team as a teenager before turning professional with the Hammers in August 1979. He transferred to Spurs for £400,000 in June 1985, scoring on his debut v. Watford and went on to net 30 goals in 377 senior appearances, up to September 1993 when he switched to Southampton for a fee of £550,000. An FA Cup winner again in 1991, Allen was capped three times by England at Under-21 level. Later on he assisted Luton Town and Stoke City (both on loan), Swindon Town and Bristol City.

ALLEN, RORY WILLIAM

England Under-21 international striker who scored four times in 28 appearances for Spurs before moving to Portsmouth for £1 million in July 1999, having spent some time on loan with Luton Town. Rory Allen was born in Beckenham on 17 October 1977.

ALMOND, WILLIAM

Attacking half-back Billie Almond was a Lancastrian, born in Blackburn on 5 April 1869. He played for Witton (a local team), Blackburn Rovers, Accrington Stanley, Middlesbrough and Millwall Athletic before joining Spurs at the start of the 1895-96 season. He only played in 28 competitive games for Spurs (61 outings in all) and scored three first-class goals before moving back to Millwall in May 1897. Later he assisted Clapton and Wandsworth. In 1889 Almond was selected to play for England but he refused his first cap, choosing instead to turn out for Blackburn in a rather one-sided FA Cup -tie against Aston Villa which Rovers won 8-1.

ALSFORD, WALTER JOHN

Wing-half Wally Alsford played in exactly 100 first team games for Spurs and scored two goals. He joined the club as a professional in August 1930 (after being nurtured for two years in the club's junior ranks) and remained at White Hart Lane until January 1937 when he switched to Nottingham Forest where he stayed until the outbreak of the Second World War. He won one full England cap (v. Scotland in 1935) and guested for a handful of clubs during the hostilities but didn't appear when League football returned in 1946. Born in North London on 6 November 1911, Alsford was only 56 when he died in Bedford on 3 June 1968.

ALTRINCHAM

Spurs playing record against Altrincham:

Competition	P	W	D	L	F	A
FA Cup	3	2	1	0	7	1

After being held to a 1-1 home draw in the 3rd round of the FA Cup in January 1979 by non-League Altrincham in front of 31,081 fans, Spurs travelled to Maine Road for the replay six days later. This time a Colin Lee hat-trick saw them make safe progress through to the next stage with a comfortable 3-0 victory before an audience of 27,878.

The third meeting between the two clubs took place at the same stage of the competition in January 1995 and again Spurs came out on top, winning 3-0 at White Hart Lane in front of just over 25,000 spectators.

Player with both clubs: Bill Felton

AMAR, MOHAMED ALI (NAYIM)

Spanish under-21 international Amar, affectionately known as Nayim, joined Spurs from CF Barcelona, initially on loan in October 1988, making the move a permanent one the following June for £300,000 which was part of the deal that also saw Gary Lineker leave the Nou Camp Stadium for White Hart Lane.

A positive midfielder, born in Morocco on 5 November 1966,

Nayim remained at White Hart Lane until the summer of 1993 when he joined Real Zaragoza. Two years later Nayim scored a dramatic 120th minute winning goal for the Spanish club against Arsenal in the European Cup-winners Cup Final, netting with a brilliant 50 yard 'looper' over 'keeper David Seaman's head.

He replaced the injured Paul Gascoigne early in the 1991 FA Cup Final victory over Nottingham Forest and went on to claim 16 goals in 134 senior appearances for Spurs

AMATEURS

Spurs took part in the FA Amateur Cup competition during the mid-1890s, shortly before they became a professional club. (See also under FA Amateur Cup).

Over the years several amateur footballers have played for Spurs at senior level, including Fred Milnes, an England Amateur international.

Outside-left George Robb (ex-Finchley) played for England's Amateur and senior sides, winning one full cap, in that 6-3 home defeat by Hungary in 1953.

Walter Bellamy, also an England Amateur international, played for the Amateurs v. Professionals in the 1925 and 1926 FA Charity Shield matches before joining Spurs.

Harry Milton played for Cambridge University and the Casuals, Bob Stevens assisted the Old Carthusians and Alex 'Sandy' Tait coached the Corinthians.

Vic Buckingham was coach of Pegasus in 1948 and later Oxford University.

In September 1952, Spurs fielded two amateur wingers - Vic Groves and George Robb - in a 3-1 win at home to Liverpool. Groves (ex-Walthamstow Avenue and Leytonstone), who was making his debut, scored twice.

Laurie Brown won 14 caps as an amateur centre-forward for England and represented Great Britain in the Rome Olympics of 1960 before establishing himself as a Football League centre-half. He joined Spurs from Arsenal in 1964.

Lycurgus Burrows was a prominent amateur defender with Spurs from October 1894 to December 1897, likewise full-back Tommy Cable who starred in two FA Amateur Cup winning sides for Leyton in 1927 and 1928 as well as playing for England.

Vic Groves

Centre-forward George Gemmell was an England Amateur international who made one FA Cup appearance for Spurs v. Leicester Fosse in 1914.

Sid Crowl was an England Amateur international trialist before joining Spurs from Enfield in 1913 while full-back William Hay was a prominent amateur full-back in Scotland with Partick Thistle and Rangers before joining Spurs in the late 1890s.

Frank Hartley won both Amateur and senior caps for England on the international scene. An inside-forward with Oxford City and the Corinthians during the 1920s, he scored five goals in 13 games during two brief spells with Spurs (1922 and 1928). He actually signed professional forms (for Spurs) at the age of 32.

Billy Cook won FA Amateur Cup winners' medals with Bishop Auckland in 1921 and 1922.

Walter Tull helped Clapton win the FA Amateur Cup in 1909. Two years earlier, Charlie Rance, a Spurs player from 1910-21, gained an FA Amateur Cup winners medal with Clapton.

The Reverend Kenneth Reginald Gunnery Hunt, who guested for Spurs during the First World War, was capped by England at both Amateur and senior levels and gained an FA Cup winners' medal with Wolves in 1908.

Len Worley (capped seven times by England) was an FA Amateur Cup winner with Wycombe Wanderers (v Bishop Auckland) in 1957.

Ted Powell, Spurs' 2001 Academy Education & Welfare Officer, won 51 Amateur international caps for England, many as captain - and he also skippered the Great Britain Olympic soccer team between 1964-74.

Old Boot Story

Spurs almost lost their Amateur status in the early years over a pair of football boots!

The club's second XI were scheduled to play in a match on 21 October 1893 with outside-left Ernie Payne set to make his debut. Payne, who had been virtually snubbed by Fulham the previous season, had accepted Spurs' invitation to play for them but when he arrived at the Northumberland Park ground he had no kit with him (having called in at Fulham only to find it missing). Spurs fixed him up with everything he required except for a pair of boots! Instead they handed him ten shillings (50p) to go out and purchase a pair. He did just that, returned, played in the game and went on to score 62 goals in 140 appearances for the club up to 1898 when he retired. However, having learnt about the handing over of the money to Payne to buy his footwear, Fulham complained to the London FA that Spurs had illegally 'poached' the player and, in fact, were also guilty of 'professionalism.' Spurs - who claimed that the boots remained the property of the club and were not actually given to Payne for him to keep - were acquitted of the poaching allegations, but were found guilty of misconduct, having induced Payne to play for them. As a result, Spurs' ground was closed for two weeks and Payne himself was suspended for seven days. Spurs became a professional club two years later, while Payne retained his amateur status by repaying Spurs the ten shillings.

AMBLER, CHARLES JAMES

Goalkeeper Charlie Ambler made 132 first team appearances for Spurs whom he served between October 1894 and the summer of 1900. Born in London in 1868, he played for Royal Arsenal, Clapton and Luton Town, among others, before taking over from Cuthbert Monk in the Spurs goal. He gained several honours during his time with the club and was eventually replaced by Joe Cullen. Later he assisted Gravesend, New Brompton, West Ham United and Millwall Athletic. Ambler died in 1952, aged 84.

ANDERLECHT (RSC)

Spurs' playing record against Anderlecht:

Comp	P	W	D	L	F	A
UEFA Cup	2	0	2*	0	2	2

* Spurs won two-legged tie on penalties.

The 1983-84 UEFA Cup Final featured Spurs against the Belgium side RSC Anderlecht and what a pulsating contest it turned out to be.

Spurs played the first leg away and in front of 38,000 fans forcing a 1-1 draw thanks to Paul Miller's goal.

The second leg, a fortnight later on 23 May went into extra-time and attracted 46,258 spectators to White Hart Lane. Again the contest finished level at 1-1, Graham Roberts equalising for Spurs six minutes from the end of normal time

So it was all down to a penalty shoot-out....and what a nail-biting ten minutes they were!

THE OFFICIAL ENCYCLOPAEDIA OF TOTTENHAM HOTSPUR F.C.

6

Spurs hero was goalkeeper Tony Parks. He saved Anderlecht's first spot-kick and then saw his side edge into a 4-3 lead with conversions by Roberts, Mark Falco, Gary Stevens and Steve Archibald. Up stepped Danny Thomas to try and clinch the game for Spurs but he missed and then Parks pulled off a tremendous save to ensure victory.

ANDERSON, JAMES

Jimmy Anderson joined Spurs' groundstaff as a 15 year-old in 1908. He did every job possible within the club - office-boy, kit-man, trainer, coach, assistant-boss and caretaker-manager (March-May 1949) - before taking over as club manager in July 1955 - on Arthur Rowe's resignation. He held office until October 1958 when Bill Nicholson (formerly his assistant & coach) took over the reins. Perhaps too old to have any real impact Anderson did his best, introduced a few useful-looking players and under his guidance Spurs reached the FA Cup semi-final in1956 but also struggled against relegation. Ill-health eventually caught up with Anderson who died on 23 August 1970

ANDERTON, DARREN ROBERT

Born in Southampton on 3 March 1972, Darren Anderton scored 13 goals in 77 senior games for Portsmouth before transferring to Spurs for £1.75 million in June 1992.

He made rapid progress in the Premiership and went on to establish himself in the England side as well as making a name for himself in the top Division of English soccer. Able to perform as a positive, direct winger or midfield play-maker, he passed the 250 appearance mark (almost 40 goals scored) for Spurs during the early part of the 2000-01 season, having struggled with injuries over the previous two years. A League Cup winner with Spurs in 1999, he has now gained 29 full caps for his country, plus others at 'B', Under-21 and Youth team levels.

ANGLO-ITALIAN LEAGUE CUP-WINNERS CUP

Spurs' record in this competition:

P	W	D	L	F	A
2	2	0	0	3	0

Having defeated Aston Villa 2-0 at Wembley to win the League Cup in February1971, Spurs met the Italian League Cup winners Torino over two legs the following September. A crowd of 28,000 saw a Martin Chivers goal give Spurs a 1-0 victory in Italy and there were 34,103 spectators present at White Hart Lane as Chivers again found the net along with Alan Gilzean as Spurs clinched the trophy with a comfortable 2-0 home win.

ANGLO-SCOTTISH FLOODLIT CUP

Spurs entered this short-lived competition 1955 -56 (one game) and 1956 - 57 (6 games). They played against three Scottish clubs, Heart of Midlothian, Hibernian and Partick Thistle, fulfilling a total of seven matches, two against Hearts and Hibs and three v Patrick.

This was Spurs full record:

P	W	D	L	F	A
7	3	1	3	18	13

The matches went as follows:

Partick Thistle (h) lost	0-1			10,000
Hibernian (a) won	5-1	Blanchflower, Harmer, Smith (2), Dyson	15,000
Partick Thistle (h) won	4-1	Medwin, Stokes (2), Smith	26,210
Hearts (a) lost	2-3	Harmer (pen), Dyson	17,000
Hibernian (h) drew	3-3	Hopkins, Medwin, Brooks	16,561
Hearts (h) won	4-2	Smith (3), Stokes	17,542
Partick Thistle (a) lost	0-2		9,000

APPEARANCES

Listed here are the top appearance-makers for Spurs in all major competitions plus other games including both Wartime periods.

Football League
(Qualification: 250)
655 Steve Perryman
477 Gary Mabbutt
472 Pat Jennings
418 Ted Ditchburn
401 Cyril Knowles
400 Jimmy Dimmock
377 Glenn Hoddle
357 Maurice Norman
343 Alan Gilzean
337 Danny Blanchflower
333 Phil Beal
331 John Pratt
324 Arthur Grimsdell
321 Jimmy Greaves
318 Tommy Clay
318 Cliff Jones
314 Bill Nicholson
312 Alan Mullery
300 Mike England
299 Peter Baker
297 Ron Burgess
297 Chris Hughton
296 Eddie Baily
295 Harry Clarke
292 Paul Allen
291 Bert Smith
278 Martin Chivers
277 David Howells
274 Len Duquemin
272 Les Bennett
271 Bobby Smith
268 Dave Mackay
259 Ian Walker
252 Taffy O'Callaghan

Premiership
(qualification: 100)
255 Sol Campbell
240 Ian Walker
224 Darren Anderton
188 Justin Edinburgh
166 Teddy Sheringham
164 Stephen Carr
163 Colin Calderwood
143 David Howells
141 Chris Armstrong
138 Gary Mabbutt
124 Dean Austin
106 Ruel Fox
106 Steffen Iversen
100 David Ginola

FA Cup
(qualification 30)
69 Steve Perryman
48 Glenn Hoddle
47 Gary Mabbutt
43 Pat Jennings
42 Cyril Knowles

40 Alan Gilzean
39 Cliff Jones
38 Jimmy Dimmock
38 Tom Morris
37 Maurice Norman
36 Jimmy Greaves
36 Arthur Grimsdell
36 Chris Hughton
35 Sandy Tait
34 Ted Ditchburn
33 Danny Blanchflower
33 Tommy Clay
33 Len Duquemin
33 Dave Mackay
33 Alan Mullery
32 Ossie Ardiles
32 Mike England
32 Bobby Smith
31 Paul Miller
30 Phil Beal
30 Ted Hughes
30 John L Jones

League Cup
(qualification: 25)
66 Steve Perryman
62 Gary Mabbutt
44 Paul Allen
44 Glenn Hoddle
39 Pat Jennings
38 Ray Clemence
35 Chris Hughton
33 Martin Chivers
33 Cyril Knowles
32 Ossie Ardiles
31 David Howells
31 John Pratt
31 Vinny Samways
30 Mike England
29 Justin Edinburgh
29 Mitchell Thomas
28 Sol Campbell
28 Alan Gilzean
27 Phil Beal
27 Jimmy Pearce
27 Steve Sedgley
25 Graham Roberts
25 Erik Thorstvedt

European Competitions
(qualification: 25)
64 Steve Perryman
36 Pat Jennings
35 Mike England
32 Martin Chivers
32 Martin Peters
30 Phil Beal
30 Chris Hughton
30 Cyril Knowles
28 Alan Gilzean
27 Ray Clemence
26 Ralph Coates
26 Graham Roberts

25 Ray Evans
25 Mark Falco
25 Tony Galvin
25 Gary Mabbutt
25 John Pratt

Southern League
(qualification: 100)
238 Tom Morris
204 Sandy Tait
152 Ted Hughes
152 John Kirwan
143 David Copeland
128 Harry Erentz
127 John L Jones
112 John Cameron
105 Walter Bull
105 Vivian Woodward
104 John Watson
102 John Walton
101 James McNaught

Other Competitions
(incl. Charity Shield)
(Qualification: 6)
11 Jimmy Dimmock
11 Steve Perryman
8 Gary Mabbutt
8 Bobby Smith
7 Paul Allen
7 Danny Blanchflower
7 Ray Clemence
7 Mike England
7 Alan Gilzean
7 Chris Hughton
7 Joe Kinnear
7 Alan Mullery
6 Pat Jennings

All Major Competitions
(not Wartime)
(qualification: 415)
865 Steve Perryman
620 Gary Mabbutt
596 Pat Jennings
492 Glenn Hoddle
484 Cyril Knowles
460 Jimmy Dimmock
457 Ted Ditchburn
428 Tom Morris
425 Phil Beal
421 Sandy Tait
418 Alan Gilzean

World War I
(qualification: 65)
130 Charlie Rance
120 Jim Elliott
105 Jimmy Banks
105 Tommy Clay
103 Bill Jacques
100 Andy Ralston
87 Percy Barton

71 Ted Bassett
70 Jabez Darnell
66 Billy Hawkins
64 Bert Bliss

World War II
(qualification: 50)
231 Ralph Ward
170 George Ludford
164 Roy White
133 Willie Hall
131 Ron Burgess
122 Bill Whatley
119 Percy Hooper
113 Jack Gibbons
105 Arthur Hitchins
91 Pat Beasley
86 Les Howe
83 Ivor Broadis
77 Andy Duncan
73 Jack Chisholm
73 Arthur Willis
60 Les Medley
54 Ted Ditchburn
50 Sonny Walters

All first team matches
(inc. friendlies)
(qualification: 300)
1,021 Steve Perryman
675 Pat Jennings
640 Gary Mabbutt
590 Glenn Hoddle
574 Ted Ditchburn
568 Cyril Knowles
522 Tom Morris
508 John Pratt
507 Ron Burgess
506 Alan Gilzean
505 Tommy Clay
502 Chris Hughton
491 Jimmy Dimmock
483 Phil Beal
453 Maurice Norman
437 Danny Blanchflower
434 Mike England
428 Alan Mullery
421 Sandy Tait
419 Jimmy Greaves
418 Cliff Jones
417 Arthur Grimsdell
416 Ossie Ardiles
415 Martin Chivers
407 Ray Clemence
406 Paul Allen
402 Peter Baker
394 Bill Nicholson
393 Bill Whatley
383 Paul Miller
381 Eddie Baily
380 Harry Clarke
378 Terry Naylor
378 Ralph Ward

377 Les Bennett
375 Tony Galvin
375 Willie Hall
374 Graham Roberts
373 Len Duquemin
368 Bert Smith
364 Dave Mackay
359 Bobby Smith
356 Bert Middlemiss
346 Sonny Walters
342 Ron Henry
340 Ian Walker
336 John L Jones
335 Mark Falco
325 Sol Campbell
323 Fanny Walden
318 Ted Hughes
317 Tony Marchi
315 Bert Bliss
314 Darren Anderton
313 Taffy O'Callaghan
313 Bob Steel
310 Vic Buckingham
305 Ralph Coates
303 Harry Erentz
302 David Copeland
Totals include substitute appearances but not abandoned matches.

Consecutive Appearances
Players with excellent runs of consecutive appearances for Spurs:

Football League:
247 Ted Ditchburn+
189 Steve Perryman
162 Pat Jennings
122 Cyril Spiers
116 Tony Marchi
114 Cyril Knowles
108 Billy Minter
107 Steve Perryman*
105 Ron Henry
103 Ray Clemence
102 Keith Osgood
102 Danny Blanchlower
100 Jimmy Dimmock
* Second spell
+ Ditchburn also played in one abandoned game.
FA Cup
69 Steve Perryman
29 Ted Ditchburn

League Cup
36 Steve Perryman
NB - Goalkeeper Ted Ditchburn also played in 23 FA Cup matches and one FA Charity Shield match during his 247-match unbroken League run,

bringing his total number of consecutive appearances to 271. Steve Perryman's FA Cup run was between Jan 1970 and March 1986

Consistency

Between 27 April 1946 and 6 November 1955 (inclusive) Spurs fulfilled a total of 392 first team games, playing goalkeeper Ted Ditchburn in 385 of them, missing only seven (five in the Football League and two in the Coronation Cup).

Steve Perryman - from his debut day on 27 September 1969 until 4 March 1986 - appeared in 865 out of the 915 competitive first team matches played by Spurs during that time (missing only 50). He did not figure in 37 out of a possible 692 League games; appeared in all 69 FA Cup matches; missed nine out of 75 League Cup fixtures, was sidelined from just two out of 66 European encounters and appeared in 11 out of a possible 13 other matches.

Other consistent performers in League Football: Eddie Baily made 295 appearances (out of 342) for Spurs between 1947-56. Right-back Peter Baker appeared in 288 games (out of 336) between 1956-64. Between 1954-6, skipper Danny Blanchflower played in 337 out of 375 First Division games for Spurs. Over a 12-year period (1965-77) goalkeeper Pat Jennings made 443 appearances for Spurs out of a possible 475. Left-back Cyril Knowles missed 40 games, starring in 357 out of 397 between 1964-74. Midfielder Martin Peters played in 189 out of 207 games for Spurs (1970-75). Full-back Alf Ramsey appeared in 226 out of 249 matches between 1949-55. Terry Venables missed only 11 games (out of 126) between 1966-69. Sandy Tait made 205 Southern League appearances (out of a possible 260) between 1899-1907 and John White made 183 First Division appearances for Spurs (out of 198) from 1959 until his tragic death in 1964.

One Match Wonders

Here are the names of players who made just one senior appearance for Spurs (in all major competitions). Wartime football and abandoned matches have not been included but substitute outings have:

Joe Allen (1933 - scored), Percy Austin (1927), Tommy Bing (1957), Robert Brace (1984), George Brewster (1907), Noel Brotherston (1976), Roy Brown (1966), Walter Bugg (1903), Ray Clarke (1973), Alf Coleman (1894), Sid Crowl (1914), Dicky Dowsett (1954 - scored), Frank Drabble (1909), Brian Farley (1951), P Finch (1901), Tom Fitchie (1902), Peter Garland (1991), CG Gaudson (1905), George Gemmell (1914, FAC), Tommy Gipps (1907), George Goldsmith (1934), Ellis Hargreaves (1897), Billy Hay (1896), Bill Hacking (1906), Hobson (1897), Hudson (1899), George Jeffrey (1937- scored), Leon Joseph (1947), Tommy Jull (1897), Eddie King (1934), John Knight (1929), J Lee (1907), Terry Lee (1974), AK Leigh (1901), Archie Lyle (1909), LH McKenzie (1895), F McMullan (1906), Harry Marshall (1932), George Montgomery (1901), Charlie Morgan (1905), Aled Owen (1954), ML Owen (1895 - scored FAC), Ron Piper (1963), Steve Pitt (1965), Andy Polston

(1990), Charlie Regan (1897), Jock Robertson (1897), Harry Robshaw (1951), Sands (1901), Tom Soulsby (1901), Graeme Souness (1971, UEFA Cup), Peter Southey (1979), Alex Steel (1910),Vaughan (1903), Claude Watson (1906), Bob Wilkie (1957), T Williams (1895), Roy Woolcott (1969) and Len Worley (1959).

Ever-presents (League only):

Players who were ever-present for Spurs during a complete League season (figures given in brackets indicate the number of matches played by team):
1908-09 (38) Bert Middlemiss, Danny Steel
1909-10 (38) Bob Steel, Billy Minter
1910-11 (38) Jabez Darnell, Billy Minter
1912-13 (38) Bert Middlemiss, Billy Minter
1914-15 (38) Tommy Clay, Fanny Walden
1919-20 (42) Bert Bliss
1921-22 (42) Jimmy Dimmock
1922-23 (42) Jimmy Dimmock
1924-25 (42) Bill Hinton
1925-26 (42) Matt Forster
1927-28 (42) Taffy O'Callaghan
1929-30 (42) Cyril Spiers
1930-31 (42) Bill Davies, Cyril Spiers
1932-33 (42) Willie Evans
1933-34 (42) Willie Hall, Joe Nicholls, Arthur Rowe
1937-38 (42) Fred Sargent, Ralph Ward
1948-49 (42) Les Bennett, Ted Ditchburn
1949-50 (42) Ted Ditchburn, Les Medley
1950-51 (42) Harry Clarke, Ted Ditchburn
1951-52 (42) Ted Ditchburn
1952-53 (42) Ted Ditchburn
1955-56 (42) Tony Marchi
1956-57 (42) Tommy Harmer, Tony Marchi
1960-61 (42) Les Allen, Danny Blanchflower, Ron Henry, John White
1962-63 (42) Ron Henry
1963-64 (42) Maurice Norman
1964-65 (42) Alan Mullery
1966-67 (42) Mike England, Cyril Knowles
1967-68 (42) Pat Jennings, Cyril Knowles
1968-69 (42) Jimmy Greaves, Pat Jennings
1970-71 (42) Martin Chivers, Steve Perryman, Martin Peters
1974-75 (42) Steve Perryman
1975-76 (42) Keith Osgood
1976-77 (42) Keith Osgood, Steve Perryman
1977-78 (42) Barry Daines, Neil McNab, Steve Perryman
1978-79 (42) Steve Perryman
1980-81 (42) Steve Perryman
1981-82 (42) Steve Perryman
1984-85 (42) Ray Clemence, Mark Falco, Steve Perryman
1985-86 (42) Ray Clemence
1988-89 (38) Gary Mabbutt, Chris Waddle
1989-90 (38) Gary Lineker
1993-94 (42) Steve Sedgley
1994-95 (42) Teddy Sheringham (41+1)
1995-96 (38) Teddy Sheringham, Ian Walker
1996-97 (38) Sol Campbell
1997-98 (38) Stephen Carr (37+1)
1999-00 (38) Ian Walker
* Steve Perryman has been ever-present most times (8); Ted Ditchburn (5) and Billy Minter (3) follow on.

Players who appeared for Spurs before, during & after the two World Wars:

1914-20 - Jimmy Banks, Bert Bliss, Jimmy Cantrell, Tommy Clay, Bill Jacques, Harry Lowe, Bert Middlemiss, Billy Minter, John Pearson and Fanny Walden.

1939-46 - Vic Buckingham, Ron Burgess, Freddie Cox, Jackie Gibbons*, Albert Hall, Jack Hall*, George Ludford, Colin Lyman*, Jimmy McCormick*, Les Medley, Johnny Morrison*, Bill Nicholson, Bert Page, Fred Sargent*, George Skinner, Ralph Ward*,

* These players all represented Spurs in 1946.

Appearance-Talk

Goalkeeper Ray Clemence made the 1,000th appearance of his career (various levels) when he lined up for Spurs against Newcastle United on 7 September 1985. His predecessor, Pat Jennings, accumulated 1,095 first-class appearances during his playing days.

Clemence himself amassed 1,116 appearances in competitive match action (including his international outings). Together the two goalkeepers gained a total of 186 full caps for their respective countries (at senior level) and taking into account all first-team appearances at club and international level (friendlies included) they played in no fewer than 2,348 football matches (at various levels) between them. Some record!

Clemence with 758 games to his credit, is currently 13th in the list of all-time Football League appearance-makers. Jennings is one place below him in 14th spot with a total of 757. Together they made 712 League appearances for Spurs alone, Jennings 472 and Clemence 240.

Jennings also played in 60 first team matches for Watford, 378 for Arsenal and 596 for Spurs.

ARCHER, ARTHUR

Strapping full-back Arthur Archer, born in Ashby-de-la-Zouch in 1877, played for Burton Wanderers, Small Heath (170 games), New Brompton and QPR before 'guesting' for Spurs in 1903-05, making eight first team appearances. He later served with Norwich City, Brighton & Hove Albion and Millwall. He died in Derby in 1940.

ARCHIBALD, JAMES MITCHELL

Scottish-born half-back Jimmy Archibald made 25 appearances at competitive level for Spurs (one goal) after signing from Motherwell in 1919. He left the club three years later for Aberdare Athletic and played for Clapton Orient and Southend United after that.

ARCHIBALD, STEVEN

Born in Glasgow on 27 September 1956, striker Steve Archibald, formerly with East Stirling and Clyde, was four months short of his 24th birthday when he joined Spurs from Aberdeen for £800,000 in May 1980. Having helped the Dons win two Scottish League Cup Finals and the Scottish League championship in his two-and-half-years at Pittodrie he quickly bedded into the Spurs attack to form a fine partnership with Garth Crooks. He collected an FA Cup winners' medal at the end of his first season in English football, adding a second twelve months later and in 1984 was a member of Spurs' UEFA Cup winning side.

Archibald went on to score 97 goals in 216 first team appearances for Spurs, and he also gained one Under-21 and 22 senior caps for Scotland before he left White Hart Lane for Barcelona in the summer of 1984, former Spurs player Terry Venables paying £1.25 million for his signature. He continued to serve his country while

in Spain but when Messrs Lineker and Hughes (Mark) appeared at the Nou Camp, Archibald departed company with the Spanish giants, transferring to Hibernian in August 1988 (after a loan spell with Blackburn Rovers with his former Spurs colleague Ossie Ardiles). Between 1990 and 1993 Archibald played for Espanyol (in Spain), St Mirren, Reading (on trial) Ayr United and Fulham (non-contract basis). He then retired to become manager of East Fife.

ARDILES, OSVALDO CESAR

Ossie Ardiles had a fine career as a player, being capped 52 times by Argentina (eight goals scored) and helping his country win the 1978 World Cup (with another future Spurs player Ricky Villa). Ardiles (and Villa) joined Spurs together in readiness for the start of the 1978-79 season, Ardiles costing just £325,000 from the Huracan club.

Born in Cordoba on 3 August 1952, he had previously played for two clubs in his home town - Red Star Cordoba and Cordoba Instituto - before making his mark with Huracan. Regarded by many as one of the best midfield players in the 1978 World Cup Finals, he became an instant success at White Hart Lane. A huge favourite with the fans, he helped Spurs win the FA Cup in 1981, reach the League Cup Final and FA Cup Final a year later and gained a UEFA Cup winners medal in 1984. He scored 37 goals in 416 first-team games for Spurs (25 in 310 major League and Cup matches) before joining London rivals Queen's Park Rangers in August 1988, having earlier been loaned out to both Paris St Germain and Blackburn Rovers. After a brief spell with Fort Lauderdale Strikers in the NASL, Ardiles tasted soccer management for the first time when he took charge of Swindon Town in July 1989. Between March 1991 and February 1992 he was boss of Newcastle United and then, in 1993, he guided West Bromwich Albion to promotion from Division Two.

He left The Hawthorns a month after that Wembley triumph to return to Spurs as team manager in succession to Doug Livermor. Ardiles failed to make much headway in the White Hart Lane hot-seat and he left Spurs, second time round, on 1 November, 1994, allowing Steve Perryman to take charge of team affairs until the appointment of Gerry Francis. Since then Ardiles has managed and/or coached the following clubs (all abroad): Deportivo Guadalajara (Mexico), Shimizu S-Pulse (Japan - to January 1999), Croatia Zagreb and Yokohama F Marinos (Japan), the latter from December 1999 to June 2001 when he was sacked. Ardiles is a qualified lawyer.

ARMSTRONG, CHRISTOPHER PETER

Striker Chris Armstrong made his Football League debut for Wrexham in 1989. He scored 16 goals in 70 appearances for the Welsh club before joining Millwall for £50,000 in August 1991. He never really established himself with the Lions and in September 1992 he moved again, this time to Crystal Palace for £1 m. He did very well with the Eagles, netting 57 times in 136 senior appearances - an achievement that led to several big-named clubs enquiring about his availability.....and it was Spurs who stepped in, boss Gerry Francis (a former Palace player himself) paying £4.5 million to bring Armstrong to White Hart Lane in June 1995.

Born in Newcastle on 19 June 1971 and capped by England 'B'. Armstrong helped Palace win the First Division title in 1994. Fast and direct, he has struggled with injuries and loss of form of late but his overall record for the club is still very satisfying - 62 goals in 173 senior appearances.

ARMSTRONG, GERARD JOSEPH

A Northern Ireland international inside or centre-forward, born in Belfast on 23 May 1954, Gerry Armstrong joined Spurs from Bangor in November 1975. He did exceedingly well for the second XI before going on to score 32 goals in 133 first team appearances for the club, 10 in 84 League outings. He was then transferred to Watford for £250,000 in November 1980, having lost his place in the side following the arrival of Steve Archibald and Garth Crooks. Between 1983 and 1985 Armstrong played for the Spanish side Real Mallorca. He then had a brief spell with West Bromwich Albion and played on loan with Chesterfield before joining the Spireites on a permanent basis in 1986. Thereafter he served with Brighton & Hove Albion and Millwall prior to securing an appointment as player-coach with non-League side Crawley Town, later assisting Southwick and then Worthing, the latter as player-manager (1991-92). Armstrong, well built, with a powerful right-foot shot, had the pleasure of scoring for his country in the 1982 World Cup Finals in Spain. He won a total of 63 caps for Northern Ireland and made 234 League appearances as a professional (29 goals).

ARMSTRONG, JAMES WILLIAM

An inside or centre-forward, Jimmy Armstrong joined Spurs from Chelsea in May 1927 and had to wait seven months before making his debut for the club in a 3-2 defeat at Birmingham. Born on Tyneside on 6 September 1901, he signed for Chelsea in 1922 but never really made his mark at Stamford Bridge. He went on to score five goals in 33 League and FA Cup games for Spurs before transferring to Luton Town in June 1930. He ended his senior career with Bristol Rovers. Armstrong died in Gateshead in August 1977.

ARSENAL (WOOLWICH, ROYAL)

Spurs playing record against the Gunners:

Comp	P	W	D	L	F	A
Premiership	18	5	8	5	16	18
F. League	110	40	24	46	158	168
FA Cup	5	2	0	3	5	7
League Cup	7	2	1	4	6	8
Other Leagues	14	6	3	5	25	18
Other Cups	11	4	3	4	14	16
Wartime	36	14	9	13	61	55
Summary	201	73	48	80	285	290

Spurs' first match against (Royal) Arsenal took place on 10 November 1887 at Northumberland Park. The visitors turned up late and as a result the friendly was abandoned in the 75th minute due to fading light with Spurs leading 2-1.

Two years later at Royal Arsenal's Manor Ground, Spurs crashed to a 10-1 defeat in another pre-arranged friendly.

The first League meeting between the two clubs was staged at Plumstead on 4 December 1909 (Division 1) and in front of 18,000 fans the Woolwich Arsenal won 1-0.

Both clubs were involved in a relegation battle at the end of that 1909-10 season; both survived the drop, Woolwich Arsenal finishing third from bottom while Spurs took 15th position.

Spurs' first League victory over Woolwich Arsenal followed on 3 December 1910 when they triumphed 3-1 at White Hart Lane.

Despite Spurs understandable protestations to the Football League the Woolwich club was allowed to move to Islington becoming The Arsenal.

When football resumed in 1919 the Football League made the surprising decision to relegate Tottenham and promote Arsenal despite having finished in fifth place!

There was a break of fifteen years (from 1935) before Spurs and Arsenal met each other again in the Football League and at Highbury in August 1950, a bumper crowd of 64,638 witnessed the 2-2 draw, Ron Burgess and Sonny Walters netting for Spurs. Wally Barnes scored a second-half penalty equaliser for the Gunners.

Beaten 4-1 by Arsenal at home in front of almost 70,000 fans in October 1953, Spurs gained revenge with a 3-0 victory at Highbury some four months later when the turn out was 64,311. George Robb scored twice in the second game.

After five defeats and a draw, Spurs finally recorded their first League win of the 1955-56 season at Arsenal's expense, beating the Gunners 3-1 at home on 10 September in front of 51,029 fans. Alf Stokes scored twice.

A real humdinger-of-a-game at Highbury in February 1958, witnessed by 59,116 fans, ended in a nail-biting 4-4 draw. Tommy Harmer and Bobby Smith both scored twice for Spurs (with one of Harmer's efforts coming via the penalty spot) while Ron Henry's early own-goal had given the Gunners the lead. Spurs in fact scored twice in the last four minutes to share the points, Cliff Jones, making his debut for Spurs following his transfer from Swansea Town, had a hand in three of his side's goals.

Arsenal were beaten twice in 1960-61 as Spurs won the double. They lost 3-2 at Highbury and then went down 4-2 at White Hart Lane.

A crowd of 59,371 saw Terry Dyson become the first Spurs player (and indeed the only one so

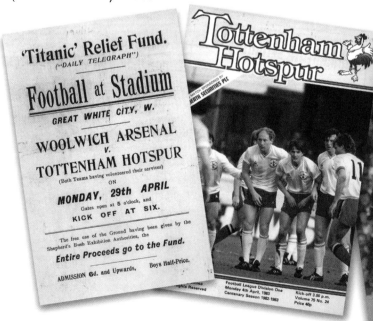

far) to score a hat-trick in a League game against Arsenal, his treble helping his side gain a 4-3 home victory in August 1961.

There was another 4-4 draw between the two North London clubs in October 1962. This time it was at White Hart Lane where the turnout was 61,749. Cliff Jones scored twice for Spurs while David Court did likewise for the Gunners.

A third post-War 4-4 draw between the clubs was played out in October 1963 at Highbury. A crowd of 67,857 attended the contest and there were 57,261 present for the return game at White Hart Lane in February which Spurs won 3-1.

In September 1965, Roy Low came on for Derek Possee to become Spurs' first League substitute during the 2-2 draw with Arsenal at White Hart Lane. The Gunners were 2-0 up after 20 minutes before Alan Gilzean and Frank Saul brought the scores level.

A crowd of 55,237 saw the first-ever League Cup encounter between Arsenal and Spurs - the 1st leg of the semi-final at Highbury in November 1968. The Gunners won 1-0 and a fortnight later, 55,923 fans saw them force a 1-1 draw at White Hart Lane to got through to the Final on aggregate. John Radford scored both of Arsenal's goals.

On 3 May 1971, Arsenal visited White Hart Lane and won 1-0 to get one hand on the League and Cup double. A crowd of almost 52,000 saw Ray Kennedy head home the decisive goal two minutes from time in that crucial League encounter. They thus emulated Spurs' success from a decade earlier.

Willie Young, who moved to Highbury in March 1977, became the first Spurs player to be sent-off in a North London derby when he took an early bath in the 2-2 draw at White Hart Lane in December 1976.

In April 1983 Spurs went to town on the Gunners, firing them down to the tune of 5-0. Mark Falco and Chris Hughton were the goalscoring heroes with a brace apiece.

Spurs' run of 14 straight League wins at White Hart Lane came to an end when Arsenal won 2-1 on 18 October 1987.

Spurs beat the Gunners in the 1991 FA Cup semi-final at Wembley in front of almost 78,000 spectators. Two years later it was Arsenal's turn to proceed into the Final when they beat Spurs at the same stage on the same pitch in front of 76,263 fans. Eight years after that, in April 2001, it was Arsenal again who went through to the Final after winning 2-1 at neutral Old Trafford just as Glenn Hoddle had taken over as Spurs' manager!

* A record crowd of 14,000 assembled at Spurs' Northumberland Park ground to witness a United League game against Woolwich Arsenal on 8 April 1898 (0-0 draw).

Players with both clubs include: Clive Allen, Charlie Ambler, David Black, Jimmy Brain, Laurie Brown, Walter Bugg, Lycurgus Burrows, Sol Campbell, Freddie Cox, James Devlin, Jack Eggett, Tom Fitchie, Vic Groves, Tom Hatfield, George Hunt, David Jenkins, Pat Jennings, Bill Julian, Peter Kyle, Neil Lacy (Gunners trialist, Spurs junior) Tom Meade, Billy Minter (Arsenal Amateur), Terry Naylor (Gunners' trialist), Tim O'Shea (Arsenal Schoolboy), George Payne, Ron Piper (Arsenal Amateur), Tom Pratt, Jimmy Robertson, Andrew Swan, Walter Thomas (Arsenal trialist, Spurs junior), Erik Thorstvedt (Arsenal trialist), Steve Walford, Charlie Williams, Willie Young.

Wartime guests (with either or both clubs): Wally Alsford, Pat Beasley, Frank Boulton, Stanley Briggs, Harry Brown, Bernie Bryant, Jim Evans, Harry Ferrier, Len Flack, Bobby Flavell, Fred Ford (Arsenal amateur), Harry Harris, Les Henley, Percy Hooper, Archie Hughes, Eric Jones, Phil Joslin, David Nelson, Les Stevens, Ralph Ward, Bill Whatley, Jack Whent, Tim Williamson, Albert Young.

Also associated: George Graham & Terry Neill (managers of both clubs, and both Arsenal players), Herbert Chapman (Spurs player, Arsenal manager), Joe Hulme (Arsenal player, Spurs manager & assistant manager chief scout assistant-secretary), Theo Foley (Arsenal assistant-manager, Spurs reserve team manager), Wilf Dixon (Spurs assistant-manager & trainer, Arsenal trainer), Peter McWilliam (Spurs manager, Arsenal scout), Stewart Houston (assistant-manager of both clubs), Bill Lane (Spurs player, Arsenal scout), Ernie Walley (Spurs player, Arsenal coach), Bob Arber (Arsenal player, Spurs reserve team manager).

ASTON VILLA

Spurs playing record against the Villa:

Competition	P	W	D	L	F	A
Premiership	18	3	6	9	17	27
Football League	98	43	19	36	176	158
FA Cup	11	6	1	4	12	8
League Cup	4	2	0	2	8	5
Charity Shield	1	0	1	0	2	2
Wartime	2	1	0	1	4	5
Summary	134	55	27	52	219	205

Spurs' 2nd round FA Cup -tie with Aston Villa on 20 February 1904 was abandoned after 20 minutes following a crowd over-spill. In front of a record attendance of 32,000, Villa were ahead at the time by 1-0. The re-arranged game was staged at Villa Park and this time Spurs won 1-0.

The first League game between Spurs and Villa took place on 20 November 1909 (Division 1) in front of 25,000 fans at Villa Park, the home side winning 3-2.

In the first FA Cup competition after the Great War (1919-20), Spurs were beaten 1-0 by the eventual winners that season, Aston Villa. In the following year Spurs then dumped out the holders in the 4th round, winning 1-0 at White Hart Lane in front of a record 56,991 crowd.

In January 1934, Spurs went to Villa Park and won 5-1. They were 4-0 up after 35 minutes and went into a 5-0 lead

Bobby Smith in action against the Villa

before the home side had Pongo Waring sent-off.

Later that year - on 22 September 1934 - the East Stand at White Hart Lane was opened to the public for the first time, but Villa spoiled the party by winning 2-0 in front of 42,088 spectators - and this time Waring was one of the scorers! Eddie King made his debut for Spurs in this game but failed to manage the 90 minutes, being led off injured. He never appeared again for Spurs!

Spurs completed the League double over Villa in 1950-51, winning both games 3-2.

Spurs' first goal of the 1953-54 season came courtesy of the Villa defender and future director Harry Parkes in a 1-0 home win in front of 50,202 supporters.

It was case of *deja vu* in August 1954 when once again Villa were Spurs' opening day opponents this time the League game was at Villa Park where Spurs won 4-2 in front of 44,193 fans, Les Bennett scoring twice. Dickie Dowsett 'kneed' a goal for Spurs on his debut - his only game for the club.

In April 1956 a crowd of 36,235 saw a thrilling League game at

Jimmy Greaves scores Spurs' second against Villa in 1964

White Hart Lane finish Spurs 4 Villa 3. Five months later (in September) Spurs won 4-2 at Villa Park and then doubled up with a 3-0 victory at home just as Villa were setting out on the Wembley trail which culminated in an FA Cup Final triumph over Manchester United.

Rampant Bobby Smith scored four times when Spurs beat Villa 6-2 at White Hart Lane in March 1958.

Spurs beat Villa 6-2 at home (they were 4-0 up at the interval) and 2-1 away when they claimed the double in 1960-61.

Spurs were undefeated against Villa in 22 League games (home & away) between September 1950 and February 1962. They also came through two FA Cup matches during that same period.

On 16 September 1963, nine days after conceding seven goals in their previous away game at Blackburn, Spurs beat Aston Villa 4-2 in Birmingham, Jimmy Greaves scoring twice.

Spurs were 5-1 up on Aston Villa in their home First Division match in March 1966, but some slack defending plus some great attacking by the visitors saw them pull back to 5-5, the equaliser coming in the 87th minute. Tony Hateley scored four goals for Villa.

A year later the teams shared six goals at Villa Park when the Midland club was battling unsuccessfully against relegation.

Villa won only one League game out of 18 played on Spurs' soil in 30 years from 1936.....a 1-0 victory on 29 October 1966.

Five different Spurs players figured on the scoresheet when Villa

were beaten 5-2 at White Hart Lane in March 1976.

Clive Allen netted a hat-trick in Spurs' 3-0 win at Villa Park on the opening day of the 1986-87 season. Halfway through the campaign Spurs repeated that scoreline when completing the double at White Hart Lane.

On 4 April 1992 Spurs led Villa 2-0 in a home League game only to lose the contest 5-2.

Earlier in the season Villa had knocked Spurs, the holders, out of the FA Cup in the 3rd round.

Spurs' run of seven straight Premiership defeats came to an end when they were held to a 1-1 home draw by Villa in March 1994.

Spurs were 2-0 up on Villa in a Premiership home game in April 2000, but lost the contest 4-2 as the visitors scored four times in the space of 12 minutes in the second-half.

Players with both clubs include: Gudni Bergsson (Villa trialist), Danny Blanchflower, Mark Burke (Spurs trialist), Colin Calderwood, Jimmy Cantrell, Billy Cook, Ronnie Dix, David Ginola, Andy Gray, James Gray, Steve Hodge, Bob Iverson (Spurs junior), Peter Kyle, Tommy Muldoon (Spurs reserve), Ernie Phypers (Villa reserve), Vic Potts (Spurs reserve & scout), Gordon Smith, Cyril Spiers, Tom Tebb (Villa & Spurs reserve), Frank Wilson (Villa reserve).

Wartime guests (with either one or both clubs): Simon Beaton, Billy Brawn, Jack Finch (Villa trialist), Jackie Martin, Frank O'Donnell, Joe Parsons, Haydn Price (Villa reserve), Andy Ralston (Villa junior), George Travers, Joey Walters.

Also associated: George Graham (Villa player, Spurs manager), Jack Tresadern (Spurs manager, Villa scout).

* Spurs centre-forward Len Duquemin scored in two FA Cup semi-finals against Blackpool, both at Villa Park, and was a loser each time - in 1948 by 3-1 and 1953 by 2-1.

ATHERTON, THOMAS HENRY

Liverpool-born inside-forward, signed from Hibernian in 1898, Tom Anderson scored four goals in 13 games for Spurs before transferring to Partick Thistle in 1899. Later he served with Dundee (his first club), Grimsby, Brentford and Motherwell.

ATLETICO MADRID

Spurs playing record against the Spanish side:

Competition	P	W	D	L	F	A
EC-winners Cup	1	1	0	0	5	1

Spurs became the first British team to win a major European competition when they defeated Atletico Madrid 5-1 in the final of the Cup-winners Cup in Rotterdam on 15 May 1963.

In front of an all-ticket crowd of 40,000, Atletico made Spurs battle every inch of the way and they never deserved to be on the receiving end of such a big scoreline. Terry Dyson (2), John White and Jimmy Greaves (2) scored for Spurs on a memorable night in Holland.

Player with both clubs: Quinton Fortune (Spurs junior).

ATTENDANCES
Highest

The all-time record crowd at White Hart Lane is 75,038 v. Sunderland, FA Cup 6th round on 5.3.1938.

The biggest League crowd ever to assemble on the ground is 70,882 v. Manchester United (Division 1) on 22.8.1951.

In the Football League Cup, the best crowd at White Hart Lane to date has been 55,923 v. Arsenal semi-final, 2nd leg on 4.12.1968.

In European Cup football, the biggest single attendance for a Spurs home game is 64,448 v. Benfica, European Cup semi-final, 2nd leg on 5.4.1962.

Lowest

The lowest attendance at White Hart Lane has been 500 - Spurs v. Bristol Rovers (Western League) on 9.9.1907.

In the FA Cup, Spurs' lowest crowd is 1,300 v. Vampires on 16 November 1895. The lowest at White Hart Lane is 16,859 v. Sunderland on 9.1.1915

At League Cup level, the lowest attendance for a Spurs home game is 12,299 v. Barnsley on 8.10.1986.

In major European Competitions, the lowest attendance for a Spurs home game has been 18,105 against Grasshopper-club Zurich UEFA Cup on 3.10.1973.

This is how the White Hart Lane attendance record has been broken:

11,000 v. Queen's Park Rgs (Southern League)	09.09.1899
18,000 v. Gravesend United (Southern League)	02.10.1899
20,250 v. Bury (FA Cup)	23.02.1901
27,000 v. Millwall Athletic (Southern League)	07.09.1901
32,000 v. Aston Villa (FA Cup)*	20.02.1904
33,000 v. Portsmouth (Southern League)	25.12.1905
40,000 v. Oldham Athletic (Division 2)	26.12.1908
47,109 v. Arsenal (Division 1)	25.12.1911
47,642 v. West Ham United (FA Cup)	21.02.1920
52,179 v. Aston Villa (FA Cup)	06.03.1920
54,500 v. Newcastle United (Division 1)	27.12.1920
56,991 v. Aston Villa (FA Cup)	05.03.1921
61,195 v. Newcastle United (FA Cup)	26.01.1935
70,347 v. Bolton Wanderers (FA Cup)	16.02.1935
71,913 v. Preston North End (FA Cup)	06.03.1937
75,038 v. Sunderland (FA Cup)	05.03.1938

* Game abandoned

Attendances of 65,000+ for Spurs home games at White Hart Lane

75,038 v. Sunderland (FA Cup)	05.03.1938
71,913 v. Preston North End (FA Cup)	06.03.1937
71,853 v. West Bromwich Albion (FA Cup)	24.01.1948
70,882 v. Manchester United (Division 1)	22.09.1951
70,347 v. Bolton Wanderers (FA Cup)	16.02.1935
70,302 v. Southampton (Division 2)	25.02.1950
70,026 v. Newcastle United (Division 2)	18.11.1950
69,821 v. Arsenal (Division 1)	10.10.1953
69,718 v. Queen's Park Rangers (Division 2)	16.10.1948
69,265 v. Southampton (Division 2)	02.04.1949
69,247 v. Arsenal (Division 1)	20.09.1952
69,111 v. West Ham United (FA Cup)	03.03.1956
69,049 v. Southampton (FA Cup)	07.02.1948
69,009 v. Newcastle United (FA Cup)	02.02.1952
67,633 v. Norwich City (FA Cup)	14.02.1959
67,088 v. Portsmouth (Division 1)	12.04.1952
66,880 v. Hull City (Division 2)	07.04.1950
66,796 v. Wolverhampton Wanderers (Div 1)	20.01.1951
66,438 v. Arsenal (Division 1)	09.02.1952
66,402 v. Portsmouth (Division 1)	04.11.1950
66,398 v. Chelsea (FA Cup)	26.01.1957
66,246 v. Sunderland (FA Cup)	28.01.1950
65,681 v. Stoke City (FA Cup)	11.01.1947
65,032 v. Chelsea (Division 1)	31.03.1961

Lowest attendances for Spurs home Football League games at White Hart Lane (under 10,000):

5,000 v. Sunderland	19.12.1914
6,000 v. Manchester City	15.03.1915
6,292 v. Swansea Town	27.01.1947

Spurs fans parade the arena before kick off against Sunderland in a Cup tie in 1950

7,000 v. Notts County	12.10.1912*
7,500 v. Sheffield United	19.04.1915
7,716 v. Everton	01.10.1927
8,000 v. Birmingham	20.03.1909
8,000 v. Middlesbrough	13.02.1911
8,000 v. Sheffield Wednesday	26.12.1914
8,000 v. Leeds United	09.03.1925
8,500 v. West Bromwich Albion	28.09.1914
8,545 v. Stoke City	09.10.1929
9,000 v. Everton	02.09.1914
9,103 v. Hull City	21.12.1929
9,359 v. Birmingham City	16.04.1986
9,436 v. Leicester City	22.09.1927
9,454 v. Southampton	24.12.1938

* This game was abandoned through fog.

Spurs' lowest away Football League crowds:

3,000 v. Bolton Wanderers	23.04.1910
3,000 v. Sheffield Wednesday	14.03.1910
3,000 v. Glossop North End	24.10.1908
3,560 v. Doncaster Rovers	17.04.1937
7,256 v. Blackburn Rovers	09.05.1966
7,917 v. Wimbledon	22.04.1987

The lowest Cup crowds at White Hart Lane:

7,548 v. Everton (SSSC)	05.02.1986
11,600 v. Reading (FA Cup)	28.03.1901
12,299 v. Barnsley (League Cup)	08.10.1986
18,105 v. Grasshopper Zurich (Europe)	03.10.1973

Other low crowds at White Hart Lane:

500 v. Bristol Rovers (Western League)	09.09.1907
1,000 v. Swindon Town (Western League)	27.02.1901
1,000 v. Brentford (Western League)	29.03.1903
1,000 v. West Ham Utd (Western League)	26.03.1906

Lowest 'other' crowds away from home:

4,680 v. Southampton (SSS Cup)	17.12.1985
5,000 v. Torquay United (League Cup)	23.09.1987
7,668 v. Leeds United (Football League)	04.05.1935
8,500 v. Margate (FA Cup)	13.01.1973

Attendances of over 70,000 at Spurs matches (home, away and neutral grounds)

114,815 v. Sheffield United (CP), FA Cup Final	20.04.1901
100,000 v. Leicester City (W), FA Cup Final	06.05.1961
100,000 v. Liverpool (W), League Cup Final	13.03.1982
100,000 v. Chelsea (W), FA Cup Final	20.05.1967
100,000 v. Queen's Park R (W), FA Cup Final	22.05.1982
100,000 v. Burnley (W), FA Cup Final	05.05.1962
100,000 v. Manchester City (W), FA Cup Final	09.05.1981
98,000 v. Coventry City (W), FA Cup Final	16.05.1987
97,446 v. Norwich City (W), League Cup Final	03.03.1973
97,024 v. Aston Villa (W), League Cup Final	27.02.1971
95,000 v. Real Madrid (a) UEFA Cup	20.03.1985
92,500 v. Manchester C (W), FA Cup Final replay	14.05.1981
92,445 v. Aston Villa (W) Charity Shield	22.08.1981
92,000 v. Queen's Park R (W), FA Cup Final replay	27.05.1982
81,945 v. Liverpool (W) Charity Shield	21.08.1982
80,000 v. G Rangers (a) ECWC	11.12.1962
80,000 v. Barcelona (a) ECWC	21.04.1982
79,776 v. Nottingham F (W) FA Cup Final	18.05.1991
77,893 v. Arsenal (W) FA Cup semi-final	14.04.1991
77,892 v. Leicester C (W) League Cup Final	21.03.1999
76,263 v. Arsenal (W) FA Cup semi-final	04.04.1993
76,000 v. Chelsea (a) League	16.10.1920
75,038 v. Sunderland (h) FA Cup	05.03.1938
74,000 v. Lokomotiv Leipzig (a) UEFA Cup	10.04.1974
72,921 v. Everton (a) FA Cup	11.02.1950
72,805 v. Wolverhampton W (SB), FA Cup Final	23.04.1921
72,164 v. Arsenal (a) League	29.09.1951
71,913 v. Preston North End (h) FA Cup	06.03.1937
71,853 v. West Bromwich A (h) FA Cup	24.01.1948
70,882 v. Manchester United (h) League	22.09.1951
70,687 v. Blackpool (n) FA Cup semi-final	13.03.1948
70,347 v. Bolton Wanderers (h) FA Cup	16.02.1935
70,336 v. Newcastle United (h) League	18.11.1950
70,302 v. Southampton (h) League	25.02.1950
70,123 v. Chelsea (a) FA Cup	08.01.1964
70,054 v. Red Star Belgrade (a) UEFA Cup	13.12.1974.
70,000 v. Benfica (a) European Cup	21.03.1962

(CP)-Crystal Palace   (W)-Wembley   (SB)-Stamford Bridge

Spurs' post WW2 average home League attendances:

Division Two

1946-47	34,636
1947-48	37,726
1948-49	48,441
1949-50	54,085
1977-78	33,416

Division One

1950-51	55,508	1976-77	30,173
1951-52	51,133	1978-79	34,902
1952-53	44,104	1979-80	32,018
1953-54	41,632	1980-81	30,724
1954-55	38,678	1981-82	35,099
1955-56	38,042	1982-83	30,654
1956-57	43.280	1983-84	28,754
1957-58	43,226	1984-85	28,932
1958-59	40,453	1985-86	20,859
1959-60	47,948	1986-87	25,910
1960-61	53,601	1987-88	25,909
1961-62	45,538	1988-89	24,469
1962-63	47,342	1989-90	26,991
1963-64	43,488	1990-91	30,630
1964-65	39,391	1991-92	27,742
1965-66	38,320		
1966-67	41,988	**Premiership**	
1967-68	42,393	1992-93	27,964
1968-69	38,607	1993-94	27,321
1969-70	34,407	1994-95	26,752
1970-71	35,240	1995-96	30,517
1971-72	38,833	1996-97	31,067
1972-73	32,318	1997-98	29,144
1973-74	26,124	1998-99	34,149
1974-75	26,457	1999-00	34,902
1975-76	27,836	2000-01	35,231

Attendance facts & figures

* The one million barrier has been broken on five occasions in respect of the aggregate number of fans attending Spurs home League games at White Hart Lane: in the 1948-49 season (1,017,264), 1949-50 (1,135,781), 1950-51 (1,165,667), 1951-52 (1,073,806) and 1960-61 (1,115,612).

* The biggest average home League attendance figure in a season for Spurs has been 55,508 (from 21 First Division matches in 1950-51).

* The lowest post-World War Two average League crowd at White Hart Lane has been 20,859 in season 1985-86.

* For their first season of League Football (1908-09 in Division 2) Spurs' average home attendance was 20,315 (from 19 matches).

* Their average League attendance in their first season in Division One (1909-10) was 27,266.

* When Spurs won the Second Division championship in 1919-20, their average home League gate was an impressive 34,038 (from 21 matches). In 1921-22 it rose to almost 35,000.

* When Spurs won promotion from Division Two in 1932-33 the average League attendance at White Hart Lane was 34,579.

* The biggest-ever crowd to watch a Second Division League game - 70,302 - packed into White Hart Lane for the Spurs v. Southampton contest on 25 February 1950.

* Over 470,000 spectators saw the seven FA Cup matches at White Hart Lane in the 1960-61 season - average 67,166.

* The lowest attendance at White Hart Lane during Spurs' double-winning season of 1960-61 was 35,743 v. Nottingham Forest on 26 April. The lowest away from home was 21,567 at Preston's Deepdale ground on 10 December.

* The three FA Cup matches between Birmingham City and Spurs in 1953 drew an aggregate attendance figure of 162,692 (average 54,321).

* During the Second World War, the biggest attendance at White Hart Lane for a Spurs home game was 44,510 v. Arsenal (League South) on 16.2.1946.

* The lowest senior competitive crowd at White Hart Lane since the Second World War has been 6,200 v Swansea Town 27 January 1947.

* The lowest in recent times has been 7,548 v. Everton in the Screen Sport Super Cup on 5 February 1986.

* The attendance figure of just 9,574 versus Birmingham City on 16 April 1986 was the lowest for a League game (Divisions 1 & 2) at White Hart Lane since 1947.

* The record attendance at Gresty Road, Crewe was set on 30 January 1960 when Spurs were the visitors for a 3rd round FA Cup tie. That day the official turnout was 19,897.

* The biggest crowd to assemble at Derby County's former home (The Baseball Ground) was 41,826 for a First Division game v. Spurs on 20 September 1969.

* Leicester City's Filbert Street housed a record crowd of 47,298 when Spurs visited there for a 5th round FA Cup tie on 18 February 1928.

* The 3rd round FA Cup encounter between Halifax Town and Spurs on 15 February 1953 drew a record crowd to The Shay of 36,885.

* Before redevelopment, the record crowd at Upton Park was 42,322 for the West Ham United v. Spurs First Division game on 17 October 1970.

* A crowd of 67,583 witnessed Spurs' game versus Manchester United at Old Trafford on 2 December 2000. This was the biggest attendance for a Spurs fixture in the Premiership and the club's biggest League audience for 67 years - since the 67,650 gate at Goodison Park on 26 October 1963.

* The last 50,000 plus crowd to assemble at The Hawthorns was for the 5th round FA Cup -tie between West Brom and Spurs in February 1962.

AUSTIN, DEAN BARRY

Right-back Dean Austin started his career with Southend United in March 1990. He played in more than 100 games for the Shrimpers before moving to White Hart Lane for £375,000 in June 1992. Over the next six seasons he appeared in exactly 150

first-class matches for Spurs. He chose to remain in London when, in July 1998, he switched across the city to Crystal Palace and in 2001 he took his overall appearance tally in senior football to past the 350 mark. Austin was born in Hemel Hempstead in April 1970.

AUSTRIA (FK)

Spurs have yet to meet the Austrian club in an official competition. A crowd of 30,000 attended White Hart Lane in May 1951 to see the Austrians win a hard-fought contest by a goal to nil in a Festival of Britain tournament.

Spurs and FC Austria drew 2-2 in Brussels in March 1952 (Len Duquemin and Les Bennett the scorers).

Just over three years later, in May 1955, Spurs were beaten 6-2 in a friendly tour match by FC Austria in Vienna. Duquemin scored both Spurs goals on this occasion.

The Austrians were the second team to play a friendly game against Spurs under the White Hart Lane floodlights. They lost 3-2 on 28 October 1953 and the 'Duke' scored again!

The last meeting between the two clubs was also in the form of a friendly, in Austria in August 1968. It ended level at 2-2.

A mixed Rapid/FCAustria XI beat Spurs 3-0 in a tour game in Vienna in May 1980.

AUSTRIA VIENNA

Spurs playing record against the Austrian side:

Competition	P	W	D	L	F	A
UEFA Cup	2	1	1	0	4	2

Spurs met Austria Vienna over two legs in the fourth round of the UEFA Cup in 1983-84.

The first game was staged at White Hart Lane on 7 March and in front of 34,069 fans Spurs gained an important 2-0 advantage with goals by Steve Archibald and Alan Brazil.

Two weeks later in Vienna, 21,000 spectators saw Ossie Ardiles and Brazil score a goal apiece to earn Spurs a 2-2 draw to confirm an overall victory of 4-2 on aggregate.

AWAY FROM HOME

(See also under Defeats and Wins & Overseas Matches & Tours & Friendlies etc)

Spurs won 16 of their 21 away League games in their 'double-winning' season of 1960-61. They scored 50 goals in the process. In contrast, Spurs registered only one win on the road in their League campaigns of 1909-10, 1914-15, 1928-29 and 1964-65.

Spurs have never won a League game on the grounds of the following clubs: Carlisle United, Doncaster Rovers, Glossop, Leeds City, Lincoln City, Mansfield Town, Rotherham United and Swindon Town.

Spurs have not lost a League game at Bristol Rovers, Gainsborough Trinity, Glossop, (Leyton) Orient, Lincoln City, Mansfield Town, Newport County, Northampton Town, Oxford United, Rotherham United, South Shields and Tranmere Rovers.

B

AARDSEN, ESPEN

Born to Norwegian parents in San Rafael, USA, on 7 December 1977, goalkeeper Epsen Baardsen gained one Under-18 cap for the USA before being rewarded with Under-21 and full caps for

Norway. A player with the San Francisco All Blacks, he joined Spurs in July 1996 as understudy to Ian Walker and in the games he played he looked confident, was calm under pressure, capable of becoming a quality 'keeper in the highest grade of football. Unfortunately he was allowed top leave White Hart Lane in the summer of 2000 when Neil Sullivan was lined up to move across from Wimbledon. Baardsen went to Watford with team-mate Allan Nielsen in a £2.5 million deal. He made 29 senior appearances for Spurs.

BADENOCH, GEORGE HUNTLY

Outside-right George Badenoch played twice for Spurs in 1906-07. Signed from Watford, having previously been with Hearts and Glossop, he joined Northampton Town on leaving the club. He was killed serving in France in 1915, aged 33.

BADGE & SHIELD

The official Spurs club badge was first seen in 1956, and depicts the environment of Tottenham Hotspur Football Club. The top left-hand corner of the badge shows the 16th century Bruce Castle. Today the same building houses the local history and archive collection belonging to the London Borough of Haringey. Top right are the seven trees, planted at Page Green by the seven sisters of Tottenham, hence the London district of Seven Sisters. It was back in 1909 when the cockerel and ball first appeared. A former Spurs player, W Scott, is believed to have cast a copper centrepiece to perch on the new West Stand at White Hart Lane. The design of the two lions is taken from the official crest of the Northumberland family (from the area surrounding Tottenham). Indeed, the said family lived at the Black House - later called Percy House - which was situtated on the High Road, oppositie to White Hart Lane. It is quite feasible that the Northumberland family hold the key to the club being called Hotspur. (See under Hotspur). The club's motto 'Audere-Est-Facere' is a Latin inscription meaning 'To Dare Is To Do'..or 'unless you try you will never achieve!' The badge - depicting the two lions, the cockerel and ball, the castle and motto - was first introduced as recently as 1983 and was updated in 1992 in readiness for the new Premier League. The motif returned to the players' shirts for the 1999-2000 season.... for two years prior to that the full crest had appeared on the club's official kit.

BADGER, HERBERT OSBORNE

A 1904-05 guest from Ilford, amateur centre-half/centre-forward Bert Badger netted three goals in nine games for Spurs before going on to assist Watford and Brentford.

BAILY, EDWARD FRANCIS

Inside-left Eddie Baily appeared in 296 League games for Spurs and in 381 first team matches overall (including friendlies). He scored 90 goals (69 in League and Cup).

Nicknamed 'The Cheeky Chappie', he was born in the East End of London on 6 August 1925 and represented Hackney and Middlesex Schools and Tottenham Juniors before signing for Finchley. He then registered as an amateur with Spurs and also for Chelsea before returning to White Hart Lane in February 1946,

Eddie Baily (far right) with the Division 1 Championship trophy of 1950-51

finally taking professional status in October of that year. He made his League debut in January 1947 in a 2-0 home win over West Bromwich Albion in front of more than 40,000 spectators and his second outing followed ten months later v. Brentford. But thereafter he became a star performer in Spurs' 'push and run' team, gaining successive Second Division and First championship medals in 1950 and 1951 when he partnered Les Medley on the left-flank.

A positive little player, always seeking to create openings for his colleagues, he won three England 'B' caps, appeared in nine full internationals (his debut coming in the heat of Rio De Janeiro against Spain in the 1950 World Cup Finals). He also represented the Rest of the UK against Wales, played for the Football League on five occasions and in 1957 starred in the eve of Cup Final encounter for England against Young England.

In January 1956 Baily moved from Spurs to Port Vale for a record fee, for the Potteries club, of £7,000. Nine months later he switched to Nottingham Forest, also for £7,000 (sold because he was too much of an individualist) and in December 1958 he teamed up with Leyton Orient as player-coach. He returned to White Hart Lane as coach and assistant to manager Bill Nicholson (a former playing colleague) in October 1963.

Later Baily acted as scout for West Ham United and was also England's regional scout in the south.

* Baily was reported 'missing' during the War while serving with the Royal Scots Fusiliers. Spurs, on hearing the news, did not re-register him as a player.....until he walked into White Hart Lane to show his face!

BAKER, PETER RUSSELL BARKER

Right-back Peter Baker made 342 senior appearances for Spurs between April 1953 and March 1965. A key member of the double-winning side, he won a second FA Cup medal in 1962 and added a European Cup-winners Cup medal to his tally in 1963. He formed a fine partnership with Ron Henry and linked up superbly with right-half Danny Blanchflower. A strong player, Baker was born in Hampstead, London on 10 December 1931. An England Youth international, he joined Spurs from Enfield in June 1949, turned 'pro' a year later and established himself in the first XI in 1956-57. In May 1965 his contract with Spurs was cancelled and he moved to South Africa where he joined Durban City. He later managed that club before taking a coaching positon with Abbinton FC (also in South Africa).

BANKS, JAMES ANDREW

Jimmy Banks was born deep in Rugby League territory at Wigan on 28 April 1893. He played for four intermediate clubs before joining Spurs as an inside or centre-forward in December 1913. He made his debut the following February but didn't really establish himself in the first XI until during the Great War - and then two years after the hostilities he was turned into a purposeful outside-right. Banks, who helped Spurs win the Second Division championship in 1920 and FA Cup twelve months later, went on to score 90 goals in more than 200 first team matches, but only ten in 78 in League and FA Cup encounters. In September 1923, after spending almost 10 years at White Hart Lane, he was transferred to Norwich City and after assisting Luton Town (1927-29), he became player-coach of the London Public Omnibus football team, later taking a coaching position with Worthing Town (1938-40). Banks died in Chelsea on 25 August 1942.

BANN, WILLIAM EDWARD

Full-back Bill Bann, a native of West Lothian, joined Spurs in 1923 and spent seven years with the club, making only 12 League appearances before moving to Brentford. He later played for Bristol Rovers and Aldershot.

BARCELONA (CF)

Spurs playing record against the Spanish side:

Competition	P	W	D	L	F	A
European Cup	2	0	1	1	1	2

Spurs met the Spanish club over two legs in the semi-final of the 1981-82 European Cup-winners Cup competition, but after two dogged battles they went out 2-1 on aggregate.

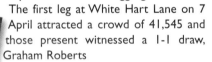

The first leg at White Hart Lane on 7 April attracted a crowd of 41,545 and those present witnessed a 1-1 draw, Graham Roberts scoring for Spurs. Then, a fortnight later, 80,000 fans assembled inside the Nou Camp Stadium to see Barcelona win 1-0 to end Spurs' hopes of another European Final.

Players with both clubs include: Steve Archibald, Gary Lineker, Nayim.

Also associated:
Vic Buckingham (Spurs player, Barcelona manager), Terry Venables (Spurs player & manager, Barcelona manager/coach), Allan Harris (assistant-manager both clubs).

Harry Lowe was a Spurs player and coach, who also coached the Barcelona side Deportivo Espanol.

BARKING

Spurs playing record against Barking:

Competition	P	W	D	L	F	A
Other Cup	2	2	0	0	6	1

Spurs' only competitive games against Barking were in a preliminary round of the London Senior Cup in November 1890 (won 2-0) and in the first round of the London FA Charity Cup in October 1920 (won 4-1).

BARLOW, JOHN

Lancashire-born inside-forward, formerly of Everton and Reading, Jack Barlow scored eight goals in 20 first-claass games for Spurs between 1901-03. He left the club for Leicester Fosse.

BARMBY, NICHOLAS JONATHAN

Born in Hull on 11 February 1974, attacking midfielder (and occasional striker) Nicky Barmby joined Spurs as a trainee in the summer of 1989 and turned professional in April 1991. Over the next four years he scored 27 goals in 108 senior appearances, winning two England caps and also reprsenting his country three times at Under-21 level having earlier played for the Schoolboy and Youth teams. His keeness and flair, anticipation and teamwork earned him praise from many fellow professionals.

Unfortunately Spurs couldn't hold on to him and in August 1995 he was transferred to Middlesbrough for £5.25 million. He only spent fifteen months at The Riverside Stadium before switching south to Everton in a £5.75 million deal in Noveember 1996. He did much better at Goodison Park and netted 24 times in 133 games for the Merseysiders before he moved across Stanley Park to neighbouring Liverpool in the summer of 2000. At this juncture he had taken his tally of England caps to 15, while also adding two at 'B' team level to his collection. At Anfield Barmby continued to prosper, collecting a handful of more caps as well as helping the Reds to a remarkable 'Cup winning treble'. When the 2000-01 season ended Barmby had amassed in excess of 300 senior appearances and more than 65 goals....and there are more to come.

BARNET

Spurs have yet to meet Barnet in League or Cup football.

Players with both clubs: Martin Chivers (player-manager of Barnet), Ross Darcy, Kevin Dearden, Willie Evans, Terry Gibson, Jimmy Greaves, Lee Hodges, John Lacy, Bill Lane, David McDonald, Billy Manuel (Spurs junior), Gerry McMahon, Destin Makumbu (Barnet trialist, Spurs junior), Stuart Nethercott, Taffy O'Callaghan, Mark Stimson, Kevin Watson, Simon Webster.

BARNETT, FREDERICK WILLIAM

A former Bolton Wanderers trialist, outside-right Fred Barnett netted once in 16 League games for Spurs between 1923-29. He also played for Northfleet, Watford and Southend.

BARNSLEY

Spurs playing record against the Tykes:

Competition	P	W	D	L	F	A
Premiership	2	1	1	0	4	1
Football League	26	13	4	9	47	34
FA Cup	3	1	1	1	3	4
League Cup	2	2	0	0	8	5

Spurs first met Barnsley in the Football League on 12 September 1908 (Division 2). They beat the Tykes 4-0 in front of 20,000 spectators.

The two Premiership matches were played in 1997-98. Over 28,000 fans saw Spurs win 3-0 at White Hart Lane and there were

18,692 spectators present at Oakwell late in the season to witness the 1-1 draw.

In this same campaign the Tykes knocked Spurs out of the FA Cup with a 3-1 win in the 4th round after visiting midfielder Stephen Clemence had been sent-off. He was only the second Spurs player to take an early bath in this competition - Joe Kinnear being the first in 1968 v. Manchester United.

David Ginola scored a quite brilliant individual goal to earn Spurs a 1-0 FA Cup win at Barnsley in 1999 to ensure them their 18th semi-final appearance.

Players with both clubs include: Danny Blanchflower, John Collins, Tom Forman, Phil Gray, Bob Hewitson, Bert Hodgkinson, Doug Hunt, Fred Mearns, Ian Moores, Joe Scott, Andrew Swan, David Tuttle, Alex Wright.

Wartime guests (with either one or both clubs): Joe Davis, George Travers

Also associated: Jim Iley (Spurs player, Tykes manager)

BARROW

No match action between Spurs and the ex-Football League club from Cumbria.

Player with both clubs: Tony Parks.

Wartime guest player: Fred Hall (with Spurs).

Also associated: Ben Ives (Barrow player, Spurs assistant-trainer & chief scout).

BARTON, KENNETH REES

Welsh Schoolboy international from Caernarvon, full-back Ken Barton was handed four League outings by Spurs in the 1960s. He later assisted Millwall and Luton Town.

BAUCHOP, JAMES RAE

Scottish inside-forward, previously with Alloa, Celtic, Norwich City, Crystal Palace and Derby County, inside-forward Jimmy Bauchop joined Spurs in 1913 and scored six goals in 10 League games for the club before moving to Bradford Park Avenue. After the Great War he played for Doncaster Rovers and Lincoln City.

BAYERN MUNICH

Spurs' European record against the German side:

Competition	P	W	D	L	F	A
ECW Cup	2	0	1	1	2	5
UEFA Cup	2	1	0	1	2	1
Summary	4	1	1	2	4	6

Spurs were knocked out of the 1982-83 European Cup-winners Cup by the German Bundesliga side Bayern Munich, who comfortably won a second round tie 5-2 on aggregate.

The first leg at White Hart Lane on 20 October ended 1-1 in front of 36,488 spectators, Steve Archibald scoring for Spurs. But then a fortnight later inside the Olympic Stadium in Munich, the second leg belonged exclusively to the Bundesliga side who ran out convincing 4-1 winners in front of 55,000 fans, Chris Hughton netting the Spurs goal.

The following season, however, it was Spurs who took the honours, eliminating the German outfit in the third round of the UEFA Cup .

After losing the first leg 0-1 in Munich on 23 November when only 20,000 fans were present, Spurs triumphed 2-0 at White Hart Lane a fortnight later, Steve Archibald and Mark Falco scoring the vital goals in front of 41,977 spectators.

Players with both clubs: Jurgen Klinsmann, Allan Nielsen, Christian Ziege

BEAL, PHILIP

Defender Phil Beal spent fifteen years at White Hart Lane. He joined Spurs as an amateur in May 1960, turned professional in January 1962 and eventually moved on in July 1975 to Brighton & Hove Albion. He appeared in 483 first team matches for the club, including 333 in the Football League, 30 in the FA Cup, 27 in the League Cup and 30 in European competitions.

Born in Godstone, Surrey on 8 January 1945, he had represented Surrey Schools before being recruited by Spurs. An England Youth international, he made his first team debut in September 1963 and gained a regular place in the side halfway through the 1965-66 season but was then struck down by an injury which resulted in him missing the 1967 FA Cup Final victory over Chelsea. He bounced back, however, and went on to gain two League Cup winning medals and played in two UEFA Cup Finals in 1972 and 1974, picking up a winners' prize in the former.

He was at Hove for two years and then after a brief sojourn in the NASL with Memphis Rogues he signed as a non-contract player with Crewe Alexandra in August 1978, finally retiring from first-class football at the end of that season.

BEAVON, MICHAEL STUART

Reserve midfielder from Wolverhampton, Stuart Beavon was associated with Spurs for five years: 1975-80. He made five first-class appearances before moving to Reading, later assisting Northampton Town. He also played on loan for Notts County

BEDMINSTER

Spurs' playing record against Bedminster:

Competition	P	W	D	L	F	A
Southern League	4	1	1	2	7	6

Spurs' only Southern League win over Bedminster came in February 1900 when they triumphed 5-1 at home, Tom Pratt (3) and John Kirwan (2) scoring the goals in front of 7,000 spectators.

BEESTON

Spurs' playing record against Beeston:

Competition	P	W	D	L	F	A
Amateur Cup	1	1	0	0	2	0

Goals by Bill Julian and Peter Hunter gave Spurs a comfortable win over Beeston in the first round of the FA Amateur Cup in February 1895.

BELL, SAMUEL

Scorer of six goals in 16 games for the club (1935-37) inside-forward Sam Bell also played for Norwich City and Luton (before Spurs) and Southend and Millwall afterwards.

BELLAMY, WALTER RICHARD

Walter Bellamy was an all-action winger who loved to run at his opponent. He joined Spurs in February 1927, having previously played Amateur football with Leysian Mission, Tufnell Park and Dulwich Hamlet, while also starring in representative matches for the FA, Middlesex and Isthmian XIs.

He played for the Amateurs side v. the Professionals in both the 1925 and 1927 FA Charity Shield matches and had also gained a cluster of Amateur Caps for England. After making his debut for Spurs in the 1926 London Charity Cup defeat by Millwall he had to wait seven months before appearing in his first League match, on the left-wing against Liverpool. He went on to make 84 appearances for the club, scoring 11 goals, nine of them coming in 70 League games. Released in May 1935, he signed for Brighton & Hove Albion and during the Second World War he assisted New

Camp FC in Gibraltar. He did not figure after 1945. Bellamy was born in Tottenham on 6 November 1904 and died in Hertfordshire on 19 October 1978.

BENEFIT, CHARITY & TESTIMONIAL MATCHES

Here are details of the various benefit, charity, testimonial & memorial matches featuring a Spurs side over the years:

1898-99
Spurs 2 New Brompton 1   (Billy Joyce)

1899-1900
Spurs 4 Players of South 1   (John L Jones &
                                            Bob Stormont)
Thames Ironworks 0 Spurs 3   (Harry Bradshaw's family)

1900-01
Spurs 2 Millwall Athletic 1   (Tom Smith &
                                            Jim McNaught)
Spurs 4 CW Brown's XI 2   (Jack Oliver)

1903-04
Spurs 3 QPR 0 (Western League)   (Harry Erentz)

1904-05
Spurs 2 Plymouth Argyle 0   (Ted Hughes, Tom Morris)
Spurs 1 West Ham 0   (David Copeland,
                                            John Kirwan)
Spurs 2 George Robey's XI 1   (John 'Bristol' Jones'
                                            Dependants)

1906-07
Spurs 1901 XI 1 Team of South 4   (For trainer Sam Mountford)

1907-08
Spurs 2 West Ham 1   (John Watson)

1920-21
Spurs 5 Chelsea 0 (F/League)   (Bert Bliss, Jimmy Cantrell,
                                            Jimmy Dimmock)

1938-39
Millwall 3 Spurs 0   (John Joyce)

1945-46
Spurs 4 FA XI 1   (Willie Hall)

1948-49
Chelmsford City 1 Spurs 5   (Fred Sargent)

1964-65
Spurs 2 Scotland XI 6   (John White memorial)

1972-73
Spurs 2 Feyenoord 1   (Jimmy Greaves)

1973-74
Spurs 2 Bayern Munich 2   (Phil Beal)

1974-75
Spurs 2 Red Star Belgrade 0   (Alan Gilzean)

1975-76
Spurs 2 Arsenal 2   (Cyril Knowles)
Brighton & HA 1 Spurs 6   (Joe Kinnear)

1976-77
Spurs 3 Arsenal 2   (Pat Jennings)

1977-78
Spurs 3 Arsenal 5   (John Pratt)

1978-79
Spurs 2 West Ham United 2   (Steve Perryman)
Wolves 2 Spurs 1   (John McAlle)

1979-80
Spurs 0 Crystal Palace 2   (Terry Naylor)

1980-81
Spurs 2 West Ham United 3   (Barry Daines)

1981-82
Luton Town 2 Spurs 2   (Paul Price)

1983-84
Spurs 1 West Ham United 1   (Bill Nicholson)
Spurs 2 England XI 2   (Keith Burkinshaw)

1984-85
Spurs 3 Fulham 1   (Peter Southey Memorial)
Arsenal 2 Spurs 3   (Pat Jennings)

1985-86
Spurs 1 Arsenal 1   (Glenn Hoddle)
Spurs 2 Inter Milan 1   (Ossie Ardiles)

1986-87
Spurs 1 Glasgow Rangers 1   (Paul Miller)

1987-88
Spurs 2 West Ham United 2   (Tony Galvin)
Spurs 3 Arsenal 1   (Chris Hughton)
Spurs 2 Manchester United 3   (Danny Thomas)
West Brom Albion 4 Spurs 1   (Mick Brown)

1988-89
Dundee United 1 Spurs 1   (David Narey)
Reading 2 Spurs 1   (Martin Hicks)
Chelsea 0 Spurs 0   (Colin Pates)
West Ham United 2 Spurs 0   (Alvin Martin)
Swansea City 0 Spurs 3   (Michael Hughes)
Charlton Athletic 4 Spurs 3   (Steve Gritt)

1989-90
Leicester City 2 Spurs 5   (Paul Ramsey)
Plymouth Argyle 0 Spurs 3   (Geoff Crudgington)
Brighton & HA 0 Spurs 3   (Graham Moseley)
Spurs 2 Northern Ireland XI 1   (Danny Blanchflower)

1990-91
Spurs 4 West Ham United 1   (Ray Clemence)
Arsenal 2 Spurs 5   (Graham Rix)
West Ham United 4 Spurs 3   (Billy Bonds)

1991-92
Cardiff City 0 Spurs 2   (Harry Parsons)
Hull City 2 Spurs 6   (Garreth Roberts)
Spurs '92 XI 2 Spurs '82 XI 2   (Cyril Knowles Memorial)

1992-93
Crystal Palace 3 Spurs 3   (Malcolm Allison)
Enfield 1 Spurs 5   (Eddie Baily)
Swansea City 3 Spurs 3   (Harold Woollacott)

1993-94
Hartlepool Utd 1 Spurs 3   (Cyril Knowles tribute)
Brentford 0 Spurs 0   (Keith Millen)
Lyn Oslo 0 Spurs 0   (Tom Sundby)

1994-95
AFC Bournemouth 0 Spurs 5   (Richard Cooke)

1995-96
Spurs 0 Newcastle United 2   (Gary Mabbutt)

1996-97
Charlton Athletic 1 Spurs 3   (Colin Walsh)

1997-98
Spurs 0 Fiorentina 2   (David Howells)

1999-2000
Portsmouth 4 Spurs 2   (Justin Edinburgh)

2000-01
Fulham 0 Spurs 0   (Simon Morgan)
QPR 0 Spurs 2   (Danny Maddix)

2001-02
Leyton Orient 0 Spurs2   (Steve Castle)
Millwall 1 Spurs 2   (Keith Stevens)
Spurs 3 Fiorentina 0   (Bill Nicholson)

Benefit Countdown
Billy Joyce (v. New Brompton, October 1898), Harry Erentz (v. QPR, October 1903), Ted Hughes/Tom Morris (v. Plymouth Argyle, September 1904), David Copeland/John Kirwan (v. West Ham United, January 1905), John Watson (West Ham United, October 1907) and Bert Bliss/Jimmy Cantrell/Jimmy Dimmock (v. October 1920) all chose League games (in various competitions) for their benefit matches - and the players concerned received the gate receipts (or a share of same).

Bob Stormont and John L Jones shared their benefit match in 1899, likewise Jim McNaught and Tom Smith (1900).

Glenn Hoddle, Pat Jennings (1976 & 1985), Cyril Knowles and John Pratt all had their testimonials against Arsenal.

A crowd of 45,799 attended Jimmy Greaves' testimonial match against Feyenoord in October 1972. Spurs won 2-1, Greaves scoring the winner!

Gary Mabbutt's testimonial match (Spurs v. Newcastle United in August 1996) attracted 17,288 fans to White Hart Lane, but United spoilt the party, winning 2-0.

Fiorentina visited White Hart Lane for David Howells' testimonial match in August 1997 - a crowd of 14,605 saw the Italian side win 2-0.

A crowd of 35,877 saw Les Ferdinand, Gus Poyet and Steffen Iversen scored the goals as Spurs beat Fiorentina in Bill Nicholson's second testimonial match on 8 August 2001.

Spurs have also taken part in several charity & fund-raising matches over the years, and here are some of the many fixtures fulfilled:

May 1919	Spurs 2 Fulham 2	(National War Fund)
Sep 1919	Arsenal 0 Spurs 1	(LPF Charity Fund)
Oct 1920	Spurs 2 Arsenal 0	(LPF Charity Fund)
Sep 1921	West Ham 1 Spurs 0	(LPF Charity Fund)
Oct 1922	Spurs 2 West Ham 1	(LPF Charity Fund)
Oct 1923	Spurs 1 Clapton O. 3	(LPF Charity Fund)
Nov 1924	Clapton O. 2 Spurs 1	(LPF Charity Fund)
Nov 1925	Spurs 1 QPR 0	(LPF Charity Fund)
Nov 1926	Clapton O.1 Spurs 3	(LPF Charity Fund)
Nov 1927	Spurs 4 Clapton O.3	(LPF Charity Fund)
Dec 1928	Clapton O. 2 Spurs 4	(LPF Charity Fund)
Nov 1929	Spurs 5 Crystal Pal 1	(LPF Charity Fund)
Nov 1930	Crystal Pal 2 Spurs 2	(LPF Charity Fund)
Aug 1938	Arsenal 0 Spurs 2	(Jubilee Trust Fund)
Aug 1939	Spurs 0 Arsenal 1	(Jubilee Trust Fund)
May 1947	Norwich C 0 Spurs 2	(Hospital Charity Cup)
May 1950	Norwich C 2 Spurs 2	(Hospital Charity Cup)
May 1952	Ipswich T 2 Spurs 2	(Hospital Charity Cup)
Aug 1964	Celtic 4 Spurs 2	(Glasgow Charity Cup)*

Key: LPF - London Professional Footballers'
*Game played at Hampden Park in front of 58,768 spectators.
The gate receipts from each of the FA Charity Shield matches involving Spurs were all in respect of various named charities.

BENFICA
Spurs' playing record against the Portuguese side:

Competition	P	W	D	L	F	A
European Cup	2	1	0	1	3	4

Spurs met the Portuguese side in the two-legged semi-final of the 1961-62 European Cup.

The first leg was played in Lisbon on 21 March and in front of 70,000 spectators, ended in a 3-1 win for Benfica, Bobby Smith netting Spurs' consolation goal.

Anticipating a Spurs 'fight back', the attendance for the second leg at White Hart Lane on 5 April, was 64,448 - the biggest turnout on record for a Spurs European home fixture. But despite a gallant effort in winning 2-1, Spurs failed to overturn the two-goal deficit and went out 4-3 on aggregate. Skipper Danny Blanchflower (penalty) and Bobby Smith scored for Spurs.
Player with both clubs: Jose Dominguez

BENNETT, LESLIE DONALD
Inside-right Les Bennett made 377 first team appearances for Spurs, 272 of which came in the Football League. He scored 170 goals, 104 at League level.

A Londoner and Wartime baby, born in Wood Green on 10 January 1918, he represented both London and Middlesex Schools before joining Spurs via Tottenham Juniors and Northfleet in May 1939. During the Second World War he guested for Distillery, Millwall and Torquay United while also serving Spurs in 25 League South and Cup matches.

Tall, upright with a galloping stride, he was a vital cog in the

mechanism of Arthur Rowe's 'Push and Run' Spurs side during the late 1940s, early '50s. He made goals aplenty for his colleagues as well as scoring his fair share himself. He was top-scorer for Spurs in three of his eight with the club and contributed greatly with 14 goals when the Second Division championship was won in 1950, and he did his bit the following year when Spurs won the First Division crown.

In December 1954 he left White Hart Lane for West Ham United and after skippering the Hammers for a short while he linked up with Romford before becoming player-manager of Clacton Town in July 1956. Bennett died in London on 29 April 1999.

BENTLEY, FRANK WILLIAM

Half-back Frank Bentley, strong and resilient, made exactly 50 first team appearances for Spurs between October 1908 and August 1912. Born in Butt Lane, Staffordshire on 9 October 1886, he played for his local club and Stoke (five outings) before moving south to Spurs in readiness for the 1908-09 season. He struggled at times to hold down a position in the side and in the end was transferred to Brentford where he stayed two seasons before returning to the Potteries. Bentley died in Stoke-on-Trent in October 1958.

BERGSSON, GUDNI

Icelandic international defender Gudni Bergsson celebrated his 36th birthday two months prematurely by leading Bolton Wanderers back into the Premiership via the First Division Play-offs in May 2001..

Born in Reykjavik, Iceland on 21 July 1965, he played for FC Valur with whom he won both domestic League and Cup honours in 1987 and 1988 respectively. Before that he was an unsuccessful trialist with Aston Villa (in 1985) and had served a loan spell with the German Bundesliga side TSV 1860 Munich (March 1988). He joined Spurs, initially on trial in November 1988 while attending Reykjavik University. He impressed during the next three months and was duly signed as a full-time professional by the club in February 1989.

Making rapid progress, he won his first Icelandic cap (and 25th in total) as a Spurs player v. England 'B' in May 1989. He has now appeared in 77 internationals for his country as well as making in excess of 325 club appearances in England alone.

Known as the 'Iceman', his reading of the game and his positional sense are second to none and he often comes up with a vital goal or two (certainly with Bolton).

Handed 87 outings by Spurs (two goals scored) he was subsequently transferred to Bolton for £115,000 in March 1995. Two years later he won a First Division championship medal but then suffered the anguish of being relegated at the first attempt from the Premiership only to return to the top flight four years later as Bolton's skipper.

BERRY, FRANK

Winger Frank Berry played in two first-class games for Spurs in season 1900-01.

BERRY, WILLIAM ALEXANDER

Centre-forward Bill Berry scored 13 goals in 38 games for Spurs before joining Manchester United in 1906, later serving Stockport County.

BERTI, NICOLA

Capped 39 times by Italy (three goals) central midfielder Nicola Berti (6ft 1in tall and over 12 stone in weight) joined Spurs initially on a six-month loan deal from Inter Milan in January 1998.

After helping the team successfully stave off the threat of relegation, he made the move permanent in August, but following the arrival of manager George Graham (October 1998) Berti became surplus to requirements at White Hart Lane. After making just 23 senior appearances for the club (two goals scored) he moved to the Spanish club Deportivo Alaves in January 1999.

Born in Parma, Italy on 14 April 1967, he had played for Parma and Fiorentina in Serie 'A' before moving to Inter where he became a firm favourite with the fans.

BING, THOMAS EDWARD

Former Margate winger, Tom Bing made one League appearance for Spurs v. Bolton in 1957. He returned to the Kent club in 1959.

BIRMINGHAM CITY

Spurs' playing record against Blues:

Competition	P	W	D	L	F	A
Football League	68	33	12	23	110	76
'39-40 League	1	0	1	0	1	1
FA Cup	10	4	5	1	21	12
League Cup	2	1	0	1	6	3
Wartime	2	0	0	2	0	9
Summary	83	38	18	27	138	101

The first League game between the two clubs took place at White Hart Lane on 14 November 1908 (Division 2). Spurs won 4-0 in front of 25,000 spectators. The return fixture that season ended in a 3-3 draw.

Jimmy Cantrell made his final appearance for Spurs in the 2-0 home win over Blues in April 1923.

Spurs' first League game after World War Two was against Blues at White Hart Lane on 31 August 1946. A crowd of 51,256 saw the visitors record a 2-1 victory, George Foreman netting Spurs' consolation goal.

On 1 May 1948, Johnny Jordan played his first Football League game for Spurs in the goalless draw with Blues. In August 1948 he left White Hart Lane for Juventus and later moved to St Andrew's (March 1949).

Spurs ran up their 200th First Division draw when sharing the spoils at 0-0 with Blues on 1 December 1956

Alf Stokes was the star performer against Blues on a warm September evening in 1957. He scored five times in Spurs' 7-1

Blues keeper Colin Withers (on his debut) sticks out a leg to thwart Dave Mackay at White Hart Lane Div 1, November 1960. Spurs won 6-0!

handsome home win. Blues' keeper Gil Merrick went off with a gashed forehead when the score was 4-1 and England winger Gordon Astall took over between the posts, Merrick returning to hug the right-hand touchline!

Spurs' sixth goal in this victory was, in fact, their 1,500th in League football.

In season 1958-59, Blues made up for that seven-goal mauling by doubling-up over Spurs - winning 4-0 at White Hart Lane and 5-1 at St Andrew's.

In the game in London, full-back Peter Baker replaced John Hollowbread in the Spurs goal for the second-half and in clash at St Andrew's Jim Iley made a rather innocuous debut for Spurs!

When the double was won in 1960-61, Spurs beat Blues 6-0 at White Hart Lane and 3-2 at St Andrew's.

Spurs doubled-up again over Blues in 1963-64, winning 6-1 at home in early October (Jimmy Greaves 3) and then 2-1 at St Andrew's at the end of February. That win, in October, brought Spurs their 2,000th Football League point.

When losing 3-1 at Blues on 17 April 1976, Spurs conceded their 2,000th away goal in the Football League.

A meagre White Hart Lane crowd of just 9,359 saw Spurs beat Blues 2-0 in April 1986. A month earlier, only 9,394 fans had seen Spurs win 2-1 at St Andrew's.

Spurs were well and truly hammered 8-0 by Blues in a Football League South game at St Andrew's in October 1946.

Players with both clubs include: Arthur Archer, David Brown (Spurs & Blues trialist), Bob Cain, John Cheeswright (Spurs YTS), Richard Cooke, Kevin Dearden, Jose Dominguez, Jack Elkes, Ian Hendon, Danny Hill, John Jones, Johnny Jordan, Peter Murphy, Gary O'Reilly, Gary Poole (Spurs junior & reserve), Vinny Samways, Pat Van den Hauwe, Tony Want.

Wartime guests (with either one or both clubs): Jack Acquroff, Percy Barton, Pat Beasley (also co-manager of Blues), Sammy Brooks, Ted Ditchburn, Ray Ferris, Billy Hughes, Bob Iverson,

Birmingham's goalkeeper Merrick clears from Duquemin of Spurs

Jimmy McCormick, Jackie Martin, Sid Ottewell, Tommy Pearson, Charlie Revell.

Also associated: Dave Mackay and Sir Alf Ramsey (Spurs players, Blues managers, Ramsey also Blues director), Len Thompson (Blues player, Spurs reserve team manager), Ernie Hoffman (Blues scout, Spurs WW1), George Travers (WW1, both clubs).

BIRNIE, EDWARD LAWSON

Half-back Ted Birnie played for Newcastle United, Crystal Palace and Chelsea before joining Spurs in 1910. After scoring once in four League games for the club he became player-coach-secretary of the German team Mulheim in 1911. Later he played for Rochdale, was coach at Sunderland and managed Southend United (1921-34) before returning to Germany.

BLACK, DAVID GIBSON

Born in Hurlford, Ayrshire on 22 January 1870, David Black played his early football for his home town club, Hurlford and in 1889 was transferred to Grimsby Town. Two years later he switched to Middlesbrough and moved south to Wolverhampton Wanderers in July 1893. He was already a Scottish international when he arrived at Molineux, having gained, what was to be his only cap, four years earlier against Ireland.

Able to play at inside or outside-left, he was a small but strong runner, good on the ball who was perhaps too greedy at times, but nonetheless was quite a handful for his opponents.

Ten months after scoring for Wolves in the 1896 FA Cup Final defeat by Sheffield Wednesday, Black left the club for Burnley from where he switched to Spurs in May 1897. He did very well in both the Southern and Western Leagues, scoring almost a goal every two games, ending up with 25 in 56 first team appearances for Spurs before moving on to neighbouring Woolwich Arsenal in May 1898. He ended his career in Scotland with Clyde, retiring in the summer of 1900. Black died in Wolverhampton on 14 December 1951, aged 83. His great grandson, Malcolm, is currently living at Bishop's Castle, near Wolverhampton.

BLACKBURN ROVERS

Spurs playing record against the Rovers

Competition	P	W	D	L	F	A
Premiership	14	6	2	6	19	16
Football League	60	28	11	21	117	95
FA Cup	9	2	4	3	11	15
League Cup	3	2	1	0	3	1
Summary	86	38	18	30	150	127

It took Spurs three attempts to knock Rovers out of the FA Cup in 1906-07. Following successive 1-1 draws, the second after extra-time, the third encounter was staged at Villa Park where Spurs triumphed 2-1.

The first League meeting between the two clubs attracted a crowd of 15,000 to Ewood Park on 1 January 1910 (Division 1). Spurs, though, failed to produce the goods and lost by a goal to nil.

The return game at White Hart Lane in March 1910 ended in a romping 4-0 win for Spurs and Billy Minter had the pleasure of scoring the club's first League hat-trick.

Spurs suffered their first six-goal defeat in the Football League when losing 6-1 at Blackburn in September 1912.

When Spurs beat Rovers 1-0 at home in April 1935 it brought to an end a club record run of 16 League games without a win.

Les Miller scored four goals when Spurs beat Rovers 5-1 in a home Second Division match on 28 December 1936. This win completed the double over the Lancastrians who had been beaten

4-0 at Ewood Park three days earlier.

Spurs lost 5-0 at Blackburn in August 1958 - their third League defeat on the trot.

On their way to the 1960 FA Cup Final showdown with Wolves, Rovers beat Spurs 3-1 at White Hart Lane in round 5.

When Spurs completed the double in 1960-61, they won both League games v. Blackburn: 4-1 away and 5-2 at home.

Spurs lost 3-0 at Ewood Park on 20 May 1963 and then succumbed to a 7-2 defeat on the same pitch four months later. However, some pride was restored when Rovers lost 4-1 at White Hart Lane in January 1964.

On New Year's Eve 1977 Spurs beat Rovers 4-0 in a Second Division game at White Hart Lane. Colin Lee scored twice. Earlier in the season the game at Ewood Park had finished goalless.

Players with both clubs include: Bill Almond, Steve Archibald, Ossie Ardiles, Noel Brotherston, George Crompton, Ronnie Dix, Mike England, Ted Harper (also Rovers coach), Archie Hughes, John 'Tiny' Joyce, Bobby Mimms, Tim Sherwood.

Wartime guests (with either of both clubs): Fred Hall, Jack Hall, Harry Jackson, Bill McIvor, Sid Ottewell, Tommy Pearson, Bob Pryde.

Also associated: Jim Iley & Graeme Souness (Spurs players, Rovers managers), Joe Hulme & Percy Smith (Rovers players, Spurs managers), Jesse Carver (Spurs coach, Rovers player).

BLACKPOOL

Spurs playing record against the Seasiders:

Competition	P	W	D	L	F	A
Football League	50	26	13	11	103	63
FA Cup	5	2	1	2	10	7
League Cup	1	1	0	0	2	0
Summary	56	29	14	13	115	70

The first League encounter between the two clubs was played at Blackpool on 10 October 1908 (Division 2) and in front of 6,000 fans it ended all-square at 1-1.

Ted Harper netted a hat-trick when Spurs beat the Seasiders 6-1 in a home Second Division match in January 1930.

The 1947-48 FA Cup semi-final between Spurs and Blackpool at Villa Park, which drew a crowd of over 70,000, went into extra-time before the Seasiders won 3-1.

Five years later, in this same competition, the Seasiders, Stanley Matthews included, again knocked Spurs out at the semi-final stage, winning 2-1 at Villa Park. Blackpool went on to beat Bolton 4-3 in a classic Final.

Spurs centre-forward Len Duquemin scored in both of those semi-final encounters.

Spurs had beaten Blackpool 4-0 in a home League game in October 1952 (Eddie Baily scored twice) but had lost the return 2-0 at Bloomfield Road only a fortnight before the semi-final encounter.

Jimmy Greaves' hat-trick helped Spurs to a 5-2 home win over the 'Pool in December 1961 - this after the Seasiders had been beaten 2-1 at Bloomfield Road earlier in the season.

In September 1963, a week after losing 7-2 at Blackburn, Spurs returned to Lancashire and beat Blackpool 6-1 at Bloomfield Road. Jimmy Greaves grabbed a hat-trick.

Players with both clubs include: Alfie Conn, Alan Hall, Cyril Knowles ('Pool trialist), Tony Parks, Tom Pratt, Jimmy Smailes, Paul Stewart.

Wartime guests (with either one or both clubs): Davie Colquhoun, Ronnie Dix, Frank O'Donnell, Sid Hoad ('Pool Amateur), Tommy Manley, Sid Ottewell, Tommy Pearson, Charlie Revell.

Also associated: Graham Carr ('Pool manager, Spurs scout), Peter Suddaby ('Pool player, Spurs Academy Director).

BLAIR, JOHN GUTHRIE

Scottish inside-forward, born in Neilston on 23 August 1905, John Blair played for Third Lanark before joining Spurs in March 1926. He scored 16 goals in 32 first team appearances during his eighteen-month stay at White Hart Lane, which ended in November 1927 when he transferred to Sheffield United. Later he assisted non-League Fordsons (1929-30). Blair scored on his debut for Spurs against West Ham in a friendly just a few days after joining the club and did likewise when making his first appearance in the Football League v. Everton the following August. In fact, he netted nine times in his first ten League outings. Blair died in Kilmarnock on New Year's Day, 1972.

BLAKE, HERBERT EDWIN

Goalkeeper Bert Blake made 62 first team appearances for Spurs (51 in the Football League) before moving down the footballing ladder to Kettering Town in June 1925.

Born in Bristol on 26 August 1894, he played for Gloucestershire County, Bristol City, Preston North End (on trial) and Mid-Rhondda before signing for Spurs in February 1922 as added cover following the shock news of Bill Jacques' sudden illness. He made his debut two months after joining the club and held his position virtually unchallenged through to April 1923 when George Maddison took over between the posts.

He remained a virtual reserve over the next two seasons and was eventually released on a free transfer. Blake died in Bristol on 21 January 1958.

BLAKE, JOHN JOSEPH

Outside-right who scored once in three Western League games for Spurs in 1905, Joe Blake also played for Southampton up to and through the Great War.

BLANCHFLOWER, ROBERT DENNIS

Born in Belfast on 10 February 1926, Danny Blanchflower's footballing career started at Belfast Technical College in 1938. He then played, in turn, for Blossomfield United (East Belfast, 1939-44), Connsbrook (Gaelic football, 1940), RAF (while serving in Scotland), Glentoran (Amateur, December 1945, professional January 1946), Swindon Town (as a Wartime guest), Barnsley (signed for £6,000 in April 1949), Aston Villa (bought for £15,000 in March 1951) and Tottenham Hotspur (secured for £30,000 in October 1954 - becoming the most expensive half-back in the game at that time - and he almost joined Arsenal for £28,000). He retired as a League player in June 1964 but turned out for the Showbiz XI at various times and then managed Northern Ireland (from June 1976 to November 1978) and Chelsea (December 1978 to September 1979). After that he continued to be a successful sports journalist working mainly for the Sunday Express until 1988 (after first penned a column in 1964).

A very talented wing-half, he developed fast after leaving the forces and scouts came flooding into Yorkshire once he had settled in at Oakwell. On the transfer deadline of March 1951, Aston Villa boss George Martin swooped to take him to the Midlands to fill the right-half berth vacated earlier in the season by Ivor Powell. Blanchflower, cool and composed, a thinker and tremendous passer of the ball, spent three-and-a-half years at Villa Park, appearing in over 150 senior games and scoring 10 goals. He also skippered the side. Three months into the 1954-55 season, Arthur Rowe, the Spurs manager, who was in the process of strengthening his side, enticed Blanchflower to White Hart Lane for what was to prove a bargain fee of just £30,000. The Irishman, a master tactician with the ability to spot weaknesses in the opposition defence and exploit them visibly, became a member of one of the greatest midfield units in post-War football, linking up with two Scots, Jimmy White and Dave Mackay. Blanchflower - described by writer and author Julian Holland as 'a footballing cornucopia' - was twice voted 'Footballer of the Year' in 1958 and 1961, the latter after Spurs had won the coveted League and FA Cup double. He then lifted the European Cup-winners Cup in 1963 and went on to gain 50 full caps for Northern Ireland. He toured Canada with the Irish FA in 1953 (eight games played out of 10) and in 1955 represented Great Britain against the Rest of Europe. He also played for the Football League against the Irish League in October 1960 and captained London versus Basle and Barcelona in the semi-final and Final of the Inter Cities Fairs Cup in 1958. Blanchflower who had been troubled by a knee injury, retired in the summer of 1964 after appearing in 720 competitive matches as a professional (384 for Spurs - 437 in all games). After retiring he was out of the game for quite a while, but continued his love for football by becoming a journalist with the Sunday Express, displaying in his writing the same innovative, forceful and at times controversial attributes that had marked his career as a player. For two-and-a-half years he managed the Northern Ireland national team before taking charge

of Chelsea. In May 1990, Blanchflower received an honour never open to him in his playing days when Spurs met a Northern Ireland XI in a benefit match for one of their all-time greats in the club's history. Blanchflower died in Surrey on 9 December 1993.

* Blanchflower was the first player to skipper two successive FA Cup winning teams, leading Spurs in the 1961 and 1962 Finals against Leicester City and Burnley respectively.
* During the War he played rugby union, Gaelic football, soccer, hockey, cricket, golf, squash, table tennis and badminton.
* Danny's brother, Jackie, centre-half of Manchester United, was seriously injured in the Munich air disaster in 1958.

BLISS, HERBERT

Bert Bliss appeared in 315 first team games for Spurs (194 in the Football League) and scored 168 goals - an exceptionally fine record for a very useful inside or centre-forward.

Born in Willenhall, Staffordshire on 29 March 1890, he was 'missed' by Wolverhampton Wanderers while playing for Willenhall Pickwick and Willenhall Swifts and joined Spurs in April 1912, making his League debut immediately against Manchester City in front of 20,000 spectators - having played his last game for the Swifts a fortnight earlier when only 150 fans turned up!

Able to use both feet, Bliss would try his luck at goal from all angles and from any distance, shooting on sight, often catching the 'keeper unaware! He was positive in everything he did and simply loved scoring goals!

He was leading scorer in 1919-20 when Spurs won the Second Division title and the following season he gained an FA Cup winners medal. He also played in two England trial matches but was selected for just one full international against Scotland in April 1921

Bliss left White Hart Lane in December 1922 for Clapton Orient and after spending the 1925-26 season with Bournemouth he hung up his boots at the age of 36.

He died in Wood Green, North London on 14 June 1968.

BLYTH, JAMES

Centre-half Jim Blyth made 11 League appearances for Spurs during his time with the club (1936-37). A Scotsman from Midlothian, he also played for Hull City, Hearts, Falkirk and St Johnstone.

BOHEMIANS PRAGUE

Spurs' playing record against Bohemians:

Competition	P	W	D	L	F	A
UEFA Cup	2	1	1	0	3	1

Spurs were involved in a tough third round UEFA Cup-tie with Bohemians in 1984-85 but they came through with flying colours after registering a 3-1 aggregate victory.

Spurs began well enough with a 2-0 home win on 28 November when goals by Gary Stevens and Ondra (og) were cheered by almost 28,000 fans.

But it was hard going in Czechoslovakia two weeks later where Mark Falco's goal earned a 1-1 draw in front of 17,500 spectators.

BOLAN, LEONARD ARTHUR

Outside-right from Suffolk, Len Bolan netted three times in 110 League games for Spurs in the 1930s. He joined the club after serving as an amateur with Norwich and West Ham and later played for Southend, Coventry City and Northampton Town, the latter two during WW2.

BOLTON WANDERERS.

Spurs' playing record against the Trotters:

Competition	P	W	D	L	F	A
Premiership	4	2	2	0	7	5
Football League	62	29	8	25	99	85
FA Cup	8	2	4	2	9	9
League Cup	1	0	0	1	1	6
Summary	75	33	14	28	116	105

The first League game against the Trotters was staged at White Hart Lane on 19 September 1908 (Division 2) and it ended in a 2-1 win for Spurs in front of 25,000 fans.

Later in the season Spurs won 1-0 at Burnden Park to complete their first 'League' double.

Spurs beat FA Cup finalists Bolton 3-2 at home in April 1953 in front of more than 40,000 fans and the following season they repeated that scoreline on the same ground.

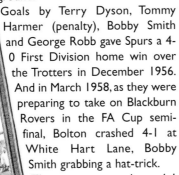

Goals by Terry Dyson, Tommy Harmer (penalty), Bobby Smith and George Robb gave Spurs a 4-0 First Division home win over the Trotters in December 1956. And in March 1958, as they were preparing to take on Blackburn Rovers in the FA Cup semi-final, Bolton crashed 4-1 at White Hart Lane, Bobby Smith grabbing a hat-trick.

There was another 4-1 victory for Spurs in April 1963, followed by a double in 1963-64 when Bolton were relegated from the top flight.

When they returned to First Division football in 1978-79 Bolton again suffered at the hands of Spurs, losing both games, 2-0 at White Hart Lane and 3-1 at Burnden Park.

A League Cup 4th round tie at The Reebok Stadium in November 1996 saw Spurs crash 6-1 - their heaviest defeat in this competition so far.

Former Spurs defender Gudni Bergsson skippered Bolton back into the Premiership via the First Division Play-offs in May 2001.

Players with both clubs include: Fred Barrett, Gudni Bergsson, Frank Drabble, Chris Fairclough, George Goldsmith, Bill Hinton, George Hunt (also Wanderers' coach), Gordon Jones, Ernie Jones, Bill Joyce, Don McAllister, Neil McNab, Ian Moores, Bob Tannahill, Wilf Waller.

Wartime guests (with either one or both clubs): Jack Hall, Tommy Pearson, Bert Pryde, Ken Smith (also Bolton Amateur).

Also associated: Frank Brettell (Bolton secretary, Spurs manager), Bert Sproston (Spurs player, Wanderers' coach & scout).

BOND, DENNIS JOSEPH THOMAS

Born in Walthamstow on 17 March 1947, midfielder Dennis Bond didn't quite reach the heights many people had predicted. Nevertheless, he was still a very capable footballer who certainly enjoyed his best days with Watford whom he served at the start and end of his career.

Bond had represented Walthamstow Boys and gained four England Schoolboy caps when he joined the Hornets as a junior in June 1962. Adding three Youth caps to his collection, he signed professional forms in March 1964 and went on to make over 100 first team appearances for the Vicarage Road club before transferring to Spurs for a fee of £27,000 in March 1967. Owing to an abundance of midfield talent, he was given just 36 outings in Spurs' first eleven (three goals scored) before being sold to Charlton Athletic in October 1970 for £25,000. He played 86 games for the Addicks (netting five goals) before returning to Watford, initially on loan, in February 1973, making the move a permanent one five months later. He ended his senior career in August 1978 when he switched to Dagenham, having accumulated 370 League appearances in total (41 goals scored).

BOOKS

Over the years there have been several books (hardback & paperback) published with a Spurs connection. Here are some of those publications:

History-related

* History of Tottenham Hotspur, plus How The Spurs got to the Cup Final (1921)
* The History of Tottenham Hotspur: 1882-1946 (1947).
* Spurs (1956, republished, 1957).
* Spurs Supreme (1961)
* Spurs - 'The Double' (1961)
* Spurs Go Marching On (1963)
* Spurs Again (1971)
* The Tottenham Hotspur Story (1971)
* The Official History of Tottenham Hotspur FC: 1882-1972 (1972)
* The Glory Game (1972, updated 1985)
* The Tottenham Hotspur Story (1980)
* And The Spurs Go Marching On (1982, republished 1985, 1988, updated 1996, 1997)
* Spurs A Complete Record: 1882-1988 (1988, updated 1993)
* Tottenham Hotspur Greats (1990)
* The Spurs Alphabet... Who's Who of Tottenham Hotspur FC (1992)
* Tottenham Hotspur Player by Player (1993, updated 1998))
* The Dream Double (1994)
* An Illustrated History of Tottenham Hotspur (1995)
* Tottenham Hotspur Official Illustrated History 1882-1995 (1995)
* Great Derby Matches - Arsenal v Tottenham (1996)
* Winning Their Spurs (1996)
* The Double (1996)
* The Pride of North London, the definitive history of Arsenal-Tottenham 'derby' matches (1997)
* Spurs, Day-To-Day Life at White Hart Lane (1998)

Autobiographies/biographies

* Clive Allen - There's Only One Clive Allen (1987)
* Osvaldo Ardiles - Ossie My Life in Football (1983)
* The Double and Before...Danny Blanchflower (1961)
* A Biography of a Visionary (Danny Blanchflower) (1997)
* Ron Burgess - Football My Life (1952)
* Herbert Chapman: Football Emperor (1980s)
* Terry Fenwick - Earning My Spurs (1989)
* Les Ferdinand - Sir Les (1997, paperback update 1998).
* Paul Gascoigne - Gazza Daft as a Brush (1989).
* Gazza A Biography (1990)
* Gazza My Life in Pictures (1990)
* El Magnifique, David Ginola (2000)

* Jimmy Greaves - A Funny Thing Happened On My Way To Spurs (1962)
* My World of Soccer, Jimmy Greaves (1966)
* Let's Be Honest, Jimmy Greaves (1972)
* This One's On Me, Jimmy Greaves (1979)
* It's a Funny Old Life, Jimmy Greaves (1990)
* The Sixties Revisited, Jimmy Greaves (1992)
* Glenn Hoddle - An Autobiography (1982)
* Spurred To Success, Glenn Hoddle (1987, paperback update 1988).
* Pat Jennings - An Autobiography (1983)
* Cliff Jones - Forward With Spurs (1962)
* Jürgen Klinsmann - Klinsmann (1995)
* Danke, Das War's, Jurgen Klinsmann (1999)
* Gary Lineker - Lineker, Golden Boot (1987)
* Strikingly Different, Gary Lineker (1993)
* Gary Mabbutt - Against All Odds (1989)
* Dave Mackay - Soccer My Spur (1961)
* Alan Mullery - In Defence of Spurs (1969)
* Giants of Football, No.4, Alan Mullery (1971)
* An Autobiography - Alan Mullery (1985)
* Terry Neill - Revelations of a Football Manager (1985)
* Bill Nicholson - Glory, Glory, My Life With Spurs (1984)
* Steve Perryman - A Man For All Seasons (1985)
* Martin Peters - Goals From Nowhere (1969)
* Alf Ramsey - Talking Football (1952)
* Anatomy of a Football Manager - Sir Alf Ramsey (1970)
* Hell Razor - Neil Ruddock (1999)
* Graham Roberts - When The Going Gets Tough (1988)
* Jimmy Seed - Soccer From The Inside (1947).
* The Jimmy Seed Story (1957)
* Hans Segers - The Final Score...Story of Soccer's Trial of the Century (1998)
* Bobby Smith - The Bobby Smith Story in Pictures (1965)
* Terry Venables - Son of Fred by Fred Venables (1990)
* Venables: The Inside Story (1994)
* The Autobiography - of Terry Venables (1994, paperback 1995).
* Chris Waddle - Waddle, The Authorised Biography (1988)

Others:
* Tottenham Hotspur Football Handbook: 1897-98 to 1914-15, 1919-20 to 1939-40, 1948-49 to date.

Annuals
* Spurs in Action 1961-62
* Spurs in Action 1962-63
* Spurs in Action 1963-64
* The Tottenham Hotspur Football Book, annually from 1967 to 1974.
* Tottenham Hotspur Official Annual 1980-89 inclusive and 1992 onwards
* Stop the Game I want to Get On! - Jimmy Greaves (1983)
* The Programme & Handbook Guide 1946-1992 (1992, reproduced 1993).
* Away The Spurs - Away Programme Guide (1994)
* The White Hart Lane Encyclopedia (1996)
* Glenn Hoddle (World Cup Diaries) 1998
* Soccer My Way Danny Blanchflower (1955)
* Clemence on Goalkeeping - Ray Clemence (1977)

BOOTLE
Spurs never competed against Bootle at any level.
Players with both clubs include: Bob Cain, John L Jones

BOREHAM, FREDERICK
Goalkeeper Fred Boreham made 35 first team appearances for Spurs - 20 in the Football League - during his two-year stay at White Hart Lane (May 1908 to May 1910).
Born in Rye, Sussex on 8 July 1885, he played for Tunbridge Wells Rangers and Leyton before being engaged by Spurs as cover for Bob Hewitson. He found himself 'out in the cold' following the arrival of John 'Tiny' Joyce from Millwall and Tommy Lunn from Wolves, and duly returned to Leyton at the end of his second season.
Boreham died in Hastings, Sussex circa July 1951.

BORUSSIA DORTMUND
Spurs playing record against the German side:

Competition	P	W	D	L	F	A
Festival of Britain	1	1	0	0	2	1

A crowd of 29,000 saw Eddie Baily and Peter Murphy give Spurs victory in this Festival of Britain encounter at White Hart Lane in May 1951. Player with both clubs: Steffen Freund.

BOSTON UNITED
Spurs' playing record against United:

Competition	P	W	D	L	F	A
FA Cup	1	1	0	0	4	0

A crowd of 46,185 at White Hart Lane saw Spurs beat the Lincolnshire club in the 3rd round of the FA Cup in Jan 1956. Len Duquemin, Bobby Smith (2) and George Robb scored the goals.

BOURNEMOUTH (AFC)
Spurs playing record against the Cherries:

Competition	P	W	D	L	F	A
FA Cup	1	0	0	1	1	3
Wartime Cup	2	2	0	0	10	2
Summary	3	2	0	1	11	5

Third Division (South) side Bournemouth, caused a major upset by knocking Spurs out of the FA Cup in the 5th round at Dean Court in February 1957. A crowd of 25,892 attended the game in which Terry Medwin netted for Spurs.
Players with both clubs include: Ken Bennett (Spurs junior), Bert Bliss, Shaun Close, Richard Cooke, Phil Holder, Alf Messer (Bournemouth player-coach), Paul Miller, Jimmy Neighbour, Jamie Redknapp (Spurs junior), Jack Richardson, Graham Roberts (Bournemouth junior), Steve Robinson, Brian Statham, Neil Young (Spurs junior).
Wartime guests (with one or both clubs): Charlie Burke, Alf Day, Bill Edrich, Wilf Mannion, Tom Paton, Jack Rowley, Alf Whittingham.
Also associated: Freddie Cox & Harry Lowe (both Spurs players, Cherries' managers, Lowe also Spurs coach), Trevor Hartley (Bournemouth player & manager, Spurs assistant manager & caretaker-manager), Doug Livermore (Bournemouth player, Spurs manager, assistant-manager/coach, reserve team manager, chief scout), John Sainty (Spurs reserve, Cherries' player-coach), Pat Holland (Bournemouth player, Spurs Youth & reserve team manager), Dickie Dowsett (Spurs reserve, Cherries' commercial manager: 1968-83),

BOWEN, MARK ROSSLYN
Full-back/midfielder Mark Bowen made only 21 League and Cup appearances (two goals) for Spurs during eight years at the club.
Born in Neath, Glamorgan on 7 December 1963, he commenced his career at White Hart Lane in June 1980, as an apprentice, turning professional in December 1981. In July 1987 - after struggling to get into the first XI owing to the presence of Chris

Spurs v victorious Third Division Bournemouth in the 5th Round of the FA Cup 1957

Hughton, Danny Thomas, Gary Stevens and Mitchell Thomas he moved to East Anglia to sign for Norwich City for a fee of £97,000. Bowen went on to appear in 399 senior games for the Canaries, gaining 41 senior caps for Wales. This followed those he had won as a Schoolboy and Youth team player plus the two full and three at Under-21 level he had collected with Spurs.

From Carrow Road, Bowen switched to West Ham United in July 1996 and after a brief spell in Japan with Shimizu S-Pulse, he returned to England to serve with Charlton Athletic, Wigan Athletic and Reading. He taken his overall senior appearance tally to 553 (in both club and international competitions) before his appointment as coach to the Welsh Under-21 squad in 2000-01.

BOWERING, ERNEST GEORGE

Local half-back George Bowering (from Wandsworth) made seven League appearances for Spurs between 1910-12. He later played for Fulham and Merthyr Town.

BOWLER, GEORGE HENRY

Signed from Derby County in 1913, reserve half-back George Bowler made four appearances for Spurs before joining Luton Town in 1919.

BRACE, ROBERT LEON

Forward Robert Brace made just one substitute appearance for Spurs v. Southampton in 1984. Later played in Belgium with Waterschei and in Germany with IFC Saarbrucken.

BRADFORD CITY

Spurs playing record against the Bantams:

Competition	P	W	D	L	F	A
Premiership	4	1	3	0	7	6
Football League	28	11	7	10	39	38
FA Cup	4	2	1	1	11	3
League Cup	1	1	0	0	2	1
Summary	37	15	11	11	59	48

The first League encounter between Spurs and Bradford City took place on 18 September 1909 (Division 1) and in front of 25,000 fans City eased to a comfortable 5-2 victory.

Spurs doubled up over City in season 1934-35, winning 4-0 at home and 1-0 away.

Johnny Morrison netted a hat-trick as Spurs beat City 5-1 in a home Second Division match in October 1936.

Players with both clubs include: Stan Alexander, Alan Hall, George Hutchinson, David McDonald, Fred Mearns, James Morton, Shaun Murray (Spurs trainee), Dean Richards, Jimmy Smailes.

Wartime guests (with either one or both clubs): Bill Adams, Davie Colquhoun, Almer Hall, Ernie Goldthorpe, Billy Grimes, Sid Ottewell, Bert Page, Taffy Spelman, Bill Sperrin, Ralph Ward, Alf Whittingham.

Also associated: Terry Yorath (Spurs player, City assistant-manager/coach & manager)

BRADFORD PARK AVENUE

Spurs playing record against Park Avenue:

Competition	P	W	D	L	F	A
Football League	32	16	8	8	75	50
Southern League	2	1	1	0	2	1
FA Cup	2	1	1	0	2	1
Summary	36	18	10	8	79	52

The first of the 32 League games between the two clubs was played at Park Avenue on 19 December 1908 (Division 2) and it was Spurs who celebrated with a 2-0 victory in front of just 5,000 fans.

Spurs completed the League double over Park Avenue in 1935-36, winning 4-0 at White Hart Lane and 5-2 in Yorkshire. Willie Evans and Johnny Morrison scored in both matches. (Spurs also beat Bradford City twice in this same season).

Morrison was again the hero with a hat-trick when Spurs clipped Park Avenue 5-1 at home in September 1936.

Ron Burgess scored twice when Spurs beat Park Avenue 5-1 in front of 47,955 spectators at White Hart Lane in October 1948 and almost a year later, the Yorkshire club lost 5-0 on the same ground, Les Medley netting twice on this occasion before almost 55,000 fans.

Players with both clubs include: Jimmy Bauchop, Laurie Brown (Avenue player-manager), Chris Carrick, Arthur Dixon, Frank Drabble, Jim Freeborough, Mel Hopkins, Joe Meek, Charlie Morgan, Les Stevens, Ralph Ward, Roy White, Alex Wright.

Wartime guests (with either one or both clubs): Charlie Briggs, Ivor Broadis, SA Clayton, Ronnie Dix, Jack Gibbons, Jimmy Smailes, Alf Whittingham.

Also associated: Vic Buckingham (Avenue manager), Graham Carr (Avenue player, Spurs scout).

BRADSHAW, THOMAS HENRY

Before becoming a Spurs player, outside-left Harry Bradshaw (some referred to him as Tom) had spent five years with Liverpool, winning two League championships, starring twice for the Football League and gaining a full England cap while also hitting 54 goals in 138 appearances. Surprisingly he spent just the one season at White Hart Lane (May 1898 to May 1899) during which time he scored 18 goals in 69 first team matches. He also represented the United League, the South v. the North in an international trial and played for an England XI in a fund-raiser against Scotland.

Born in Liverpool on 24 August 1873, Bradshaw assisted Northwich Victoria before moving to Anfield in October 1893. After leaving Spurs he spent a season with Thames Ironworks before being taken ill. He died of pneumonia, Christmas Day, 1899.

BRAIN, JAMES

Born in Bristol, on 11 September 1900 and a former coalminer, Jimmy Brain was a free-shooting centre or inside-forward, rejected by Cardiff City who, after doing well with Ton Pentre in the Welsh League, went on to net 139 goals in 232 competitive games in seven splendid seasons with Arsenal before joining Spurs in September 1931.

He had played in the 1927 FA Cup Final defeat by his boyhood heroes Cardiff, appeared in an England international trial and at one time held the scoring record at Highbury for most goals in a season (34 in 1925-26).

He notched just 10 goals in 45 League and FA Cup outings for Spurs with whom he remained until May 1935, coaching the youngsters for the last two years before taking over as manager of Kings Lynn, later taking a similar post with Cheltenham Town. He then returned to Highbury as a senior scout. Brain died in Barnet in October 1971.

BRAZIL, ALAN BERNARD

Alan Brazil is the only player so far to have scored five goals in a League game for Ipswich, doing so v. Southampton at Portman Road (Division 1) 16 February 1981. Two years later he was a Spurs player, signed for £450,000 in March 1983.

A Scotsman, born in Simshill, Glasgow on 15 June 1959, he represented Glasgow Schools and played for the Celtic Boys Club before being engaged as a professional by manager Bobby Robson at Portman Road in May 1977. A loan spell with Detroit Express in the NASL in the summer of 1978, punctuated Brazil's career with the Suffolk-based club for whom he went on to claim 80 goals in 210 appearances. His spent just over a season at White Hart Lane, scoring 13 goals in 38 competitive games before transferring to Manchester United for £700,000 in June 1984.

From Old Trafford he switched to Coventry City (June 1986) with an old Spurs colleague of his, Terry Gibson, going in the opposite direction. Then, after spells with Queen's Park Rangers, Witham Town, Chelmsford City (three separate spells), FC Baden (Switzerland), Southend Manor, Bury Town, Stamford and Saffron Walden Town, he retired to become a soccer pundit on both radio and TV.

Capped 21 times by Scotland (eight at under-21 level and 13 by the senior side) Brazil notched 89 goals in 235 League appearances for his five English clubs.

BREARLEY, JOHN

A Liverpudlian, born circa October 1875, the versatile John Brearley occupied several positions during a very interesting career, including those of inside-right, centre-forward and right-half.

Starting out with Kettering, he played one game for Notts County in 1897-98, served with Chatham the following season and then signed for Millwall in July 1899, switching back to Notts County in May 1900. He then assisted Middlesbrough and Everton before signing for Spurs in May 1903. Selected to represent the

Professionals against the Amateurs at White Hart Lane in January 1905, he went on to appear in 133 first team games for Spurs, scoring 24 goals, finishing up on the left-wing prior to his transfer to Crystal Palace in May 1907. He was appointed player-coach of Millwall in the summer of 1909 and ended his playing career by coaching Berlin Victoria in Germany.

When the Great War broke out, Brearley was still based in Germany and was interned at Ruhleben prison camp along with several other well-established footballers and sportsmen, one being his former Spurs manager, John Cameron.

He later returned to England and died in Southend in 1944.

BRENTFORD

Spurs playing record against the Bees:

Competition	P	W	D	L	F	A
Football League	6	3	2	1	12	5
FA Cup	3	1	1	1	4	4
League Cup	6	5	1	0	15	7
Other Leagues	26	13	9	4	42	22
Other Cups	4	1	1	2	6	9
Wartime	25	13	7	5	53	39
Summary	70	36	21	13	132	86

Spurs' first-ever League game against the Bees ended in a comprehensive 4-0 home victory on 1 November 1947. Len Duquemin scored his first hat-trick for the club in front of 42,362 fans. Later in the season the Bees won 2-0 at Griffin Park.

Spurs goalkeeper Neil Sullivan was sent-off in the 0-0 draw with the Bees at Griffin Park in a League Cup 2nd round, 1st leg encounter in September 2000.

Players with both clubs include: Tom Atherton, Bert Badger, Bill Bann, Frank Bentley, A Bird (Bees junior), Garry Brooke, Johnny Brooks, Jimmy Brown, Jack Chisholm, Allan Cockram (Bees non-contract), Billy Cook, Arthur Crompton, Harry Crump, Kevin Dearden, Jim Elliott, Les Ferdinand, Jack Gibbons (Bees Amateur, later manager-secretary: 1949-52), Alex Glen, Jim Hartley, Baden Herod, Jimmy Holmes, Chris Hughton, David Jenkins, Bill Lane (also Bees manager), Charlie Lanham, Richard McElhaney, Dave McEwen (Bees trialist), Bob McTavish, Billy Manuel (Spurs junior), Paul Miller, John Moncur, Tony Parks, Steve Perryman (also Bees assistant-manager & manager), Andy Sinton, Steve Slade, Simon Spencer (Spurs reserve), Brian Statham, Sid Tickridge, Cyril Toulouse, Archie Turner (Bees trialist), Kevin Watson, Fred Webster, Charlie Williams, Kevin Watson.

Wartime guests (with either one or both clubs): Harry Brown, Albert Chester, John Davie, Frank Drabble, Harry Dukes, Andy Duncan, Stan Eastham, Harry Ferrier, Jack Finch, Bobby Flavell, Jim Fulwood, Les Henley, Jack Hoffman (Bees junior), Doug Hunt, Jakey Jackson, Eric Jones, Tommy Manley, Alex Muir, David Nelson, Taffy O'Callaghan, Frank O'Donnell, WA Saunders (Bees junior), Tommy Simmons, Bill Sperrin.

Also associated: Phil Holder (Spurs player, Bees assistant-manager, caretaker-manager, manager), Stewart Houston (Bees player, Spurs assistant-manager), Colin Lee (Spurs player, Bees Youth development officer), Billy Brawn (Spurs WWI, Bees manager & director), Roger Cross (Bees player, Spurs assistant-manager).

BRETTELL, FRANK

Born in Liverpool circa 1854, and player-secretary of the St Domingo club in Liverpool from 1875, Frank Brettell signed as a professional for Everton in 1878, being one of the club's founder members. He played in virtually every position for the Merseyiders in the early days before retiring to work on the Liverpool Mercury as a reporter. He quickly returned to football, however, as assistant-secretary and finally secretary at Goodison Park. He moved in the same capacity to Bolton Wanderers for the 1896-97 season before being appointed secretary-manager of Spurs in February 1898 - although he did not actually take office until mid-March....and then played an important part in the formation of a Limited Company He introduced some quality players to White Hart Lane, he retained his position for just twelve months, handing in his notice in early February 1899 to take effect on 1 April. He passed over his duties to the man he signed as a player, John Cameron, while he contemplated a new role as manager of Portsmouth, having been offered a substantial wage rise to leave Spurs for the south coast!

A universally respected manager, Brettell officially moved in at Fratton Park in April 1899 and stayed there until June 1901 having seen Pompey rise to become a prominent force in the Southern League (like he had done with Spurs). He then took over the reins at Plymouth Argyle, leaving the Pilgrims in the summer of 1905 after he had again made them a respected outfit in Southern League circles.

BRIGHTON & HOVE ALBION
Spurs playing record against the Seagulls:

Competition	P	W	D	L	F	A
Football League	10	5	2	3	15	10
Southern League	10	3	4	3	13	13
League Cup	2	1	1	0	2	1
Wartime	4	2	0	2	7	7
Summary	26	11	7	8	37	31

The first Football League meeting was played at White Hart Lane on 19 November 1977 (Division 2). It finished goalless in front of 48,613 fans. The fixture at The Goldstone Ground that season saw Albion win 3-1.

Spurs finally recorded their first League win over the Seagulls in September 1979, winning 2-1 in the top flight at White Hart Lane. Players with both clubs include: Gerry Armstrong, Phil Beal, Walter Bellamy, Ken Bennett (Spurs junior), Martin Chivers, Ray Clarke, Allan Cockram (Albion trialist), Jimmy Collins, Ian Culverhouse, Ally Dick, Matt Edwards (Spurs reserve), Harry Gilberg, Pat Gilhooley, Almer Hall, Mel Hopkins, Leon Hyde, Jimmy Kennedy, Joe Kinnear, George Leach, Jack Lee, Harry Lowe, Neil McNab, Jeff Minton, Gary O'Reilly, Andy Polston, Art Rule, Jack Skinner, Bobby Smith, Gary Stevens, Jimmy Townley, Steve Walford, Willie Young.
Wartime guests (with either one or both clubs): George Coomber, John Davie, Alf Day, Doug Flack, Fred Ford, Willie Hall, Percy Hooper, Frank O'Donnell, Bob Pryde, Bill Sperrin, Jack Whent, Joe Wilson.
Also associated: Alan Mullery, (Spurs player, Albion manager), Bill Lane (Spurs player, Brighton manager & coach), Peter Suddaby (Albion player, Spurs Academy Director)

BRIGHTON UNITED
Spurs' playing record against United:

Competition	P	W	D	L	F	A
Other Leagues	6	5	0	1	16	5

Two of Spurs' five wins over United - those of 6-1 at home and 3-0 away in season 1899-1900 - were not recorded in the final Southern League table as the Brighton club resigned from the competition.
Player with both clubs: Jock Davidson.

BRISTOL CITY
Spurs playing record against the Robins:

Competition	P	W	D	L	F	A
Football League	20	10	5	5	28	18
FA Cup	3	3	0	0	5	1
League Cup	2	1	1	0	3	1
Other Leagues	14	6	4	4	24	24
Summary	39	20	10	9	60	44

The first League game between the two clubs was played on 2 October 1909 (Division 1) and ended in a goalless draw in front of 20,000 fans.
Players with both clubs include: Jamie Attwell (Spurs reserve), Peter Beadle, Herbert Blake, Terry Boyle (Spurs reserve), Joe Brough, Andy Burke (Spurs reserve), Jason Cundy, Clayton Fortune (Spurs reserve), David Howells, Bill Jones, Bill Lane, Colin Lee, Walter Moles, Archie Turner, Kevin Watson.
Wartime guests (with either one or both clubs): Pat Beasley, Frank Boulton, Ronnie Dix, Fred Ford (also City manager), Cyril Williams.
Also associated: Jimmy Seed (Spurs player, City advisor & caretaker-manager), Ernie Jones (City player/coach).

BRISTOL ROVERS
Spurs playing record against the Pirates:

Competition	P	W	D	L	F	A
Football League	2	2	0	0	12	2
FA Cup	2	2	0	0	10	3
Other Leagues	32	17	4	11	71	35
Summary	36	23	4	11	93	40

Spurs were leading Rovers 1-0 in a home Southern League game in October 1899 when thick fog caused the fixture to be abandoned ten minutes after the break. The 'replay' resulted in a 5-1 win for Spurs.
When Spurs crushed the ten men of Rovers 6-2 in an FA Cup-tie in 1921 all eight goals came from different players with Tommy Clay almost bursting the net with his penalty for Spurs. The attendance was 35,175. Spurs of course went on to lift the trophy that season.
Spurs were 3-0 up at half-time in their home Second Division match against Rovers on 22 October 1977. They went on to win 9-0, scoring five times in the last 15 minutes. This is Spurs' best-ever Second Division victory and it was also the first Football League meeting with the Pirates. (See under goalkeepers).
Players with both clubs include: Jimmy Armstrong, Bill Bann, Peter Beadle, Jim Chalmers, Jamie Clapham, Allan Cockram, George Crompton, Ronnie Dix, , James Gray, John Hills, John Jones, Gary Mabbutt, Joe Nicholls, John Scales, Harry Stansfield, Bob Walker, Harry Wilding
Wartime guests (with either one or both clubs): Fred Ford (also Rovers manager), Jack Skinner
Also associated: Gerry Francis (manager of both clubs, also Rovers player and director), Percy Smith (manager of both clubs), John Chaplin (Spurs player, Rovers trainer).

BRITTAN, COLIN

A wing-half, born in Bristol on 2 June 1927, Colin Brittan played for Bristol North Old Boys before joining Spurs as an Amateur in January 1948, turning professional nine months later. Over the next ten years he played in just 55 first team games for the club (41 in the First Division), scoring one goal, although he did become a valuable member of the second XI, helping along the stars of the future before transferring to Bedford Town in November 1958.

BRITTAIN, CHARLES RICHARD

Charlie Brittain made 51 first team appearances for Spurs between October 1911 (when he made his Football League debut against Notts County) and November 1913 when he was transferrd to Cardiff City.

Born on the Isle of Wight on 7 August 1887, he played initially for Portsmouth and then under manager and former Spurs player Herbert Chapman at Northampton Town before joining Spurs, having represented the Southern League on five occasions whilst a 'Cobbler.' Brittain, who skippered Cardiff City into the Football League in 1920, retired in 1924 after making two appearances for the Welsh League as well as helping Cardiff twice win the Welsh Cup (in 1920 and 1922). He later became a prominent member of the Cardiff City Council. He died on 31 July 1949.

BRITTON, JOHN

Goalkeeper Jock Britton played in 40 Football League matches for Spurs during his two seasons at White Hart Lane: 1926-28.

Born in Lennoxtown on 18 March 1900 and now deceased, he played for Albion Rovers and Dundee before moving south and when he left Spurs (following the arrival of Cyril Spiers) he signed for Celtic.

BROADIS, IVAN ARTHUR

Inside-forward 'Ivor' Broadis was born in Poplar, London on 18 December 1922 and was an amateur with Spurs during World War Two. He scored 38 goals in 83 Football League South games before joining Carlisle United as player-manager at the age of 23 in August 1946. He later played for Sunderland (February 1949 to October 1951), Manchester City (until October 1953) and Newcastle United to July 1955 when he returned to Carlisle for a second spell, this time as player-coach. He later served as a player and coach at Queen of the South (1959-62) and thereafter worked as a sports journalist for the Carlisle Evening News & Star until the mid 1980s.

Capped 14 times by England, Broadis scored 136 goals in 442 League appearances for his four English clubs.....and is certainly listed as one who 'got away' from Spurs!

* Broadis was the first manager to transfer himself - from Carlisle to Sunderland for £18,000 in 1949.

BROMLEY

Spurs playing record against Bromley

Competition	P	W	D	L	F	A
Other Cups	1	1	0	0	3	0

Spurs 3-0 win over Bromley was achieved in the first round of the London FA Charity Cup in September 1912. Just 2,000 fans saw Billy Minter rattle in a hat-trick.

BROOKE, GARRY JAMES

Almost a third of midfielder Garry Brooke's 129 first time appearances for Spurs were made as a subsitute.

He was, in fact, drawn off the bench 45 times as he battled to earn,

and hold down, a regular place in the League side during the period: 1978-85. Indeed, three of his 'sub' outings came in FA Cup Finals - the first game of the 1981 showdown with Manchester City and both 1982 encounters against QPR. He scored 45 goals all told, 15 in the League.

Born in Bethnal Green, London on 24 November 1960, he represented Waltham Forest District, McEntree Seniors and Essex County Boys before joining Spurs as a junior in the summer of 1977, taking professional status in October 1978. He made his League debut two years later (after a loan spell with GAIS in Sweden) and was having his best season when, in February 1983, Brooke was involved in a serious car crash. He recovered full fitness but was never the same player after that mishap. He left White Hart Lane for Norwich City in May 1985 for a fee of £50,000. From Carrow Road he went to Holland to assist FC Groningen (December 1986) and then played for Wimbledon, Stoke City (on loan), and Brentford before leaving the League scene (albeit temporarily) to join Baldock Town in January 1991. In that same month Brooke was loaned out to Colchester United and following a trial with Reading a few weeks later, he rounded off his career with Wivenhoe Town and St Albans City. He played alongside two other former Spurs players, John Lacy and Paul Price at Wivenhoe and with Price at St Albans.

BROOKS, JOHN

Inside-forward Johnny Brooks had a good scoring record with Spurs - 51 goals in 179 League and FA Cup appearances. He also netted 21 times in 43 'other' games.

Born in Reading on 23 December 1931, he joined the Elm Park club as an Amateur in February 1949 and turned professional two months later. In February 1953 he was transferred to White Hart Lane (in a deal that took Dennis Uphill and Harry Robshaw to Reading). His debut for Spurs arrived on 6 April of that same year. The departure of Eddie Baily to Port Vale early in 1956 opened the door for Brooks to establish himself in the first XI and he did just that, also gaining three England caps in the process, scoring in his first two against Wales and Yugoslavia.

Brooks was eventually transferred to Chelsea in a £20,000 deal that brought Les Allen to Spurs in December 1959. He remained in League action until October 1964, playing also for Brentford and Crystal Palace. He then dropped down the ladder to join Stevenage Town, and after spells with Cambridge City and FC Toronto in Canada, he took his last job in football as player-manager of Knebworth Town. After that Brooks was employed in the City of London as a broker's messenger.

BROOKS, SAMUEL ERNEST

Outside-left Sammy Brooks had scored 53 goals in 246 games for Wolves and had played for England in 1919 before joining Spurs in 1922. He netted once in ten League outings during his brief spell at White Hart Lane, leaving to sign for Southend United in 1923. He was 70 when he died in 1960.

BROTHERSTON, NOEL

Northern Ireland international winger who sadly died at the age of 38 in 1995, Brotherston played in only one League game for Spurs v. Aston Villa in 1976. He then spent ten years with Blackburn Rovers, making over 300 appearances, winning 27 caps.

BROUGH, JOSEPH

Half-back Joe Brough played for Burslem Port Vale and Stoke before making two senior appearances for Spurs in 1908-09. He returned to Vale and later assisted Liverpool, Bristol City and Vale (again).

BROWN, ALEXANDER

Alex 'Sandy' Brown was a terrific marksman, not a great footballer but a specialist at snapping up the half chance with either head or foot. He scored 96 goals in 113 appearances for Spurs, 67 coming in 85 competitive matches and 15 alone being recorded in Spurs' successful FA Cup campaign of 1900-01 (including a fourtimer in the semi-final v. West Bromwich Albion).

Born at Glenbuck, Ayrshire, on 7 April 1879 he played for three Scottish-based clubs before entering the Football League with Preston North End in the summer of 1896. Three years later he switched to Portsmouth and arrived at White Hart Lane in May 1900 - ready to bulge a few nets like he had done regularly during the previous six or seven seasons! After two terms with Spurs, Brown returned to Portsmouth and in August 1903 he diverted some 400 miles north to join Middlesbrough, moving south once again in June 1905 to play for Luton Town, finally calling it a day with Kettering in 1907-08.

* Brown was capped by Scotland as a Middlesbrough player v. England in 1904, having represented his country, also against England, in that ill-fated international at Ibrox Park in April 1902 when part of the congested West Stand collapsed. A total of 25 fans lost their lives while another 517 were injured, some seriously.

BROWN, CHARLES

Half-back Charlie Brown scored once in 36 games for Spurs in two years with the club: 1902-04. Signed from Everton, he later played for Hull City, Reading and Luton Town.

BROWN, DAVID CRICHTON

Scottish-born centre-forward, Davey Brown played in one League game for Spurs v. Liverpool in 1910. After trials with Birmingham, Reading and Merthyr Town, he signed for Morton in 1911.

BROWN, IVOR RONALD JOHN

A centre-forward from Derbyshire, Ivor Brown (born Ivor Erwin) spent two years with Spurs: 1909-11. He played in 12 League games before leaving for Coventry City, later serving with Reading, Port Vale and Swansea Town.

BROWN, JAMES

Jimmy Brown, a former Manchester United and Brentford inside-forward, made four League appearances for Spurs in 1936-37.

BROWN, LAURENCE

Centre-half Laurie Brown was an apprentice cabinet-maker before taking up football.

He served in the National Service as a PT Instructor and played at intermediate level for Shildon Workers Juniors FC, All Saints Rovers, Shildon Town, Woking Town, Fulham (as an Amateur), Bishop Auckland and Darlington (also as an Amateur) before signing as a professional for Northampton Town in October 1960. He moved to Arsenal in August 1961 and on to Spurs in February 1964, after having 109 senior outings for the Gunners. He ironically made his debut for Spurs against Arsenal, the first of 65 appearances at competitive level for the club (three goals scored, all in the League). When Mike England was recruited from

Blackburn Rovers in August 1966 Brown slipped into the reserves and the following month he was transferred to Norwich City. Later he assisted Bradford Park Avenue, Altrincham and Kings Lynn (all as player-manager) before becoming boss of Stockton. After taking a job as a publican in 1971, he returned to his native Durham where he became a milkman.

Brown was born in Shildon, County Durham on 22 August 1937.

BROWN, ROY ERIC

Goalkeeper Roy Brown's only League game for Spurs was against Blackpool in 1946. He later assisted Reading, Notts County and Mansfield Town.

BROWN, ROBERT SAMUEL

Full-back Bob Brown made 45 League and FA Cup appearances for Spurs over a six-year period: 1919-25. Born in Southampton 16 October 1895, he joined the club from Thorneycrofts FC and on leaving White Hart Lane he decided to retire and became a publican on the Isle of Wight where he died circa April 1980.

BROWN, WILLIAM DALLAS FYFE

Goalkeeper Bill Brown had already been honoured by Scotland when he joined Spurs from Dundee for £16,500 in June 1959. He went on to win 28 full caps for his country and made 262 appearances for Spurs, missing only one League game when the double was achieved in 1960-61. A tremendous performer between the posts, he helped Spurs retain the FA Cup the following season and was in the side that won the European Cup-winners' Cup in 1963. Replaced in the first XI at White Hart Lane by Pat Jennings, Brown left Spurs in 1966 to join Northampton Town and in 1967-68 he assisted Toronto Falcons of Canada in the outlawed American NPSL. He retired to live in Toronto and later worked in the real estate business.

Born in Arbroath, Angus on 8 October 1931, Brown played his early football for Arbroath Cliffburn, Carnoustie Juveniles and Carnoustie Panmure before signing for Dundee in September 1949. He was also capped by his country at Schoolboy, Under-23 and 'B' team levels and was named a reserve for the senior side no fewer than 22 times before he finally gained his first cap against France in the summer of 1958.

BRUGES (FC)

Spurs' playing record against the Belgium side:

Competition	P	W	D	L	F	A
UEFA Cup	2	1	0	1	4	2

Spurs defeated the Belgium club Bruges in the second round of the 1984-85 UEFA Cup competition - winning 4-2 on aggregate. The first leg in Bruges resulted in a 2-1 win for the home side in front of 27,000 fans, Clive Allen grabbing the all-important away goal for Spurs who had Glenn Hoddle sent-off. Two weeks later, on 7 November, 34,356 fans inside White Hart Lane saw Spurs win 3-0 with goals by Graham Roberts, Allen (again) and Micky Hazard to set up a next round clash with Bohemians (Prague). Players with both clubs: Ray Clarke, Nico Claesen.

BUCKINGHAM, VICTOR FREDERICK

Vic Buckingham played in 309 first XI games for Spurs, 207 in the Football League.

A very competent full-back who could also play in any defensive position, he was strong in the tackle and always looked at ease no matter what the circumstances.

Born in Greenwich, London on 23 October 1915, he represented Tottenham Juniors and England Schoolboys before joining Bromley from where he switched to Spurs as a professional in May 1935, making his first team debut at home to Bury in November of that same year. During the War Buckingham, like so many other players, guested for several clubs and after the hostilities with various defenders ready to show their mettle in at competitive level, he retired from the game in 1949. At that point he was appointed coach at White Hart Lane, having already tasted that line of sport in Norway (with Moss FC), Stanmore and Oxford University during the previous three years.

After coaching Pegasus albeit briefly in 1950, Buckingham was given the manager's job at Bradford Park Avenue in June 1951. Less than two years later (in February 1953) he was placed in charge of First Division West Bromwich Albion whom he guided to the runners-up spot in the League and to FA Cup glory in 1954. He remained at The Hawthorns until June 1959 when he took over as coach of the crack Dutch side, Ajax Amsterdam whom he guided to League and Cup success, in 1960 and 1961 respectively. He later managed Sheffield Wednesday, Fulham, the Greek club Ethnikos and two Spanish clubs, CF Barcelona (from March 1970) and Sevilla (March 1972-73), steering Barcelona to a Cup Final victory in 1971.

Buckingham, who won two Wartime caps for England, died in January 1996, aged 79.

BUGG, WALTER JAMES

Centre-half Walter Bugg was a Millwall reserve and played for Arsenal before joining Spurs in 1902. After one game for the club he moved to Norwich City in 1905.

BULL, WALTER

After spending ten excellent years with Notts County, the versatile Walter Bull was signed by Spurs in May 1904. He remained at White Hart Lane for six seasons, making 182 first-team appearances and scoring 15 goals.

Born in Nottingham on 19 December 1897, he played for St Andrew's Church team before joining the Magpies in the summer of 1894. Appearing in practically every outfield position, but preferring a half-back role, he made well over 300 appearances for County (282 in the League) and scored in excess of 50 goals.

He played for the Football League side in 1901 and appeared in four international trials (three during his time with Spurs).

He left Spurs in June 1910 for Heanor Town. At the end of the 1910-11 season he travelled halfway round the world to take up a coaching position in Buenos Aires and in July 1912 he returned to England to become manager of Northampton Town, replacing former Spurs player Herbert Chapman who had taken over at Leeds City.

Bull died in Nottingham on 28 July 1952.

BUNJEVCEVIC, GORAN

A defender, born in Karlovac, Yugoslavia on 17 February 1973, Goran Bunjevcevic played for Graficar Belgrade; Rad Belgrade (from 1994) and Red Star Belgrade (signed in 1997); before joining Spurs for £1.4 million in May 2001.

Capped 12 times at senior level - winning his first in 1998 v. Israel - he was a member of Red Star's League and Cup double-winning side in 2000, having gained his first Cup winners' medal a year earlier.

He has made more than 200 club appearances (League and Cup) and has scored over 20 goals. He faced Leicester City in UEFA Cup competition in 2000-01.

BURGESS, WILLIAM ARTHUR RONALD

Wing-half Ron Burgess totalled 505 first team appearances for Spurs, with 297 coming in the Football League; he also scored 63 goals.

A tremendous competitor, rated as one of the greatest Spurs players of all-time, he joined the club as an amateur in May 1936 and turned professional two years later while being groomed in the Northfleet side. Returning to White Hart Lane for the start of the 1938-39 campaign, he remained with the club until May 1954, skippering the side on many occasions.

Born in Cwm, South Wales on 9 April 1917, as a teenager he used to kick a ball around with his mates on the slag-heaps overlooking the River Ebbw in South Wales. He represented Ebbw Vale Schools and played for Cwm Villa before signing as an Amateur for the team he supported, Cardiff City, in 1933.

He was working as a pit boy when Spurs came along and invited him to join their junior ranks but after a year or so he was told that he wouldn't make the grade.

A disappointed Burgess contemplated returning home but before he did he went along to watch a Spurs 'A' team game. With only ten men at the ground, he was asked to fill in at right-half. He did well, was taken on the groundstaff and he never looked back after that!

He made his Football League debut for Spurs at Norwich in February 1939 and during the Second World War guested for five major clubs while also playing in 10 internationals for Wales. He also represented the RAF and the FA and amassed well over 130 appearances for Spurs during the hostilities.

An attacking player, always ready to back up his forwards, Burgess captained Spurs to both the Second and First Division League titles in successive seasons (1950 and 1951) and he also led his country on several occasions while gaining 32 full caps between 1946 and 1954. He also played for the Football League side and for Great Britain against the Rest of Europe.

On leaving White Hart Lane at the end of the 1953-54 season Burgess

was appointed player-coach of Swansea Town. He later took over as player-manager at Vetch Field and in March 1959 was placed in charge of Watford, guiding the Hornets to promotion from Division Four in 1960. He later accepted managerial positions with non-League side Hendon (1963-65) and Bedford Town (1966-67) while acting as Fulham's trainer in between times. Under his charge, Hendon beat Whitby Town 3-1 to win the FA Amateur Cup Final at Wembley in 1965.

BURKINSHAW, KEITH H.

Born in Higham, Yorkshire on 23 June 1935, Keith Burkinshaw played as a wing-half for Wolverhampton Wanderers (Amateur), Denaby United, Liverpool and Workington before taking over as player-manager of the latter club in November 1964. He remained at Borough Park until March 1965 and two months later he signed as a player for Scunthorpe United, although he later acted as caretaker-manager of the club during his three-year stay. Coach at Newcastle United for seven years from 1968, Burkinshaw (after a spell as Spurs' coach from May 1975) applied successfully for the manager's job at White Hart Lane. He held office from July 1976 until the end of the 1983-84 season, resigning after becoming disillusioned following a boardroom take-over.

During his reign at White Hart Lane Burkinshaw guided Spurs to two FA Cup Final triumphs (1981 and 1982) and victory in the 1984 UEFA Cup Final as well as reaching the League Cup Final. He signed several quality players, including the Argentinian duo of Ossie Ardiles and Ricky Villa.

On leaving the club (on good terms it must be said) he became Bahrain national coach and then held a similar position in Portugal with Sporting Lisbon before returning to England to manage Gillingham (October 1988-April 1989). After acting as Swindon Town's chief scout he was appointed assistant-manager to Ossie Ardiles at West Bromwich Albion in May 1992 and after the Argentinian had left The Hawthorns to return as boss of Spurs, Burkinshaw took his place in the hot seat (July 1993). Replaced by Alan Buckley early in the 1995-96 season, he then ventured north to serve Aberdeen as Director of Football.

BURNLEY

Spurs playing record against the Clarets is:

Competition	P	W	D	L	F	A
Football League	88	32	22	34	159	138
FA Cup	7	4	1	2	13	10
League Cup	3	1	1	1	4	5
Charity Shield	1	1	0	0	2	0
Summary	99	38	24	37	178	153

The first League meeting between the two clubs was played at White Hart Lane on 12 December 1908 (Division 2) when six goals were scored, Spurs winning 4-2 in front of 10,000 spectators.

In 1924-25, Spurs triumphed 4-1 at Burnley to record their best away win of the season. The Clarets played with 10 men for biggest part of the game after an injury to centre-forward Tom Roberts.

After beating Reading 7-1 on the opening day of the 1930-31 season, Spurs then whipped Burnley 8-1 at White Hart Lane in their second match, Billy Cook scoring a hat-trick.

Another hat-trick hero against the Clarets was Johnny Morrison

who helped Spurs to a convincing 4-0 home win in August 1937. Burnley failed to win any of their seven Second Division matches at White Hart Lane in the 1930s; Spurs were victorious on six occasions.

Burnley completed an early season double over Spurs in 1953-54, winning 4-2 at Turf Moor and 3-2 at White Hart Lane.

In December 1960, Spurs were 4-0 up at home to Burnley after 35 minutes play. It was 4-1 at half-time - but the visitors stormed back during the second period and with a late flurry, gained a point from a 4-4 draw.

Spurs beat Burnley 3-0 in the semi-final of the FA Cup at neutral Villa Park in March 1961. Then, just over a year later, as holders of the trophy, they again defeated the Clarets, this time by 3-1 in the Final itself, skipper Danny Blanchflower getting on the scoresheet with a penalty, one of the few players to score from the spot in such an important game.

However, a third round tie played on a treacherous, icy pitch at White Hart Lane the following season, went Burnley's way to the tune of 3-0.

On a Tuesday evening in April 1964, Spurs (4-0 down at the break) crashed 7-2 to Burnley at Turf Moor - having earlier in the season beaten the Clarets 3-2 at White Hart Lane.

A first-half hat-trick by ace marksman Jimmy Greaves helped Spurs crush Burnley 7-0 at White Hart Lane in September 1968, and the corresponding League games over next two years both produced 4-0 scorelines in favour of Spurs.

When losing heavily in November 1970, it was Burnley's fifth successive visit to White Hart Lane without scoring a goal.

Playing for Spurs against Burnley at White Hart Lane on 5 October 1974, Mike England and John Pratt both conceded own goals in the first-half and then after the break they both scored for Spurs - but the Clarets still won 3-2.

When Spurs defeated Burnley 3-2 in a competitive League Cup-tie at White Hart Lane in October 1993 they had midfielder Darren Caskey sent-off.

Players with both clubs include: David Black, Ralph Coates, Jock Davidson, Arthur Dixon, Frank Drabble, David Haddow, Ellis Hargreaves, Harry Hargreaves, Jim Hartley, Mark Kendall, Doug McFarlane, Paul Mahorn, Tony Parks, Tom Roberts, Max Seeburg, Paul Stewart, Mitchell Thomas, Chris Waddle (Burnley player & manager).

Wartime guests (with either or both clubs): Harry Jackson, Joe Meek, Fred Sargent.

Also associated: Jack Tresadern (Burnley player, Spurs manager), John Sainty (Spurs reserve, Burnley coach), Theo Foley (Burnley reserve, Spurs reserve team manager).

BURROWS, LYCURGUS

A Lancastrian, born in Ashton-under-Lyne on 26 June 1875, tough-tackling full-back Ly Burrows played his early football in the Glasgow area with the Govan-based club, Melrose. He then attended and represented a school in Sheffield and on moving south to London he promptly joined Woolwich Polytechnic, switching to Woolwich Arsenal in January 1892.

Spurs came along and secured his services in October 1894 and over the next three years he played in 119 first team games for the club, scoring three goals.

In December 1897, he returned to Yorkshire to fulfil business requirements and assisted Sheffield United's reserve team (as well as participating in a handful of games for Spurs) before ending his serious playing career in 1899.

Burrows died in Gosforth on 23 August 1952.

BURTON ALBION/UNITED/TOWN/WANDERERS

Spurs have never met any of the main clubs from Burton-on-Trent.

Players with both clubs include: Bill Joyce and Haydn Price (Spurs WW1) (United); Arthur Archer (Wanderers) and Keith Osgood (Albion).

BURTON, JOHN HENRY

Having failed to make his mark with Derby County, half-back John Burton joined Chatham in the summer of 1899 and spent almost two seasons with the Kent club before switching to Spurs in March 1901. He went on to scored three goals in 72 first team outings for Spurs, replacing the injured John L Jones for most of the 1902-03 campaign. He was transferred to Preston North End in October 1906 and later returned south to play for West Ham United (1908-09).

Burton was born in Derby on 13 August 1875 and he died in the same town on 13 May 1949.

BURTON, OLIVER

Able to play as an orthodox full-back or defensively-minded half-back, Olly Burton (John's elder brother) appeared in 163 first team matches for Spurs. He made his debut in a friendly against Cambridge University in November 1902 and played his last game in October 1909 versus Notts County in the First Division.

Born in Derby on 27 May 1879, he came to Spurs on trial in October 1901 and his performances certainly impressed those watching for he was signed as a full-time professional a month later. He remained at the club until the end of the 1909-10 season, missing the last five games of Spurs' first season of League football (1908-09). He retired on leaving White Hart Lane and died at St Pancras, London, on 20 January 1929.

BURY

Spurs playing record against the Shakers is:

Competition	P	W	D	L	F	A
Football League	40	18	8	14	67	66
FA Cup	1	1	0	0	2	1
Summary	41	19	8	14	69	67

In February 1901, Spurs, on their way to the Final, beat the holders Bury 2-1 at home in the 2nd round of the FA Cup.

A crowd of 30,000 attended the first League game between the Shakers and Spurs which was played at White Hart Lane on 9 October 1909 (Division 1). It ended in a 1-0 victory for the Londoners, Bert Middlemiss the goalscorer.

On 26 March 1937 Spurs lost 5-3 at Bury but three days later they gained revenge with a 2-0 victory at White Hart Lane.

Spurs won their last 'valid' home League game before WW2 against Bury - beating the Shakers 4-3 on 22 April 1939 in front of 16,279 spectators. George Ludford and Andy Duncan both scored twice.

Players with both clubs include: Noel Brotherston, Bill Dow, Bill Fleming, Ken Hancock, Fred Mearns, Tom Pangbourne, John Shackleton.

Wartime guests (with either one or both clubs): Jack Acquroff, Len Flack (Bury player-coach), Ernie Jones, Billy Peake, Charlie Revell. Also associated: Percy Smith (manager of both clubs), Jim Iley (Spurs player, Bury manager), Jesse Carver (Spurs coach, Bury player).

BUTTERS, GUY

A strong-tackling central defender, born at Hillingdon on 30 October 1969, Guy Butters represented both Hillingdon & District Boys and Middlesex Schools before joining Spurs as a trainee in July 1986, turning professional in August 1988. He scored once in 39 first-team outings for Spurs before transferring to Portsmouth for £375,000 in September 1990, having had a loan spell with Southend United earlier that year. After 186 appearances for Pompey and another loan spell, this time with Oxford United in November 1994, Butters moved from Fratton Park to Gillingham for £225,000 in October 1996. He did well at the Priestfield Stadium and helped the Kent club gain promotion to the First Division in 2000. Capped three times by England at Under-21 level whilst at White Hart Lane, he was fast approaching the 450 appearance mark when the 2000-01 season came to an end.

C

CABLE, THOMAS HENRY

Having made his name as a fearless England Amateur international centre-half with Barking, Leyton (two spells), Queen's Park Rangers and Middlesex Wanderers, Tommy Cable signed as a professional for Spurs in July 1928.

Twice an FA Amateur Cup winner with Leyton (in 1927 & 1928), Clay was born in Barking, East London on 27 November 1900. He struggled early on at White Hart Lane but eventually settled in and made 49 first team appearances before joining Southampton in September 1932. He was later employed as player-manager by Kettering and then became team manager of Leyton before taking a similar position with Grays Athletic (July 1950-September 1951). He died in Southend-on-Sea on 23 May 1986.

CAIN, ROBERT

Scottish-born full-back Bob Cain played for Airdrieonians, Everton, Bootle and Sheffield United before joining Spurs in May 1898, remaining with the club for just the one season. Having failed to make much of an impression with any of his first three clubs, he appeared in over 175 competitive games for the Blades (164 in the Football League) before adding a further 69 outings to his tally with Spurs (one goal scored).

He was well into his 30s when he moved from White Hart Lane in the summer of 1899 to sign for Albion Rovers, later joining Small Heath as a reserve for half-a-season.

CALDERWOOD, COLIN

Born in Glasgow on 20 January 1965, Colin Calderwood played for Mansfield Town (juniors, June 1980, professional March 1982) and Swindon Town (£30,000, June 1985) before joining Tottenham Hotspur for £1.25 million in July 1993 (a record incoming fee for the Wiltshire club at that time).

He made 117 appearances whilst at Field Mill and then added over 400 more outings to his tally during his time at The County Ground. His performances for the Robins didn't go unnoticed and was signed by Spurs manager Ossie Ardiles in the summer of 1993. He quickly gained the first of his 36 full caps for Scotland and went on to play almost 200 games for the club before transferring to Villa Park in March 1999 for £225,000. After a bright enough start as part of a three-man defence alongside Ugo Ehiogu and Gareth Southgate, Calderwood then lost his place to young Gareth Barry. He became unsettled and after 30 appearances for Villa was eventually sold to Nottingham Forest - signed by ex-Villa star David Platt for £70,000 in March 2000. A year later he had a spell across the River Trent with Notts County.

CAMBRIDGE UNITED

Spurs playing record against United:

Competition	P	W	D	L	F	A
League Cup	1	1	0	0	3	1

Spurs defeated United in the League Cup in season 1986-87, winning a 4th round tie at the Abbey Stadium in front of 10,033 fans. Clive Allen, Shaun Close and Chris Waddle were the scorers. Players with both clubs include: Kevin Dearden, Mike Flanagan (Spurs Youth), Roger Gibbins (Spurs Youth), Danny Greaves & Billy Manuel (both Spurs juniors), John Moncur, Ollie Morah (Spurs reserve), Paul Moran, Keith Osgood, Andy Polston, Martin Robinson, Andy Sinton, Les Stevens, Clive Wilson.
Wartime guest: Wilf Mannion (Spurs).
Also associated: Allan Harris (United player, Spurs coach).

CAMERON, JOHN

One of many Scottish players recruited by Spurs by manager Frank Brettell, John Cameron himself later became boss at White Hart Lane.

Born in Ayr on 13 April 1872, Cameron was a centre or inside-forward who attended Ayr Grammar School before playing junior football for Ayr Parkhouse. He then joined the famous amateur side, Queen's Park before having a spell as a professional with Everton (signed in September 1895). He moved from Merseyside to Spurs in May 1898 and the following February was appointed player-manager at White Hart Lane, taking over from Brettell when he departed to take charge of Portsmouth. Cameron successfully regained amateur status for himself in January 1906. A goal scorer as well as goal maker, Cameron led the Spurs attack when they won the Southern League title in 1900 and then he scored a vital equaliser in the replay of the 1901 FA Cup Final defeat of Sheffield United twelve months later. He was also a key member of the side that finished second in the Southern League in 1902 and 1904. He went on to score 139 goals in 293 first team appearances for the club and was a key figure when the Players' Union (the current PFA),
He resigned as Spurs' manager in 1907 and after a spell as coach to the German club, Dresden FC, he went on to manage his home-town club Ayr United after the Great War before returning to football journalism in 1921, having started writing a column or two in various newspapers prior to the hostilities.
Cameron died in Glasgow on 20 April 1935.

CAMPBELL, SULZEER JEREMIAH

Born in Newham on 18 September 1974, Sol Campbell had two outstanding seasons at the heart of the Spurs defence (and indeed, as a regular in the full England side) before a spate of injuries interrupted his game during the 2000-01 season - which in fact, was to be his last as a Spurs player. When the curtain came down on that campaign Campbell had talks with the club and demanded far too much money (in wages) and as a result moved controversially across the city to Spurs' arch rivals Arsenal.
Twelve months earlier Chairman Sir Alan Sugar and Director of Football David Pleat, had hinted that they would break the bank to keep Campbell at White Hart Lane. They did just that for a while but in the end the club simply couldn't afford to pay the £80,000-a-week demanded by Campbell.
Signed as a trainee in the summer of 1990 and taken on the professional staff in September 1992, Campbell won 40 caps as a Spurs player. He also represented his country in one 'B' international, played eleven times for the Under-21 side and starred in nine youth games for his country.
Physically strong, sound in defence and commanding in the air, he certainly added steel to the Spurs back division and in total made 315 senior appearances for the club (15 goals scored) before leaving in June 2001. He gained a League Cup winners' medal in 1999 (v. Leicester City).

CANTRELL, JAMES

Born in Sheepbridge, Chesterfield on 7 May 1882, Jimmy Cantrell starred for Chesterfield Schools before making an impact with Bulwell Red Rose. He developed further with Bulwell White Star and Hucknall Constitutionals before joining Aston Villa as a professional in July 1904, switching to Notts County in March 1908. Four years later (Oct 1912) he was recruited by Spurs and spent 11 years at White Hart Lane before ending his playing days with Sutton Town (from Aug 1923), retiring in May 1925.
An inside-right or centre-forward, Cantrell scored on his League debut for Villa in a 4-0 win over his future club Notts County in November 1904. A subtle, dainty player, smart and alert with an excellent right-foot he remained at Villa Park for almost four seasons, scoring 23 goals in 52 appearances. He became a Spurs player in 1912 after netting over 60 times in 131 League games for the Magpies, top-scoring at Meadow Lane in three of his four seasons there. At White Hart Lane he continued to rattle in the goals - amassing 95 in almost 200 competitive matches, bagging 19 in 29 outings when Spurs won the Second Division title in 1919-20. Surprisingly Cantrell never gained a full England cap, but one has to remember that there were several high-class marksmen in the game at the same time. During the First World War he guested for his former club Notts County and, with his best years behind him, he still continued in League soccer right up until 1923 when he joined Sutton. The oldest player ever to don a Spurs jersey, he was 40 years and 349 days old when he lined up in a League match against Birmingham in April 1923. After leaving football Cantrell became a professional golfer. He died in Basford on 31 July 1960.

CAPTAINS

Here are some of the many players (listed in A-Z order) who have captained Spurs down the years (some much longer than others): Danny Blanchflower (1950s/60s), Bobby Buckle (elected the club's first captain in 1882), Ron Burgess (1940s/50s), Sol Campbell (1990s), Tommy Clay (1919-20), Tom Collins (1913-15), Bill Felton (1930s), Richard Gough (1986-87), Arthur Grimsdell (early 1920s), Glenn Hoddle (1980s), John (Jack) L Jones (early1900s), Jack Jull (1880s), James McNaught (early 1900s), Dave Mackay (1960s), Gary Mabbutt (1980s), Alan Mullery (late 1960s), Bill Nicholson (1950s), Steve Perryman (1970s), Martin Peters (1970s), Jim Randall (1880s), Graham Roberts (1980s) and Sandy Tait (early 1900s).

Others who have held the job temorarily include: Mike England (1970s), Harry Erentz (late 1890s/early 1900s).

Captain's Log

- Jack Jones led Spurs to victory in the 1900-01 FA Cup Final. Arthur Grimsdell did likewise in 1920-21 and Danny Blanchflower collected the trophy in 1960-61 and 1961-62, as well as leading Spurs to the League championship (and of course the double) in 1960-61 and European Cup-winners Cup glory in 1962-63.
- The 1966-67 winning captain was Dave Mackay.
- Steve Perryman was skipper in 1980-81 and again in 1981-82 and then Gary Mabbutt lifted the star prize in 1990-91.
- The League Cup was collected by Alan Mullery in 1971; two years later a delighted Martin Peters stepped forward to receive the trophy, and in 1999 the silver prize was presented to Spurs' skipper Sol Campbell.
- Ron Burgess captained Spurs to the Second Division championship in 1949-50 and was skipper again the following season when the First Division title came to White Hart Lane.
- When the UEFA Cup was won in 1971-72, Alan Mullery led Spurs from midfield and it was hard man Graham Roberts who was team captain when the same trophy was won in 1983-84.

CARDIFF CITY

Spurs playing record against the Bluebirds:

Competition	P	W	D	L	F	A
Football League	40	20	10	10	60	37
FA Cup	4	2	1	1	6	5
Wartime	2	1	1	0	6	5
Summary	46	23	12	11	72	47

The first of the 40 League games played between the two clubs so far took place at Ninian Park on 27 August 1921 Division 1) and a crowd of 50,000 saw Spurs win 1-0, Jimmy Banks the scorer.

George Robb (3) and Alf Stokes (2) scored the goals when Cardiff were defeated 5-0 at White Hart Lane in October 1956.

Players with both clubs include: Terry Boyle (Spurs reserve), Charlie Brittan, Ron Burgess (City amateur), Willie Davies, Willie Evans (amateur), Danny Hill, Roger Hoy, David Gwilan Jones (Spurs reserve), Terry Lee, Bill Rees.

Wartime guests (with either one or both clubs): Ken Bennett, Eric Jones, Ernie Marshall, Albert Tomkin

Also associated: Gerry Francis (City player, Spurs manager), Cyril Spiers (Spurs player, City manager), Terry Medwin (Spurs player, City coach), Doug Livermore (City player, Spurs manager, assistant-manager/coach, reserve team manager, chief scout).

CARLISLE UNITED

Spurs playing record against the Cumbrians:

Competition	P	W	D	L	F	A
Football League	2	0	1	1	1	2
League Cup	2	2	0	0	5	2
Summary	4	2	1	1	6	4

The two League games between the clubs were played in 1974-75 (Division 1). United drew 1-1 at White Hart Lane after beating Spurs 1-0 at Brunton Park. Only 12,813 fans saw the game in London, Spurs' lowest crowd of the season whereas. there were 18,426 present for the game in Cumbria.

Players with both clubs include: Bill Adams, Ivor Broadis (Carlisle player-manager), Archie Burgon, John Gorman, Tom Smith.

Also associated: Fred Ford (Carlisle player-coach/trainer, Spurs Wartime guest).

Burnley line up to greet captain Danny Blanchflower and the Spurs League Championship winning team of 1960-61 before their match at Turf Moor

CARR, STEPHEN

Born in Dublin on 29 August 1976, right-back Stephen Carr joined Spurs as a trainee in the summer of 1991 and turned professional in September 1993. A player who loves to get forward, he has scored some cracking goals already and there are more to come from the Republic of Ireland international who has now represented his country 18 times while also gaining honours at Schoolboy, Youth and Under-21 levels, collecting 12 caps in the latter category. When the 2000-01 season ended, Carr's appearance record for the club stood at 199 first-class games (with seven goals scored).

CARRICK, CHRISTOPHER

Outside-left Chris Carrick was born in Stockton-on-Tees on 8 October 1882 and played for Middlesbrough and West Ham United before joining Spurs in April 1905. He scored five goals in 24 first team appearances for the club before transferring to Reading in the summer of 1906. Later he assisted Bradford Park Avenue and Glentoran.

* Carrick was involved in a 'misdemeanour' with Spurs colleague Peter Kyle whilst down in the West Country for games against Bristol Rovers and Plymouth in March 1906 and as a result neither played for the club again!

CARTWRIGHT, WILLIAM

Between 1906-20 full-back Bill Cartwright played for Gainsborough Trinity, Chelsea, Spurs (1913-19) and Swansea Town. He then became coach at Southend United. He appeared in 15 first-class games for Spurs

CASKEY, DARREN MARK

Hard-working midfielder who, on leaving Spurs for Reading for £700,000 in February 1996, became the Royals' most expensive signing.

Born on 21 August 1974 in Basildon, he joined the apprentice ranks at White Hart Lane in 1990, signed professional forms in March 1992 and over the next four years made 43 League and Cup appearances for Spurs, scoring five goals. Capped by England at Schoolboy and Youth team levels, Caskey assisted Watford on loan before moving to Reading. He did very well with the Royals but a month or so after sitting on the bench as an unused substitute watching his team lose the Second Division Play-off Final against Walsall in May 2001 he left Reading for Notts County.

CASTLE, SIDNEY ERNEST ROWLAND

A guest for Reading and Crystal Palace during WWI, right-winger Sid Castle played in five League games for Spurs in 1920-21 before transferring to Charlton Athletic later joining Chelsea.

CASUALS

Spurs record against the Casuals:

Competition	P	W	D	L	F	A
LAC	2	0	0	2	0	9

The famous London amateur side, Casuals, beat Spurs twice in the London Association Cup competition - first by 8-0 in a second tie in November 1885 and then by 1-0 in round five in January 1893.

CENTENARY

Spurs celebrated their centenary in season 1981-82 - and they retained the FA Cup (at Queens Park Rangers' expense) to bring the curtain down on a memorable campaign.

Surprisingly, there was not a match arranged by the club to celebrate the 100th birthday!

CHAIRMEN

Here is a list of Spurs Chairmen in order of holding office:

John Oliver	March, 1898 to November, 1898
Charles D. Roberts	November, 1898 to July, 1943
Fred J. Bearman	August, 1943 to October, 1961
Fred Wale	October, 1961 to October, 1969
Sidney A. Wale	October, 1969 to March, 1980
Arthur Richardson	June, 1980 to December, 982
Douglas A. Alexiou	December, 1982 to 16 July, 1984
Irving A. Scholar	16 July, 1984 to 22 June, 1991
Tony G. Berry	22 June, 1991 to June, 1992
Alan M. Sugar	June, 1992 to 28 February, 2001
Daniel Levy	Since 28 February, 2001

CHALMERS, JAMES

Outside-left Jim Chalmers played for Morton, Sunderland, Preston, Notts County and Watford before making 26 senior appearances for Spurs (1902-04). He later served with Swindon Town, Norwich City and Bristol Rovers.

CHAMPIONSHIPS

Spurs have won the Football League championship twice: in 1950-51 and 1960-61.

The Second Division title was won in 1919-20 and 1949-50.

Prior to entering the Football League in 1908, Spurs won the Southern League title in 1899-1900; the London League in 1902-03 and the Western League in 1903-04.

During World War Two they were Regional League (South) champions in 1939-40 and winners of the Football League (South) in 1943-44 and 1944-45.

CHANNELL, FREDERICK CHARLES

Full-back Fred Channell played for the amateur side Harwich & Parkeston and Haywards FC before joining the groundstaff at White Hart Lane in February 1928, turning professional in August 1930. He went on to make 113 first team appearances for the club, his debut coming against Sunderland in October 1933 and his final outings versus West Ham United in March 1936. He broke a leg against the Hammers and was forced to retire two months later.

Born in Edmonton on 5 May 1910, Channell assisted Clapton Orient (as a trialist), Peterborough & Fletton United and Northfleet before signing 'pro' forms. In 1935 he played in an England trial at West Bromwich and also for an English XI v. the Anglo-Scots at Highbury. A cool, competent defender, he looked set for full international honours before that crushing injury just before his 26th birthday.

Channell, who later ran a pub in Ponders End, Middlesex, died in Colchester on 6 August 1976.

CHAPLIN, JONATHAN FOWLER

Strong and stocky full-back Jock Chaplin was signed by Spurs' boss Frank Brettell from Dundee in May 1905, having gained Scottish League representative honours. He made 102 first team appearances before returning to the Scottish club in May 1908. Born in Dundee on 10 October 1882, Chaplin played initially for Dundee Arnot and then Dundee Wanderers, and after his second spell at Dens Park he switched back to the Football League to sign for Manchester City (November 1910). He was later employed as a trainer by four different clubs, Leeds City (November 1913), Bristol Rovers (March 1920), Sheffield Wednesday (August 1920) and Huddersfield Town (April 1921). He was also assistant-manager of Leeds City and became manager of Huddersfield in August 1926 (following in the footsteps of Herbert Chapman)

Spurs Second Division Title squad of 1949-50

and, in fact, he guided the Terriers to the FA Cup Final in 1928. He returned to his job as spongeman at Leeds Road in May 1929, retiring in 1935.

Chaplin, whose playing career was ended by a serious knee injury, died in Doncaster on 15 April 1952.

* Chaplin's two brothers, Alex and George, were both professional footballers. George won full caps for Scotland while Alex guested for Spurs during the Great War.

CHAPMAN, HERBERT

As a player Herbert Chapman was of average ability, as a manager he was outstanding, some say great!

A Yorkshireman, born in Kiveton near Sheffield on 19 January 1878, he was something of a soccer nomad and served with 12 different clubs (at various levels) including Rochdale, Swindon Town, Grimsby Town, Sheffield United and Notts County before joining Spurs from Northampton Town in March 1905. An inside-forward, he scored 22 goals in 71 first team appearances during his two-year stay at White Hart Lane. He then returned to Northampton as player-manager in April 1907, became manager of Leeds City in May 1912 and was then appointed secretary of Huddersfield Town in September 1920, moving into the manager's chair in March 1921 after a month acting as assistant to Ambrose Langley.

It was here, at Leeds Road, where he became an acknowledged, highly-respected and admired manager. He quickly guided the Terriers to victory in 1922 FA Cup Final (beating Preston 1-0) and then led them to successive League championship triumphs in 1924 and 1925.

After that second success he moved south to take over the reins at Highbury and in the space of nine years saw the Gunners win the First Division title in 1931 and 1933, finish runners-up in 1926 and 1932, carry off the FA Cup in 1930 and lose the 1927 and 1932 Cup Finals to Cardiff City and Newcastle United respectively.

The Gunners were, in fact, well on their way to clinching a second successive League title when, on 6 January 1934, Chapman sadly died of pneumonia in a Hendon hospital.

Chapman could be and undoubtedly was at times, ruthless (very

ruthless) with certain footballers. When Third Division (South) side Walsall knocked Arsenal, the reigning League champions, out of the FA Cup in 1933, he singled out one player - Tommy Black - for not pulling his weight and indeed, for giving away a crucial goal. Black was sent home, told to stay well clear of Highbury - and was eventually sold to Plymouth. He also sacked one of his coaches for undermining his instructions.

* Today a bust of Herbert Chapman stands in the main entrance hall to Highbury Stadium - an epitaph to one of football's greatest-ever managers!

CHARLTON ATHLETIC

Spurs playing record against the Addicks:

Competition	P	W	D	L	F	A
Premiership	4	1	2	1	6	4
Football League	34	18	6	10	67	40
FA Cup	4	3	1	0	10	6
Other Cups	2	2	0	0	11	3
Wartime	19	12	0	7	40	31
Summary	63	36	9	18	134	84

The first time Spurs met Charlton in the Football League was on 14 December 1929 (Division 2). A crowd of 17,350 at The Valley saw the Addicks win 1-0 before Spurs gained revenge with a 3-0 victory at White Hart Lane in mid-April, Ted Harper netting twice.

On Christmas Day 1931 Spurs lost 1-0 at home to Charlton but 24 hours later they gained revenge with a 5-2 victory at The Valley, George Hunt scoring a hat-trick.

When Spurs beat Charlton 6-2 at White Hart Lane in a First Division game in April 1957, all five forwards found the net, Tommy Harmer scoring twice.

The teams weren't to meet again at League level until 1977-78 (Division 2) and then the Addicks won 4-1 at The Valley before losing the return fixture 2-1 at White Hart Lane.

Spurs completed the double over Athletic in 1989-90, winning 3-0 at home and 3-1 away.

Two goals in the last 90 seconds helped Spurs beat Charlton 4-1 at The Valley in a Premiership game in April 1999. The Addicks had led 1-0 at half-time.

And on their way to reaching the FA Cup semi-finals in 2001,

Spurs knocked their London rivals out of the competition with a 4th round win on Charlton soil.

Players with both clubs include: Dennis Bond, Sid Castle, Garth Crooks, Mike Flanagan (Spurs Youth), Matt Forster, Clayton Fortune (Athletic trialist), Abraham Goodman, Richard Gough, John Hendry, Baden Herod, Scott Houghton, Neil Johnson, Chris Jones, David Kerslake (briefly with the Addicks), Don McAllister, Paul Miller, Terry Naylor, Martin Robinson, Mark Robson, Neil Ruddock, Paul Walsh, Simon Webster, Len Worley (Amateur).

Wartime guests (with either one or both clubs): Ted Bassett, Pat Beasley, John Davie, Fred Ford, Harry Gilberg, Charlie Hannaford, Charlie Harbridge, John Oakes, Charlie Revell (also Athletic coach & scout), Jack Skinner, George Smith, Les Stevens, Charlie Whitchurch.

Also associated: Alan Mullery & Jimmy Seed (Spurs players, Athletic managers), Peter Shreeves (Charlton coach, Spurs Youth, reserve and first team manager), Theo Foley (Charlton player, coach, manager & chief scout, Spurs reserve team manager), Jim Iley (Spurs player, Athletic coach), Daniel H Clark (Spurs amateur, Charlton director).

CHATHAM

Spurs playing record against Chatham:

Competition	P	W	D	L	F	A
Other Leagues	13	8	0	5	29	22

Beaten 4-2 away by Chatham in a Southern League game on 29 January 1898, Spurs won the return fixture in early April by 2-1, David Black scoring the winner, having also netted in the first fixture.

Spurs crashed to successive Thames & Medway League defeats at the hands of Chatham in January 1899, losing 5-0 away and 4-0 at home in the space of eight days!

Spurs' 5-0 home win over Chatham in a Southern League fixture in 1900-01 was not recorded in the final table as the Kent club resigned from the competition.

Player with both clubs: Bob Clements.

CHIEDOZIE, JOHN OKAY

Born in Owerri, Nigeria on 18 April 1960, right-winger John Chiedozie was educated in Newham and represented London Schools as a teenager before joining (Leyton) Orient as an apprentice, turning professional in April 1977. Four-and-a-half years later he was transferred to Notts County from where he switched to Spurs in August 1984, manager Peter Shreeves paying £375,000 for his services. Fast and direct with some fine skills, he scored 19 goals in 103 first team outings for Spurs (12 coming in 53 First Division games, including one on his debut against Everton at Goodison Park). A series of niggling injuries led to him leaving White Hart Lane on a free transfer to Derby County in August 1988. He later went back to Meadow Lane (as a non-contract player) and after a loan spell with Chesterfield (in March 1990) he wound down his playing career with Bashley and Banks of Barking.

Capped before, during and after his days with Spurs, Chiedozie appeared in a total of 23 internationals for Nigeria and he played in 319 League games for his five different clubs.

CHELSEA

Spurs playing record against the London club:

Competition	P	W	D	L	F	A
Premiership	18	0	7	11	13	35
Football League	88	40	17	31	150	115
FA Cup	7	4	1	2	11	7
League Cup	4	0	2	2	4	8
Other Cups	2	2	0	0	5	1
Wartime	28	15	5	8	46	49
Summary	147	61	32	54	229	214

The first Football League encounter between the two clubs was played at Stamford Bridge on 18 December 1909 (Division 1). A crowd of 50,000 saw the Blues win 2-1.

On the last day of that season Spurs and Chelsea met in a relegation battle at White Hart Lane. A victory for either side would ensure First Division survival, defeat would be disastrous!

Ted Ditchburn punches clear from Billy Gray in Spurs' 3-2 defeat in 1953

Chelsea keeper Reg Matthews thwarts Alf Stokes in the 1-1 draw in August 1957

Cliff Jones sees his header tipped over the bar in the 2-0 win at Stamford Bridge in December 1961

Vivian Woodward, much to the chagrin of the Spurs' supporters, was in the visitors; line-up while Percy Humphreys, a former Chelsea centre-forward was in the Spurs line-up. A crowd of 35,000 witnessed a tense match, which Spurs won 2-1 with Humphreys scoring the winning goal. Chelsea went down with Bolton, while Spurs stayed up with Arsenal!

Spurs beat Chelsea 5-0 at home and 4-0 away in 1920-21. The game at White Hart Lane was also a benefit match for players Bert Bliss, Jimmy Cantrell and Jimmy Dimmock and 47,000 fans turned out to see Bliss score a terrific hat-trick. A record crowd of 76,000 packed into Stamford Bridge to see Spurs complete the double. Towards the end of the season Spurs returned to Stamford Bridge to beat Wolves 1-0 in the FA Cup Final.

After losing 2-0 at Stamford Bridge in season 1955-56, Spurs defeated the reigning League champions 4-0 in the return fixture, Johnny Brooks scoring twice.

Alf Stokes was Spurs' hero in their 4-2 win at Stamford Bridge in October 1956, but he could only net once in the return leg as the Blues gained revenge with a 4-3 victory in front of a meagre mid-week derby day crowd of just 20,849.

On 27 August 1958 Spurs lost 4-2 at Chelsea. A week later they beat the Blues 4-0 at White Hart Lane, Terry Medwin netting a hat-trick.

Spurs collected four points off neighbours Chelsea when they won the double in 1960-61. They beat the Blues 4-2 at home and 3-2 at Stamford Bridge.

It was as you were twelve months later as Spurs doubled-up again, winning 2-0 away and 5-2 at home. Jimmy Greaves scored once at the 'Bridge' against his former club while Cliff Jones netted a hat-trick at White Hart Lane. In 1967 the first all-London FA Cup Final ended Spurs 2 Chelsea 1.

Spurs lost 4-3 at Chelsea in a thrilling Premiership encounter in February 1994 and they crashed to an alarming 6-1 home defeat at the hands of the Blues in December 1997 - Spurs' heaviest home reverse in the Premiership.

When Spurs lost 2-0 at Stamford Bridge in December 1998 they had striker Chris Armstrong sent-off.

As it stands, Spurs have not yet recorded a single win over their London rivals in Premiership football, their latest embarrassment was to lose 3-0 at White Hart Lane in April 2001 when Willem Korsten was shown the red card.

In senior competition, Spurs have not beaten Chelsea in 26 attempts between 1989 and 2001 (six in the old First Division, two League Cup games in 1991 and 18 encounters in the Premiership). Having been defeated 1-0 at White Hart Lane in August 1987, Chelsea were then relegated from the top flight at the end of that season. They returned for the start of the 1989-90 campaign and as yet Spurs haven't beaten them in a competitive match!

Players with both clubs include: Clive Allen, Les Allen, Jimmy Armstrong, Eddie Baily (Chelsea amateur), Ted Birnie, Derek Brazil (Chelsea trial), Johnny Brooks, Bill Cartwright, Sid Castle, David Copeland, Jason Cundy, Kerry Dixon (Spurs Youth player), Gordon Durie, Mark Falco, Lee Gardner (Chelsea trialist), Jimmy Greaves, Frode Grodas, Micky Hazard, Percy Humphreys, Steve Kelly (Chelsea trialist), John Kirwan, Colin Lee, Gustavo Poyet, Graham Roberts (Chelsea player-coach), Max Seeburg, Buchanan Sharp, Bobby Smith, Sid Tickridge, Jimmy Townley (Chelsea trialist), Keith Weller, Harry Wilding, Clive Wilson, Vivian Woodward (also Spurs and Chelsea director).

Wartime guests (with either one or both clubs): Alex Anderson, Frank Boulton, Billy Brawn, Bernie Bryant, Harry Ferrier, Alf Fitzgerald, James Fulwood, Jakey Jackson, Eric Jones, Tom Kiernan,

George Ludford, Charlie Revell, Albert Sibley, Reg Smith, Bill Sperrin, Les Stevens, Alf Whittingham, Vic Woodley, Tim Worrall, Albert Young.

Also associated: Danny Blanchflower (Spurs player, Chelsea manager), Glenn Hoddle (player & manager, Spurs and Chelsea), George Graham (Chelsea player, Spurs manager), Tommy Harmer & Andy Thompson (Spurs players, Chelsea coaches), Stewart Houston (Chelsea player, Spurs assistant-manager), Allan Harris (Chelsea player, Spurs assistant-manager), Ernie Walley (Chelsea assistant-manager), Peter Suddaby (Chelsea U-15/16 coach, Spurs Academy Director).

CHELTENHAM TOWN

No competitive have taken place between Spurs and Town as yet. Player with both clubs: Bill Adams.

Associated: Jimmy Brain (Spurs player, Town manager), David Gwilan Jones (Spurs reserve).

CHESHAM

Spurs playing record against Chesham:

Competition	P	W	D	L	F	A
WDCC	2	1	1	0	5	3

Spurs' only win at first team level over Chesham was achieved in the Wolverton & District Charity Cup in season 1893-94. After a 2-2 draw at home, Spurs won the 1st round replay 3-1 with goals by Archie Cubberley, Jock MacLaughan and Ernie Payne.

CHESTER (CITY)

Spurs playing record against Chester:

Competition	P	W	D	L	F	A
League Cup	2	2	0	0	7	1

Chester were Spurs 2nd round League Cup victims in 1995-6. It was 4-0 at home and 3-1 away.

Players with both clubs include: Foster Hedley, Baden Herod, Harry Skitt, Andy Thompson, Clive Wilson.

Wartime guests (with either or both clubs): Harry Blackburn, Ronnie Dix, Tom Howshall, Ernie Jones, Jimmy McCormick, Tommy Manley, Sid Ottewell.

Also associated: Charlie Hewitt (Spurs player, Chester manager), John Sainty (Spurs reserve, Chester coach & manager), Doug Livermore (Chester player, Spurs manager, assistant-manager/coach, reserve team manager, chief scout).

CHESTERFIELD

Spurs playing record against the Spire-ites:

Competition	P	W	D	L	F	A
Football League	20	9	6	5	45	28
FA Cup	2	1	1	0	4	3
Summary	22	10	7	5	49	31

The first time Spurs met Chesterfield at League level was on 17 October 1908 (Division 2) and in front of 14,000 fans at White Hart Lane they won comfortably by four goals to nil.

When Spurs beat Chesterfield 4-0 at White Hart Lane in September 1948 it was their second successive result with that scoreline in five days.

Players with both clubs include: Gerry Armstrong, John Chiedozie, Ed Downie, George Hunt, Mark Kendall, Jimmy McCormick, Les Miller, Bob Tannahill, Walter Tattersall.

Wartime guests (with either one or both clubs): John Davie, Colin Lyman, David Nelson, Sid Ottewell, Vic Woodley.

Also associated: John Duncan (Spurs player, Chesterfield manager; three spells).

CHIPPERFIELD, JOHN JAMES

London-born forward Jimmy Chipperfield played for Luton Town and Arsenal (WWI) before joining Spurs in 1919. After scoring six goals in 15 League games for the club he switched to Notts County in 1921. Later he assisted Northfleet and Charlton Athletic.

CHISHOLM, JOHN RICHARDSON

Scorer of just one goal in 81 first-team outings for Spurs, made between May 1942 and August 1947, centre-half Jack 'The Boy' Chisholm went on to greater things after leaving White Hart Lane. Born in Enfield, Middlesex on 9 October 1924, he was a Tottenham junior before joining Spurs in October 1941.

Besides playing many times for Spurs during the War (when he served as a guardsman in the Army) he also guested for Fulham and Millwall but after the hostilities he struggled to get into the first XI at White Hart Lane and finally left for Brentford in December 1947. He assisted Sheffield United (from March to December 1949) and then, as captain, made 187 senior appearances for Plymouth Argyle, helping them regain their Second Division status, before ending his career in non-League circles with Helston and then Romford, the latter as manager. A fine cricketer in his time - he played for Middlesex as well as Bedfordshire and Devon - Chisholm, with his neatly-trimmed beard, later managed a betting shop in Edmonton.

He died in Waltham Forest in August 1977.

CHIVERS, MARTIN HARCOURT

Martin Chivers so desperately wanted to play for Southampton that he wrote a handful of letters to The Dell asking for a trial. He was successful - and after a game or two for CPC Sports (Saints' nursery team) he was taken on as a full-time professional in September 1962. Playing alongside Welsh international Ron Davies, he went on to score 107 goals in 189 League and Cup games over the next five-and-a-half years, helping Saints win promotion from the Second Division for the first time in the club's history.

Using Frank Saul, valued at around £45,000 as bait, plus £125,000 (a British record at the time), Spurs manager Bill Nicholson enticed Chivers to White Hart Lane in January 1968 (a move viewed with gloom by the ardent Saints' supporters). But it had to happen, Spurs needed a proven goalscorer to accompany Alan Gilzean and Jimmy Greaves - and Chivers fitted the bill to a tee. Unfortunately an injury suffered against Nottingham Forest in September 1968 (after he had already netted 16 times in 34

major competitive matches) set him back somewhat but once he had regained full fitness he struck back with a vengeance and slowly but surely piled up the goals and international honours. He took his overall tally to 202 for Spurs in 415 first-team outings, including 118 in 278 League games and 56 in various Cup matches. He won 24 full caps for England plus five at Under-23 level, having earlier gained 12 in the latter context with Saints. He helped Spurs win the 1971 League Cup Final with two late goals against Aston Villa, followed up with a UEFA Cup triumph in 1972 v. Wolves and then added a second League Cup winners' prize to his collection in 1973. He was also a member of Spurs' beaten 1974 UEFA Cup Final side.

Chivers, who was blessed with a terrific long throw (he hurled the ball some 45 yards in one game) left White Hart Lane for the Swiss side Servette in an £80,000 deal in July 1976. Two years later he returned to the UK to sign for Norwich City and after a spell with Brighton & Hove Albion he was appointed player-manager of Dorchester Town in August 1980. He then acted as player-coach to the Norwegian side FC Vard (1981-82) before ending his footballing days as player-manager of Barnet (from October-December 1982). He then took on a hotel/restaurant business in Hertfordshire and when time allowed, worked as a soccer analyst on BBC Radio 5.

* Surprisingly, in the first 29 League games of Saints' Second Division promotion-winning campaign of 1965-66, Chivers scored 30 goals and then failed to net at all in the last 13!

CHRISTMAS DAY

Spurs have played 54 games on Christmas Day. Here is the full list.
Football League

1908 v. Oldham Athletic	(a)	0-1
1909 v. Nottingham Forest	(h)	2-2
1911 v. Woolwich Arsenal	(h)	5-0
1912 v. Manchester City	(a)	2-2
1914 v. Sheffield Wednesday	(a)	2-3
1919 v. Hull City	(h)	4-0
1920 v. Newcastle United	(a)	1-1
1922 v. Sheffield United	(h)	2-1
1923 v. Huddersfield Town	(h)	1-0
1924 v. Bury	(h)	1-1
1925 v. Birmingham	(a)	1-3
1926 v. Manchester United	(h)	1-1
1928 v. Reading	(h)	2-2
1929 v. Southampton	(h)	3-2
1930 v. Southampton	(h)	1-3
1931 v. Charlton Athletic	(h)	0-1
1933 v. Huddersfield Town	(h)	1-3
1934 v. Grimsby Town	(a)	0-3
1935 v. Plymouth Argyle	(h)	1-2
1936 v. Blackburn Rovers	(a)	4-0
1937 v. Bury	(a)	2-1
1946 v. Coventry City	(a)	1-3
1947 v. Chesterfield	(h)	3-0
1948 v. Leicester City	(a)	2-1
1950 v. Derby County	(a)	1-1
1951 v. Charlton Athletic	(a)	3-0
1952 v. Middlesbrough	(h)	7-1
1953 v Portsmouth	(h)	1-1
1954 v. Bolton Wanderers	(a)	2-1
1956 v. Everton	(h)	6-0
1958 v. West Ham United	(a)	1-2

Southern League

1896 v. Millwall Athletic	(a)	4-0
1899 v. Portsmouth	(h)	3-0
1900 v. Portsmouth	(h)	4-1
1901 v. Portsmouth	(h)	1-2
1902 v. Portsmouth	(h)	2-2
1903 v. Portsmouth	(h)	1-1
1905 v. Portsmouth	(h)	3-1
1906 v. Millwall	(h)	3-1
1907 v. Northampton Town	(h)	2-0

United League

1897 v. Woolwich Arsenal	(a)	3-2

London Combination

1915 v. Croydon Common	(h)	3-0
1916 v. Brentford	(a)	5-1
1917 v. Millwall	(a)	6-0
1918 v. Queens Park Rangers	(a)	1-1

Football League (South)

1939 v. Millwall	(a)	1-5
1940 v. Millwall	(h)	3-3
1941 v. Millwall	(a)	2-1
1942 v. Brentford	(h)	1-1
1943 v. Fulham	(h)	2-0
1944 v. Queens Park Rangers	(h)	4-2
1945 v. Derby County	(h)	2-5

Friendlies

1894 v. Sheffield & District League (h) 7-1
1895 v. Millwall Athletic (a) 3-5

Summary of Christmas Day fixtures

P	W	D	L	F	A
54	27	13	14	129	77

Xmas Cheer

- Bill Dryburgh scored on his Southern League debut for Spurs against Portsmouth on Christmas Day, 1902.
- A Christmas Day crowd of over 47,000 saw Spurs beat Woolwich Arsenal 5-0 in the First Division game at White Hart Lane in 1911.
- Les Bennett scored four goals in Spurs' 7-1 home win over Middlesbrough in 1952.
- Jimmy Banks netted a hat-trick when Spurs beat Millwall (away) in 1917.
- Spurs lost five Christmas Day games on the trot between 1930 and 1935.
- Portsmouth have played Spurs most times on 25 December - total six (all in the old Southern League days).
- Spurs' last Christmas Day game was a visit to Upton Park for a First Division game in 1958. The Hammers won 2-1 in front of 26,178 fans - and Bobby Smith had the honour of scoring Spurs' last Yuletide goal!

CITY RAMBLERS

Spurs' playing record against the Ramblers:

Competition	P	W	D	L	F	A
Amateur Cup	1	1	0	0	6	1

Goals by Peter Hunter (2) and Ernie Payne (2) helped Spurs to a comfortable second qualifying round win over the Ramblers in the FA Amateur Cup in November 1894.

CLAESEN, NICOLAS PIETER JOSEF

Striker Nico Claesen was signed by Spurs manager David Pleat for £600,000 from the Belgian side Standard Liege in October 1986. For practically two seasons he did very well, scoring 28 goals in 77 first-team appearances for the club (netting 18 times in exactly 50 outings in Division One) and playing as a substitute in the 1987 FA Cup Final. But when Terry Venables took over the reins at White Hart Lane, Claesen became unsettled and in August 1988 he returned to his homeland to sign for RSC Antwerp for £550,000.

Born in Lent, Belgium on 1 October 1962, he played initially for Patro Eisden and then Seraing (of Liege) before teaming up with German club Vfb Stuttgart from where he joined Standard Liege in 1985. Capped over 50 times by his country, he helped Belgium reach the semi-finals of the 1986 World Cup and he also played in the 1990 World Cup Finals.

CLAPTON

Spurs playing record against Clapton:

Competition	P	W	D	L	F	A
FA Cup	3	2	1	0	7	3

The first time Spurs met Clapton at competitive level was in the 3rd qualifying round of the FA Cup on 24 November 1894 and in front of 2,500 spectators Spurs raced through to the 4th stage with a competent 4-0 victory, Scotsman Jock Eccles scoring twice. Another two-goal hero was John Cameron who achieved the feat when Spurs defeated Clapton 2-1 in a 2nd qualifying round replay at home in November 1898.

Players with both clubs include: Don Goodall, William Hay, Charlie Rance, Charlie Regan, Alf Stokes, Walter Tull, Jack Welham.

CLAPTON ORIENT

Spurs played Clapton Orient several times at various levels and in several competitions before the London club changed its name to Leyton Orient in 1946 and then Orient in 1966 before reverting back to Leyton Orient in 1987. (See under Leyton Orient for all the relevant match and player details).

CLARKE, HENRY ALFRED

Almost a year after helping Lovells Athletic win the Welsh Cup, 6ft 3in centre-half Harry Clarke was snapped up by Spurs for what was described as 'peanuts' in March 1949. Replacing Horace Woodward in the No.5 position, he quickly established himself in the side, helping Spurs win both the Second and First Division championships in successive seasons while taking his total of appearances at first-team level slowly towards the 100 mark. His final tally was to reach 380 (including 295 in the Football League and 27 in the FA Cup) before he was replaced in the team by John Ryden in December 1956. He remained at White Hart Lane as a coach before taking over as player-manager of Llanelli in February 1959, later managing Romford. Clarke was capped once by England against Scotland in front of 135,000 spectators at Hampden Park in 1954 - a month after representing his country's 'B' team v. West Germany.

Clarke was born at Woodford, Essex on 23 February 1923 and he died on 16 April 2000.

CLAWLEY, GEORGE

Efficient goalkeeper George Clawley broke his leg early in the 1900-01 season but made a full recovery and starred in Spurs' FA Cup Final replay victory over Sheffield United later in the campaign. In fact, he was involved in a controversial incident during the first game of that Final when a goal was allowed to stand despite claims by Clawley and his fellow defenders that the ball never crossed the line! Clawley had dropped the ball when under pressure from two United forwards. Born in Scholar Green in Staffordshire on 10 April 1875, he played for Crewe Alexandra, Stoke and Southampton St Mary's before returning to the Potteries' club for a second spell in May 1898. He moved to White Hart Lane twelve months later and over the next four seasons appeared in 186 first-class matches, helping Spurs win the Southern League title in 1900 before following up with his Cup medal.

On leaving White Hart Lane in May 1903, he returned to Southampton and retired in 1907. Clawley died in the Hampshire town on 16 July 1920.

CLAY, THOMAS

OUR FOOTBALL BOYS—No. 2

TOM CLAY (Spurs' right-back). Five feet ten high, eleven stone ten in weight, and every bit of him brilliant. Has several caps but still has room for more.

Full-back Tommy Clay made 505 first-team appearances for Spurs over a period of 15 years. Born in Leicester on 19 November 1892, a former bricklayer, he joined Leicester Fosse in April 1911 and actually made his debut against Spurs as a 19 year-old before switching south to White Hart Lane (with his colleague Harry Sparrow) in January 1914, signed by manager Peter McWilliam. Strong, confident and reliable, a cultured thinker and fine passer of the ball, he was admired by the young supporters of the club. He guested for Notts County during the Great War and then starred in the 1920 promotion side and FA Cup-winning team the following season. He was capped four times by England, played in an international trial and also represented the Football League. In March 1921 he was chosen to keep goal against Sunderland at Roker Park. He did well as Spurs won 1-0.

When he retired in June 1929 Clay was appointed player-coach of Northfleet, later taking over as trainer/coach of St Albans City where he was also a publican. He went back to being a bricklayer before passing away in Southend on 21 February 1949, aged 56.

CLAYTON, EDWARD

Able to play equally as well in either a wing-half or inside-forward position, Eddie Clayton scored 26 goals in 133 first team appearances for Spurs (20 coming in his 92 outings in the First

Division). Born in Bethnal Green, North London on 7 May 1937, he was a player with Eton Manor before joining the amateur ranks at White Hart Lane in 1955, turning professional in December 1957. With so many fine players around him, he struggled to hold down a place in the senior side, his best season coming in 1965-66 when he missed only four League matches. In March 1968 he was transferred to Southend United and two years later moved to Margate before ending his career with Aylesbury. He later became a PE teacher at a school in Hornchurch, Essex.

CLEAN SHEETS.

Pat Jennings kept a club record 20 clean sheets in 40 League games for Spurs in season 1970-71. He also kept five blank sheets in Cup matches.

The previous record-holder, Bill Jacques, was not passed in 19 of his 42 League games in the 1919-20 season.

Ian Walker holds the Spurs record for most clean-sheets in a Premiership season - 13 in 1996-97. Neil Sullivan had nine blanks to his name in 2000-01

CLEMENCE, RAYMOND NEAL, MBE

During an exceptionally fine career, goalkeeper Ray Clemence made 1,116 competitive appearances (for clubs and country). He played in 407 first-team matches for Spurs alone, 240 coming in the First Division and 80 in various Cup competitions. He also won 61 full and four Under-23 caps for England and made two appearances for the Football League.

Born in Skegness on 5 August 1948, he was rejected by Notts County as a teenager before signing professional forms for Scunthorpe United in August 1965. Two years and 50 appearances later (most of them made under the managership of Keith Burkinshaw, later to be boss at White Hart Lane) he moved to Liverpool for just £15,000. At Anfield he became a star in a star-studded team, gaining medals galore.

He was a member of five victorious League Championship-winning teams, a winner in two FA Cup Finals, triumphed in three European Cup Finals, celebrated two UEFA Cup Final successes, appeared in one League Cup Final win and was a champion in the European Super Cup .He also rejoiced in three outright FA Charity Shield victories. And one cannot fail to mention that he was also rewarded with a handful of runners-up medals as well!

He made 662 competitive appearances for Liverpool (in the Football League, FA Cup, League Cup, in Europe and in the FA Charity Shield). Only two players, Emlyn Hughes and Ian Callaghan (both team-mates of his) have made more.

Clemence left Anfield (to be replaced by Bruce Grobbelaar) in August 1981 when he signed for Spurs for £300,000. He made his debut for the club at Wembley later that same month - in the 2-2 FA Charity Shield draw with Aston Villa - and then he went majestically on until retiring in March 1988 following a serious knee injury suffered six months earlier. At that point he became goalkeeping coach at White Hart Lane, later taking over as reserve team manager and then reverting to assistant first team coach (May 1992). He has also been goalkeeping coach to the full England squad over the past few years.

In his first season with Spurs, Clemence won an FA Cup winners medal and received a League Cup runners-up when beaten by his former club Liverpool. He also collected second prize in the 1987 FA Cup Final, receiving the MBE that same year for services to football.

CLEMENCE, STEPHEN NEAL
Son of Ray (above) Stephen Clemence, unlike his father is a central midfield player, and a good one at that. Strong and mobile, he passed the 100-mark in senior appearances for the club during the latter stages of the 2000-01 season when he was also a member of the England Under-21 side, having earlier represented his country at both Schoolboy and Youth team levels.
Born in Liverpool on 31 March 1978, he joined Spurs as a trainee in June 1994 and turned professional in April 1995.

CLEMENTS, ROBERT WILLIAM
Bob 'Topsy' Clements scored Spurs' first goal in Southern League football, in a 3-1 away win at Sheppey on 5 September 1896. He went on to net another 70 times for the club in a total of 128 appearances before transferring to Chatham at the end of the 1897-98 season. Born in Greenwich on 14 May 1875, he was still a teenager when he joined Spurs in March 1895. A regular in the side for two years, until the arrival of Bob Stormont, Clements later played for Grays United (November 1900-May 1903). He died in Greenwich circa April 1940.

CLOSE, SHAUN CHARLES
Half of forward Shaun Close's 12 first-class appearances for Spurs came as a substitute. He scored two goals. Signed as a junior in 1983, he left the club in 1988 for Bournemouth having had a loan spell with Halmstad in Sweden two years earlier. He later joined Swindon Town.

COACHES
Details of the coaches employed by Spurs:

Harry Lowe	1938-47	
Bill Whatley	1948-54	(also scout)
George Ludford	1954-55	
Bill Nicholson	1954-55	(first team)
Keith Burkinshaw	1975-76	(first team)
Jesse Carver	1958-59	(first team)
Ray Clemence	1988-93	(goalkeeping)
John Lyall	1989-90	(technical co-ordinator, overseas scouting)
Chris Hughton	1993-94	(U21 manager), since April, 2001 (first team)
Doug Livermore	1993-94	(also chief scout)
Pat Jennings	Since 1993	(part-time goalkeeping consultant)
Hans Segers	Since July 1998	(full-time goalkeeping coach)

* Also Spurs have had the following all act as a coach in some capacity: Jimmy Anderson, Jimmy Brain and John Pratt.

Coach's Clipboard
Jimmy Elliott, a Spurs player from 1911 to 1920, coached and trained football teams in the Balkans, Switzerland and Sweden as well as Guatemala and Turkey after retiring. He actually spent ten years as coach of the Fenerbahce first XI that won the Turkish League title three times in four attempts in the late 1930s.
Ray Evans, a former Spurs full-back, later became a prominent coach in the Seattle area of the USA.
Ray Clemence has also acted as goalkeeping coach to the England national team.

COATES, RALPH

A one-time centre-forward, fluffy-haired Ralph Coates turned into an international right-winger/wide midfielder who was the hero of the 1973 League Cup Final when, as substitute, he came on and scored the only goal of the game to earn Spurs victory over Norwich City at Wembley. Born in Hetton-le-Hole, County Durham on 26 April 1946, Coates was spotted by Burnley playing for a local coalmine team (Eppleton Colliery Welfare). He turned professional at Turf Moor in June 1963 and made over 260 senior appearances for the Clarets (32 goals scored) before transferring to White Hart Lane for £190,000 in May 1971. He was capped twice by England at senior level and eight times by by the Under-23s as well as representing the Football League on four occasions whilst at Turf Moor but failed to add to his international collection with Spurs despite some exceptionally fine performances. He starred in the club's 1972 UEFA Cup winning team and was a member of the 1974 losing side. When he left Spurs for Leyton Orient on a free transfer in November 1978 (after a loan spell with the Australian club St George's FC of Sydney) Coates had netted 30 goals in 305 first team appearances during his seven-and-a-half years at White Hart Lane. He retired from League football in May 1981 and wound down his career with Hertford Heath, Ware and Nazeing FC before becoming a manager of a leisure complex in Hertfordshire, maintaining a wide variery of sporting interests.

COCKEREL & BALL
The Cockerel & Ball, which has looked over the White Hart Lane ground from its lofty perch for much of the last 103 years or so, has a history all of its own.
The contract was carried out by F. Braby & Co., Coppersmiths, Euston Road, London and cost £35. The total structure measured 9ft 6in tall, the ball was 31 ins in diameter and the bird itself 5 ft high. The span from beak to tail was 3ft 6in and overall was 15 ins thick. The copper centrepiece was made and fixed to the mock-Tudor gable of the new West Stand in November 1909 by one WJ Scott of Edmonton who had played for Spurs during the club's amateur days.
It remained there until the summer of 1934 when the West Stand roof was renewed. A group of local dignitaries were photographed with the cockerel when it was temporarily brought down and given a spring-clean on the order of club secretary Arthur Turner. Additional floodlighting necessitated the removal of the cockerel and ball from the West Stand gable during the summer of 1957. It was not until December 1958 that it re-appeared on the opposite side of the ground, perched on top of the East Stand.
On 28 April 1989, with work underway on the refurbishment of the east side, the trusted friend made its final journey to discover if it did, indeed, contain coinage and items of interest from 1909. On being opened all that was found was one very soggy handbook for the 1909-10 season!
The cockerel and ball has spent the last few years in well earned retirement, away from all that the elements could throw at it,

housed within the East Stand executive area. Two offspring still face all weathers, the fibreglass replicas which were cast from the original in 1989 now stand on top of the East and West Stand roofs.

COCKRAM, ALLAN CHARLES
Midfielder Allan Cockram made two appearances for Spurs in the early 1980s. After leaving the club he played for Bristol Rovers, San Jose Earthquakes, Brentford, Brighton & Hove Albion and Reading, amongst others.

COLCHESTER UNITED
No competitive games as yet between Spurs and United:
Players with both clubs include: Garry Brooke, Simon Brown, Ray Bunkell (Spurs reserve) Jason Dozzell, Terry Dyson, David Leworthy, Bert Page, Steve Pitt.
Wartime guests (with either one or both clubs): Ken Burditt, Len Duquemin, Steve Grenfell (Spurs junior & later community officer and part-time coach), Jack Finch.
Also associated: Stewart Houston (United player-coach, Spurs assistant-manager).

COLDSTREAM GUARDS (2ND)
Spurs' playing record against the Guards:

Competition	P	W	D	L	F	A
FA Cup	1	1	0	0	7	0
Other Cups	3	2	1	0	13	7
Summary	4	3	1	0	20	7

Frank Cottrell scored twice when Spurs defeated the Guards 3-2 in a 2nd round London Senior Cup-tie in October 1892.
The 4th qualifying round FA Cup clash between the two clubs on 30 October 1897 should have taken place on the Guards' ground, but by mutual consent it was switched to Spurs territory and 4,000 fans saw the seven-goal romp.
Player with both clubs: Officer Hobson

COLERAINE
Spurs' playing record against the Irish club:

Competition	P	W	D	L	F	A
ECW Cup	2	2	0	0	7	0

Spurs commenced their 1982-83 European Cup-Winners Cup campaign with a first round tie against the Irish club, Coleraine - and they eased through 7-0 on aggregate.
The first leg, played in Ireland on 15 September, drew a crowd of 12,000 and resulted in a 3-0 win for Spurs, Steve Archibald and Garth Crooks (2) the scorers.
Thirteen days later just under 21,000 fans saw Spurs tidy things up with a 4-0 second leg victory at White Hart Lane, Garry Brooke, Gary Mabbutt, Terry Gibson and Crooks on target this time.

COLLINS, JOHN LINDSAY
After just two League outings for Spurs, full-back John Collins went on to serve Portsmouth, Halifax Town, Sheffield Wednesday and Barnsley through the 1970s.

COLLINS, PETER JOHN
Central defender Peter Collins made 117 appearances for Spurs (83 in the Football League). Born in Chelmsford, Essex on 29 November 1948, he played local Schoolboy and Youth team football before joining Chelmsford City from where he switched to Spurs in January 1968 for £5,500 with a further payment of £4,000 following later in the year. He remained at White Hart Lane for almost seven years before arthritis in his ankle forced

him to retire from League soccer in November 1974 when he became player-manager of Folkestone, later taking charge of Maldon Town and coaching at both Southend United and Chelmsford City.
Making his League debut in a North London derby v. Arsenal in August 1968, he was a well built, strong-tackling defender, quick in recovery, who battled hard and long to win a first team place alongside either Mike England or Phil Beal. He finally took over from the injured England, having his best season in 1970-71 when he started in 31 senior matches.

COLLINS, THOMAS
Full-back Tom Collins was born in Leven, Fife on 16 April 1882 and played for Leven Thistle, Heart of Midlothian, Bathgate (on loan), East Fife and Hearts again before moving south to join Spurs in November 1910. He went on to make 133 first team appearances for Spurs, scoring one goal - a block-busting penalty in a 2-1 defeat at Derby in September 1912. North of the border he had appeared twice for the Scottish League in 1909 and 1910 and had also won a full cap versus Wales. After moving to London he represented the Anglo Scots against the Home Scots in international trial matches in 1911 and 1912. One of the first Spurs players to join the forces at the outbreak of the Great War, Collins suffered horrific injuries on the battlefield, which resulted in the loss of both an arm and a leg. His last game for the club was in March 1915, in a 2-1 home League win over Manchester City. Collins died at Edmonton on 13 July 1929.

COLOGNE (1 FC)
Spurs' playing record against the German club:

Competition	P	W	D	L	F	A
European Cup	2	2	0	0	5	1

Spurs' 50th game in a European Cup competition was against the German side Cologne in the UEFA Cup in March 1974. It was a fourth round, first leg clash away from home which resulted in an excellent 2-1 victory in front of 28,000 fans. Chris McGrath and Martin Peters were the scorers.
A fortnight later, with a place in the semi-finals awaiting the winners, Spurs played very well to record a 3-0 victory to go through 5-1 on aggregate. Close on 41,000 saw the game at White Hart Lane when Martin Chivers, Peters (again) and Ralph Coates breached the Cologne defence.
Spurs crashed 8-0 away to Cologne in a UEFA InterToto Cup-tie in July 1995. For this fixture Spurs fielded their third XI as the 22 senior squad members were on tour in Denmark.

COLOURS
During their early years, Spurs' players wore mainly dark blue shirts with a scarlet shield incorporating the letter 'H'. The club changed to blue and white halved shirts in 1885-86 in 1890-91 then switched to wearing red shirts and navy blue shorts.
In 1896-97 the club's colours were chocolate and gold but since 1898-999 Spurs have played in the now traditional and familiar strip of white shirts and dark blue (navy blue) shorts....except for a brief spell from 1985-87 when the team wore an all-white strip. The team's change strip (in the early days) was generally white. They changed into dark blue tops once they had chosen white shirts and blue shorts, but for over 30 years (perhaps longer) up to 2001, yellow was used predominantly when the team has had to make a change owing to a clash of colours.
For the 2001-02 season a new light blue change strip was introduced (the only previous time a pale blue shirt was used was in the club's centenary season of 1982-83),

COLQUHOUN, DAVID WILLIAM

Wing-half Davie Colquhoun was on the brink of playing for Scotland when Spurs stepped in and enticed him to White Hart Lane in July 1931.

The former Blantyre Victoria and St Mirren star, who was born in Motherwell on 23 January 1906, had just played in an international trial when he was signed to take over the right-half berth from Harry Skitt allowing Wally Alsford to switch to the left.

He didn't have the greatest of debuts, Spurs being on the receiving end of a 4-0 defeat at Wolves on the opening day of the 1931-32 season, but Colquhoun soon bedded himself in and went on to make 91 first team appearances for the club (three goals scored). He moved to Luton Town in March 1935, switching to Rochdale in May 1936. And during the Second World War he guested for Blackpool, Bradford City, Stockport County and Walsall. He did not re-appear when League football resumed in 1946.

COMEBACKS

Spurs' most famous comeback was in their 5th round FA Cup replay with Everton on 22 February 1937. In front of a White Hart Lane crowd of almost 47,000, they found themselves a goal down within 120 seconds and two adrift by the 20th minute before pulling back to 2-1 before the half-time break. Everton then went 3-1 ahead on 63 minutes, but Spurs again reduced the deficit to a single goal within two minutes and were still 3-2 down with four minutes to play. But a tremendous finish produced two goals within the space of a couple of minutes as Spurs stormed through to record a splendid 4-3 victory.

Another epic fight back from that era came during the Second Division home fixture with Bury on 16 November 1935. The visitors raced into a 3-0 lead after 28 minutes through goals from Bill Graham, Ernie Matthews and a Fred Channell own goal. Spurs pulled one back before the interval and then produced a terrific second-half performance to win the game 4-3, Johnny Morrison scoring the winner just eight minutes from time. Jimmy McCormick, Willie Hall and Willie Evans were Spurs' other scorers in front of 32,176 excited fans.

Spurs' best comeback overall has probably been in their first-ever European Cup-tie against the Polish champioins Gornik Zabrze in September 1961. Spurs were 4-0 down soon after half time in the first leg in Poland. But two precious goals in the last 20 minutes by Cliff Jones and Terry Dyson eased the agony. Spurs scored three more at White Hart Lane to lead 5-4 on aggregate before the Poles netted their fifth goal to level things up. In the end Spurs finished the stronger and ran out 8-1 winners on the night, taking the tie 10-5 on aggregate.

In recent times the FA Cup-tie at Southampton in March 1995 will take some beating. Spurs fell 2-0 behind after 40 minutes but then scored twice themselves in as many minutes just before the hour mark. The game went into extra-time and Spurs claimed a further four goals to secure an impressive 6-2 victory, Ronny Rosenthal netting a sparkling hat-trick.

Then there was that tremendous effort against Charlton Athletic in a 4th round tie at The Valley on 7 February 2001. The Addicks led 2-0 after 49 minutes, but an own-goal by Richard Rufus in the 57th minute set Spurs on their way. Darren Anderton equalised halfway through the half, Oyvind Leornhardsen made it 3-2 fifty seconds later before Sergei Rebrov sewed things up with a fourth goal seven minutes from time.

Spurs, two-nil down, bounced back in style to beat Sunderland 3-2 at The Stadium of Light in a Premiership game on 14 April 2001, Gary Doherty netting the winner two minutes from time.

Burnley were 4-0 down to Spurs in a League game at White Hart Lane in December 1960 but fought back to draw 4-4.

Spurs led Aston Villa 5-1 at home in a League game in March 1966' but the Midland club stormed back to force a 5-5 draw.

Villa have twice fought back from two goals down to beat Spurs at White Hart Lane...in April 1992 they won 5-2 and in April 2000 they triumphed 4-2.

West Brom trailed 2-0 to Spurs at The Hawthorns in October 1976, but the Baggies, inspired after the break by Willie Johnston's wing play, raced to a 4-2 victory..

COMMERCIAL DEPARTMENT

A Commercial Department was first established within Tottenham Hotspur Football Club during the 1960s, but the first Commercial Manager was not appointed until the summer of 1978 when Mike Lewis, formerly of Newport County, took office. Over the years there have been several other 'Commercial Managers', the latest being Mike Rollo, who was employed in various roles at White Hart Lane from 1983 until 2000, Scot Gardiner was Sales Manager at White Hart Lane in 2001-02.

COMMITTEE

Initially - when first formed in 1882 - Spurs were run by a committee, a chosen group of men who looked after the club's affairs - taking care of the internal paperwork, organising training sessions, team selection, arranging the fixtures and ensuring everything was running efficiently, smoothly and legally.

The committee in the early 1880s comprised Bobby Buckle, Sam Casey, John (Jack) Thompson senior and John Thompson.

CONN, ALFRED JAMES

Inside-forward Alfie Conn followed in his father's footsteps by playing international football for Scotland.

Born in Kirkcaldy, Fife on 5 April 1952, Conn junior joined Glasgow Rangers from Musselburgh Windsor, turning professional in October 1969, having already represented his country as an amateur. Earlier he had toyed with the idea of becoming a Rugby Union player and, indeed, had starred for East of Scotland in both the oval and round ball codes. But he chose soccer and proved he had made the right decision by enjoying a fine career. He made his senior debut for Rangers aged 16 and by the time he reached his 21st birthday he had already won a European Cup-Winners Cup medal and had been a winner in both the Scottish League Cup and Cup Finals of 1971 and 1973 respectively.

After leaving Ibrox Park for White Hart Lane in a £140,000 deal in June 1974, he went on to net 10 goals (including a hat-trick against Newcastle United early in 1975) in 59 first team appearances for Spurs, winning two full and three Under-23 caps for his country.

After a loan spell with Celtic (making him one of the elite band of players to serve with both Glasgow giants) Conn joined the Parkhead club on a permanent basis in April 1977 for £60,000. Starring in the Bhoys' Scottish Cup winning team at the end of that season, he also helped them lift the Scottish League title before adding another League championioin medal to his collection in 1979. Loan spells in the NASL with Pittsburgh Spirit and San Jose Earthquakes preceded his transfer to Heart of Midlothian in July 1980 and after assisting Blackpool on loan he switched to Motherwell in 1981. Retiring three years later, Conn then became manager of Coatbridge whom he guided to victory in the Scottish Amateur Cup Final of 1986.

COOK, GEORGE WILLIAM

Inside or centre-forward Billy Cook had already scored 58 goals in 186 League games before joining Spurs from Aston Villa in June 1929. In his two seasons at White Hart Lane he added a further 22 to his tally in 63 Second Division matches, netting 30 in 73 first-class outings for the club in total.

Born at Evenwood in County Durham on 27 February 1895, he played his first competitive football while serving with the Royal Artillery.

After an excellent spell with Bishop Auckland (whom he helped win successive FA Amateur Cup Finals), he joined Rotherham County in May 1922, transferring to Huddersfield Town in May 1923 (signed by former Spurs player Herbert Chapman). He became a key figure in the Terriers' attack, teaming up with fellow striker George Brown as three League championship titles were won in succession (1924-25-26). He continued to find the net on a regular basis for Aston Villa and then he did the business with Spurs before transferring to Brentford at the age of 36 in August 1931. Cook ended his playing days in the Welsh League with Colwyn Bay. Cook chose to live the remainder of his life in North Wales, passing away in Colwyn Bay on 31 December 1980 at the age of 85.

COPELAND, DAVID CAMPBELL

Inside or centre-forward David Copeland scored 110 goals in a total of 302 first team appearances for Spurs. A Scotsman, born in Ayr on 2 April 1875, he played for Ayr Parkhouse before joining Walsall in October 1893. Only 5ft 7ins tall and weighing less than 12 stone, he was an aggressive footballer with a powerful right-foot shot who scored a goal every three games for the Midland club. Injured playing against Newton Heath in October 1897, his career was seriously threatened, He was subsequently released by the Saddlers at the end of that season when he joined Bedminster. He surprised even himself by regaining full-fitness and in May 1899 he was signed by Spurs whom he helped win the Southern League championship in his first season, adding an FA Cup winners medal to his collection twelve months later. Selected to represent the Anglo-Scots against the Home Scots, one feels that Copeland was certainly of international class, but there were so many other talented forwards around at the time that he unfortunately missed out on a full cap. On leaving Spurs in May 1905, Copeland joined London rivals Chelsea (with John Kirwan) and played in the Blues' first-ever League game at Stockport County. Having been appointed Chelsea's captain, he broke a leg in November 1906 and after recovering he joined Glossop North End in September 1907. He returned to Walsall in September 1910, but found it hard going in the Birmingham League and decided to retire the following May at the age of 36. Copeland later worked at the Rose & Crown Hotel in Erdington, Birmingham and he was still employed there when he died of a heart attack on 16 November 1931 whilst chopping wood in the back garden of his home.

COQUET, ERNEST

Combative full-back Ernie Coquet appeared in well over 100 first team games for Spurs (76 in the Football League). Signed from Reading in March 1907, having previously played for Sunderland, he stayed with the club for three seasons before transferring to Burlsem Port Vale in May 1911, later assisting Fulham before retiring in 1919.

Born at Durnston-upon-Tyne on 6 January 1883, he was spotted by Sunderland while playing local football for Seaham White Star and made rapid progress. He helped Vale win the Staffordshire Cup in 1912. He died in Gateshead on 26 October 1946.

CORINTHIANS

Spurs' playing record against the Corinthians

Competition	P	W	D	L	F	A
Dewar Shield	3	3	0	0	19	8

The biggest of Spurs' three Dewar Shield wins over the famous amateur side was achieved in November 1934 when they ran up a 7-2 scoreline at White Hart Lane. Almer Hall (3), Johnny Morrison (2), Fred Sargent and Foster Hedley scored the goals in front of 5,117 spectators..

Players with both clubs include: Frank Hartley, Foster Hedley, John Knight, Allan Leach-Lewis, Vivian Woodward.

Also associated: Sandy Tait (Spurs player, Corinthians coach).

CORONATION CUP

Spurs' record in the Coronation Cup

P	W	D	L	F	A
2	0	1	1	2	3

In May 1953, to celebrate Queen Elizabeth's ascendancy to the throne, Spurs competed in the Coronation Cup and played the Scottish club Hibernian. The first game at Ibrox Park drew a crowd of 43,000 and finished level at 1-1 after extra-time, Sonny Walters scoring for Spurs. The 'replay' was staged at Hampden Park and this time Hibs won 2-1 in front of 13,000 fans, Syd McClellan the Spurs marksman on this occasion.

COVENTRY CITY

Spurs playing record against the Sky Blues:

Competition	P	W	D	L	F	A
Premiership	18	7	3	8	25	25
Football League	64	30	19	15	110	76
FA Cup	2	1	0	1	5	4
League Cup	4	2	0	2	10	8
Wartime	2	2	0	0	3	0
Summary	90	42	22	26	153	113

Coventry City's first Football League game was against Spurs at Highfield Road (Div 2) on 30 August 1919 - Spurs won 5-0 with Jimmy Chipperfield scoring twice on his debut. A week later Spurs completed the double over City, winning 4-1 at White Hart Lane (Chipperfield again on target).

Spurs lost 2-0 at Coventry on 23 August 1948 but a week later the tables were turned as the Sky Blues succumbed to a 4-0 defeat at White Hart Lane, Len Duquemin scoring twice in front of 31,768 fans.

Spurs completed their first 'top flight' double over the Sky Blues in 1967-68 - winning 3-2 at Highfield Road before gaining a 4-2 victory at White Hart Lane. Greaves scored twice in each game.

Spurs' caretaker-boss (again) David Pleat celebrated with a 3-0 St Patrick's Day Premiership victory over relegation-threatened City at White Hart Lane in March 2001.

A crowd of 22,536 saw Spurs beat Coventry 4-3 in a thrill-a-minute First Division game at White Hart Lane in February 1980. Glenn Hoddle scored with two penalty kicks.

Garry Brooke's only hat-trick for Spurs was claimed in the 4-0 home win over the Sky Blues in October 1982.

At Wembley in May 1987, after taking an early lead through Clive Allen, Spurs eventually lost 3-2 after extra-time to the Sky Blues in the FA Cup Final. Gary Mabbutt is on record as having scored at both ends in that game!

Gordon Durie scored a hat-trick when Spurs beat City 4-3 at home in March 1992. Earlier in the season at Highfield Road Spurs had won 2-1.

The Sky Blues inflicted upon Spurs their first defeat in the Premiership, winning 2-0 at White Hart Lane on 19 August 1992.

In mid-December 1997, a week after losing 6-1 at home to Chelsea in a Premiership game Spurs travelled to Highfield Road and were whipped 4-0 by Coventry.

Players with both clubs include: Alan Brazil, Ivor Brown, Will Buckingham, Randolph Galloway, Terry Gibson, Jimmy Holmes, Bill Jacques, Don McAllister, Peter Murphy (later City coach), Keith Osgood, Tommy Roe, Steve Sedgley, John Smith, Danny Thomas, Dennis Uphill, Charlie Wilson (did not appear for City), Terry Yorath.

Wartime guests (with either one or both clubs): Len Bolan, Colin Lyman, Bert Middlemiss

Also associated: Gerry Francis (City player, Spurs manager), Jesse Carver (Spurs coach, Coventry manager), Allan Harris (City player, Spurs Asst. Manager), Graham Carr (scout for both clubs).

COWES

Spurs' playing record against the Isle-of-Wight club:

Competition	P	W	D	L	F	A
Southern League	1	1	0	0	6	1

This victory was not registered in the final Southern League table in 1899-1900 as Cowes resigned from the competition.

For the record, David Copeland, with a hat-trick, Tom Smith (2) and Tom Pratt scored the goals in front of 500 spectators on the Isle of Wight.

COX, FREDERICK JAMES ARTHUR

Freddie Cox spent 36 years in football - as a player, coach, assistant-manager and manager. He was born in Reading on 1 November 1920 and on leaving school played on the right-wing (and occasionally at centre-forward) for St George's Lads' Club before joining Spurs as an amateur in 1936, turning professional in August 1938, having had a decent spell with the club's nursery side, Northfleet. A scorer on his senior debut in the Second Division v. Swansea Town in November of that year, he went on to net a total of 26 goals in 144 first team appearances for Spurs (15 coming in 99 League outings).

Awarded the DFC during the war, Cox guested for Fulham, Reading, Manchester City and Swindon Town between 1939-45 before leaving White Hart Lane for neighbouring Highbury in a £12,000 deal in September 1949. He remained with the Gunners until July 1953 when he was appointed player-coach of West Bromwich Albion, later acting as assistant-manager under his former team-mate at Spurs, Vic Buckingham.

Cox left The Hawthorns in April 1956 to become team manager at Bournemouth. Two years later he stepped into the hot-seat at Portsmouth. He bossed Gillingham from June 1962 to December 1965 (leading the Kent club to the Fourth Division title in 1964) and then returned for a second spell in charge at Dean Court, staying there until April 1970 when he retired from the game.

While in charge of Bournemouth, Cox guided the Cherries, based in the Third Division (South) to a sensational FA Cup victory over Spurs in February 1957. He later ran a successful newsagents shop in the seaside town where he died on 7 August 1973.

CREWE ALEXANDRA

Spurs playing record against the Alex:

Competition	P	W	D	L	F	A
FA Cup	3	2	1	0	20	5
League Cup	2	2	0	0	5	1
Summary	5	4	1	0	25	6

After a 2-2 draw at Gresty Road, Spurs led Crewe 10-1 at half-time in their 4th round FA Cup replay in February 1960. They eventually won the game 13-2, Les Allen (5), Bobby Smith (4) and Cliff Jones (3, one penalty) all scoring hat-tricks in front of 64,365 fans.

On the morning of this replay the Crewe party arrived at Euston Station on platform 2 and departed late that evening from platform 13. They arrived back home at Crewe Station just after 13 minutes past two in the morning! Does that say something?

Players with both clubs include: Phil Beal, George Clawley, Bert Hodgkinson, Fred Latham, Jimmy Robertson, Ralph Ward (also Crewe manager).

Wartme guests (with either one or both clubs): Vic Buckingham, Les Howe, Eric Jones, Jimmy McCormick and Joey Walters. The latter sadly died of pneumonia without playing a single game for Crewe.

CRICKETING-FOOTBALLERS

Among the many sportsman who have played both football and cricket and have been associated with Spurs we have England Test opener Bill Edrich, all-rounder George Leach and quality batsman Fanny Walden.

Edrich, an all-rounder, played for Middlesex and England (1934-58). In a fine career he scored over 40,000 runs (36,965 in the County Championship), claimed 92 centuries (86 for Middlesex) and snapped up 520 wickets (479 at County level). In international quarters, he appeared in 39 Test Matches, notched 2,440 runs for an average of 40 with a top score of 219. He also claimed 41 Test wickets and helped England win the Ashes in 1953.

Leach spent eleven years with Sussex (1903-14). He scored 5,788 runs and took 413 wickets in 225 matches. He also played for Hailsham CC.

Walden was a Northamptonshire cricketer who scored 7,462 runs and took 114 wickets, in 258 first-class matches. He later became a first-class umpire and was on the Test Match Board.

Other Cricketing-footballers

Joe Hulme, who managed Spurs for four years (1945-49) was also a very capable cricketer with Middlesex whom he served for ten years from 1929 to the outbreak of the Second World War. He scored 8,103 runs including 12 centuries.

Jack Chisholm played for Bedfordshire, Devon and Middlesex, appearing in one County Championship match for the latter in 1947 (with Denis Compton and Bill Edrich).

Ian Crook was a trialist with Essex County Cricket Club.

Frank Hartley, an amateur and senior England international forward, played cricket for the Minor Counties and Oxfordshire.

John L Jones, Spurs' first full international, played cricket for Whitburn CC (Durham) and he also coached the sport at Rugby Public School, in Leinster (Ireland) and Durban, South Africa.

Another Spurs player, Bill Julian, also coached cricket in later life.

Gary Lineker is a very capable cricketer and often turns out for local club sides (in the Leicester area).

Charlie McGahey, a Spurs player and committee member, was a very useful county cricketer with Essex.

Winger Roger Morgan played cricket for Essex & District Schools but he, too, tuned down the chance to play at a higher level, choosing the larger ball game!

Bob Pilch was a key figure at the Norfolk County Cricket Club while also acting as Director (and Chairman) of Norwich City FC.

John Polston was a useful all-round cricketer with the Waltham Forest Schoolboy team.

Spurs WW2 guest Charlie Revell was a qualified cricket coach and often guided youngsters through their paces at The Oval.

Vinny Samways played cricket for East London and London Schools and was asked to go to Surrey for trails - but he chose to kick a ball instead!

After ending his soccer days, Tom Smith played club cricket for Maryport and was chosen as 12th man for Cumberland &

Westmorland.

Vivian Woodward enjoyed a game of cricket and he turned out regularly for the Spencer CC.

Some eleven of twelve schoolboy founder-members of Tottenham Hotspur had also been members of the Hotspur Cricket Club.

CROMPTON, ARTHUR

Birmingham-born outside-right, Arthur Crompton played for Devon County before scoring three goals in 15 League appearances for Spurs between 1927-30. Later he assisted Southend, Brentford, Crystal Palace and Tranmere Rovers.

CROOK, IAN STUART

Midfielder Ian Crook scored once in 24 first-class games for Spurs before leaving the club for Norwich City in 1986. He went on to make almost 350 appearances for the Canaries up to 1997.

CROOKS, GARTH ANTHONY, OBE

Born in Stoke-on-Trent on 10 March 1958, striker Garth Crooks made his name with his home-town club, Stoke City whom he joined as an apprentice straight from school - after kicking a tennis ball against the wall of manager Tony Waddington's office at The Victoria Ground! He signed professional forms in March 1976 and went on to score 53 goals in 264 competitive games for the Potters before transferring to Spurs for £650,000 in July 1980 after falling out with new boss Alan Durban. He was capped four times by the England Under-21 side while with Stoke, whipping in a hat-trick on his debut against Bulgaria at Filbert Street in November 1979. He settled into the Spurs side immediately and with Ossie Ardiles, Ricky Villa and Glenn Hoddle creating the openings, Crooks gleefully scored the goals - 22 in his first season at White Hart Lane as Spurs win the FA Cup. He followed up with 16 more goals in 1981-82 when he gained a second Cup winners medal but had to settle for a loser's prize in the League Cup Final. After striking 105 goals in 238 first team appearances for Spurs (48 in 105 League games) and having a loan spell with Manchester United, Crooks was transferred to West Bromwich Albion for £100,000 in July 1985. He left The Hawthorns for Charlton Athletic in March 1987 and retired in November 1990 having amassed a fine record of 168 goals in 468 club appearances.

Crooks was Chairman of the PFA in 1989-90, but resigned his position after suffering a back injury. In later years he joined BBC TV as a soccer interviewer and summariser.

He was awarded the OBE in June 1999.

CROWD DISTURBANCES

During a Southern League fixture between Spurs and Luton Town on 2 February 1898 three Hatters' players were assaulted by unruly spectators. The game ended in a 2-2 draw.

Two players - Andy Duncan and Alf Hawley - both walked off the pitch during certain games in their respective Spurs careers....annoyed at the behaviour of the spectators!

When Spurs visited Argentina in 1908, a troop of cavalrymen came onto the pitch and used the flat part of their swords in an attempt to beat back scores of spectators who had forced their way into the ground illegally. They wanted them outside - so that they had to pay to get back in!

There were separate crowd disturbances (involving rival supporters) when Spurs played Feyenoord in the UEFA Cup in Holland in both 1974 and 1983.

After the violence at the 1974 Final in Rotterdam, which at times was described as being 'savage and terrifying' manager Bill Nicholson called the rampaging Spurs supporters 'Hooligans' saying:"You are a disgrace to Tottenham Hotspur and a disgrace to English football, this is football not a war".

CROYDON COMMON

Spurs' playing record against the Croyd Common:

Competition	P	W	D	L	F	A
Other Cups	1	1	0	0	7	1
Wartime	4	2	2	0	8	3
Summary	5	3	2	0	15	4

Players with both clubs include: Ted Bassett, Ken Bennett, Albert Chester (all Spurs WW1), Jack Eggett, John George, Abraham Goodman, Bob Hewitson, Harry Sparrow, Tim Williamson (Spurs WW1).

Also associated: Sandy Tait (Spurs player, CC manager).

CRUMP, HAROLD WILLIAM

Born in Smethwick in 1870, half-back Harry Crump played for Smethwick Centaur, West Smethwick and Wednesfield before joining Wolverhampton Wanderers in September 1894. He remained at Molineux for just nine months, making one League appearance before transferring to Hereford Thistle in May 1895. Twelve months later - after brief spell with Bloxwich - he had a trial with Spurs, did well and was signed full-time. After one season with the club he switched his allegiance to Luton Town but returned to White Hart Lane in September 1899 and went on to make 105 first team appearances, scoring 13 goals for Spurs. Having guested for Thames Ironworks he moved to Brentford in May 1900 before ending his career with Watford in 1901-02. Crump died in Coventry in 1943.

NB - Some reference books show that there was also a Winston Howard Crump playing at the same time as Harry Crump (possibly a brother).

CRUSADERS

Spurs' playing record against Crusaders:

Competition	P	W	D	L	F	A
LCC	2	1	0	1	6	7

Spurs played two 1st round London Charity Cup -ties against Crusaders - the first in December 1893, lost 5-2 at home, the second in December 1894, won 4-2, also at home.

CRYSTAL PALACE

Spurs playing record against the Eagles:

Competition	P	W	D	L	F	A
Premiership	6	2	3	1	9	6
Football League	20	11	6	3	34	18
FA Cup	4	1	1	2	4	3
League Cup	2	1	1	0	3	1
Other Leagues	6	4	0	2	8	4
Other Cups	8	2	2	4	13	17
Wartime	29	14	7	8	62	51
Summary	75	35	20	20	133	100

The first League game between the two clubs took place at Selhurst Park on 23 August 1969where, in front of 39,494 fans

Spurs won 2-0 with goals by Jimmy Pearce and Martin Chivers. The return fixture that season ended with the same scoreline.

A total of thirteen goals were scored in the two League games between Spurs and Palace, played in August and October 1980. Spurs won the first by 4-3 at Selhurst Park and doubled up with a 4-2 victory at White Hart Lane. Garth Crooks netted five goals overall, three in the latter encounter.

In a League Cup-tie at Selhurst Park in between those two League games, the usually subdued Glenn Hoddle was sent-off as Spurs crashed to a 3-1 defeat.

Spurs defender Neil Ruddock, later to play for Palace, was sent-off in the 2-2 First Division draw at White Hart Lane in September 1993.

Players with both clubs include: Clive Allen, Dean Austin, Chris Armstrong, Jimmy Bauchop, Ken Bennett (Spurs junior), Ted Birnie, Terry Boyle (Spurs reserve), John Brearley, Johnny Brooks, Arthur Crompton, Jason Cundy, Chris Day, Bill Dodge, Dickie Dowsett, Terry Fenwick, Mike Flanagan (Spurs Youth), Johnny Gavin, Andy Gray, Bob Hewitson, Charlie Hewitt, Phil Holder, Roger Hoy, Archie Hughes, Chris Jones, John Lacy, David Levene, Jimmy McCormick, Bobby Mimms, Gary O'Reilly, George Payne, Derek Possee, Neil Ruddock, Charlie Rundle, Neil Sullivan, Paul Stewart, Peter Taylor, Andy Turner, David Tuttle, Dennis Uphill, Terry Venables (also manager of both clubs and coach of Palace), Claude Watson.

Wartime guests (with either one or both clubs): Simon Beaton, Frank Boulton, Charlie Briggs, Harry Brown, Charlie Burke, Sid Castle, John Davie, Andy Duncan, Harry Ferrier, Jack Finch, Bobby Flavell, George Foreman, Les Henley, Bill Hill, Arthur Hitchins, Percy Hooper, Rev. Kenneth Hunt, Eric Jones, Phil Joslin, Bill Lawrence (also Palace amateur), Reg Mogford, David Nelson, Bert Page, Tom Paton, Charlie Revell (also Palace coach & scout), Albert Sibley, George Smith, Alf Spencer, Les Stevens, Ed Tunney, Albert Young.

Also associated: Jack Tresadern (manager of both clubs), Alan Mullery (Spurs player, Palace manager), Gerry Francis (Palace player & manager, Spurs manager), George Graham (Palace player, Spurs manager), Arthur Rowe (Spurs player & manager, Palace assistant-manager, caretaker-manager, team manager & director), Cyril Spiers (Spurs player, Palace manager), Ron Reynolds (Spurs player, Palace scout), Ernie Walley (Spurs player, coach and caretaker-manager of Palace).

CULLEN, JOSEPH

Glaswegian goalkeeper Joe Cullen made 126 first team appearances for Spurs following his transfer from Celtic in the summer of 1897.

Born north of the border circa 1866, he had been at Parkhead for several seasons and had represented the Scottish League against the Irish League in 1894. A fine positional 'keeper, he was a good shot-stopper and was chosen to play for the United League against the Thames & Medway League at Northumberland Park in 1898. Released by Spurs in May 1899, he ended his career with Lincoln City, retiring in 1900.

Cullen died after a short illness in Glasgow on 27 October 1905.

FA Cup Final 1962. The victorious Spurs team run around the pitch at Wembley with the FA Cup after the game against Burnley

CULVERHOUSE, IAN BRETT

Born in Bishops Stortford on 22 September 1964 and a junior with Southampton, defender Ian Culverhouse signed apprentice forms for Spurs in May 1981 and turned professional in September 1982. An England Youth international, he made only two League appearances for the club before transferring to Norwich City in October 1985 for £50,000. Over the next 15 years he amassed almost 550 senior appearances playing for the Canaries, Swindon Town (1994-98) and Brighton & Hove Albion, as well as assisting Kingstonian. On the bench when Spurs won the UEFA Cup in 1984, he won Second Division championship medals with Norwich in 1986 and Swindon ten years later.

CUNDY, JASON VICTOR

Born in Wimbledon on 12 November 1969, 6ft 1in and 13st 13lb defender Jason Cundy joined Chelsea on leaving school and turned professional at Stamford Bridge in August 1988. He made 57 first team appearances for the Blues and gained three England Under-21 caps before transferring to Spours for £750,000 in March 1992. Unable to hold down a regular place in the first XI and with injuries disrupting his game, he was loaned out to Crystal Palace and Bristol City before transferring to Ipswich Town for £200,000 in October 1996. He was given 72 outings at Portman Road and in July 1999 he switched to Portsmouth. Cundy made just 28 first team appearances for Spurs (one goal scored).

CUP FINALS

Spurs played in four major Cup Finals in successive years: League Cup 1971 & 1973, UEFA Cup 1972 &1974. The club's teenagers also reached the 1970 Youth Cup Final.

CURTIS, JOHN JOSEPH

Right-winger John Curtis had hoped to make his mark with Sunderland whom he joined in 1905, but he failed to gain a place in the side and dropped into non-League football with Shildon Athletic. In May 1908 he returned with Gainsborough Trinity and a year later he signed for Spurs. Born in Southbank on 13 December 1888, Curtis played for two local sides before trying his luck on Wearside. He was a lively footballer who scored on his debut for Spurs and eventually netted 12 goals in 114 first team appearances (five in 82 Football League fixtures) before joining Fulham at the end of the 1912-13 season. Later he assisted Brentford and after the Great War he signed for Middlesbrough, returning to Shildon Athletic in October 1920. Curtis died in Wimbledon in February 1955.

D

AINES, BARRY RAYMOND

Almost 150 of goalkeeper Barry Daines' 236 first-team appearances for Spurs came in the Football League. An England Youth international, he made his senior debut against West Bromwich Albion in November 1971 and played his last game for the club almost a 10 years later in April 1981. Understudy to Pat Jennings for some considerable time, he made barely a dozen or so appearances in the first team during his initial five years as a professional. But when the big Irishman departed to Arsenal, he bedded himself in as the club's number one and held the position until Milija Aleksic arrived at the club.

Born in Witham, Essex on 30 Septmber 1951, Daines represented Chelmsford, Middlessex and Essex Schools before enlisting as a junior at White Hart Lane in July 1968, turning professional in September 1969.

After missing out on FA Cup Final glory in 1981 despite playing in the first four rounds, Daines joined the Hong Kong club Bulova for the start of the next season and later he signed as a non-contract player with Mansfield Town (October 1983).

DARLINGTON

No competitive matches between Spurs and the Quakers so far. Players with both clubs include: Laurie Brown (Darlington amateur), Bert Gosnell, Neil McNab, John Shackleton, Willie Young.

Wartime guests (with either one or both clubs): George Burchell, Ernie Hoffman, Fred Hopkin, Archie Hughes, Bill Nicholson (also Spurs manager), Taffy Spelman.

DARNELL, JABEZ

Despite standing only 5ft 5in tall, the robust tackling of wing-half Jabe Darnell was a terrific competitor who never gave up the fight, refusing to be beaten and always coming up for more! He made 323 first team appearances for Spurs (150 in the Football League). He was signed from Northampton Town in the summer of 1905 and retired in May 1919 when he was appointed assistant-trainer, a position he held until 1946, giving him more than 40 years service at White Hart Lane.

Born in the Bedfordshire village of Potton on 28 March 1884, the smart-looking Darnell, with his dapper moustache, who replaced Ted Hughes in the Spurs side, missed only one game during the club's first season of League football (1908-09). Later on, having dropped out of the limelight, his vast experience rubbed off on several up-and-coming youngsters in the reserves. Darnell died in Edmonton in December 1950.

DARTFORD

Spurs playing record against the Kent club:

Competition	P	W	D	L	F	A
T&M League	2	2	0	0	12	2

Spurs met their Kent counterparts in the Thames & Medway League in season 1898-99. After a 3-2 away win, Spurs raced to a 9-0 home victory on the last day of the campaign. Billy Joyce scored five times while John Cameron and George Leach both netted twice.

DARWEN

No competitive match action to report between Spurs and the Lancashire cotton mill town club of Darwen.

Associated with both clubs: Harry Jackson (Spurs WW2 guest).

DAVIDSON, JAMES

After spells with Celtic, Burnley and Lincoln City (on loan) inside-forward Jock Davidson, a Scotsman, born in Edinburgh in 1873, was recruited by Spurs in May 1897. He scored 15 goals in 46 first team appearances for the club before transferring to the newly-established professional side Brighton United in in May 1898. He returned to Burnley in April 1900 and retired in May 1902 after having 67 senior outings for the Clarets. Before joining Spurs he had helped the Imps win the Lincolnshire Senior Cup.

DAVIES, SIMON

Born in Haverfordwest on 23 October 1979, Simon Davies was signed by Spurs manager George Graham from Peterborough United for £700,000 in January 2000, along with his club colleague Matthew Etherington. Already capped by Welsh at Youth, 'B' and Under-21 levels the attacking, goal-seeking midfielder certainly made his mark in the Premiership during the 2000-01 campaign with a series of excellent performances which resulted in him being selected by his country as a full international. He had made 19 first-team appearances and scored four goals for Spurs prior to the commencement of the 2001-02 campaign. He had netted six times in 75 League and Cup outings for Posh whom he joined initially as a trainee in 1995, turning professional at London Road in July 1997.

DAVIES, WILLIAM

Welsh international right-winger Willie Davies had already represented his country on 17 occasions and played for the Welsh League v. the League of Ireland when he joined Spurs from Notts County in February 1930.

Born in the village of Troedrhiwfuwch near Bargoed in Glamorgan on 16 February 1900, Davies played for his local team Troedrhiwfuwch FC and then Rhymney before joining Swansea Amateurs for the first season after the Great War (August 1919). Moving to Swansea Town as a professional in May 1921 he remained at The Vetch Field for three years before switching to Cardiff City for just £25 in June 1924. He won three caps with the Swans and added eight more to his tally with the Bluebirds before moving to Meadow Lane in March 1928. He was sidelined with a serious chest infection for a year but still managed almost 100 senior appearances for the Ninian Park club, appearing in the 1925 FA Cup Final.

Six further caps came his way with the Magpies before Spurs paid £3,000 for his signature in 1930. He served the very club well, being described as 'the speedy, orthodox Welshman who played many good games and never any bad'. Davies appeared in 123 first-team matches and scored 24 goals during his three-and-a-half years at White Hart Lane. In September 1933, shortly after helping his side gain promotion from Division Two, he returned to Swansea Town and rounded off his career by having a season with Llanelli (1936-37). He later became a caretaker of a Pontarddulais School complex in South Wales. Davies died in Llandielo, Carmarthenshire on 6 August 1953.

DAY, ALFRED

Alf Day made his international debut for Wales before he had appeared in a League game. A half-back, born in Ebbw Vale in 1907, he joined Spurs in 1931 and went on to play in 14 first-class games for the club before moving to Millwall in 1936. After serving with Southampton, Tranmere Rovers and Swindon Town, he then guested for Bournemouth, Brighton & Hove Albion, Ipswich Town, Lincoln City and Reading during WW2. He retired in 1944.

DEARDEN, KEVIN

Goalkeeper Kevin Dearden passed the milestone of 400 competitive appearances in 2001 - having been given away after having two first-class games for Spurs. Born in Luton in 1970, he was loaned out to Cambridge United, Hartlepool, Swindon, Peterborough, Hull City, Rochdale and Birmingham City before switching to Brentford on a free transfer in 1993. After the Bees he served Barnet (on loan), Wrexham and Torquay United (since September 2001)

DEATHS

Scottish international inside-forward John White was tragically killed while sheltering under an oak tree during a thunderstorm on the Crews Hill golf course, Enfield, Middlesex on 21 July 1964. The tree was struck by lightning. He was only 27.

Another player to die on a golf course was Walter Bellamy in Hertfordshire in October 1978. He was registered with Spurs from 1927 to 1935.

During the Great War of 1914-18, several Spurs players lost their lives.

Centre-forward John Fleming (who had earlier scored a hat-trick when making his first appearance for Spurs in a friendly against Red Star Amical in Paris in May 1913), died aged 26 on 21 March 1916.

Another centre-forward, Walter Tull, lost his life on the battlefield on 15 March 1918 at the age of 29.

Glasgow-born half-back Findlay Weir was badly wounded and died of his injuries on 9 July 1918, also aged 29 and fellow wing-half Ted Lightfoot was tragically killed whilst serving his country in France on 20 July 1918. He was 28 years of age.

Fred Griffiths also lost his life on a French battlefield on 30 October 1917 and George Badenoch was killed while serving with the Canadian Regiment in France on 15 June 1915.

Full-back Peter Southey died of leukaemia at the age of 21 at Ham in Surrey on 28 December 1983. He had joined Spurs in 1978 and appeared in one League game for the club.

While still an active player, goalkeeper Bill Jacques was taken ill in 1922 and two years later he died, aged 36.

John 'Bristol' Jones died of typhoid fever on 13 September 1904 whilst still a registered player with Spurs. He was only 29.

Harry Bradshaw, the Spurs and England international outside-left, died prematurely on Christmas Day 1899 aged 26....likewise James Melia who passed away at the age of 30 in February 1905.

John Stephenson died in January 1908 of pneumonia. He was 33.

Spurs' defender Cyril Knowles, also a full-back, died from an incurable a brain illness in Middlesbrough on 31 August 1991. He was 47.

Former Spurs and Northern Ireland star Noel Brotherston died in 1995 after a short illness. He was only 38. And ex-Spurs striker Ian Moores died at the age of 44 in 1998.

Spurs full-back of the early 1900s, Bob Stevens, was tragically killed in a car crash in February 1928 whilst on his way to his daughter's wedding.

DEBUTS

- These were the eleven players who made their Football League debuts for Spurs v. Wolves on 1 September 1908: Bob Hewitson; Ernie Coquet, John Burton; Tom Morris, Danny Steel, Jabez Darnell; Joe Walton, Vivian Woodward, Doug McFarlane, Bob Steel, Bert Middlemiss.

- The first side to play a Premiership game v. Southampton in August 1992 (when in fact, all the players were making their debuts in the competition), was: Ian Walker; Justin Edinburgh, Terry Fenwick; David Howells, Jason Cundy, Neil Ruddock;

Andy Turner, Gordon Durie, Vinny Samways, Darren Anderton and Paul Allen, with Andy Gray as substitute (on for Turner). Erik Thorstvedt and Dean Austin were the other two subs.

- Spurs' first FA Cup line-up versus West Herts on 13 October 1894 was: Cuthbert Monk; Jack Jull, Jack Welham; Jack Shepherd, Stanley Briggs, Bill Julian; Archie Cubberley, Don Goodall, Peter Hunter, Jock Eccles, Ernie Payne.

- Spurs' first League Cup line-up versus West Ham United in September 1966 was: Pat Jennings; Joe Kinnear, Cyril Knowles; Alan Mullery, Phil Beal, Eddie Clayton; Jimmy Robertson, Jimmy Greaves, Alan Gilzean, Terry Venables and Frank Saul.

- For their first 'European' game against Gornik Zabrze in Poland in the European Cup in September 1961, Spurs fielded: Bill Brown; Peter Baker, Ron Henry; Danny Blanchflower, Maurice Norman, Dave Mackay; Cliff Jones, John White, Bobby Smith, Les Allen and Terry Dyson.

- In 1898, inside-right Ken McKay had the distinction of scoring on his first appearance for Spurs in four different categories of matches: a hat-trick in a friendly v Gainsborough on 1 September, one goal in the Thames & Medway League clash with Thames Ironworks on 3 September, another goal in the United League match with Luton Town on 5 September and then a strike in the FA Cup-tie with Wolverton on 29 October.

- Striker Colin Lee scored four goals on his League debut for Spurs in a 9-0 home win over Bristol Rovers (Division 2) in October 1977.

- Jimmy Greaves netted a hat-trick on his Spurs debut in a 5-2 win over Blackpool in mid-December 1961.

- Goalkeeper Jock Eadon was beaten seven times on his debut for Spurs away at Middlesbrough on 13 February 1915. The game produced 12 goals overall, Spurs losing 5-7.

- Another 'keeper - John Hollowbread - conceded five goals on his League debut for Spurs v. Blackburn Rovers (a) on 30 August 1958.

- Norwegian goalkeeper Erik Thorstvedt (replacing Bobby Mimms) had a nightmare debut for Spurs - filmed live on TV - and his blunder allowed Nottingham Forest to sneak a 2-1 League victory at White Hart Lane on 15 January 1989.

- Almer Hall scored a hat-trick on his first team debut for Spurs against the Corinthians in the Dewar Shield game in November 1934 and followed up by netting twice when making his Football League debut v. Grimsby on Boxing Day of that same year.

- Goalkeeper Ray Clemence made his senior debut for Spurs at Wembley v. Aston Villa in the 1981 FA Charity Shield game (2-2).

- Gary Stevens was on associated Schoolboy forms with Ipswich Town but was not taken on board at Portman Road. Later he made both his senior debuts for Brighton and Spurs against Ipswich Town!

DEFEATS

Details of heavy defeats suffered by Spurs in various competitions (first XI only):

Premiership

1-7 v. Newcastle United	(a)	28.10.1996
0-6 v. Sheffield United	(a)	02.03.1993
1-6 v. Chelsea	(h)	06.12.1997
2-6 v. Liverpool	(a)	08.05.1993
0-5 v. Leeds United	(a)	25.08.1992
2-5 v. Manchester City	(a)	22.10.1994

Football League

2-8 v. Derby County	(a)	16.10.1976
0-7 v. Liverpool	(a)	02.09.1978
2-7 v. Liverpool	(a)	31.10.1914
2-7 v. Newcastle United	(a)	01.09.1951
2-7 v. Blackburn Rovers	(a)	07.09.1963
2-7 v. Burnley	(a)	21.04.1964
5-7 v. Middlesbrough	(a)	13.02.1915
0-6 v. Sunderland	(a)	21.02.1934
0-6 v. Arsenal	(h)	06.03.1935
0-6 v. Leicester City	(a)	28.03.1935
1-6 v. Leicester City	(a)	24.12.1927
1-6 v. Sheffield United	(a)	06.05.1939

FA Cup

1-6 v. Huddersfield Town	(a)	03.03.1928
1-6 v. Newcastle United	(a)	22.12.1999
0-5 v. Stoke	(a)	01.02.1896

League Cup

1-6 v. Bolton Wanderers	(a)	27.11.1996
0-4 v. Middlesbrough	(h)	11.9.1974

European Cup-winners Cup

1-4 v. Manchester United	(a)	10.12.1963

UEFA Cup

1-4 v. Bayern Munich	(a)	03.11.1982

Southern League

0-5 v. Chatham	(a)	02.01.1899
0-5 v. Norwich City	(a)	26.01.1907
4-5 v. New Brompton	(a)	10.04.1899
0-4 v. Portsmouth	(a)	24.04.1901
1-4 v. Southampton	(a)	23.10.1897

Wartime

0-8 v. Birmingham City	(a)	06.10.1945
1-8 v. Chelsea	(a)	04.12.1915
1-7 v. Brentford	(a)	09.11.1918
1-7 v. Queens Park R	(a)	15.02.1919
1-6 v. Watford	(a)	30.12.1939

London Association Cup

0-8 v. Casuals	(a)	07.11.1885
0-6 v. Upton Park	(a)	16.10.1886

London Senior Cup

2-8 v. Old Etonians	(h)	13.10.1888

United League

5-6 v. Millwall   (a)   19.09.1894

Friendly/tour games

1-10 v. W. Arsenal	(a)	21.09.1889
0-9 v. Luton Town	(a)	10.02.1896
1-8 v. Latymer	(a)	06.01.1883
3-7 v. Chelsea	(h)	21.02.1914
2-7 v. England XI	(h)	23.11.1954

Most Defeats in a League season

22 League Division 1	1934-35
21 League Division 1	1953-54
21 League Division 1	1974-75
21 League Division 1	1976-77
20 League Division 1	1912-13
20 League Division 1	1955-56

* Most in Premiership: 19 in season 1993-94.

Fewest Defeats in a League season

4 Division 2	1919-20
6 Division 2	1977-78
7 Division 2	1932-33
7 Division 1	1950-51
7 Division 1	1960-61

Fewest Defeats in the Premiership

9 in season   1995-96.

Losing Habit

- The most League defeats suffered by Spurs in a season is 22 in 1934-35.
- The most home reverses in a campaign is 9 in 1974-75.
- The most away defeats is 17 (in 21 games) in 1934-35.
- The fewest defeats in a season is four in Division 2 in 1919-20.
- The least number of away defeats in a season is four in 1919-20 & 1960-61.
- The fewest home defeats is nil (achieved on four occasions).
- Spurs have lost seven League games in a row on three separate occasions: in October 1955, February/March 1975 and January/February 1994.

Defensive Records

The fewest goals conceded by Spurs in a complete League season has been 32 - in 1908-09 (their first in the competition). They let in 33 in 1970-71 and 35 in 1949-50.

Their best defensive record in the Premiership has been 38 conceded in 1995-96.

Spurs conceded only four goals in a spell of 11 games during the course of the 1990-91 season.

Spurs did not concede a single goal in five Premiership games during November and December 1995.

DERBY COUNTY

Spurs playing record against the Rams:

Competition	P	W	D	L	F	A
Premiership	10	4	3	3	13	12
Football League	50	16	14	20	71	86
FA Cup	3	0	1	2	4	7
League Cup	2	1	0	1	2	2
Wartime	2	0	0	2	2	7
Summary	67	21	18	28	92	114

The first League game between the two clubs took place at White Hart Lane on 3 October 1908 in front of 25,000 fans - and it ended goalless after a rather drab 90 minutes.

Jack Bowers, the Derby centre-forward, scored all his side's goals when County 'rammed' Spurs 4-3 at The Baseball Ground in April 1934. Earlier that season County had won 2-1 in London.

As reigning League champions, Spurs beat the Rams 5-0 at home but lost 4-2 away in the two First Division games played in 1951-52.

A Thursday afternoon attendance of 13,933 - the lowest of the season - saw Spurs beat County 5-2 in a League game on 12 March 1953. The Rams were struggling at the time and were eventually relegated to the Second Division.

When the teams met again at League level - September 1969 - it was one-way traffic as County cantered to a 5-0 home win.

Scottish international Bruce Rioch scored four times when the Rams hammered lowly Spurs 8-2 at The Baseball Ground on 16 October 1976. It was the club's heaviest defeat in the Football League (in terms of goals conceded).

Players with both clubs include: Jimmy Bauchop, George Bowler, John Burton, John Chiedozie, Ally Dick, Ronnie Dix, John Duncan, Randolph Galloway, David Haddow, Bill Hickling, Dave Mackay (also manager of County), Keith Osgood, Charlie Rance, Archie Turner, Simon Webster.

Wartime guests (with either one or both clubs): Pat Beasley, Frank Boulton, Harry Brown, Billy Grimes, Ernie Hoffman, Colin Lyman, Jimmy McCormick, Cecil Potter (also County manager), Charlie Revell, Ron Staley.

DEVLIN, JAMES

Scotsman half-back Jimmy Devlin spent seventeen months with Spurs during which time he scored four goals in 59 first-class matches.

Born north of the border, circa 1874, he played for Dundee, Airdrieonians and Hereford Thistle (on loan) before joining Spurs in June 1896. He was a regular in the side up until April 1897 when, along with his team-mates Richard McElhaney, Jimmy Milliken and Frank Wilson, he was suspended for 'acts of insubordination.'

However, despite this misdemeanour, Devlin was re-signed by the club for the next campaign but not the other three. In the meantime Devlin had arranged his own transfer - choosing to switch to neighbours Millwall (unbeknown to Spurs). He was quickly found out, suspended again, and when the situation was finally sorted out between the respective clubs, Devlin was transferred officially to Millwall after wilfully disobeying training instructions laid down by the club. In November 1897 Devlin was in trouble again - this time he was sent to prison for two months for assaulting the landlord of the Sussex Arms public house in Woolwich (Arsenal territory).

He left the Lions for Sunderland but stayed in the north-east barely a month before returning south to sign for Woowich Arsenal (December 1897). He ended his career back in Scotland with Airdrie, whom he rejoined in August 1898.

DICK, ALISTAIR JOHN

When he made his debut for Spurs against Manchester City on 20 February 1982, winger Ally Dick became the youngest player ever to don a first team jersey for Spurs at Football League level. He was just 16 years and 301 days old at the time.

A Scotsman, born in Stirling on 15 April 1965, he represented Scotland Schools before signing as an apprentice at White Hart Lane in July 1981, turning professional in May 1982. After starring for his country's Youth team, he went on to appear in 43 first team games for Spurs (15 as a substitute, including one in the second leg of the victorious 1984 UEFA Cup Final) and scored six goals before transferring to Ajax Amsterdam in the summer of 1986. After trials with Derby County and Southampton, he teamed up with Wimbledon in July 1989. The following March he switched to Brighton & Hove Albion, and then had an unsuccessful trial with Sheffield Wednesday in 1992.

DILLON, MICHAEL LESLIE

'Matt' Dillon, an England Youth international defender, made 29 appearances for Spurs and assisted Montreal Olympic, Millwall, Swindon Town and New York Cosmos all on loan before joining the latter club on a permanent contract in 1975. He ended his career with Washington Diplomats in 1980. He played with Pele in the New York Cosmos side.

DIMMOCK, JAMES HENRY

Scorer of 100 goals in 400 League games and 138 in a total of 491 first team matches overall, outside-left Jimmy Dimmock was one of the great Spurs players of the twenties, helping the club race away with the Second Division title in the first season after the Great War.

Born only a tram ride from White Hart Lane, at Edmonton on 5 December 1900, he was signed from Edmonton Ramblers as an amateur in 1916 and was taken on the professional pay-roll in May 1919 having guested for Clapton Orient during the hostilities.

After establishing himself in the side by making 34 appearances in his first full season, Dimmock then became the hero of all Spurs fans when he netted the winning goal in the FA Cup Final against Wolves at Stamford Bridge in April 1921.

Described by one soccer reporter as being 'a player of graceful skills, explosive reflexes and subtle imagination' he had balance and strength to match plus a fluid bodyswerve and booming shot. Despite his elaborate on-the-ball skills, when he occasionally tried to be too clever for his own good (to the annoyance of his colleagues but not the fans) Dimmock was certainly a quality footballer. Surprisingly, he lined up in only three full internationals for England (spread over a period of five years: 1921-26) having played in two international trials beforehand.

After a marvellous innings Dimmock left Spurs for Thames FC in August 1931. In September of the following year he transferred to Clapton Orient and played for non-League Ashford from March to May 1934 before retiring. For some years prior to his death in Enfield on 23 December 1972, Dimmock had worked in the road haulage business.

DIRECTORS (& TOTTENHAM HOTSPUR FC, PLC)

From a membership of 100 plus during the 1890's to the 13,000 shareholders today, here you will read about the changes in the infrastructure of the football club from its humble beginnings.

First there are the men who have guided the club, as directors, since the Limited Company was formed towards the end of the 19th century.

It was back in 1898 that the first moves to transform Tottenham Hotspur FC into a Limited Company were made. A special meeting of club members was called at The Red Lion Hotel, High Road on Wednesday, 2 March. The vast majority of the 112 members of Tottenham Hotspur Football Club were present.

A 15-man committee was formed which selected five men to take their place on the first board of directors. Jack Oliver (then club president), Charles D Roberts (vice president), Bobby Buckle (general secretary), Jack Thompson junior (financial secretary) and Ralph Bullock (senior committee man) had all held office under the old regime. A committee had overseen the club affairs since being founded by a group of cricket playing schoolboys in 1882.

A prospectus was distributed at Spurs' Northumberland Park ground on April 8 prior to the match with Woolwich Arsenal. An allowance of 2s 6d (13 pence) was given against the purchase price of a season ticket to encourage the sale of shares at £1 each. A total of 8,000 were made available with the share list due to close on April 30. As it happened the list remained open for several years. Initially a total of 1,552 shares were taken up by 296 people. By June 1901, a total of 2,340 shares had been issued with 123 of those surrendered or forfeited due to lack of full payment. The Tottenham Hotspur Football & Athletic Company Limited was incorporated in England, registered number 57186, on 2 May 1898. When the centenary passed in 1998 the club received a special certificate confirming the 100th anniversary.

It was nearly a year later, during March 1899 that share certificates were first issued by the club. The introduction of a shareholders' stand, the central one of three on the west side of the new High Road Ground, was suggested by Morton Cadman and agreed by the board.

When building work and leasehold problems arose in 1905 the club took the unusual step of an appeal for further shareholders through the club handbook raising much of the finance needed to fulfil their ambitions but the issued capital of the club was still well below the 8,000 maximum. By 1915 the share capital had risen to 4,892 shares and this figure remained static until 1983.

In 1931 the Tottenham Weekly Herald revealed that of the 812 shareholders the largest was not on the board of directors. Mrs Cadman, wife of Morton, held 374 shares, followed by secretary Arthur Turner (222), Fred Bearman (188) and Mrs. Deacock (150).

Tottenham Hotspur PLC

In 1983, Spurs became the first publicly quoted football club in the UK.

Whilst preparing for the floating of Tottenham Hotspur plc, further shares were created to be added to the 4,892 previously in existence. As a result, on 14 March 1983, Nailage plc was set up and its name changed two months later to Tottenham Hotspur plc.

Six months later, on 13 October 1983 trading commenced with 3.8 million shares being made available at £1 each. The minimum acceptance was for 100 shares. The offer was nearly four-and-a-half times over-subscribed with 12,859 applicants for 16,939,100 shares. Since then, the number of shares has multiplied to a current total of 100,738,310 at 25 pence each.

Here are the men who served as Directors of Tottenham Hotspur FC (in order of their appointment to the board)

1898

Bobby Buckle had been involved with the club since its inception in September 1882, first as a player, then as secretary and also as a hard-working and enthusiastic committee member. He worked in the office of a London-based firm of solicitors and served as director for just over two years, until his retirement, from March 1898 until June 1900. Buckle was 90 when he died in 1959.

1898

Charles David Roberts has been the longest serving chairman in the club's history, holding office for almost 45 years from November 1898 until his death in July 1943. An original board member, he had been involved in local rugby and later played baseball stateside for the well-supported Nassau club at Brooklyn. Roberts had many business interests including cooperage on the Tottenham High Road.

1898

Ralph Bullock first served on the club committee in 1893 and it was he who compiled the initial Tottenham Hotspur Football Handbook (1897). He was a club director for four years, one month, until choosing to emigrate to the USA in April 1902. A keen supporter, Bullock later became a commander and returned to England (and Tottenham), serving as an auditor for the shareholders from June 1931 until his death in December, 1946, aged 77.

1898

Jack Thompson, the fourth member of the original board, appointed in March 1898, had been the founding secretary of the club in 1882. He continued to work behind the scenes with Buckle throughout the amateur years. He resigned as a director in July 1899 and died in February 1909.

1898

Jim Hawley was a key member of the club during the amateur days. He was employed as a rate collector by the Middlesex Council and served as a director from November 1898 until his death in May 1907. His son, Alf, played for the club in Southern League matches.

1898

Jack Oliver the first club chairman, he served on the board for eight months between March and November 1898. Proprietor of the Athletic World newspaper, he had succeeded John Ripsher as club president in 1894. Later became involved at the Leeds City club.

1899

Tom Deacock served as a director from July 1899 until his death in June 1924 at the age of 58. During that period, however, he did have two breaks in service - the first from March to September 1903 and the second from October 1912 until the summer of 1913. Deacock sold his chain of eleven provisions shops to John Sainsbury. A Football League and FA Councillor, he was linesman for the Amateur international between England and Ireland at White Hart Lane in 1907 and six years later changed his black uniform for a white one when he represented England against Scotland at bowls.

1900

Morton Cadman joined the club as a playing member in December 1888 and captained the reserve team during the 1890-91 season. He was elected to the board in June 1900 and held office until he retirement in April 1943 He was employed for 40 years as a rate collector by the Edmonton Council (1889- 1929) and he also served on the Football League Committee and FA Council throughout the 1930s. Cadman, whose wife was a shareholder, became vice-president and thereafter a life vice-president of Tottenham Hotspur FC until his death in December 1948.

1902

George Cox had two separate spells as a Spurs director - the first spanned six years from November 1902 until 1908 and the second lasted much longer, from December 1917 until July 1949. He then became vice-president until retiring in October 1950 at the age of 94. Cox ran a building firm on Holloway Road for many years and as a youngster he played rugby union for Highbury Utd.

1907

Henry D Carter had been connected with football for more than 30 years - as both player and supporter - prior to his election to the board in May 1907. He had business at Finsbury Park and remained a member of the board until 1913.

Club staff from the late 1920's

1909

Fred Bearman was opted onto the Spurs board in October 1909 and became chairman in August 1943, holding office until his retirement in October 1961 at the age of 88. He then served as club president until his death in April 1964. Managing-director of the family brewery at Notting Hill, Bearman also played centre half for the works team! He was later chairman of a malt extract firm and legend has it that his association with Spurs started in 1901 when he went out and purchased some beer barrels from a local cooper - Mr. Roberts, who was in fact, the club's chairman.

1907

Vivian Woodward, the most celebrated Amateur international footballer of his day, was first associated with the club as a player in 1901. He became a Spurs director in June 1907 and was still a member of the board when he won a gold medal at the 1908 Olympic Games. He also had the pleasure - and honour - of scoring Spurs' first-ever Football League goal against Wolves, also in 1908. Woodward resigned in July 1909 to concentrate on his profession as an architect but he later returned to football as a director of Spurs' near neighbours, Chelsea.

1912

Dr. JF Mackenzie served the club in a dual role as medical officer and director for just over five years, from October 1912 until December 1917. Torpedoed on a ship in the Mediterranean Sea during the Great War, he retired to his native Scotland.

1924

When George Wagstaffe Simmons joined the board of directors at White Hart Lane in July 1924, he had a wealth of football experience behind him, having served as chairman of the Herts County FA and as an FA Councillor (since 1901). He had also worked on the editorial staff of the Sporting Life (covering football in the main), was an international selector and had found time to run the line in a 1906 Spurs FA Cup-tie! He compiled the first comprehensive history of the club, published in 1947, and became a vice-president on retiring in July 1949. Wagstaffe passed away in January 1954 on the same day as former player and fellow director Vivian Woodward.

1943

Bill Heryet, who had a long association with the Spartan League, joined the Spurs board of directors in August 1943, retiring in 1950. He worked for 40 years as a solicitor's managing clerk and was also an FA Councillor, a position he filled until his death in November 1957.

1950

John Bearman took the place of Bill Heryet on the Spurs board. The son of Fred, he served as a director for more than ten-and-a-half years - from October 1950 until July 1961.

1943

Eddie Dewhurst Hornsby moved south to London (and Tottenham) in 1913 and was employed as the district manager for the Whitbread brewery firm based on Tottenham High Road. He served on the Council of the London FA and also as Spurs director for over eleven years, from August 1943 until his death in November 1954.

1943

Fred Wale, a fully trained engineer, worked at one of the family firms, Brown's of Tottenham. He was an active member of the

Council of the London FA and was elected to the board of directors at White Hart Lane in August 1943. He took over as club chairman in October 1961 and retained that position until his death in October 1969, aged 82.

1948

Lord Robert 'Bob' Morrison had a brief spell as a Spurs director between December 1948 and March 1949, later holding the position of club president until his death in December 1953. He also served as Mayor of Tottenham.

1949

Harry Taylor replaced Lord Morrison on the board in March 1949. He remained as a director until his death in January 1954 and often used his linguistic skills to good effect as translator on several of the club's overseas tours.

1957

Sidney Wale, educated at Tottenham Grammar School, succeeded his father as chairman of Spurs in 1969. A chartered accountant and director of several engineering firms, he joined the board of directors in November 1957, resigning his position in June 1980. He was a life president until his death in October 1986.

1957

Douglas Deacock, the youngest son of Tom, served on the board from November 1957 until his death in September 1968, aged 67.

1961

Charles Cox, son of George (above) was a sales promotion manager of a London-based car sales firm. He served as a Spurs director for almost 20 years - from July 1961 until April 1981. He then held the title of life vice-president until his death three years later, aged 87.

1961

Arthur Richardson had a trial for London Schoolboys. He was chairman and managing director of a waste paper firm when he joined the board of directors in October 1961. He was chairman of the club from June 1980 until December 1982 and then acted as a life vice-president until March 1983. He passed away in April 1990 at the age of 84.

1968

Godfrey Groves, Tottenham born and bred, attended the local Grammar School. He was a quantity surveyor by profession and served on the Spurs' board of directors from December 1968 until his death in June 1978.

1970

Geoffrey Richardson was only 29 years of age when he was elected to the board in April 1970, making him the youngest man ever to serve as a Spurs director. Like his father, Arthur (above) he held office until December 1982 and was vice-president until March 1983. Richardson was also a director of the family's waste paper company.

1978

Ken Kennard served as a Spurs director from August 1978 until December 1982. The son-in-law of Charles Cox, he continued to attend White Hart Lane right up until his death in June 1994.

1980

Douglas Alexiou was elected to the board of directors in June 1980. He later had a spell as chairman (from December 1982 until July 1984). Since resigning from the board in August 1998 he has been a club vice president. The senior partner in a firm of London solicitors, Alexiou is a son-in-law of Sidney Wale.

1981

A Spurs supporter since the thirties, Frank Sinclair became a director of the club in July 1981 and was made a vice-president on his retirement from the board in August 1991. He worked as managing director of Mountview Estates PLC and passed away in November, 1994 at the age of 78.

1982

Paul Bobroff was the man who manufactured the takeover of the club with Irving Scholar from the Richardson family in December 1982. He remained as a director at White Hart Lane until June 1991. He was appointed chairman and managing director of the firm Markheath Securities when the club was floated in 1983.

1982

Peter Leaver was a practising barrister during his time as a Spurs director which lasted from December 1982 until July 1984. Now a QC and deputy High Court Judge, Leaver was formerly the Chief Executive of the FA Premier League.

1984

Irving Scholar was just 35 years of age when he became the major shareholder in the club in December 1982. However, he did not take up the position of club chairman until July 1984. Scholar worked for a property division of European Ferries PLC and served as an FA Councillor. He left the club board in Sept 1991.

1987

Tony Berry played for Spurs' youth team during the 1958-59 season. A schoolboy boxing champion and later opening bat for Edmonton Cricket Club, he had a spell as chairman of St. Albans City FC prior to joining the board of directors at White Hart Lane in March 1987. Berry was club chairman during the 1991-92 season and has been a club vice-president since leaving the board in August 1998.

1991

Sir Alan Sugar joined the board in June 1991 and took the position of club chairman a year later. He built up the Amstrad Electronics firm from humble beginnings in North London and was knighted in the 2000 New Year's Honours List for his services to the electronics and computer industry. He left the board in February 2001.

1991

Terry Venables played for the club from 1966 to 1969 and returned as manager in 1987. He joined the board in June 1991 and sold his shareholding in September 1993. Venables also served Queen's Park Rangers as a director during the early eighties.

1991

Igal Yawetz has served as a director of the club since June 1991. During his teenage years he played as a centre forward for the Tel Aviv-based Haifa Club in his native Israel. Yawetz is now an established London-based architect whose designs can be seen in the north and south stands at White Hart Lane.

1991

Colin Sandy, a certified accountant who was finance director for four years from August 1991, is a non-executive director of the club. He's also a director of companies under the Amshold Group.

1995

John Sedgwick, a chartered accountant, joined the Spurs board as a finance director in August 1995. He had previously held various finance positions for a number of high street retailers.

1998

Sam Chisholm served as a director at White Hart Lane between August and November 1998 and was then re-appointed to the board in October 2000. He is a former Chief Executive and Managing-Director of British Sky Broadcasting and MD of the Nine Network in Australia.

1998

Claude Littner was the club's Chief Executive for five years until November 1998. He is now a non-Executive Director, having previously worked for Unilever PLC and later for Amstrad PLC in France, Spain and Denmark.

1998

Martin Stanford Peters, MBE, the former West Ham United, Spurs, Sheffield United and England midfield player, joined the board as a non-executive director during August 1998. Peters, who scored in England's 1966 World Cup Final triumph, was a star at White Hart Lane for five years during the '70s

1998

David Pleat was appointed as the club's first Director of Football during January 1998. With a wealth of football knowledge gathered from 40 years as a player, coach and manager, including a spell in the latter role at White Hart Lane from May 1986 until October 1987, he has already proved invaluable to the club. (See also: Pleat, David).

2000-01

David Buchler joined the board as executive vice-chairman in February 2001.

Sam Chisholm was re-appointed as a board member in October 1999, but resigned again in December 2000.

David Levy was appointed as a non-executive chairman in February 2001.

Claude Littner was a non-executive director of the club until December 2000 and Colin Sandy was a non-executive director until July 2001.

Sir Alan Sugar remained as the club's chairman until February 2001 and five months later (in July) Igal Yawetz stood down as a director of the club.

In addition to the lengthy list of directors of Tottenham Hotspur Football Club, there have also been some who served only on the PLC board. These include Derek Peter (financial controller for seven years: 1983 to 1990), Peter Day, Colin Wooldridge, Bob Holt, Ian Gray, Nat Solomon - currently a club vice president - and Jonathan Crystal.

Committee (The)

Without the assistance of the committee members, who steered the club through the first 16 years, it is unlikely that Tottenham Hotspur would have survived. The major force was John Ripsher, who was club president from 1883 until 1894 and a club patron thereafter. It was he who formed the first committee during the summer of 1883 comprising of TW Bumberry, WG Herbert, F Dexter and W Tyrell. In addition, by 1885, the club had five vice-presidents.

Others to serve on the committee during the 1880s include Sam Casey, Stuart Leaman, F Cottrell, JG Randall, JH Avery, W Lomas, FJ Powell, Jack Jull, G Rochford, Henry Turner, John Jull, Billy Mason and Frank Hatton.

Those in office during the 1890s included W Pilbrow, Frank Scott Walford, J Baxter, Tom Purdie, J Hurry, CV Monk, J Smallbone, JW Welham, Stanley Briggs, T Hacking, AS Petter and Charlie McGahey - the latter a well known Essex cricketer. The vast majority of these were playing members of the club at one time or another during the formative years.

By 1895 the number of vice-presidents had increased to 25 with three patrons, local MPs Joseph Howard and Major Bowles in addition to John Ripsher.

Directors' Minutes

*In 1901, when Spurs won the FA Cup for the first time, the Board was made up of Charles D Roberts (Chairman), James Hawley, Thomas Deacock, Morton Cadman and Ralph Bullock. John Cameron was secretary-manager and worked in conjunction with the board.

* Player to Director.... The following Spurs players later became football club directors: David H Clark (Spurs amateur) Charlton Athletic director 1925-32, Morton Cadman (Spurs), Gerry Francis (Bristol Rovers), Arthur Grimsdell (Watford), Alf Ramsey (Birmingham City), Martin Peters (Spurs), Jimmy Seed (Charlton Athletic), Terry Venables (Chief Executive) & Vivian Woodward (Spurs and Chelsea).

DITCHBURN, EDWIN GEORGE

A brilliant goalkeeper, Ted Ditchburn made 572 first team appearances for Spurs, 418 in the Football League between August 1946 and August 1958. By coincidence he played his first and last matches against Chelsea!

Born in Gillingham, Kent on 24 October 1921, the son of a boxer, Ditchburn represented Kent Schools and Northfleet Paper Mills FC before joining the groundstaff at White Hart Lane in 1937. He signed amateur forms in June 1938, was sent to play for he club's nursery side Northfleet and then returned to put pen to paper to become a professional in May 1939. Unfortunately the War disrupted his progress considerably (like it did many other footballers) although he did make guest appearances for Aberdeen, Birmingham and Dartford during the hostilities.

When peace returned Ditchburn went straight into Spurs' first XI for the start of the 1946-47 season and he held his position, unchallenged, for eight years up to November 1954 when Ron Reynolds took over between the posts. During that period he hardly missed a match, appearing in 377 out of a possible 382 at competitive level (League, FA Cup & Charity Shield). From 17 April 1948 to 17 March 1954 inclusive, he made a club record 247 consecutive League appearances, plus 23 games in the FA Cup and one in the Charity Shield. An ever-present for five seasons running from 1948, he was one of the stars of Spurs' successive Second Division and First Division championship winning sides in 1950 and 1951.

Daring, agile, alert, confident, a safe handler (but not a puncher) and clean striker of a dead ball, Ditchburn was a wonderful 'keeper. It was a pity that there were so many other fine custodians around at the same time (Bert Williams, Frank Swift, Gil Merrick) for he would certainly have won many more England caps than the paltry six he did gain. He did though represent his country's 'B' team and played twice for the Football League.

A Spurs man through and through, Ditchburn suffered serious injuries during the 1958-59 season and he eventually moved on to assist Romford (April 1959), later taking over as manager (to March 1962). He announced his retirement from football in April 1965 only to come back for more as an occasional 'keeper for Brentwood Town FC four months later, finally quitting in 1966 - so that he could sit and watch England win the World Cup in peace! In later life Ditchburn ran a successul sports outfitters/games shop in Romford and was also involved in the printing business.

DIX, RONALD WILLIAM

Born in Bristol on 5 September 1912, Ronnie Dix attended and played for South Central School (Bristol) and represented Bristol Schools, Gloucestershire Schools and England Schools (the latter at the age of 13). He joined Bristol Rovers as an amateur in July 1927 and became the youngest player ever to score a League goal, aged 15 years, 180 days old) for Rovers against Norwich City in a Third Division (South) game in March 1928. He turned professional eighteen months later and moved into a higher grade when he signed for Blackburn Rovers in May 1932. From Ewood Park he switched to Aston Villa (with Arthur Cunliffe in March 1933) and four years later transferred to Derby County (February 1937). He found his way to Spurs in June 1939 but the War came and severely interrupted his progress. Dix guested for Blackpool, Bradford PA, Bristol City, Chester, Liverpool, Wrexham and York City during the hostilities and then moved to Reading in November 1947, announcing his retirement in June 1949. Dix joined Aston Villa after a proposed move to Everton had fallen through. He was a fine footballer, a clever, constructive inside-forward of high consistency who made the ball do the work! He scored 30 goals in just over 100 games in his four years at Villa Park, appeared in almost 100 first XI matches for Spurs (19 goals) and during his career netted almost 140 times in 442 League and FA Cup matches. Capped by England against Norway in 1939, he had earlier represented the Football League (1938) and in 1943 won a League North Cup winners medal with Blackpool, following on with a runners-up medal twelve months later when the Seasiders lost to his old club Aston Villa in the two-legged Final. Dix died on 2 April 1998.

DIXON, ARTHUR

Full-back Archie Dixon played in 11 games for Spurs in season 1907-08, in between spells at Burnley and Bradford Park Avenue. He also assisted Nelson.

DODGE, WILLIAM CHARLES

Half-back Bill Dodge was with Spurs at the same time as Blanchflower and Mackay. He made just ten first-class appearances before moving to Crystal Palace in 1962.

DOHERTY, GARY MICHAEL THOMAS

The versatile Republic of Ireland international made his Football League debut for Luton Town in 1997 and went on to appear in 83 first-class matches for the Hatters (15 goals scored) before transferring to Spurs for £1 million in April 2000.

Born in Cardonagh on the Emerald Isle on 31 January 1980, he is equally at home in defence or attack.

Tottenham goalkeeper Ted Ditchburn gets the ball away from Preston North End's Foster at White Hart Lane in 1954

Skipper of the Republic of Ireland Under-18 team in the European Youth Championship in Sweden, in the summer of 1999, he established himself in both the Eire and Spurs senior sides during the 2000-01 season. He has now made over 40 first and second team appearances during his time at White Hart Lane.
Doherty won his first full cap v. Greece in April 2000.

DOMINGUEZ, JOSE MANUEL MARTINS

Preferring to occupy a position wide on the flank, darting Portuguese star Jose Dominguez is one of the smallest players ever to don a Spurs' first team jersey. Skilful with a a powerful shot he played initially for Benfica before making his English debut with Birmingham City in 1994 following his £180,000 transfer to St Andrew's. He played 45 games for Blues having loan spells with Sintrense and Fafe, before switching to Sporting Club de Portugal in a £1.8 million deal in August 1995. He then joined Spurs for £1.6 million in August 1997 but during his four years at White Hart Lane he managed only 58 first team appearances, 42 as a substitute. Born in Lisbon on 16 Feb 1974 and capped three times by his country at senior level and once for the U-21s, Dominguez helped Blues win the Second Division championship in 1995.

DONCASTER ROVERS

Spurs playing record against Rovers:

Competition	P	W	D	L	F	A
Football League	6	3	2	1	10	5
FA Cup	1	1	0	0	2	0
League Cup	1	1	0	0	7	2
Summary	8	5	2	1	19	7

The first Spurs v. Doncaster Rovers League game took place at White Hart Lane on 12 December 1936 and resulted in a 2-0 win for the Londoners.

Players with both clubs include: Jimmy Bauchop, Kerry Dixon (Spurs reserve, Rovers player-manager), Jack Eggett, Ian Gilzean (Spurs reserve), Warren Hackett (Spurs Youth), Alan Hall, Bob Hewitson (Rovers reserve), Leon Hyde, Arthur Jones, John Moncur, Tony Parks, Ernie Phypers, Vic Potts (Spurs reserve & scout), Micky Stead (Rovers player-coach), Andy Turner, Charlie Woodruff.
Wartime guests (with either of both clubs): Wally Alsford, Cliff Parker, Tommy Simmons.
Also associated: Dave Mackay (Spurs player, Rovers manager), Joe Kinnear (Spurs player, Rovers coach, assistant-manager & manager). They were at Belle Vue together. Also Jimmy Neighbour (Spurs player & coach, Rovers assistant-manager).

DOUBLE WINNERS

Results in Spurs' double-winning campaign of 1960-61.

Football League

Opponents	H	A
Arsenal	4-2	3-2
Aston Villa	6-2	2-1
Birmingham City	6-0	3-2
Blackburn Rovers	5-2	4-1
Blackpool	3-1	3-1
Bolton Wanderers	3-1	2-1
Burnley	4-4	2-4
Cardiff City	3-2	2-3
Chelsea	4-2	3-2
Everton	2-0	3-1
Fulham	5-1	0-0
Leicester City	2-3	2-1
Manchester City	1-1	1-0
Manchester United	4-1	0-2
Newcastle United	1-2	4-3
Nottingham Forest	1-0	4-0
Preston North End	5-0	1-0
Sheffield Wednesday	2-1	1-2
West Bromwich A	1-2	3-1
West Ham United	2-0	3-0
Wolverhampton W	1-1	4-0

FA Cup

Rd 3 v. Charlton Athletic	(h)	3-2
Rd 4 v. Crewe Alexandra	(h)	5-1
Rd 5 v. Aston Villa	(a)	2-0
Rd 6 v. Sunderland	(a)	1-1
Rep. v. Sunderland	(h)	5-0
S/f v. Burnley	(VP)	3-0
Final v. Leicester City	(W)	2-0

Summary: Football League

Venue	P	W	D	L	F	A	Pts
Home	21	15	3	3	65	28	33
Away	21	16	1	4	50	27	33
Totals	42	31	4	7	115	55	66

Seasonal Facts

Spurs finished eight points clear of runners-up Sheffield Wednesday and 11 ahead of third-placed Wolves. Bottom club Preston North End netted only 30 points, 36 fewer than Spurs.
Spurs claimed 11 successive League wins at the start of the season. The run ended with a 1-1 home draw against Manchester City on 10 October.

The first defeat was suffered in match number 17, away at Sheffield Wednesday (2-1).

Spurs ran up eight successive away wins, commencing with a 3-1 victory at Blackpool on 22 August.

They completed eleven doubles; beat the FA Cup holders Wolves 4-0 at Molineux in October and conceded eight goals against Burnley (drawing 4-4 at home and losing 4-2 away).

Bobby Smith with 33 goals (28 League, five FA Cup) was top-scorer, followed by Les Allen with 27 (23 League) and Cliff Jones (19).

Allen, skipper Danny Blanchflower, left-back Ron Henry, and John White were all ever-present. Goalkeeper Bill Brown missed one game and kept ten clean-sheets.

DOW, WILLIAM

Former Leith Athletic outside-left Bill Dow joined Spurs from Bury in 1906. He spent one season at White Hart Lane, making 14 first-class appearances (three goals).

DOWSETT, GILBERT JAMES

Outside-left Dicky Dowsett scored on his League debut for Spurs v. Aston Villa in 1954 - his only senior appearance for the club. He left White Hart Lane at the end of that season and went on to net over 100 goals in more than 250 first-class appearances during the next ten years playing for Southend, Southampton, Bournemouth and Crystal Palace.

DOZZELL, JASON ALVIN WINANS

A £1.9 million buy from Ipswich Town in August 1993, midfielder Jason Dozzell became the youngest goalscorer in the First Division when, at the age 16 years, 56 days, on his debut, he netted for Ipswich against Coventry City on 4 February 1984. Strong and confident, 6ft 1in tall, he appeared in over 400 games for the Portman Road club (71 goals), gained four Youth and nine Under-21 caps for England and helped the Suffolk club win the 1992 Second Division title before making the move to White Hart Lane. He spent a little over four years with Spurs, playing in 99 League and Cup games and netting 14 times. In October 1997 he returned to Ipswich but within two months had signed for Northampton Town, later joining Colchester United (October 1998).

Dozzell was born in Ipswich on 9 December 1967.

DRAWS

Spurs drew a record 17 League games in season 1968-69 (42 matches played).

Sixteen games were drawn in 1948-49, 1977-78 and 1990-91 while there were 15 level scorelines in 1932-33, 1975-76, 1978-79 and 1980-81.

The most in the Premiership so far in a season has been 14 - in 1994-95 and 1998-99.

In 1957-58 Spurs had two successive 3-3 draws in December and January against Newcastle United and Preston. Soon afterwards they drew 4-4 with Arsenal.

Spurs played out four successive 0-0 draws during the month of September 1980 - three in the First Division with Manchester United, Leeds United and Sunderland and one in the League Cup v. Crystal Palace.

Spurs drew six Premiership games on the trot during January and February 1999, four of them by 0-0 and two at 1-1.

Tottenham Hotspur FC Double Winning Team 1960-61

Between 13 January and 3 February 2001 Spurs had four successive goalless draws in the Premiership - the first time this had happened at Football League level (since 1908).

DROGHEDA UNITED

Spurs playing record against the Irish club:

Competition	P	W	D	L	F	A
UEFA Cup	2	2	0	0	14	0

Spurs started their charge towards UEFA Cup glory in 1983-84 with a comfortable 14-0 aggregate victory over the Irish part-timers Drogheda in the opening round, played in September. Gary Mabbutt (2), Mark Falco (2), Tony Galvin and Garth Crooks scored in the 6-0 win in Ireland when the attendance was just 7,000. A fortnight later full-back Chris Hughton, Graham Roberts (2), Steve Archibald, Falco (2) and Alan Brazil (2) netted in the rather one-sided second-leg 8-0 victory when the turnout was just 19,831.

DRYBURGH, WILLIAM

Outside-right Bill Dryburgh had two spells with both Cowdenbeath and Sheffield Wednesday as well as serving Millwall Athletic before joining Spurs in 1902. He netted three goals in 32 senior games for the club, leaving in May 1903.

DUKLA PRAGUE

Spurs playing record against the Czech club:

Competition	P	W	D	L	F	A
European Cup	2	1	0	1	4	2

Spurs have met the Czech side twice - in the second round of the 1961-62 European Cup competition. The first leg, played in Prague on St Valentine's Day, attracted a crowd of 64,000 and resulted in a 1-0 win for Spurs, courtesy a Cliff Jones goal.

The return leg, played 12 days later, ended in a comfortable 4-1 victory for Spurs, Dave Mackay (2) and Bobby Smith (2) obliging with the goals in front of 55,388 spectators.

DUMITRESCU, ILIE

Midfielder Ilie Dumistrecu cost Spurs £2.6 million when signed from Steaua Bucharest in September 1994. He went on to make just 20 senior appearances for the club (five goals scored) before transferring to West Ham United for £1.5 million in January 1996. There was an initial hold up and the deal wasn't completed until early March. Hammers' boss Harry Redknapp later cursed his luck for failing to obtain a work permit for the Romanian international beyond the end of that 1995-96 season - and he regretted it for years afterwards! Dumitrescu subsequently left Upton Park (bitterly disappointed) and joined the Mexican side, Clube de Futbol (January 1997). He retired to take a coaching position with the Otelul Galati club (early 2001).

Born in Bucharest in January 1969, respected and talented, Dumitrescu was loaned by Spurs to the Spanish side Sevilla in December 1994, but a proposed move from White Hart Lane on a permanent basis never materialised.

He won more than 60 caps for Romania at senior international level.

DUNCAN, ANDREW

A £6,000 signing from Hull City in May 1935, inside-forward Andy Duncan scored 45 goals in 184 first team appearances for Spurs before leaving the club in April 1946 for Chelmsford City for whom he had guested during the Second World War.

Born in Renton, Dumbartonshire on 25 January 1911, he had two separate spells with Renton Thistle and also assisted Dumbarton before joining the Tigers as a professional in May 1930. Plagued by injuries from time to time, Duncan left the team playing with only 10 men when he walked off the pitch during a home game with Crystal Palace in August 1942 - because he couldn't stand the barracking from irate supporters. He didn't play for Spurs again. Duncan, who also assisted Brentford and Palace during the hostilities, died in Southall, Middlesex on 10 October 1983.

DUNCAN, JOHN PEARSON

£150,000 striker John Duncan was Terry Neill's first signing after he had taken over as Spurs manager in October 1974. A Scotsman, born in Dundee on 22 February 1949, Duncan had played for Morgan Academy, Butterburn Youth Club, Broughty Thistle and Dundee north of the border, as well as representing the Scottish League against the Football League in March 1973 and gaining a Scottish League Cup winners' medal with Dundee (1974). He quickly made his mark in England, scoring 12 goals in 30 League and Cup games during that 1974-75 season. He went on to notch a total of 75 goals in 145 first team outings for the club (including 53 in 103 Football League matches) before transferring to Derby County for £150,000 in September 1978....soon after Spurs had crashed 7-0 at Liverpool!

In June 1981 Duncan switched to Scunthorpe United and was appointed manager of the Iron in February 1983. He later managed Hartlepool United (from April 1983), Chesterfield (two spells: the first from June 1983 to June 1987, steering the Spire-ites to the Fourth Division title in 1985; the second from February 1993 to May 2000) and Ipswich Town, whom he bossed for three seasons from 1987 to 1990.

Duncan also assisted England as team 'observer' from August 1992 before returning to Saltergate.

DUNDALK

Spurs playing record against the Irish club:

Competition	P	W	D	L	F	A
ECW Cup	2	1	1	0	2	1

Spurs made hard work of eliminating the Irish club side Dundalk from the second round of the European Cup-winners Cup in 1981-82. They eventually scraped through 2-1 on aggregate after two difficult encounters. The first leg played in Ireland on 21 October ended 1-1, Garth Crooks the Spurs scorer. For the return fixture on 4 November, 33,455 fans were present to see Crooks find the back of the net again as Spurs squeezed home 1-0.

Players with both clubs include: Alex Anderson & John Smith (player-manager).

DUNFERMLINE ATHLETIC

Spurs playing record against the Scottish side:

Competition	P	W	D	L	F	A
Texaco Cup	2	2	0	0	7	0

The two Texaco Cup games were played in 1970-71, Spurs winning 4-0 at home and 3-0 away. Martin Chivers netted a hat-trick in the victory at White Hart Lane.

Player with both clubs: Hans Segers.

DUNMORE, DAVID GERALD IVOR

Born in Whitehaven, Cumbria on 8 February 1934, centre-forward

Dave Dunmore played for Cliftonville Minors FC before joining York City on a part-time basis in May 1952. In February 1954, having netted 41 goals in 123 League and Cup games for the Minstermen, he was signed by Spurs manager Arthur Rowe for £10,500. Over the next six years Dunmore, strong and mobile, who made his First Division debut against Arsenal in front of more than 64,000 fans, hit a further 34 goals in 97 first team appearances up to March 1960, before he transferred across London to West Ham United for £20,000.

He later helped Leyton Orient win promotion to the First Division (1962) before returning to Bootham Crescent where he ended his senior career prior to winding down with spells at Wellington and Bridlington Trinity.

DUQUEMIN, LEONARD STANLEY

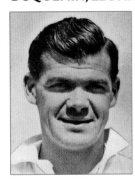

A terrific centre-forward, not all that skilful but a great marksman who had the knack of being in the right spot at the right time, Len Duquemin netted 184 goals in 373 first-team games for Spurs, 114 coming in 274 League appearances.

A Channel-Islander, born in the village of Calvo on Guernsey on 17 July 1924, he joined Spurs as a trialist from Vauxbelet FC (Guernsey) in December 1945. He impressed and was duly taken on as an amateur a month later, turning professional in September 1946, having guested for Chelmsford City and Colchester United during the war.

Over the next twelve years 'the Duke' certainly did the business, helping Spurs win the Second Division and First Division championships in successive seasons (1949-51). He was the perfect partner in attack for Les Bennett and between them they bagged well over 200 goals in League and FA Cup action before Bennett dropped out of the forward-line to be replaced by Johnny Brooks.

A scorer and loser in two FA Cup semi-finals, Duquemin left White Hart Lane for Bedford Town in November 1958 (three years after Bobby Smith's arrival in the camp). Later he assisted Romford and Hastings United before hanging up his boots to run a newsagents' shop on Northumberland Park prior to becoming landlord of the Haunch of Venison in Cheshunt.

DURHAM CITY

No competitive games between Spurs and City as yet.
Players with both clubs include: Fred Mearns, Tommy Roe.

DURIE, GORDON SCOTT

Striker Gordon Durie had the honour of scoring Spurs' first Premiership goal, in a 2-2 home draw with Crystal Palace in August 1992. His final tally for the club - in 78 senior appearances - was 17 before he left White Hart Lane for Glasgow Rangers in November 1993 for £1.2 million.

Born in Paisley on 6 December 1965, he played for the Hill o'Beath club before turning professional with East Fife in 1983, moving next to Hibernian and then on to Chelsea for £380,000 in April 1986.

A fast, well built and brave striker, operating through the middle or down the flanks, Durie netted 49 goals in more than 150 competitive games north of the border, being something of a 'folk hero' at Easter Road. At Stamford Bridge he notched another 62 in 152 outings before moving to Spurs for £2.2 million in August

1991.

Capped four times at Under-21 level by Scotland (when a Chelsea player) Durie went on to represent his country in 43 full internationals (seven goals scored), gaining his last cap in 1998 with Rangers whom he helped win five League championships, two Scottish Cups and three League Cups.

DYNAMO TBILISI

Spurs playing record against the Russian club:

Competition	P	W	D	L	F	A
UEFA Cup	2	1	1	0	6	2

After accounting for Grasshoppers (Zurich) and Aberdeen in the early stages of the 1973-74 UEFA Cup competition, Spurs met the Soviet club Dynamo Tbilisi in the third round and promptly dismissed them in style with a 6-2 aggregate scoreline.

The first leg ended 1-1 in Georgia on 28 November when 45,000 fans saw Ralph Coates score a vital away goal, and then just 18,602 hardy supporters turned up at White Hart Lane a fortnight later to see Spurs finish the job with a 5-1 victory. On target this time were Chris McGrath, Martin Chivers (2) and Martin Peters (2).

DYSON, TERENCE KENT

At 5ft 3ins tall Terry Dyson was a darting left-winger with good pace and powerful shot who struck Spurs' second goal in the 1961 FA Cup Final victory over Leicester City to clinch the double. Unfortunately he missed the 1962 Cup Final win over Burnley but then hit two goals when the European Cup-Winners Cup was lifted a year later. A Yorkshireman, born in Malton on 29 November 1934, Dyson played for Scarborough before joining Spurs as an amateur in December 1954, turning professional four months later (April 1955). After notching 55 goals in 209 first-class matches for Spurs (68 in 244 first team matches overall) he moved to Fulham for £5,000 in June 1965. Later Dyson assisted Colchester United (August 1968-70), Guildford City and Wealdstone before taking over as manager of Kingsbury Town, holding a similar position with Wingate and then acting as assistant-boss of Dagenham. He retired from football to become a games instructor at Hampstead School prior to opening his own sports shop.

E

EAST END CUP

Spurs entered this London competition in season 1886-87 and reached the semi-final by knocking out Phoenix 6-0, Park 2-0 and St Luke's 2-1 - all at home - before losing 1-0 to Caledonian (at Tottenham).

EDINBURGH, JUSTIN

Full-back Justin Edinburgh made 270 League and Cup appearances for Spurs (one goal scored) during his ten years with the club. Signed from Southend United for £150,000 in July 1990, he was an FA Cup and League Cup winner in 1991 and 1999 respectively. A totally committed defender, his pace down the left and his extraordinary tenacity made him a firm favourite with the fans.

Born in Basildon, Essex on 18 December 1969, he was a trainee at Roots Hall before signing as a professional for the Shrimpers in August 1988. On leaving White Hart Lane in March 2000, Edinburgh joined Portsmouth for £150,000. He holds a UEFA 'B' coaching badge.....which sets him up for when he retires.

EDRICH, WILLIAM JOHN

Best known as a Test Match cricketer rather than a footballer, left-winger Bill Edrich played in 20 first team games for Spurs. He served the club from October 1934 (initially as an amateur) until the outbreak of the war, and remained a registered player until 1947 when he decided to hang up up his brown boots for a pair of white cricketing shoes.

Born in Lingwood on 26 March 1916, Edrich was a County player with Norfolk and an Amateur with Norwich City before moving to White Hart Lane, playing initially for Spurs' nursery side, Northfleet and signing as a professional in August 1935. He then assisted Chelmsford City (from August 1939), Bournemouth, Chelmsford and Lincoln City during the War.

A Squadron Leader during WW2, he won a DFC but always preferred to play cricket and it was as an aggressive top-order batsman with Middlesex where he made his name. Between 1937-58 and playing with Denis Compton most of the time, he appeared in 389 County matches and in 39 Tests.

He scored 86 centuries in a total of 36,965 runs at County level, obtaining a top-score of 267 not out v. Northants in 1947 when all grounds were packed as Middlesex raced away with the County championship. His batting average was 42.39. He also claimed 479 wickets for an average of 33.31 with a best haul of 7-48. He appeared in 39 Test Matches, stroked 2,440 runs for an average of 40 with a top innings of 219 v. South Africa in Durban. He also took 41 Test wickets (4-68 being his best return). He captained Middlesex from 1951-57 and later did likewise when playing for Norfolk.

Edrich died at Chilton, Buckinghamshire on 23 April 1986.

EGGETT, JOHN HENRY

Jack Eggett was a competent goalkeeper who made 119 first-team appearances for Spurs (including 66 in the Southern League and eight in the FA Cup) during his three seasons at White Hart Lane. Born in Wisbech on 19 April 1874, he played his early football with Doncaster Rovers before joining Woolwich Arsenal in the summer of 1903, moving to West Ham United in January 1904 and onto Spurs at the end of that season. He was in command of the number one position when a knee injury allowed Matt Reilly to take over. Eggett never reclaimed his place and was transferred to Croydon Common in April 1907. He died in Doncaster in the summer of 1943.

EINTRACHT FRANKFURT

Spurs playing record against the German club:

Competition	P	W	D	L	F	A
ECW Cup	2	1	0	1	3	2

Spurs entered the semi-final of the 1981-82 European Cup-Winners Cup competition after beating the German side Eintracht Frankfurt in the third round 3-2 on aggregate.

Both matches were tight. The first at White Hart Lane on 3 March attracted a crowd of 38,172 as Spurs won 2-0 with goals by defender Paul Miller and midfielder Micky Hazard. And then for the return clash a fortnight later, around 45,000 fans packed into the Waldstadion in Frankfurt to see Glenn Hoddle's goal take Spurs through despite a 1-2 defeat.

ELKES, ALBERT JOHN

Jack Elkes was born in Snedshill, Shropshire on New Year's Eve 1894; he played as an inside-right for two local amateur sides as well as Stalybridge Celtic and Shifnal Town before joining Birmingham in January 1918. He spent four years at St Andrew's, scoring 18 goals in 35 League and Cup appearances before transferring to Southampton in March 1922. He scored twice on his debut for Saints but broke his collarbone in his second game. Then he started to attract the attention of the bigger clubs and in May 1923 signed for Spurs for £1,000. For a tall man (6ft 2in) Elkes was a clever dribbler and at one time was regarded as one of the best forwards in the country. He assembled a fine record during his time at White Hart Lane, netting 57 goals in 213 first team outings. He played in four international trials for England, represented the Football League XI on three occasions, toured Australia with the FA party in 1925 and lined up for the Professionals against the Amateurs in the FA Charity Shield game in that same year. He left White Hart Lane for Middlesbrough in August 1929; four years later he joined Watford (August 1933) and ended his career with spells at Stafford Rangers and Oakengates Town, retiring in 1937. Best known as a forward, in later years Elkes became a competent centre-half and after hanging up his boots he took up coaching, initially with the Ford Motor Works team at Dagenham. He died in Rayleigh, Essex on 22 January 1972.

ELKIN, BERTIE HENRY WEST

Previously with Fulham and Luton Town, full-back Bert Elkin joined Spurs from Stockport County in December 1909. He played in 34 first team matches for the club before being released in May 1911. Born at Neasden, London on 14 January 1886, Elkin emigrated to South Africa four months after leaving Spurs, where he died on 3 June 1962.

ELLIOTT, JAMES E

Able to play either as a wing-half or centre-forward Jimmy Elliott scored 15 goals in 147 first team games for Spurs whom he joined in October 1911 from Peterborough City.

Born in Essex in 1891, he remained at White Hart Lane until May 1920 when he moved to Brentford He spent four years at Griffin Park and after a spell out of the game he was later appointed manager of the Spanish club Valencia in August 1927. Later he coached in the Balkans, Switzerland and Sweden and also prepared Guatemala City for the 1935 Central American Olympic Games. Prior to the Second World War Elliott, well respected, moved to Turkey where he was employed by the Fenerbahce Spor Kluba who ran ten different teams. He helped coach the first XI to three League championships during a period of four years. It is believed that Elliott died in Turkey in 1939.

ENGLAND, HAROLD MICHAEL, MBE

An inside-forward at school (when he played alongside Ron Davies) and even when he first signed for Blackburn Rovers, Mike England developed into an international-class centre-half who gained 24 caps for his Wales and appeared in 505 League games. Born in Greenfield, North Wales on 2 December 1941, he represented Hollywell and Flint Schools before joining the amateur ranks at Ewood Park in 1957, turning professional in April

1959. After 184 outings (21 goals scored) for Rovers he was transferred to Spurs for £95,000 in August 1966 - having already represented his country in 11 Under-23 and 20 full internationals.

Rated among the best half-dozen central defenders in world football, England was teak-tough, had excellent heading ability and could use the ball well, and he even played up front in an emergency!

He netted 20 times in his 434 first team appearances for Spurs, gaining an FA Cup winners medal in 1967, a UEFA Cup winners medal in 1972 and runners-up prize in 1974 and a League Cup winners' tankard in 1973. He also took his tally of full caps to 44 before choosing to retire in March 1975 after suffering a series of painful ankle injuries. However, he was enticed back into football by Seattle Sounders two months later and even returned to the Football League scene with Cardiff City in August 1975, helping the Bluebirds gain promotion from the Third Division. After four separate summer spells back in the NASL with the Sounders, and an outing for Team American in the 1976 Bi-Centennial Tournament which also featured Brazil and England, he was appointed manager of the Welsh national team in May 1980, holding the position until February 1988.

In 1984 England was awarded the MBE for services to football.

ERENTZ, HENRY BERNT

A Scotsman of Danish extraction, born in Dundee on 17 September 1874, full-back Harry Erentz played for his home town club (Dundee), Oldham Athletic and Newton Heath (Manchester United) before joining Spurs in May 1898. He was a great favourite with the supporters and went on to appear in 303 first team games for the club, scoring two goals. Nicknamed 'Tiger' he was as hard as a rock, tackled positively and was totally reliable, giving very little away. He helped Spurs win the Southern League title in 1899-1900 and was a key member of the FA Cup-winning side the following season. Unfortunately niggling injuries began to upset his rhythm, so at the end of the 1903-04 season he was released by the club, eventually joining Swindon Town in December 1904. Unfortunately after just 16 games for the Wiltshire club he fractured his right leg and was forced to retire at the age of 29. Erentz later returned to his native Dundee where he died on 19 July 1947.

ERITH

Spurs playing record against Erith:

Competition	P	W	D	L	F	A
S. Alliance	2	1	0	1	4	4

These games were played in season 1892-93, Spurs won 3-2 at home but lost 2-1 away.

EUROPEAN COMPETITIONS

Spurs' records in the three major European club competitions are:

European Cup

P	W	D	L	F	A
8	4	1	3	21	13

European Cup-winners Cup

P	W	D	L	F	A
33	20	5	8	65	34

UEFA Cup

P	W	D	L	F	A
29	24	4	1	85	13

Summary

P	W	D	L	F	A
99	59	19	21	219	89

European Cup Fact File

- First game: Gornik Zabrze (a) 13.9.1961 (lost 2-4)
- Biggest win: 8-1 v. Gornik Zabrze (h) 20.9.1961
- Heaviest defeat: Gornik Zabrze (a) (above)
- Biggest aggregate win: 10-5 v. Gornik (above)
- Biggest attendance: 70,000 v. Benfica (a) 21.3.1962
- Lowest attendance: 55,388 v. Dukla Prague (h) 26.2.1962
- Leading scorer: Bobby Smith, 6 goals
- Hat-trick: Cliff Jones v. Gornik Zabrze (h) (above)
- Spurs lost in the semi-final in 1961-62 to Benfica (going down 3-4 on aggregate, 1-3 away, 2-1 at home). They hit the woodwork three times and had a goal disallowed in the second leg at White Hart Lane.
- Spurs won three of their four home European Cup matches, 1961-62, conceding one goal in each game.
- Terry Dyson scored in each of four consecutive European Cup games for Spurs.
- Spurs were 4-0 down to Gornik in their first European Cup game but two late goals gave them a fighting chance in the second leg.
- The only time Spurs have played in this competition.

European Cup-winners Cup Fact File

- First game: Glasgow Rangers (h) 31.10.1962 (won 5-2).
- Biggest win: 6-0 v. Slovan Bratislava (h) 14.3.1963
- Heaviest defeat: 1-4 v. Manchester United (a) 10.12.1963
- Biggest aggregate win: 8-4 v. Glasgow Rangers 1962-63 (3-2 away)
- Biggest attendances: 80,000 v. Glasgow Rangers (a) 11.12.1962 and v. Barcelona (a) 21.4.1982.
- Biggest attendance (home): 61,504 v. Slovan Bratislava on 14.3.1963
- Lowest attendance: 7,000 v. Hajduk Split (a) 17.9.1991
- Lowest attendance (home): 20,925 v. Coleraine on 28.9.1982
- Leading scorer: Jimmy Greaves, 9 goals
- Hat-tricks: none
- Spurs beat Atletico Madrid 5-1 in Rotterdam to win the ECWC on 15 May 1963. Their team that night was: Brown; Baker, Henry; Blanchflower, Norman, Marchi; Jones, White, Smith, Greaves, Dyson. A crowd of 40,000 saw White, Greaves (2) and Dyson (2) score the goals. This victory is the biggest by a British club in any of the major European Finals. Spurs took the lead in the 16th minute through Jimmy Greaves and added a second in the 32nd minute via Terry Dyson. But a penalty, conceded by Ron Henry and scored by Collar, reduced the deficit, and for at least 20 minutes after this set-back Spurs struggled against the Spaniards who came close on a number of occasions to an equaliser. Then, totally against the run of play, Dyson got past full-back Rivilla and whipped over a teasing cross from near the left-hand corner flag. The Atletico 'keeper Madinabeytia somehow lost his bearings, flapped at the ball and then in amazement saw it drop behind him into the net. After this Spurs took control and on 80 minutes Greaves pounced to make it 4-1 before 'Man of

the Match' Dyson ended the scoring with a stunning long-range effort after a fabulous 30-yard dribble. One coincidental point relating to the respective teams in this game was that both clubs had a player named Jones appearing at outside-right!

- Spurs have played in this competition on six occasions, in 1962-63, 1963-64 (as holders) 1967-68, 1981-82, 1982-83 and 1991-92.
- Spurs scored in each of their first 15 home European Cup-winners Cup games before drawing 0-0 with Feyenoord on 18.3.1992.
- Spurs lost to the French club Olympique Lyonnais on the away goal rule in the 2nd round of the Cup-Winners Cup in 1967-68 (won 4-3 at home, lost 0-1 away). Alan Mullery was sent-off in the away leg - the second Spurs player to take an early bath in this competition, following Jimmy Greaves' dismissal in the semi-final clash against OFK Belgrade (away) in April 1963.
- Spurs have never lost a home game in the European Cup-Winners Cup competition: their full home record is: played 16, won 13, drawn 3, goals for 42, against 12.
- The team recorded nine straight wins from the first game in 1962.
- Spurs scored 14 goals in their first three European Cup-winners Cup games at White Hart Lane (5,6 & 3).

UEFA Cup Fact File
- First game: Keflavik (a) 14.9.1971 (won 6-1)
- Biggest win: 9-0 v. Keflavik (h) 28.9.1971
- Heaviest defeat: 0-2 v. Feyenoord (a) Final, 2nd leg, 29.5.1974
- Biggest aggregate win: 15-1 v. Keflavik (see above)
- Biggest attendance: 95,000 v. Real Madrid (a) 20.5.1985
- Biggest attendance (home): 54,303 v. Wolves (Final 2nd leg) 17.5.1972
- Lowest attendances: 7,000 v. Drogheda (a) 14.9.1983; 7,000 v. Zimbru Chisinau (a) 30.9.1999
- Lowest attendance (home): 18,105 v. Grasshoppers, Zurich on 3.10.1973
- Leading scorer: Martin Chivers, 22 goals
- Hat-tricks: Martin Chivers v. Keflavik (h) see above, and Lyn Oslo (h) 27.9.1972 and Garth Crooks v. Sporting Braga (h) 3.10.1984.
- Spurs have won the UEFA Cup twice. In 1971-72, they beat Wolverhampton Wanderers 3-2 on aggregate (winning 2-1 away with a brace from Martin Chivers and 1-1 at home, Alan Mullery on target). In 1983-84 they defeated RSC Anderlecht 4-3 in a penalty shoot-out after the two-legged Final had finished level at 2-2 on aggregate (1-1 away, 1-1 home). Paul Miller scored in the first leg in Belgium and Graham Roberts in the second. The crowds were 38,000 and 46,258 respectively. The players who netted in the shoot-out were Roberts, Mark Falco, Gary Stevens and Steve Archibald, while goalkeeper Tony Parks saved the crucial last spot-kick.
- Spurs lost in the 1973-74 Final to Feyenoord, 4-2 on aggregate (2-2 at home, 2-0 away). A crowd of 46,281 saw

Mike England and Van Deele (og) score for Spurs at White Hart Lane and there were 62,988 fans present in Holland for the second leg.

- In 1974, Spurs created a unique record by becoming the first British club to reach three major Finals of European Cup competitions.
- Spurs have entered this competition on six occasions: in 1971-72 (the first season it was changed from the Fairs Cup), 1972-73 (as holders), 1973-74, 1983-84, 1984-85 (as holders) and 1999-2000..
- Spurs lost to Liverpool on the away goal rule in the semi-final of the UEFA Cup in 1972-73 (lost 1-0 at Anfield, won 2-1 at White Hart Lane). In the quarter-final Spurs had defeated Vitoria Setubal on the away goal rule (won 1-0 at home, lost 2-1 in Portugal).
- In 1983-84, Spurs went through to the Final of the UEFA Cup after beating Hajduk Split on the away goal rule (lost 2-1 in Yugoslavia, won 1-0 at White Hart Lane).
- Spurs' full home record in the UEFA Cup is impressive and reads: played 27, won 22, drawn three and lost one, goals for 79, against 13. They won 10 games in succession over a period of 18 months from 27 September 1972 to 24 April 1974
- Spurs played 26 home games in the UEFA Cup (scoring at least once in every one) before suffering their first defeat - 1-0 in the first leg of a 4th round tie against Real Madrid on 6 March 1985.
- Jimmy Pearce was the first Spurs player to be sent-off in the UEFA Cup, taking an early bath in the 2-0 away win over Rapid Bucharest in December 1971.
- Two of Spurs' greatest-ever players - Glenn Hoddle and Steve Perryman - also received their marching orders in this competition; the former against FC Bruges in Belgium in 1984 and the latter versus Real Madrid in the Bernabeu Stadium in 1985.
- Season 1999-2000 saw Spurs account for Zimbru Chisinau (Moldova) 3-0 (h) and 0-0 (a) in the first round before going out to the German side, FC Kaiserslautern, losing 2-1 on aggregate. In front of 35,177 fans, Spurs claimed a one-goal lead from the first leg (via Steffen Iversen's 34th minute penalty) but succumbed to a 2-0 defeat in the second when the crowd was 29,044.

InterToto Cup Fact File
Spurs took part in this UEFA-arranged competition in July 1995. They were in group 'A' and fielded their third team in their four games as follows v. Lucerne (h)* lost 2-0, attendance 2,497; v. Rudar (a) won 2-1 (Simpson, Hendry) attendance 1,000; v. Osters (h)* lost 2-1 (McMahon) attendance 2,143 and v. Cologne (a) lost 8-0, attendance 2,000
*Both home games played at Brighton.

Spurs Euro Statistics:
- Most appearances in European Competitions: Steve Perryman 64, Pat Jennings 36, Mike England 35, Martin Chivers 32, Martin Peters 32.
- Most goals scored: Martin Chivers 22, Mark Falco 13, Alan Gilzean 13, Martin Peters 13, Bobby Smith 10.

EVANS, RAYMOND LESLIE
Full-back Ray Evans made 203 first team appearances for Spurs, 136 in the Football League.
Born at Edmonton on 20 September 1949, he represented

Middlesex Schools before joining the apprentice ranks at White Hart Lane in July 1965, turning professional in May 1967 - just as Spurs lifted the FA Cup ! He made his senior debut in the local derby against Arsenal in March 1969 and never looked back after that. An England Youth international, Evans was a strong, purposeful footballer who operated like an engine down the right-hand touchline, his overlapping being a feature of many of his performances.

He unfortunately missed out in 1971, 1972 and 1973 when Spurs reached won three successive Cup Finals but did make the second UEFA Cup Final in 1974 only to finish up on the losing side.

After Terry Naylor had taken over the right-back berth, Evans moved on to join Millwall in January 1975. In March 1977 he switched to neighbours Fulham and after loan spells with St Louis Stars and California Surf in the NASL, he signed for Stoke City in a £120,000 deal in August 1979. He later returned to the NASL and helped Seattle Sounders reach the Super Bowl Final. After spending a short time playing in the American Indoor Soccer League he announced his retirement in 1984 and became a coach in the States where he still resides.

EVANS, THOMAS

Half-back Tommy Evans scored five goals in 108 first team games for Spurs. A Welshman, born in Ton Pentre on 25 November 1907, he played for his local team (Ton Pentre) and Leytonstone before joining Spurs as an amateur in May 1927. Evans then had a spell with Northfleet and re-signed for Spurs in 1929, making his senior debut that same year before having a few games with Haywards Sports, finally turning professionalism at White Hart Lane in May 1931. Over the next six seasons he battled hard and long for a

place in the League side and had his best seasons in 1933-34 and 1934-35. Unfortunately Spurs were relegated from the First Division at the end of that second campaign and after that Evans struggled to get back into the team. He transferred to West Bromwich Albion in April 1937, but retired a year later after failing to make the Baggies first XI. He died in Enfield in March 1993.

EVANS, WILLIAM

Willie Evans netted practically a goal every two games for Spurs - 96 in 203 first team outings. Born in Waunllwyd near Ebbw Vale, Monmouthshire on 7 November 1912, he attended the same school as Taffy O'Callaghan and Bill Whatley who also played for Spurs. Before moving to White Hart Lane as a young amateur he had worked as a pit lad. He was given his football grounding at Haywards Sports and Northfleet (Spurs' two nursery clubs) and also played as amateur for Cardiff City on loan in July-August 1930 before turning professional in May 1931. He made his Football League debut six months later, scoring twice in a 6-2 win over Swansea Town...the team he had supported as a youngster! Evans had splendid ball control, perfect timing and a powerful shot in both feet. He

never seemed to have an off day and when he was in full flow heading for goal, there was a buzz of excitement from the crowd. He helped Spurs regain their First Division status in 1932-33 when he netted 28 goals in 42 games, forming an excellent front-line partnership with George Hunt (33 goals). His reputation for accuracy (especially from the penalty spot) was second to none. A collision with the England goalkeeper Harry Hibbs while playing for Wales in September 1934 left him badly injured and led to a loss of confidence. But he bounced back only to suffer another

Spurs European Cup-Winners Cup Winning Squad 1963

bad injury, this time to his right knee against Aston Villa in November 1936. He underwent a cartilage operation from which he never really recovered and was released at the end of that season, joining Fulham. He never played a single game for the Cottagers, injury resulting in an early retirement in May 1938. He was only 26 years of age.

Evans, who represented the Spartan League, Middlesex and the London FA before turning professional with Spurs, went on to gain six full caps for his country (one goal scored). In later years he was a reporter for the Daily Mirror.

EVERTON

Spurs playing record against the Goodison Park club:

Competition	P	W	D	L	F	A
Premiership	18	10	7	1	27	13
Football League	110	36	33	41	170	160
FA Cup	10	4	1	5	14	15
SS Super Cup	2	0	1	1	1	3
Summary	150	50	42	48	211	191

In January 1908 Spurs met Everton, the FA Cup winners of two years previous and the beaten finalists of 1907, in a 1st round tie on Merseyside. A crowd of 21,000 saw Everton win 1-0.

The first League meeting between the two clubs took place at Goodison Park on 4 September 1909 (Division 1) ending Everton 4 Spurs 2 in front of 20,000 fans.

Everton beat Spurs 5-2 at White Hart Lane and 4-2 at Goodison Park in successive League games in April 1924.

In that initial seven-goal encounter in London, Everton's right-winger Sam Chedgzoy decided to expose a loophole in the laws of the game which then allowed for the taker of a corner to play the ball more than once without it touching another player. Chedgzoy, in fact, dribbled the ball along the bye-line after tapping a corner-kick to himself - and SCORED. The law was suitably amended almost straightaway!

Four goals by Taffy O'Callaghan helped Spurs to a convincing 5-3 League win in front of 29,149 fans against the League champions-elect Everton at Goodison Park in February 1928.

In January 1934, a 3rd round FA Cup-tie against the holders Everton resulted in a 3-0 win for Spurs in front of 45,637 fans at White Hart Lane. Three years later, in February 1937, Spurs again eliminated the Merseysiders from the same competition, pipping them 4-3 in a terrific 5th round encounter in London. On this occasion nearly 47,000 fans saw Tommy Lawton (aged 17) score after two minutes for the visitors. Dixie Dean made it 2-0 and the same player later put his side 3-1 ahead before Spurs stormed back to take the tie, John Morrison scoring twice in the last five minutes.

On 25 December 1956, Everton were defeated 6-0 at White Hart Lane - this being the Spurs last Christmas Day fixture at home. A crowd of 27,761 saw the action.

Almost two years later (in October 1958) Spurs were 6-1 up at half-time before going on to beat the Merseysiders 10-4 at home in another League game. Five goals were scored in the last ten minutes, the scoreline going from 7-2 to 10-4. Jimmy Harris was an unfortunate loser with Everton, claiming a worthless hat-trick! Prior to this game, the Everton 'keeper Albert Dunlop had conceded four goals in a friendly against a South African XI.

Later in the season Spurs were defeated 2-1 at Goodison Park - such is football!

In between times (1957-58) Spurs had completed the double over the Merseysiders, winning 2-1 at home and 4-3 away.

Everton defenders gave away a penalty and conceded two own-goals to earn Spurs a 3-0 home League win in November 1959.

The First Division game between the two clubs at White Hart

Spurs deprived of another goal against Everton in 1964

Lane in December 1969 stood at 0-0 when the floodlights failed. There were almost 28,500 fans inside the ground at the time. The 'replay' ended in a 1-0 win for the Merseysiders.

Spurs drew 3-3 at home with Everton and lost 4-0 at Goodison Park in their 1976-77 relegation season. Spurs, in fact, were 3-1 up in that six-goal thriller before conceding two late goals to drop a point!

In February 1983 and again in March 1986 Spurs went out of the FA Cup to Everton, losing in the 5th round on both occasions. Spurs were the Cup holders in 1983.

John Chiedozie scored on his debut for Spurs in a 4-1 win at Everton on the opening day of the 1984-85 League season.

In 1985-86 (after all English clubs had been banned from European competitions) Spurs and Everton met in the semi-final of the Screen Sport Super Cup. After a 0-0 draw at White Hart Lane, the Merseysiders went through to the Final with a 3-1 victory after extra-time at Goodison Park.

Nayim's late strike earned Spurs a 3-3 League draw at home to Everton in April 1991.

Four years later the two teams met in the FA Cup semi-final at Elland Road. Spurs had Jurgen Klinsmann in attack but he had a quiet afternoon as the Merseysiders eased through to Wembley with a comfortable 4-1 victory.

Striker Chris Armstrong scored a second-half hat-trick when Spurs beat Everton 4-1 at White Hart Lane in the Premiership in December 1998.

Players with both clubs include: Jamie Attwell (Everton trialist),

John Barlow, Nick Barmby, John Brearley, Charlie Brown, Bob Cain, John Cameron (also Spurs manager), Paul Gascoigne, Richard Gough, Charlie O'Hagan, Ted Hughes, Pat Jennings, (Everton on loan as cover), Steve Kelly (Everton trialist), John Kirwan, Gary Lineker, Bobby Mimms, Charlie Morgan, Robert Pilch, Vinny Samways, Pat Van den Hauwe, John Watson, Alex Young. Wartime guests (with either one or both clubs): Warney Cresswell, Charlie Crossley, Ed Tunney.

Also associated: Frank Brettell (Everton player, assistant-secretary and secretary, Spurs manager).

EXETER CITY

Spurs playing record against the Devon club:

Competition	P	W	D	L	F	A
FA Cup	1	1	0	0	2	0
League Cup	1	1	0	0	6	3
Summary	2	2	0	0	8	3

Jimmy Greaves hit a hat-trick when Spurs beat the Grecians 6-3 at home in a 3rd Rd League Cup tie in September 1968.

Players with both clubs include: George Crompton, Mark Robson, Peter Taylor (City non-contract), Simon Webster.

Wartime guests (with either one or both clubs): Harry Brown, John Dockray, Stan Eastham, Eric Jones, Phil Joslin.

Also associated: Jim Iley & Cyril Spiers (Spurs players, City managers), Gerry Francis & David Pleat (City players, Spurs managers, Pleat also Spurs caretaker-manager and Director of Football), Ben Ives (Exeter player, Spurs assistant-trainer & chief scout), Harry Evans (Exeter player, Spurs assistant-manager), Theo Foley (City player, Spurs reserve team manager).

F

FAIRCLOUGH, COURTNEY

In April 2000 centre-half Chris Fairclough reached the personal milestone of 400 League appearances and he also passed the 500 mark in major competitions.

Born in Nottingham on 12 April 1964, he joined Nottingham Forest as a trainee in June 1979 and turned professional at The City Ground in October 1981.

After 134 appearances for the Reds, and five England Under-21 caps, Fairclough was transferred to Spurs for £385,000 in July 1987. He made his senior debut against Coventry City (who a few months earlier had beaten Spurs in the FA Cup Final) on the opening day of the season - the first of 70 League and Cup outings for the club (97 in all). He scored six goals and added two more Under-21 caps to his tally, also playing for England 'B' against Malta. A strong, athletic defender, Fairclough was injured in November 1988. Guy Butters took over his position and when he regained full fitness he was played as a full-back before being loaned out to Leeds United in March 1989, joining the Elland Road club on a permanent basis the following month in a £500,000 deal.

In his three years with Leeds he gained both Second and First Division championship medals (in 1990 and 1992 respectively) and also played in a victorious Charity Shield winning side, as well as making 241 appearances before switching across the Pennines to Bolton Wanderers for £500,000 in July 1995. After helping the Wanderers clinch a place in the Premiership (1997) further moves took Fairclough to Notts County (in July 1996) and then to York City (in March 1999).

FALCO, MARK PETER

Six-foot striker Mark Falco had a wonderfully successful career as a goalscorer, netting 166 times in 537 competitive matches at club level alone. His Spurs record was 153 goals in 335 first team outings, 90 coming in 236 League and Cup encounters.

Born near Hackney Marshes on 22 October 1960, he represented both Middlesex and London Schools before joining Spurs as an apprentice in July 1977, turning professional twelve months later. An England Youth international (4 caps), he scored on his Football League debut for Spurs against Bolton in May 1979, but found it difficult to hold down a regular place in the first XI at White Hart Lane. A strong-running player, he manfully battled on and scored twice for Spurs in the 1981 FA Charity Shield draw with Aston Villa at Wembley. After a loan spell with Chelsea (in November 1982) he eventually established himself in the side in 1983-84, collecting a UEFA Cup winners medal at the end of that campaign. However, he did not fit into David Pleat's managerial plans and was subsequently transferred to Watford for £350,000 October 1986. A spell in Scotland with Glasgow Rangers followed (from July 1987) before he rounded off his career by serving with Queen's Park Rangers and Millwall, finally hanging up his boots in June 1992 after suffering a painful injury.

FAMILY CONNECTIONS
Brothers In Arms

The three Steel brothers of Newmilns in Ayrshire, Alex (born July 1886), Bob (born June 1888) and Danny (born May 1884), were playing colleagues together at Spurs between 1908-12. All three had played junior football for Newmilns FC and it was Danny who arrived at Spurs first, in May 1906 from Glasgow Rangers. He was followed in May 1908 by Bob, who came via Kilwinning and Port Glasgow and finally Alex who was signed in August 1908 after spells with Ayr United and Manchester City.

On 29 January 1910, all three appeared in the same League side against Bradford City.

Alex left for Kilmarnock in the summer of 1911; Danny followed in July 1912, moving to Third Lanark while Bob stayed much longer. He was finally released by Spurs in 1919 when he teamed up with Gillingham. Between them Bob and Danny appeared in 361 League games for Spurs and starred in 479 first-team matches in all.

A further seven sets of brothers have been together on Spurs' professional staff since the club adopted professionalism at the end of 1895, but only two other pairs can claim to have played together at the highest possible level - the McTavish clan from Govan, Glasgow and the Polstons from London.

John and Rob McTavish had played together for three years in Falkirk's forward-line before going their separate ways in June 1910. John went to Oldham Athletic whilst Rob came to Tottenham. It did not take long for them to be reunited, John, capped against Ireland in March 1910, coming south in December after just ten games for Oldham. Their only League game as Spurs team-mates was in the final fixture of the 1910-11 campaign, a 3-0 defeat at Blackburn Rovers on April 22.

Both departed White Hart Lane during the early months of 1912. John, with three goals in 39 senior outings for us, led a nomadic career with stints at Newcastle United, Partick Thistle, York City, Goole Town and Falkirk (again) before the Great War and East Fife, Dumbarton and East Stirling in the immediate aftermath. Rob, who notched two goals in a dozen senior games, joined Southern League Brentford and later served Third Lanark. His son John played around 100 senior games as a centre half for Manchester City during the fifties.

John and Andy Polston progressed through the intermediate set-up at White Hart Lane and played together for Spurs against Crystal Palace in the top flight on March 3, 1990. John lasted the whole game whilst Andy came on as a substitute for John Moncur after 70 minutes. The two formed Spurs' centre half pairing for the remaining 20 minutes. For Andy that proved to be his only senior game in Spurs' colours whilst John had 28 outings and scored one goal. After four years together at Spurs John departed for Norwich City in the summer of 1990.

Andy, who had made his League debut whilst on loan to Cambridge United in October 1989, had a similar spell at Gillingham during 1990-91 before being released by Spurs. He later served with Brighton & Hove Albion, Fulham, Hendon and St. Albans City.

The Burtons from Derby formed Spurs earliest brotherly partnership as a professional outfit. Both joined the club during 1901; John in April and Oliver in October. John had spent two years with Derby County prior to joining Chatham in 1899, but for Oliver it was his first taste of senior football.

Both were half-backs, virtually competing for each others' place in the Spurs first team.

For four years they were together at Tottenham yet they never played alongside one another in the senior competition, the Southern League. It was only in the Western and London Leagues that they were team-mates and even then only on four occasions. John made 30 senior appearances for Spurs, scoring twice, before leaving in 1905. He subsequently served Preston North End. Oliver stayed on until 1910, totting almost 100 senior games in Spurs' colours and featuring in the first two seasons of Football League action.

Ralph and Albert Wetton both arrived at Tottenham via Cheshunt. Born at Rowland Gill, County Durham, they were both on Spurs' books for the 1950-51 campaign. Ralph, the elder by 16 months, went on to make 46 first team appearances for the club while Bert progressed no further than the reserve side. They featured together in the 'A' team and later found League experience elsewhere; Bert, who arrived at Tottenham in 1949 - twelve months before Ralph - at Brighton & Hove Albion and Crewe Alexandra and Ralph at Plymouth Argyle and Aldershot.

Similarly, only one of the Stead brothers, Mickey and Kevin, made it into Spurs' first team during their time with the club. Both featured in the 1974-75 Youth team and were together as professionals from April, 1976 until July, 1977, but whereas Mickey played 15 senior games in defence, striker Kevin got no further than the second XI. His only League experience was two outings for Arsenal. Mickey later played for Southend United and Doncaster Rovers and later entered non-League with Dagenham & Redbridge, Chelmsford City, Heybridge Swifts, Halstead Town and Fisher '93.

Glenn Hoddle was joined at White Hart Lane by his brother, Carl, for a two-year period 1983 to 1985. Again, the younger brother found difficulty following in the footsteps of a famous elder and it was after spells with Norwich City and Bishops Stortford that Carl eventually played in the Football League for Leyton Orient and Barnet. He also had spells at Woking, Enfield, Baldock Town and Aylesbury United in the ICIS League Premier Division.

David Howells' brother Gareth spent four years at White Hart Lane between 1986 and 1990. Much of his two years on Spurs' professional staff were spent on loan elsewhere, including spells at Farnborough Town, FF Malmo, Enfield, Swindon Town and Leyton Orient. He eventually made his League bow at Torquay United and later turned out for Dorking, Farnborough (again), Stockport County, Kettering, the South African club Hellenic and St. Albans City.

David went on to receive a testimonial at White Hart Lane before moving to Southampton and then Bristol City. He made 337 appearances for Spurs up to 1998.

A handful of brothers played for Spurs' first team during both World Wars. The Great War saw the Croft brothers, known only by their initials T and W, both feature in the team during the 1916-17 season. They made two and three appearances respectively but did not play together.

The Second World War saw several brothers feature. The Bennetts from Wood Green were both products of Ben Ives' Tottenham Juniors side. Les, who first signed as an amateur in August 1935, was joined by Ken in May 1939 on the same day that Les himself signed professional for the club. Ken played in the team during the 1940-41 campaign but never alongside Les. He went on to serve Southend United, Bournemouth, Brighton & Hove Albion and Crystal Palace. Les, meanwhile, spent most of his career at Tottenham, rounding off with a spell at West Ham United.

Bobby and Billy Sainsbury were colts from Wales who also progressed through the Tottenham junior ranks. They played for Enfield and turned out for Spurs in the early War years but not together.

The Sperrin brothers, Bill and Jimmy, also hailed from Wood Green. They twice played together during the 1940-41 campaign. Bill subsequently served with Finchley and Brentford and his son Martyn played for Luton Town during the seventies.

Jimmy played for St. Albans City during the late forties and early fifties.

From the club's inception in 1882 there has seemingly always been a brotherly link. Amongst the founder members were three sets - Lindsay and Hamilton Casey, John and Tom Anderson and Jack and P. Thompson. Soon they were joined by Jack and Tom Jull, And by

Danny Blanchflower with brother Jackie of Manchester United training for Ireland

the time amateur status was relinquished in December 1895, another three sets had been associated with the club.

There were the Randalls, the Markhams and the Monks. GJ Randle (possibly George Joseph) and his brother JT (possibly Joseph Thomas) were Londoners who failed to hit the heights. Ernie 'Bunks' Markham and his two brothers, Dick and Wall, all played together for Robin Hood FC, Shaftsbury Rovers and Ilford, as well as for Spurs in at least one game v. Windsor & Eton in a Southern Alliance fixture in 1893. Dick was also an Essex County cricketer. Cuthbert Monk was joined at Spurs by his brother Steve in the late 1890s. The latter played only two reserve team games while Cuthbert made almost 70 appearances in the first team.

Spurs' Joe Moffatt played with his brother Bobby for Manchester City at reserve team level. Bobby later became a coach with Kilmarnock.

Others to feature in the lower ranks at White Hart Lane include the Bulling brothers from Nottingham. Edward was taken on after a three match trial in our South Eastern League team during 1908-09, whilst his brother, initial C (possibly for Charles), returned to the Notts Olympic club. Phil and Jimmy Holder played in the 1968-69 Youth team together and a year later the Dillon brothers, Mike and Tom, did likewise. The Greene twins Dennis and David, later at Harlow Town, had a trial spell at Tottenham in January, 1989. Their only game together in Spurs' colours was a reserve team friendly at Hertford Town.

Cyril Knowles was joined briefly by his brother Peter - a former Wolves player - in October 1975 for his testimonial match against Arsenal.

Eleven years previously, Tom White, brother of John, scored for Spurs in the memorial match against a Scotland XI staged at White Hart Lane. Tom, then of Aberdeen, later turned out for Crystal Palace, Blackpool, Bury and Crewe Alexandra in the Football League.

Several brothers have followed in the footsteps of their elders to wear our colours. Jim Moles captained Spurs' reserve side in 1905-06, a few years after utility man Walter had served us.

Bill Fleming, brother of Spurs' centre-forward John Fleming, joined the playing staff at White Hart Lane in 1914 but did not re-appear after the Great War.

In 1915-16, Alec Chaplin, later a coach at Northfleet, guested for Spurs, while his brother Jock had played for Spurs in the club's final Southern League campaign, 1907-08.

The brothers of Spurs wingers Fanny Walden and Jimmy Dimmock played for Spurs second XI in the immediate post-war period, as did those of Billy Lane in 1926 and Darkie Lowdell in 1930. In between times, the Hayward brothers of Blaina, Monmouthshire saw Frank follow Bill through the ranks at White Hart Lane. Bill later played for Leyton Orient. Fred Channell, a 1930s full back, had a brother on Spurs' professional staff briefly during the early twenties.

Annis Willis, brother of 1940s full-back Arthur, had a brief spell on Spurs' books; and the Barney brothers formed a left-wing partnership for the Youth team in 1956 while David Culverhouse followed brother Ian through the Spurs Youth set up. David later joined Dagenham & Redbridge while Ian did very well at Norwich, Swindon Town and Brighton.

Darren Anderton's brother Ben, also a former Portsmouth trainee, was injured in his only outing for Spurs' South East Counties Division Two side in February, 1994.

Luke Young followed his brother Neil into League football; Luke of course with Spurs while Neil made his mark with AFC Bournemouth afer leaving White Hart Lane in October 1994.

Like Father and Son (and Other Family Connections)

Here we take a look at the father and son combinations who have featured for Spurs over the years, plus an assortment of other inter-related personalities involved both on and off the pitch.

Of the father and son theme, the Allen family from Essex can claim the strongest connection with Les playing an important role in Spurs' double-winning success while his son Clive created the club record number of goals in a season some 26 years later.

The Allen dynasty were first associated with the club in 1953 when Les, just out of school, was an amateur on Spurs books. It was Chelsea, however, who signed him on professional forms and Spurs had to wait until 1959 to secure his services in a swap deal involving Johnny Brooks. Les went on to net on average a goal almost every two games for Spurs, including many important strikes during the 1960-61 campaign.

Clive, like his father, spent much of his career in the capital. His four years at White Hart Lane yielded plenty of goals (over 80) and saw him create a club record with 49 strikes in all competitions in the 1986-87 season.

In 1985 Clive was joined at Tottenham by his cousin, Paul, and in the next three years they played alongside each other on 98 occasions. Paul went on to surpass the combined tally of Les and Clive with his tally of senior apprearances in his eight year at Spurs.

Les later played for Queens Park Rangers whom he also managed as well as Swindon Town.

Clive had two spells at Loftus Road, plus stints at Arsenal, Crystal Palace, Bordeaux, Manchester City, Chelsea and West Ham, and he also played for the London Monarchs at American football! Paul, signed from West Ham, later assisted Southampton, Swindon Town, Stoke City, Luton Town and Bristol City.

Only one other family can claim a father and son in Spurs' first team goalkeeper Ray Clemence and his midfield son, Stephen. Ray also played for Scunthorpe United and Liverpool and made over 300 senior appearances for Spurs before joining the coaching staff in 1988.

The Gibbins family came close to producing the first father and son combination. Eddie was on Spurs' books, initially as an amateur, for ten years from 1944. His made five first team appearances, three of them Cup games.

Eddie later worked in the White Hart Lane offices. His son Roger was on Spurs' books for four years from 1971, spending two in the apprentice ranks, but failed to make the first XI. He later turned out for Oxford United, Norwich City, Cambridge United, Cardiff City, Swansea City, Newport County and Torquay United, amongst others.

Ian Gilzean spent six years at White Hart Lane from 1986 but, again, could not find a way through to the senior side. Ironically, when he left he joined his father's old club Dundee and later turned out for Doncaster Rovers, Ayr United, Northampton Town and Sligo Rovers. Alan Gilzean spent ten years at Tottenham from 1964, notching over 130 goals in more than 400 senior games.

Several other sons had brief spells at Tottenham; JW Julian, son of 1890's amateur Bill, turned out for the 'A' team in 1909 and in the early 1920s, the sons of Jock Montgomery and Tom Smith were given trials in in Spurs' second XI. Montgomery senior had been one of the first professional players at Tottenham, whilst Smith featured in the 1901 FA Cup-winning side. During the latter part of the 'twenties, Jabez Darnell, then assistant trainer at the club and formerly a long-serving player, was in charge of the 'A' team which, on a couple of occasions, included his son!

When goalkeeper John Hollowbread came to Spurs in 1952, he followed in the footsteps of his father, who had kept goal for the club's nursery team Northfleet United twenty years previously. John went on to make over 70 senior appearances for the club and later played for Southampton.

Bobby Scarth, the son of former Spurs star Jimmy, made light of his disabilities in his two years as an apprentice at White Hart Lane in the early seventies, alongside another son, Roger Gibbins. Scarth junior was born deaf and dumb.

Danny Greaves played in Spurs' junior team during the 1978-79 season and later had spells at Southend United and Cambridge United. Following in the footsteps of father, Jimmy, was a tall order for any youngster. After 13 years on the Southend coaching staff, mainly in charge of the Shrimpers' touth team, Danny left to take over as manager of Halstead Town.

When Steve Sedgley, then a Schoolboy, turned out for Spurs' junior side in the early 1980s, he followed his father, Gordon, who had played for the club at as an amateur in the Youth set-up in the late 'fifties. Sedgley senior went on to play for Enfield and Steve for Coventry City prior to rejoining Spurs in 1989. He moved to Ipswich Town in 1994.

Leon Hughton, son of Chris, was on Spurs' books as an associated schoolboy.

Lewis Sykes was the son of EJ, a club vice-president during Spurs' amateur days. Both went into the medical profession.

Alf Hawley, who scored twice in three outings for Spurs' Southern League team in 1901, was the son of Jim Hawley, a club director from 1898 to 1907.

Eddie and Derek King, who both played in Spurs' first XI, were cousins. Full back Eddie was associated with the club from his junior days in 1929 until forced to retire through injury seven years later. He was injured on his only senior appearance for the club. Derek also progressed through the junior ranks to play 19 senior games at centre half after the War and later had a spell at Swansea Town.

Toni Marchi followed in the footsteps of his uncle, George Dorling. Again, both went through the junior network at White Hart Lane, Dorling in the pre-War era with a spell at Northfleet and Marchi with the juniors in the late 1940's. Dorling's eleven senior outings for Spurs came in the 1939-40 Wartime season, although he later turned out for Gillingham in the Football League. Marchi spent 15 years at White Hart Lane, divided by a two-year spell in Italy.

The Smart cousins each had two-year spells as a trainee at Tottenham. Steve was with the club from 1986 and has since turned out for Wealdstone, Sutton United, Aylesbury United and Hendon whilst Lee left Spurs in 1992 and has played for Welling, Kingstonian and Hendon since

During the Great War, Mr A. Bearman, described by the Weekly Herald as "a young relative of the club director Fred Bearman" played in Spurs' first team. The same lad re-emerged, as a student at Charterhouse, to play for the clubs reserve team in 1922.

Keep It In The Family

Roger Morgan and his twin brother, Ian, played for Queen's Park Rangers in the 1967 League Cup Final. Roger moved to Spurs in February 1969.

The Blanchflower brothers - Jackie of Manchester United and Danny of Barnsley, Aston Villa and Spurs - played together for Northern Ireland at full international level.

Frank Osborne's brother, Reg, was an England amateur international who also won two full caps for his country. Another Osborne brother, Harold, played for Chelmsford City and Norwich City.

Richard Gough's father, Charles Storrar Gough, was a junior footballer with West Ham United before signing as a professional for Charlton Athletic in 1963. He later assisted Highlands Park FC after emigrating to South Africa early in 1965.

Gary Mabbutt's father Ray, was a very useful player with Bristol Rovers and Newport County, while another brother, Kevin, served with Bristol City and Crystal Palace.

Danny Thomas' brother, Valmore, was a player with Danny at Coventry City and he also assisted Hereford United.

Andy Keeley's brother, Glenn, was a defender with Ipswich Town, Newcastle United, Blackburn Rovers and Oldham Athletic.

Tony Galvin's kid brother Chris played professionally for Hull City, Leeds United and Stockport County in the 1970s.

Angus Seed, Jimmy Seed's brother, played for Aldershot, Barnsley and Workington.

Jimmy Bauchop's brother, Willie, played for Alloa Athletic, Plymouth Argyle, Hearts, Carlisle United, Stockport County, Leicester City and Norwich City.

Tommy Bing's brother played for Margate and West Ham United.

Charlie Rundle's brother, Sid, was with Plymouth Argyle in the 1940s.

John Ryden's two brothers - George and Hugh - were both professional footballers, the former with Dundee and the latter with Chester, Stockport County and Leeds United.

Walter Moles' brother John was also on Spurs' books at one time, but he failed to make the grade at White Hart Lane and later served with Birmingham and Leyton.

Jock Montgomery, probably the first professional footballer to register with Spurs had a brother, Archie, who was a 'pro' with Bury. Spurs' centre-forward Willie Newbigging's brother, Alex, kept goal for Aberdeen, Coventry City, Nottingham Forest, QPR, Rangers and Reading.

Rio Ferdinand (Leeds United) is the cousin of Spurs' striker Les Ferdinand.

Cliff Jones' father, Ivor, played for Swansea Town, West Bromwich Albion and Wales in the 1920s; his uncle Bryn served with Norwich City, Wolves, Arsenal and Wales (either side of World War Two) and his brother Bryn (junior) was a player with Swansea, Newport County, Bournemouth, Northampton Town and Watford.

Alfie Conn's father, also named Alfie, played for Hearts and Scotland.

The father of Spurs' 1920s inside-forward Jimmy Townley was Bill Townley, the England international centre-forward who scored a hat-trick for Blackburn Rovers in the 1890 FA Cup Final.

Bert Lyons, the 1930s Spurs full-back was the son of Tommy Lyons who played in the same position for Aston Villa and England (1907-22).

Between 1971 and 1985, Chris Waddle's cousin, Alan Waddle, played as a forward for Halifax Town, Leicester City, Newport County, Swansea City, Liverpool, Mansfield Town, Hartlepool and Peterborough United as well as in Hong Kong.

Goalkeeper Ian Walker is the son of the former Cochester United and Watford 'keeper Mick Walker who was also coach and manager of Norwich City.

Jack Over was head groundsman at White Hart Lane for 25 years and was followed into the job by his eldest son Will.

John Moncur's father was Youth Development Officer at White Hart Lane when his son joined Spurs as a junior in 1983.

The son of 1920s Spurs goalkeeper Geordie Maddison, who was

also named George, was, like his father, a goalkeeper with Aldershot and York City between 1948 and 1953.

Stuart Beavon's father, Cyril, played League football for Wolves and Oxford United.

Johnny Brooks' son, Shaun, was a midfield player with Crystal Palace, Orient and Bournemouth.

Spurs' Scottish-born full-back Gordon Smith's father, Neil, played for Kilsyth Rangers, whilst his grandfather, Willie Salisbury, served with Partick Thistle and Liverpool.

Tom Smith's son, Ed Smith, refereed the 1946 FA Cup Final at Wembley. Tom played for Spurs between 1898 and 1902.

Harry Gilberg's father, played for Tunbridge Wells Rangers and had trials with Charlton Athletic.

George Hunt's grandfather, Sam, was a professional footballer with Barnsley (St Peter's).

Johnny Jordan's cousin, Clarrie, was a goalscorer with Doncaster Rovers and Sheffield Wednesday in the late 1940s/early '50s.

Neil Woods, the son of Spurs' 1950s wing-half Alan Woods, was a professional with Doncaster Rovers, Ipswich Town, Grimsby Town, Bradford City, Scunthorpe United, Mansfield Town and Glasgow Rangers between 1983 and 1998.

Sandy Tait, Spurs' Scottish-born full-back (1899-1908), had no fewer than twelve brothers and sisters!

FANZINE/SUPPORTERS' MAGAZINE

The Spurs monthly magazine has been available to suppoprters since July 2000. The contact is: editorial@footballworld.co.uk

FELTON, WILLIAM

Full-back Bill Felton was capped by England against France seven years before he joined Spurs from Manchester City in March 1932. He had also helped Sheffield Wednesday win the First Division championship in 1926.

Born in Heworth near Gateshead on 1 August 1900, he played for Pelaw Town (two spells), Pandon Temperance FC, Wardley Colliery and Jarrow before signing professional forms for Grimsby Town in January 1921, switching to Hillsborough in January 1923 and onto Maine Road in March 1929. He skippered Spurs' Second Division promotion-winning side in 1932-33 and went on to appear in 75 League and FA Cup games for the club prior to his release in the summer of 1934 when he joined Altrincham. Felton made 347 League appearances in total, scoring one goal - a penalty for Spurs in the 1-1 derby draw with Arsenal in September 1933 before 56,610 spectators at White Hart Lane. He died in Manchester on 22 April 1977.

FENWICK, TERENCE WILLIAM

Born in the North-East, the hot-bed of English football, in the village of Camden, County Durham on 17 November 1959, Terry Fenwick represented Durham Schools before moving south to sign apprentice forms for Crystal Palace in June 1975, turning professional at Selhurst Park in December 1976.

A defender able to occupy a variety of positions in front of his goalkeeper, including that of sweeper, Fenwick gained England Youth international honours before adding three Under-21 caps to his wardrobe during his four years with the Eagles. He helped them win the Second Division title in 1979 as well as claiming two FA Youth Cup winning medals (1977 and 1978).

He was transferred to neighbouring Queen's Park Rangers in December 1987 for £110,000 (re-joining Terry Venables) and added a further eight Under-21 caps top his collection whist at Loftus Road. He helped Rangers reach the 1982 FA Cup Final when they lost in a replay to Spurs, and, in fact, it was Fenwick

who scored a dramatic equaliser in the first encounter. Four years later he was another unfortunate Wembley loser when QPR lost to Oxford United in the League Cup Final.

Honoured for the first time by England at senior level in 1984, Fenwick went on to gain a total of 19 full caps for his country and soon after joining Spurs for £550,000 in December 1987 he collected his 20th cap as a substitute against Israel in Tel Aviv.

After breaking his leg in a League Cup-tie against Manchester United in October 1989, Fenwick went on loan to Leicester City as he battled to regain full fitness. However, following his return to White Hart Lane he agonisingly fractured an ankle in the pre-match warm-up prior to an FA Cup-tie at Portsmouth in February 1991. He failed to recapture his form with Spurs and eventually left the club on a free transfer to Swindon Town in September 1993, having appeared in 118 competitive games (10 goals scored). In February 1995 Fenwick put his first foot on the managerial ladder when he took over the reins at Fratton Park, holding the position for three years before losing in job to Alan Ball.

FERDINAND, LESLIE

Having produced some exciting goalscoring performances for non-League Hayes, striker Les Ferdinand entered the big-time with Queen's Park Rangers when signed for £15,000 in March 1987. Over the next five years he netted 90 goals in 184 first team appearances for Rangers, also having loan spells with Besiktas (whom he helped lift the Turkish Cup in 1989) and Brentford before transferring to Newcastle United for £6 million in June 1995, signed by Geordies' manager Kevin Keegan. He continued to bulge the net at St James' Park, rattling in excatly 50 goals in only 84 games up to August 1997 when he moved to White Hart Lane, again for £6 million which constituted a Spurs record fee at the time (subsequently topped by £5 million when Rebrov arrived in 2000).

Capped 17 times by England at senior level and once by the 'B' team, Ferdinand ended the 2000-01 season with a Spurs record of 103 appearances and 22 goals, injuries having ruined the 1999-2000 season when he managed only nine Premiership outings. Voted PFA Footballer of the Year in 1996 (with Newcastle), he was a League Cup winner with Spurs in 1999. Ferdinand was born in Paddington on 8 December 1966 and played intermediate football for Viking Sports and Southall before joining Hayes in 1986.

Ferdinand's cousin, Rio, is the current Leeds United and England centre-back.

FESTIVAL OF BRITAIN
Summary of matches

P	W	D	L	F	A
2	1	0	1	2	2

In May 1951 Spurs played two Festival of Britain matches at White Hart Lane - the first against FC Austria in front of 30,000 spectators, ended in a 1-0 defeat whilst the second, versus the German side Borussia Dortmund, resulted in a 2-1 victory watched by 29,000 fans. Eddie Baily and Peter Murphy scored Spurs' goals against the German side.

FEYENOORD
Spurs playing record against the Dutch club:

Competition	P	W	D	L	F	A
European Cup	2	1	1	0	4	2
ECW Cup	2	0	1	1	0	1
UEFA Cup	4	2	1	1	8	6
Summary	8	3	3	2	12	9

The first of Spurs' four two-legged encounters against the Dutch club took place in Holland in November 1961. It was a first round, first leg encounter in the European Cup when in front of 61,719 fans they triumphed by three goals to one with Frank Saul (2) and Terry Dyson the scorers.

The return fixture later in the month ended 1-1 at White Hart Lane, Dyson again on target in front of a crowd of 62,144, as Spurs went through 4-2 on aggregate.

It was 12 years before the third and fourth matches took place, this time in the Final of the 1973-74 UEFA Cup. Feyenoord came out on top, winning 4-2 on aggregate. After a 2-2 draw at White Hart Lane on 21 May when 46,281 fans saw Mike England and Van Deele (og) score for Spurs, Feyenoord won the return leg in Rotterdam eight days later 2-0 in front of almost 63,000 spectators.

Ten years on - again in the second round of the UEFA Cup in October/November 1983 - Spurs and Feyenoord clashed again. A brace of goals apiece from Tony Galvin and Steve Archibald gave Spurs a 4-2 home win before they duly completed the two-legged triumph with a 2-0 victory in Rotterdam, Chris Hughton and Galvin the marksmen this time. The respective attendances were 35,404 and 45,061.

Matches seven and eight were contested in the quarter-final of the European Cup-Winners Cup competition of 1991-92 and on this occasion Feyenoord took the honours with a 1-0 aggregate victory, achieved from their home leg in March in front of 38,385 spectators. Spurs battled hard and long when the teams met a fortnight later at White Hart Lane but the scoreline finished blank, much to the disappointment of the Spurs fans in the near 30,000 crowd.

* Spurs won the 1963 European Cup-Winners Cup Final at the Feyenoord Stadium in Rotterdam (Holland).
Player with both clubs: Johnny Metgod.

FINALS & SEMI-FINALS
Spurs have appeared in 16 major Cup Finals and in 28 semi-finals.

The details are as follows:
Finals
FA Cup: 1901, 1921, 1961, 1962, 1967, 1981, 1982, 1987, 1991 (eight wins).
League Cup: 1971, 1973, 1982, 1999 (three wins)
European Cup-winners Cup: 1963 (won)
UEFA Cup: 1972, 1974, 1984 (two won)

Semi-finals
FA Cup: 13
League Cup: nine
European Cup: one - 1962
European Cup-winners Cup; one
UEFA Cup: four (two won, two lost)

FINES
Spurs (the club) received a hefty fine for fielding a relatively weakened side (made up mainly of reserve and squad members) for a League game against Southampton on 7 May 1984 - prior to their UEFA Cup Final clash with RSC Anderlecht. Robert Brace made his only appearance for Spurs in this game as a substitute as the Saints won 5-0!

Aston Villa's Australian-born goalkeeper Mark Bosnich was fined £1,000 and severely reprimanded by the FA after his 'Hitler style' salute to the Spurs fans during the Premiership game at White Hart Lane in 1996.

FIORUCCI CUP
On 27 April 1993, Spurs, Real Madrid and Inter Milan participated in the Fiorucci Cup at White Hart Lane. Each team played the other once with all the games lasting for just 45 minutes. Spurs were defeated 1-0 by Real and then drew 0-0 with Inter, eventually losing to the Italian club 6-5 in a penalty shoot-out.

FIRSTS
Here are some of the many footballing firsts involving Spurs (listed in date order):

- Bobby Buckle was appointed Spurs' first captain and club secretary in 1882.
- Mr John Ripsher was named as the club's first Chairman in 1883.
- The first known reported game played by Spurs was a friendly against Radicals on 30 Sept 1882 (lost by two goals).
- Jack Oliver was appointed the club's first chairman in March 1898.
- The first known competitive match took place on 17 October 1885 when Spurs played and beat St Albans 5-2 in the first round of the London Association Cup. They fielded this team: Bumberry; Jull, Tyrell; Bull, Lovis, Casey; Buckle, Hartson, Mason, Amos, Cottrell.
- In the 1880s Jack Jull became the first Spurs player to receive representative honours.
- Peter Hunter scored Spurs' first FA Cup goal in their first-ever game and victory in the competition v. West Herts in 1894.
- Frank Brettell was appointed the first secretary-manager of Spurs in 1898.
- Bob Clements had the pleasure of scoring Spurs' first Southern League goal in 1896 v Sheppey United.
- Jock Montgomery was the first professional registered by Spurs, also in 1896.
- In January 1897 Ly Burrows netted Spurs' first penalty....in a Southern League game v Wellingborough.
- Jack Jones became Spurs' first senior international player when he was capped by Wales in 1898.
- The first senior game at White Hart Lane was a friendly between Spurs and Notts County in Sept. 1899.
- Spurs were the first non-League side to win the FA Cup, doing so in 1901.

- Vivian Woodward was the first Spurs player to win a full England cap scoring twice on his debut against Ireland in 1903.
- In 1905 Spurs went on their first major overseas tour to the Austro-Hungarian Empire.
- Vivian Woodward scored the first League goal at White Hart Lane - in the first League game staged there for Spurs against Wolverhampton Wanderers in September 1908 (won 3-0). In this same year Spurs also suffered their first League defeat and played out their first League draw, while in January 1909 Spurs registered their first Football League 'double' over Bolton Wanderers.
- Bob Steel netted Spurs' first League hat-trick in 1911.
- Spurs were relegated for the first time at the end of the 1914-15 season.
- Johnny Blair was the first Spurs player to get sent-off in a Football League game, taking an early bath in 1928.
- Floodlights were first switched on at White Hart Lane in 1953.
- Dave Mackay was the first Scottish-born player to win a full cap for his country as a Spurs player, doing so in 1957.
- In 1960-61 Spurs became the first team in the 20th century to complete the League and FA Cup double.
- In 1961 Spurs played their first competitive game in a major European competition against the Polish side Gornik Zabrze.
- In 1962 Spurs' wing-half Danny Blanchflower became the first player to skipper successive FA Cup winning teams and in 1963 he made it three Final victories as captain when he led Spurs to victory in the European Cup-winners Cup Final. This latter success gave Spurs the honour of being the first British team to lift a major European trophy.
- The first substitute called into action by Spurs in a League game was Roy Low v. Arsenal in 1965.
- West Ham were Spurs' first League Cup opponents in 1966. Striker Alan Gilzean was sent-off as Spurs suffered their first defeat in the competition.
- In 1968 Spurs' first six-figure transfer took place when Martin Chivers was signed from Southampton for £125,000.
- Also in 1968 Joe Kinnear became the first Spurs player to be sent-off in the FA Cup and Alan Mullery was the first England player to be dismissed in a full international v. Yugoslavia.
- First all-London FA Cup Final was between Chelsea and Spurs in 1967.
- In 1972 Spurs became the first English (British) team to win both the First and Second Division League championships, the FA Cup, the League Cup, the European Cup-Winners Cup and the UEFA Cup.
- In 1977 Willie Young became the first Spurs player to be sent-off in a North London derby v. Arsenal.
- In 1981 the first FA Cup Final replay to be staged at Wembley took place when Spurs met Manchester City.
- In 1981-82 Steve Perryman became the first Spurs' player to reach the milestone of 500 League appearances. In 1986 he played his 1,000th first team game for the club.
- The first Football League game played by Spurs on a Sunday (v Nottingham Forest) took place in 1983.
- Paul Stewart became Spurs' first seven-figure capture when he joined the club from Manchester City for £1.5 million in 1988.
- Also in 1988 Spurs made their first 'official' loan signing - goalkeeper Bobby Mimms from Everton.
- Spurs played their first Premiership match in 1992 at Southampton (0-0). The same year Gordon Durie scored the club's first Premiership goal; the first win was recorded (v Crystal Palace) and the first defeat suffered (v Coventry City).

FLEMING, JOHN

A month after joining Spurs from Newcastle United, centre-forward John Fleming scored a hat-trick on his first-team debut in a friendly match against Red Star Amical in Paris in May 1913. He went on to net five more goals in a total of 29 appearances for the club before transferring to Armadale Thistle in the summer of 1915. Almost a year later (21 March 1916) Fleming was killed. He was only 26.

Born circa 1890, he played for St Bernard's before switching to St James' Park in April 1911.

FLOODLIGHTS

Floodlights were first seen at White Hart Lane in 1953, They were mounted on four enormous poles (not pylons) situated at each corner of the ground. They were just a few feet higher than the East Stand and could be seen for miles around. There were additional sets of lights fitted on two gantries - to give the spectators excellent coverage of evening matches.

The first time the lights were used (for a senior game) was when Spurs entertained the French side, Racing Club de Paris in a friendly match on 29 September 1953.

The band of the Grenadier Guards provided the pre-match entertainment for a crowd of 28,070.

The first goal under the lights was scored by a Frenchman, Jean Courteaux, who put Racing Club ahead on 33 minutes.

The second-half was televised live and it was only two minutes old when Spurs drew level through Len Duquemin who converted George Robb's low cross with aplomb.

Les Bennett drove Spurs in front in the 55th minute then George Hutchinson made it 3-1 seven minutes later with a low angled drive. Ron Burgess shot through a crowd of players to net Spurs' fourth goal on 67 minutes and with 20 minutes remaining Bennett claimed his second goal and Spurs' fifth.

Substitute Claude Bruey and Courteaux (again) made the scoreline look more respectable with two late strikes from the French side as Spurs ran out winners by 5-3.

The Spurs side that night was: Ditchburn; Ramsey, Withers; Wetton, Farley, Burgess; Hutchinson, Bennett, Duquemin, Harmer, Robb.

Racing Club fielded: Pivois; Lelong, Arnadeau (Jacowski); Dubreucq, Jurilli, Boulet; Courteaux, Amalfi (Bruey), Cisowski, Schap, Curyl.

The match was refereed by the former League official Arthur Blythe from Edmonton.

Rays of Light

- Prior to that initial first team game under the White Hart Lights, the previous week a private match was staged under the lights between two teams of Spurs amateur players. Onlookers included shareholders and local electrical technicians, who were on hand to make sure everything ran smoothly and to make any adjustments to the alignment of the lights in readiness for the official opener against the Racing Club side.
- Further floodlit matches soon followed the 'Paris' game including one featuring an FA XI against the RAF and Spurs v. FC Austria. By the end of the decade night games against overseas opposition were a regular feature at White Hart Lane and among the visitors were two top class sides from Brazil, Canto do Rio and Bela Vista plus Torpedo Club Moscow, as well as several sides from mainland Europe.
- In 1989, the four-pylon system of floodlighting at White Hart Lane was changed to a state-of-the-art spotlighting system.

- Tony Marchi had the pleasure of scoring the first goal under floodlights at a competitive level in England in a Football Combination game for Spurs v Southampton on 1 October 1951 at The Dell.
- Ernie 'Alphabet' Jones (ex-Spurs) helped design and erect the floodlights at Rhyl Town FC in 1954-55.

FA AMATEUR CUP
Spurs' full record in the FA amateur Cup:

P	W	D	L	F	A
9	6	2	1	34	12

Spurs were invited to compete in the FA Amateur Cup in its inaugural season of 1893-94. They received a bye in the first round, beat Vampires 3-0 at home in the second, but after being paired with Clapham Rovers in the third, when they were banned from the competition (owing to the Ernie Payne 'boots' affair) but were back again the following season doing much better.

This time they progressed through five stages before losing in the second round proper.

Prior to that, Spurs had defeated, in turn, Old Harrovians (h) 7-0 (seven different players found the net in this tie), City Ramblers (h) 6-1 (two goals apiece for Peter Hunter and Ernie Payne) and Romford (a) 8-0 (a hat-trick for Hunter on this occasion) before meeting London Welsh in the Division Final. The first two games ended in draws (1-1 and 3-3) before Spurs went through 4-2 on a neutral ground - the Spotted Dog. They then beat Beeston (h) 2-0 before succumbing to the former FA Cup winners Old Carthusians 5-0 at home in March 1895 in front of 5,000 spectators.

The Old C's were a formidable force at the time and fielded five full England internationals including the great GO Smith at centre-forward and the Walters brothers, AM and PM (known affectionately as morning and afternoon).

The following season (1895-96) Spurs were drawn against Chatham in the opening round but withdrew when the club decided to turn professional.

FA CHARITY SHIELD
Spurs have competed for the FA Charity Shield on nine occasions:

1920	v. West Bromwich Albion (h) 0-2
1921	v. Burnley (h) 2-0
1951	v. Newcastle United (h) 2-1
1961	v. FA XI (h) 3-2
1962	v. Ipswich Town (a) 5-1
1967	v. Manchester United (a) 3-3*
1981	v. Aston Villa (n) 2-2*
1982	v. Liverpool (n) 0-1
1991	v. Arsenal (n) 0-0*

* Trophy shared.

Summary of Charity Shield Matches:

P	W	D	L	F	A
9	4	3	2	17	12

Charity Shield Facts
- Spurs were defeated by the League champions, WBA, in 1920 in front of 38,168 fans at White Hart Lane.
- Only 18,000 fans saw Spurs, the Second Division champions, beat Burnley in 1921.
- Spurs had already played ten League games at the start of the 1951-52 season before they met the FA Cup winners Newcastle United in the Charity Shield match.
- A crowd of 36,593 saw Les Allen score twice when a strong FA XI was defeated in 1961.
- Jimmy Greaves scored twice when Spurs won 5-1 at League champions Ipswich Town in 1962. Former player Alf Ramsey was manager at Portman Road at the time.
- Spurs 'keeper Pat Jennings scored a goal in the 3-3 draw at Old Trafford in 1967 when the turnout was 54,106.
- Mark Falco (Spurs) and Peter Withe (Villa) both scored twice in the 2-2 Wembley draw in 1981.
- Ian Rush's 32nd minute goal decided the 1982 Final in Liverpool's favour in front of almost 82,000 fans at Wembley.
- And after a 0-0 stalemate in 1991, both Arsenal and Spurs agreed to hold the shield for six months each.

FA CUP
Spurs full record in this competition reads:

Venue	P	W	D	L	F	A
Home	177	113	45	19	431	173
Away	160	58	44	58	241	235
Neutral	37	21	4	12	66	43
Totals	374	192	93	89	738	451

NB - Away games switched to a home fixture have been classed as a 'home' match.

Spurs have played in nine Finals and a total of 17 semi-finals. Here are reports on their eight winning Final victories.

- Spurs are the only non-League team to have won the FA Cup since the league was formed in 1888, doing so on 27 April 1901, when members of the old Southern League. Fielding a team comprising five Scots, two Welshman, three Englishmen and an Irish-born player - none of them born within at least 100 miles of White Hart Lane - they beat Sheffield United in the Final after a replay. The first game at The Crystal Palace which had a 3.30pm kick-off, drew a massive crowd of 114,815 (gate receipts were over £8,500) and those present saw an enthralling contest finish level at 2-2. Sandy Brown scored both goals for Spurs to keep up his record of netting in very round. Fred Priest scored the opening goal for United on 12 minutes with a 20 yard drive that flew past 'keeper George Clawley. Brown equalised with a smart header from John Kirwan's free-kick in the 25th minute and six minutes after the resumption, John Cameron set up Brown for his and Spurs' second goal, whipped past the huge 18-stone frame of United 'keeper Billy 'Fatty' Foulke, the ball going in off the underside of the crossbar. Playing against a strong wind, United hit back immediately and within a minute they had drawn level with a disputed goal. Clawley fumbled a shot from from Lipsham on his line. As Bennett rushed in, Clawley diverted the loose ball around his goalpost. The Spurs' keeper appealed for a goal-kick, Bennett for a corner. The referee (Mr Kingscott) awarded neither, pointing to the centre spot for a 'goal' much to the annoyance of the Spurs' players and indeed their supporters. The match was the first ever filmed in full (by Pathe News) and clearly shows that the ball was at least a foot from the goal-line.....it never crossed it!

• Thomas Cook, the travel agents, offered a conducted tour of London for the travelling Sheffield United supporters, visiting principal places of interest on the morning on the Final. They linked the bus ride with train excursions run by the Midland Railway. A meat breakfast was guaranteed on arrival in the capital, followed by a leisurely drive around London. Lunch was served at the Crystal Palace ground and the all-inclusive charge of the day's outings was 6s 6d (33p).

• The 1901 replay was staged at a damp and dreary Burnden Park the following Saturday 27 April, but on this occasion only 20,470 hardy supporters bothered to turn up (due to the Lancashire & Yorkshire Railway Company's refusal to issue cut-price travel tickets, whilst Bolton station was under reconstruction). Spurs, unchanged, won a scrappy game by 3-1. The first half was dour and it was United who struck first, taking the lead - against the run of play - five minutes from half-time through Priest. Ten minutes after half-time John Cameron found space to equalise and shortly afterwards, with United defenders watching each other, Tom Smith pounced to make it 2-1. Sandy Brown tied things up for Spurs with a third goal seven minutes from the end.
After this 1901 success, the wife of the Spurs' director, Morton Cadman, tied navy blue and white ribbons on the handles of the trophy for the first time - a custom which has since become tradition.

• Stamford Bridge, home of Chelsea, was the venue for the 1921 FA Cup Final between Spurs and Wolverhampton Wanderers (kick-off 2.55pm). The game took place on a miserable, rainy afternoon on 23 April, yet despite the atrocious weather conditions, a crowd of 72,805 packed into the ground to witness a lively contest. With players slip-sliding around, the ball shooting all over the place, passes going astray and the soggy pitch not helping in any way, Wolves looked the stronger, although Jimmy Seed missed the first clear-cut chance for Spurs. Wolves 'keeper Noel George then pulled off excellent saves from Seed, and the two Jimmys, Dimmock and Cantrell while George Edmonds went close for the Wanderers. At half-time all the Wolves outfield players changed their shirts as did some of the Spurs men, and eight minutes into the second period Spurs scored the decisive goal. Maurice Woodward back-pedalled into the danger-zone as Dimmock bore down on goal. The Spurs man only half-hit his shot through the mud but the ball was cleared back to him and this time he drove it past the diving figure of George and into the net. After this both sides could have scored, Seed and Dimmock went close for Spurs, as did Edmonds and the lively Sammy Brooks who hit a post for Wolves, but in the end Dimmock's goal decided the outcome in Spurs favour - just! The gate receipts for the Final amounted to £13,414.

• Spurs 2 Leicester City 0 was the outcome of the 1961 FA Cup Final at Wembley on 6 May - and victory also gave Spurs the coveted League and Cup double, previously won by Aston Villa way back in 1896-97. The Final itself was something of a let-down for a full-house crowd of 100,000. City's full-back Len Chalmers became a limping passenger from the 19th minute onwards, yet with only ten fit men, one a makeshift defender, City had no trouble in holding Spurs at bay and, indeed, they may well have scored at least one, even two goals. The breakthrough came in the 67th minute, Bobby Smith controlling the ball on the right side of the

penalty area before turning and firing a shot past Gordon Banks. Plucky Leicester still battled on and it wasn't until Terry Dyson headed home Spurs' second goal (from Smith's precise cross) in the 77th minute that the Foxes finally conceded defeat.

• The 1962 Final against Burnley was played on 5 May in front of 100,000 spectators (recs. £53,837). The Clarets, along with Ipswich Town, had been fighting it out with Spurs for the League championship that season and it was Ipswich (managed by former Spurs right-back Alf Ramsey) who won the title. Burnley had to be content with the runners-up spot while Spurs finished third. At Wembley the Turf Moor club again finished second - beaten by an enthusiastic and more purposeful side. The 3-1 scoreline could and should have been far wider. Although second favourites on the day, Spurs dominated the game for long periods (despite not playing all that well). A third minute goal by ace marksman Jimmy Greaves quickly settled the nerves and although chances went begging after that (at both ends) Jimmy Robson equalised (against the flow) in the 48th minute. Spurs though, always seemed to have something in hand and a second strike by Bobby Smith a minute later (after a great run down the right by John White) restored the lead. A third goal followed in the 82nd minute courtesy of a sweetly converted penalty by skipper Danny Blanchflower (after Tommy Cummings had handled) to ensure the Cup returned to White Hart Lane.

• May 1967 saw the first all-London Final between Spurs and Tommy Docherty's Chelsea and despite having by far the better of the exchanges, dictating play for long periods and creating many chances, Spurs just scraped home by two goals to one. Skippered by that tough Scotsman Dave Mackay, they should have triumphed by a far bigger margin, so much were they on top. But they only had one first-half goal scored by Jimmy Robertson (a snap-shot past Peter Bonetti after Alan Mullery's effort had bounced off Ron Harris) and a second-half strike by Frank Saul (who swivelled to bury a right-foot shot inside an upright) to show for their efforts. Bobby Tambling headed in a late consolation goal for the 'Pensioners'. The attendance of 100,000 realised gate receipts of £109,649 (a record at the time).

• Manchester City were Spurs' opponents, in the Centenary Cup Final, the game taking place at Wembley Stadium on 9 May 1981 in front another 100,000 crowd. It turned out to be an exciting affair that ran into extra-time. Spurs, confident on the day, played well and perhaps deserved to win but they had to settle for a 1-1 draw - thanks to Tommy Hutchison! The Scottish international put City ahead in the 29th minute and he could have scored a second before he inadvertently diverted Glenn Hoddle's free-kick past his own 'keeper ten minutes from time for Spurs' equaliser. Extra-time produced no further scoring and, in fact, very few chances were created as the players became rather tired and cautious!

• The replay - the first to take place at Wembley - went ahead five days later, on a Thursday evening, and it turned out to be one of the most exciting Finals ever seen inside the Empire Stadium. A restricted crowd of 92,500 saw Spurs win a classic encounter by the odd goal in five. The Argentinian international Ricky Villa gave Spurs an eighth minute lead but three minutes later Steve Mackenzie banged home a terrific equaliser. A Kevin Reeves penalty edged City in front on 50 minutes before Garth Crooks levelled things up ten minutes later. Then in the 66th minute, came one of the finest individual goals ever seen, live or on TV, as the

raven-haired Villa weaved his way through a tightly packed City defence to score with a low right-foot shot past 'keeper Joe Corrigan. He was mobbed by his team-mates, and rightly so...it was a marvellous effort, worthy of winning any football match, not only the 1981 FA Cup Final replay!

● Queen's Park Rangers from Division Two - managed by the club's former midfielder Terry Venables and conquerors of West Bromwich Albion in the semi-final - were Spurs' opponents in the 1982 Final, played on 22 May before a capacity crowd of 100,000. Having been beaten in the semi-final of the European Cup-Winners Cup by Barcelona and by Liverpool in the League Cup Final, Spurs found a resilient Rangers outfit a hard nut to crack. Both Ardiles and Villa were left out of the Spurs line-up due to circumstances surrounding the Falklands War, Villa being told that he wouldn't figure in the action at 11.30am on the morning of the game. This allowed Micky Hazard to partner Hoddle and Graham Roberts in midfield, the latter having been pushed forward from the back. Rangers were stubborn throughout and it was goalless at the end of 90 minutes. Ray Clemence who was equalling Pat Jennings' goalkeeping record of appearing in four FA Cup Finals, had a fairly quiet 90 minutes and he wasn't troubled at all in the early stages of extra-time. He saw Hoddle (after exchanging passes with Roberts) put Spurs ahead in the 110th. His 20 yard well struck right-foot shot skimmed through the legs of Tony Currie and took a slight deflection before eluding 'Man of the Match' Peter Hucker in the Rangers' goal. But then with the ribbons being unfolded in readiness to drape over the handles of the trophy, Rangers somehow conjured up an equaliser five minutes later to earn a second chance they hardly deserved. The Spurs defence was caught out as Terry Fenwick, later to play for Spurs, beat Clemence, with a smartly taken header after defender Bob Hazell had touched on Simon Stainrod's long throw-in.

● The 1982 replay - played the following Thursday, 27 May - attracted 92,000 spectators. And it was decided as early as the sixth minute when Glenn Hoddle put away a penalty after Rangers' skipper Currie (who had taken over the armband from the suspended Glenn Roeder) had brought down Roberts inside the area. Rangers played far better than they had done in the first game and this time they certainly deserved a draw (at least) despite Steve Archibald striking a post late on. But Clemence played well, as did his defenders, and it was a delighted Steve Perryman who held aloft the silver prize for the second season running, thus equalling the feat of skipper Danny Blanchflower 20 years earlier.

● There was a dramatic opening sequence of events when Spurs (now managed by Terry Venables) took on Nottingham Forest at Wembley in the 1991 FA Cup Final, played on 18 May in front of nearly 80,000 spectators. Paul Gascoigne, the Spurs midfielder committed two early fouls, the second on Gary Charles, resulting in him being carried off with serious ligament damage. Forest were the better side early on and they took the lead with a cracking free-kick by Stuart Pearce in the 15th minute (awarded for Gascoigne's second foul) as referee Roger Milford failed to notice the 'wall' being pulled apart by Lee Glover who heaved out Gary Mabbutt. Thereafter, it was basically all Spurs, but they had to wait until the 52nd minute before Paul Stewart struck home an equaliser with aplomb from a tight angle. It was four minutes into extra-time when England centre-half Des Walker - with a mistimed header - conceded an own-goal to give Spurs victory. A missed penalty by Gary Lineker (who also had a 'goal' disallowed) had put the pressure on Spurs but they held out and it was the smiling Gary Mabbutt who went up to collect the trophy.

One Final defeat:
Spurs were defeated 3-2 by Coventry City in a classic Final played at Wembley on 16 May 1987 before a crowd of 98,000. After just 112 seconds Clive Allen swooped to give Spurs an early lead with his 49th goal of the season and for the next few minutes the football produced by David Pleat's side was superb. But Coventry drew level in the seventh minute Downs crossed, Keith Houchen's head flicked the ball into the path of Dave Bennett who found the net past Spurs' 39 year-old goalkeeper Ray Clemence. Spurs had the better of an exciting football-packed first-half and went in at the break 2-1 up courtesy of City's centre-half Brian Kilcline. He technically conceded an own-goal in the 41st minute when the ball bounced off his chest and over the line after Glenn Hoddle's measured free-kick had caught Steve Ogrizovic in two minds, although Gary Mabbutt later staked claim to the goal and was awarded it by the FA! The same pace was continued in the second period and it was the Sky Blues who grabbed an equaliser in the 63rd minute - and what a beauty it was, headed in by the diving Houchen from Bennett's right-wing cross. Both sides had half-chances afterwards as the game went into extra-time - the third time in three Finals for Spurs. It was Coventry who proved the stronger, grabbing the winning goal in the 96th minute. Substitute Graham Rodger (on for the injured Kilkline) sent McGrath racing clear down the right and his cross was inadvertently kneed past his own 'keeper by the unlucky Gary Mabbutt. Spurs battled on after that but failed to penetrate a tight defence- and so their unbeaten run in FA Cup Finals came to a sad end.

● Old Moore's Almanac had predicted that a team wearing blue and white stripes would win the FA Cup - and that's precisely what happened despite Spurs being odds-on with the bookies to lift the trophy for the eighth time.

FA Cup action against the Minnows
Since entering the Football League in 1908 Spurs have opposed the following non--League teams in the FA Cup competition:

Date	Rd	Opponents	Score/Venue
1909-10	1	Plymouth Argyle	1-1 (a) 7-1 (h)
1909-10	3	Swindon Town	2-3 (a)
1910-11	1	Millwall	2-1 (h)
1912-13	2	Reading	0-2 (a)
1914-15	2	Norwich City	2-3 (a)
1919-20	1	Bristol Rovers	4-1 (a)
1919-20	2	West Stanley	4-0 (h)
1922-23	1	Worksop Town	0-0 (h) 9-0 (h)
1955-56	3	Boston United	4-0 (h)
1972-73	3	Margate	6-0 (a)
1978-79	3	Altrincham	1-1 (h) 3-0 (n)
1992-93	3	Marlow	5-1 (h)
1994-95	3	Altrincham	3-0 (h)

Spurs FA Cup Dossier
● Spurs' first FA Cup-tie was a 1st round qualifying game against West Herts (forerunners to Watford FC) on 13 October 1894. They won 3-2 with goals by centre-forward Peter Hunter (the opener on his debut) and Don Goodall (2). The attendance was 2,000.
● Spurs suffered their first FA Cup defeat at the hands of Luton Town (away) in a 4th round qualifying tie on 12 December 1894, going down 0-4 after a 2-2 draw. Again the attendance was given as 2,000.
● Spurs gained revenge over the Hatters in the 1st qualifying round of the 1895-96 competition, winning 2-1 away. Their next qualifying tie against Vampires (away) ended in a 4-2 defeat, but

Spurs protested that the pitch had been wrongly marked out. A committee sat and ordered a replay to take place and this time Spurs won 2-1 at home. However, after beating Ilford 5-1 and Old St Stephen's 2-1, they failed to get past the first round proper, crashing out 0-5 at Stoke.

• Spurs were again knocked out of the Cup by Luton in January 1897 (0-3 away) after earlier having accounted for Old Stephen's FC 4-0 and Maidenhead 6-0.

• Amazingly Spurs were defeated again by Luton in a 2nd qualifying round tie in 1897-98. They lost 4-3 at home on this occasion in front of 12,000 spectators.

• The last FA Cup-tie to be staged at Spurs' Northumberland Park ground was against Sunderland on 11 February 1899. Spurs won 2-1 before a crowd of 12,371.

• Spurs went on to reach the 3rd round proper in 1898-99 - their best run in the competition at that time. They lost 1-4 at Stoke in their tenth match.

• The first FA Cup-tie at White Hart Lane saw Spurs play Preston North End on 9 February 1901. A crowd of 15,223 witnessed the 1-1 draw before Spurs went north to win the replay 4-2, 'Sandy' Brown scoring a hat-trick.

• Spurs went on to win the trophy in 1900-01, becoming the first non-League side to achieve this feat. Since the league's formation in 1888. After beating Preston North End, they put out Bury, Reading (after a replay) and West Bromwich Albion, whom they crushed 4-0 in the semi-final at Villa Park where Brown again took the scoring honours with all his side's goals (two headers and two shots, one from fully 30 yards). This was a record at the time and it wasn't until 1934 when Fred Tilson bagged a fourtimer for Manchester City in the semi-final against Aston Villa that Brown's record was equalled. In the Final Spurs met Sheffield United at a packed Crystal Palace and were held to a 2-2 draw before going north to win the replay at Bolton. 'Sandy' Brown scored in every round of the competition (15 goals in total). Against Reading in the third round at Elm Park in front of a record 14,417 crowd, Spurs were decidedly lucky! With the scores level at 1-1 and time running out, Sandy Tait punched the ball off his own goal-line. None of the officials saw it and the referee awarded a goal-kick, much to the dismay of the Reading players!

• Holders of the trophy, Spurs went out in the first round of 1901-02, beaten 3-2 at Reading by fellow Southern League side Southampton (after 1-1 and 2-2 draws).

• Spurs' first FA Cup defeat at White Hart Lane was suffered at the hands of Aston Villa in March 1903. They went down 3-2.

• The following year (February 1904) Villa were leading 1-0 in a 2nd round tie on the same ground, but 20 minutes into the game hundreds of spectators spilled on to the pitch, the referee eventually abandoned the action, a replay was ordered (at Villa Park) and Spurs won 1-0. (See Abandoned Matches).

• In February 1905, Spurs suffered their heaviest FA Cup defeat up to that time when they lost 4-0 at Newcastle United, who went on to reach the Final.

• Knocked out in 1905-06 by Birmingham, 2-0 after-extra-time in a 3rd round replay, Spurs then took three games to oust both Hull City and Blackburn Rovers from the 1906-07 competition before they lost in the 3rd round 4-0 away to Notts County.

• Over a period of eight seasons (between 1907-08 and 1914-15) Spurs failed to reach the fourth round, going out twice in round one, four times in round two and twice in round three.

• They beat Plymouth Argyle 7-1 (h) in January 1910, lost to the eventual beaten finalists West Bromwich Albion in January 1912 and defeated Blackpool 6-1 at home in January 1913 (after the Seaside club had agreed to switch the 3rd round tie to White Hart Lane).

• In January 1914 Spurs were involved in a thrilling 5-5 draw away to Leicester Fosse in the 3rd round. They won the replay 2-0 but then lost 2-1 at Manchester City.

• Spurs' first FA Cup defeat after the Great War saw them beaten 1-0 at home by Aston Villa in January 1920 in front of 52,179 fans. The only goal was scored by Spurs full-back Tommy Clay who sliced a clearance into his own net. His blunder, however, did not prevent him from gaining his first of four England caps days later.

• On their way to winning the trophy in 1921, Spurs put out Bristol Rovers (h) 6-2, Bradford City (h) 4-0, Southend United (a) 4-1, Aston Villa (h) 1-0 (sweet revenge this in front of 52,179 spectators who paid £6,992 at the gate - both new club records) and Preston North End 2-1 in the semis. They conquered Wolves 1-0 at muddy Stamford Bridge in the Final. Jimmy Seed scored a hat-trick in that smart victory over Bradford City, two of his goals coming in the space of just 30 seconds. And in the game with Third Division Southend at their ground in Kursaal Gardens, the scores were level at 1-1 when Albert Fairclough missed a penalty for the home side and Spurs somehow scraped a draw.

• As holders, Spurs reached the semi-final stage in 1922 only to lose 2-1 to Preston at Hillsborough in front of 50,095 fans.

• Spurs played Worksop Town at home in the 1st round in January 1923 after the non-League club had sold the rights to transfer the game to White Hart Lane. Spurs capitalised on home advantage to win 9-0, Alex Lindsay (4) and 'Tich' Handley (3) leading the goal chase in front of 23,122 spectators. Handley scored a hat-trick in the next round when Manchester United were defeated 4-0, and he found the net against Cardiff City but missed out in round four as Spurs lost to Derby County.

• After beating West Ham United 5-0 in the first round in January 1926, Spurs succumbed 2-0 to Manchester United after a replay in the next round.

• An Upton Park crowd of 44,417 (a record at that time) saw the Hammers gain revenge with a 3-2 win over Spurs in January 1927.

• After looking good in the previous rounds, Spurs crashed 6-1 to Huddersfield Town in the quarter-finals in 1927-28.

• Spurs went out of the FA Cup in the third round in 1928-29 and 1931-32, beaten by Reading and Sheffield Wednesday respectively, and fell at the fourth fence in 1929-30 (to Manchester City), 1930-31 (to West Bromwich Albion, the winners of the trophy) and 1932-33 (to Luton Town). George Hunt had earlier scored a hat-trick when Spurs won 6-0 at Oldham in January 1933.

• Spurs played three home ties in 1933-34 beating Everton 3-0 and West Ham 4-1 before losing 1-0 to Aston Villa in round five.

• Spurs lost 2-0 to Bolton Wanderers at the third attempt at neutral Villa Park 1934-35, having earlier defeated Manchester City and Newcastle United.

• After drawing 4-4 with Southend United at home and winning the replay 2-1 Spurs made progress into the quarter-finals in 1935-36 where they lost 3-1 to Sheffield United at Bramall Lane.

• Spurs knocked out two 'Ps'...Portsmouth (a) 5-0 and Plymouth Argyle (h) 1-0 before going on to reach the 6th round in 1936-37 when they lost to another 'P' Preston North End 3-1 at Deepdale. In the 5th round against Everton, Spurs 'keeper John Hall played a blinder saving a penalty from Dixie Dean in the 1-1 draw. Spurs won the replay 4-3.

• Spurs overcame three hard matches with Blackburn Rovers (won 3-2), New Brighton (won 5-2 after a 0-0 draw) and Chesterfield (3-2, also after a draw 0-0) before losing again in the quarter-finals to Sunderland in March 1938 in front of the biggest-ever crowd at White Hart Lane, 75,038. In this game Colin Lyman scored what appeared to be a good goal for Spurs but just to make sure, his colleague Alex Gibbons punched the ball into the net to make sure! The referee thought otherwise, stating that in his mind Lyman's effort hadn't crossed the line and he awarded a free-kick for handball against Gibbons!

● In the last season before the Second World War, Spurs beat Watford 7-1 at home in the third round but then lost to London rivals West Ham United 2-1 (at the third attempt) following 3-3 and 1-1 draws.

● In 1945-46, for the first (and so far) only time, the FA Cup featured two-legged ties up to and including the sixth round. Spurs, though, went out in round three, beaten 4-2 on aggregate by Brentford (2-0 to the Bees at Griffin Park after a 2-2 draw at White Hart Lane).

● It was out in round three again in 1946-47, beaten in an away replay by Stoke City. The following season Spurs reached the semi-final stage, ousting Bolton Wanderers 2-0 away (after extra-time), West Bromwich Albion 3-1 at home in front 71,853 fans, Leicester City 5-2, also at home and Southampton 1-0 at The Dell. However, with their sights firmly set on Wembley, Spurs went down 3-1 to Blackpool after extra-time in the Villa Park semi-final. Spurs were 1-0 up in this game before Stan Mortensen scored a hat-trick for the Seasiders in front of almost 67,500 spectators.

● North London rivals Arsenal put paid to Spurs' FA Cup hopes in 1948-49; the following season, after winning 1-0 at Stoke before a crowd of 47,000, an audience of 66,246 saw Spurs defeat Sunderland 5-1 in round four. Then almost 73,000 spectators packed into Goodison Park to see Everton win a 5th round tie 1-0.

● Eliminated in the third round by Huddersfield Town at Leeds Road in January 1951 and dumped out of the competition by Newcastle United 3-0 at home in the fourth round in February 1952, Spurs then progressed through to the semi-finals in 1952-53. But after beating Tranmere Rovers and Preston North End (both after a replay), Halifax Town, in front of a record crowd at The Shay of close on 37,000 and Birmingham City (at the third attempt) they once again found neutral Villa Park an unlucky ground. They slumped to a 2-1 defeat at the hands of a Stanley Matthews-inspired Blackpool side - Alf Ramsey admitting that he handed the Seasiders' their second goal with a weak back-pass to 'keeper Ted Ditchburn, Jackie Mudie nipping in to score.

● After edging out Leeds United, Manchester City and Hull City, Spurs were beaten 3-0 by the eventual winners West Bromwich Albion at the Hawthorns in the 6th round in March 1954. Then twelve months later they had the indignity of losing to Third Division (North) giant-killers York City in a 5th round tie at Bootham Crescent. Earlier Spurs had seen off two other Division Three North sides in Gateshead and Port Vale.

● In March 1956, for the third time since the War, Spurs travelled to Villa Park to contest an FA Cup semi-final, losing this time 1-0 to Manchester City on a soggy pitch. Unfortunately, Dave Dunmore, preferred to Alf Stokes, was a misfit at outside-right. In the earlier rounds, non-League side Boston United (4-0), Middlesbrough, Doncaster Rovers and neighbours West Ham United (after a replay) had all been defeated. Spurs were 3-1 down with time running out at Upton Park, but Maurice Norman was pushed up front and his massive frame helped in the two goals to earn a 3-3 draw. Spurs won the replay 2-1.

● Humiliation for Spurs in 1956-57 as they surrendered to Third Division side Bournemouth at Dean Court in round five - having earlier beaten Chelsea 4-0 at home in front of 66,398 spectators.

● Spurs went out of the competition early in 1957-58 to Sheffield United, 1958-59 to semi-finalists from Division Three South, Norwich City and 1959-60 to Blackburn Rovers - the latter dismissal coming after a sensational 13-2 replay win over luckless Crewe Alexandra at White Hart Lane.

● At long last it was joy in 1960-61 with both the League championship and FA Cup triumphs making it a double celebration for Spurs. On their way to winning the Cup, Spurs accounted for Charlton Athletic (3-2), the unfortunate Crewe Alexandra again (5-1), Aston Villa (2-0), Sunderland (5-0 after a replay) and Burnley 3-0 in the semi-final at Villa Park in front of almost 70,000 spectators. Leicester were beaten 2-0 at Wembley. An aggregate total of 530,000 spectators watched Spurs' seven Cup matches this season - averaging 75,661.

Jimmy Greaves (second from left on one knee) puts the ball beyond five Burnley players to score Spurs' first goal in the early minutes of the FA Cup Final of 1962.

Gary Mabbutt lifts the F.A.Cup for
Tottenham Hotspur v Nottingham Forest 18/5/91

● Spurs went back to Wembley twelve months later and retained the FA Cup, beating Burnley 3-1. In earlier rounds, Bill Nicholson's side had ousted Birmingham City 4-2 (after a replay), Plymouth Argyle (5-1), West Bromwich Albion (4-2 at The Hawthorns), Aston Villa (2-0) and Manchester United (3-1 at Hillsborough). Jimmy Greaves scored in every round except the Villa clash.

● As so often happens, as Cup holders, Spurs were knocked out of the competition in the opening round in 1962-63 by previous season's beaten finalists Burnley winning 3-0 at White Hart Lane.

● Spurs went out in the 4th round in 1963-64 and the 5th round the following season, beaten on each occasion by Chelsea, the latter departure coming after two healthy wins over Torquay United by 5-1 and Ipswich Town 5-0. In 1965-66 Spurs succumbed to Preston North End before going on to gain sweet revenge over Chelsea with a 2-1 victory in the Final of 1967.

● En-route to Wembley Spurs defeated Millwall, Portsmouth, Bristol City, Birmingham City and Nottingham Forest (at Hillsborough).

● As holders, Spurs saw off the threat of both Manchester United and Preston North End in 1967-68 before losing out to Liverpool in round five. In the 1968-69 tournament three Midland clubs - Walsall, Wolverhampton Wanderers and Aston Villa - were all disposed of before Manchester City ended Spurs' glory bid in the quarter-finals at Maine Road (1-0).

● Neighbours Crystal Palace ended Spurs' hopes in 1969-70 with a 4th round victory and a year later it was Liverpool again who sent Spurs packing in a quarter-final replay - this after Sheffield Wednesday, Carlisle United and Nottingham Forest had all been beaten (in that order).

● Spurs reached the last eight again in 1971-72 but this time they lost to Leeds 2-1 at Elland Road after Carlisle United, Rotherham United and Everton had fallen by the wayside before hand.

● A rousing 6-0 third round win at non-League Margate in 1972-73 was followed by a 1-1 draw at Derby. But the Rams came to North London and won the replay 5-3 after extra-time of a thrilling contest, seen by 52,3736 fans.

● Spurs, much to the annoyance of their faithful supporters, went out of the FA Cup at the first hurdle five seasons running 1973-74 to 1977-78 inclusive, losing in turn to Leicester City, Nottingham Forest, Stoke City, Cardiff City and Bolton Wanderers.

● Things picked up a bit in 1978-79 when Altrincham, Wrexham, Oldham Athletic were all dismissed before Man United ended Spurs' Final ambitions with a 6th round replay win at Old Trafford.

● A year later Spurs again failed at the quarter-final stage, beaten this time by Liverpool, having earlier seen off Manchester United, Swindon Town and Birmingham City. Ossie Ardiles' superb goal won the 3rd round replay at Old Trafford.

● Then it was 'double' success again for Spurs in the early 1980s as first the FA Cup found its way back to White Hart Lane in 1981 and stayed their for a further twelve months after a second victory at Wembley in 1982. En-route to their first final for 14 years Spurs beat QPR, Hull City, Coventry City, Exeter City and Wolverhampton Wanderers. Garth Crooks scored twice in the 3-0 semi-final replay win at Highbury over the latter club after a disputed late penalty by Kenny Hibbitt had denied Spurs a 2-1 victory in the initial game at Hillsborough. Then it took two attempts to over come Manchester City at Wembley to win the trophy for the sixth time.

● The 1982 Final also went to a replay, Spurs eventually taking the prize away from QPR with a 1-0 victory courtesy of Glenn Hoddle's early penalty after an initial 1-1 draw. On their way to glory this season Spurs defeated Arsenal, Leeds United, Aston Villa,

Chelsea and Leicester City (the latter by 2-0 in the semi-final at Villa Park).

● After these successive triumphs, Spurs did not do too well in the next four campaigns, losing to Everton (round 5), Norwich City (round 4), Liverpool (round 4) and Everton (round 5) in that order. But then it was back to Wembley for the 1987 showdown with Coventry City.

● David Pleat was Spurs' manager against the Sky Blues and he forecast that the Final itself would be a showpiece - and that's how it proved, Coventry pipping Spurs 3-2 after extra-time providing terrific entertainment. On the way to Wembley in 1987 Spurs accounted for Scunthorpe Utd, Crystal Palace, Newcastle Utd, Wimbledon and Watford, the Hornets crashing to a 4-0 semi-final defeat at Villa Park where Steve Hodge scored twice.

● Oldham Athletic were defeated 4-2 by Spurs in the 3rd round of the 1987-88 tournament but deeat soon came as Port Vale pulled off a shock 2-0 victory in the Potteries at the next hurdle.

● It was early exits for Spurs in 1988-89 (beaten by Bradford City) and 1989-90 (ousted by Southampton) before it was back to Wembley once again to meet Brian Clough's Nottingham Forest in the 1991 Final. This time Spurs, despite losing Paul Gascoigne early on and Gary Lineker fluffing a penalty, won 2-1 in extra-time thanks to an own-goal by Forest defender Des Walker. Spurs had won through to their ninth FA Cup Final by eliminating Blackpool, Oxford Utd, Portsmouth, Notts County and Arsenal, the semi-final being played at Wembley in front of 77,893 spectators.

● As holders, it was goodbye to Spurs in the 3rd round in 1991-92 (beaten by Aston Villa in a home replay). Then it was back to Wembley once more a year later, only to lose this time to arch rivals Arsenal in the Cup semi-final watched by another useful crowd of 76,263. Spurs were confident of reaching their tenth Final after good wins over Marlow (5-1), Norwich City, Wimbledon and Manchester City, but it was not to be as the Gunners fired in one bullet too many!

● A tension-packed 5-4 penalty shoot-out victory over plucky Peterborough Utd saw Spurs squeeze through to the 4th round in 1993-94, but they went no further, beaten 3-0 at Ipswich Town.

● In 1994-95 Spurs won through to yet another semi-final. Yet once more joy turned to sadness as Everton comfortably beat them 4-1 at neutral Elland Road. Early on, Altrincham (3-0), Sunderland (4-1 on Wearside), Southampton (6-2 in a tremendous 5th round replay at The Dell) and Liverpool (2-1 at Anfield) had all been defeated by a very purposeful and confident Spurs side which contained the German international Jurgen Klinsmann.

● After withstanding the threats of lowly Hereford United (5-1 in a replay, thanks mainly to a Teddy Sheringham hat-trick) and Wolverhampton Wanderers (also after a replay) Spurs went out of the 1995-96 competition at the hands of Nottingham Forest, losing 3-1 on penalties after 2-2 and 1-1 draws.

● A third round exit followed - beaten by Manchester United in January 1997 - and then Barnsley won in round 4 a year later before Spurs reached their 16th FA Cup semi-final in 1998-99. This time they played and beat Watford 5-2, Wimbledon 3-0 (after a replay), Leeds United 2-0 (also after a replay) and Barnsley 1-0 at Oakwell (thanks to a stunning David Ginola goal) before losing 2-0 to Newcastle United at Old Trafford.

● Then by coincidence, Spurs were drawn against the Geordies in the 3rd round of the 1999-2000 competition and had the chance of gaining revenge. But it was not to be and after a 1-1 draw at White Hart Lane, Spurs were slammed 6-1 in the replay at St James' Park - equalling their heaviest defeat in the competition to date, an identical scoreline at Huddersfield in 1928.

● Thankfully, that crushing defeat at Newcastle was soon

forgotten as Spurs went on the FA Cup march again in 2000-01. They progressed through to the semi-final stage after beating London rivals Leyton Orient 1-0 at Brisbane Road and Charlton Athletic 4-2 at The Valley, Stockport County 4-0 at White Hart Lane and another London club, West Ham United 3-2 at Upton Park. Next up were their arch enemies from the capital city, Arsenal, the venue Old Trafford, and in front of 63,541 spectators Spurs, with Glenn Hoddle installed as manager, Spurs despite taking the lead, were defeated 2-1 by the Gunners.

FA Cup Facts & Figures

● Spurs went a club record 14 FA Cup games without defeat during seasons 1960-61 and 1961-62. The run came to an end when losing 3-0 at home to Burnley in the 3rd round in Jan 1963.

● The previous best unbeaten spell was 12 matches - 1966-68.

● Steve Perryman, with 69, has made most FA Cup appearances for Spurs. Glenn Hoddle made 48, Gary Mabbutt 47, Pat Jennings 43, Cyril Knowles 42 and Alan Gilzean 40.

● Jimmy Greaves with a total of 32, has scored most FA Cup goals for Spurs. Bobby Smith netted 22, Alan Gilzean 21 and Len Duquemin 20.

● The first Spurs player to be sent-off in an FA Cup-tie was Joe Kinnear, in the 1-0 3rd round home victory over Manchester United in January 1968.

FOOTBALL COMBINATION

Spurs' first XI participated in the London Combination for four seasons during the Great War (1915-19 inclusive). Thereafter the second XI took over the fixtures, and Spurs' reserves went on to lift the championship a record 19 times before the club moved out to join the newly-formed FA Premier Reserve League, South in 1999-2000. They finished runners-up to Charlton in 1998-99 (beaten by three points: 60-57) and then finished in third place at the end of that initial season of the Premier League, behind Derby County and Charlton (again).

The Spurs 1st team record in the London Combination:

P	W	D	L	F	A	Pts
148	75	26	47	320	249	176

Best wins:

10-0 v. Portsmouth	(n)	31.03.1917
8-0 v. Clapton Orient	(a)	28.04.1917
8-0 v. Crystal Palace	(n)	16.02.1918
7-2 v. Queens Park R	(a)	02.02.1918
7-4 v. Luton Town	(h)	26.02.1916
6-0 v. Millwall	(a)	25.12.1917
6-1 v. Brentford	(n)	10.11.1917

Heaviest defeats:

1-8 v. Chelsea	(a)	04.12.1916
1-7 v. Brentford	(a)	09.11.1918
1-7 v. Queens Park R	(a)	15.02.1919
3-6 v. Crystal Palace	(a)	14.12.1918

* Jimmy Banks scored five goals in the 10-0 win over Portsmouth in 1917 and Bert Bliss netted most Combination goals for Spurs, total 44.

FA YOUTH CUP

This is Spurs full record in the FA Youth Cup: 1952-2001:

Venue	P	W	D	L	F	A
Home	90	61	16	13	277	85
Away	93	43	15	35	152	127
Totals	183	104	31	48	429	212

Youth Cup Facts & Figures

The competition was first launched in 1952-53, Spurs entering at the outset, reaching the fourth round of that inaugural campaign before losing 2-1 away to QPR.

Spurs have since won the trophy on three occasions, having lost in two other Finals and been eliminated in the semi-finals three times.

The first game was played on 18 September 1952 against Welwyn Garden City at home (Cheshunt, Spurs winning comfortably by 4-0, Grace and Cliss both scoring twice.

The first defeat was suffered against QPR (above) on 27 December 1952.

Spurs' biggest Youth Cup victory is 15-0, achieved against Terrington lads (a Kings Lynn-based Youth Club) on 10 September 1960 in a preliminary round encounter, again at Cheshunt. Lloyd (5), Roffman (4) and R Smith (4) were the key marksman.

Six years earlier, on 16 October 1954, Spurs' youngsters had beaten Holbrook United 14-1 at home in a first round tie when Titt netted a double hat-trick (six goals) while Iley scored three times.

On 9 November 1966 the Metropolitan Police under 18 side were crushed 14-0 by Spurs in another first round clash at Cheshunt. Shoemark (5) and Clancy (4) top-scored on this occasion.

Spurs' best away win in the competition is 7-0 - claimed twice, at Eastbourne United in round 4 on 9 February 1957 and at Wealdstone in a second round clash on 4 December 1979. Lee and Bolton scored hat-tricks in those respective games.

Spurs' heaviest home defeat is 6-0 - suffered at the hands of London rivals Crystal Palace in the second-leg of the semi-final on 13 April 1977.

Their heaviest away defeat is also 6-0 - at Southampton in round 5 on 6 March 1956.

Spurs' youngsters have crashed out of the FA Youth Cup at the first attempt on nine occasions, twice as holders, in 1970-71 to Charlton Athletic and 1990-91 to Birmingham City.

* Spurs utilised the Cheshunt ground for most of their home FA Youth Cup games from 1952 to 1965. The first match in the competition to be staged at White Hart Lane was against QPR in a 3rd round replay on 29 January 1964, when a crowd of 1,623 saw Rangers win 2-1 after extra-time.

Final Triumphs

On reaching the Final in season 1969-70, Spurs eliminated, in turn, Leyton Orient 2-0, Arsenal 1-0, Reading 2-0, Stoke City 2-0 and Bristol City 3-0 on aggregate in the semi-final. Their opponents in the two-legged Final were Coventry City. Crowds of 10,700 fans at White Hart Lane and 9,968 at Highfield Road saw both teams win their respective home game by 1-0, resulting in a 1-1 aggregate score. The replay at Coventry City ended level at 2-2 (in front of 14,926 spectators) before Spurs triumphed 1-0 in front of 7,560 fans at White Hart Lane on 1 May 1970, Graeme Souness scoring the vital goal.

The winning line-up was: Daines; Almond, Jones; Dillon, Edwards, Souness; Olive, Turner, Clarke, Perryman, Flanagan.

Spurs won the trophy for the second time in 1973-74, beating Huddersfield Town 2-1 on aggregate in the Final.

En-route to that showdown with the Terriers, Spurs knocked out West Ham United 2-0 (in a replay), Leyton Orient 2-1 (also after a replay), Birmingham City 1-0 at St Andrew's, Ipswich Town 2-1 at Portman Road and neighbours Arsenal 2-0 on aggregate in the semis (both games finishing 1-0). A crowd of 4,182 saw the first leg of the Final at White Hart Lane on 11 May which ended in a 1-1 draw, but there was a massive audience of 15,300 at Leeds

Road for the return leg which Spurs won 1-0 after-extra time, Gibbins the goalscoring hero.

The victorious team on this occasion was: Cranstone; Smith, Stead; Keeley, Cegielski, Anderson; Brotherston, Margerrison, C Jones, Gibbins, McNab.

Spurs' third triumph came in 1989-90 against Middlesbrough whom they beat 3-2 (2-1 away, 1-1 at home). Spurs were given a walkover in the opening round when Bournemouth scratched from the competition. They then ousted Colchester United (a) 3-0, Wolves (h) 4-1, Manchester City (a) 2-1 and Manchester United 3-1 in the semi-final (winning 2-0 at home and drawing 1-1 away). There were 8,297 fans present for the first leg of the Final at Ayresome Park, which saw Scott Houghton net Spurs' winning goal in a 2-1 victory. The return leg was seen by 5,579 spectators and finished 1-1, Paul Moran the Spurs scorer.

The players who starred in the first leg of the 1990 Final were: Walker; Hendon, Hackett; N Smith, Tuttle, Hardwicke; Howell (Nethercott), K Smith, Morah, Potts, Houghton (Fulling).

For the second leg Fulling replaced Howell who then came off the bench as a sub for the same player whilst Nethercott was a substitute for Morah.

Spurs' two Final defeats were suffered at the hands of West Ham United in 1980-81 (beaten 2-1 on aggregate) and Manchester United in 1994-95 (defeated 4-3 on penalties after a 2-2 aggregate score). A record crowd for a Spurs FA Youth Cup game of 20,190 saw the second leg of the Final at Old Trafford which United won 1-0 to ensure a penalty shoot-out.

Spurs' three semi-final defeats came in 1976-77 (beaten by Crystal Palace 8-0 on aggregate); in 1987-88 (eliminated by Doncaster Rovers 3-2 on aggregate) and 1991-92 (lost 5-1 on aggregate to Manchester United).

FOOTBALL LEAGUE

Spurs full Football League record: 1908-09 to 1991-92:

Div	P	W	D	L	F	A	Pts
1	2356	964	563	829	3812	3441	2683
2	668	311	172	185	1253	851	794
Totals	3024	1275	735	1014	5065	4292	3477

Breakdown of League games (Division 1 & 2):

Venue	P	W	D	L	F	A	Pts
Home	1512	851	343	318	3171	1796	2164
Away	1512	424	392	696	1894	2496	1313

Spurs' record in their first League season of 1908-09:

Venue	P	W	D	L	F	A	Pts
Home	19	12	5	2	42	12	29
Away	19	8	6	5	25	20	22
Totals	38	20	11	7	67	32	51

* Spurs finished runners-up in Division 2 behind Bolton Wanderers (52 pts).

Champions/runners-up/relegtion:

Spurs have won the First Division championship just twice, in 1950-51 and 1960-61.

They have finished runners-up on four occasions, in 1921-22, 1951-22, 1956-57 and 1962-63.

They have also won the Second Division title twice, in 1919-20 and 1949-50 and have finished runners-up on two occasions, in 1908-09 and 1932-33. In 1977-78 they took third place in the Second Division to gain promotion.

Spurs have suffered relegation from the top flight four times: in 1914-15, 1927-28, 1934-35 and 1976-77.

When they went down in 1927-28 they heard the news while on tour to Holland!

Still To Play

Of the current members of the Nationwide Football League, Spurs have still to play the following clubs at League level: AFC Bournemouth, Barnet, Cambridge United, Cheltenham Town, Colchester United, Crewe Alexandra, Darlington, Exeter City, Gillingham, Halifax Town, Hartlepool United, Kidderminster Harriers, Macclesfield Town, Peterborough United, Rochdale, Rushden and Diamonds, Scunthorpe United, Shrewsbury Town, Southend United, Torquay United, Walsall, Wigan Athletic, Wrexham, Wycombe Wanderers and York City.

Football League Pot Pourri

● Spurs first applied to join the Football League for the 1896-97 season, but they received only two votes, falling way behind Blackpool (19 votes), Walsall (16), Gainsborough Trinity (15) and Burlsem Port Vale and Luton Town (10 each).
● They were finally accepted into the competition in July 1908.
● Spurs recorded their first League win on 1 September 1908, beating Wolves 3-0 at White Hart Lane in front of 20,000 fans. Vivian Woodward had the pleasure of scoring the club's first League goal.
● Leeds City, on 5 September 1908, inflicted the first League defeat on Spurs when winning 1-0 at Elland Road.
● West Bromwich Albion inflicted upon Spurs their first home League defeat, winning 3-1 at White Hart Lane on 13 March 1909 (Division 2). The Baggies were also the first team to register a League double over Spurs (that same season).
● The first League draw contested by Spurs was against Derby County (home) on 3 October 1908 (0-0). And later that season, on 27 February 1909, they recorded their first 3-3 draw v. Glossop (also at White Hart Lane).
● In 1912-13 Spurs made their worst-ever start to a League season when they failed to win any of their opening thirteen First Division matches (losing ten and drawing three). They finally broke their duck with a 1-0 home victory over Newcastle United on 23 November. (Spurs had lost their last League game at the end of the previous season).
● Spurs had five spells in the First Division of the Football League: 1909-15, 1920-28, 1933-35, 1950-77 and 1978-92. Spurs celebrated the club's 50th anniversary in 1932-33 by gaining promotion from Division Two.
● Spurs finished bottom of the First Division in 1914-15 and when League Football returned at the start of the 1919-20 campaign, the First Division was extended from 20 to 22 clubs. Chelsea who had finished 21st stayed up and were joined by Spurs' arch rivals Arsenal (who had finished 5th in Division 2 in 1915). The Division 2 champions Derby County and runners-up Preston North End were also promoted.
● Spurs claimed their first double over a League club in their first season (1908-09), beating Bolton Wanderers 2-1 at home and 1-0 away.
● Spurs last Football League game was played on 2 May 1992 when they lost 3-1 at Manchester United in front of 44,595 spectators. Gary Lineker scored the Spurs goal.
● On 18 December 1991, Spurs were defeated 2-1 at home by Liverpool in their 3,000th Football League game and this time 27,434 fans were present.
● Spurs' 5,000th goal in the Football League was scored by John Hendry in a 2-1 defeat at Norwich on 10 April 1991.
● The following clubs have never won a Football League game at White Hart Lane - Bradford Park Avenue, Brentford, Bristol Rovers, Carlisle Utd, Doncaster Rovers, Gainsborough Trinity, Glossop, Hull City, Leeds City, Mansfield Town, Millwall, Newport

Couty, Northampton Town, Oldham Athletic, Oxford Utd, Port Vale, Reading, Rotherham Utd, South Shields, Stockport County, Swansea Town (City), Swindon Town and Tranmere Rovers.
● The team that has recorded most Football League wins at White Hart Lane is Arsenal, with 19
● Manchester United - with 20 - have gained most Football League draws on Spurs' soil while Nottingham Forest 28, Sheffield Wednesday 27, Aston Villa 26, Everton 26 Stoke City 26 and Wolves 26 have suffered the most defeats.
● Spurs suffered a record 34 League defeats away to Manchester United. They failed 32 times at West Bromwich Albion.
● Spurs drew 17 Football League games at Everton, while the most away League wins achieved by Spurs against one single club is 20 at Leicester City.
● In terms of goals - Spurs have scored the most Football League goals at home against Burnley (109) and Everton (108) while away their best haul has been 76 at Newcastle. In contrast, Aston Villa have scored most at White Hart Lane (80) while on the road Spurs have conceded a record 114 at West Brom, followed by 104 at Manchester United and 95 at Liverpool.
● The most Football League goals scored against Spurs (at home and away) is 171 by Manchester United. West Brom have netted 170 and Arsenal 168.
● Spurs have scored a record 176 Football League goals against Aston Villa (H & A). They notched 170 v. Everton, 169 v. Newcastle and 168 v. Arsenal.

FOR PREMIERSHIP: 1992 ONWARDS, SEE UNDER 'P' (PREMIER LEAGUE)

FOOTBALL LEAGUE CUP

This competition has been sponsored since 1982 and since then it has also been known as the Milk Cup (to 1986), Littlewoods Cup (from 1987 to 1990), the Rumbelows Cup (1991 and 1992), the Coca-Cola Cup (1993 to 1998) and the Worthington Cup (from 1999 to date).

Spurs first entered this competition in 1966-67 and this is their full record in the League Cup (to the end of the 2000-01 season):

Venue	P	W	D	L	F	A
Home	79	52	11	16	168	79
Away	71	34	16	21	109	83
Neutral	4	3	0	1	5	3
Totals	154	89	27	38	282	165

Spurs have won the trophy three times (in 1971, 1973 and 1999) and lost in one other Final (1982). They have reached the semi-final stage on nine occasions.

Here are details of those four Final appearances:

● Spurs' first appearance in the Final came at Wembley was in February 1971. They played Third Division Aston Villa, who were the underdogs, but it never showed on the day as the accustomed 100,000 spectators (paying £132,000 in gate money) came close to witnessing an upset as Villa matched their top Division opponents kick for kick in an enthralling contest. Andy Lochead knows he should have scored for Villa to give them a deserved lead and Pat McMahon clipped the crossbar. But somehow a hesitant Spurs survived and two late goals (in the 78th and 81st minutes) by Martin Chivers saw them 'pinch' the trophy from under Villa's noses.
● Two years later - on 3 March 1973 - Spurs re-visited Wembley to play relegation-threatened Norwich City in their second

Spurs ended the season as League Champions of 1961 and were presented with the trophy at White Hart Lane

League Cup Final. It was not a great game, far too many mis-placed passes and in the end it took a 72nd minute goal by substitute Ralph Coates (following a long throw-in by Martin Chivers and touched on by Martin Peters) to maintain Spurs' record of never losing a major Final. A happy Mike England went up to collect the trophy again. The official attendance was given 100,000.

● The 1982 Final (played on 13 March in front of another 100,000 crowd) saw Spurs beaten 3-1 by Liverpool after extra-time. The scores were level at 1-1 at the end of 90 minutes but the Merseysiders were far superior after that and won well. Steve Archibald gave Spurs the lead on 11 minutes but after that it was only some great defending that kept the Reds out - until Ronnie Whelan deservedly equalised with just three minutes remaining. The Irishman then gave Liverpool the lead in the 111th minute before Ian Rush hammered a third nail into Spurs' coffin with 90 seconds remaining.

● Spurs played Leicester City in their fourth League Cup Final on 21 March 1999 - a repeat of the 1961 FA Cup Final at the same venue (Wembley). This time 77,892 fans saw Allan Nielsen's late, late goal (headed home from three yards in the second minute of added time) decide the issue in Spurs' favour 1-0 after a fairly even contest. Spurs' defender Justin Edinburgh was sent-off in the 63rd minute - one of the few players to be dismissed at Wembley in a competitive game.

Football League Cup Fact File

● Spurs' first League Cup opponents were West Ham United (away) in their opening game (round two) on 14 September 1966. They lost 1-0 in front of 34,068 fans. In this heated encounter, striker Alan Gilzean became the first Spurs player to receive his marching orders in the competition.

● Spurs registered their first win in the League Cup on 4 September 1968, beating Aston Villa 4-1 away in a 2nd round tie. Martin Chivers scored a hat-trick.

● Spurs reached the semi-final stage in 1968-69, but lost over two legs to arch rivals Arsenal (beaten 1-0 away, 1-1 home). Over

111,000 fans witnessed the two matches. Earlier Jimmy Greaves had netted a hat-trick in a 6-3 third round win over Exeter City.

● After going out in the second round to Wolves in 1969-70, Spurs went on to win the trophy for the first time the following season, ousting Swansea, Sheffield United, West Bromwich Albion (5-0), Coventry City and Bristol City (in the semi-finals) before taking on and beating Aston Villa at Wembley.

● Spurs reached the semi-final stage of the League Cup on four occasions in the space of five years (1968-73). They qualified for the Final twice (in 1971 and 1973) and won the trophy each time.

● As holders, Spurs reached the semi-final stage in 1971-972, but lost to London neighbours Chelsea 4-3 on aggregate.

● Spurs won the Cup for the second time in three years in 1973. On the way to the Final they knocked out Huddersfield Town, Middlesbrough (after three tries), Millwall, Liverpool (in a replay) and Wolves (after extra-time in the two legged semi-final).. Norwich were beaten in the Final.

● As holders once more, Spurs succumbed to QPR in the second round in 1973-74 and went out at the same stage to Middlesbrough twelve months later.

● A place in the last four was gained in 1975-76 after wins over Watford, Crewe Alexandra, West Ham Utd (after a replay) and Doncaster Rovers. Spurs couldn't get past Newcastle who came back from a goal down to win 3-2 in the two-legged semi-final.

● Over a period of four seasons - 1976-77 to 1979-80 - Spurs were disappointing in the League Cup, going out to in turn to Wrexham (round 3), Coventry City (round 3), Swansea City (round 2) and Manchester United (round 2). They were beaten at home by the first three named clubs.

● In 1980-81, West Ham United defeated Spurs 1-0 at Upton Park in a 5th round tie - after three other London clubs had fallen by the wayside in earlier rounds: Leyton Orient, Crystal Palace (when Glenn Hoddle was sent-off) and Arsenal.

● Manchester United, Wrexham, Fulham, Nottingham Forest and West Bromwich Albion were Spurs' victims prior to their 3-1 extra-time defeat in the 1982 Final by Liverpool. Tony Galvin

(Spurs) and Dutch midfielder Maarten Jol (WBA) were both sent-off in a first leg semi-final flare-up at The Hawthorns which ended 0-0, Spurs winning the return game 1-0 thanks to Micky Hazard's fine goal.

● Burnley won a 5th round tie by 4-1 at White Hart Lane in 1982-83 - Spurs' heaviest home defeat in the competition so far.

● In 1983-84 Spurs went out to Arsenal (beaten 2-1 at home in round 3); they fell to Sunderland in round 4 in 1984-85 (after beating Hartlepool United 9-1 on aggregate in the previous round) and lost to Portsmouth (at the third attempt) also in round 4, in 1985-86.

● Arsenal were again Spurs' destroyers in the 1986-87 tournament, winning the semi-final replay 2-1 after an initial two-legged aggregate scoreline of 2-2. In earlier rounds Spurs had taken out Barnsley, Birmingham City (5-0), Cambridge United and West Ham United.

● After defeating lowly Torquay United in the second round in 1987-88, Spurs fell at the next hurdle to Aston Villa.

● In 1988-89 victories over Notts County and Blackburn Rovers preceded a 4th round exit at the hands of Southampton.

● Spurs went one round further in 1889-90, losing to Nottingham Forest 3-2 at home after eliminating Southend United (on away goals), Manchester United (3-0 away) and Tranmere Rovers. Paul Stewart was sent-off against the Shrimpers in the 3-2 second leg defeat at Roots Hall.

● Wins over Hartlepool Utd (7-1 on aggregate), Bradford City and Sheffield Utd had set Spurs up for a possible Final place in 1990-91 but they were beaten by Chelsea 3-0 at home in round 5.

● Wins over Swansea City (5-2 over two legs), Grimsby Town, Coventry City and Norwich City took Spurs into the last four in 1991-92, but they were denied a trip to Wembley by their previous season's FA Cup opponents Nottingham Forest, who won the two-legged semi-final 3-2 on aggregate.

● Forest again put Spurs out of the League Cup in 1992-93, winning a 4th round tie 2-0.

● Another Midland club - Aston Villa - ended Spurs' run in 1993-94, after earlier round victories over Burnley (when Darren Caskey saw 'red'), Derby County and Blackburn Rovers.

● Notts County (by 3-0 after Ilie Dumistrescu's dismissal)) and Coventry City (by 3-2) both beat Spurs in 3rd round ties in the 1994-95 and 1995-96 competitions respectively. In the former Spurs had whipped Watford 8-6 over two legs with Jurgen Klinsmann scoring a hat-trick in the 6-3 win at Vicarage Road.

● Spurs suffered their heaviest League Cup defeat to date when they crashed 6-1 at Bolton in the 4th round in 1996-97 and the following season they were dismissed in the 3rd round by Jim Smith's Derby County who won 2-1 at White Hart Lane.

● After a break of 17 years Spurs reached the League Cup Final for a fourth time in 1998-99....and they duly claimed their third success at Leicester City's expense, thanks to Allan Nielsen's late, late goal and despite Justin Edinburgh becoming one of only a handful of players sent-off at Wembley. In the 2nd, 3rd, 4th and 5th rounds Spurs defeated Brentford, Northampton, Liverpool and Manchester United in that order, before accounting for Wimbledon over two tough legs in the semi-final, Steffen Iversen scoring in the second leg at Selhurst Park to decide the issue.

● As holders of the Cup, Spurs were dismissed 3-1 by London rivals Fulham - then members of the Nationwide League Division One - at Craven Cottage in a 3rd round encounter in 1999-2000. A year later they lost to First Division Birmingham City 3-1 at White Hart Lane after dismissing Brentford over two legs in the previous round (Neil Sullivan was sent-off in the 0-0 draw at Griffin Park).

● Steve Perryman (66), Gary Mabbutt (62), Paul Allen (44), Glenn Hoddle (44) and Pat Jennings (39) have made most League Cup appearances for Spurs, whilst Martin Chivers (23), Clive Allen (13)

Spurs, winners of the Football League Cup in 1999 beating Leicester City with a late goal from Allan Nielsen

and Martin Peters (12) have scored most goals.
- Allen scored a record 12 League Cup goals in the 1986-87, netting in every round up to Spurs' defeat in the semi-finals at the hands of their arch rivals Arsenal.

FOOTBALL LEAGUE JUBILEE FUND
Summary:

P	W	D	L	F	A
2	1	0	1	1	2

Spurs, like vitually every other club in the country, played two Football League Jubilee Fund games in the late 1930s and both were against their arch rivals from Highbury:

Aug 1938 Arsenal 0 Spurs 2 (Morrison, Lyman)   Att. 41,997
Aug 1939 Spurs 0 Arsenal 1 (Drury)   Att. 32,702

Bert Sproston, signed from Leeds United, made his debut at right-back for Spurs in the 1938 game and only four players - Percy Hooper, Vic Buckingham, Johnny Morrison and Colin Lyman - played in both matches for Spurs.
Hooper was injured in the second game when saving a penalty taken by Arsenal's Alf Kirchen.

FOREIGN (OVERSEAS) BORN PLAYERS
Here is an unofficial list of players, all of whom were born 'overseas' (in a foreign country) who have been associated with Spurs at various levels, whether on trial, as a guest, on loan or as an amateur:

Player	Country of Birth
Mark Arber	South Africa
Ossie Ardiles	Argentina
Espen Baardsen	USA
Gudni Bergsson	Iceland
Nicola Berti	Italy
Goran Bunjevcevic	Yugoslavia
John Chiedozie	Nigeria
Nico Claesen	Belgium
Maurizio Consorti	Italy
Jose Dominguez	Portugal
Ilie Dumitrescu	Romania
Quinton Fortune	South Africa
Steffen Freund	Germany
Luigi Galetti	Italy
Len Garwood	India
David Ginola	France
Richard Gough	Sweden
Frode Grodas	Norway
Luca Di Giuliantonio	Italy
Steffen Iversen	Norway
Jon Jonsson	Sweden
Yannick Kamanan	France
Kasey Keller	USA
Jurgen Klinsmann	West Germany
Willem Korsten	Holland
Oyvind Leonhardsen	Norway
Destin Makumbu	Congo DR
Johnny Metgod	Holland
Nayim (Amar)	Morocco
Allan Nielsen	Denmark
Roger Nilsen	Norway
Ludwig Norbert	France
Jonatan Partin	Sweden
Jimmy Pass	India
Gica Popescu	Romania
Gustavo Poyet	Uruguay
Sergei Rebrov	USSR
Ronny Rosenthal	Israel
Moussa Saib	Algeria
Max Seeburg	Germany
Hans Segers	Holland
Brian Statham	Zimbabwe
Mauricio Taricco	Argentina
Erik Thorstvedt	Norway
Paolo Tramezzani	Italy
Pat van den Hauwe	Belgium
Ramon Vega	Switzerland
Ricky Villa	Argentina
Wilf Waller	South Africa
Christian Ziege	Germany

- Despite their foreign-sounding names, players Milija Aleksic, Len Duquemin (Guernsey), Harry Erentz and Tony Marchi were, in fact, all born in the U.K.
Spurs' head coach Christian Gross was born in Switzerland.

FOREIGN CONNECTION
The following personnel (including reserve and senior players, trialists, Amateurs, Wartime guests, managers, coaches, trainers, internal staff, etc) were associated with 'foreign' clubs in various capacities before or after serving with Spurs.

Jack Acquroff	Metro & Caledonioans (Tasmania), Tasmania FA
Milija Aleksic	South African Rebel Tour
Clive Allen	Bordeaux
Joe Allen	Racing Club De Roubaix
Les Allen	Greek Club (manager)
Arthur Archer	Coach/trainer of FC Ghent (Belgium) and also in Germany
Steve Archibald	CF Barcelona, Espanyol
Ossie Ardiles	(as a player): Cordoba Instituto, FC Huracan, Red Star Cordoba (all Argentina), Fort Lauderdale Strikers & Paris St Germain; (as a manager/coach): Deportivo Guadalajara (Mexico), Shimizu S-Pulse (Japan), Croatia Zagreb & Yokohama F Marinos (Japan).
Gerry Armstrong	Real Mallorca
Espen Baardsen	FC Grodan (Norway), San Francisco All-Blacks
Peter Baker	Abbinton FC, South Africa (coach), Durban United (player & manager)
Phil Beal	Los Angeles Aztecs, Memphis Rogues
Walter Bellamy	FC New Camp, Gibraltar
Gudni Bergsson	TSV 1860 Munich, FC Valur
Nicola Berti	Parma, Fiorentina, Inter Milan, Deportivo Alaves (Spain)
Ted Birnie	Mulheim, Germany (player-coach)
Mark Bowen	Shimizu SP (Japan)
Robert Brace	Waterschei (Belgium), Saarbrucken (W Germany)
Alan Brazil	Detroit Express, FC Baden (Switzerland)
John Brearley	Berlin Victoria (coach)
Garry Brooke	GAIS Gothenburg (Sweden), Groningen (Holland)
Johnny Brooks	Toronto FC (Canada)
Noel Brotherston	Montola (Sweden)

Bill Brown	Toronto Falcon (Canada)		and Israel.
Jimmy Brown	Bayonne Rovers (New Jersey), New	Roger Gibbins	New England Teamen
	York Giants, Newark Skeeters,	Terry Gibson	GAIS (Sweden)
	Brookline Wanderers, coach at	Alan Gilzean	Highland Park FC (South Africa)
	Brunswick Senior School	David Ginola	Paris St Germain, Toulon, Racing Club
	& Greenwich		de Paris, Brest
	High School, Connecticut (USA),	John Gorman	Tampa Bay Rowdies
	Greenport United, USA (player &	Richard Gough	Southern Transvaal, San Jose,
	president), Polish Falcons (manager)		Wits University team (S Africa),
Vic Buckingham	Coach of Moss FC (Norway),		Northern Spirit (Australia N/C)
	manager of Ajax, Amsterdam,	George Graham	California Surf
	CF Barcelona, Ethnikos (Greece) &	Phil Gray	Fortuna Sittard (Holland),
	Sevilla (Spain)		Nancy (France)
Goran Bunjevcevic	Red Star Belgrade, Graficar Belgrade,	Jimmy Greaves	AC Milan
	Rad Belgrade	Frode Grodas	Lillestroem, FC Schalke 04
Keith Burkinshaw	Bahrain (national coach), Sporting	Christian Gross	Player with SV Hongg,
	Lisbon (coach)		Grasshopper-Club Zurich,
Walter Bull	Buenos Aires (coach)		Laussanne-Sports, Xamax
John Cameron	Dresden FC (Germany) (Coach)		Neuegburg, Vfl Bochum, FC St Gallen
Jesse Carver	Coach/manager of Italian clubs AS		(1982) & FC Lugano. Head coach of
	Roma, Genoa, Inter Milan, Juventus,		FC Wil & Grasshopper-Club Zurich
	Lazio and Torino. Also coach in		& FC Basel
	Netherlands, Portugal & USA.	Luca Di Giuliantonio	SS Lazio (trialist)
Wayne Cegielski	FC Schalke 04	Charlie Handley	Berne, Switzerland (coach)
Martin Chivers	Servette (Switzerland),	Allan Harris	Barcelona (assistant-manager)
	Vard (of Norway) (player-coach)	Trevor Hartley	Singapore (Director of Coaching)
Nico Claesen	RSC Antwerp, Patro Eisden,	Ricky Hill	Le Havre
	FC Seraing,	Glenn Hoddle	AS Monaco
	Standard Liege, Vfb Stuttgart	Phil Holder	Memphis Rogues
Ray Clarke	Ajax Amsterdam, RFC Bruges,	Jimmy Holmes	Vancouver Whitecaps
	Sparta (Holland)	Gareth Howells	Malmo FF, Hellenic (South Africa)
Shaun Close	Halmstad (Sweden)	Roger Hoy	Palm Beach (Australia)
Ralph Coates	St George's FC (Sydney)	Percy Humphreys	Coach in Switzerland
Allan Cockram	San Jose Earthquakes	Steffen Iversen	Astor, FC Nationalkam,
Alfie Conn	Pittsburgh Spirit,		Rosenborg BK
	San Jose Earthquakes	David Jenkins	South African football
Maurizio Consorti	SS Lazio (junior trialist)	Jon Jonsson	FC Hasslehom (Sweden)
Pat Corbett	Finland (player), GAIS (Sweden)	Johnny Jordan	Juventus
Peter Crouch	FC Hassleholm (Sweden)	Bill Julian	Coach in Holland
Barry Daines	Bulova (Hong Kong)	Yannick Kamanan	FC Le Mans
Ally Dick	Ajax Amsterdam	Kasey Keller	University of Portland FC,
Matt Dillon	Montreal Olympic,		Portland Timbers,
	New York Cosmos,		Rayo Vallecano (Spain)
	Washington Diplomats	Joe Kinnear	Malaysia (national team
Jose Dominguez	Benfica, Sporting Club de Portugal,		manager/coach),
	Sintrense, Fafe.		Nepal (trialist manager),
Ilie Dumitrescu	Steaua Bucharest, Sevilla (Spain),		Sharjah, of UAE, (manager/coach)
	Clube de Futbol (Mexico),	John Kirwan	Coach in Holland &
	Otelul Galati (coach)		FC Livorno (Italy)
Jim Elliott	Coach in the Balkans, Guatemala,	Jurgen Klinsmann	Bayern Munich, AS Monaco,
	Sweden & Switzerland, Fenerbahce		Inter Milan, Sampdoria
	(Turkey), Valencia (manager)	Willem Korsten	Geen FC, Vitesse Arnhem, NEC
Mike England	Seattle Sounders, Team America		Nijmigen
Ray Evans	California Surf, St Louis Stars, Seattle	John Lacy	FC Stanunsgund (Norway)
	Sounders (USA)	Terry Lee	North Island (New Zealand)
Les Ferdinand	Besiktas	Oyvind Leonhardsen	FC Clausenengen, FC Molde,
Jack Finch	Iceland (as coach)		Rosenborg
Bobby Flavell	Marios Club, Bogota (Colombia)	David Levene	Northern France
Quinton Fortune	Atletico Madrid	Gary Lineker	CF Barcelona, Grampus 8 (Japan)
Steffen Freund	Borussia Dortmund, FC Motorsud,	Harry Lowe	Deportivo Espanol,
	FC Stahl Brandenburg, FC Schalke 04		Barcelona (coach)
Steve Hodge	Hong Kong Football	Don McAllister	Tampa Bay Rowdies, Washington
Paul Gascoigne	SS Lazio		Diplomats
Jack Gibbons	Coached in Belgium, South Africa	Jim McCormick	Sliema Wanderers of Malta (coach),

	Turkey (national coach)
Chris McGrath	South China, Tulsa Roughnecks
Dave Mackay	Al Arabi Sporting Club, Kuwait (manager), Alba Shabab, Dubai (manager), Zamalek of Egypt (manager)
John Madden	Slavia Prague (player-coach)
Tony Marchi	Lanerossi Vicenza, Torino
Les Medley	Toronto Greenbacks, Ulster United (Canada), Randfontein, South Africa (player-coach)
Johnny Metgod	AZ 67 Alkmar, DWS Amsterdam, Feyenoord, Haarlem, Real Madrid
Les Miller	Souchaux (France)
Paul Miller	Skied Oslo
Fred Milnes	USA football
Ian Moores	Western Suburbs (Sydney), Apoel (Tel Aviv), Lanskrona Bols (Sweden)
Nayim	Barcelona Athletico, CF Barcelona, Real Zaragoza
Jimmy Neighbour	Seattle Sounders
Allan Nielsen	Brondby IF, FC Esbjerg, Bayern Munich, FC Sion, Odense, FC Copenhagen
Roger Nilsen	Viking Stavanger, Grazer AK (Austria)
Ludwig Norbert	Paris St German, Red Star FC (France)
John Oakes	Sweden (coach)
Charlie O'Hagan	Coach in Germany (FC Berlin)
Keith Osgood	Helsinki
Tim O'Shea	Hong Kong
Jonatan Partin	Edsbyns IF
Steve Perryman	Manager of IK Start (Norway) & Shimizu S-Pulse (Japan); also assistant-manager of latter club. Kashiwa Reysol (coach)
Gica Popescu	PSV Eindhoven, Barcelona, Galatasaray
Derek Possee	Vancouver Whitecaps, Canadian FA (coach)
Gustavo Poyet	Bella Vista, River Plate, Grenoble, Real Zaragoza
John Pratt	Portland Timbers
Paul Price	Minnesota Kicks
Sergei Rebrov	Shakhter Donetsk, Dynamo Kiev
Matt Reilly	Freemantle (Australia)
Jimmy Robertson	Seattle Sounders
Mark Robson	FC Rosenburg
Ronny Rosenthal	Maccabi Haifa, FC Bruges, Standard Liege
Jack Rowley	Ajax (manager)
Moussa Saib	Jeunesse Sportive Kabylie, AJ Auxerre, Valencia, Al Nasr
Vinny Samways	Las Palmas
Arthur Sanders	Rosario (Argentina)
Hans Segers	PSV Eindhoven
George Skinner	Finnish Olympic Team (manager)
Bert Smith	Young Boys of Berne (player-coach)
Reg Smith	Durban City (player-coach), Addington FC (player, coach manager), Cape Town City (manager)... all in South Africa.

Graeme Souness	Montreal Olympic, Sampdoria, Galatasaray (manager)
Robbie Stepney	Bahrain FA & National coach; coach to IFK Osterund and Haggenas (Sweden)
Mauricio Taricco	Argentinos Juniors
Alton Thelwell	FC Hassleholm (Sweden)
Erik Thorstvedt	AIK (Norway), IFK Gothenburg, Viking Stavanger, Borussia Mönchengladbach
Jimmy Townley	Borussia Mönchengladbach, Hamburg Victoria, IFK Gothenburg, St Gall (Switzerland) & coach in Switzerland
Paolo Tramezzani	FC Prato, Cosena, Lucchesse, Inter Milan (2 spells), Venezia, Cesena, Picenza, Pistoese (all clubs in Italy).
Ramon Vega	FC Trimbach (two spells), FC Olten, Grasshopper Club Zurich (Switzerland), Cagliari
Tery Venables	Australia (national coach), CF Barcelona (manager)
Ricky Villa	Athletico Tucuman (Argentina), Colombia, Fort Lauderdale Strikers (NASL), Quilmes FC (Argentina), Racing Club Buenos Aires (Argentina), Deportivo Cali (Colombia), Defensa y Justicia (Argentina). Also coach of Quilmes & Defensa y Justicia
Chris Waddle	Olympique Marseille
Steve Walford	Lai Sung (Hong Kong) & Turkey
Des Walker	Sampdoria

Tony Want	Minnesota Kicks, Philadelphia Atoms
Jack Whent	Canadian football
Keith Weller	New England Teamen, Fort Lauderdale Strikers, Tacoma Stars, Dallas Sidekicks (coach)
Charlie Williams	Danish Olympic National Team coach, Olympique Club, Lille (manager), Le Havre, Holland (coach), Rio Grande De Sol , Brazil (trainer)
Igal Yawetz	Haifa Club Tel Aviv (Spurs director)
Terry Yorath	Vancouver Whitecaps
Christian Ziege	Sudstern 08, TSV Rudlow, Hertha 03 Zehlendorf, AC Milan, Bayern Munich

FOREMAN, GEORGE ALEXANDER

George Foreman guested for Spurs during the Second World War and did very well, scoring 21 goals in only 15 League South games. He was signed on a permanent basis by the club in February 1946 and remained at White Hart Lane until the summer of 1949 when he was released (having been replaced by the Channel Islander Len Duquemin). His Spurs record (at first team level) was 39 goals in 56 appearances.

Born in Walthamstow on 1 March 1914, Foreman was a hard-shooting centre-forward who played for Leyton, Walthamstow Avenue and West Ham United (signed in March 1938) before the War. He also guested for Clapton Orient and Crystal Palace during the hostilities and won a Football League War Cup medal in 1940 with the Hammers.

Foreman died in his home district of Walthamstow on 19 June 1969.

FORMATION OF CLUB

The exact date or precise details of when Tottenham Hotspur Football Club was founded or formed has never really been clarified. Suffice to say it was probably either in late August or the early part of September 1882 as Hotspur FC.

It is known, however, that subscriptions to join were received by the club on 5 September 1882.

These were the eleven founder members, most of them local cricketers, who wanted something to do in the cold winter months - E Beaven, Bobby Buckle (the club's first appointed secretary), Fred Dexter, Stuart Leaman (the first registered goalkeeper), E Wall and three sets of brothers, the Andersons (J & T), the Caseys (LR & Ham, the latter was also called Sam) and the Thompsons (Jack & Peter).

An uncle of the Thompson brothers loaned Spurs his cricket pitch to train on and contest their early matches, at the start of 1882-83, shortly after the cricket season had ended.

In no time at all, eight more members were recruited and things began to happen quickly, Spurs playing their first challenge/friendly match against Radicals on 30 September 1882. They lost by two goals but the players weren't too downhearted as they knew they had started the ball rolling.

LR Casey was appointed the club's first treasurer, his father providing the first set of goal-posts which were painted blue and white! When not in use, these were stored in the nearby railway station. The first ball also came via the Casey family and the local YMCA hostel (Percy House) was used as changing rooms.

The following season Spurs fulfilled at least 20 fixtures, starting off with a 9-0 home win over Brownlow Rovers (this being recorded as the club's first-ever victory). The team that participated in this

game which was staged on The Marshes (a strip of public land between The River Lea and the Great Eastern railway line) was: Leaman; Tyrell, Dexter, H Casey, Lovis, Lomax, Cottrell, Watson, Fisher, Harston and Buckle.

The club's first Annual General Meeting (under the presidency of John Ripsher) had taken place in August 1883 (seemingly held under a gas light on Tottenham High Road) when 21 players turned up. The meeting was organised by Jim Randall, clerk of the Edmonton County Court. He joined the club as a player and was made captain, with Billy Harston his understudy, although he (Randall) did not appear in the first game. Harston, an inside-forward, had a fine career with Spurs and later became the club's assistant-secretary. In the early 1940s he was still working at White Hart Lane as a press steward.

After the name Tottenham had been added to Hotspur (circa 1884) Dorset Villas now became Spurs' changing rooms, then using the Red House (number 748 High Road) from 1886 to 1891, this being their first real secure HQ. In fact the Red House later became the club's offices at the White Hart Lane ground. Spurs also hired rooms from time to time (for big matches especially) in three other pubs, the Milford Inn, The Park and Northumberland Arms.

Now established, Spurs made rapid progress...an enclosed ground (Northumberland Park), entry into the Southern League, knockout Cup football and much more.

FORSTER, MATTHEW

Matt Forster was a reliable, strong-tackling full-back who joined Spurs in October 1919 from Newburn FC in the North-East of England. He was understudy to Messrs Clay and McDonald for practically three years before establishing himself in the first XI at White Hart Lane, taking over the left-back slot halfway through the 1922-23 campaign. He held firm and went on to appear in 271 first team matches (236 in the Football League) up to July 1930 when he was transferred to Reading. He later returned to London to assist Charlton Athletic, retiring from the game after one season at The Valley. He then became coach at Goldsmith's College (New Cross) and later assisted Bexleyheath & Welling before rounding off his footballing days as scout for Fulham (1938-39).

Born in Newburn-on-Tyne on 24 August 1900, a Northumberland Schools representative player, he signed for Scotswood FC as a 15 year-old before joining Newburn. Forster died at St Albans, Herts on 18 October 1976.

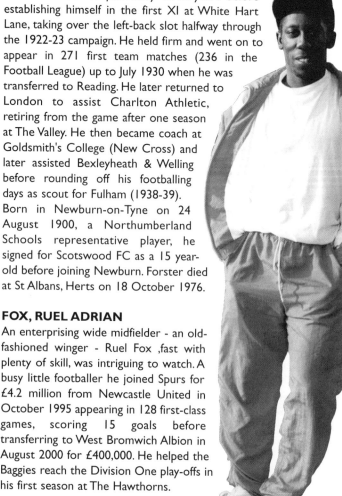

FOX, RUEL ADRIAN

An enterprising wide midfielder - an old-fashioned winger - Ruel Fox ,fast with plenty of skill, was intriguing to watch. A busy little footballer he joined Spurs for £4.2 million from Newcastle United in October 1995 appearing in 128 first-class games, scoring 15 goals before transferring to West Bromwich Albion in August 2000 for £400,000. He helped the Baggies reach the Division One play-offs in his first season at The Hawthorns.

Born in Ipswich on 14 January 1968, he joined his neighbours Norwich City as an apprentice in June 1984, turning professional at Carrow Road a week after his 18th birthday. He went on to net 25 goals in more than 200 appearances for the Canaries who then sold him to Newcastle for £2.25 million in February 1994. Capped twice by England 'B', Fox had 70 outings and scored 14 goals during his time at St James' Park.

FRANCIS, GERRY CHARLES JAMES

As a bustling midfield player, Gery Francis made over 500 League appearances (69 goals scored) between 1968 and 1986, while serving with Queen's Park Rangers (two spells), Crystal Palace, Coventry City, Exeter City, Cardiff City, Swansea City, Portsmouth and Bristol Rovers. He also served Wimbledon as a player-coach and gained 12 full caps for England, plus another six at Under-23 level.

He was appointed player-manager of Bristol Rovers in July 1987 retaining his position as manager until May 1991, also assuming the role of club director. He guided Rovers to the Third Division title in 1989-90 and took them to Wembley for the Leyland Daf Trophy that same season. He then returned to his first club, QPR, as team manager (June 1991) and stayed at Loftus Road until taking over the hot seat at White Hart Lane in November 1994, Ray Wilkins replacing him as Rangers' boss. He failed to bring any success to Spurs and left the club in November 1997, allowing Christian Gross to move into office (after Chris Hughton had held the fort on a temporary basis).

In October 1998, Francis went back to Queen's Park Rangers once again, but couldn't refloat a sinking ship and with a relegation fight imminent and the Second Division of the Nationwide League looming, he called it a day and moved upstairs! Returned to Bristol Rovers as manager (July 2001)

Francis was born in Chiswick on 6 December 1951.

FREEBOROUGH, JAMES

Defender Jimmy Freeborough played for Stockport County before making 14 first-class appearances for Spurs (one goal scored) in a two-year spell at White Hart Lane (1904-06). Later he assisted Leeds City and Bradford Park Avenue.

FRIENDLY MATCHES

On 30 September 1882, Spurs played their first-ever game as an organised football team, losing by two goals in a friendly against a local team called the Radicals.

The following season (1883-84) more friendly matches were arranged (at least 20 were started) and the first win was recorded, 9-0 over Brownlow Rovers (at home) on 6 October. Spurs also gained revenge over Latymer, beating them twice by the same score of 2-0.

In the 1884-85 season a total of 29 friendly matches were fulfilled and among the many victories were those of 4-0 v. Remington, 5-0 v. Grange Park (this was a 60-minute contest), 4-0 and 5-0 v. Sekforde Rovers, 4-0 v. Tottenham (a local club) and 5-0 v. Woodgrange (this game was of 40 minutes duration).

A nine-goal thriller ended Spurs 4 Woodgrange 5 in mid-October. Since then Spurs have played many more friendly matches, at home and away in the UK, and also overseas, and listed here are some of the fixtures fulfilled (given in order of play).

* Note some testimonial/benefit matches, tours (etc) have been listed elsewhere.

1885-86

v. Silesia College	(h)	won 4-3
v. Westminster Rovers	(h)	won 3-2
v. South Hackney	(a)	won 3-1
v. Dalston Rovers	(h)	won 3-0
v. St Martin's	(h)	won 3-0
v. South Hackney	(h)	won 8-0
v. Ilford	(h)	won 6-1
v. Rutland	(h)	won 5-0
v. Enfield Lock	(h)	won 7-0
v. Park	(h)	won 8-0

1886-87

v. South Hackney	(h)	won 13-1
v. Fillebrook	(a)	lost 1-4
v. Oana	(a)	won 5-0
v. Dreadnought	(h)	won 6-0
v. Park	(h)	won 4-1
v. Enfield Lock	(h)	won 7-1

1887-88

v. Buckhurst Hill	(h)	won 6-1
v. Priory	(a)	won 3-0
v. Luton Town	(a)	won 2-1
v. St Bride's	(h)	won 3-2
v. St Bride's	(a)	won 3-0

1888-89

v. Royal Arsenal	(a)	won 1-0
v. Clapton	(h)	lost 2-5
v. Plaistow	(h)	won 4-0
v. Old St Mark's	(h)	won 5-1
v. Upton Excelsior	(h)	drew 3-3
v. Bowes Park	(a)	won 4-0
v. Orion Gymnasium	(h)	won 6-1

1889-90

v. Westminster	(h)	won 13-0
v. Vulcan	(h)	won 5-1
v. Edmonton	(h)	lost 1-4
v. Maidenhead	(a)	won 3-2

1890-91

v. Hampstead	(h)	won 6-3
v. Luton Town	(a)	lost 1-4
v. Old St Stephen's	(h)	won 3-0

1891-92

v. Hampstead	(h)	won 6-2
v. Uxbridge	(h)	won 3-0
v. Clapton	(a)	won 2-0
v. Grenadier Guards	(h)	won 9-0
v. Casuals	(h)	won 3-1

1892-93

v. Paddington	(h)	won 10-0
v. Royal Arsenal Ath	(h)	won 3-0
v. 2nd Coldstream Gds	(h)	won 6-0
v. University	(h)	won 5-4
v. Caledonian Thistle	(h)	won 5-0
v. London Welsh	(h)	won 4-1

1893-94
v. Enfield (a) lost 1-5
v. Casuals (h) lost 0-1
v. South'ton St Mary's (a) lost 0-1
v. Polytechnic (h) won 5-0
v. 2nd Scots Guards (h) won 3-1
v. Slough (h) won 2-0
v. New Brompton (a) drew 3-3

1894-95
v. Casuals (h) won 3-1
v. Sheffield & D.L. (h) won 7-1
v. West Liverpool (h) won 3-0
v. Vampires (h) won 4-1
v. London Caledon's (h) won 5-1
v. Liverpool Casuals (h) won 6-0
v. Bristol South End (a) won 7-0

1895-96
v. Royal Engineers (a) won 3-0
v. Casuals (h) won 3-2
v. Clapton (a) lost 4-5
v. Ilford (h) won 2-0
v. Royal Artillery (h) lost 1-2
v. Luton Town (h) lost 0-2
v. Casuals (h) won 3-1
v. Millwall Athletic (a) lost 3-5
v. Accrington (h) won 3-0
v. Freemantle FC (h) won 2-0
v. Reading (h) won 2-1
v. Millwall Athletic (h) drew 1-1
v. Notts County (h) lost 1-5
v. Luton Town (a) lost 0-9
v. Clapton (h) won 4-0
v. Burslem Port Vale (h) won 4-0
v. 1st Scots Guards (h) won 8-0
v. Uxbridge (h) won 4-0
v. Woolwich Arsenal (a) won 3-1
v. Manchester Reg (h) won 8-0
v. London Caledonians (a) won 5-0
v. Reading (a) won 3-2
v. Middlesbrough (h) won 5-0
v. Swindon Town (h) lost 2-3
v. Aston Villa (h) lost 1-3
v. Swindon Town (a) won 2-0
v. South'ton St Mary's (a) lost 1-4
v. Woolwich Arsenal (h) won 3-2

1896-97
v. Rossendale (h) won 7-0
v. London Caledonians (h) drew 3-3
v. Casuals (h) won 4-0
v. Casuals (a) won 4-1
v. 1st Coldstream Grds (h) won 4-0
v. Royal Scots Greys (h) won 5-0
v. South'ton St Mary's (h) won 3-1
v. Luton Town (a) lost 0-3
v. Blackpool (h) lost 0-2
v. Clapton (a) won 2-1
v. Vampires (h) won 4-0
v. Northfleet (h) won 4-0
v. Aston Villa (h) drew 2-2

v. 3rd Grenadier Grds (h) won 9-3
v. South'ton St Mary's (a) lost 0-2
v. Nottingham Forest (h) drew 1-1
v. Blackburn Rovers (h) lost 1-2
v. Everton (h) lost 1-2

1897-98
v. Glossop North End (h) won 3-2
v. Royal Scots Fuslrs (h) won 12-0
v. Chorley (h) won 3-1
v. 2nd Scots Guards (h) won 4-1
v. 3rd Grenadier Grds (h) won 4-0
v. Reading (h) won 2-1
v. New Brompton (h) won 3-0
v. Gravesend United (a) lost 0-3
v. Kettering (h) won 1-0
v. Ilkeston Town (h) won 4-2
v. Stockton (h) won 3-0
v. Sussex County (a) won 2-1
v. Sheffield United (h) drew 1-1
v. St Barnard's (h) won 4-0
v. Chesham (a) won 4-2
v. Tunbridge Wells (a) won 5-0
v. Sunderland (h) lost 0-2
v. Lincoln City (h) won 2-1
v. Reading (a) drew 3-3
v. Aston Villa (h) lost 2-3
v. Woolwich Arsenal (a) lost 0-3
v. Bolton Wanderers (h) drew 2-2

1898-99
v. Gainsborough Tr. (h) won 6-2
v. Surrey Wanderers (h) won 5-0
v. Burton Wanderers (h) won 5-2

1899-1900
v. Notts County (h) won 4-1
v. Clapton (a) won 4-1
v. Southampton (a) lost 1-2
v. Southampton (h) won 4-3
v. Ilkeston Town (h) won 7-0
v. Bolton Wanderers (h) won 4-0
v. Corinthians (h) won 5-1
v. The Kaffirs (h) won 6-4
v. HR Burke's XI (h) won 12-2
v. Middlesbrough (a) drew 2-2
v. Sunderland (a) won 3-1
v. Oxford University (h) won 6-0
v. Chesterfield (h) won 7-2
v. Aston Villa (a) lost 3-4

1900-01
v. Bristol Rovers (a) lost 0-1
v. Southampton (a) won 3-1
v. Reading (h) drew 3-3
v. Millwall Athletic (a) won 2-1
v. Richmond Assoc. (h) won 8-0
v. Notts County (a) lost 1-4
v. Reading (h) drew 1-1
v. Notts County (h) drew 1-1
v. Corinthians (h) drew 2-2
v. Luton Town (h) lost 1-3
v. QPR (h) won 7-0

v. Portsmouth	(a) won 3-1	
v. Luton Town	(a) lost 0-1	
v. Preston North End	(h) drew 1-1	
v. Clapton	(h) won 3-0	
v. German Assoc.	(h) won 9-6	
v. Oxford University	(h) won 5-2	

1901-02

v. Heart of Midlothian	(h) drew 0-0
v. Sheffield United	(a) lost 1-2
v. Rest of Southern Lge	(h) won 2-0
v. Cambridge Univ.	(h) won 3-1
v. Army Association	(h) won 2-1
v. Corinthians	(a) lost 0-3
v. Everton	(a) lost 1-3
v. Heart of Midlothian	(a) lost 1-3
v. Sheffield United	(h) won 3-2
v. Portsmouth	(a) won 2-0

1902-03

v. Cambridge Univ.	(h) won 2-1
v. Corinthians	(a) won 3-1
v. London FA XI	(h) drew 2-2
v. West Norwood	(a) won 9-0
v. Corinthians	(h) drew 2-2
v. Queen's Park	(h) won 1-0
v. Nottingham Forest	(h) won 2-1

1903-04

v. New Brompton	(a) lost 0-3
v. Burnley	(h) won 4-0
v. Corinthians	(h) won 5-1

1904-05

v. Brighton & HA	(h) won 3-1
v. London FA XI	(h) won 4-1
v. Littlehampton	(a) won 7-0
v. Corinthians	(h) lost 0-2
v. Cambridge Univ.	(a) drew 4-4
v. Sheffield United	(h) drew 0-0

1905-06

v. Cambridge Univ.	(h) won 2-1
v. Corinthians	(h) won 2-0
v. Cambridge Univ.	(a) lost 1-4

1906-07

v. London Caledonians	(h) won 6-4
v. Ilford	(h) drew 4-4
v. Cambridge Univ.	(h) won 4-2
v. Corinthians	(a) lost 1-6
v. Oxford University	(h) won 2-1
v. Corinthians	(h) won 5-0
v. CW Brown's XI	(h) won 2-1

1907-08

v. Woolwich Arsenal	(h) lost 0-1
v. Chelsea	(a) drew 1-1
v. Clapton Orient	(a) lost 0-2

1908-09

v. Clapton Orient	(a) won 3-2

1909-10

v. Reading	(a) won 3-2

1911-12

v. Clapton Orient	(h) won 3-2
v. Northampton Town	(a) lost 0-2

1912-13

v. Watford	(h) drew 0-0

1913-14

v. Chelsea	(h) lost 3-7

1914-15

v. Chelsea	(a) drew 1-1
v. Fulham	(h) drew 2-2

1915-16

v. Clapton Orient	(h) lost 0-1
v. Clapton Orient	(a) lost 2-3

1916-17

v. West ham United	(a) drew 3-3

1918-19

v. Clapton Orient	(a) lost 1-6
v. Crystal Palace	(a) lost 0-3

1919-20

v. Corinthians	(h) won 4-1
v. Norwich City	(a) won 4-0

1920-21

v. Fulham	(n) won 4-0

1921-22

v. Partick Thistle	(a) lost 1-3
v. Inverness Cal'dns	(a) lost 3-6
v. Corinthians	(h) won 2-1

1922-23

v. Corinthians	(a) won 2-1
v. Llanelli	(a) lost 1-2
v. West Ham United	(h) won 5-2
v. Chelsea	(n) drew 1-1

1923-24

v. Norwich City	(a) won 3-2
v. Chelsea	(a) drew 0-0
v. West Ham United	(a) drew 1-1
v. Inter-Varsities XI	(h) won 7-1

1925-26

v. Norwich City	(n) lost 2-3
v. Hull City	(a) lost 0-5
v. West Ham United	(a) drew 1-1

1927-28

v. Ebbw Vale	(a) won 7-3

1929-30

v. Yeovil & Petters	(a) won 6-4

1930-31

v. West Ham United	(a) won 2-1
v. Huddersfield Town	(h) lost 2-4

1933-34

v. Luton Town	(a) drew 2-2

1934-35

v. Burton Town	(a) drew 2-2

1938-39

v. Arsenal	(n) lost 1-2

1939-40

v. Chelmsford City	(a) lost 2-4
v. Chelsea	(a) lost 2-4
v. West Ham United	(h) lost 0-2

1941-42

v. Crystal Palace	(a) won 5-3

1942-43

v. QPR	(a) drew 1-1
v. Charlton Athletic	(h) won 2-1
v. Fulham	(h) won 3-0
v. Clapton Orient	(h) won 4-3
v. Arsenal	(h) lost 1-2

1943-44

v. Millwall	(a) drew 0-0

1944-45

v. Coventry City	(a) lost 1-3
v. Crystal Palace	(a) lost 1-3
v. Arsenal	(h) won 4-0
v. Fulham	(h) drew 2-2

1945-46

v. Chelsea	(h) won 4-2

1946-47

v. Arsenal	(h) won 2-0

1948-49

v. Middlesbrough	(h) won 4-1
v. Hibernian	(h) lost 2-5
v. Cornwall County	(n) won 2-0

1949-50

v. Chelmsford City	(a) won 4-1
v. Hibernian	(h) lost 0-1

1950-51

v. Lovells Athletic	(a) won 8-0
v. Cardiff City	(a) won 3-2
v. Combined Liege XI	(a) won 4-1
v. Hibernian	(a) drew 0-0
v. Chelmsford City	(a) won 7-3
v. Racing Club de Paris	(a) won 4-2

1951-52

v. Copenhagen Com XI	(h) won 2-1
v. FC Austria	(n) drew 2-2
v. Hibernian	(h) lost 1-2
v. Racing Club de Paris	(a) won 2-1
v. Crittalls Athletic	(n) won 8-1

1952-53

v. West Ham United	(a) lost 1-2
v. Reading	(a) won 4-0
v. Arsenal	(a) won 2-0
v. Heart of Midlothian	(a) lost 0-2
v. Racing Club de Paris	(a) drew 1-1

1953-54

v. Hibernian	(a) won 1-0
v. Racing Club de Paris	(h) won 5-3
v. Millwall	(a) won 2-0
v. FC Austria	(h) won 3-2
v. Hibernian	(h) won 3-2

1954-55

v. Lille Olympique	(a) drew 1-1
v. QPR	(a) lost 1-2
v. Sportklub Wacker	(h) lost 1-2
v. Rot-Weiss Essen	(h) won 4-2
v. England XI	(h) lost 2-7
v. Arsenal	(h) lost 1-4
v. Racing Club de Paris	(h) won 6-0

| v. Hibernian | (a) drew 1-1 |
| v. FC Servette | (h) won 5-1 |

1955-56

v. Arhus Gymnastik.	(a) won 4-3
v. FC Vasas	(h) lost 1-2
v. Plymouth Argyle	(a) drew 0-0
v. Partick Thistle	(h) lost 0-1
v. Swansea Town	(h) won 4-1

1956-57

v. Racing Club de Paris	(h) won 2-0
v. Red banner MTK	(h) won 7-1
v. Comb. Antwerp XI	(a) won 2-1

1957-58

| v. Vfb Stuttgart | (a) won 2-1 |
| v. Hibernian | (a) lost 2-5 |

v. Swiss National XI	(a) won 5-4
v. Bristol City	(a) won 4-3
v. Vfb Stuttgart	(h) won 3-2
v. Partick Thistle	(h) won 4-1
v. Rotterdam Select	(a) won 4-1
v. Hibernian	(h) won 4-0
v. Canto Do Rio	(h) won 4-1

1958-59

v. Bela Vista	(h) won 3-1
v. Hibernian	(h) won 5-2
v. Bucharest Select XI	(h) won 4-2

1959-60

v. Reading	(a) won 5-2
v. Torpedo Moscow	(h) won 3-2
v. Crystal Palace	(a) drew 2-2
v. Juventus	(a) lost 0-2

1960-61

| v. Dynamo Tbilisi | (h) won 5-2 |

1961-62

v. Zamalek Sporting Club	(a) won 7-3
v. Arsenal	(h) won 3-1
v. Portsmouth	(a) won 3-1

1963-64

| v. Coventry City | (a) won 6-5 |

1964-65

v. Feyenoord	(a) lost 3-4
v. Copenhagen Select	(a) lost 1-2
v. Leytonstone	(a) won 5-0
v. RSC Anderlecht	(a) lost 2-4
v. Coventry City	(a) won 3-0

1965-66

v. Walton & Hersham	(a) won 8-1
v. Hungary Select XI	(h) won 4-0
v. WKS Legia Warsaw	(a) lost 0-2

1966-67

| v. Dundee | (a) won 3-2 |
| v. Polish Select XI | (h) won 2-1 |

1967-68

| v. Celtic | (n) drew 3-3 |

1968-69

| v. Glasgow Rangers | (h) won 3-1 |
| v. FK Austria | (a) drew 2-2 |

1969-70

| v. Heart of Midlothian | (a) drew 1-1 |
| v. Glasgow Rangers | (a) won 1-0 |

1970-71

| v. Glasgow Rangers | (h) won 2-0 |

1971-72

| v. Heart of Midlothian | (a) lost 1-2 |
| v. Glasgow Rangers | (a) lost 0-1 |

1972-73

v. Bournemouth	(a) won 4-2
v. Aston Villa	(a) drew 0-0
v. Celtic	(a) lost 0-1

1973-74

v. Ajax Amsterdam	(a) lost 1-4
v. Cardiff City	(a) won 3-1
v. Sunderland	(a) won 1-0

1974-75

v. Heart of Midlothian	(a) drew 1-1
v. Portsmouth	(a) won 2-0
v. Fulham	(a) won 1-0
v. Watford	(a) won 3-2
v. Red Star Belgrade	(a) won 1-0

1975-76

v. Bristol Rovers	(a) won 4-1
v. La Stade Rennais	(a) drew 1-1
v. Millwall	(a) lost 1-3

1976-77

v. Swindon Town	(a) lost 1-3
v. Royal Antwerp	(h) drew 1-1
v. Arsenal	(a) won 2-1
v. Nepredac Krusevac	(a) lost 0-4

1977-78

v. Arsenal	(a) lost 1-3
v. Truro City	(a) won 8-2
v. Orient	(a) won 3-1

1978-79

v. Aberdeen	(a) lost 1-3
v. Royal Antwerp	(a) won 3-1
v. VV Venlo	(a) lost 0-1
v. Bohemians	(a) won 4-0
v. Aldershot	(a) drew 1-1
v. IFK Gothenburg	(a) lost 0-1
v. Saudi Arabia XI	(a) won 4-2
v. West Ham United	(a) lost 2-4
v. El Nasar	(a) won 7-0
v. QPR	(a) won 3-1
v. Gillingham	(a) won 3-2

1979-80

v. Gillingham	(a) drew 1-1
v. Oxford United	(a) lost 1-2
v. Dundee United	(a) lost 2-3
v. Aberdeen	(a) lost 0-2
v. Orient	(a) drew 1-1
v. Widad, Morocco	(a) won 4-2
v. Crystal Palace	(a) won 3-2
v. Bournemouth	(a) won 2-1
v. Hertford Town	(a) won 4-0

1980-81

v. Southend United	(a) drew 1-1
v. Portsmouth	(a) won 2-1
v. PSV Eindhoven	(n) lost 2-4
v. Glasgow Rangers	(a) lost 1-2
v. Dundee United	(a) lost 1-4

v. Swansea City	(a) lost 0-1
v. Weymouth	(a) won 6-1
v. Jersey Select XI	(a) won 5-0

1981-82

v. Glentoran	(a) drew 3-3
v. Limerick	(a) won 6-2
v. Norwich City	(a) drew 2-2
v. Aberdeen	(a) won 1-0
v. Israel Select XI	(a) won 3-2
v. Plymouth Argyle	(a) drew 1-1
v. Sporting Lisbon	(a) lost 2-3
v. Jersey Select XI	(a) won 8-3

1982-83

v. Scunthorpe United	(a) won 5-0
v. FC Lausanne	(a) lost 0-3
v. Glasgow Rangers	(a) won 1-0
v. Barnet	(a) lost 1-2
v. Borussia M'gladb'h	(n) lost 0-2
v. Israel Select XI	(n) drew 2-2
v. Northerners, Jersey	(a) won 6-1
v. Bristol Rovers	(a) won 3-2
v. Trinidad & Tobago	(a) won 3-2
v. ASL Trinidad	(a) won 2-1
v. Charlton Athletic	(a) drew 4-4
v. Aslund, Norway	(a) won 3-2

1983-84

v. Enfield	(a) won 4-1
v. Brentford	(a) won 4-2
v. Portsmouth	(a) won 3-1
v. Brighton & HA	(a) drew 0-0
v. Celtic	(a) drew 1-1
v. Dundee United	(a) drew 1-1
v. Vale Rec. Jersey	(a) won 4-2
v. Wimbledon	(a) won 5-0
v. West Ham United	(a) lost 1-4

1984-85

v. Enfield	(a) won 7-0
v. Nice, France	(a) drew 1-1
v. Brentford	(a) won 3-0
v. Manchester City	(a) won 2-0
v. Sheffield United	(a) won 3-0
v. Real Madrid	(a) lost 0-1
v. Malta National XI	(a) won 1-0
v. Sutton United	(a) won 5-3
v. Kuwait National XI	(n) won 1-0
v. Guernsey FA XI	(a) won 5-0
v. Bristol Rovers	(a) won 6-2

1985-86

v. Wycombe Wands	(n) won 4-1
v. Chesterfield	(a) won 4-2
v. AFC Bournemouth	(a) won 3-1
v. Plymouth Argyle	(a) lost 0-1
v. Exeter City	(a) drew 2-2
v. Norwich City	(a) drew 1-1
v. Fareham Town	(a) won 6-3
v. Maidstone United	(a) won 2-1
v. Jersey Select XI	(a) won 7-0
v. Glasgow Rangers	(a) won 2-0

v. Chelmsford City	(a) won 8-2
v. Brentford	(a) lost 3-4
v. West Ham United	(a) lost 1-5

1986-87

v. Aldershot	(a) won 3-2
v. Brighton & HA	(a) won 4-0
v. Gillingham	(a) drew 1-1
v. PSV Eindhoven	(n) drew 1-1*
v. AC Milan	(n) won 2-1
v. SV Hamburg	(h) won 5-1
v. Bermuda National XI	(a) won 3-1
v. Linfield	(a) won 3-2
v. Marios Club	(n) lost 0-1

* Spurs lost 3-4 on penalties

1987-88

v. Exeter City	(a) won 1-0
v. AFC Bournemouth	(a) drew 4-4
v. Brentford	(a) drew 0-0
v. AS Monaco	(h) lost 0-4
v. Hull City	(a) lost 1-2
v. Crystal Palace	(a) drew 3-3
v. Barnet	(a) won 2-1

1988-89

v. Dundee United	(a) drew 1-1
v. Reading	(a) lost 1-2
v. Chelsea	(a) drew 0-0
v. West Ham United	(a) lost 0-2
v. Swansea City	(a) won 3-0
v. Arsenal	(n) lost 0-4+
v. AC Milan	(n) lost 1-2+
v. Home Farm	(a) won 4-0
v. AS Monaco	(h) lost 1-3
v. IFK Gothenburg	(h) won 3-0*
v. Bordeaux	(h) lost 1-2
v. Charlton Athletic	(a) lost 3-4

+ Wembley International tournament
* Played on training ground

1989-90

v. Fulham	(h) won 3-1
v. Bohemians	(a) won 2-0
v. Cork City	(a) won 3-0
v. AFC Bournemouth	(h) won 6-0*
v. Swindon Town	(h) lost 0-1*
v. Viking	(a) won 5-1
v. SK Brann	(a) won 2-0
v. Dinamo Bucharest	(n) lost 1-2+
v. Atletico Madrid	(n) lost 0-1+
v. SM Caen	(n) won 2-1
v. Leicester City	(a) won 5-2
v. Plymouth Argyle	(a) won 3-0
v. Brighton & HA	(a) won 3-0
v. Valerengen	(a) drew 1-1
v. Northern Ireland XI	(h) won 2-1

* Played at training ground
+ Madrid Tournament

1990-91

| v. Ipswich Town | (n) won 3-0* |
| v. Maidstone United | (n) lost 0-1* |

v. Shelbourne	(a) won 3-0
v. Derry City	(a) won 3-0
v. Heart of Midlothian	(a) drew 1-1
v. Southend United	(a) won 4-1

* Played at Chase Lodge ground

1991-92

| v. Celtic | (a) lost 0-1 |

1992-93

v. Reading	(h) won 3-1*
v. Gillingham	(h) won 2-0*
v. Heart of Midlothian	(a) won 2-1
v. Brighton & HA	(a) drew 1-1
v. Glenavon	(a) won 1-0
v. West Brom Albion	(a) won 2-0
v. Sunderland	(a) won 3-0+
v. Watford	(a) won 1-0
v. Portsmouth	(a) lost 2-4
v. SS Lazio	(a) lost 0-3**
v. SS Lazio	(h) lost 0-2
v. Real Zaragoza	(a) lost 0-2
v. Real Madrid	(h) lost 0-1++
v. Inter Milan	(h) drew 0-0

* Games played at Chase Lodge ground
+ City Celebration match
** Capital Cup games
++ Fiorucci Cup games (Inter Milan won 6-5 on pens)

1993-94

v. Shelbourne	(a) won 4-2
v. Drogheda United	(a) won 3-1
v. SS Lazio	(h) won 3-2*
v. Chelsea	(h) lost 0-4*
v. Peterborough Utd	(a) won 2-1
v. Brann	(a) lost 0-2
v. Atletico Madrid	(n) won 2-1+

* Makita Tournament
+ Game played in Jerez in front of 500 fans.

1994-95

v. Cambridge United	(a) won 3-0
v. Bristol City	(a) won 3-1
v. Brighton & HA	(a) won 3-0
v. Watford	(a) drew 1-1
v. Shelbourne	(a) won 1-0

1995-96

v. Sampdoria	(n) lost 0-2*
v. Steaua Bucharest	(n) lost 2-3*
v. Derby County	(a) lost 0-1
v. Watford	(a) won 2-0

* Ibrox International Tournament

1996-97

v. Brentford	(a) won 3-0
v. Reading	(a) won 1-0
v. Southend United	(a) won 3-1*

* CTA International Trophy

1997-98

| v. Leyton Orient | (a) won 1-0 |

v. Swindon Town   (a) drew 2-2
v. Oxford United   (a) won 3-2*
* Bill Halsey Memorial Cup game

1998-99
v. Grasshopper Club   (a) lost 1-3
v. Peterborough United (a) won 6-0
v. IF Brondby   (a) lost 0-3
v. Birmingham City   (a) lost 2-4
v. Celtic   (a) lost 1-2
v. Norwich City   (a) won 3-1
v. QPR   (a) drew 0-0
v. St Albans City   (a) won 6-2

1999-2000
v. Heart of Midlothian (a) drew 2-2
v. QPR   (a) drew 2-2
v. Wolves   (a) drew 1-1
v. Bishop Stortford   (a) won 6-0*
* Official opening of Woodside Park Stadium

2000-01
v. Birmingham City   (a) won 1-0
v. Peterborough United (a) won 2-1
v. Vitesse Arnhem   (a) won 2-1

2001-02
v. Stevenage Borouigh (a) won 8-1
v. Swindon Town   (a) won 3-1
v. Leyton Orient   (a) won 2-0
v. Wycombe Wanderers (a) won 2-1
v. Portsmouth   (a) won 5-2
v. Reading   (a) won 2-0
v. Millwall   (a) won 2-1
v. Luton Town   (a) drew 1-1
v. Fiorentina   (h) won 3-0

Friendly Gossip
● Peter Hunter scored a hat-trick when defeating a selected Sheffield & District League XI 7-1 on Christmas Day 1894.
● In the nine-goal thriller at Clapton in October 1895, Bob 'Topsy' Clements scored a hat-trick in Spurs' 5-4 defeat.
● Charlie Lanham & Dick Logan both scored four times in an 8-0 friendly win over the 1st Scots Guards in March 1896.
● When Spurs beat the 3rd Grenadier Guards team 9-3 in February 1897, nine different players figured on the scoresheet (six for Spurs).
● Three players scored hat-tricks when Spurs beat the Royal Scots Guards 12-0 in September 1897 - Jock Davidson (4), Billy Joyce (3) and Tom Meade (3).
● Billy Joyce netted another treble later in the season when Spurs beat Tunbridge Wells 5-0 in early March 1898.
● The reigning League and FA Cup double winners, Aston Villa, defeated Spurs 3-2 in a friendly in April 1898.
● John Kirwan scored four times when Spurs beat HR Burke's XI 12-2 at home in December 1899. He had earlier scored twice in each of the two previous matches v. the Corinthians and the touring Kaffirs.
● Tommy Pratt hit a hat-trick in Spurs' 6-0 win over Oxford University in February 1900. He followed up with a fourtimer in the next match against Chesterfield (won 7-2) and repeated that feat with four goals in the 6-0 win over Stoke on 5 March.
● 'Sandy' Brown, preparing himself for his exploits in the FA Cup,

scored four goals in Spurs' 8-0 friendly win over the Richmond Association side in September 1900.
● Fifteen goals were scored when Spurs met the German Association XI at home in January 1901. The result was a 9-6 win for Spurs, Alex Tait led the scoring with a hat-trick.
● Alf Warner scored four times when Spurs defeated a weak West Norwood side 9-0 in December 1902 and the same player netted twice, along with John Cameron when Spurs and Cambridge University drew 4-4 in January 1905.
● Spurs played seven friendly matches in 1906-07 producing no fewer than 42 goals. Jimmy Reid scored a hat-trick in the 6-4 win over London Caledonians.
● Spurs suffered one of their biggest defeat at White Hart Lane in February 1921 when they lost 7-3 to rivals Chelsea in a friendly.
● Jimmy Dimmock netted three times in Spurs 7-1 home win over the Inter-Varsities side in April 1924 and he repeated that feat in the 7-3 victory away to Ebbw Vale in March 1928.
● In the 1942-43 Wartime season Spurs played five friendlies, all against fellow London clubs.
● Over the years Spurs have played 14 'other' matches against the Scottish side Hibernian (at home and away). They won five, drew four and lost five.
● Len Duquemin netted three times and Syd McClellan scored a fourtimer when Spurs beat Lovells Athletic 8-0 and Chelmsford City 7-3 respectively in the 1950-51 season.
● When Spurs beat the Essex side Crittalls Athletic 8-1 at Braintree in May 1952, the nine goals were distributed between eight players, Len Duquemin scoring twice.
● Full-back Alf Ramsey scored twice (one from the penalty spot) when Spurs beat Rot-Weiss Essen 4-2 at home in Nov 1954.
● Danny Blanchflower had a hand in four of the goals (scoring one himself) when Spurs beat Red Banner MTK (Hungary) 7-1 at White Hart Lane in December 1956. Alf Stokes scored a hat-trick in this same game.
● Bobby Smith, with four goals, set Spurs up for a thrilling 5-4 win in Basle against the Swiss National side in October 1957.
● Winger Cliff Jones (with three goal) helped Spurs beat Reading 5-2 at Elm Park in October 1959.
● The two 'Ms' Dave Mackay and Terry Medwin both netted twice when Spurs beat the Russia side Dynamo Tbilisi 5-2 at home in November 1960.
● The first Egyptian side to play at White Hart Lane were the Zamalek Sporting Club (Cairo) who were beaten 7-3 by Spurs in a friendly in November 1962. Jimmy Greaves and Terry Dyson both scored twice.
● Les Allen hit a hat-trick when Spurs won 6-5 at Highfield Road against Coventry City in April 1964 and in September 1965 Alan Gilzean went one better with a fourtimer when Walton & Hersham succumbed to an 8-1 defeat.
● Scotsman Gilzean weighed in with another hat-trick when the Hungarian Select XI lost 4-0 at White Hart Lane in Nov 1965.
● Over 50,000 saw a six-goal thriller at Hampden Park between Celtic and Spurs in Aug 1967. Jimmy Greaves scored two goals.
● Spurs beat the Scottish giants Glasgow Rangers three times in three seasons (1968-71 inclusive) before losing a fourth game 1-0 at Ibrox in August 1971.
● Chris Jones had the pleasure of scoring Spurs' winning goal in Yugoslavia against red Star Belgrade in February 1975 and Gerry Armstrong was on target in the 1-1 draw in Belgium against Royal Antwerp in August 1976.
● Glenn Hoddle and Colin Lee both struck twice in Spurs 7-0 win over El Nasar in December 1978. The temperature for this game was given as 90 degrees fahrenheit.

● The two Argentinians, Ossie Ardiles and Ricky Villa, both scored twice when Spurs beat Weymouth 6-1 (away) in November 1980, and Steve Archibald followed up with a hat-trick as Spurs beat a Jersey XI 5-0 in February 1981.

● As FA Cup holders, Spurs travelled to Ireland to start their preparations for the 1981-82 season with a 3-3 draw against Glentoran. In the next game they beat Limerick 6-2 when Glenn Hoddle netted four times-his best scoring of his entire career!

● Mick Hazard had the pleasure of netting his first hat-trick for Spurs in a 3-2 win over an Israeli XI (away) in November 1981 and when Spurs returned to Jersey in March 1983, Steve Archibald led with a treble in a 6-1 win over the Northerners side.

● Mark Falco scored all Spurs' goals in the 4-4 friendly draw with Charlton Athletic on 23 May 1983 and Garth Crooks struck a hat-trick in the 3-2 win in Norway over Alesund a week later.

● Archibald was again top man as far as Spurs were concerned when his fourtimer helped his side beat the Vale Recreation side 7-2 on the island of Guernsey in October 1983 while Garth Crooks followed suit with four goals in Spurs' 7-0 victory at Enfield in August 1984.

● Ally Dick's goal was enough to beat the Maltese Select XI 1-0 in October 1984 and Crooks was again 'too hot to handle' with another hat-trick in a 5-3 win at Sutton the following month.

● And indeed it was Crooks, in the stifling heat of Jordan, who scored the only goal when Spurs beat the Kuwait National team in Amman by a goal to nil in March 1985.

● David Leworthy had the pleasure of scoring two hat-tricks for Spurs in five months in 1985 - his first when Bristol Rovers were humbled 6-2 at Eastville in April and his second in September when Fareham Town were defeated 6-3.

● Mark Falco went nap with five goals as a full-strength Spurs side crushed hapless Chelmsford City 8-2 in April 1986 and he netted twice in a 4-0 win at Brighton the following August.

● After drawing 1-1 with PSV Eindhoven in a tournament in Barcelona in August 1986, the Dutch side won a penalty shoot-out by 4-3. Spurs' next game resulted in a 2-1 win over the Italian giants Inter Milan, Falco and Gary Mabbutt the scorers.

● The Orange Bowl, Miami was the venue for the clash between the Colombian side Millonarios and Spurs in May 1987. The result was a 1-0 win for the Millonarios.

● The Spurs v. Northern Ireland XI encounter at White Hart Lane on 1 May 1990 (for the benefit of Danny Blanchflower) was attended by 6,769 fans, the Irish line-up featuring Gerry Armstrong and Phil Gray, both former Spurs stars. Spurs themselves utilised 20 players on the night and one their subs, Matt Edwards, came on for the Irish!

● A crowd of around 30,000 saw Spurs beaten 2-0 in Spain by Real Zaragoza in April 1993.

● Les Ferdinand (3), David Ginola (penalty), Ruel Fox and Steve Carr scored six goals when Spurs beat St Albans City in Aug 1998.

● Tiny winger Jose Dominguez scored twice when Bishop's Stortford were defeated 6-0 in September 1999 in game arranged to mark the official opening of the new Woodside Park Stadium. The attendance was 3,109.

FREUND, STEFFEN

Strong-tackling German midfielder Steffen Freund joined Spurs in December 1998 from Borussia Dortmund, having previously played for FC Motor Sud, Brandenburg (two spells), FC Stahl and FC Schalke 04.

Born in Brandenburg on 19 January 1970, he won two Bundesliga championship medals in 1995 and 1996 (with Dortmund) and was a Football League Cup winner with Spurs in 1999. On the international scene Freund has been capped 21 times at senior level and has also represented his country in two Olympic Games matches and played once for the East German Under-21 side as well as winning Schoolboy and Youth caps as a teenager.

When the 2000-01 season ended he had appeared in 87 first-class matches for Spurs.

FULHAM

Spurs playing record against their London rivals:

Competition	P	W	D	L	F	A
Football League	44	22	18	4	78	49
FA Cup	4	3	1	0	6	1
League Cup	2	1	0	1	2	3
Other Leagues	14	6	3	5	18	13
Other Cups	5	3	0	2	12	12
Wartime	26	15	3	8	52	34
Summary	95	50	25	20	168	112

Spurs first met their London neighbours in the Football League on 5 December 1908 (Division 2). The venue was Craven Cottage and in front of 35,000 fans, Spurs won 3-2.

Fulham recorded their ONLY League win at White Hart Lane on 10 April 1948 when they triumphed 2-0. Their full record on Spurs' soil at League level is played 22, won one, drawn nine and lost 12, goals scored 21, goals conceded 41.

In 1948-49 Fulham and Spurs were going hard for promotion from Division Two. Both games ended in 1-1 draws, the second-last game of the season at White Hart Lane attracting a crowd in excess of 50,000. The Cottagers went up as champions, Spurs finished 5th. seven points behind.

Spurs beat Fulham 3-0 at home but lost 4-1 away in 1964-65 and the following season a Cliff Jones treble earned Spurs a 4-3 home win to complete the double having won 2-0 at Craven Cottage.

Spurs doubled-up again in 1966-67, winning 4-3 away and 4-2 at home - and in 1967-68, when Fulham were relegated, Spurs were held 2-2 at home but won 2-1 by the River Thames.

● When Jimmy Neighbour played on the left-wing for Spurs against Fulham in a reserve match in October 1970, his opposite number was named Barry Friend!

Players with both clubs include: Steve Archibald, Ernie Bowering, Laurie Brown (Fulham amateur), John Curtis, Terry Dyson, Bert Elkin, Ray Evans, Willie Evans, Tom Fitchie, Phil Gray, Cliff Jones, David Gwilan Jones (Spurs reserve, Fulham trialist), John Lacy, Harry Lowe, Ken McKay, Tom Meade, Paul Mahorn, John Margerrison (Spurs reserve), Alan Mullery, Taffy O'Callaghan (also Fulham coach & assistant-manager), Tim O'Shea (Fulham trialist), Frank Osborne (also Fulham manager & director), Tony Parks, Ernie Payne, Tom Pratt, Jimmy Reid, Neil Smith, Bob Stevens, Alf Stokes, Bob Tannahill, Charlie Walters.

Wartime guests (with either one or both clubs): Jack Acquroff, Pat Beasley, Frank Boulton, Alex Chaplin, Jack Chisholm, Freddie Cox, John Davie, Frank Drabble, Harry Dukes, Jim Evans, Harry Ferrier, Jack Finch, Doug Flack, Len Flack, Fred Ford, Jack Gibbons, Les Henley, Les Howe, Doug Hunt, Jimmy Jinks, Eric Jones, Phil Joslin, Tom Kiernan, George Ludford, Jimmy McCormick, Tommy Manley, Alex Muir, Matt Muir, Bill Nicholson (also Spurs manager), Frank O'Donnell, Sid Ottewell, Bob Pryde, Charlie Revell, Fred Sargent, Albert Sibley, Jack Skinner, Tommy Simmons, Taffy Spelman, Billy Sperrin, Sid Tickridge, Walter Tull, Ralph Ward, Bill Whatley, Roy White, Joe Wilson, Albert Young.

Also associated: Vic Buckingham (Spurs player, Fulham manager and WW2 guest), Harry Evans (Fulham player and Spurs assistant-manager), Ron Burgess (Spurs player, Fulham trainer), Terry Medwin (Spurs player, Fulham coach), Roger Cross (Fulham player,

Spurs assistant-manager), Theo Foley (Spurs reserve team manager, Fulham Youth team manager), Matt Forster (Spurs player, Fulham scout)

FULLWOOD, JAMES

Full-back Jimmy Fullwood was a miner in Derbyshire before having trials with Spurs in October 1934. These proved successful and he was signed as a professional the following month. Basically a reserve (understudying Bill Whatley) he went on to appear in 39 first team games for the club (one goal scored) before transferring to Reading in August 1938. He assisted Brentford, Chelsea and Clapton Orient during the War but did not re-appear after the hostilities, choosing to retire at the age of 35.

Born in Ilkeston on 17 February 1911, he worked at Thorne Colliery on leaving School. Fullwood died in 1981.

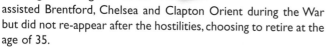

GAINSBOROUGH TRINITY

Spurs playing record against Trinity:

Competition	P	W	D	L	F	A
Football League	2	1	1	0	3	1

Both of these League games were played in season 1908-09 (Division 2), the first at Gainsborough on 21 November when 6,000 fans saw Spurs win 2-0...their first away success in the Football League. The return fixture ended all-square at 1-1.

Players with both clubs include: Bill Cartwright, John Curtis, Albert Hall, John Madden, Tom Morris, John Raby, Jimmy Reid, Fred Webster, Chris Young.

GALVIN, ANTHONY

A Yorkshireman, born in Huddersfield on 12 July 1956, Tony Galvin was a wide midfielder with pace, energy and a telling shot. He represented both Yorkshire and England Schools and obtained a Bachelor of Arts Degree in Russian Studies whilst at Hull University allowing him to attend teacher's training college before joining Goole Town. Spotted by an eagle-eyed scout, he moved to Spurs for just £30,000 in January 1978 - although he did complete his teacher-training course before becoming a full-time professional at White Hart Lane. Eleven years later he switched to Sheffield Wednesday for £130,000 in August 1987, after scoring 47 goals in 375 first-class matches for the club. A member of the 1981 and 1982 FA Cup-winning teams, Galvin was also on the losing side in the League Cup Final in the latter year before adding a UEFA Cup winners' medal to his collection in 1984. Thanks to his grandfather, Galvin qualified to play for the Republic of Ireland.and he gained 20 senior caps before leaving for Hillsborough. From there he moved to Swindon Town (July 1989). There he acted as assistant-manager to Ossies Ardiles and also

had a spell as caretaker-boss at The County Ground (prior to Gelnn Hoddle's arrival) before rejoining the little Argentinian at Newcastle United. Whilst at St James' Park (March 1991-February 1992), Galvin turned out occasionally for Gateshead. He was dismissed (with Ardiles) after a board-room reshuffle.

GAMES PLAYED

The most first-class games played by Spurs in one single season is 68 in 1971-72. They contested 42 in the First Division, five in the FA Cup, seven in the League Cup, 12 in the UEFA Cup and two in the Anglo-Italian League Cup Winners' Cup. Spurs also played two friendly matches and a tour game in the course of this campaign.

GASCOIGNE, PAUL

A true North-Eastern Geordie, born in Gateshead on 25 May 1967, Paul Gascoigne at his peak, was one of the finest attacking midfield players in world soccer.

Signed in July 1988, for a then British record fee of £2 million by Spurs' manager Terry Venables (having spent five years with Newcastle United, the first two as an apprentice) Gazza quickly made his mark at White Hart Lane. Ironically his League debut for Spurs was against his former team (Newcastle)... the first of 143 appearances for the club (92 in the First Division). He scored 46 goals and made many more for his colleagues!

When he joined Spurs he was already an England Under-21 player (first capped in June 1987). He went on to appear in another 12 games for his country at that level, as well as starring in one 'B' and 57 full internationals, having gained Youth honours as a teenager.

An FA Youth Cup winner with Newcastle in 1985, Gazza - although he went off injured following a reckless challenge on Gary Charles, the Nottingham Forest wing-back - then collected an FA Cup winners' medal with Spurs in 1991. He left White Hart Lane for the Italian club, SS Lazio, for £5.5 million in May 1992 and spent three excellent seasons in Serie 'A' before returning to Britain in July 1995 to sign for Glasgow Rangers for £4.3 million. At Ibrox he became a folk hero, idolised by the younger supporters especially. He had his hair dyed white, had his own fan club and proceeded to take the Scottish League by the scruff of the neck, helping the 'Gers win the Scottish Cup, the League Cup and two Premier League titles in the space of two seasons. In March 1998 Gascoigne re-entered the League scene in England when he joined his former England team-mate Bryan Robson at Middlesbrough for £3.45 million. He struggled off and on with injuries at The Riverside Stadium until in July 2000 he became an Everton player. Unfortunately again, he had to battle to stay fit, spending more time in the treatment room than he did on the pitch. Nevertheless, Gazza - the Pied Piper of football - reached three personal milestones during the 2000-01 season....his 300th League appearance (in England and Scotland); his 400th appearance in all club matches and his 500th appearance as a professioinal for club and country (at various levels). He also took his tally of goals past the 120 mark.

*Gazza's Euro 98 number 8 shirt was sold at auction for £6,400 on 16 October 1999.

GATE RECEIPTS

How the gate receipts records have been broken at White Hart Lane (to the nearest £)

£115	Spurs v. Notts County, friendly	04.09.1899
£329	Spurs v. Queen's Park Rangers, Southern League	09.09.1899
£415	Spurs v. Portsmouth, Southern League	25.12.1899
£443	Spurs v. Southampton, Southern League	13.04.1900
£510	Spurs v. Preston North End, FA Cup	09.02.1901
£720	Spurs v. Bury, FA Cup	23.02.1901
£1,200	Spurs v. Millwall, Southern League	07.09.1901
£1,223	Spurs v. Southampton, FA Cup	01.01.1902
£1,276	Spurs v. West Brom Albion, FA Cup	07.02.1903
£1,305	Spurs v. Aston Villa, FA Cup	07.03.1903
£1,324	Spurs v. Aston Villa, FA Cup	20.02.1904
£2,100	Spurs v. Fulham, FA Cup	06.02.1909
£2,180	Spurs v. Arsenal, Football League	25.12.1911
£4,100	Spurs v. West Ham United, FA Cup	06.03.1920
£4,975	Spurs v. Newcastle United, Football L	27.12.1920
£6,992	Spurs v. Aston Villa, FA Cup	04.03.1921
£7,683	England v. Germany, international	00.12.1933
£10,400	Spurs v. Sunderland, FA Cup	05.03.1938
£18,100	Spurs v. West Bromwich Albion, FA Cup	24.01.1948
£19,300	England v. Italy, international	30.11.1949
£30,080	Spurs v. Manchester United, ECWC	02.12.1963
£47,998	Spurs v. Wolves, League Cup Final s/f	17.05.1972
£49,920	Spurs v. Feyenoord UEFA Cup Final 2nd leg	21.05.1974
£136,408	Spurs v. West Bromwich Albion, League Cup s/f	10.02.1982
£245,632	Spurs v RSC Anderlecht, UEFA Cup Final	23.05.1984
£336,702	Spurs v. Manchester United, League Div. 1	28.09.1991

Money Talk

£2,016,000 was taken in gate receipts from the 1991 FA Cup Final between Spurs and Nottingham Forest and when the TV revenue was added the overall take was given as £2.89 million. This was a British record take at the time.

Record gate receipts of £162,314 were taken at Griffin Park when Spurs played Brentford there in a 2nd round League Cup encounter on 15 September 1998.

Record gate receipts of £146,000 were banked from the Carlisle United v. Spurs League Cup clash at Brunton Park on 30 September 1997.

The Northampton Town-Spurs League Cup clash at The Sixfields Stadium on 27 October 1998 produced record gate receipts of £102,979.

The Hartlepool United v. Spurs League Cup game on 9 October 1990 realised record gate receipts for The Victoria Ground of £42,300.

The record amount of money taken from a major game at Elland Road is £780,697 from the Leeds United v. Spurs FA Cup-tie played there on 13 February 1999.

Wimbledon's record home gate receipts of £531,976 were banked from their League Cup semi-final encounter with Spurs at Selhurst Park on 16 February 1999.

The first time a five-figure sum was taken at the gate for an FA Cup Final was in 1921 when £13,414 was banked from the Stamford Bridge encounter between Spurs and Wolves clash.

Then, 41 years later, the first £50,000 'take' was recorded (£53,837) for the Spurs-Burnley FA Cup final of 1962.

GATESHEAD (SEE SOUTH SHIELDS)

Spurs played Gateshead (formerly known as South Shields) in an FA Cup third round tie in January 1955, Johnny Brooks scored both goals in a 2-0 win in front of 18,842 fans at Redheugh Park.

Players with both clubs include (Gateshead): Tony Galvin, Allan Taylor and (South Shields) Foster Hedley, Joe Knowles, Joe Meek (Amateur). Wartime guests (with either one or both clubs): Taffy Spelman, Ernie Hoffman, Archie Jack, George Wilbert.

* Paul Gascoigne and Chris Waddle were both born in Gateshead!

GAVIN, JOHN THOMAS

Outside-right Johnny Gavin was born in Limerick on 20 April 1928 and after a spell with Jamesborough United, he joined Norwich City from his home town club for £1,500 in August 1948. He remained at Carrow Road until October 1954 when he was transferred to Spurs, returning to the Canaries' nest in November 1955 (as part of the Maurice Norman deal) after scoring 16 goals in 34 League and FA Cup games during his 13-month stay at White Hart Lane. He went on to secure a fine record with Norwich - registering 112 goals in 338 games up to July 1958 when he switched to Watford, later assisting Crystal Palace, Cambridge City and finally Newmarket, as player-coach.

Capped seven times by the Republic of Ireland (twice as a Spurs player in May/June 1955) Gavin became a publican in Cambridgeshire after retiring from football.

GIBBONS, ALBERT HENRY ('JACK')

Jack Gibbons, an England amateur international inside or centre-forward, played for Uxbridge, Kingstonian, Brentford, Spurs (two spells: July 1937-July 1938 & during the War from August 1939) and Bradford Park Avenue before returning to Griffin Park in May

1947, later becoming manager-secretary of the Bees (May 1949-August 1952). He also guested for Bradford PA, Brentford, Fulham and Reading during the hostilities. He was an outstanding marksman and netted 109 goals in 148 first-team games for Spurs, the majority during WW2 when he also represented the RAF, the FA and England v. Wales in 1942. He was capped seven times as an amateur for his country. Gibbons was born in Fulham on 10 April 1914. He was, in fact, never referred to as Albert or Henry, he was always called Jack ...to avoid confusion with four other sporting colleagues, all named Gibbons (Bert, Bertie, Albert and Herbert Gibbons) who were members of the local gymnasium club. Even Jack's family adopted his nickname!

GIBSON, TERENCE BRADLEY

A nippy little striker, short and stocky with good pace and powerful right-foot shot, Terry Gibson - a real jack-in-the-box - was never afraid to mix it with the tough-tackling defenders of his day. Born in Walthamstow on 23 December 1962, he represented Waltham Forest, London, Essex and England Schools before joining Spurs as an apprentice in April 1979, turning prrofessional in January 1980. Despite winning a handful of England Youth caps he was never a regular in the first XI at White Hart Lane - there were so many other talented players around at the same time. After scoring 16 goals in 43 first team appearances, as well as having a loan spell in Sweden with GAIS, he was transferred to Coventry City in August 1983 for £100,000. He netted a goal every two games for the Sky Blues before moving to Manchester United in a swap deal involving Alan Brazil. Sadly things didn't work out for him at Old Trafford and in August 1987 he returned to London to sign for Wimbledon, helping the Dons to that shock 1988 FA Cup Final victory over Liverpool. After a spate of niggling injuries, he teamed up as a loan player with Glenn Hoddle at Swindon Town (March 1992) and following stints with Peterborough United and Barnet he announced his retirement as a player at the end of the 1994-95 season. At that juncture he took up coaching and later linked up with his old Wimbledon colleague Lawrie Sanchez as assistant-manager/coach at Wycombe Wanderers, helping them reach the semi-finals of the FA Cup in 2001. Gibson scored 72 goals in 267 League games for the seven major clubs he served.

GILHOOLEY, PATRICK

A Scotsman from Lanarkshire (born in 1878) inside-forward Pat Gilhooley scored seven goals in 50 first-class games for Spurs during his three years with the club: 1901-04. He also played for Celtic and Sheffield United before moving to White Hart Lane, then Brighton & Hove Albion when he left.

GILLINGHAM (ALSO NEW BROMPTON)

Spurs record against the Gills:

Competition	P	W	D	L	F	A
League Cup	1	1	0	0	4	2
Other Leagues	26	18	3	5	47	23
Summary	27	19	3	5	51	25

A nine-goal thriller went New Brompton's way by 5-4 in a Southern League game in Kent in April 1899. Spurs then won six of the next seven meetings and ten of the next 12.
Spurs' best win so far is 6-0 over New Brompton, in a home Southern League game in October 1905.
Spurs' League Cup clash with Gillingham was a 3rd round tie at The Priestfield Stadium in November 1982. A crowd of 14,366 saw Steve Archibald and Garth Crooks both score twice in a 4-2 win.

Players with both clubs include: Charlie Ambler, Arthur Archer, Peter Beadle, Guy Butters, Wally Eames, Abraham Goodman, Bert Gosnell, Fred Griffiths, Jim Hartley, Scott Houghton, John 'Tiny' Joyce, Jimmy Kennedy (also Gills trainer), Terry Lee, Tom Leslie, Bill McCurdy, David McDonald, Billy Manuel (Spurs reserve), Tim O'Shea, Tom Pangbourne, Tony Parks, Jimmy Pass, Arthur Pickett, Andy Polston, Martin Robinson, Jimmy Scarth, Jack Skinner, Neil Smith, Jimmy Reid, Alex Steel, Bobby Steel, Mark Stimson, Andrew Swan, Steve Walford, Bob Walker, John Watson, Alf Whyman, Roy Woolcott.
Wartime guests (with either one or both clubs): Tom Caldwell, George Dorling, Pat Glen, Percy Hooper, Gil Piper, George Travers.
Also associated: Keith Burkinshaw (manager of both clubs, also Spurs coach), Freddie Cox (Spurs player, Gills manager), John Gorman (Spurs player, Gills coach).

GINOLA, DAVID DESIRE MARC

Born in Gassin near Toulon, France on 25 January 1967, David Ginola's career took him to FC Toulon (1985), Racing Club de Paris (1988), Brest (1990), Paris St Germain (1992), Newcastle United (£2.5m, July 1995) Tottenham Hotspur (£2m July 1997) and Aston Villa (£3m, August 2000). When he joined Villa in readiness for the 2000-01 season, he immediately received £40,000-a-week to become the highest-paid player in the Midland club's history. He helped PSG win their first French League title in eight years in 1994 when he was also named both France's 'Player of the Year' and the 'Players' Player of the Year.' After appearing in more than 200 French League games (25 goals scored) and gaining international recognition, Ginola signed for Newcastle and spent two seasons at St James' Park (scoring seven goals in 76 outings for the Geordies). After his move to Spurs, he immediately became a star at White Hart Lane and gained a League Cup winners' medal in 1999. He appeared in 100 Premiership games for Spurs (12 goals) and starred in 27 various Cup matches (nine goals) before joining Aston Villa in a blaze of publicity! A player with tremendous on-the-ball skill, splendid body-swerve, stunning right foot shot and a great deal of charisma, he was voted both the Football Writers' and PFA 'Player of the Year' in 1999 and was also selected in the Premiership representative side.. A celebrity both on and off the field, he unfortunately fell out with the management of the French national team in the mid-90s and after attempting to settle his differences, failed to get a recall and subsequently missed out on his country's World Cup and European Championship triumphs. He has 17 caps to his credit (his first came in 1990 as a 'sub' against Albania in a European Championship qualifier). Ginola suffered with injury problems during his first half-season with Villa and when the 2000-01 campaign ended his record with the club was 22 goals scored in 137 first-class appearances (100 in the Premiership, 13 goals).
* Ginola's book: 'El Magnifique' was a best seller in the year 2000.

GILZEAN, ALAN JOHN

Scorer of 173 goals in more than 500 first-ream games for Spurs (133 of them coming in 439 League and Cup matches) Alan Gilzean proved himself to be one of the finest strikers in the game during nine-and-a-half years at White Hart Lane (December 1964-May 1974). Born in the village of Coupar Angus in Perthshire on 22 October 1938, he played his early football with the local Juveniles Club before assisting Dundee Violet. He then joined Dundee as an amateur in January 1956, turning professional at Dens Park in August 1957. He was always eager to play football and whilst serving in the Army he guested for Aldershot in a couple of reserve team games. He went on to score over 100 goals for Dundee, helping the win the Scottish League title in 1961-62, reach the semi-final of the European Cup twelve months later and then finish runners-up in the Scottish Cup in 1963-64. He also played in three Under-23 internationals for his country, represented the Scottish League on three occasions and won five full caps, later taking that tally to an impressive 22. He moved to Spurs for £72,500 halfway through the 1964-65 season and took no time whatsoever in drawing up a fine understanding with Jimmy Greaves. Indeed, the dynamic duo netted over 50 goals between them that season. They added 31 more to their tally in 1965-66 and then jointly did the business the following term as Spurs lifted the FA Cup for a fifth time, Gilzean contributing four goals during that triumphant run (plus 17 in the League). Following the arrival of Martin Chivers, Gilzean - an expert with the flicked header, he still produced the goods and starred in two League Cup and UEFA Cup winning teams respectively in 1971-72-73. He left the club to join Highlands Park FC in South Africa but made an emotional return to White Hart Lane to score in his testimonial match shortly afterwards. Gilzean managed Stevenage Athletic from May-August 1975 and in later life he worked for an Enfield-based transport company.

GLASGOW RANGERS (RANGERS FC)

Spurs playing record against the Scottish club:

Competition	P	W	D	L	F	A
ECW Cup	2	2	0	0	8	4

Spurs knocked the Scottish giants out of the 1962-63 European Cup-winners Cup competition in the first round - beating them 8-4 on aggregate after two excellent performances.

The first leg, played at White Hart Lane on 31 October, was witnessed by 58,859 fans and resulted in a comprehensive 5-2 win for Spurs, Maurice Norman, John White (2), Les Allen and Bobby Shearer (og) the scorers.

There were 80,000 spectators present for the return leg at Ibrox Park on 11 December and this time Spurs won 3-2, Smith (2) and Jimmy Greaves on target this time. Ralph Brand netted in both games for Rangers.

Players with both clubs include: Alfie Conn, John Duncan, Gordon Durie, Mark Falco, Paul Gascoigne, Richard Gough, David Haddow, Billy Hay, John McConnachie, Graham Roberts, Jocky Smith, Danny Steel, Alex Tait.

GLASGOW XI

On 5 August 1964 Spurs played a Glasgow XI for the Glasgow Charity Cup. The venue was Hampden Park and in front of 58,768 fans, the 'Scots' won 4-2. Frank Saul and Jimmy Robertson netted for Spurs.

GLEN, ALEXANDER

Versatile Scottish forward Alex Glen scored 24 goals in 65 first team games for Spurs during his two years with the club: May 1904-May 1906.

Born in Kilsyth, Stirlingshire on 11 December 1878, a medical student at the Glasgow Royal Infirmary, he was a surgical dresser when serving his country in the Boer War. On his return to Britain he commenced his career as a footballer with Fitzhugh Rovers (Stirling) and Glasgow Parkhead before joining Clyde from where he switched to Grimsby Town in July 1902. He spent a season with the Mariners and likewise with Notts County before moving south to White Hart Lane.

Described as a 'dextrous, neat and elegant dribbler for a tall man' he signed for Southampton on leaving Spurs and after acting as vice-captain at The Dell, he had spells with Bournemouth and Brentford before returning to Scotland in 1909.

Fluent in German, Glen acted as Southampton's official interpreter when the club toured Germany in 1907.

GLOSSOP (NORTH END)

Spurs playing record against Glossop:

Competition	P	W	D	L	F	A
Football League	2	0	2	0	4	4

These two Second Division fixtures took place in 1908-9, the first at Glossop on 24 October which ended 1-1 in front of 3,000 spectators and the second at White Hart Lane which finished 3-3 before a crowd of 12,000.

Players with both clubs include: George Badenoch, David Copeland, Tom Fitchie, Billy Grimes & Tom Knighton (both Spurs WW1), John Montgomery, Charlie Regan.

Alan Gilzean in action

GOALKEEPERS

Goalkeeper Bob Hewitson made his senior debut for Spurs in the club's first-ever football League game v. Wolves at White Hart Lane on 1 September 1908. Seven months earlier he had been suspended by the FL for allegedly throwing mud at the referee.

Pat Jennings is the only 'keeper to appear in more than 600 first team games for Spurs and in fact, is only the second (with Ted Ditchburn) to play in more than 500 competitive first XI matches.

Goalkeeper John Joyce (nicknamed 'Tiny') scored for Spurs in a League game v. Bolton Wanderers on 10 April 1914 and he also netted from the penalty spot in a friendly against Bayern Munich the following month.

Two other Spurs 'keepers have also found the net whilst with the club. Pat Jennings netted in the 3-3 draw with Manchester United in the FA Charity Shield game at Old Trafford in August 1967 - his long clearance bounced over the head the United 'keeper Alex Stepney in front of mote than 54,000 fans. Fellow England international Ray Clemence scored from the penalty spot when a Guernsey Select XI were beaten 5-0 (away) in April 1985.

Making his League debut for Spurs, 'keeper Jock Eadon conceded seven goals (in a 7-5 defeat) at Middlesbrough in February 1915. In contrast, on 22 October 1977, Glyn Jones, an 18 year-old novice, conceded nine goals at Spurs when playing in only his third senior game for Bristol Rovers. Nine days later he was back at White Hart Lane, playing for Rovers' reserves in a 1-1 draw with Spurs' second XI.

Frank Smith's career as a goalkeeper at Spurs up to 1962 consisted of eight years without a senior appearance, never once being named as 12th man and never being included on an overseas tour. He was then sold to QPR and made 71 League and Cup appearances for the Loftus Road club before moving into non-League football in August 1966.

On 2 October 1965, Spurs provided both goalkeepers - Pat Jennings and Bill Brown - for the respective Northern Ireland and Scotland teams in a Home international match.

Goalkeeper Tony Parks was the Spurs hero in the 1984 UEFA Cup Final victory over RSC Anderlecht. The Final went to a penalty shoot-out (after a 2-2 aggregate score) and Parks saved two vital spot-kicks to help Spurs win 4-3.

England international right-back Tommy Clay kept goal for Spurs throughout their away First Division League game at Sunderland in March 1921. Spurs won 1-0.

Half-back Alex Hall played one game in goal for Spurs v. Thames Ironworks (in the Thames & Medway League) on 3 September 1898. Spurs won 3-0.

GOALS & GOALSCORERS

Over the years Spurs have had some splendid goalscorers and indeed goalscoring teams! Listed here are details of Spurs' top leading marksmen in the various competitions at first team level.

All Matches (inc. friendlies, abandoned games, tours) (qualification: 100 goals)

306 Jimmy Greaves
251 Bobby Smith
202 Martin Chivers
184 Len Duquemin
176 Cliff Jones
173 Alan Gilzean
169 Les Bennett
168 Bert Bliss
155 Billy Minter
153 Mark Falco

150 George Hunt
139 John Cameron
138 Jimmy Dimmock
132 Glenn Hoddle
132 Johnny Morrison
122 Taffy O'Callaghan
112 Clive Allen
110 David Copeland
109 Jack Gibbons
109 Sonny Walters
105 Garth Crooks
100 Vivian Woodward

Football League

(qualification: 50 goals)
220 Jimmy Greaves
176 Bobby Smith
135 Cliff Jones
124 George Hunt
118 Martin Chivers
114 Len Duquemin
102 Les Bennett
100 Jimmy Dimmock
95 Billy Minter
93 Bert Bliss
93 Alan Gilzean
93 Taffy O'Callaghan
88 Glenn Hoddle
88 Johnny Morrison
78 Willie Evans
78 Frank Osborne
74 Jimmy Cantrell
68 Mark Falco
67 Gary Lineker
66 Sonny Walters
65 Terry Medwin
64 Jimmy Seed
64 Eddie Baily
63 Ted Harper
60 Clive Allen
58 Steve Archiblad
53 John Duncan
53 George Robb
52 Bert Middlemiss

Premiership

(qualification 20)
75 Teddy Sheringham
48 Chris Armstrong
31 Steffen Iversen
30 Darren Anderton
29 Jurgen Klinsmann
22 Les Ferdinand

FA Cup

(qualification: 15 goals)
32 Jimmy Greaves
22 Bobby Smith
21 Alan Gilzean
20 Len Duquemin
16 Cliff Jones
15 Sandy Brown

League Cup
(qualification: 10 goals)
23 Martin Chivers
13 Clive Allen
12 Martin Peters
10 Chris Armstrong
10 Glenn Hoddle
10 Teddy Sheringham

European Cups
(qualification: 10 goals)
22 Martin Chivers
13 Mark Falco
13 Alan Gilzean
13 Martin Peters
10 Bobby Smith

FA Charity Shield
(qualification: 2 goals)
2 Les Allen
2 Mark Falco
2 Jimmy Greaves

Southern League
(qualification: 20 goals)
46 David Copeland
45 Vivian Woodward
41 John Cameron
37 John Kirwan
29 William Joyce
27 Sandy Brown
23 John Walton
21 Tom Morris
20 Tom Pratt

Wartime (1915-19)
(qualification: 15 goals)
67 Jimmy Banks
44 Bert Bliss
36 Ted Bassett
16 Billy Minter

Wartime (1939*-46)
(qualification: 20 goals)
90 Albert Gibbons
76 George Ludford
42 Ron Burgess
31 Pat Beasley
28 Johnny Morrison
21 George Foreman
24 Jack Rowley
21 Andy Duncan
* Including Div.2, August/September 1939

All Competitive Matches (not friendlies etc)
(qualification: 125 goals)
268 Jimmy Greaves
215 Bobby Smith
181 Martin Chivers
159 Cliff Jones
138 George Hunt
134 Len Duquemin

Most goals in a game (for Spurs):
9 Syd McClellan v. Saskatchewan FA XI (Canadian tour) May 1952
7 Jack Rowley v. Luton Town (League South) February 1944
6 George Hunt v. Jersey (tour) May 1932
5 *Ted Harper v. Reading (Division 2) August 1930
5 *Alf Stokes v. Birmingham City (Division 1) September 1957
5 *Les Allen v. Crewe Alex (FA Cup replay) February 1960
5 Frank Cottrell v. Coldstream Guards (Luton Charity Cup) November 1891
5 Mark Falco v. Chelmsford City (friendly) April 1986
5 Billy Joyce v. Dartford (Thames & Medway) April 1899
5 Jack Jull v. Iona (London Senior Cup) October 1889
5 Ken McKay v. Royal Engineers (Thames & Medway) November 1898
5 Bobby Smith v. Ontario All Stars (Canadian tour) May 1957
5 Alf Stokes v. Manitoba All Stars (Canadian tour) June 1957
5 Vivian Woodward v. West Ham United (s/f S.C.C.) January 1905
*Spurs League record against these three players

Spurs' top League scorers (season by season)
1908-09 Billy Minter 16
1909-10 Billy Minter 15
1910-11 Billy Minter 19
1911-12 Billy Minter 17
1912-13 Jimmy Cantrell 12
1913-14 Jimmy Cantrell 16
1914-15 Bert Bliss 21
1919-20 Bert Bliss 31
1920-21 Bert Bliss 17
1921-22 Charlie Wilson 11
1922-23 Alex Lindsay 11
1923-24 Alex Lindsay 20
1924-25 Jimmy Seed 17
1925-26 Frank Osborne 25
1926-27 Jimmy Dimmock 19
1927-28 Taffy O'Callaghan 19
1928-29 Frank Osborne 19
1929-30 Ted Harper 14
1930-31 Ted Harper 36
1931-32 George Hunt 24
1932-33 George Hunt 33
1933-34 George Hunt 32
1934-35 Willie Evans 12
1935-36 Johnny Morrison 25
1936-37 Johnny Morrison 29
1937-38 Johnny Morrison 22
1938-39 Albert Hall 10
1946-47 Les Bennett 16
1947-48 Len Duquemin 16
1948-49 Les Bennett 19
1949-50 Les Medley 18
1950-51 Sonny Walters 15
1951-52 Les Bennett 20
1952-53 Len Duquemin 18
1953-54 George Robb 16
1954-55 Johnny Gavin 13
1955-56 Johnny Brooks/Bobby Smith 10
1956-57 Bobby Smith/Alf Stokes 18
1957-58 Bobby Smith 36
1958-59 Bobby Smith 32
1959-60 Bobby Smith 25

1960-61 Bobby Smith 28
1961-62 Jimmy Greaves 21
1962-63 Jimmy Greaves 37
1963-64 Jimmy Greaves 35
1964-65 Jimmy Greaves 29
1965-66 Jimmy Greaves 15
1966-67 Jimmy Greaves 25
1967-68 Jimmy Greaves 23
1968-69 Jimmy Greaves 27
1969-70 Martin Chivers 11
1970-71 Martin Chivers 21
1971-72 Martin Chivers 25
1972-73 Martin Chivers 17
1973-74 Martin Chivers 17
1974-75 John Duncan 12
1975-76 John Duncan 20
1976-77 Chris Jones 9
1977-78 John Duncan 16
1978-79 Peter Taylor 11
1979-80 Glenn Hoddle 19
1980-81 Steve Archibald 20
1981-82 Garth Crooks 13
1982-83 Steve Archibald 11
1983-84 Steve Archibald 21
1984-85 Mark Falco 22
1985-86 Mark Falco 19
1986-87 Clive Allen 33
1987-88 Clive Allen 11
1988-89 Chris Waddle 14
1989-90 Gary Lineker 24
1990-91 Gary Lineker 13
1991-92 Gary Lineker 28
1992-93 Teddy Sheringham 21
1993-94 Teddy Sheringham 14
1994-95 Jurgen Klinsmann 20
1995-96 Teddy Sheringham 16
1996-97 Teddy Sheringham 7
1997-98 Jurgen Klinsmann 9
1998-99 Steffen Iversen 9
1999-00 Chris Armstrong 14
2000-01 Les Ferdinand 10

Top Scorers in the Southern League: 1896-1908
1896-97 Bob Clements 14
1897-98 Billy Joyce 20
1898-99 Billy Joyce 13
1899-00 Tom Pratt 24
1900-01 Sandy Brown 12
1901-02 Sandy Brown 18
1902-03 David Copeland/Alf Warner 8
1903-04 John Jones 15
1904-05 Alex Glen 10
1905-06 Herbert Chapman 11
1906-07 Jimmy Reid 18
1907-08 Vivian Woodward 10

Top Scorers in the Western League: 1900-1908
1900-01 Sandy Brown/John Cameron 6
1901-02 Sandy Brown/John Kirwan 9
1902-03 John Barlow 5
1903-04 John Jones 7
1904-05 David Copeland 5
1905-06 Frank Berry/Peter Kyle 6
1906-07 Alf Whyman 3

1907-08 Jimmy Reid 5

Top Scorers in the United League: 1896-1899
1896-97 Frank Clements 5
1897-98 Billy Joyce 13
1898-99 Billy Joyce 8

Top Scorers in the London League: 1901-04
1901-02 Sandy Brown 7
1902-03 John Jones 3
1903-04 Alf Walton 4

Top Scorers in the Thames & Medway League
1898-99 John Cameron/Billy Joyce/Ken McKay, all 9

Top Scorer in the Southern District Combination
1898-99 John Cameron 10

Top Scorer in the South East Counties League
1903-04 John Jones 4
Top Scorers in Wartime
1915-16 Bert Bliss 22
1916-17 Jimmy Banks 30
1917-18 Jimmy Banks 23
1918-19 Billy Minter 11

1939-40 Johnny Morrison 28
1940-41 Jack Gibbons 24
1941-42 Jack Gibbons 19
1942-43 George Ludford 20
1943-44 Jack Rowley 22
1944-45 Jack Gibbons 16
1945-46 Jack Gibbons 14

Most first-class goals scored in a season by players:
49 Clive Allen   1986-87
42 Jimmy Greaves 1962-63
42 Ted Harper   1930-31
38 Bobby Smith   1957-58
35 Bobby Smith   1958-59
33 Bert Bliss   1919-20
33 Bobby Smith   1960-61

Most goals scored in a season by the team:
115 League Division 1	1960-61 (42 games)
112 London F/Combination	1916-17 (40 games)
111 League Division 1	1962-63 (42 games)
104 League Division 1	1956-57 (42 games)
102 League Division 2	1919-20 (42 games)

* Most goals scored in Premiership - 66 in 1994-95.

Lowest number of goals scored in a season (by the team):
38 League Division 1	1987-88 (40 games)
44 Premiership	1996-97 (38 games)
44 Premiership	1997-98 (38 games)
45 League Division 1	1973-74 (42 games)
45 League Division 1	1912-13 (38 games)

Most goals conceded in a season (by the team):
95 League Division 1	1958-59 (42 games)
93 League Division 1	1934-35 (42 games)
90 League Division 1	1914-15 (38 games)
81 League Division 1	1963-64 (42 games)
81 Football League (S)	1945-46 (42 games)

* Most in Premiership - 66 in 1992-

Fewest goals conceded in a season (by the team):

29	Southern League	1905-06 (34 games)
32	League Division 2	1908-09 (38 games)
32	League Division 2	1919-20 (42 games)
33	League Division 1	1970-71 (42 games)
35	League Division 2	1949-50 (42 games)
38	Premiership	1995-96 (38 games)

Own Goals

A breakdown of the own-goals in Spurs' favour at senior level:

Premiership	14
Football League	68
FA Cup	14
League Cup	7
European Games	4
Others	24

● Mike England and John Pratt both conceded first-half goals when Spurs played host to Burnley in October 1974. They quickly made amends by scoring at the right end after the interval but their efforts were in vain as the Clarets won 3-2.

● Gary Mabbutt scored at both ends (for Spurs and Coventry City) in the 1987 FA Cup Final.

● Nottingham Forest defender Des Walker (a former junior at White Hart Lane) conceded the winning own-goal when Spurs won the 1991 FA Cup Final at Wembley.

● An own-goal by Terry Phelan (Manchester City) gave Spurs a 1-0 win at Maine Road on November 1992. This was Spurs' first own-goal in the Premiership.

● Future Spurs wing-half Alan Mullery once conceded an own-goal after just 14 seconds when playing for Fulham.

● The first 'away' goal scored at White Hart Lane came courtesy of a Spurs player - Sandy Tait - who conceded an 'og' in the friendly with Notts County in September 1899.

Rapid/quick scoring

● On 7 February 1993, Spurs were a goal down at half-time at home to Southampton but they stormed back in the second-half and scored four times in four minutes 44 seconds (between the 54-59th minutes) to eventually win 4-2.

● Ledley King scored for Spurs after just ten seconds play in the away game against Bradford City on 9 Dec 2000....the fastest so far ever recorded in the Premiership.

● That King strike may well have been the fastest ever goal scored by a Spurs player in any match. Other Spurs players who have secured 'quick' goals include Peter Taylor in the League v. Sunderland at home on 22 April 1978 (26 seconds); Foster Hedley for Spurs' reserves against The Army on 5 March 1934 (27 secs); Bill Nicholson on his debut for England v. Portugal at Everton on 19 May 1951 (28 seconds) and Jimmy Lee for the club's Academy Under-17 side v. Queen's Park Rangers on 19 Nov 2000 (47 secs).

● Clive Allen put Spurs ahead after 112 seconds of the 1987 FA Cup Final v. Coventry City.

Goal-talk

● Clive Allen scored a club record 49 goals for Spurs in season 1986-87 (33 League, 12 League Cup, four FA Cup).

● The previous record holders were Jimmy Greaves (who netted 42 in 1962-63, 37 in the First Division) and Ted Harper, also with 42 in 1930-31.

● Greaves was Spurs' top goalscorer in each of his eight seasons at White Hart Lane (1961-62 to 1968-69).

In total, hot-shot Greaves scored 266 first-class goals for Spurs

(1961-70). He netted 220 in the First Division, hit 32 in the FA Cup, claimed five in the League Cup and claimed nine in European competitions. He also notched 40 goals in other matches....to finish with a total of 306 (in 419 outings).

Greaves scored in five successive League games for Spurs in 1968 (at the end of one season and at the start of the next).

During his career Greaves - the goal-machine - netted 357 times in League games for Chelsea, Spurs and West Ham - all in the First Division. In English club football, he scored well over 450 goals in close on 500 games plus a few more in Italy's Serie 'A'.

Greaves scored against 36 of the 38 League clubs he played against (the exceptions being Crystal Palace and Huddersfield Town). His only appearance against the latter club was his 516th and final League game in 1971 (West Ham lost 1-0). He claimed two five-timers in his career - both for Chelsea v. PNE in 1959 and WBA the following year. Prior to signing professional forms for Chelsea in 1957, Greaves had already notched 114 goals for the club's junior and intermediate sides.

● Billy Minter was Spurs leading scorer in each of the club's first four League seasons (from 1908-09). He was runner-up (with 11 goals) in 1912-13.

● Bert Bliss was Spurs' top marksman in the last season before the Great War (1914-15) and the first after it (1919-20).

● Ted Harper's tally of 36 goals in 1930-31 included two hat-tricks and a fourtimer. He also netted in five successive League games: 17 January to 14 February inclusive. Harper established individual scoring records for three clubs in eight seasons - 43 goals for Blackburn Rovers in 1925-26, 36 for Spurs in 1930-31 and 37 for Preston North End in 1932-33. Jimmy Greaves later bettered his Spurs record.

● Harper scored more goals per games for Spurs than any other player - 83 in 78 outings, including 62 in 63 League appearances.

● Johnny Morrison netted in six successive League games for Spurs between 12 October and 16 November 1935 (his overall tally was 10 goals). Then, during April and May 1940 Morrison netted in each of seven consecutive Wartime games. He scored 17 goals in total including three hat-tricks.

● Garth Crooks found the net in each of six successive League games between 18 December 1984 and 12 January 1985. He also scored in one FA Cup-tie during the same period.

● Clive Allen scored nine times in five successive League games in 1986. Allen also scored in every League Cup game played by Spurs in season 1986-87 (12 goals in nine outings).

● In seven home League games played between September and November 1935 Spurs scored 31 goals: 3, 5, 5, 4, 7, 4, 3.

● During the months of October, November & December 1950, a total of 26 goals were scored in four League games at White Hart Lane; Spurs winning 6-1, 5-1 and 7-0 and drawing 3-3.

● Spurs netted 27 goals (4, 9, 4, 6, 4) in five home League games during a six-week period from mid-September to early November 1962. Jimmy Greaves netted nine.

● Tom Pratt was Spurs' top-scorer in a Southern League season, netting 24 goals in 1899-1900. Billy Joyce hit 20 in 1897-98 and Sandy Brown claimed 18 in 1901-02. Brown also scored nine goals in the Western League, seven in the London League and one in the Dewar Shield in that same 1901-02 campaign for an overall total of 35 at senior level. He also netted five goals in 'other' matches.

● Brown scored 15 FA Cup goals for Spurs in 1900-01 (a record). He netted in every round to become only the second player to achieve that feat (behind Aston Villa's utility forward Archie Hunter in season 1886-87).

● Spurs striker Clive Allen, with a total of 12 in season 1986-87, holds the record for most goals in a League Cup competition.

● Teddy Sheringham (with 22 goals) finished up as the Premiership's top-scorer in its first season of 1992-93.

● Spurs scored 15 goals in successive League games in August/September 1930, beating Reading 7-1 and Burnley 8-1.

● Over a period of five-and-a-half weeks in October/November 1932, Spurs scored 29 goals in seven League games, including a haul of 24 in five successive home matches.

● Spurs scored 14 goals in their last three homes games in 1933-34 (they registered two 5-1 wins).

● Equalled 52 years later, scoring 14 times in their last three home First Division games at the end of the 1985-86 season.

● Spurs netted 16 goals against Clapton Orient in a week in December 1940, beating their London neighbours 9-0 and 7-0 in League South matches. In between times they drew 3-3 with Millwall to claim 19 goals in eight days.

● Spurs played Clapton Orient four times in three weeks during 1940-41 season & scored 28 goals, winning 9-0, 7-0, 3-0 and 9-1.

● At the end of the 1962-63 season (in April) and between August-October at the start of the next campaign, Spurs scored 38 goals in eight home League games.

● Spurs' last five League games of 1964-65 produced 25 goals including wins of 7-4 and 6-2.

● Spurs netted 11 goals in their opening three games at the start of the 1965-66 campaign and it was 38 scored in their first eight matches at White Hart Lane.

● Alan Gilzean did not score a single 'away' goal for Spurs between February 1965 and October 1966 despite playing in 28 games. In that same period, however, he did oblige with 26 goals at home. He eventually ended his blank spell on opposing grounds by getting six goals in six away matches, starting off with two against Blackpool on 5 November 1966.

● One of the most unusual (and perhaps fortunate) goals scored was the winner at home to Huddersfield Town in a First Division match on 2 April 1952. Eddie Baily took a corner but the ball struck the referee and rebounded to the Spurs inside-left who then delicately chipped a pass into the penalty-area where Len Duquemin headed home the only goal of the game. Huddersfield protested vigorously to the referee and linesman, to no avail. The Spurs player had certainly infringed the law 17 which states that a player cannot play the ball a second time without any other player doing so from a dead-ball situation. The referee was clearly at fault yet, after the game the Football League allowed the result to stand despite Huddersfield's complaints! Spurs went on to claim the runners-up spot in the First Division on goal-average from Arsenal.

● Spurs failed to score in any of six successive home and away League games during January and February 1986.

● Spurs played out 602 minutes of Premiership football between 18 November and 23 December 1995 without conceding a goal - a club record. Their best shut-out period in the Football League is 576 minutes - between 4 January and 25 March 1987.

● Jimmy Seed scored around 80 goals for Whitburn FC (Durham League) in season 1913-14. He was snapped up by Sunderland and finally moved to Spurs in 1920.

● Les Miller scored 60 goals for the French club Souchaux in 1935-36. He joined Spurs for the start of the next campaign!

GORMAN, JOHN

A full-back, born in Winchburgh near Edinburgh on 16 August 1949, John Gorman played for Celtic and Carlisle United before joining Spurs in November 1976. He had made 32 first-class appearances for the club up to March 1979 when he signed for Tampa Bay Rowdies. He then became Gillingham coach and

afterwards was trainer/coach at Leyton Orient prior to taking over as assistant-manager (to Glenn Hoddle) at Swindon Town. Gorman has since been assistant-manager at West Bromwich Albion, Southampton and Spurs, with Hoddle again manager at the latter two clubs. He also held a similar post during Hoddle's spell as England manager.

GORNIK ZABRZE

Spurs playing record against the Polish club:

Competition	P	W	D	L	F	A
European Cup	2	1	0	1	10	5

Gornik Zabrze were Spurs' first opponents in a major European Cup tie. The Polish side were defeated 10-5 over two legs in a Preliminary Round of the European Cup in 1961-62.

The first leg was played in Poland on 13 September when Gornik won 4-2 in front of 70,000 fans.

Cliff Jones and Terry Dyson scored for Spurs who fielded: Brown; Baker, Henry; Blanchflower, Norman, Mackay; Jones, White, Smith, Allen, Dyson.

The return leg at White Hart Lane a week drew a crowd of 56,737 and this time Spurs overwhelmed their opponents to the tune of 8-1 (after leading 5-0 at half-time).

Danny Blanchflower, Jones (3), John White, Bobby Smith (2) and Dyson scored the goals to clinch Spurs' first victory in a European competition. The team remained unchanged from the first game.

GOUGH, CHARLES RICHARD

Born in Stockholm, Sweden on 5 April 1962, the son of a Scottish mother and a former professional footballer (Charlie), Richard Gough was brought up in South Africa. Educated at Wits University, he played for the University team and Southern Transvaal and was also chosen to play for South Africa Schoolboys before spending a few months with Charlton Athletic in 1978. He failed to make the grade with the Addicks and in June 1979 was signed as an apprentice by Dundee United, turning professional in March 1980.

He quickly established himself north of the border and collected five Scottish Under-21 caps and also gained the first of his 61 senior caps when he lined up against Switzerland in 1983. That same year he helped Dundee United win the League championship and finish runners-up in both the Scottish Cup and League Cup Finals. In 1986 Gough was voted Scotland's 'Player of the Year' and skippered his country - a few weeks later he joined Spurs for £750,000 and at the end of his first season at White Hart Lane he played in the FA Cup Final defeat by Coventry City. Having been selected to represent the Football League against the Rest of the World in the Centenary Match at Wembley in 1988, he went on to score twice in 65 League and Cup games for Spurs. He played in 76 first team matches overall before transferring to Glasgow Rangers for £1.5 million in October 1987. He left Goodison Park to sign briefly for the Australia club Northern Spirit in the summer of 2001.

He lined up initially alongside his former White Hart Lane colleague Graham Roberts as the Ibrox Park side started to assert their superiority on the Scottish footballing scene. He went on to win nine more League championships, five Skol Cup Finals and three Scottish Cup Finals.

Gough was again voted Scotland's 'Footballer of the Year' (by the SFWA) in 1989 and was a key member of Scotland's 1990 World Cup squad - having had a disappointing campaign four years earlier. He made well over 400 appearances for the 'Gers (35 goals scored) prior to having a decent spell in the USA with San Jose, from May 1998 to March 1999. On his return to England Gough signed for Nottingham Forest but failed to settle at The City Ground and in June 1998 (at the age of of 37) he was snapped up on a free transfer by his former Ibrox boss, Walter Smith for Everton. He skippered the Merseysiders in the Premiership before a calf injury started to disrupt his fitness. In 2001 Gough agreed to play for Northern Spirit in Australia. He left Goodison Park in June 2001.

* In February 1987, a Scottish brewery company presented Gough with an award to 'honour the performance of the Scottish-born player'...who was, of course, born in Sweden!

GRAHAM, GEORGE

George Graham was born in Bargeddle, Lanark on 30 November 1944. He attended Coatbridge Schools and played for Swinton FC (West Scotland) and Coatbridge Boys before joining Aston Villa's groundstaff in 1959, turning professional in December 1961. He was transferred to Chelsea for £5,950 in July 1964 and switched across London to Arsenal for £50,000 plus Tommy Baldwin in September 1966. From Highbury he went north to Manchester United for £120,000 (December 1972), then to Portsmouth in November 1974, had a spell with Crystal Palace from November 1976 to May 1980 and assisted California Surf (NASL) on loan for four months from March-July 1978. He retired as a player in the summer of 1980 and was appointed Youth team coach/assistant-manager at Selhurst Park. He became coach at Queen's Park Rangers in 1981 and took over as manager of Millwall in December 1982, a position he held for three-and-a-half years, until May 1986 when he took over at Arsenal. He spent nine successful seasons in the hot-seat at Highbury (up to May 1995). Then he accepted the manager's job at Leeds United (September 1996-September 1998) before becoming boss of Tottenham Hotspur in October 1998. He retained that position until March 2001 when he was dismissed by the new owners who brought in ex-player Glenn Hoddle.

Nicknamed 'Stroller', Graham - a runner-up with Villa in the 1963 League Cup Final against - won a League Cup prize himself with Chelsea two years later. He gained League championship and FA Cup winning medals in 1971, earned a runners-up prize in the latter competition in 1972 and also helped Arsenal win the Fairs Cup in 1970. He also collected two loser's prizes in the League Cup Finals of 1968 and 1969. During his League career, Graham made 455 appearances and notched 95 goals. Capped as a Schoolboy and Youth player by Scotland, he also represented his country twice at Under-23 level and appeared in 12 full internationals.

As a manager he led Millwall to victory in the Final of the Football League Trophy (1983) and then he guided the Lions to promotion from Division Three two years later.

As boss of Arsenal, Graham saw two League titles won (in 1989 & 1991) and victory claimed in the League Cup Final of 1987. He tasted glory of completing the FA Cup and League Cup double in 1993. After leaving Highbury he guided Leeds into Europe in 1998 before moving back to North London to take charge Spurs Unfortunately he failed to bring success to White Hart Lane and was dismissed a week or so before Spurs met his former club Arsenal in the FA Cup semi-final in March 2001.

GRASSHOPPER-CLUB ZURICH

Spurs playing record against the Swiss club:

Competition	P	W	D	L	F	A
UEFA Cup	2	2	0	0	9	2

Spurs were paired with the Swiss side Grasshopper-Club Zurich in the first round of the 1973-74 UEFA Cup competition and they went through comfortably, winning the tie 9-2 on aggregate after two comfortable victories.

The first game was played in Zurich on 19 September in front of 11,200 fans and goals by Ray Evans, Martin Chivers (2) and Alan Gilzean (2) gave Spurs an impressive 5-1 victory.

A fortnight later 18,105 spectators attended White Hart Lane to see Spurs confirm their superiority with a 4-1 second leg triumph when Mike England, Martin Peters (2) and Lador (og) found the back of the Grasshopper's net.

Associated with both clubs: Ramon Vega (player) & Christian Gross (manager of both Spurs and Grasshopper-Club).

GRAVESEND UNITED

Spurs playing record against United:

Competition	P	W	D	L	F	A
Other Leagues	12	10	0	2	38	11
Wellingboro' C Cup	1	1	0	0	3	2
Summary	13	11	0	2	41	13

Spurs average over three goals a game in the various League & Cup encounters with United. Their best wins of the eleven recorded were those of 6-2 in March 1900, 5-0 in April 1901, 4-0 in October 1896 and October 1899 (all in the Southern League)

GRAY, ANDREW ARTHUR

Born in Lambeth, London on 22 February 1964, midfielder Andy Gray's footballing career started with Lambeth & London Borough Schools. He then assisted Corinthian Casuals and Dulwich Hamlet before joining Crystal Palace as a professional in November 1984 for £2,000). He transferred to Aston Villa for £150,000 in November 1987, returned to London with Queen's Park Rangers for £425,000 in February 1989 and then had a second spell with Crystal Palace, re-signed for £500,000 in August 1989. He found his way to White Hart Lane in a £900,000 deal in February 1992, but never really settled down with Spurs and after a loan spell with Swindon Town (December 1992-January 1993) he quit League football in 1994. A forceful player, able to turn his hand to any request, Gray was capped twice by England at Under-21 level before gaining a full cap. In 1991 he helped Palace win the Zenith Data Systems Cup (v Everton). Gray made 335 appearances and scored 61 goals in League and Cup football. His record with Spurs was two goals in 16 first team outings.

GRAY, JAMES A

Born in Bristol circa 1878, Jimmy Gray played for Bristol Rovers, Aston Villa (August 1904) and Glasgow Rangers (April 1905) before joining Spurs in May 1907. He remained at White Hart Lane for just the one season, making 24 first team appearances as a half-back before moving to Leyton where he remained until May 1912 when he retired. A very useful footballer, Gray did well with Bristol Rovers before making seven first team appearances for Villa. He was a regular choice for Rangers for two years before making his Spurs debut against his old club, Bristol Rovers!

Gray (with a team-mate Bob Walker) was suspended by Spurs after a 'breach of club discipline' in February 1907. A further indescretion followed (while still under suspension) and as a result an indefinite ban was imposed on the player who was released by the club at the end of the 1907-08 campaign.

GRAYS UNITED

Spurs playing record against United:

Competition	P	W	D	L	F	A
T&M League	2	1	0	1	2	2

These two matches in the Thames & Medway League took place in season 1898-99.

GREAVES, JAMES PETER

Born in East Ham, London on 20 February 1940, inside-forward Jimmy Greaves started scoring goals (at competition level) for the Lakeside Manor Boys Club and Dagenham Schools. He then continued to bulge the net playing for London Schools and Essex Boys before signing as a junior for Chelsea at the age of 15, turning professional at Stamford Bridge in May 1957. He never looked back and continued to savage goalkeepers for the next 20 years! A tremendous striker - a goal poacher of the highest calibre - Greaves was lethal anywhere around the penalty area! One of the finest marksmen ever to grace a football pitch (world-wide) Greaves seemed to skate through First Division defences at will. He netted some stunning individual goals. Indeed, most of his efforts came from inside the 18-yard area - very rarely did he smash an effort from any distance. He used to feed superbly off capable target men and he did this for club and country, rattling in goals left, right and centre, at all levels. There is not an exact figure available to show how many goals Greaves actually scored as a professional footballer. Suffice to say it was well over 500 with 357 of them coming in the First Division alone - fired and sometimes headed home past some of the greatest goalkeepers in the country! He netted 132 in 169 first-class games for his first club Chelsea. Followed on with nine for AC Milan in Italy; whipped in a staggering 268 (in 381 competitive games for Spurs) Spurs (306 in 419 first team games in total); weighed in with 13 for West Ham United and followed up quite a few more for his four non-League clubs....And don't forget he also scored 44 goals in only 57 games for England at full international level, netted 11 in 12 appearances for the Under-23 side, potted two more for Young England, registered five for the Football League XI in representative matches, knocked in one for England against Young England and grabbed four for England's Youth team. Greaves also scored in front of a 20,000 gate when he made his first appearance in a Spurs shirt, in a Combination game at Plymouth just after joining the club. Even before he signed as a full-time professional for Chelsea, he had notched no fewer than 114 goals as a junior for the club...apart from what he had achieved earlier as a Schoolboy and down the park with his local team on Saturdays and Sundays! Greaves left Chelsea for AC Milan in June 1961 for £80,000. He returned to England in December 1961 to sign for Spurs for a fee of £99,999 (manager Bill Nicholson refusing to acknowledge him as being the first £100,000 footballer).

A member of Spurs' 1962 and 1967 FA Cup winning sides, he scored twice to help seal victory over Atletico Madrid in the European Cup-winners Cup Final of 1963, and was part of the England squad that won the World Cup in 1966. He did not figure in the Final, having lost his place in the side to Geoff Hurst after playing in the opening three matches.

In March 1970 Greaves moved from White Hart Lane to West Ham United in a £200,000 package deal that saw his England colleague Martin Peters end up with Spurs (Greaves was valued at £54,000 and Peters at £146,000). From Upton Park he switched to Barnet (May 1971) before rounding off a magnificent career with Chelmsford City, Brentwood Town and Woodford Town. After hanging up his boots Graeves sadly became an alcoholic and was in fact serious ill at one stage. Thankfully, he overcame the problem and for many years worked very successfully on ITV (with Ian St John) before falling ill again.

* A crowd of almost 46,000 attended Greaves' testimonial match at White Hart Lane in October 1972
* Greaves still holds the individual scoring records for most League goals in a season at Chelsea 41 (in 1960-61) and Spurs 37 (in 1962-63).

GREENFIELD, GEORGE JOHN WILLIAM

A broken leg, suffered against Fulham at Craven Cottage in December 1932, effectively ended what could have been a sparkling international career for inside-forward Jack 'Nobby' Greenfield. Highly-rated at the time, it seemed inevitable that he

A shot from Greaves is deflected by Blackburn right back Taylor in a League game at White Hart Lane.

would gain full England recognition. Unfortunately it was not to be, and after more than two years of treatment (and only a handful more first team outings) he was forced to retire from competitive football in February 1935 at the age of 27. He was retained for a while as a member of the White Hart Lane groundstaff. Born in Hackney on 4 August 1908 and now deceased, Greenfield joined Spurs as a professional in November 1930 after playing for the Lea Bridge Gasworks club. He scored 13 goals in 34 first team games for Spurs before injury struck

GRICE, FRANK

Perhaps Frank Grice's greatest claim to fame in the world of football came in April 1949 when, as manager of the Irish club Glentoran, he sold Danny Blanchflower to Barnsley. And we know what the Irishman did after that!

As a player himself Grice was also a wing-half who served in the Army before joining Linby and then Notts County, first as an amateur in June 1931, turning professional two months later. He moved from Meadow Lane to Spurs in March 1936 and appeared in 55 first team games (one goal scored) before being released at the end of the 1938-39 season when he signed as a player for Glentoran, later taking over as manager of the Irish League club. After the War he took charge of Cambridge City.

Grice had a good innings: he was born in Derby on 13 November 1908 and died in Dundee on 29 April 1988.

GRIFFITHS, FRANK

Welsh goalkeeper Frank Griffiths from Derby was 27 when he joined Spurs from Millwall in April 1901. He appeared in 21 games for the club before moving to Preston in March 1902. Later he assisted West Ham and New Brompton before losing his life on a French battlefield in October 1917.

GRIMSBY TOWN

Spurs playing record against the Mariners:

Competition	P	W	D	L	F	A
Football League	14	8	1	5	27	24
League Cup	1	1	0	0	3	1
Summary	15	9	1	5	30	25

Spurs met the Mariners for the first time at League level on 28 November 1908 (Division 2), a crowd of 14,000 at White Hart Lane seeing Spurs register a 2-0 victory.

Spurs beat the Mariners 5-2 in a home Second Division match in April 1949, Les Bennett and Len Duquemin both scoring twice.

Players with both clubs include: Tom Atherton, David Black, Herbert Chapman, Bill Felton, Alex Glen, Leon Hyde, John L Jones, Tom Pratt, Max Seeburg, Jimmy Smailes.

Wartime guests (with either one or both clubs): Tom Howshall, Joe Meek, Haydn Price (also Grimsby manager), Chris Young (Amateur).

GRIMSDELL, ARTHUR

Half-back Arthur Grimsdell was an aggressive player, always totally committed, a real competitor who had a marvellous career in the game.

Born in Watford on 23 March 1894, he attended the local school and played for Watford St Stephens while also representing Watford Boys and England Schools as a teenager. In the summer of 1909, he signed as an amateur for Watford, turning professional in November 1911. Less than four months later he was transferred to Spurs and over the next 17 years gave the club tremendous service, appearing in 417 first team games and scoring 38 goals, some netted from well outside the penalty area.

He made 324 League appearances and also played in 36 FA Cup matches, captaining the winning side in 1921 when Spurs defeated Wolves 1-0 at Stamford Bridge.

He scored twice for England against Scotland in one of two 1919 Victory Internationals he took part in and later, after coming steadfastly through the pre-arranged England trials, he added six senior caps to his tally while also representing the Football League.

A key performer for Spurs, Grimsdell broke his leg in a 5-3 defeat at Leicester City in October 1925 and was out of first team action until April 1927. He regained his fitness to a certain extent, but was never quite the same again and left White Hart Lane in August 1929 to become player-secretary-manager of Clapton Orient, later joining the Orient Board of Directors, a position he later held at Watford (1945-451). Grimsdell died in his native Watford on 12 March 1963.

GROSS, CHRISTIAN

Spurs' head coach (team manager) from 25 November 1997 until 5 September 1998, Christian Gross left the Grasshopper-Club Zurich to take up his position at White Hart Lane six days after the departure of Gerry Francis (Chris Hughton having held things together in the interim period).

Unfortunately under his guidance Spurs struggled and won only ten League and Cup matches before Gross departed company to be replaced by David Pleat.

Born in Zurich, Switzerland on 14 August 1954, he was a player (midfield) with SV Hongg, Grasshopper-Club Zurich (1967), Laussanne-Sports (1975), Xamax Neuegburg (1978), Vfl Bochum (1980), FC St Gallen (1982) and FC Lugano (1985-88). On his retirement he was appointed head coach of FC Wil, a position he held for five years until taking over in the same capacity at his former club, Grasshopper-Club Zurich. He was there for four years prior to moving to England.

Gross represented his country once in a full international v. East Germany in March 1978. He also won five 'B' caps at Youth team level as a teenager. He gained a Swiss coaching certificate & German 'A' certificate (Deutscher Fussballbund) in 1982.

As coach he guided FC Wil from the Swiss Fourth Division into the Second and took Grasshopper Club to a Swiss Cup Final victory in 1994 and two League championships in 1995 and 1996. Gross was in line to take over as coach/manager of the Switzerland national team in 2000, but missed out on the job at the last minute. Gross is now coach of FC Basel (Switzerland).

GROUNDS

Spurs have played competitive football (League and/or Cup matches) on the following 'home' grounds:

1882-88	Tottenham Marshes
1888-99	Northumberland Park
Since 1899	White Hart Lane

(The ground was originally called 'The High Road Ground')
(See also under separate categories).

Ground Facts

Spurs have also used their 'training' ground at Cheshunt for various matches (including reserve and Youth team games and pre-season first team friendlies) and they occupied the The Goldstone Ground (home of Brighton & Hove Albion) for two InterToto Cup home ties in July 1995. Spurs moved out of their Cheshunt training ground in 1987, present training ground is Spurs Lodge at Chigwell.

GUEST PLAYERS (SEE UNDER PLAYERS)

HADDOW, DAVID

Goalkeeper David Haddow was a vastly experienced professional when he joined Spurs in November 1899 at the age of 30. He remained at the club until May 1901, making 57 first team appearances.

A Scotsman, born in Dalserf, Lanarkshire on 12 June 1869, he played junior football in Coatbridge before registering with Albion Rovers in 1888. From there he switched to Derby County (1890), moved to Albion Rovers (early in 1901), transferred to Glasgow Rangers (mid-1891), teamed up with Motherwell (in 1895), diverted south to Burnley (halfway through the 1985-96 season) and spent fifteen months with New Brighton Tower (from August 1898) before becoming a 'Spur.'

At Ibrox Park he was capped by Scotland (v. England) and also represented the Scottish League, gaining a Scottish Cup winners' medal in 1894. He helped Burnley win the Second Division title in 1898 and was recruited by Spurs after George Clawley had suffered a broken leg. When Clawley was fit again, Haddow was released.

HAJDUK SPLIT

Spurs' playing record against Split is:

Competition	P	W	D	L	F	A
ECW Cup	4	3	0	1	8	4
UEFA Cup	2	1	0	1	2	2
Summary	6	4	0	2	10	6

In 1967-68 Spurs defeated the Yugoslavian side Hajduk Split 6-3 on aggregate in the 1st round of the European Cup-winners Cup competition.

A crowd of 25,000 saw Spurs win 2-0 in Split on 20 September (Jimmy Robertson and Jimmy Greaves the scorers) and there were 38,623 fans present for the return leg a week later when Robertson (2), Alan Gilzean and Terry Venables gave Spurs a hard-earned 4-3 victory.

The third and fourth meetings between the two clubs took place in the semi-final of the 1983-84 UEFA Cup and again Spurs came out on top, winning on the away goal rule after two titanic battles. On 11 April, a crowd of 40,000 saw Mark Falco's first-half strike give Spurs a great chance with a vital 'away' goal in the first leg in Yugoslavia, Split winning 2-1. And then in front of almost 44,000 ecstatic fans at White Hart Lane a fortnight later, Micky Hazard's vital sixth minute effort took Spurs through to meet RSC Anderlecht in the Final.

When Spurs last entered a European competition - the Cup-winners Cup in 1991-92 - they met Split over two legs in the 1st round proper, defeating them 2-0 at home on 2 October after losing the opening game 0-1 in front of only 7,000 spectators a fortnight earlier. This attendance figure is the smallest Spurs have ever played in front of at European level.

A crowd of 24,297 witnessed the return game at White Hart Lane when early goals by Dave Tuttle and Gordon Durie took Spurs through to meet FC Porto in the next round.

HALF-TIME SCORES

* Spurs trooped off the pitch with a 14-0 half-time lead in their Canadian tour game against Saskatchewan in 1952. In the dressing room the respective managers got together and agreed that Ted Ditchburn, the Spurs 'keeper who had hardly touched the ball during the first 45 minutes, should take over between the posts for the host club. He did just that and only conceded four goals as Spurs ran out winners by 18-1.

* At half-time in the Spurs v. Crewe Alexandra FA Cup replay at White Hart Lane in February 1960, the visitors trailed 10-1 - and eventually lost 13-2.

* When Spurs beat Everton 10-4 at home in a League game in October 1958, they went in at the interval with a 6-1 lead.

* Spurs were also 6-1 in front at the break in their home First Division game against Nottingham Forest in September 1961. They eventually won 9-2.

* Spurs were 5-0 up at half-time against Sheffield United in a home League game in 1949 (they finally won 7-0).

* Spurs led Southampton 5-0 at the break in their home Second Division match in March 1936. They went on to win 8-0.

* After being 4-2 down from the first leg of their first-ever European Cup-tie against the Polish side Gornik Zabrze, Spurs raced into a 5-0 half-time lead at White Hart Lane and went on to win the return leg 8-1 in front of 56,737 fans.

HALIFAX TOWN

Spurs record against the Shaymen:

Competition	P	W	D	L	F	A
FA Cup	1	1	0	0	3	0
League Cup	2	2	0	0	9	1
Summary	3	3	0	0	12	1

A record crowd of 36,995 packed into The Shay to watch a 5th round FA Cup-tie between Halifax and Spurs in February 1953 and two goals by Les Bennett helped Spurs to a comfortable 3-0 victory.

Players with both clubs include: John Collins, Sid Helliwell, George Hutchinson, Bobby Mimms, Tony Parks. Wartime guests (with either one or both clubs): Charlie Briggs, Harry Jackson, Tommy Simmons, Alf Whittingham.

HALL, ALBERT EDWARD BENJAMIN

Scorer of 21 goals in 81 first team outings for Spurs, Albert Hall was born at Barry Island, South Wales on 3 September 1918. He gained a handful of Welsh Schoolboy international caps as a teenager before joining the professional ranks at White Hart Lane in October 1935, following a spell at the club as a junior.

Able to play in any position in the front-line, he eventually lost his place in the side to Ronnie Dix and was transferred to Plymouth Argyle in June 1947 (signed by former Spurs manager Jack Tresadern). Moving into non-League football with Chelmsford in August 1948, Hall had guested for Norwich City and Millwall during the War when, as a serving gunner in the Royal Artillery, he was captured by the Japanese in Singapore (February 1942) and remained a prisoner for two-and-a-half years. He was then released and eventually picked up in the Pacific Ocean!

HALL, ALEX R

A versatile Scotsman, signed from Dundee in the summer of 1897, half-back Sandy Hall played in 74 first team games for the club (one in goal v. Thames Ironworks in the Thames & Medway League in September 1898). He was suspended by the club for 'neglect of training rules' in January 1899 and announced his retirement four months later.

HALL, GEORGE WILLIAM

Spurs handed Willie Hall an early Christmas present on 20 December 1932 - giving him his Football League debut against his former club Notts County in place of broken leg victim 'Nobby' Greenfield. That was the first of 375 appearances Hall made for the club, up to February 1944, when he announced his retirement. He scored 45 goals.

W. HALL (TOTTENHAM HOTSPUR)

Born in Newark, Nottinghamshire on 12 March 1912, he represented Nottinghamshire Schools and played for Ransome & Marles FC before signing professional forms at Meadow Lane in November 1930, switching to White Hart Lane just over a year later.

A clever footballer, Hall helped Spurs win promotion in his first season with the club and was quickly capped by England (1934). Indeed, a fee of £500 was paid to Notts County as soon as Hall stepped into the international arena. He went on to gain ten full caps, scoring nine goals in the process - five in one game against Ireland in November 1938 - quite unusual for a player who was known as a creator of chances rather than a marksman himself.

He overcame a few injury worries and continued to play for Spurs deep into the War years when he was forced to retire just before his 32nd birthday. In 1946, having served as a coach and manager of Clapton Orient, he was awarded a deserved testimonial before taking over as manager of Chelmsford City, later taking a similar position with Chingford Town (August 1949-51).

In later life the unfortunate Hall had the lower part of both legs amputated. He died in his native town of Newark on 22 May 1967.

HALL, JOHN

After 73 first team appearances for Manchester United, agile goalkeeper Jack Hall was transferred to Spurs in June 1936. He remained a registered player at White Hart Lane until May 1946 when he moved north to Stalybridge Celtic for the first of two spells with the Cheshire club, playing for Runcorn in between times. He guested for Blackburn Rovers, Bolton Wanderers, Hartlepool United, Nottingham Forest, Oldham Athletic, Rochdale and Stockport County during the War. He lined up in 67 first-team games for Spurs.

Born in Failsworth, Lancashire on 23 October 1912, he played for the local team before assisting Newton Heath Loco FC, from where he switched to Old Trafford in September 1932. He actually conceded six goals on his debut for United's reserve side against Huddersfield but helped the Reds win the Second Division championship in his last season with the club. It was a surprise when he left United, having performed exceedingly well in 1935-36, conceding only 43 goals. He was Spurs' first choice 'keeper for a year before handing back the gloves to Percy Hooper.

Hall was a qualified electrician and worked in that trade before and after playing professional football.

HANCOCK, KENNETH PAUL

Potteries-born goalkeeper Ken Hancock started his career with Stoke City. He made over 250 appearances for Port Vale and more than 170 for Ipswich Town before joining Spurs in 1969 as cover (with Barry Daines) for Pat Jennings. He moved to Bury in 1971.

HISTORY OF THE SPURS HANDBOOK

The 2001-02 edition of the Spurs handbook is the 93rd issue since it first appeared in 1897. Eighteen editions appeared prior to the Great War, 21 were produced between the Wars and 54 have been published since the 1939-45 conflict.

The first edition - 'The Tottenham Hotspur Football Hand-Book' - published for the 1897-98 season, contained 40 pages, 18 of which were basically adverts.

At 71 x 112mm, with a salmon pink cover, it was compiled & published by Ralph Bullock & Harry Goddard and printed by C Coventry of Tottenham. The cover price was 2d (1p).

The contents included 'The Progress of the 'Spurs', biographies of the new players, fixtures for the coming season, hints to supporters and all of the previous season's League tables. There were two pages appertaining to the laws of the game.

Photographs first appeared in the handbook in 1900-01 and by 1902-03 the number of pages had been increased to 56.

The 64-page issue for the 1907-08 season gave details of the previous season's results for the first time and in 1909-10 players' appearance records from the previous campaign were listed.

After a four-year gap, the 32-page 1919-20 handbook contrained hardly any adverts at all and by the end of the 1920s, the publication comprised 56 pages. This format remained the norm, with similar dimensions and salmon pink cover until the Second World War when there was one produced for the aborted 1939-40 season.

The first price increase to the handbook came in 1948-49 when it went up to 6d (3p) and contained 60 pages, each measuring 103mm by 147mm - dimensions that remained uniform for the next 30 years with a different design adorning the cover each season.

Biographies of all the current playing staff first appeared in 1957-58; photographs were added in 1959-60 and first team line-ups were first listed in 1974-75. In recent years details of all four of Spurs' teams (seniors, reserves, youths and juniors etc) have featured in depth....moreso since Premiership football came into being in 1992-93.

Nowadays, the Official Spurs Handbook is one of the best productions in the country.

HANDLEY, CHARLES HAROLD JAMES

Able to play inside or outside-left, Charlie 'Tich' Handley had to battle for a place in the League side at White Hart Lane, but he stuck to his guns and stayed with Spurs for eight years, scoring 49 goals in 155 first team appearances.

Born in Edmonton on 12 March 1899, he joined the club in April 1921 from Edmonton Juniors and made his League debut eleven months later against Everton. He played his last game for Spurs in September 1928 before leaving to join Swansea Town seven months later. From the Vetch Field he transferred to Sittingbourne in Kent and later played for Sheppey, Thames, Sittingbourne (again) and Norwich City (no senior first team outings) before retiring to take up a coaching position in Berne, Switzerland (November 1932), linking up with another ex-Spurs star, Bert Smith. He attempted to find a coaching job in England but failed and ended his footballing days back near the Swiss Alps. Handley died in his native Edmonton on 21 January 1957.

HARDINGE, WALTER

Club trainer Wally Hardinge was appointed caretaker-manager on 6 May 1935 following the departure of Percy Smith. He held office for barely eight weeks until 30 June when he reverted back to his duties as reserve team manager following the arrival of new boss Jack Tresadern.

HARGREAVES, HAROLD

A thrustful inside-forward with deadly shot, Harry Hargreaves was born at Higham, Lancashire on 3 February 1899 and played for Great Harwood, served in the East Lancashire Regiment and assisted Nelson (albeit for only three months) before joining Wolverhampton Wanderers in November 1921. Sent-off for the only time in his career playing against Leeds United in December 1922, he was suspended for a month (January 1923) and left Molineux at the end of that season, teaming up with Pontypridd. He was signed by Spurs just before Christmas of that same year, but had to wait until February 1924 before making his Spurs debut in the local derby against West Ham United - the first of 39 appearances for the club (13 goals scored). He left White Hart Lane in (March 1926) for Burnley and later assisted Rotherham United (from May 1928), Mansfield Town (May 1930), Rossendale United (October 1930) and Barnoldswick Town (March 1931 to April 1932). Hargreaves died in Nelson on 18 September 1975.

HARMER, THOMAS CHARLES

Tommy 'The Charmer' Harmer was a masterful footballer, clever in both mind and feet. An inside-forward, he was an artist in close ball control and created chances galore for his colleagues while scoring his fair share of goals himself, mainly with free-kicks and penalties!
Born in Hackney on 2 February 1928, he played for Spurs as a junior and served with Finchley before signing amateur forms at White Hart Lane in  August 1945, turning professional three years later. After Army service, he made his first appearance for Spurs in a friendly against Hibernian in May 1950 and his League debut followed in September 1951. Harmer, although a very talented footballer, surprisingly had to wait until 1956 before he finally established himself as a regular in the Spurs side, taking over the inside-right berth from the departed Johnny Brooks. He held his position until his transfer to Watford in October 1960 - after netting 51 times in 222 senior appearances for Spurs and gaining an England 'B' cap, his only honour with the club! Two years later he moved from Vicarage Road to Chelsea and scored a dramatic goal for the Blues against Sunderland at Roker Park that clinched promotion from the Second Division in 1963. He later became coach at Stamford Bridge and on pulling out of football (in June 1967) he took a job as a messenger for an Israeli bank in the West End of London.

HARPER, EDWARD CASHFIELD

Ted Harper was a wonderfully consistent marksman. In an exciting career he netted no fewer than 263 goals in 327 League games and in all first team matches his record was even better - 325 goals in 376 appearances. For Spurs alone he bagged 83 goals in only 78 outings and during his time with Blackburn Rovers (May 1923 to November 1927) he notched 122 goals in 177 matches. His tally of 36 goals for Spurs in 1930-31 included four hat-tricks,

a fourtimer and a fivetimer to share the club record. He also netted in five successive League games from 17 January to 14 February inclusive. In fact, he established individual scoring records for three different clubs in eight seasons - 43 goals for Blackburn Rovers in 1925-26 followed by that haul of 36 for Spurs (in just 30 matches) and then 37 for Preston North End in 1932-33.
Born in Sheerness on 22 August 1901, Harper played for Whitstable Town and Sheppey United before becoming a full-time professional at Ewood Park in 1923. After leaving Rovers he joined Sheffield Wednesday and became a Spurs player for £5,500 in March 1929, leaving White Hart Lane for Preston in December 1931 for £5,000 (and Dick Rowley). Two years later he returned to Blackburn for a second spell before retiring to become coach at Ewood Park in May 1935, holding that position until May 1948. Harper later worked for English Electrics and was still employed by that company when he died in Blackburn on 22 July 1959.

HARTLEPOOL UNITED

Spurs playing record against United:

Competition	P	W	D	L	F	A
League Cup	2	2	0	0	7	1

Paul Gascoigne destroyed the 'Pool with a fourtimer (one penalty) in Spurs' 5-1 second round 1st leg League Cup win at White Hart Lane in September 1990.
Players with both clubs include: Kevin Dearden, Charlie Hewitt, Fred Mearns, Allan Taylor.
Wartime guests (with either or boths clubs): Bill Adams, Dicky Dunn, Jack Hall, Bill Nicholson (also Spurs manager), Jack Skinner, Jimmy Smailes, Taffy Spelman, Ed Tunney.
Also associated: John Duncan & Cyril Knowles (Spurs players, 'Pool managers).

HARTLEY, JAMES

Utility forward Jimmy Hartley netted 35 goals in 65 first team games for Spurs during his two seasons with the club: 1897-99.
A Scotsman, born in Dumbarton on 29 October 1876, he played for Dumbarton and Sunderland before joining Burnley in November 1896. He had a loan spell with Lincoln City just before moving to Spurs in readiness for the 1897-98 campaign. On leaving White Hart Lane he joined Lincoln on a permanent basis and later assisted Glasgow Athletic, Brentford and New Brompton, retiring circa 1908.

HARTLEY, TREVOR

As a fast-raiding fair-haired winger, Trevor Hartley made 50 League and Cup appearances while serving with West Ham United and Bournemouth. Forced to retire in 1971, he was immediately made coach at Dean Court before taking over as manager of the Cherries in November 1973 (from John Bond). He retained that psoiton until January 1975 and the following year became director of coaching in Singapore. He returned to England as Luton Town's reserve team coach for the 1984-85 season and was then made assistant-manager to David Pleat. In May 1986, when Pleat took over the reins at Tottenham, Hartley followed on and after Pleat lost his job he stepped forward in the capacity of caretaker-manager for the last week of October 1987, prior to Doug Livermore taking over, also on a temporary basis.
Hartley was born in Doncaster on 16 March 1947.

HAT-TRICKS

Here are details of all the hat-tricks scored by Spurs players at competitive level (including Wartime). Trebles in friendly, tour, benefit matches etc, are not listed but listed are hat-tricks claimed in various domestic challenge and pre-arranged League and Cup competitions and annual shield encounters.

Premiership (from 1992)

Teddy Sheringham (3) v. Leeds United (h)	20.02.1993
Teddy Sheringham (3) v. Newcastle United (h)	03.12.1994
Steffen Iversen (3) v. Sunderland (a)	04.03.1997
Jurgen Klinsmann (4) v. Wimbledon (a)	02.05.1998
Chris Armstrong (3) v. Everton (h)	28.12.1998
Steffen Iversen (3) v. Southampton (h)	11.03.2000
Les Ferdinand (3) v. Leicester City (h)	25.11.2000

Football League (1908-1992)

Billy Minter (3) v. Blackburn Rovers (h)	28.03.1910
Billy Minter (3) v. Bristol City (h)	07-01.1911
Bob Steel (3) v. Middlesbrough (h)	13.02.1911
Ernie Newman (3) v. Preston North End (h)	28.10.1911
Jimmy Cantrell (3) v. Manchester City (h)	26.12.1912
Bert Bliss (4) v. Sheffield Wednesday (h)	26.12.1914
Jimmy Cantrell (4) v. Middlesbrough (a)	13.02.1915
Bert Bliss (3) v. Bolton Wanderers (h)	03.04.1912
Charlie Wilson (3) v. South Shields (a)	20.09.1919
Bert Bliss (3) v. Clapton Orient (a)	18.10.1919
Bert Bliss (3) v. Wolverhampton Wds (h)	02.04.1920
Bert Bliss (3) v. Chelsea (h)	09.10.1920
Jimmy Seed (3) v. Newcastle United (h)	05.11.1921
Jack Elkes (3) v. Blackburn Rovers (h)	15.12.1924
Frank Osborne (3) v. Liverpool (h)	24.10.1925
Frank Osborne (3) v. Leicester City (a)	31.10.1925
Frank Osborne (3) v. West Ham United (h)	07.11.1925
John Blair (3) v. Middlesbrough (h)	12.09.1927
Frank Osborne (4) v. Newcastle United (h)	07.01.1928
Taffy O'Callaghan (4) v. Everton (a)	11.02.1928
Ted Harper (3) v. Chelsea (h)	20.04.1929
Frank Osborne (3) v. Stoke City (h)	09.10.1929
Ted Harper (3) v. Blackpool (h)	18.01.1930
Dick Rowley (3) v. Wolverhampton Wds (h)	22.02.1930
Ted Harper (5) v. Reading (h)	30.08.1930
Billy Cook (3) v. Burnley (h)	01.09.1930
Ted Harper (3) v. Charlton Athletic (h)	01.11.1930
Ted Harper (4) v. Port Vale (h)	29.11.1930
Ted Harper (3) v. Oldham Athletic (h)	07.02.1931
Willie Davies (3) v. Port Vale (h)	21.11.1931
Doug Hunt (3) v. Charlton Athletic (a)	26.12.1931
Doug Hunt (3) v. Wolverhampton Wds (h)	02.01.1932
Taffy O'Callaghan (3) v. Southampton (h)	22.10.1932
Willie Evans (3) v. Chesterfield (h)	19.11.1932
Doug Hunt (3) v. Oldham Athletic (a)	11.03.1933
Jimmy McCormick (3) v. Leicester City (a)	09.09.1933
Doug Hunt (3) v. Chelsea (a)	30.09.1933
Doug Hunt (4) v. Sheffield United (h)	30.12.1933
Doug Hunt (3) v. Everton (h)	03.03.1934
Doug Hunt (3) v. Newcastle United (a)	24.03.1934
Doug Hunt (3) v. Leeds United (h)	31.03.1934
Willie Evans (3) v. Liverpool (h)	27.04.1935
Johnny Morrison (3) v. Port Vale (h)	01.02.1936
Willie Hall (3) v. Swansea Town (h)	02.11.1935
Johnny Morrison (3) v. Port Vale (a)	01.02.1936
Joe Meek (3) v. Southampton (h)	28.03.1936
George Hunt (3) v. Southampton (h)	28.03.1936
Johnny Morrison (4) v. Bradford Park Ave (h)	19.09.1936
Johnny Morrison (3) v. Bradford City (h)	31.10.1936

George Hunt (3) v. Chesterfield (h)	14.11.1936
Les Miller (3) v. Blackburn Rovers (h)	28.12.1936
Johnny Morrison (3) v. Norwich City (a)	02.01.1937
Andy Duncan (3) v. Swansea Town (h)	27.02.1937
Jimmy McCormick (3) v. Chesterfield (a)	20.03.1937
Johnny Morrison (3) v. Burnley (h)	30.08.1937
Johnny Morrison (3) v. Southampton (h)	23.04.1938
Johnny Morrison (3) v. West Brom Albion (a)	02.09.1939
Len Duquemin (3) v. Brentford (h)	01.11.1947
Les Bennett (3) v. Plymouth Argyle (a)	07.05.1949
Sonny Walters (3) v. Sheffield United (h)	12.11.1949
Eddie Baily (3) v. Portsmouth (h)	04.11.1950
Les Medley (3) v. Newcastle United (h)	18.11.1950
Len Duquemin (3) v. West Brom Albion (h)	17.03.1951
Les Bennett (4) v. Middlesbrough (h)	25.12.1952
Len Duquemin (3) v. Preston North End (h)	21.02.1953
Johnny Gavin (4) v. Sheffield United (h)	19.03.1955
Bobby Smith (3) v. Sheffield United (h)	28.04.1956
Alf Stokes (3) v. Chelsea (a)	06.10.1956
George Robb (3) v. Cardiff City (h)	13.10.1956
Alf Stokes (5) v. Birmingham City (h)	18.09.1957
Bobby Smith (3) v. Manchester United (a)	30.11.1957
Bobby Smith (3) v. Manchester City (h)	08.02.1958
Bobby Smith (3) v. Bolton Wanderers (h)	12.0.3.1958
Bobby Smith (4) v. Aston Villa (h)	29.03.1958
Terry Medwin (3) v. Chelsea (h)	03.09.1958
Bobby Smith (4) v. Everton (h)	11.10.1958
Terry Medwin (3) v. Leicester City (h)	07.03.1959
Bobby Smith (4) v. West Brom Albion (h)	18.04.1959
Cliff Jones (3) v. Newcastle United (a)	22.08.1959
Bobby Smith (4) v. Wolverhampton Wds (h)	10.10.1959
Cliff Jones (3) v. Sheffield Wednesday (h)	05.03.1960
Bobby Smith (3) v. Chelsea (a)	15.04.1960
Bobby Smith (3) v. Blackpool (h)	31.08.1960
Cliff Jones (3) v. Preston North End (h)	01.04.1961
Terry Dyson (3) v. Arsenal (h)	28.08.1961
Jimmy Greaves (3) v. Blackpool (h)	16.12.1961
Jimmy Greaves (4) v. Nottingham Forest (h)	29.09.1962
Jimmy Greaves (3) v. Manchester United (h)	24.10.1962
Dave Mackay (3) v. West Ham United (h)	22.12.1962
Jimmy Greaves (3) v. Ipswich Town (h)	26.12.1962
Jimmy Greaves (3) v. Liverpool (h)	15.04.1963
Jimmy Greaves (3) v. Nottingham Forest (h)	31.08.1963
Jimmy Greaves (3) v. Blackpool (h)	14.09.1963
Jimmy Greaves (3) v. Birmingham City (h)	02.10.1963
Jimmy Greaves (3) v. Blackburn Rovers (h)	11.01.1964
Cliff Jones (3) v. Ipswich Town (h)	04.04.1964
Frank Saul (3) v. Burnley (h)	02.09.1964
Cliff Jones (3) v. Wolverhampton Wds (h)	27.03.1965
Alan Gilzean (3) v. Blackburn Rovers (h)	11.04.1965
Cliff Jones (3) v. Leicester City (h)	24.04.1965
Cliff Jones (3) v. Fulham (h)	19.02.1966
Jimmy Greaves (3) v. Burnley (h)	07.09.1968
Jimmy Greaves (3) v. Leicester City (h)	05.10.1968
Jimmy Greaves (4) v. Sunderland (h)	16.11.1968
Martin Peters (4) v. Manchester United (a)	28.10.1972
Martin Chivers (3) v. Birmingham City (h)	06.02.1972
Alfie Conn (3) v. Newcastle United (a)	11.01.1975
Ian Moores (3) v. Bristol Rovers (h)	22.10.1977
Colin Lee (4) v. Bristol Rovers (h)	22.10.1977
Glenn Hoddle (3) v. Coventry City (h)	27.02.1980
Garth Crooks (3) v. Crystal Palace (h)	12.11.1980
Ricky Villa (3) v. Wolverhampton Wds (h)	06.02.1982

Graham Roberts (3) v. Southampton (h) — 20.03.1982
Garry Brooke (3) v. Coventry City (h) — 09.10.1982
Steve Archibald (3) v. Stoke City (h) — 14.05.1983
Mark Falco (3) v. Leicester City (a) — 05.04.1986
Tony Galvin (3) v. Southampton (h) — 05.05.1986
Clive Allen (3) v. Aston Villa (a) — 23.08.1986
Clive Allen (3) v. Norwich City (h) — 04.04.1987
Paul Stewart (3) v. Millwall (a) — 29.04.1989
Gary Lineker (3) v. Queen's Park Rangers (h) — 30.09.1989
Gary Lineker (3) v. Norwich City (h) — 04.02.1990
Paul Gascoigne (3) v. Derby County (h) — 08.09.1990
Paul Walsh (3) v. Sheffield United (h) — 20.10.1990
Gary Lineker (4) v. Wimbledon (a) — 21.09.1991
Gordon Durie (3) v. Coventry City (h) — 28.03.1992
Gary Lineker (3) v. West Ham United (h) — 01.04.1992

FA Cup (from 1894)
Sandy Brown (3) v. Preston North End (a) — 13.02.1901
Sandy Brown (4) v. West Bromwich Albion (s/f) — 08.04.1901
Percy Humphreys (3) v. Plymouth Argyle (h) — 19.01.1910
Jimmy Cantrell (3) v. Bristol Rovers (a) — 10.01.1920
Jimmy Seed (3) v. Bradford City (h) — 29.01.1921
Alex Lindsay (4) v. Worksop Town (h) — 15.01.1923
Charlie Handley (3) v. Worksop Town (h) — 15.01.1923
Charlie Handley (3) v. Manchester United (h) — 03.02.1923
Jimmy Dimmock (3) v. West Ham United (h) — 09.01.1926
George Hunt (3) v. Oldham Athletic (a) — 14.01.1933
Johnny Morrison (3) v. Portsmouth (a) — 16.01.1937
Johnny Morrison (3) v. Everton (h) — 22.02.1937
Len Duquemin (3) v. Leicester City (h) — 07.02.1948
Syd McClellan (3) v. Tranmere Rovers (h) — 12.01.1953
Bobby Smith (4) v. Crewe Alexandra (h) — 03.02.1960
Cliff Jones (3) v. Crewe Alexandra (h) — 03.02.1960
Les Allen (5) v. Crewe Alexandra (h) — 03.02.1960
Jimmy Greaves (3) v. Torquay United (h) — 18.01.1965
Jimmy Greaves (3) v. Ipswich Town (h) — 30.01.1965
Alan Gilzean (3) v. Burnley (h) — 12.02.1966
Colin Lee (3) v. Altrincham (Maine Road) — 16.01.1979
Chris Jones (3) v. Wrexham (a) — 21.02.1979
Nayim (3) v. Manchester City (a) — 07.03.1993
Ronny Rosenthal (3) v. Southampton (a) — 01.03.1995
Teddy Sheringham (3) v. Hereford United (h) — 17.01.1996

Football League Cup (from 1966)
Martin Chivers (3) v. Aston Villa (a) — 04.09.1968
Jimmy Greaves (3) v. Exeter City (h) — 15.09.1968
Martin Peters (3) v. West Brom Albion (h) — 28.10.1970
Martin Chivers (3) v. Coventry City (h) — 18.11.1970
John Duncan (3) v. Doncaster Rovers (h) — 03.12.1975
John Duncan (3) v. Wimbledon (h) — 31.08.1977
Garth Crooks (3) v. Halifax Town (a) — 26.09.1984
Clive Allen (3) v. West Ham United (h) — 02.02.1987
Paul Gascoigne (4) v. Hartlepool United (h) — 26.09.1990
Jurgen Klinsmann (3) v. Watford (a) — 21.09.1994

European Cup
Cliff Jones (3) v. Gornik Zabrze (h) — 20.09.1961

UEFA Cup
Alan Gilzean (3) v. Keflavik (a) — 14.09.1971
Martin Chivers (3) v. Keflavik (h) — 28.09.1971
Martin Chivers (3) v. Lyn Oslo (h) — 27.09.1972
Garth Crooks (3) v. Sporting Braga (h) — 03.10.1984

Texaco Cup
Marin Chivers (3) v. Dunfermline Athletic (h) — 16.09.1970

Anglo-Scottish Tournament
Bobby Smith (3) v. Heart of Midlothian (h) — 12.11.1956

Southern League (1896-1908)
Bob Clements (3) v. Northfleet (h) — 13.02.1897
Tom Meade (3) v. Millwall Athletic (h) — 25.09.1897
Bill Joyce (3) v. Northfleet (h) — 15.01.1898
Bill Joyce (4) v. Wolverton (h) — 22.01.1898
Bill Joyce (4) v. Sheppey United (h) — 19.03.1898
John Cameron (3) v. Sheppey United (h) — 17.09.1898
Tom Smith (3) v. Warmley (h) — 24.09.1898
Bill Joyce (3) v. Warmley (h) — 24.09.1898
John Cameron (3) v. Swindon Town (a) — 31.12.1898
John Kirwan (3) v. Brighton United (h) — 07.10.1899
Tom Pratt (3) v. Thames Ironworks (h) — 04.11.1899
David Copeland (3) v. Cowes (a) — 16.12.1899
Tom Pratt (3) v. Sheppey United (a) — 03.02.1900
Tom Pratt (3) v. Brighton United (a) — 10.02.1900
Tom Pratt (3) v. Bedminster (h) — 17.02.1900
Sandy Brown (3) v. Chatham (h) — 15.09.1900
Sandy Brown (3) v. Watford (h) — 16.10.1901
Sandy Brown (3) v. Queen's Park Rangers (a) — 28.12.1901
Sandy Brown (3) v. Swindon Town (h) — 08.03.1902
David Copeland (3) v. Kettering (h) — 22.03.1902
Vivian Woodwatd (3) v. Reading (h) — 30.01.1904
Arthur Turner (4) v. Kettering (h) — 16.04.1904
John Jones (3) v. Wellingborough (a) — 30.04.1904
Alex Glen (3) v. Wellingborough (h) — 17.12.1904

Dewar Shield
John Cameron (3) v. Corinthians (h) — 01.03.1902
Doug Hunt (3) v. Corinthians (h) — 02.05.1934
Albert Hall (3) v. Corinthians (h) — 07.11.1934

United League
Frank Hartley (3) v. Rushden (h) — 08.01.1898
Bill Joyce (4) v. Southampton (h) — 18.03.1898
Frank Hartley (3) v. Wellingborough (h) — 24.04.1899

Southern District League
John Cameron (3) v. Queen's Park Rangers (a) — 23.10.1899
Tom Pratt (3) v. Chatham (h) — 06.11.1899

Thames & Medway League
Ken McKay (3) v. Royal Engineers (a) — 02.11.1899
Bill Joyce (5) v. Dartford (h) — 13.04.1899

Western League
Sandy Brown (3) v. Bristol Rovers (h) — 10.12.1900
Jack Brearley (3) v. Reading (h) — 07.09.1903
John Jones (3) v. West Ham United (h) — 14.12.1903
Herbert Chapman (3) v. Reading (h) — 04.09.1905
Bill Berry (4) v. Millwall Athletic (h) — 23.10.1905
Jimmy Pass (4) v. Bristol Rovers (h) — 09.09.1907

London League
Sandy Brown (3) v. Woolwich Arsenal (h) — 04.11.1901
John Jones (3) v. Brentford (a) — 06.10.1902
Joe Walton (3) v. Queen's Park Rangers (a) — 15.04.1904

London FA Charity Shield

Bob Steel (4) v. Nunhead (a)	20.09.1909
Bert Middlemiss (3) v. Nunhead (a)	20.09.1909
Bert Middlemiss (4) v. Croydon Common (h)	11.10.1909
Billy Minter (3) v. Bromley (h)	23.09.1912
Jimmy Cantrell (3) v. Metrogas (h)	22.09.1913
Jimmy Bauchop (4) v. Metrogas (h)	22.09.1913
Charlie Wilson (4) v. Millwall (h)	22.09.1919
Jack Elkes (3) v. Fulham (h)	27.10.1924
Ted Harper (3) v. Charlton Athletic (h)	13.10.1930
Billy Cook (3) v. Ilford (semi-final)	17.11.1930
George Hunt (3) v Ilford (semi-final)	17.11.1930

London Senior Cup

Jack Jull (5) v. Ioana (h)	12.10.1889
Ernie Payne (3) v. London Welsh (h)	26.01.1895

Luton Charity Cup

Frank Cottrell (5) v. Coldstream Guards (h)	14.11.1891

Southern Charity Cup

Vivian Woodward (3) v. West Ham United (h)	09.01.1905

FA Amateur Cup

Peter Hunter (3) v. Romford (a)	01.12.1894

London Professional Footballers' Charity Fund

Taffy O'Callaghan (3) v. Clapton Orient (h)	07.11.1927

Wartime

Bert Bliss (3) v. Luton Town (h)	26.02.1916
Bert Bliss (3) v. Crystal Palace (h)	21.04.1916
Fanny Walden (3) v. Queen's Park Rangers (n)	28.10.1916
Jimmy Banks (3) v. Arsenal (n)	02.12.1916
Ted Bassett (3) v. Brentford (n)	26.12.1916
Bert Bliss (4) v. Portsmouth (a)	17.02.1917
Ted Bassett (4) v. Clapton Orient (a)	17.03.1917
Jimmy Banks (5) v. Portssmouth (n)	31.03.1917
Jimmy Banks (3) v. Crystal Palace (a)	07.04.1917
Jimmy Banks (3) v. Clapton Orient (a)	28.04.1917
Bert Bliss (3) v. Clapton Orient (a)	28.04.1917
Jimmy Banks (3) v. Millwall Athletic (a)	25.12.1917
Billy Peake (3) v. Queen's Park Rangers (a)	02.02.1918
Billy Minter (3) v. Crystal Palace (n)0	8.02.1919
Les Bennett (3) v. Watford (h)	11.11.1939
Johnny Morrison (3) v. Charlton Athletic (a)	13.04.1940
Johnny Morrison (3) v. Brentford (a)	04.05.1940
Johnny Morrison (3) v. Portsmouth (h)	11.05.1940
Johnny Morrison (3) v. Southampton (a)	18.05.1940
Ron Burgess (3) v. West Ham United (a)	07.09.1940
Jack Gibbons (3) v. Clapton Orient (h)	21.12.1940
Jack Gibbons (3) v. Clapton Orient (n)	28.12.1940
Jack Gibbons (3) v. Bournemouth (a)	22.02.1941
Ivor Broadis (3) v. Cardiff City (h)	22.03.1941
Jack Gibbons (3) v. Clapton Orient (h)	04.01.1941
Jack Gibbons (3) v. Clapton Orient (a)	11.01.1941
George Ludford (3) v. Watford (h)	30.08.1941
Jack Gibbons (3) v. Clapton Orient (a)	14.02.1942
George Ludford (3) v. Charlton Athletic (h)	12.09.1942
Jack Gibbons (4) v. Aldershot (h)	03.10.1942
Jack Gibbons (3) v. Reading (a)	17.10.1942
George Ludford (3) v. Portsmouth (h)	30.01.1943
Ron Burgess (3) v. Watford (h)	20.11.1943
Jack Rowley (7) v. Luton Town (h)	12.02.1944
Ron Burgess (3) v. Luton Town (a)	21.10.1944
Pat Beasley (3) v. Aldershot (h)	04.11.1944
George Foreman (4) v. Aldershot (h)	04.11.1944
Jack Gibbons (3) v. Arsenal (n)	09.12.1944
Jack Gibbons (4) v. Aldershot (a)	17.12.1945
Jack Gibbons (3) v. Millwall (h)	01.12.1945
George Foreman (4) v. Newport County (a)	20.04.1946

Treble Chance

- Frank Osborne scored a hat-trick in three successive League games for Spurs in 1925, netting trebles against Liverpool (h) on 24 October (won 3-1), v. Leicester Fosse (a) a week later (lost 3-5) and against West Ham United (h) on 7 November (won 4-2).
- Johnny Morrison scored a hat-trick against both Bradford clubs (Park Avenue and then City) in 5-1 home League wins in September and October 1936.
- Alfie Conn scored a hat-trick on his first full outing for Spurs v. Newcastle United in January 1975.
- Spurs striker Jack Gibbons scored four hat-tricks in the same season against the same club - Clapton Orient - in 1940-41.
- Ex-Spurs player, Bill Lane, netted a hat-trick in just under three minutes for Watford, also against Clapton Orient, in a Third Division (S) encounter in December 1933. And another former Spurs forward, Jimmy Scarth, repeated that feat with a treble playing for Gillingham, also against Clapton Orient in a Third Division (S) match in November 1952.
- Spurs inside-forward Willie Hall scored five goals for England v. Ireland on 16 November 1938 including a hat-trick in just 3½ minutes (an international record).
- Harry Rainbird (v. West Norwood in 1902), Jimmy Reid (v. London Caledonians 1906), Max Seeburg (v. Ostend 1907), Almer Hall (v. Corinthians 1934) and Les Bennett (v. Watford 1939) all scored hat-tricks appearing in Spurs' first XI for the first time.

HAZARD, MICHAEL

Born in the North-East of England in Sunderland on 5 February 1960 - and no doubt 'missed' by his home town club - midfielder Micky Hazard represented Durham Schools before making the long journey south to sign apprentice forms for Spurs in July 1976, turning professional in February 1978. He made his first debut in 1980 and went on to appear in close on 200 games for the club (34 goals scored) before transferring to Chelsea for £310,000 in September 1985. Five years later he switched to Portsmouth for £100,000 (Jan 1990) before linking up again with Ossie Ardiles by signing for Swindon Town for £130,000 in September of that same year. He duly returned to White Hart Lane for a second spell in November 1993, this time for a fee of £50,000. This time round Hazard made 32 appearances and netted two more goals to finished with a club record of 228 outings and 36 goals.

A busy player, always eager for the ball, but too often in the shadows of Messrs Ardiles and Hoddle at Spurs, he gained an FA Cup winners medal in 1982 and a UEFA Cup winners medal two years later, collecting a League Cup loser's medal as well. In a generally fine career Hazard amassed a total of 442 League and Cup appearances and netted 59 goals.

HEART OF MIDLOTHIAN

Spurs' playing record against Hearts:

Competition	P	W	D	L	F	A
A/S Floodlit	2	1	0	1	6	5

Spurs met the club twice in the 1956-57 Anglo-Scottish Floodlit Tournament. At Tynecastle on 15 October, a crowd of 17,000 saw Hearts win 3-2 (Tommy Harmer penalty and Terry Dyson scoring for Spurs). In London on 12 November, a White Hart Lane audience of 17,542 witnessed a 4-2 win for Spurs, Bobby Smith (3) and Alf Stokes the home scorers on this occasion.

Players with both clubs include: George Badenoch, Jim Blyth, Tom Collins, Alfie Conn, Ed Downie, Bobby Flavell, Bob Houston, Peter Kyle, Bob McDonald, Dave Mackay, Bob Walker.

Wartime guests with either or both clubs: Warney Cresswell, Frank O'Donnell

HEDLEY, FOSTER

Outside-left Foster Hedley from Northumberland, played for South Shields, the Corinthians. Jarrow, Hull City, Nelson, Manchester City and Chester befoe joining Spurs in 1933, aged 25. In his four years at White Hart Lane he made only five senior appearances (one goal) before transferring to Millwall. He signed for Swindon before WW2 and guested for his former club, Millwall, during the hostilities. He retired in 1946.

HEIGHT

Spurs have had many players who have either stood well over six feet or have been under 5ft 4ins tall - far too many to list here. Therefore here are those regarded as the tallest and shortest players to have served the club over the years:

Tallest

6' 5"	Peter Crouch
6' 4"	Joe Nicholls, Erik Thorstvedt (both goalkeepers)
6' 3"	Guy Butters, Harry Clarke, John Lacy, Johnny Metgod, Arthur King, Jack Jull
6' 2"	Cyril Spiers (gk)

Shortest

5' 2¾"	Fanny Walden
5' 3ins	Sammy Brooks, Jose Dominguez, Terry Dyson

'Tall Story'

On 21 October 1922, Fanny Walden (9st 4lbs) and Sammy Brooks (9st) were the smallest and, indeed, lightest pair of extreme wingers ever seen in the same Football League team when they first appeared as colleagues for Spurs v. West Bromwich Albion. One of the tallest players ever to appear against Spurs was the Sheffield United goalkeeper Willie 'Fatty' Foulke who stood some 6ft 4ins tall (and weighed at times more than 22 stones).

HENRY, RONALD PATRICK

Solid, hard-tackling left-back Ron Henry made 287 appearances for Spurs during a period of twelve years. An ever-present in the double-winning season, he and his partner Peter Baker were the only local-born players in the side and, in fact, Henry missed just two League games out of a possible 171 between November 1959 and December 1963. During that time he added a second FA Cup medal to his collection plus a European Cup-winners Cup medal in 1963. Born in Shoreditch on 17 August 1934 and capped by England v. France in 1963, he was replaced in the Spurs team by Cyril Knowles and later coached the juniors at the club. Indeed, he has given Spurs long and dedicated service for almost 50 years! A junior player with Luton Town and Harpenden Town, he joined the club from Redbourne as an amateur in March 1953, turning professional in January 1955. He made his first team and League debuts later the same year and retired as a player in May 1969 to become coach at White Hart Lane.Later he developed his own garden nursery business in Hertfordshire, while also continuing to work on a part-time basis at White Hart Lane to this day.

HEREFORD UNITED

Spurs playing record against United:

Competition	P	W	D	L	F	A
FA Cup	2	1	1	0	6	2

It took Spurs two goes to dispose of lowly Hereford in a 3rd round FA Cup-tie in 1995-96. The teams drew 1-1 at Edgar Street before Spurs turned up the heat to win the replay 5-1, thanks mainly to Teddy Sheringham's hat-trick.

Players with both clubs include: Wayne Cegielski (Spurs reserve), David Jenkins, Colin Lee, Ollie Morah (Spurs reserve).

Wartime guest: Jim Evans (Spurs).

HEROD, EDWIN REDVERS BADEN

Full-back Baden Herod was a permanent fixture in the Charlton Athletic side for six years from August 1922 until June 1928 when, after 236 senior appearances, he joined Brentford for £1,500. Eight months later a record fee of £4,000 earned his transfer from Griffin Park to Spurs and he and added 59 outings to his tally whilst at White Hart Lane before moving to Chester in July 1931. After gaining a Welsh Cup winners' medal in 1933 he then had a spell with Swindon Town before ending his career with Clapton Orient (July 1935-May 1937). Born in Ilford on 16 May 1900, Herod played for Barking Town before moving to The Valley. He died in Redbridge on 9 May 1973.

HEWITSON, ROBERT

Goalkeeeper Bob Hewitson played for Morpeth Harriers, Barnsley, Crystal Palace and Oldham Athletic before joining Spurs in July 1908. Born in Blyth, Northumberland on 26 February 1884, he was a temperamental player whose stormy career hit its peak in 1907-98 when he was suspended by the FA for allegedly tossing a clod of earth at the referee during an ill-tempered match between Fulham and Oldham. Hewitson was also suspended and severely reprimanded by the Boundary Park board who subsequently transferred him to Spurs! He played in the first-ever Football League game at White Hart Lane (v. Wolves) but remained with the club for just one season, switching to Croydon Common in May 1909 after making 37 first team appearances and helping the team gain promotion. He rounded off his footballing days by having a brief spell with Doncaster Rovers. In later life he returned to the North-East where he died in 1957.

HEWITT, CHARLES WILLIAM

Inside-forward Charlie Hewitt was another player born in the North-East of England, at Greatham near Hartlepool on 10 April 1884. He started out with West Hartlepool on 1900 before moving to Middlesbrough four years later. From there he joined Spurs in May 1906 and a year later switched to Liverpool, moving to West Bromwich Albion in April 1908 and onto Spennymoor United in May 1910. Later that year he came back to London to play for Crystal Palace and after assisting Huddersfield Town during the Great War, he retired in 1917 only to return to the game two years later with Hartlepools United (May 1919). In November 1921, Hewitt was appointed manager of the Welsh League side Mold and after spending three years there, he took up a similar position with Wrexham, where he remained until December 1926. Thereafter he managed, in turn, Flint FC (1927-May 1928), Connah's Quay (from May 1928 to June 1930), Chester (until April 1936), Millwall (for four years to April 1940), Leyton Orient (from January 1946 to April 1948) and finally Millwall again (from August 1948 to January 1956).

A man of many words, sometimes abrasive, he was forthright in his methods and approach and was said to be the last of the Football League managers in the showman tradition. As a player he accumulated a pretty useful record of more than 350 League and Cup appearances and 115 goals. His Spurs tally was 15 strikes in 49 first team outings.

Hewitt guided Millwall to the Third Division (South) championship in 1938 and Wrexham and Chester to Welsh Cup Final victories in 1925 and 1933 respectively. He died in Darlington on 31 December 1966.

HIBERNIAN

Spurs playing record against the Edinburgh side:

Competition	P	W	D	L	F	A
Coronation Cup	2	0	1	1	2	3
Anglo-Scot F/Cup	2	1	1	0	8	2
Summary	4	1	2	1	10	5

Spurs entered the Coronation Cup competition in May 1953 and met Hibernian in the semi-final. A crowd of 43,000 saw the 1-1 draw (after extra time) at Ibrox Park and then just 13,000 fans attended the replay at nearby Hampden Park, which the Scottish side won 2-1.

In 1956-57 Spurs and Hibs took part in the Anglo-Scottish Floodlit Cup and after Spurs had triumphed 5-1 at Easter Road, the return leg at White Hart Lane ended all square at 3-3. Blanchflower (away) and Hopkins (home) scored rare goals for Spurs!.

Players with both clubs include: Steve Archibald, Tom Atherton, Gordon Durie, Jimmy Reid, Alex Wright.

HINTON, WILLIAM FREDERICK WESTON

Goalkeeper Bill Hinton made 70 first team appearances for Spurs, the first in August 1924 against Bolton Wanderers, two months after signing from the Lancashire club..

Born in Swindon on Christmas Day 1895, he represented Swindon Boys before joining Swindon Town as an amateur in September 1914, moving to Burnden Park in May 1920.

In September 1928, more than a year after his release from White Hart Lane, Hinton rejoined his former club Swindon Town. Hinton, who later ran his own timber and box-making company, was 80 years of age when he died in Poole, Dorset on 8 March 1976.

HITCHINS, ARTHUR WILLIAM

Centre-half Arthur Hitchins represented the Essex County side before joining Spurs as a professional in January 1935. After a breaking-in period with Northfleet, he returned to White Hart Lane prior to the start of the 1936-37 season. Replacing Bert Page in the middle line, he appeared in 155 first team games (37 in the Football League and well over 100 in the Wartime period) over the next five years. During the hostilities he also guested for Crystal Palace and Watford. He retired in 1942.

Hitchins was born in Devonport on 1 December 1913 and died on 10 October 1975.

HODDLE, GLENN

One of the most talented - and exciting - midfielders of his generation, Glenn Hoddle started to show off his footballing skills with Spinney Dynamos and after representing Harlow and Essex Schools he signed apprentice forms for Spurs in April 1974, turning professional twelve months later. He developed quickly, won England Youth recognition and then made his senior debut in August 1975 as a substitute v. Norwich City. He finally established himself in Spurs first team in 1976-77 and thereafter continued to produce skilful performances week in week out. He represented England on 12 occasions at Under-21 level and played in two 'B' team games before winning the first of his 53 full international caps in November 1979 against Bulgaria. He collected 44 of his

senior caps as a Spurs player - eight goals scored. He took his appearance tally for the club to an impressive 590 (132 goals). At competitive level alone he starred in 378 League games (88 goals), in 48 FA Cup matches, in 44 League Cup encounters and in 21 European matches. Hoddle helped Spurs win promotion from Division Two in 1977-78 (missing only one League game). He was twice an FA Cup winner (in 1981 and 1982 - his penalty deciding the latter Final against QPR in the Wembley replay) and was a loser in both the 1982 League Cup and 1987 FA Cup Finals. He was forced to miss the 1984 UEFA Cup Final victory through injury. Voted PFA 'Young Footballer of the Year' in 1980, some of his goals were stunning - far too many to list here - but the ardent Spurs fans will never forget his terrific volley against Manchester United at White Hart Lane and that memorable chip at Watford. And there were a few extra specials hammered home for England as well.

Able to swing a pass to his colleague with purposeful precision, Hoddle could manufacture a goal out of nothing - and often did! He left Spurs for AS Monaco in July 1987 for a fee of £750,000. In December 1990 (having collected a French League championship medal at the end of his first season) he came back to England after developing knee trouble and the following month signed as a non-contract player with Chelsea. He never pulled on a senior 'blue' shirt (only appearing in the second XI) and in March of that year he entered management for the first time with Swindon Town, who also registered him as a player. He took over from another ex-Spurs star, Ossie Ardiles, at The County Ground. He remained in office until June 1993 when he was enticed back by Chelsea as their manager, a position he held until the summer of 1996 when he quit to become England's coach (manager). Unfortunately things didn't turn out too well at national level for Hoddle, England failing miserably in the 1998 World Cup Finals in France. He quit shortly afterwards. In January 2000, Hoddle returned to domestic League football when he became manager of Southampton and he certainly turned things round at The Dell, steering Saints away from relegation trouble. But there had always been talk, speculation,

anticipation, that one day Hoddle would return 'home' to White Hart Lane - and that is precisely what he did, taking over from George Graham as Spurs manager in April 2001 - some 27 years after first signing for the club as a junior.

Hoddle was born in Hayes, Middlesex on 27 October 1957.

HODGE, STEPHEN BRIAN

An exceptionally skilful, hard-working left-sided midfield player, Steve Hodge had a fine career spanning 20 years. In that time he amassed well over 500 club and international appearances and scored more than 100 goals. Capped 24 times by England (the first v. USSR in March 1986), he also represented his country in two 'B' and eight Under-21 matches. Born in Nottingham on 25 October 1962, Hodge represented Nottinghamshire Boys, before joining Nottingham Forest as an apprentice in May 1978, turning professional in October 1980. He moved to Aston Villa for £450,000 in August 1985 and signed for Spurs in a £650,000 deal in December 1986. Unfortunately he was sent-off in new manager Terry Venables' opening match in charge of the London club and after that Hodge's career with Spurs was on the line! However, he suffered with injuries but still produced some useful performances and netted a few important goals before returning to Forest for £575,000 in August 1988, having claimed 12 goals in 71 outings for Spurs. He later assisted Leeds United (£900,000 July 1991), Derby County (on loan, August 1994), QPR (£300,000, October 1994), Watford (free transfer, February 1995), Hong Kong football (January 1996) and Leyton Orient (from August 1997), retiring in May 1998. Hodge was twice a League Cup winner during his second spell with Forest (1989 & 1990), gained a Simod Cup winners prize as well (1989) and played in the 1991 FA Cup Final defeat against his old club Spurs, having appeared in the Final for Spurs against Coventry City four years earlier. In 1992 Hodge helped Leeds win the last Football League championship before the Premiership was introduced. Hodge is now Notts County Academy Coach (2001-02).

HODGKINSON, HERBERT

Left-back Bert Hodgkinson was born in Penistone, Derbyshire on Boxing Day 1903. He played for the local junior team before joining Barnsley in November 1923, transferring to Spurs seven years later (Aug 1930). He spent the next two seasons at White Hart Lane, appearing in 63 first team games before switching to Colwyn Bay United in Aug 1932, later assisting Crewe Alexandra (from Aug 1933). In later life he moved to the Black Country and worked as a machinist. He died in Dudley on 1 April 1974.

HOLLIS, ROY WALTER

Centre-forward Roy Hollis, born in Great Yarmouth on Christmas Eve 1925, netted over 50 goals in almost 100 League games for Norwich City before joining Spurs in December 1952. He failed to establish himself in the first XI at White Hart Lane, despite scoring twice on his debut in the FA Cup v. Tranmere and regularly hitting the net for the reserves. He left the club for Southend in February 1954 and went on to notch 120 goals in 240 Division Three (South) games for the Shrimpers. Later he assisted Chelmsford City and Lowestoft Town.

HOLLOWBREAD, JOHN FREDERICK

Born in Enfield on 2 January 1934, goalkeeper John Hollowbread

represented both Middlesex and England Schools before joining Enfield from where he switched to Spurs, first as an amateur in June 1950, turning professional in January 1952.

With Ted Ditchburn and Ron Reynolds ahead of him he had to bide his time waiting for his first senior outing and this finally arrived in August 1958 against Blackburn Rovers, Spurs crashing to a 5-0 defeat! Undisturbed Hollowbread held his place in the side for the remainder of that season and went on to make 82 first team appearances for the club before being placed on the transfer list in May 1964 (unable to dislodge Bill Brown who had been signed in 1959).

Signed by Southampton for £3,000 within hours of being put up for sale, Hollowbread went on to appear in 40 games for Saints before retiring from League football in October 1966 after suffering a serious knee injury. He later teamed up with Mullard Sports and after settling in Hampshire he became a publican in Romsey.

HOLMES, JAMES PAUL

Born in Dublin on 11 November 1953, defender Jimmy Holmes played for Dublin and Eire Schools and the John Bosco Boys Club before joining Coventry City as an apprentice in 1968, turning professional at Highfield Road in November 1970. During his seven years with the Sky Blues he appeared in 150 competitive games and had represented his country 17 times at senior level, gaining his first cap before making his League debut. He moved to Spurs for £100,000 in March 1977 and was quickly into his stride, although relegation from the top flight was now becoming reality! A very competent full-back who liked to play football rather than use the heave-to approach, Holmes made 121 first team appearances for Spurs (4 goals scored) and added 12 more senior caps to his tally before transferring to Vancouver White Caps in February 1981. From there he switched to Leicester City (October 1982) and after serving both Brentford and Torquay United and Peterborough United he took over as player/assistant-manager of Peterborough United (November 1983). He then drifted out of League soccer to become player-manager of Nuneaton Borough, later taking charge of Hitchin Town and then Bedworth Town prior to joining the West Midlands Police Force for whom he played as well as walking the beat!

HONOURS & AWARDS

Several footballers managers & directors etc (who have been associated with Spurs) have received honours both within the game and outside. Here are details of some achievements:

SIR

1968	Alfred Ernest Ramsey
2000	Alan M Sugar

MBE

1976	Pat Jennings
1978	Martin Peters
1984	Mike England
1986	Steve Perryman
1987	Ray Clemence
1993	Johnny Wallis
1994	Gary Mabbutt

OBE

1975	Bill Nicholson
1987	Pat Jennings
1992	Gary Lineker
2000	Garth Crooks

PFA   Player of the Year

1976	Pat Jennings
1986	Gary Lineker (with Everton)
1987	Clive Allen
1996	Les Ferdinand
2001	Teddy Sheringham

FWA Footballer of the Year

1958	Danny Blanchflower
1961	Danny Blanchflower
1973	Pat Jennings
1982	Steve Perryman
1986	Gary Lineker (with Everton)
1987	Clive Allen
1992	Gary Lineker
1995	Jurgen Klinsmann
1999	David Ginola
2001	Teddy Sheringham

PFA Young Player of the Year

1980	Glenn Hoddle
1984	Paul Walsh
1987	Paul Gascoigne

SPFA Footballer of the Year

1986	Richard Gough
1995	Paul Gascoigne
1996	Paul Gascoigne

SFWA Footballer of the Year

1988	Richard Gough
1995	Paul Gascoigne
1996	Paul Gascoigne

PFA Merit Award

1984	Bill Nicholson
2000	Gary Mabbutt

Football League Long Service Medal

1939	Peter McWilliam

Chit Chat

Over the years several Spurs bosses have received the 'Manager of the Month' award.

Gary Lineker was the recipient of the famous 'Golden Boot' after scoring six goals to top the charts in the 1986 World Cup Finals.

Ex-Spurs star Teddy Sheringham was voted 2001 Player of the Year by both the PFA and the FWA.

Jack Jull was the first Spurs player to receive a representative honour when he was chosen to play for the Middlesex County side in the late-1880s.

Tony Galvin won a Bachelor of Arts Degree at Hull University (in Russian Studies).

Two Spurs players, Freddie Cox and Bill Edrich, were awarded the DFC during the World War Two.

MEL HOPKINS

HOOPER, PERCY WILLIAM GEORGE

Goalkeeper Percy Hooper made 244 first team appearances for Spurs (101 in the Football League) during his 12 years association with the club.

A Londoner, born in Lambeth on 17 December 1914, he played for Cheddington Athletic and Islington Corinthians before joining Spurs as an amateur in 1953. He was nurtured at the Northfleet nursery before signing professional forms in January 1935. During the pre-War years he and Jack Hall shared the number one position and during the hostilities Hooper was practically first choice while also guesting for Arsenal, Bath City, Brighton & Hove Albion, Crystal Palace, Gillingham and West Ham. With Ted Ditchburn in control, he left White Hart Lane in March 1947 for Swansea Town and after spells with Chingford and Kings Lynn he hung up his boots (and gloves) in 1950. He later acted as trainer of the latter club and also worked for the Electricity Board.

HOPKINS, MELVYN

Welsh international left-back Mel Hopkins joined Spurs (ahead of Manchester United) as an amateur in May 1951 and turned professional twelve months later, the same year he made his senior debut. He then found it mighty hard to get first team football owing to the presence, and fine form of Arthur Willis and Charlie Withers. In 1954 he finally got the nod and over the next five years or so made 200 competitive appearances before suffering an injury playing for Wales in 1959. Ron Henry stepped in to take over the number three shirt and after that Hopkins struggled without success to reclaim his position. Nevertheless he remained loyal to the club and stayed at White Hart Lane until October 1964 when he transferred to Brighton & Hove Albion, later assisting the Irish club Ballymena, Canterbury City and Bradford Park Avenue (January-May 1969). Between 1956 and 1963 the rangy Hopkins won 34 full caps for his country (23 in succession). He played in the 1958 World Cup Finals and also appeared in one Under-23 international. Born in Ystrad in the Rhondda Valley (Glamorgan) on 7 November 1934, Hopkins played for the local boys club from the age of 12. And when he hung up his boots at the age of 36, he became a sports master and football coach as was also secretary to the Sussex coaches association.

HOTSPUR

The name Hotspur was used by Spurs for two seasons: 1882-83 and 1883-84.

Tottenham was then added in the summer of 1884, after secretary Sam Casey had become rather frustrated at receiving mail addressed to another club, London Hotspur! As a result Tottenham Hotspur has been the club's full name ever since.

Seemingly the name Hotspur derived from the character 'Harry Hotspur' who featured in many William Shakespeare plays.

It certainly came from the Percy family, Henry Percy, the First Earl of Northumberland, who owned most of the land around the Tottenham area of London in the late 1870s, early 1880s.

The son of Henry Percy, Harry, presumably acquired the name 'Harry Hotspur' because of his regular use of spurs when out riding or maybe following his deeds on the battlefields. And spurs were also seen to be attached to cockerels when they fought against each other in the back streets of London in the Edwardian days.....hence the cockerel (and Spurs) still being strongly associated with the football club of today.

● According to ancient history books, the young Harry Percy was slain at Shrewsbury in 1403.

● The Schoolboys who first created the Hotspur Cricket Club in

1880 - from which the football club was formed two years later - no doubt looked up to the character (Harry Hotspur) as their hero and duly named the club after him.

Was the name chosen for the popular boys' comic, I wonder?

HOWE, LESLIE FRANCIS

If the Second World War hadn't disrupted football like it did then the versatile Les Howe would surely have made 500 appearances for Spurs. As it was he had 284 first team outings, including 165 in the Football League and 17 in the FA Cup. He scored 44 goals. Born in Bengeo, Herts on 4 March 1912, he represented England Schools, Tottenham Argyle, Tottenham Juniors and Enfield before playing for Spurs' nursery team, Northfleet. In August 1930 he was taken on the professional register at White Hart Lane and remained with the club until announcing his retirement in May 1947. During the hostilities he guested for Bath City, Chelmsford City, Crewe Alexandra, Fulham, Hull City, Middlesbrough, Millwall, Nottingham Forest, Reading, Rotherham Utd and Swansea Town. In the late 1940s he was trainer-coach of Edmonton Borough. Howe made his debut for Spurs against Southampton on Boxing Day 1930. Able to play anywhere and often did, but preferring the right-half berth if possible, he was a certainly an adaptable footballer and was a regular in the Spurs side until injury forced him out in 1945. He never recovered full fitness.

HOWELLS, DAVID

Born in Guildford, Surrey on 15 December 1967, and originally a striker when representing Guildford and Surrey Schools and England Youths, David Howells developed into an exceptionally fine and reliable midfield player, performing splendidly alongside Paul Gascoigne in the engine room. He joined Spurs on YTS forms in July 1984 and signed as a professional in January 1985. His senior debut was against Sheffield Wednesday at Hillsborough in February 1986 and he struck his first goal for the club to celebrate the occasion. He went on to appear in a further 326 competitive games (277 in the League/Premiership) and netted 26 more goals, collecting an FA Cup winners' medal in 1991, before transferring to Southampton on a free in July 1998. Injuries upset his progress at The Dell and although he gallantly fought his way back to fitness, having a loan spell with Bristol City in March 1999, Howells finally called it a day in June 2000.

HUDDERSFIELD TOWN

Spurs playing record against the Terriers:

Competition	P	W	D	L	F	A
Football League	36	9	13	14	44	50
FA Cup	3	1	0	2	3	8
League Cup	1	1	0	0	2	1
Summary	40	11	13	16	49	59

The first League meeting between the two clubs was in Division Two on 24 January 1920 and it ended in a 1-1 draw at Leeds Road. Three weeks later Spurs beat the Terriers 2-0 at White Hart Lane in front of 35,000 fans.

A crowd of 20,880 saw a thrilling ten-goal League encounter at White Hart Lane in September 1925. It finished Spurs 5 Huddersfield (the reigning champions) 5.... Alex Jackson scoring a hat-trick for the Terriers while Jack Elkes netted twice for Spurs. Spurs were 5-3 ahead with time fast running out but the ten men of Huddersfield (who also had three players limping) stormed back to grab a point with two late goals.

On 29 January 1928 when Spurs lost 2-0 at Leeds Road, they had Johnny Blair sent-off - the first player from the club to be dismissed in a Football League game.

In 1928 Huddersfield beat Spurs 6-1 in the 6th round of the FA Cup at Leeds Road. The Terriers went on to reach the Final where they surprisingly lost 3-1 to Blackburn.

The Terriers were relegated from the First Division at the end of the 1951-52 season - a fate helped by a disputed Len Duquemin goal in Spurs' 1-0 win at White Hart Lane in early-April (a crucial stage in the campaign).

Players with both clubs include: Andy Booth, Billy Cook, Archie Hughes, George Hutchinson, Neil McNab, Tom Meads, John Shackleton, Bert Smith, Jimmy Smailes, Bert Sproston (Town trialist), Andy Turner, Simon Webster, Charlie Wilson.

Wartime guests (with either one or both clubs): Simon Beaton, Ron Burgess, Charlie Crossley, Charlie Hewitt, Reg Mogford, Alf Whittingham

Also associated: Herbert Chapman (Spurs player, Town secretary, assistant-manager & manager), Joe Hulme (Huddersfield player, Spurs manager & assistant-secretary), Cecil Potter (Spurs WW1, Town manager), Jock Chaplin (Spurs player, Town trainer & manager), Jesse Carver (Spurs coach, Huddersfield asst.-trainer).

HUGHES, EDWARD

Defender Ted Hughes played in 318 first team games for Spurs, including 152 in the Southern League (the fourth highest for the club) and 30 in the FA Cup, gaining a winners' medal in the latter competition in 1901.

A Welshman, born in Ruabon, Clwyd in 1876, he played for the Liverpool club Formby for two seasons from 1894 before signing as a professional for Everton. He moved from Merseyside to Spurs in July 1899 and spent seven years at White Hart Lane before transferring to Clyde in June 1908. He won two caps whilst with Everton and went on to add a further twelve to his tally as a Spurs player, gaining his last against England in 1907. Not very tall, Hughes, a 'stopper' centre-half, was spotted by Spurs secretary-manager John Cameron and brought down to London where he excelled after taking over from the injured Jim McNaught. Hardworking, brainy and fearless, Hughes was also a very fine header of the ball and was 'a keen supporter of the forwards' never hestitating to try his luck at goal. He retired from soccer in 1910 and emigrated to the USA, settling in Springfield, Massachusetts. He later returned to England and died in Tottenham in 1936.

HUGHTON, CHRISTOPHER WILLIAM GERARD

Full-back Chris Hughton had 502 first team outings for Spurs, placing him 12th in the club's all-time list of appearance-makers. He made just three less than 300 in the League, 36 in the FA Cup, 35 in the League Cup and 30 in European football. He is also the second-best cap winner in Spurs' history, winning 51 (out of 53) for the Republic of Ireland during his time at White Hart Lane. Hughton also acted as caretaker-manager for five days during November 1997, following the departure of Gerry Francis and before the arrival of Christian Gross. He was an FA Cup winner in both 1981 and 1982 and was also part of the 1984 UEFA Cup triumph. Born in Forest Gate, London on 11 December 1958, signing associated Schoolboy forms at White Hart Lane (1972-73), he represented Newham Schools before joining Spurs as a part-time professional in May 1977, turning professional in June 1979. He was loaned out to neighbours West Ham United in November 1990 before making the move a permanent one the following month. He helped the Hammers win the Second Division title that year. In February 1992 (after Julian Dicks had returned to the West Ham side after injury) Hughton was transferred to Brentford and assisted the Bees in claiming the Third Division championship that season before announcing his retirement as a player in May 1993 (through injury). At that point he returned to White Hart Lane as manager of the Under-21 side, later taking charge of the reserves before becoming assistant-manager.

HULL CITY

Spurs playing record against the Tigers:

Competition	P	W	D	L	F	A
Football League	14	5	4	5	18	13
FA Cup	6	3	3	0	6	1
Summary	20	8	7	5	24	14

Season 1908-09 saw the first League meeting between the two clubs, Spurs losing 1-0 in a Second Division encounter at Hull on 26 September in front of 12,000 spectators.

When Spurs lost 2-0 at Hull on 4 October 1977 it was their first Second Division defeat since April 1950 when they went down 1-0 at Swansea.

Players with both clubs include: Stan Alexander (also City junior coach), Jim Blyth, Charlie Brown (City trialist), Kevin Dearden, Andy Duncan, George Goldsmith, Foster Hedley, George Maddison.

Wartime guests (with either one or both clubs): Jack Acquroff, Les Howe, Cecil Potter, Fred Sargent.

Also associated: Terry Neill (manager of both clubs, also City player), Wilf Mannion (Spurs World War Two guest, City player).

HULME, JOSEPH HAROLD ANTHONY

During an excellent playing career with York City, Blackburn Rovers, Arsenal (1926-38) and Huddersfield Town, as well as for England (nine caps won), right-winger Joe Hulme amassed a fine record, appearing in well over 500 competitive matches, 374 for the Gunners for whom he also scored 125 goals. He was a member of the Arsenal side that won three League championships, two FA Cup Finals, two Charity Shields and numerous other local Cups and runners-up prizes in his twelve years at Highbury. He retired as a player in 1938, a week after playing in the losing FA Cup Final v. Preston North End. Six years later, in February 1944, he was appointed assistant-mamager at White Hart Lane, taking over as team manager in January 1946 and holding that position until May 1949 when he quit football to become a journalist with The People. He took Spurs to the FA Cup semi-final in 1948 and no doubt it was he who formed the basis of the side which won the Second Division title in 1950 under his successor Arthur Rowe. Hulme, was also a very capable cricketer with Middlesex whom he served for ten years (1929-39), scoring 8,103 runs including 12 centuries. He died at Winchmore Hill on 26 September 1991.

HUMPHREYS, PERCY

Centre or inside-forward Percy Humphreys was born in Cambridge on 3 December 1880. He played for Cambridge St Mary's and represented Cambridgeshire County before joining Queen's Park Rangers in the summer of 1900. A year later he was transferred to Notts County and after spells with Leicester Fosse and Chelsea (signed for £350 in February 1908) he moved to Spurs in December 1909. He scored a goal every two games (29 in 54 first team outings) during his time at White Hart Lane that ended in October 1911 when he went back to Leicester for a second spell. In June 1913 Humphreys was appointed player-manager of Hartlepool United and after holding a brief coaching position in Switzerland, he returned to England to assist Norwich City during the last season before the Great War. Indeed, Humphreys was all set to return to Switzerland to take up his coaching post but Hitler's Army prevented that from happening! Humphreys represented the Football League in March 1903 and played for England against Scotland at Sheffield a month later, when he had Vivian Woodward alongside him in the forward-line. He died in Stepney, London on 13 April 1959

HUNT, GEORGE SAMUEL

Centre-forward George Hunt scored 151 goals in 205 first team games for Spurs - a tremendous return for the £500 paid to Chesterfield for his services in June 1930.

A real tough Yorkshireman, born overlooking a colliery in Barnsley on 22 February 1910, he played for Regent Street Congregationalists before having unsuccessful trials at Oakwell, Sheffield United and Port Vale. In Sept 1929 he signed professional forms for Chesterfield and despite Arsenal seeking to secure his signature, Hunt - known as the 'Chesterfield Tough' - chose to join Spurs instead. He was certainly one of manager Percy Smith's finest signings, and during his seven years at White Hart Lane became a huge favourite with the supporters. He helped the team win promotion from Division Two in 1933 (netting 33 goals in 41 League games alone - 36 in total) and collected three England caps. But once Jack Tresadern had taken over as boss, hot-shot Hunt was never the same and in October 1937 he eventually found his way to Highbury, only to move to Bolton Wanderers within six months. War arrived and Hunt guested for Liverpool, Luton Town and Rochdale during the fighting, transferring to Sheffield Wednesday in November 1946. He announced his retirement two years later when he returned to Burnden Park as first team coach, a position he held for 20 years. Hunt died in 1996.

HUNTER, PETER J

Aggressive centre-forward Peter Hunter, with his neatly trimmed moustache, scored 53 goals in only 77 first team games for Spurs whom he served between June 1894 and May 1896 and again in April 1897. He had the pleasure of netting the club's first-ever FA Cup goal against West Herts on 13 October 1894, a month after making his debut. Born in London circa 1870, he played for London Caledonians before his first spell with Spurs and he was still associated with the Callies when he returned to assist the club for a second time. He also played for London Welsh in 1898-99. Hunter, a prolific marksman wherever he played, represented both London and Middlesex and certainly did his part in helping Spurs establish themselves as a professional club.

HYDE, LEONARD JOSEPH

Winger Leon Hyde played for two Birmingham sides, Summerfield Eclipse of Hockley and Harborne before joining Kidderminster Harriers in 1896. From there he switched to Grimsby Town (July 1897) but was released by the Mariners after only six months, signing for Wellingborough just prior to the 1898-99 season. At the end of that campaign he was secured by Spurs for whom the netted nine goals in 45 first team appearances before moving back to Wellingborough in April 1902. Later he assisted Brighton & Hove Albion and Doncaster Rovers, eventually quitting the game in 1906. Hyde was born in Birmingham on 6 May 1876 and died on 30 December 1932.

Spurs
MEMORY LANE

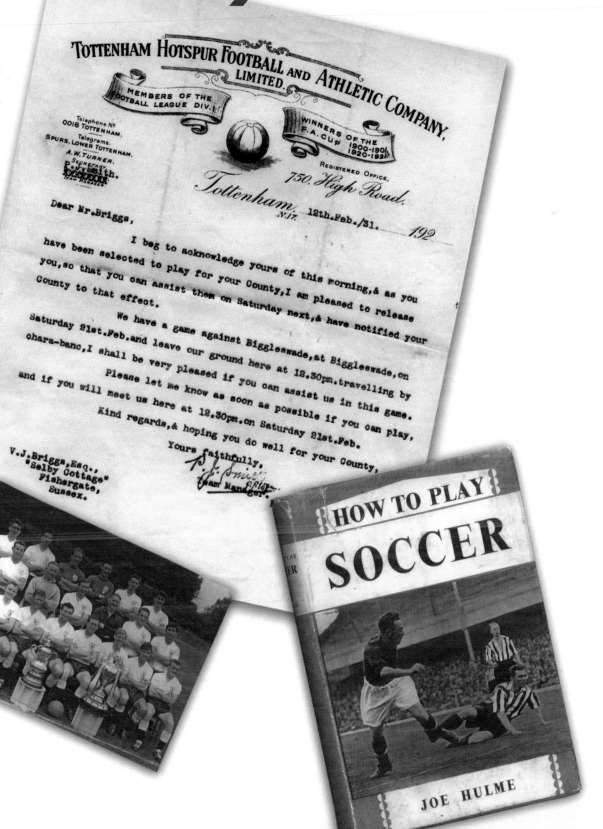

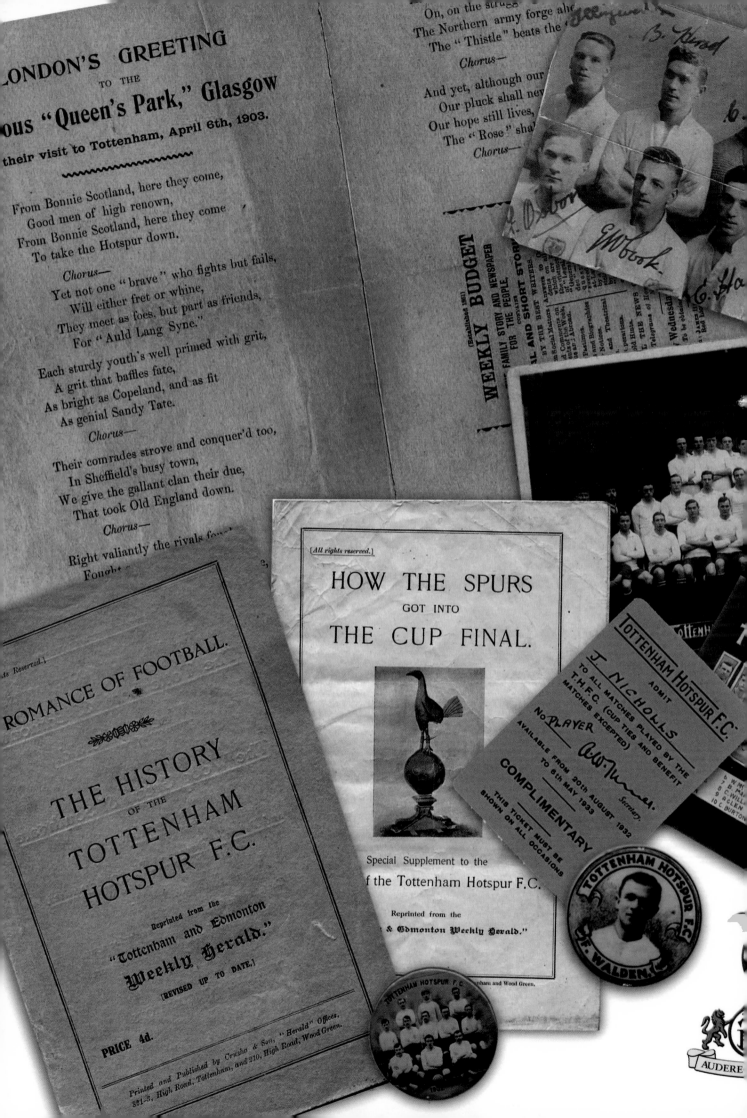

TOTTENHAM HOTS
DOUBLE WINNI

D. Blanchflower   R. Henry   M. Norman
C. Jones   J. White   R. J

UR FOOTBALL CLUB

TEAM 1960-61

Brown   P. Baker   D. Mackay   W. Nicholson

ith   L. Allen   T. Dyson

Danny Blanchflower

Bobby Smith

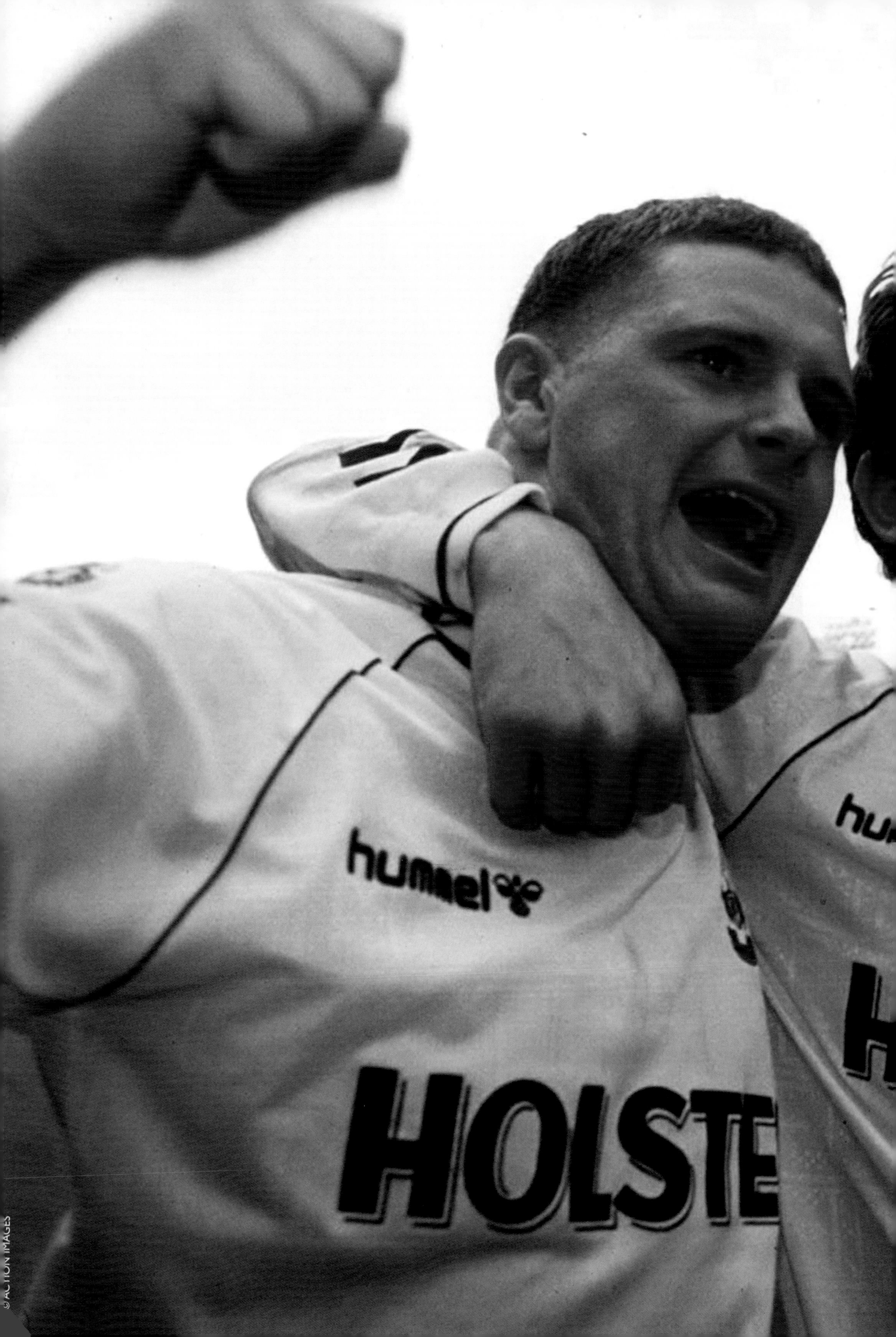
hummel
HOLSTE

Paul Gascoigne and Gary Lineker

Ray Clemence

Les Ferdinand

ILEY, JAMES

A Yorkshireman, born at Kirkby on 15 December 1935, wing-half Jim Iley represented East Yorkshire and Yorkshire County Schools, along with a couple of local teams, plus the National Association of Boys Clubs before having a few games with Pontefract in 1951-52. At the end of that season he had trials with Sheffield United and after a spell at Bramall Lane as a junior he signed professional forms for the Blades in June 1953. His career was up and running....and he continued in football until 1987. After more than 100 appearances for United, Iley moved to White Hart Lane in August 1957 for £16,000, signed to replace Tony Marchi. He struggled early on but gradually bedded himself in and played in 66 first team games, scoring one goal, before the arrival in the camp of a certain Dave Mackay. Iley was then transferred to Nottingham Forest in July 1959 - just after the East Midland club had lifted the FA Cup. From The City Ground he switched to Newcastle United in Septembver 1962. Seven years later he was appointed player-manager of Peterborough United. He acted as Cambridge United scout for a short time before taking the reins at Barnsley (1973-78). He was in charge of Blackburn Rovers for just seven months after that, staying in League management with Bury from July 1980 until February 1984 when he switched in the same capacity, to Exeter City where he remained for just one season. He later coached at Charlton Athletic. In 1958, Iley won an England Under-23 cap v. Wales and also represented the Football League v. the Scottish League. During his playing career Iley amassed a total of 545 League appearances, 31 goals scored.

ILFORD

Spurs' playing record against Ilford:

Competition	P	W	D	L	F	A
FA Cup	1	1	0	0	5	1
London FA CC	1	1	0	0	8	1
Summary	2	2	0	0	13	2

Spurs were 5-1 victors over Ilford in the 3rd qualifying round in November 1895. Harry Pryor and Ernie Payne both scored twice in front of 2,000 spectators at Ilford's ground.
Some thirty-five years later hat-tricks by George Hunt and Billy Cook helped Spurs to a comfortable 8-1 win over the non-League side in the semi-final of the London FA Charity Cup at Upton Park in November 1930
Player with both clubs: Ernie 'Bunks' Markham

INJURY & ILLNESS

● Nine senior Spurs' players broke legs whilst with the club.
● In March 1936, during a reserve team game against Bristol City, Fred Channell fractured his right leg. He retired at the end of that season, having also suffered with cruciate ligament and cartilage trouble. He was 26.
● Micky Dulin was forced to retire after breaking his leg in 1959, age 23..A year or so earlier he suffered a serious leg injury which had threatened to end his career then.
● England international centre-half Maurice Norman broke his leg in a friendly against the Hungarian Select XI at White Hart Lane in November 1965 and as a result was forced to retire.
● Goalkeeper George Clawley fractured his right leg against QPR in a Southern District Combination game in October 1899. He was sidelined for almost six months.
● Arthur Grimsdell broke his leg in October 1925 at Leicester. He got back into the first team but was never quite as positive as he was before his mishap and left the club in 1929.

● Outside-right Fred Sargent broke his right leg playing for Spurs against Chelsea in a Wartime game in February 1940. He never regained full fitness and although he remained on the club's books throughout the hostilities, his contract was cancelled by mutual consent in May 1946.
● Dave Mackay fractured his left leg twice within a matter of nine months (v. Manchester United in the European Cup-winners Cup game in December 1963 and v. Shrewsbury Town reserves in September 1964). He recovered from both mishaps and continued to play on until 1972 - despite going through the pain barrier on many occasions.
● Full-back Joe Kinnear broke his leg in January 1969 in the home League game against Leeds United. Although out of action for almost a year he regained full fitness and continued playing (with Spurs and Brighton & Hove Albion) until 1976.
● The three other players who broke legs whilst with Spurs were Jack 'Nobby' Greenfield (1932), Terry Medwin (on tour in South Africa in May 1963) and Terry Fenwick (against Manchester United in the League Cup in 1989). Fenwick also fractured an ankle. All recovered full fitness and continued playing.
● Defender Paul Price broke his leg twice during his time as a youngster at Luton Town. He regained full-fitness, joined Spurs and went on to win a total of 25 caps for Wales.
● Paul Gascoigne suffered a serious knee injury early in the 1991 FA Cup Final v Nottingham Forest when he challenged Gary Charles in a reckless manner on the edge of the penalty area.
● Alan Mullery badly ricked his back in 1964 while cleaning his teeth and as a result was forced to miss England's trip to Brazil!
● Phil Beal missed the 1967 FA Cup Final with a broken arm.
● Spurs full-back Tom Collins, a Scottish international capped in 1909, lost both an arm and a leg after being severely wounded during the First World War.
● Full-back Danny Thomas was forced to retire through injury at the age of 26 in 1988. He later qualified as a physiotherapist!
● Former Spurs player Albert Ringrose broke his leg when making his debut for Notts County in August 1939....three months after leaving White Hart Lane. He recovered and guested for Clapton Orient during the War and later played for the RAF and Gravesend & Northfleet.
● Eddie King injured a knee when making his Football League debut for Spurs against Aston Villa on 22 September 1934. He never played again, retiring in May 1936.
● Arthur Lowdell retired after failing to recover from a cartilage injury in February 1932.
● Gary Stevens' career ended prematurely in 1992 after suffering a serious leg injury. He was approaching his 30th birthday.
● The entire duration of Gary Mabbutt's illustrious career saw the great player suffering from diabetes. The fact that his career spanned over 600 matches is a great tribute to the player's resilience.

INTERNATIONAL SECTION

Here are details of players who gained representative honours at various levels whilst serving with Spurs. Figures in brackets indicate the number of caps won/appearances made in the various categories, including those as a substitute.
Note that guest players (during the two respective World wars of 1915-19 and 1939-46) have anot been included in the statistics as technically there were not 'officially' registered with Spurs.

FULL/SENIOR INTERNATIONALS
Algeria
Moussa Saib (5)

Argentina
Ossie Ardiles (8)
Belgium
Nico Claesen (9)
Denmark
Allan Nielsen (30)
England
Clive Allen (2), Wally Alsford (1), Darren Anderton (29), Eddie Baily (9). Nick Barmby (2), Bert Bliss (1), Johnny Brooks (3), Sol Campbell (40), Martin Chivers (24), Harry Clarke (1), Tommy Clay (4), Ray Clemence (5), Ralph Coates (2), Jimmy Dimmock (3), Ted Ditchburn (6), Terry Fenwick (1), Les Ferdinand (4), Paul Gascoigne (20), Jimmy Greaves (42), Arthur Grimsdell (6), Willie Hall (10), Ron Henry (1), Glenn Hoddle (44), Steve Hodge (4), George Hunt (3), Cyril Knowles (4), Gary Lineker (38), Gary Mabbutt (16), Les Medley (6), Alan Mullery (35), Bill Nicholson (1), Maurice Norman (23), Frank Osborne (2), Steve Perryman (1), Martin Peters (34), Alf Ramsey (31), George Robb (1), Graham Roberts (6), Arthur Rowe (1), Jimmy Seed (5), Teddy Sheringham (28), Tim Sherwood (3), Bert Smith (2), Bobby Smith (15), Bert Sproston (2), Gary Stevens (7), Paul Stewart (3), Chris Waddle (36), Fanny Walden (2), Ian Walker (3), Arthur Willis (1), Vivian Woodward (21).
Germany
Jurgen Klinsmann (17)
Iceland
Gudni Bergsson (30)
Ireland
Jack Kirwan (12), Charlie O'Hagan (5)
Israel
Ronny Rosenthal (19)
Northern Ireland
Gerry Armstrong (27), Danny Blanchflower (41), Pat Jennings (75), Chris McGrath (6), Gerry McMahon (7), Paul McVeigh (1), Dick Rowley (2)
Nigeria
John Chiedozie (3)
Norway
Espen Baardsen (4), Frode Grodas (8), Steffen Iversen (24), Oyvind Leonhardsen (11), Erik Thorsvedt (47).
Republic of Ireland
Stephen Carr (18), Gary Doherty (8), Tony Galvin (19), Johnny Gavin (2), Jimmy Holmes (12), Chris Hughton (51), Joe Kinnear (24).
Romania
Ilie Dumitrescu (8), Gica Popescu (6)
Scotland
Steve Archibald (22), Alan Brazil (2), Sandy Brown (1)*, Bill Brown (24), Colin Calderwood (32), Alfie Conn (2), Gordon Durie (13), Alan Gilzean (17), Richard Gough (8), Dave Mackay (18), Jimmy Robertson (1), Neil Sullivan (6), John White (18)
Switzerland
Ramon Vega (6)
Ukraine
Sergei Rebrov (7)
Wales
Mark Bowen (2), Ron Burgess (32), Simon Davies (2), Alf Day (1), Mike England (24), Willie Evans (6), Mel Hopkins (34), Ted Hughes (12), Cliff Jones (41), John L Jones (12), Ernie Jones (2), Terry Medwin (27), Taffy O'Callaghan (11), Paul Price (14), Bill Rees (1), Bill Whatley (2), Terry Yorath (8).
* This international v. England at Ibrox Park on 5 April 1902 was later declared void after a crowd disaster left 25 spectators dead and more than 500 injured.

Rest of The United Kingdom
Eddie Baily (1)

Great Britain (v Rest of Europe)
Ron Burgess (1)

'B' Internationals
England
Darren Anderton (1), Eddie Baily (3), Nick Barmby (1), Sol Campbell (1), Harry Clarke (1), Ted Ditchburn (1), Chris Fairclough (1), Les Ferdinand (1), Paul Gascoigne (4), Tommy Harmer (1), Glenn Hoddle (2), Gary Mabbutt (9), Tony Marchi (1), Bill Nicholson (3), George Robb (3), Graham Roberts (1), Paul Stewart (5), Alfie Stokes (1), Mitchell Thomas (1), Ian Walker (1), Sonny Walters (1), Charlie Withers (1).
Northern Ireland
Gerry McMahon (2), Steve Robinson (1)
Republic of Ireland
Ross Darcy (1), Neale Fenn (1), Peter Gain (1), David McDonald (1)

Under-23 Internationals
England
Les Allen (1), Martin Chivers (5), Jimmy Greaves (1), Jim Iley (1), Cyril Knowles (6), Roger Morgan (1), Maurice Norman (3), Steve Perryman (17), Alf Stokes (1)
Northern Ireland
Phil Gray (1), Richard Johnston (1)
Norway
Espen Baardsen (6), Steffren Iversen (4)

Scotland
Alfie Conn (3), Jimmy Robertson (3), John White (1)
Wales
John Collins (4), Mel Hopkins (1), Cliff Jones (1)

Under-21 Internationals
England
Paul Allen (1), Rory Allen (3), Darren Anderton (12), Nick Barmby (3), Guy Butters (3), Sol Campbell (11), Stephen Clemence (1), Richard Cooke (1), Chris Day (3), Chris Fairclough (2), Ian Hendon (7), Danny Hill (4), Glenn Hoddle (12), Chris Jones (1), Ledley King (7), Gary Mabbutt (4), Stuart Nethercott (8), Vinny Samways (5), Steve Sedgley (1), Steve Slade (4), Brian Statham (3), Gary Stevens (6), Alton Thelwell (1), Danny Thomas (2), Ian Walker (9), Luke Young (10).

Northern Ireland
Gerry McMahon (1), Paul McVeigh (11), Steve Robinson (1), Ciaran Toner (9)
Norway
Espen Baardsen (20), Steffen Iversen (2)
Republic of Ireland
Stephen Carr (12), Owen Coll (5), Ross Darcy (6), Gary Doherty (5), Neale Fenn (9), Peter Gain (1), Eddie Gormley (3), David McDonald (5), Kevin Maher (5), Andy Turner (8)
Scotland
Steve Archibald (1), John Hendry (1), Neil McNab (1)
Wales
Mark Bowen (3), Simon Davies (5), Ian Hillier (3), Mark Kendall (1), Gareth Knott (1)

UNDER-20
England
John Piercy, Brian Statham

YOUNG ENGLAND (v. England)
Cyril Knowles (1), Frank Saul (1)

ENGLAND (v Young England)
Eddie Baily (1)

ANGLO SCOTS (v Home Scots)
Sandy Brown (1), Tom Collins (1), David Copeland (1), Alex Lindsay (1), James McNaught (1), Jock Montgomery (1), Bobby Steel (1), Danny Steel (3).

FA XI
Eddie Baily (1), Les Bennett (1), Harry Clarke (1), Ted Ditchburn (3), Jack Gibbons (2), Tommy Harmer (2), Johnny Jordan (1), Tony Marchi (3), Bill Nicholson (1), Ron Reynolds (1), Bobby Smith (1), Sid Tickridge (1), Sonny Walters (2), Ralph Wetton (1), Charlie Withers (1)

NORTHERN IRELAND REG. LEAGUE (v Lge of Ireland)
Les Bennett (1)

RAF
Arthur Rowe (1)

ARMY
Eddie Baily (7), Dave Dunmore (2) Mel Hopkins (2), Tony Marchi (1), Arthur Rowe (2), John Smith (1), John White (1)

FA TOUR (to Australia, 1925)
Cecil Poynton (1), Willie Sage (4)

FA TOUR (to South Africa 1929)
Jimmy Seed (5)

FA TOUR (to Canada, 1930)
Stan Alexander (2)

UEFA XI (v Scandinavia)
Jimmy Greaves (1)
PROFESSIONALS (v. Amateurs)
John Brearley (1), Cecil Poynton (1)

INTERNATIONAL TRIALS (including South v North and the Rest v England)
England
Wally Alsford (1), Bert Bliss (1), Walter Bull (3), Harry Bradshaw (1), Tommy Clay (1), Jimmy Dimmock (2), Arthur Grimsdell (3), Tom Morris (2), Joe Nicholls (1), Bert Smith (2)
Scotland
Tom Collins (2), David Copeland (1), Sandy Tait (1)

ENGLAND XI
Harry Bradshaw (1), Jimmy Greaves (1), James McNaught (1), Maurice Norman (2), Tom Smith (1)

SCOTLAND XI (v. Scottish League)
Bill Brown (1)

TEAM AMERICA
Mike England (1)

FOOTBALL LEAGUE
Les Allen (1), Eddie Baily (5), Danny Blanchflower (1), Tommy Clay (1), Ted Ditchburn (5), Jack Elkes (2), Richard Gough (1), Jimmy Greaves (6), Arthur Grimsdell (1), Willie Hall (2), Jim Iley (1), Cliff Jones (3), Cyril Knowles (1), Tommy Lunn (1), Dave Mackay (2), Les Medley (1), Johnny Metgod (1), Bert Middlemiss (1), Alan Mullery (1), Bill Nicholson (1), Maurice Norman (1), Martin Peters (2), Alf Ramsey (5), George Robb (1), Bert Smith (1), Cyril Spiers (1), Bert Sproston (1), Alf Stokes (1), Fanny Walden (1), John White (1), Vivian Woodward (2).

FOOTBALL LEAGUE XI
Matt Forster (1), Bert Middlemiss (1), Jimmy Seed (1)

FOOTBALL LEAGUE (v. Rest of the World)
Clive Allen (1)

REST of the WORLD (v. The Americas)
Pat Jennings (1)

SOUTHERN LEAGUE
James Melia (1), John Montgomery (1)

UNITED LEAGUE
Harry Bradshaw (1), Joe Cullen (1)

SPARTAN LEAGUE
Willie Evans (1)

LONDON FA XI
Jimmy Allen (5), Willie Evans (1), Bill Julian (1), Jack Jull (2)
MIDDLESEX (County XI)
Willie Evans (1), Lee Gardner (1), Chris Herron (1), Bill Julian (1), Jack Jull (3)

TOTTENHAM (Representative side)
Jack Jull (1)

WARTIME REPRESENTATIVE HONOURS
(1915-19)
England
Arthur Grimsdell (2)
(1939-46)
England
Vic Buckingham (2), Ted Ditchburn (2), Jack Gibbons (1), Willie Hall (2),
Wales
Ron Burgess (10), Bill Whatley (1)
Wales XI
Ron Burgess (1)
Welsh Services XI
Bill Whatley (1)
FA XI
Ivor Broadis (1), Vic Buckingham (4), Ron Burgess (1), Jack Chisholm (3), Jack Gibbons (1), Willie Hall (2), Colin Lyman (1), Johnny Morrison (1), Roy White (2)
RAF XI
Vic Buckingham (9), Ron Burgess (9), Ted Ditchburn (2), Jack Gibbons (3), Colin Lyman (1), Jimmy McCormick (2)
RAF Amateurs
Jack Gibbons (1)
Northern Command
George Dorling (1), Bill Nicholson (5)

Western Command
Ronnie Dix (5)
Combined Services
Vic Buckingham (1), Ron Burgess (3), Ted Ditchburn (1), Bill Whatley (1), Roy White (2)
Football League XI
Ron Burgess (1), Willie Hall (2)
Army XI
Jack Chisholm (2), Ronnie Dix (2)
Police Professional XI
Taffy O'Callaghan (1)
London & District XI
Jack Chisholm (2), Archie Hughes (2), Roy White (2)

AMATEUR INTERNATIONALS
England
Arthur Kerry, John Knight, Fred Milnes, Vivian Woodward, Len Worley

AMATEURS of the SOUTH
Harold Milton (1)

UNITED KINGDOM (AMATEUR)
Vivian Woodward (1)

YOUTH INTERNATIONALS (1949-2001)
England
Nick Barmby, Phil Beal, Ben Bowditch, Terry Boyle, Ray Bunkell, James Bunn, Sol Campbell, Darren Caskey, Ray Clarke, Stephen Clemence, Richard Cooke, Pat Corbett, Derek Crossman, Peter Crouch, Ian Culverhouse, Barry Daines, Chris Day, Alan Dennis, Matt Dillon, Ray Evans, Mark Falco, John Field (Amateur), Mike Flanagan, Peter Garland, Terry Gibson, Mark Gower, Jason Hall, Geoff Hayzelden, Ian Hendon, Danny Hill, Glenn Hoddle, Lee Hodges, Phil Holder, Scott Houghton, David Howells, Johnnie Jackson, Andy Keeley, Ledley King, Chris Landon, Tony Marchi*, Andy Marlowe, Jeff Minton, John Moncur, Ollie Morah, Shaun Murray, John Oliver, Keith Osgood, Steve Perryman, John Piercy, John Polston, Neil Ruddock, Vinny Samways, Frank Saul, Robert Simpson, Ian Smith, Simon Spencer, Brian Statham, John Sutton, Andy Turner, David Tuttle, Steve Walford, Ian Walker, Tony Want, Alan Woods, Luke Young.
France
Yannick Kamanan, Ludwig Norbert
Northern Ireland
Noel Brotherston, Brendan Conroy, Tommy Fitzgerald, Phil Gray, Chris Herron, Mark Hughes, Richard Johnston, Steve Robinson, Ciaran Toner
Republic of Ireland
Stephen Carr, Ross Darcy, Neale Fenn, Peter Gain, Darren Grogan, Gavin Kelly, Stephen Kelly, Mike McCabe, David McDonald, Kevin Maher, Alan Mannix, Ray Morris, Kevin O'Brien, Gary O'Reilly, Tim O'Shea, Gerry Reardon, George Snee, Andy Turner, Roger Wade, Simon Webb
Scotland
Garry Brady, Tom Collins, Ally Dick, Ian Gilzean, Neil McNab, Graeme Souness
Sweden
Jon Jonsson, Jonatan Partin
Wales
Jamie Attwell, Mark Bowen, Wayne Cegielski, Darren Davies, Paul Ellis, Ian Hillier, Mark Kendall, Wayne Morley
* Listed as London, 1949.

NB - Several players have represented their country at Under 16 and Under 17 levels, having signed for Spurs either as a junior, trainee or semi-professional.

Capped Elsewhere
Several Spurs players gained international honours, at various levels, either before joining Spurs or after leaving the club. Listed below are those who won full caps for their respective country whilst elsewhere!
Wartime guests, trialists or associated Schoolboys have not been included
Algeria
Moussa Saib
Argentina
Ossie Ardiles, Ricky Villa
Belgium
Nico Claesen
Denmark
Allan Nielsen
England
Arthur Turner, Harry Bradshaw, Sammy Brooks (1919), Ray Clemence, Ralph Coates, Ronnie Dix, Kerry Dixon, Bill Felton, Paul Gascoigne, Bert Gosnell, Andy Gray, Jimmy Greaves, Ted Harper, Glenn Hoddle, Percy Humphreys, Bill Jones, John Knight, Gary Lineker, Frank Osborne, Alf Ramsey, Jamie Redknapp, Tom Roberts, Neil Ruddock, Teddy Sheringham, Andy Sinton, Bert Sproston, Peter Taylor, Danny Thomas, Arthur Turner, Chris Waddle, Wilf Waller, Des Walker, Paul Walsh, Keith Weller, Terry Venables, Paul Walsh, George Woodger & Vivian Woodward
France
David Ginola
Germany
Steffen Freund, Jurgen Klinsmann, Christian Ziege
Holland
Johnny Metgod
Ireland
Matt Reilly & Dick Rowley
Italy
Nicola Berti
Nigeria
John Chiedozie
Northern Ireland
Danny Blanchflower, Noel Brotherston, Phil Gray, Chris McGrath, Pat Jennings & Steve Robinson
Norway
Espen Baardsen, Frode Grodas, Steffen Iversen, Oyvind Leonhardsen, Roger Nilsen, Erik Thorstvedt
Portugal
Jose Dominguez
Republic of Ireland
Tony Galvin & Johnny Gavin
Romania
Ilie Dumitrescu & Gica Popescu
Scotland
David Black, Alan Brazil, Bill Brown, Sandy Brown, Colin Calderwood, Tom Collins, John Cameron, Tom Fitchie, Richard Gough, David Haddow, John McTavish, John Madden, Graeme Souness, Neil Sullivan & Sandy Young.
South Africa
Quinton Fortune
Switzerland
Ramon Vega
Ukraine
Sergei Rebrov

USA

Kasey Keller

Uruguay

Gustavo Poyet

Wales

Terry Boyle, Willie Davies, Alf Day, Mike England, Fred Griffiths, Archie Hughes, Ted Hughes, Terry Medwin, Paul Price, Bill Rees, Pat Van den Hauwe & Terry Yorath

Capped at Amateur level (with other clubs)

Walter Bellamy, Laurie Brown (14 caps), Tommy Cable, Sid Crowl, George Gemmell, Frank Hartley, the Reverend Kenneth Hunt (20 caps), Fred Milnes, George Robb (18), Vivian Woodward (10) and Len Worley - all England.

Spurs and England Players... the 54 capped by England

● Clive Allen won two full caps as a Spurs player and both games ended 0-0 versus Turkey in 1987 and Israel in 1988.

● Wing-half Wally Alsford's only cap was against Scotland in front of more than 120,000 spectators at Hampden Park in April 1935.

● Terry Venables gave Darren Anderton his England debut against Denmark in March 1994.

● Eddie Baily made his international debut against Spain in July 1950. He and Alf Ramsey played in nine England games together.

● Nick Barmby beat Andy Cole by just six minutes to become the first product of the FA National School to win a full England cap (as a substitute v Uruguay in March 1995).

● Bert Bliss was one of four Spurs players who faced Scotland in 1921 - a fortnight before the FA Cup Final.

● Johnny Brooks' three games for England (2 goals scored) came in a three-week period during November and December 1956. England were victors in all three internationals and Ted Ditchburn was in goal on each occasion.

● Sol Campbell figured as a defender and midfield player for England. He won his first cap as a substitute v. Hungary in May 1996 when another Spurs player - 'keeper Ian Walker - also made his first appearance for his country as a sub. Anderton, Les Ferdinand and Teddy Sheringham played in this same match.

● Martin Chivers made the first of his 24 appearances for England v. Malta in February 1971 and his last against Poland in October 1973 - the night England went out of the World Cup ! He scored 13 goals for his country.

● Centre-half Harry Clarke was 31 when he won his only England cap against Scotland in front 135,000 fans at Hampden Park in April 1954.

● In March 1920 Tommy Clay played behind Arthur Grimsdell against Wales - the first time two Spurs players had lined up together for England.

● Ray Clemence is the oldest Spurs player to win an England cap. He was 35 years, 103 days old when appeared in his last international in 1983.

● Ralph Coates' two England caps (as a Spurs player) were gained within eight days in May 1971.

● At the age of 20 years 125 days, Jimmy Dimmock is the youngest Spurs player to win an England cap - doing so against Scotland on 19 April 1921. It is also understood that Dimmock was the first 20th century-born player to appear for England.

● Ted Ditchburn gained his six caps in eight years. He was Spurs' first post War international in 1948 - and at the same time became the club's first England 'keeper.

● Terry Fenwick won his last cap as substitute v Israel in Feb 1988.

● Les Ferdinand won 12 England caps before moving to White Hart Lane in 1997. His first was against San Marino in 1993 and his first for Spurs came v. Moldova in 1998.

● Paul Gascoigne, capped as a Spurs player for the first time in 1988 v. Denmark, went on to make 57 full international appearances for his country.

● Jimmy Greaves is Spurs' highest scorer for England with 28 goals. He struck six hat-tricks (a record) and won 57 caps in total, the last against Austria in 1967.

● Arthur Grimsdell captained both Spurs and England.

● Willie Hall netted five goals v. Ireland in November 1938, including a hat-trick in three-and-a-half minutes. He is one of only a handful of players to claim a fivetimer in a full international for England. A 21 year-old international debutant in 1933, he hit nine goals in ten appearances for his country.

● Ron Henry had just one outing for England in a 5-2 defeat in France in February 1963, playing with his club colleagues Jimmy Greaves and Bobby Smith.

● Glenn Hoddle won 44 England caps as a Spurs player (a club record). He struck nine goals. His final tally of caps was 53.

● Steve Hodge won four of his 24 caps as a Spurs player ...and was one of a record five Spurs players who faced Turkey in a European Championship qualifier in 1987.

● George Hunt scored on his England debut v. Scotland in 1933.

● Cyril Knowles won four full caps in 1967-68. Alf Ramsey picked him at right back for his first two international outings and at left-back for his last two.

● Gary Lineker captained his country 20 times in his 38 internationals as a Spurs player. He netted 18 of his 48 England goals whilst at White Hart Lane. He won 80 caps in all.

● Gary Mabbutt won the first of his 16 full caps in 1982. He played in both defence and midfield for England and scored one goal against Yugoslavia in 1986.

● Les Medley won six England caps in just over 12 months (1950-51). He was accompanied in each international by his team-mate Alf Ramsey.

● Alan Mullery won his 35 full caps between 1964-71. He also captained his country and was the first England player to be sent-off in a major international - dismissed in the European Championship semi-final v. Yugoslavia in 1968.

● Bill Nicholson scored after just 30 seconds into his only international - a 5-2 win over Portugal in May 1951. He had previously been a regular reserve.

● Maurice Norman made his England debut in 1962. He won 23 caps in less than three years, making his final appearance in 1964.

● Frank Osborne is the only Spurs player to win an England cap having been born in another country (South Africa). He is the only England player to score a hat-trick in his last international (v. Belgium in 1926).

● Steve Perryman's international career comprised just 20 minutes - as a substitute v. Iceland in 1982

● Martin Peters, who netted nine goals in 34 games for his country as a Spurs player, is the only Englishman to play for Spurs having won a World Cup medal. In all he struck 20 goals in 67 internationals, acting as skipper on four occasions

● Alf Ramsey won 31 of his 32 England caps as a Spurs player. He skippered his country three times. His last outing was that 6-3 defeat by Hungary in 1953. Ramsey was the only Spurs player in the England side that beat Italy 2-0 at White Hart Lane in 1949.

● George Robb won 18 amateur caps for England but only one at full international level - in that heavy defeat by Hungary in 1953.

● Graham Roberts won six caps in just over a year (1983-84). Glenn Hoddle and Gary Mabbutt played in his first two games while Mickey Hazard was on the subs' bench for his last game v the Soviet Union.

● Arthur Rowe's only England cap was against France at White Hart Lane in 1933.

BILL BROWN

• Jimmy Seed's five caps were won over a four-year period. He scored one goal v. Belgium in 1923 - the first home match against foreign opposition

• Teddy Sheringham won the 500th England cap by a Spurs player, coming on as a substitute v. Japan in 1995. His debut was against Poland in 1993.

• Tim Sherwood had already made over 450 appearances as a professional before winning his first England cap, as a Spurs player v. Poland in a Euro 2000 qualifying game in 1999.

• Bert Smith lined up with five different Spurs players in his two internationals v. Scotland in 1921 and Wales the following year.

• Bobby Smith netted in each of his first five outings for England: 1960-63. He notched 13 goals in 15 games all told, many when playing alongside Jimmy Greaves.

• Bert Sproston won two of his 11 caps during his brief spell with Spurs in 1938.

• Gary Stevens was never a loser in his seven internationals for England. He did however only start in one game v. Northern Ireland in 1985.

• Paul Stewart made his international debut for England in 1991 and all his three caps came as a substitute.

• Chris Waddle struck six goals in 36 games for England as a Spurs player in mid to late '80s. Surprisingly he completed only 28 of his 62 games for his country.

• Fanny Walden was one of the smallest men ever to play for England (with WBA'a Tommy Magee). Nearly eight years separated his two caps, won v. Scotland in 1914 and Wales in 1922.

• Ian Walker followed Ted Ditchburn and Ray Clemence by keeping goal for England. His first two caps were gained as a substitute v. Hungary and China in 1996. Sol Campbell also made his England debut against the Magyars when Darren Anderton, Les Ferdinand and Teddy Sheringham all figured. Anderton, Paul Gascoigne and Nick Barmby all played against the Chinese.

• Arthur Willis won his only cap v. France in 1951 aged 31.

• Vivian Woodward, Spurs' first ever England international, scored twice on his debut against Ireland in 1903. He was captain the side on a few occasions and also led the Amateur and British Olympic teams. He netted 27 goals in his 21 outings at senior level as a Spurs player.

A United Nations of Spurs internationals.

• Steve Archibald won 22 of his 27 Scotland caps as a Spurs player. He made his international debut in 1980, his last game being in the 1986 World Cup Finals.

• Ossie Ardiles was Spurs' first continental international when capped for Argentina v. Holland in 1979. He won his first cap in 1975 and his last and 43rd in 1983.

• Gerry Armstrong made his international debut for Northern Ireland in 1977. He won 27 caps as a Spurs player (five goals). He scored a then record 12 goals in 63 outings for his country, appearing in his last game in the 1986 World Cup Finals.

• Goalkeeper Espen Baardsen played four times for Norway during his time at White Hart Lane, all his caps coming in the last two seasons with the club (1998-2000).

• Gudni Bergsson had 24 Icelandic caps to his name when he joined Spurs in 1988. He added a further 30 to his tally during his time at White Hart Lane. His international debut as a Spurs player was against England against team-mates Gary Mabbutt, Paul Gascoigne and Paul Stewart. He was first capped in 1984.

• Danny Blanchflower made his international debut for Ireland in 1949 (the Northern prefix was added in 1954). He had 15 caps to his name when joining Spurs in 1954 and later took his tally to 56. He captained the Irish team at the 1958 World Cup Finals in

Sweden and later managed his country: 1976-79.

• Mark Bowen won two caps for Wales as a Spurs player on a Canadian tour in 1986. He went on to appear in 41 internationals.

• Alan Brazil scored three goals in 13 international outings for Scotland in the space of three years. He collected only two caps as a Spurs player.

• Goalkeeper Bill Brown had four Scottish caps to his name on joining Spurs, having made his international debut in the 1958 World Cup Finals in Sweden. He took his total to 28 whilst at White Hart Lane, his last game being against Italy in 1965 aged 34.

• Alex 'Sandy' Brown was the first Spurs player to serve Scotland, lining up against England in that ill-fated international at Ibrox Park in 1902 when scores of spectators were killed after barriers and terracing collapsed.

• Former Red Star defender Goran Bunjevcevic had 12 Yugoslavian caps when he joined Spurs in the summer of 2001.

• Ron Burgess had played in several Wartime internationals prior to winning his first full cap for Wales in 1946. He went on to win 32 caps in eight years. In 1965 he acted as the Welsh team manager v. Northern Ireland when Dave Bowen was unavailable.

• Colin Calderwood was first selected for international duty in 1995. He represented his country 36 times at senior level.

• Stephen Carr gained his first cap for the Republic of Ireland in 1999 against Sweden in Dublin. He has since been a regular in the national side and has steadily added to his total of senior appearances, ending the 2000-01 season with 18 senior caps.

• John Chiedozie, was capped for his native Nigeria on three occasions whilst at White Hart Lane, facing Liberia once and Tunisia twice: 1984-85.

• Nico Claesen notched six goals in nine games for Belgium during his time at Spurs. He had six goals in 22 games to his credit when signing for the club and he took his tally to 36 caps (12 goals) with Royal Antwerp. He played against England in the 1990 World Cup Finals - his last appearance for his country.

• Alfie Conn gained his two Scottish caps as a Spurs player during a four-day spell in May 1975.

• Simon Davies won the first of what he hopes to be many full caps for Wales in 2000.

• Alf Day won his first cap for Wales in 1933 ...before he had played a League game. His team-mate Taffy O'Callaghan played in the same international v. Ireland.

• Gary Doherty won his first two Republic of Ireland caps in successive months: April-May 2000 - the first as a substitute v. Greece, the second v. USA. He's since added to his tally.

• Ilie Dumitrescu netted 17 goals in 44 internationals for Romania before joining Spurs. He scored once in eight games for his country during his stay at White Hart Lane. He was introduced to the national side in 1989.

• Gordon Durie won 12 caps for Scotland as a Chelsea player and he took his total to 25 during his time with Spurs (two goals). He was first capped by Scotland in 1987 and went on to gain a total of 43 (seven goals).

• Mike England was capped 44 times by Wales, the last 24 as a Spurs player. He netted three goals, including one on his last appearance in 1974. He captained his country and also played for Team America in the 1976 Bicentennial celebrations. He managed the Welsh national side from 1980-88.

• Willie Evans gained six caps for Wales, scoring once, all as a Spurs player. First selected in 1932, injury curtailed his international career in 1936.

• Tony Galvin qualified for the Republic of Ireland via a grandparent. First capped in 1982, he won 19 of his 29 caps as a Spurs player.

● Johnny Gavin made a goalscoring debut for the Republic of Ireland v. Finland in 1949. He gained seven caps in seven years, two coming as a Spurs player in 1955. He was the first Eire international from the club

● Alan Gilzean notched eight goals in 17 games for Scotland whilst on Spurs' books. He made his international breakthrough in 1963 and won his final cap in 1971, aged 32.

● Richard Gough won eight of his 61 caps (six goals scored) whilst at Spurs. He had appeared 26 times for Scotland prior to his arrival at White Hart Lane, initially as a 20 year-old in 1983.

● Goalkeeper Frode Grodas was capped eight times by Norway during his time with Spurs. He later took his tally of senior international appearacnes past the 50 mark.

● Jimmy Holmes is Republic of Ireland's youngest ever player - aged 17 years 200 days when making his debut in 1971. He gained 12 of his 30 full caps as a 'Spur', making his final appearance for his country in 1981.

● Mel Hopkins, first honoured by Wales in 1956, went on to gain 34 caps in a seven-year spell - all as a Spurs player.

● Teddy Hughes had two Welsh caps to his credit on joining Spurs. He took his final tally to 14 during his time at White Hart Lane, his final appearance coming in 1907.

● Chris Hughton is the second most-capped Spurs player of all-time, making 51 of his 53 appearances for Republic of Ireland during his time at White Hart Lane, his first in 1979.

● Norwegian striker Steffen Iversen, capped 24 times as a Spurs player, had already represented his country at Under-21 level before moving to White Hart Lane in 1996.

● Pat Jennings, Spurs' most capped player with 75 appearances for Northern Ireland during his two spells at White Hart Lane, is also the club's youngest and oldest international. He was 19 years, 113 days old when playing for his country in 1964 and he celebrated his 41st birthday when appearing in his last and record-breaking 119th international v. Brazil in 1986.

● Cliff Jones made his debut for Wales at the age of 19 in 1954. He had 16 caps to his credit on joining Spurs and added 41 more to his tally (plus a dozen goals) during his spell at White Hart Lane. His final tally was 15 goals in 59 games. Jones is probably the first Spurs player to be sent-off in a senior international, dismissed v. Mexico (a) in 1962.

● Welshman Jack Jones was the first Spurs player to win a full cap when facing Ireland in Llandudno in 1898. He had already won nine caps on his arrival at the club and took his tally to 21 as a Spurs player. He captained Wales v. England in 1902 and never finished on the winning side in any of his 12 internationals during his time with Spurs.

● Ernie Jones - first capped by Wales in 1946 - won two of his four caps with Spurs, Ron Burgess featuring in all the internationals.

● Republic of Ireland full-back Joe Kinnear won all but his 26th and final cap as a Spurs player (in October 1975). He gained his first in 1967 v. Turkey at the age of 20.

● Jack Kirwan was the second Spurs player to gain full international honours. First capped for Ireland v. Wales in 1900, he netted two goals in 12 games during his time at White Hart Lane, captaining his country against England in 1905. He ended his career with 17 caps to his name, the last arriving in 1909 at the age of 36.

● Jurgen Klinsmann struck 47 goals in 108 international appearances for Germany. He captained the side throughout his 17 caps as a Spurs player. First capped by the former West Germany in 1987 v. Brazil.

● Oyvind Leonhardsen had already won 62 caps for Norway when he moved to White Hart Lane in 1999. He has since added more caps to that total during his time with Spurs but missed Euro 2000 through injury.

● Dave Mackay was Spurs' first 'full' Scottish international, capped in 1959 - less than a month after signing from Hearts with whom he had already won four caps, having collected his first in 1957. He gained 22 caps in all (four goals) with his final outing in 1965.

● Chris McGrath collected the first six of his 21 caps for Northern Ireland in 1974 as a Spurs player, celebrating with a goal against Scotland. One of only a handful of teenagers to gain full international honours as a Spurs player, he was handed his debut as a 19 year-old. His last cap was won in 1979 as a Manchester United star.

● Gerry McMahon, first capped by Northern Ireland on their Canadian tour in in 1995, went on to net two goals in his 17 international outings. Spurs had to pay his previous club (Glenavon) an additional sum of money when he won his first cap.

● Terry Medwin was capped three times by Wales as a Swansea player, collecting his first in 1953 v. Northern Ireland. He netted six goals in 27 games for his country during his time with Spurs, winning his final cap in 1962.

● Allan Nielsen became the 100th player to go on Spurs' international roll of honour at White Hart Lane when playing for Denmark against Slovenia in September 1996. He had earlier scored within a minute of his international debut against Armenia in 1995 and has now appeared in well over 40 internationals for his country (30 as a Spurs player).

● Taffy O'Callaghan won all of his eleven Welsh caps as a Spurs player, scoring three goals. He was the first international produced from the club's nursery side, Northfleet when selected to face Northern Ireland in February 1929. He captained Wales on a few occasions during his six-year international career.

● Charlie O'Hagan netted once in five appearances for Ireland as a Spurs player, each when playing with team-mate Jack Kirwan. He was first capped against Scotland in 1905 and added a further six caps (one goal) to his tally during his time with Aberdeen.

● Gica Popescu scored once in six games for Romania during his brief stay at Spurs. Like fellow countryman Ilie Dumitrescu, he was introduced to the national side as a 20 year-old in 1988. He went on to appear in over 100 senior internationals.

● Gus Poyet moved across London from Chelsea to Spurs at the end of the 2000-01 season having already gained 27 caps for Uruguay at senior level.

● Paul Price qualified for Wales via his father. First capped against England in 1980 by ex-Spurs centre-half Mike England - his first game as national team manager. Price won 14 caps as a Spurs player to go with the eleven he gained at Luton Town.

● Sergei Rebrov was already an established Ukrainian international with 36 full caps to his credit when he moved to White Hart Lane in the summer of 2000 for a club record fee. He then added seven more caps to his total during his first season in English football.

● Billy Rees won four caps in twelve months for Wales, the first three whilst a Cardiff City player. His fourth came as a Spurs player in 1950. Ron Burgess played in the same four international games that Rees starred in.

● Jimmy Robertson shares with Pat Jennings the distinction of being Spurs' first teenage international at senior level. 'Robbo' (19) represented Scotland against Wales on 3 October 1964. It was his only senior appearance for his country.

● Israeli international forward Ronny Rosenthal took his tally of full caps to 60 before retiring from competitive football in June 1999. He scored over 20 goals. An international debutant at the age of 21 in 1984, his record as a Spurs player was five goals in 19 international outings.

● Dick Rowley scored twice in six international games for Northern Ireland. First capped in 1929 (with Southampton). His last two were as a Spurs player soon afterwards.

● Moussa Saib was Spurs' first ever Algerian footballer when he signed for the club in 1998. When he left White Hart Lane for Al Nasar he had taken his tally of full internationals to almost 50.

● Goalkeeper Neil Sullivan joined Spurs from Wimbledon in 2000, having already appeared in 16 full internationals for Scotland, including two Euro 2000 play-off encounters with England. He appeared in six more internationals during his first season at White Hart Lane.

● Erik Thorstvedt lies third in Spurs' all-time international honours list with 47 caps gained as a goalkeeper at White Hart Lane. First capped by Norway v. Kuwait in 1982, he played in the last of his 98 internationals against Northern Ireland in 1996. He captained his country during the early '90s.

● Switzerland international Ramon Vega had impressed greatly in Euro '96 before joining Spurs in January 1997. He had already represented his country on 20 occasions before adding six more to his tally prior to May 2001.

● Bill Whatley was capped twice by Wales - and both of his international appearances (v. England and Scotland) came within a three-week spell in late 1938.

● John White scored on his debut for Scotland v. West Germany in 1959. He had four caps to his name when arriving at White Hart Lane and he duly took his overall tally to 22 (three goals) before his tragic death in 1964 at the age of 27.

● Terry Yorath was only 19 when he won his first cap for Wales v. Italy in 1969. He went on to score twice in 59 full international appearances, several as captain, his last outing coming in 1981. Eight of his caps were awarded during his time with Spurs. He managed the Welsh national side for five-and-a-half years to November 1993.

● The German international Christian Ziege arrived at White Hart Lane (from Liverpool) in 2001 with 59 full German international caps to his name.

One step beyond - Spurs' intermediate internationals
● In 1925 Cecil Poynton and Jack Elkes toured Australia with an FA XI. They played in several matches which were not regarded as international standard and caps were not awarded.

● In 1941 Vic Buckingham played for England twice in wartime games against Wales. Jack Gibbons faced the Welsh in 1942. The only reward these two players received for their efforts in Wartime internationals was a third class rail travel ticket and an illuminated address from the Football Association detailing the games in which they participated.

● Shortly after the Second World War the FA introduced 'B' internationals, and over a period of eight years (from 1949 to 1957) England played a total of 19 such matches. Five Spurs players featured in these games - Sonny Walters the first v. the Netherlands in 1950. Tommy Harmer and Charlie Withers followed in 1952 (also against the Dutch). Toni Marchi and Alf Stokes followed on by playing against Scotland in 1957.

● A year after Under-23 internationals had come into being, Alf Stokes became the first Spurs player to win a cap at this level when he netted twice on his debut against Denmark in 1955. He was followed in 1958 by Jim Iley, also capped by England against Wales.

● Les Allen's only international honour as a Spurs player was to gain an England Under-23 cap v. Wales in 1961.

● Frank Saul - the youngest member of Spurs' double-winning squad - was selected for the Young England v. England game in 1966 and in that same year, Spurs' 17 year old John Collins won the first of his seven Under-23 caps Wales.

● Roger Morgan scored twice for England Under-23 against Bulgaria in 1970.

● In season 1976-77, Under-21 internationals came into force (in place of Under-23 games). Within two years Spurs had three players capped at this level - Neil McNab lined up for Scotland while Mark Kendall kept goal for the Wales in the same game, and Jersey-born striker Chris Jones made a substitute appearance for England v. Yugoslavia.

● Paul Allen won his third and final Under-21 cap against Romania in 1985 - soon after joining Spurs from West Ham. Shortly afterwards Richard Cooke won his only England Under-21 cap, away to Denmark.

● Three months into the 1987-88 season, Chris Fairclough and Mitchell Thomas lined up for the England 'B' team against Malta 'B', having already won Under-21 honours with their previous clubs. The England 'B' team had been re-introduced in 1978. Fairclough made two more Under-21 appearances later that season.

● Vinny Samways and Brian Statham made their England Under-21 debuts v. Switzerland in 1988. Samways won five U-21 caps while Statham gained three, all during their time at White Hart Lane.

● Another Spurs youngster, Richard Johnston, gained both Under-23 & Under-21 honours for Northern Ireland during the 1988-89 season. His fellow countryman, Tommy Fitzgerald, joined him at Under-21 level for the 1989 Toulon tournament. In 1990 he won an Under-23 cap.

● Guy Butters (England) and Eddie Gormley (Republic of Ireland) also featured in the French tournament of 1989, both players winning three caps each.

● The 1989-90 season saw Steve Sedgley and David McDonald play at Under-21 level....Sedgley collected the last of his eleven England caps while McDonald represented the Republic of Ireland. McDonald went on to gain a 'B' cap in 1991.

● Ian Hendon (as captain) and John Hendry each won their first England Under-21 caps in 1992. Hendon went on to appear in seven internationals at this level; Hendry one (v.Denmark).

● Towards the end of the 1992-93 campaign, Andy Turner gained the first of his seven Republic of Ireland Under-21 caps as a Spurs player. In March 1994 Stuart Nethercott (England) and Steve Robinson (Northern Ireland) attained their first Under-21 caps. Robinson also played for his country's 'B' team against England whilst Nethercott went on to make eight Under-21 appearances for England.

● Stephen Carr (Republic of Ireland) and Danny Hill (England) joined Spurs' list of Under-21 internationals during the 1994-95 season. Carr made the first of his 12 appearances at this level in November 1994 while Hill won four caps at Toulon in the summer of 1995.

● Chris Armstrong and Ruel Fox both arrived at White Hart Lane with England 'B' caps, whilst Jason Cundy, Jason Dozzell and David Kerslake had all won Under 21 caps with other clubs.

● In 1995-96, Spurs teenagers Owen Coll and Kevin Maher stepped into the Republic of Ireland Under-21 team, while Chris Day and Steve Slade (for England) and Gareth Knott (for Wales) all made their final appearance as Spurs players at Under-21 level. Day gained three caps, Slade four and Knott one (the latter against San Marino).

● In 1996-97, goalkeeper Espen Baardsen and Ross Darcy represented Norway and the Republic of Ireland respectively at Under-21 level, while Rory Allen won the first of his three England Under-21 caps, having previously featured in the squad as a reserve. Baardsen, in fact, broke a finger whilst playing in a 'B'

© ACTION IMAGES

© ACTION IMAGES

international against Scotland in 1999. When he left the club he had twenty Under-21 caps in his locker.

• Paul McVeigh won the first of his eleven Under-21 caps for Northern Ireland in the 1998-99 season.

International Chit-Chat

• When Ian Walker and Sol Campbell came off the bench for their full international debuts versus Hungary in May 1996, they took the club's tally of full England internationals to exactly 50.

• Since Vivian Woodward became club's first England player back in 1903, the longest peacetime gap between Spurs' players gaining a full international honours foir England was one of nearly seven years, from 1926 to 1933.

• In 1962-63, a total of eleven different Spurs players (a complete team) were capped at full international level by their respective countries - but they never all appeared together in the club's senior side. The eleven were...for England: Jimmy Greaves, Ron Henry, Maurice Norman and Bobby Smith...for Scotland: Bill Brown, Dave Mackay and John White...for Wales: Mel Hopkins, Terry Medwin and Cliff Jones ...and for Northern Ireland: Danny Blanchflower.

• Glenn Hoddle, Gary Mabbutt, Steve Hodge, Clive Allen and Chris Waddle - were all in the England team that took on Turkey in a European Championship qualifying game in April 1987. Future Spur Lineker (then of Barcelona) also played for England.

• Spurs players Alf Ramsey and George Robb, both members of the England squad in 1953, were taken to a West End cinema as part of a social function to watch the film 'The Naked Spur' starring James Stewart and Janet Leigh!

• Spurs goalkeeper Milija Aleksic went on the rebel tour of South Africa in 1982.

• Two members of Spurs double-winning team of 1960-61 - left-back Ron Henry and left-winger Terry Dyson - both played in the same Royal Artillery team, Henry as a left-winger and Dyson as a full-back!

• Arthur Rowe and Willie Hall played for England against France at White Hart Lane on 6 Dec. 1933, and both starred in a 4-1 win.

• Goalkeeper Cyril Spiers was the only 'home-based' player in the Football League side that entertained the Scottish League at White Hart Lane in November 1930.

• Spurs managers Ossie Ardiles (Argentina), Gerry Francis, Glenn Hoddle, Joe Hulme Bill Nicholson, Arthur Rowe, Jack Tresadern and Terry Venables (England), George Graham and Peter McWilliam (Scotland) and Terry Neill (Northern Ireland) all represented their country at full international level. Hoddle, Venables and Neill also managed England. Ex-Spurs right-back Alf Ramsey managed Ipswich Town, Birmingham City and England, while Danny Blanchflower took charge of Northern Ireland and both Mike England and Terry Yorath were managers of Wales.

• Chris Hughton, was also a full international with the Republic of Ireland.

• Dave Mackay was the first player to represent the Scottish League v. the Football League (with Hearts) and the Football League v the Scottish League (with Spurs).

• Vivian Woodward gained a total of 67 Amateur internationals caps for England (35 gained with Spurs) and he also played for the Great Britain and United Kingdom sides in the Olympics Games of 1908 and 1912.

• James McNaught played for an England XI and also for the Anglo-Scottish side (v the Home Scots).

• Peter Shreeves (former Spurs manager) was assistant-manager/coach of Wales for a short time in the 1990s.

• Former Spurs full-back Mark Bowen was appointed Welsh Under-21 coach in 2000.

• Spurs defender Luke Young was one of two England players sent-off in the Under-21 European championship qualifying game against Greece in June 2001.

• Up to the end of the 2000-01 season, Spurs had seen 145 players capped by their respective country whilst serving with the club. Between them they had amassed well total of 1,500 full caps. The 54 players who represented England had claimed almost 600 caps between them, while seven players who have starred for Northern Ireland had accumulated 159.

International Goals

• Vivian Woodward scored 29 goals in his 23 international outings for England at senior level. This record stood until 1958 when Preston's Tom Finney reached the 30 mark. Woodward netted four hat-tricks for his country - in 1908 against Wales (three goals) and Austria (4) and in 1909 v. Hungary (4) and Austria (3). He was only ever on the losing side once at senior international level, when England went down 2-1 to Scotland in his third game. A total of 86 goals were scored by England when Woodward was in the forward-line.

• Bobby Smith (Spurs) and Jimmy Greaves (Chelsea, later to join Spurs) scored in five successive England games in the 1960-61 season, claiming a total of 19 goals between them. Greaves went on to score 44 goals for England.

IPSWICH TOWN

Spurs playing record against the Suffolk club

Competition	P	W	D	L	F	A
Premiership	8	3	3	2	13	11
Football League	40	19	5	16	66	60
FA Cup	2	1	0	1	5	3
Charity Shield	1	1	0	0	5	1
Hospital Cup	1	0	1	0	2	2
Summary	52	24	9	19	91	77

The first League game between the two clubs took place at Portman Road on 21 October 1961 (Division 1). A crowd of 28,778 saw Spurs lose 3-2 despite a brace by Cliff Jones.

Spurs scored a total of nine goals (Jimmy Greaves five) against Ipswich in the two League games in 1962-63. It was 5-0 at White Hart Lane (Greaves hat-trick) and 4-2 at Portman Road.

Cliff Jones netted a hat-trick when Spurs beat Ipswich 6-3 at home in April 1963, while earlier in the season fellow winger Terry Dyson had scored twice in a 3-2 win at Portman Road.

After beating Ipswich 5-3 at home in December 1980, Spurs then succumbed to a 3-0 defeat at Portman Road three months later as Ipswich kept up their quest for the League championship (with Aston Villa).

Spurs' record of 16 away League games without defeat came to an end when they lost 1-0 at Ipswich on 24 August 1985.

Players with both clubs include: Milija Aleksic, Alan Brazil, Jamie Clapham, Jason Cundy, Jason Dozzell, Ken Hancock, Scott Houghton, John Moncur, Aled Owen, Jimmy Robertson, John Scales, Steve Sedgley, Gary Stevens (Ipswich Schoolboy forms), Mauricio Taricco, Ian Walker.

Wartime guests (with either one or both clubs): Alf Day, Cecil Potter, George Smith (later Town assistant-manager & manager).

Also associated: John Duncan & Alf Ramsey (Spurs players, Town managers), John Lyall (Town manager, Spurs technical co-ordinator, overseas scouting).

IRISH CONNECTION

List of Spurs personnel, including players (at various levels, trialists, amateurs, Wartime guests), managers, coaches, who have been associated with clubs in Ireland (Northern Ireland and The

Republic of Ireland):

Alex Anderson	Dundalk
Gerry Armstrong	Bangor
RD Blanchflower	Blossomfield (Belfast), Connisbrook (Belfast), Glentoran
Bobby Browne	Derry City
Chris Carrick	Glentoran
Theo Foley	Ormeau FC, Home Farm
Johnny Gavin	Jamesborough United, Limerick
Ian Gilzean	Sligo Rovers
Frank Grice	Glentoran
Len Henley	Bohemians (manager)
Mel Hopkins	Ballymena
Archie Hughes	Larne, Newry Town
Mark Hughes	Dungannon Swifts
Pat Jennings	Newry United
Arthur King	Belfast Celtic
Frank McDiarmid	Distillery
Gerry McMahon	Glenavon, FC Har
James McNaught	Linfield
Jim McVeigh	Shelbourne
Harry Marshall	Linfield
Tommy Muldoon	Athlone Town
Terry Neill	Bangor
Charlie O'Hagan	Derry Celtic
Matt Reilly	Shelbourne
John Smith	Dundalk (player-manager)
Terry Venables	St Patrick's Athletic
Sonny Walters	Derry City (WW2 guest)
Albert Young	Glentoran (WW2 guest)

IVERSEN, STEFFEN

Signed from Rosenborg for £2.7 million in December 1996 - having earlier assisted Nationalkam - Steffen Iversen ended the 2000-01 campaign with an impressive record under his belt of 39 goals in 131 senior appearances for Spurs. He is now hoping to continue to produce the goods in the Premiership as well as add to his tally of 24 senior caps, all gained during his five years at White Hart Lane. He also starred in Euro 2000.

Born in Oslo on 10 November 1976, he was capped by his country at both Youth and Under-21 levels before moving to England.

JACQUES, WILLIAM

Goalkeeper Billy Jacques made 264 first team appearances for Spurs - 123 of them in the Football League. One of the handful of players who served the club before, during and after the Great War, Jacques was born in Erith, Kent on 8 December 1888 and played for Gravesend and Coventry City (from 1911) before moving to White Hart Lane in May 1914. He remained a registered player with Spurs straight through until June 1923 when he announced his retirement due to ill-health. Sadly he never recovered and died two years later at the age of 36. He had earlier missed the 1921 FA Cup Final through injury.

Prior to his transfer to Spurs, Jacques had played in an excellent Gravesend side that included Charlie Buchan.

Jennings saves against West Bromwich Albion in a 2-0 Spurs victory in 1969

JENNINGS, PATRICK ANTHONY, MBE, OBE

Goalkeeper Pat Jennings appeared in 675 first team games for Spurs - 472 coming in the Football League. He also starred in 60 matches for Watford and 378 for Arsenal as well as making 119 full international appearances for Northern Ireland, plus one at Under-23 level. In all major competitions, Jennings lined up in no fewer than 1,095 fixtures, including 52 for the Hornets, 327 for the Gunners and 596 for Spurs (one goal scored in the 3-3 Charity Shield draw with Manchester United in 1967). His League tally was impressive too, 757 outings whilst he also made 85 FA Cup appearances.

Jennings was awarded the MBE in 1976 and the OBE eleven years later. In 1973 he was voted FWA 'Footballer of the Year' three years later collecting the PFA 'Footballer of the Year award. As a Spurs player, he won an FA Cup winners' medal in 1967, gained two League Cup winners' tankards in 1971 and 1973 and a UEFA Cup winners' prize in 1972. He later collected a second FA Cup winners' medal with Arsenal.

Jennings was born in Newry, County Down on 12 June 1945. He played his early football on the Emerald Isle with Newry United and then Newry Town before joining Watford for £6,000 in May 1963. He transferred to Spurs in June 1964 (signed by manager Bill Nicholson for a bargain fee of £27,000) and thirteen years later he switched across North London to Arsenal for £45,000, linking up with his international colleague Terry Neill, who was then boss at Highbury.

In September 1985, Jennings returned to White Hart Lane as a non-contract player, but four months after a standby loan spell with Everton (as cover) and having skippered the Rest of the World against the Americas in a FIFA/UNICEF Charity match in July 1986, he retired to take up coaching. He was re-employed by Spurs in June 1993 (as goalkeeping consultant) - and today he is still associated with the club, albeit on a part-time basis.

JOHNSON, NEIL JOHN

Seventeen of winger Neil Johnson's 52 first team appearances for Spurs came as a substitute. He netted six goals. The former Lincolnshire Schools player joined the club in May 1963 as an apprentice, signed professional forms in June 1964 and remained at White Hart Lane until July 1971 when he moved to Torquay United, having had a loan spell with Charlton Athletic five months earlier. Johnson was born in Grimsby on 3 Dec 1946.

JONES, CHRISTOPHER HARRY

Striker Chris Jones had a good scoring record with Spurs - 68 goals in 247 first team appearances. His Football League record was 37 goals in 164 outings.

Born in Jersey on 18 April 1956 - only the second Channel Islander to play for the club at that time (following in the footsteps of Len Duquemin) Jones represented Jersey and Jersey & Guernsey Schools before signing apprentice forms for Spurs in May 1971, turning professioinal two years later. He played alongside Martin Chivers in the Spurs attack for a while and also with Irish international Gerry Armstrong, John Duncan, Colin Lee and Ian Moores. After helping the team gain promotion from the Second Division in 1977-78 and receiving England Under-21 recognition, Jones became surplus to requirements following the arrival of Steve Archibald and Garth Crooks and he subsequently left White Hart Lane for Manchester City in September 1982 for £110,000. He later assisted Crystal Palace, Charlton Athletic, Leyton Orient and St Albans City before becoming manager of St Peter's FC (Jersey) in 1988. In all Jones scored 61 goals in a total of 315 Football League games.

JONES, CLIFFORD WILLIAM

Welshman Cliff Jones was a fast, direct goalscoring winger who occupied both flanks, with outstanding aerial ability.

He netted 176 goals in 418 first team appearances for Spurs between February 1958 and October 1968. He made his debut for the club v. Arsenal soon after his £35,000 transfer from Swansea Town for whom he played in two Welsh Cup Finals (1956 & 1957). On leaving White Hart Lane he switched to nearby Fulham for just £5,000. A double-winner in 1960-61, he also starred in the FA Cup and European Cup-winners Cup triumphs of the next two years and as a non-playing substitute added a third FA Cup medal to his tally in 1967. Born in Swansea on 7 February 1935, he joined Spurs from the Vetch Field club in February 1958, having signed for the Swans as a part-time professional in May 1952 after representing both Swansea and Wales as a Schoolboy. During his ten-and-a-half years at White Hart Lane, Jones, who could shoot with both feet and head a ball as powerfully and as true as some players could kick it, was capped 43 times by his country, having previously won 16 caps as a Swansea player. He played for Wales in the 1958 World Cup Finals and netted a total of 16 international goals. Jones also represented the Football League on three occasions including an outing against the Italian League, and gained one Welsh Under 23 cap. Jones completed his national service in the Royal Horse Artillery (Kings Troop) - a footballers' unit and a plum posting for the enthusiastic and sports-minded Welshman! From Fulham, Jones moved to Kings Lynn of the Southern League in July 1970 and after a spell with Wealdstone, he then served with Bedford Town and Cambridge City before becoming player-coach of Wingate (in the Athenian League) finally retiring in 1977. He later ran a butcher's shop (he learned about the trade as a 16 year-old in Swansea dry dock), was a sheet-metal worker, served in a Sports Leisure Complex and was a games master at a London School (Highbury High Grove).

* Jones followed his father Ivor and uncle Bryn into international and League soccer.

JONES, JOHN

John Jones was nicknamed 'Bristol' to distinguish him from the John L Jones who was registered with the club at the same time (see below). Born in West Bromwich in October 1874, he was an inside-forward who played initially for Small Heath (now Birmingham City) before joining Spurs from Bristol Rovers in the summer of 1902. He drew up an excellent record of 40 goals in in only 66 first-team appearances during his short time at White Hart Lane that effectively ended in July 1904 when he was struck down with typhoid fever. He never recovered from the illness and sadly died at the age of 29 on 13 September 1904.

JONES, JOHN LEONARD

Born in Rhuddlan near Rhyl, North Wales in 1866, full-back John L Jones played for his home town club and also for Bootle before joining Stockton (on Teeside) in 1889. He was transferred to Grimsby Town in May 1893 and then moved to Sheffield United twelve months later, spending three seasons at Bramall Lane before transferring to Spurs in May 1897. He went on to appear in 335 first team appearances for the club (including 131 in the Southern League and 30 in the FA Cup). Already capped nine times by Wales, Jones became Spurs' first full international player when he lined up for his country against Ireland on 19 February 1898. He went on to win a total of 21 senior caps(12, with Spurs). In 1899-1900 he helped Spurs win the Southern League title and the following year skippered the team to victory in the FA Cup Final over his former club Sheffield United! He joined Watford in May 1904 and after a brief spell with Worcester City, he quit competitive football in November 1905 to became part of a team of players at Olympia (London) putting on exhibition matches on an imitiation 'turf carpet' (the first astro-pitch!). Having coached part-time at Rugby School in Warwickshire (when given time off by Spurs) he became a cricket professionmal with Leinster (Ireland) in 1906. Later Jones took a cricket engagement in Durban, South Africa and on his return to England (in March 1923) became coach/groundsman of the Whitburn Cricket Club, who played in the Durham League. He retired from sport in 1929 to become a pattern maker in Sunderland. Whilst in this line of work he fell down a 12 foot stairway, sustaining serious head injuries from which he never recovered. Jones died in a Sunderland hospital on 24 November 1931.

JONES, WILLIAM ERNEST ARTHUR

Bill Jones was another Welshman, born in Cwmbwrle near Swansea on 12 November 1920. He was a winger with good pace and powerful shot who represented Cwmbwrle Juniors and Swansea Schools before joining Swansea Town as an amateur in 1937. He switched from the Vetch Field to Bolton Wanderers as a professional in August 1938. After guesting for Bury and Chester during the War he rejoined Swansea in 1946 before transferring to White Hart Lane in May 1947. Jones - nicknamed 'Alphabet' - scored 16 goals in 64 first team appearances for Spurs (14 in 55 outings in the Football League) up to May 1949 when he switched to Southampton, across to Bristol City as player-coach in November 1951. He broke an ankle playing for Southampton in 1950 and never really got over that injury. Later Jones assisted Rhyl Town (from April 1954, manager from April 1954 to July 1956), Poole Town (one game in January 1956), Southampton (again, this time as Youth team coach: February 1956 to June 1958). He then chose to live in Bolton and was chairman of Horwich RMI for four years: 1961-65. Also employed as an an engineer by Hawker Siddeley, Jones announced his retirement in 1980 when he became a member of the National Association of Inventors and Innovators while also designing water leisure products.

JORDAN, JOHN WILLIAM

Inside-forward, born in Romford, Essex on 8 November 1921, Johnny Jordan played for Bromley, Grays Athletic and West Ham United (as an amateur) before joining Spurs in July 1947, turning professional the following month. A very promising footballer during his amateur days, he never quite made it at a higher level and after scoring 13 goals in 28 first team games for Spurs, he was transferred to the Italian club Juventus in August 1948. He returned to English soccer with Birmingham City in March 1949 and then rounded things off with a spell at Sheffield Wednesday (September 1950-May 1951) and then Tonbridge.

JOYCE, JOHN WILLIAM

Goalkeeper John 'Tiny' Joyce scored two goals in 113 first team appearnces for Spurs.

Born in the brewery town of Burton-on-Trent on 26 June 1877, he played his early football with Burton Pioneers, Woodville and Overseal Town before joining Southampton St Mary's for £80 in May 1898. He made only seven Southern League appearances for Saints before switching his allegiance to Millwall in May 1900. Seasonal spells with Burton United and Blackburn Rovers then followed prior to him returning to Millwall in May 1903 (after a proposed move to White Hart Lane had broken down at the last minute). He eventually found his way to Spurs in November 1909 and spent the next six-and-a-half years with the club before going back to Millwall for a third time in 1916. A loan spell with Gillingham followed in November 1919 prior to his retirement later that season. The well built and physically strong Joyce was one of the most powerful kickers of a dead ball in the game and it was commonplace for him to send a clearance downfield up to a distance of 60-70 yards first bounce. His two goals were both penalties struck with power, the first against Bolton Wanderers in a home League game in April 1914 and the second in a friendly against Bayern Munich the following month. Joyce died in Greenwich in June 1956.

* Joyce made over 250 first-team appearances in his three spells with Millwall.

JOYCE, WILLIAM

Centre-forward Bill Joyce played for Spurs from May 1897 until May 1899 and during that time he scored an amazing total of 93 goals (including four hat-tricks, three fourtimers and one five) in 119 first team appearances. In his first season with the club he notched 36 in competitive matches and followed up with 35 the following year. He was then transferred to Thames Ironworks and later assisted Portsmouth and Burton United, retiring in 1903. Born in Scotland circa 1870, he played for Greenock Morton (from August 1893) and Bolton Wanderers (from March 1895) prior to joining Spurs. He was somehow overlooked when it came to representative calls, the only honour he recieved was to play for the United League v. the Thames & Medway League in November 1898 and even then he celebrated with a goal on his own patch! During his playing career Joyce netted over 200 goals in more than 350 various League and Cup matches.

JULL, JACK C

Jack Jull was the first Spurs player to win a representative honour when he lined up for Middlesex against Surrey in February 1891. He later represented the respective Tottenham (district) and London sides. A fearless full-back, Jull went on to score 24 goals in 158 first team games for the club whom he served superbly well for more than 14 years. He played in many - if not all - of the club's FIRST matches in the various competitions, lining up versus St Albans in the London Senior Cup in October 1885; competing in the first 'League' game v. Polytechnic FC in the Southern Alliance in September 1892; starring in the first FA Amateur Cup game v. Vampiers in November 1893 and then defending earnestly in FA Cup tie v. West Herts in October 1894. Born seemingly in London in 1867, he retired at the end of the 1896-97 season. Later Jull served on the club's committee, his vast knowledge and experience of the game always being acknowledged to the full. In 1895 he was appointed as the club's president and afterwards performed admirably as a linesman for many years. Jull died on 22 December 1920.

* Thomas E Jull, Jack's younger brother, was a forward with Spurs 1893-97, appearing in four first team games.

K

KAISERSLAUTERN (1FC)

Spurs playing record against the German side:

Competition	P	W	D	L	F	A
UEFA Cup	2	1	0	1	1	2

Spurs met the German Bundesliga side in the 2nd round of the 1999-2000 UEFA Cup competition. A crowd of 35,177 saw Spurs claim a narrow lead from the first leg, Steffen Iversen's 34th minute spot-kick deciding the issue played at White Hart Lane on 28 October. There were over 29,000 fans present for the return clash in the Fritz-Walter Stadion, Betzenberg a week later when the German outfit went through with a hard-earned 2-0 victory. After the game Spurs lodged a complaint that Kaiserslautern technically broke the rules of the competition regarding the handing in of their team-sheet. This was so, but instead of banning the German side, FIFA handed them a £500 fine for their indiscretion.

KEFLAVIK (IBK)

Spurs playing record against the Icelandic club

Competition	P	W	D	L	F	A
UEFA Cup	2	2	0	0	15	1

Spurs' first-ever UEFA Cup-tie was against the Icelandic side Keflavik in the 1971-72 competition - and they won hands down by an aggregate scoreline of 15-1.

The first leg of this first round encounter was played in Iceland on 14 September and in front of 18,000 supporters, ended in a 6-1 win for Spurs, Alan Mullery (2), Ralph Coates and Alan Gilzean (3) the scorers. Graeme Souness came on as a substitute in this game - his only first team outing for Spurs.

The return leg - played a fortnight later in front of 23,818 loyal spectators - finished Spurs 9 Keflavik 0 and on target this time were Cyril Knowles, Coates, Steve Perryman, Martin Chivers (3), Phil Holder (on his debut) and Gilzean (2). This is still Spurs' biggest-ever European victory and their best aggregate score of any two-legged Cup-tie.

KELLER, KASEY - See Late News

KERSLAKE, DAVID

Full-back David Kerslake - born in Stepney, London on 19 June 1966 - was an England international at both Schoolboy and Youth team levels before gaining an Under-21 cap. He turned professional with Queen's Rark Rangers in August 1983 and made more than 60 appearances for the Loftus Road club prior to moving to Swindon Town in November 1989. He lined up in 135 League matches for the Robins who then sold him to Leeds United in March 1993. He joined Spurs in six months later and was given 44 during his time at White Hart Lane that ended in August 1997 when he switched to Charlton Athletic having had a loan spell back at Swindon in November 1996. He spent only 14 days with the Addicks (no appearances), transferring to Ipswich Town. During his spell at Portman Road, Kerslake was loaned out to Wycombe Wanderers before returning to Swindon for a third spell in March 1998. He quit competitive football in May 2000, having amassed in excess of 340 senior appearances over a period of almost 17 years.

KETTERING TOWN

Spurs playing record against Town:

Competition	P	W	D	L	F	A
Other Leagues	14	7	4	3	30	17

Spurs' United League away game with Kettering in March 1897 was abandoned in the 25th minute after a home player suffered a fractured leg. It was 1-1 at the time. Kettering won the 'replay' 5-2.

Players with both clubs include: Herbert Blake, Tommy Cable (Town player-manager) and Fred Mearns.

Also associated: Graham Carr (Kettering manager, Spurs scout).

KIDDERMINSTER HARRIERS

No competitive action, as yet, between Spurs and Harriers, who entered the Football League for the 2000-01 season after winning the Nationwide Conference title.

Players with both clubs include: Sammy Brooks, Leon Hyde.

Wartime guest: Reg Mogford (Spurs).

KING, LEDLEY

Versatile defender Ledley King holds the record for scoring the fastest-ever goal in a Premiership match - after just ten seconds play for Spurs in the away game against Bradford City on 9 December 2000. Born in Bow, London on 12 October 1980, he joined the apprentice ranks at White Hart Lane in July 1997 and was upgraded to professional status twelve months later. King made his senior debut against Liverpool at Anfield in May 1999. He has already won England honours at Under-16, Under-17, Youth and Under-21 levels. When the 2000-01 season ended, his senior record with Spurs was 27 appearances and two goals scored - with plenty more to come!

KINNEAR, JOSEPH PATRICK

Full-back Joe Kinnear (capped 26 times by the Republic of Ireland) made 301 first team appearances for Spurs (196 in the Football League). He was the first player from the club to be sent-off in an FA Cup-tie, dismissed in the 1-0 third round victory over Manchester United in January 1968. Born in Dublin, on 27 December 1947, Kinnear represented both Watford and Hertfordshire Schools before joining St Albans City in 1962. From there he became an amateur with Spurs (August 1963), turning professional in February 1965 and making his League debut against West Ham United in April 1966. He won a regular place in the side during the latter stages of the 1966-67 season - after Phil Beal had broken his arm and shortly after gaining the first of his 25 full caps for the Republic of Ireland. He ended that campaign with an FA Cup winners' medal in his hand after Spurs had defeated Chelsea 2-1. He broke a leg in January 1969 and after a long, arduous struggle to regain full-fitness, he returned to the action before the end of the year and in 1971 and in 1973 collected League Cup winning prizes, in between times helping Spurs win the UEFA Cup. Kinnear, who had many other fine full-backs challenging him for a first team place, went on to serve Spurs until August 1975 when he was transferred to Brighton & Hove Albion. He retired due to injury after just one season at The Goldstone Ground. Kinnear managed Woodford Town for a short time in 1976-77 and had a trial period as coach/manager in Nepal before taking over as coach (under his old Spurs team-mate Dave Mackay) of Sharjah FC (UAE). He was then appointed national team coach of Malaysia before obtaining the position of assistant-manager of Doncaster Rovers (again under Mackay), taking over the reins at Belle Vue himself as caretaker-manager in March 1989 and holding office for just three months. At that juncture Kinnear became coach at Wimbledon (September 1989). He was upgraded to assistant-manager by the Dons in 1990 and took control as manager in January 1992. A little over seven years later Kinnear had a heart attack and on medical advice quit his position. He recovered sufficiently well to move back into management in a vain attempt to save Luton Town from relegation to the Nationwide League Div. Three in 2000-01 and was eventually appointed Luton manager on a full time basis, June 2001.

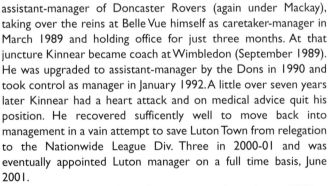

* Kinnear was the last Spurs first team squad member in 1967 to acquire a car. He purchased a Ford Corsair automatic and used to travel in it daily from his home in Watford to White Hart Lane.

KINGSTONIAN

Spurs playing record against the then amateur side:

Competition	P	W	D	L	F	A
Other Cup	1	1	0	0	5	0

Spurs comfortably accounted for Kingstonian in the 2nd round of the London FA Charity Cup in November 1924. A crowd of around 5,000 saw Frank Osborne, Harry Skitt, Jimmy Seed, Harry Hargreaves and Jack Elkes score the goals in a White Hart Lane romp.

KIRKHAM, FREDERICK

Lancashire-born Fred Kirkham was Spurs' manager for a little over 15 months, from 18 April 1907 to 20 July 1908. A former Preston-based referee, Kirkham had been in charge of the 1902 and 1906 FA Cup Finals as well as officiating in several international matches. This, in fact, was his only involvement with football prior to his appointment by Spurs. Kirkham had been working as a commercial traveller and had taken charge of Spurs' Southern League match at Watford on 13 April 1907, after which he successfully applied for the manager's job at White Hart Lane - and got it! He signed the appropriate paperwork on 18 April and took up his position four days later. He signed a three-year contract worth approximately £1,000 (£350 per-annum). Unfortunately he wasn't a liked man. Too controversial, abrasive and contradictory, he was unpopular with both the players and the supporters and often had heated arguments with first team regulars and club officials. Indeed, after a game against Brighton United in October 1907, it was alleged that he made 'inproper remarks' to the referee. A month later he was severely censured by the club. He was certainly not a success as a manager and he resigned his position in July 1908 - a month before Spurs kicked off their Football League career!

At that point Spurs decided not to seek a replacement for Kirkham, asking Arthur Turner to assist the directors with the choosing of the team and indeed the training schedule.

KIRWAN, JOHN HENRY

John Kirwan appeared in 343 first team matches for Spurs (23 in the FA Cup). He scored 97 goals (60 coming at League level). An outside-left, born in County Wicklow, Ireland in 1878, he played for Southport and Everton before joining Spurs in July 1899. He remained at White Hart Lane until May 1905 when he certainly surprised everyone by moving across London to Chelsea (with David Copeland). He figured in the Blues' first ever Football League game. Three years later Kirwan switched north to Scotland and signed for Clyde, returning to the English soccer scene with Leyton in the summer of 1909. He then took up a coaching position in Holland (September 1910) and from 1923 did a similar job with the Italian club, Livorno. Very fast, an excellent dribbler and fine passer and crosser of the ball, Kirwan was a great character and huge favourite with the fans (wherever he played). Capped 13 times by Ireland as a Spurs player (he was the club's first Irish international incidentally) he added three more to his tally whilst at Stamford Bridge and an extra one when serving Clyde. He helped Spurs win the Southern League championship in 1899-1900 and the FA Cup the following season.

Kirwan, who did very well as a coach, died on 9 January 1959.

KLINSMANN, JURGEN

German international striker Jurgen Klinsmann scored on his Premiership debut for Spurs in the 4-3 win at Sheffield Wednesday on the opening day of the 1994-95 season, just nineteeen days after signing for the club. He then netted twice on his home debut

v. Everton shortly afterwards (won 2-0)...diving along the turf to celebrate every goal! Born in Goppingen, Germany on 30 July 1964, he played for Vfb Stuttgart, Inter Milan and AS Monaco before moving to White Hart Lane for £2 million on 1 August 1994. A player with exceptional heading ability, he was fast, direct, had excellent ball control and as well as scoring plenty of goals himself, he created many more for his colleagues with his unselfish off-the-ball running and delicate passes and knock-downs.

Voted the FWA 'Player of the Year' and included in the Premiership team of the year in his first season in English Football, Klinsmann netted 29 goals in exactly 50 appearances for Spurs before transferring to Bayern Munich, also for £2 million in June 1995.

Returning to Spurs (on a permanent long-term contract from the Italian Serie 'A' club Sampdoria) for the second-half of the 1997-98 campaign, his presence in the side helped the team steer clear of relegation. He scored nine vitally important goals (in 15 Premiership games) as Spurs climbed from 19th in the table to 14th. He netted four times in a 6-2 win against Wimbledon at Selhurst Park that secured Spurs' status in the top Division. Klinsman retired in Jan 1999 with 108 senior caps in his locker for Germany (47 goals scored) plus more than 500 club appearances and a total of 200 goals.

KNOWLES, CYRIL BARRY

Full-back Cyril Knowles played in 568 first team games for Spurs (401 in the Football League). He made his debut for the club against Feyenoord in August 1964, his League bow following a fortnight later against Sheffield United and he played his last game in December 1975 v. Everton at White Hart Lane. He retired at the end of that season (mainly through injury) and almost immediately became manager of Hertford Town. He acted as Spurs' Yorkshire scout for a short while before taking a position as coach with Doncaster Roveres (1977), moving to Middlesbrough in the same capacity in 1981. He was then given the job of assistant-manager at Ayresome Park (February 1982) and fifteen months later became manager of Darlington (May 1983). He remained in office at Feethams until May 1987 when he moved south to become boss of Torquay United (June 1987). He stayed at Plainmoor until October 1989. A month later he went north again to take charge of Hartlepool United, retaining that post until the summer of 1991 when he was forced to quit - having heard the stunning news a few months earlier that he was suffering from a serious brain illness. Sadly Knowles died in a Cleveland hospital on 31 August 1991, aged 47.

A Wartime baby, born in Fitzwilliam, Yorkshire on 13 July 1944, he was on Manchester United's books as a youngster and also had a trial with Blackpool before joining Middlesbrough (from Monckton Colliery Welfare) in October 1962. He was transferred to Spurs in May 1964 for a bargain fee of just £45,000.

During his time at White Hart Lane, Knowles - tall, upright, a clean kicking, hard but fair tackling and reliable defender - won four full

and six Under-23 caps for England. He also played for Young England and represented the Football League. He was twice a League Cup winner in 1971 and 1973 and was a member of Spurs triumphant UEFA Cup winning team in between times.

As manager of Darlington, he guided the Quakers to promotion from Division Four in 1985 and Hartlepool were also in the race for promotion when he received news from his doctor about his brain illness.

● Knowles' brother, Peter, was a professional footballer with Wolves but quit the sport to become a Jehovah's Witness.

KYLE, PETER

Centre-forward Peter Kyle was born in Rutherglen, Glasgow on 7 September 1878.

He played for Glasgow & District Schools, Glasgow Parkhead (1896), Partick Thistle, Clyde (trialist), Liverpool (July 1899), Leicester Fosse (May 1900), Wellingborough, West Ham United (November 1902), Kettering Town, Heart of Midlothian (trialist), Larkhall Thistle (February 1904) and Port Glasgow Athletic (July 1904) before joining Spurs in July 1905. He spent just one season with the club and then moved to Woolwich Arsenal in April 1906. From there he switched to, Aston Villa (March 1908) and afterwards assisted Sheffield United (October 1908), Royal Albert (July 1909) and finally Watford (November 1909-May 1910). He returned to Scotland before the Great War and did not re-appear on the soccer scene after the hostilities.

With his smartly waxed moustache and black hair, Kyle was a dangerous centre-forward with an eye for goal. He had a nomadic career in the game, travelling all over Britain. He participated at various levels with 17 different clubs and made well over 200 League and Cup appearances, scoring more than 40 goals. Kyle could be somewhat temperamental at times and was suspended by Spurs for a breach of club rules in March 1906 (he never played for the club again). A Scottish international trialist, ironically his last game for Woolwich Arsenal was against Aston Villa - next month he moved to Villa Park! He scored 19 goals in 41 first team outings for Spurs.

NB - There is no firm evidence that this Peter Kyle did assist all the clubs listed above as there was another Scottish-born player bearing the same name and desription around at the same time (possibly related). However, I have listed all the clubs who had a Peter Kyle (forward) registered between 1896 and 1910.

LACY, JOHN

With a name containing just eight letters, central defender John Lacy is one of the shortest-named players ever to appear in Spurs' first team!

A Scouser, born in Liverpool on 14 August 1951, he represented Merseyside and Lancashire Schools, played for Liverpool Marine and both the London and British University sides before joining Fulham as an amateur, turning professional at Craven Cottage in June 1972. After playing with Alan Mullery and Bobby Moore and appearing in the 1975 FA Cup Final defeat by West Ham, he left Fulham to sign for Spurs for £200,000 in July 1978. He remained at White Hart Lane for five seasons, amassing 174 first team appearances (104 in the Football League) and scoring three goals

before transferring to Crystal Palace in June 1983. Fifteen months later he went over to Norway to assist Stanungsund and thereafter played for Barnet, St Albans City (as player-manager) and Wivenhoe.

LANE, WILLIAM HARRY CHARLES

Born in Tottenham on 23 October 1904, centre-forward Billy Lane was another soccer nomad who served with no fewer than 16 different teams/clubs over a period of 62 years. He started off, as a player, with London City Mission in 1918 and then assisted, in turn: Gnome Athletic, Park Avondale, Spurs (amateur, June 1920), Barnet (on loan September 1920), Northfleet, Spurs (July 1924-November 1926), Leicester Fosse for £2,250, November 1926), Walsall (1927), Reading (June 1928), Brentford (May 1929), Watford (May 1932), Bristol City (January 1936), Clapton Orient (July 1937) and Gravesend United (albeit briefly in April 1938). In August 1938 Lane went back to Brentford as assistant-manager and after guesting for Brighton & Hove Albion during the War, he served as Guildford City's boss from 1946-50. Brighton's assistant-manager from April 1950, he was employed as team manager at the Goldstone Ground from March 1951 to May 1961 and was then chief of Gravesend & Northfleet from December 1961 to May 1963. Appointed Arsenal scout in 1963-64, he held a similar position with QPR in 1968-69 and also with Brighton from 1969 until retiring from the game in 1980, at the age of 76.

A dedicated Christian, teetaller and non-smoker, Lane was quite small and dapper for a striker but he certainly had a bit about him and was never bothered by the bigger, more solid defenders who opposed him. He scored 152 League goals (in 298 appearances) including 79 in 96 outings for Brentford and 68 in124 for Watford. His record with Spurs was seven strikes in 25 matches (and 12 in 37 first team games altogether). Lane once netted a hat-trick in the space of 180 seconds playing for Watford against his future club Clapton Orient in December 1933.

As a manager he guided Guildford to runners-up spot in the Southern League in 1947 and after taking Brighton to second spot in the Third Division (S) in 1954 and 1956 he finally saw the Gulls win the championship of that section in 1958.

Lane died in Chelmsford, Essex on 10 November 1985.

LATYMER FC

The second known game played by Spurs is believed to have been another friendly against Latymer FC (away) on 6 January 1883. The result was an 8-1 defeat, but Spurs quickly gained revenge when on 22 December of that same year they won 2-0 at home (albeit against a rather weakened side) and then followed up with a second 2-0 victory on Laymer's ground on 15 March 1884.

* For many years this fixture was thought to have been Spurs very first game as a football club!

LEE, COLIN

Born in Torquay, Devon on 12 June 1956, striker Colin Lee began scoring goals for Torbay Schools. He then joined Bristol City as an apprentice before turning professional at Ashton Gate in July 1974. Loan spells with both Hereford United and Torquay United preceded his £60,000 transfer to Spurs in October 1977 - and in his first season at White Hart Lane he helped the team reclaim their Division One status by scoring eleven goals in 23 League games.

In January 1980, Lee was transferred to nearby Chelsea and on announcing his retirement from the first-class game in July 1987, he was appointed player-Youth Development Officer at Brentford (linking up with Steve Perryman). He moved to Watford as Youth team manager in July 1989 and took over as team boss at Vicarage Road in March 1990. He held that position until November of that year when he left (replaced by Perryman) to become Youth Development Officer at Reading. From Elm Park he went to Filbert Street (as assistant-manager to Mark McGhee) then followed McGhee in the same capacity to Wolverhampton Wanderers, eventually taking over as boss at Molineux in November 1998, when McGhee was dismissed. Lee then lost his job half way through the 2000-01 season and he ended that campaign by acting as caretaker-manager of Torquay - and succeeded in keeping the Gulls in the Football League. He had considered taking the job at Plainmoor on a full-time basis but rejected the offer from the Devon club.

As a player, Lee was a very useful striker, who later became a confident defender. He scored a fourtimer on his League debut for Spurs v. Bristol Rovers and went on to notch a total of 31 goals in 94 first team appearances for the club before his £200,000 to Stamford Bridge. In 1984 he helped Chelsea win the Second Division championship and followed up with a Full Members' Cup prize (at Wembley) in 1987.

LEEDS CITY

Spurs' playing record against the now defunct Yorkshire club:

Competition	P	W	D	L	F	A
Football League	2	1	0	1	3	1

These two matches were Division 2 encounters played in season 1908-09. Leeds won 1-0 at Elland Road on 5 September in front of 20,000 fans before Spurs gained sweet revenge with a 3-0 victory at White Hart Lane on 2 January when the attendance was 16,000. The defeat at Leeds was in fact, Spurs' first in the Football League.

Players with both clubs include: John Freeborough, John George, Jimmy Kennedy, Charlie Morgan, Bill Murray, George Page, Haydn Price (Spurs WW1), Fanny Walden (City W1).

Also associated: Herbert Chapman (Spurs player, City manager), Jock Chaplin (Spurs player, City trainer & assistant-manager), Jack Oliver (Leeds City committee member, Spurs Chairman, 1898)

LEEDS UNITED

Spurs playing record against United:

Competition	P	W	D	L	F	A
Premiership	18	4	5	9	21	28
Football League	64	24	20	20	92	85
FA Cup	6	3	2	1	9	6
Summary	88	31	27	30	122	119

The first League game between Spurs and United took place at Elland Road on 18 October 1924, a crowd of 25,000 seeing the Yorkshire side win 1-0. The following March, Spurs gained revenge with a 2-1 home win, Jimmy Seed and Billy Lane the scorers in front of White Hart Lane's lowest crowd of the season, just 8,000. In May 1935, just 7.668 fans attended Elland Road to see Leeds win a League game by 4-3 to confirm Spurs' relegation from the First Division.

When they lost 3-0 at Leeds on 14 January 1950, Spurs' record of 22 unbeaten League matches came to an end.

Five different Spurs players found the net (including wing-half Danny Blanchflower) when Leeds were defeated 5-1 at White Hart Lane in August 1956.

When Leeds won 3-2 at White Hart Lane in October 1958 it was their first League victory over Spurs in London in 12 attempts. Over the same period of time Spurs had only won twice at Elland Road!

John Charles (left) of Leeds fires in a cross passed Danny Blanchflower

Over a period of three days - 26 and 28 December 1959 - Spurs beat Leeds 4-2 away and then lost 4-1 at home!

Spurs played United at Boothferry Park, Hull on 25 August 1971 after Elland Road had been closed by the Football League following crowd disturbances v. WBA the previous season. The game ended 1-1 in front of 25,099 spectators.

Spurs lost 2-1 to the 1972 FA Cup winners Leeds in the 6th round of that season's competition.

Spurs had to beat Leeds, the European Cup Finalists, on the last day of the 1974-75 season to retain their First Division status. Almost 50,000 fans turned up to see them do just that - to the tune of 4-2. Full-back Cyril Knowles scored two of the goals, one a penalty.

Spurs trailed United 3-1 with 19 minutes left of their Premiership game at White Hart Lane in September 1998, but two late strikes by Steffen Iversen and Sol Campbell (three minutes into added-time) earned them a point at 3-3.

In March 2000, the FA dished out record £150,000 fines to both Leeds United and Spurs following misconduct by players during a Premiership game at Elland Road the previous month which United won 1-0.

Players with both clubs include: Chris Fairclough, Ernie Goldthorpe (Spurs WW1), Steve Hodge, George Hutchinson, David Kerslake, Willem Korsten, Neil McNab, Taffy Spelman, Bert Sproston, John Scales, Danny Thomas (United trialist), Terry Yorath.

Wartime guests (with either one or both clubs): Bobby Browne, John Davie, George Dorling, Tom Paton.

Also associated: George Graham (manager of both clubs), Theo Foley (Spurs coach, Leeds scout).

LEICESTER CITY (FOSSE)

Spurs playing record against the Foxes:

Competition	P	W	D	L	F	A
Premiership	12	3	2	7	14	21
Football League	72	36	14	22	143	120
FA Cup	9	7	1	1	25	8
League Cup	1	1	0	0	1	0
Wartime	4	3	0	1	11	7
Summary	98	50	17	31	194	156

The first League meeting between the two clubs was a Second Division contest, played at White Hart Lane on 1 September 1919 - and it ended in a 4-0 win for Spurs, Jimmy Cantrell scoring twice in front of 21,060 spectators. Spurs quickly doubled up over the Foxes, winning 4-2 at Filbert Street ten days later.

Top-of-the-table Spurs lost Arthur Grimsdell with a broken leg when going down 5-3 in an eight-goal thriller at Filbert Street in October 1925.

A record Filbert Street crowd of 47,296 saw Leicester beaten 3-0 by Spurs in a 5th round FA Cup-tie on 18 February 1928. Taffy O'Callaghan netted twice.

In March 1935 Spurs suffered a 6-0 League battering at Leicester for whom Danny Liddle scored two superb goals and Spurs right-back Fred Channell conceded a rather bizarre own-goal!

On 11 April 1936, centre-half Doug Hunt (Spurs) opposed Fred Sharman, centre-forward of Leicester City, in a drawn League game at White Hart Lane. Both players were, in fact, playing out of position and a week later they were opponents again in a London Combination fixture on the game ground, but on this occasion Sharman was City's centre-half while Hunt was the Spurs centre-forward!

On 1 May 1937 - the last day of the season - Leicester beat Spurs 4-1 in front of 22,761 fans at Filbert Street to clinch the Second Division championship.

Ron Reynolds dives to save a shot against Leicester City

A week after putting ten past Everton, Spurs defeated Leicester 4-3 at Filbert Street (October 1958) and later in the season (March) Welshman Terry Medwin (wearing the number 9 shirt) scored four times as Spurs beat the Foxes 6-0 at home to complete the double. The latter victory ended in a run of five League games without a win.

City won twice at White Hart Lane in the year 1961 - beating Spurs 3-2 in February and 2-1 in November.

In fact, Leicester enjoyed playing in London around this time; they won four out of five League games at White Hart Lane between 1957-62.

In return Spurs won 2-1 at Filbert Street in September 1960 and 3-2 on the same ground in April 1962....and of course Spurs won the 1961 FA Cup Final 2-0 to complete the double!

In April 1965 Spurs scored three goals in each half as they beat City 6-2 at White Hart Lane. Cliff Jones hit a hat-trick and Jimmy Greaves netted twice, one from the penalty spot. Earlier in the season City had won 4-2 at Filbert Street.

Spurs doubled-up over City in 1970-71, winning 4-3 at home and 1-0 away. Cyril Knowles scored twice, once from the penalty spot, in the first game.

A seven-goal thriller at White Hart Lane in December 1973 saw Spurs beat Leicester 4-3 after the scoring had gone 2-0, 2-2, 4-2 and 4-3.

On 25 October 1975 Spurs beat City 3-2 at Filbert Street to end a run of 11 games without a win. It was also their first away win in the League for seven months (eight games).

Spurs defeated the Foxes 2-0 at neutral Villa Park to reach the 1982 FA Cup Final.

Nico Claesen scored twice when Spurs beat City 5-0 at home in February 1987 to complete the double, having won 2-1 at Filbert Street earlier in the campaign.

A dramatic late goal by Allan Nielsen (scored in the 90th minute) won 10-men Spurs the 1999 Worthington Cup Final 1-0 against Leicester in front of 77,892 fans at Wembley. Defender Justin Edinburgh was sent-off - his second 'red card' in a month and his third as a Spurs player.

Towards the end of the 2000-01 season Spurs lost 4-2 at Filbert Street in a Premiership game.

Players with both clubs include: Joe Barlow, Tommy Clay, Terry Fenwick, Jimmy Holmes, Percy Humphreys, Bill Lane, Billy Leech, Gary Lineker, Jim Milliken, Fred Milnes, Paul Moran, Taffy O'Callaghan, Tom Roberts, Buchanan Sharp, Harry Sparrow, Ian Walker, Ralph Ward (City Amateur), Keith Weller.

Wartime guests (with either orr both clubs): Ken Burditt, Stan Eastham, Colin Lyman, Jimmy McCormick, George Travers

Also associated: David Pleat (manager of both clubs, also Spurs caretaker-manager & Director of Football), Peter Taylor (Spurs player, City manager), Cyril Spiers (Spurs player, City scout), Ricky Hill (Spurs Academy coach, City player).

LEONHARDSEN, OYVIND

Norwegian international Oyvind Leonhardsen had 62 full caps to his credit when he joined Spurs from Liverpool for £3 million in August 1999.

Formerly with FC Clausengengen and FC Molde, he then played for Rosenborg before transferring to Wimbledon for £660,000 in November 1994 - signed by former Spurs full-back Joe Kinnear.

Leonhardsen, an attacking, goal-seeking midfielder scored 16 goals in 102 senior games for the Dons and followed up by netting seven times in 49 outings for Liverpool after his £3.5 move from the London club. He was eventually 'frozen out' at Anfield, hence his big-money move to White Hart Lane.

He suffered with injuries during his first season with Spurs and as a result missed Euro 2000. His record with the club prior to the start of the 2001-02 campaign was 59 appearances and 11 goals scored.

LEYTON

Spurs playing record against Leyton:

Competition	P	W	D	L	F	A
Southern League	4	2	2	0	7	3

Players with both clubs include: Fred Boreham, Tommy Cable, George Foreman, James A Gray, Rev. Kenneth Hunt (Spurs WW1), John Kirwan, Tom Leslie, Fred Massey, Bert Page, George Payne, Tommy Simmons (Spurs WW1), Sandy Tait (Leyton player & manager), Jack Whitbourne.

LEYTON ORIENT (ALSO ORIENT & CLAPTON ORIENT)

Spurs playing record against Orient:

Competition	P	W	D	L	F	A
Football League	10	6	3	1	20	8
FA Cup	1	1	0	0	1	0
League Cup	4	3	0	1	8	3
Other Cups	5	1	0	4	4	8
Wartime	26	21	2	3	90	26
Summary	46	32	5	9	123	45

Spurs first met the 'Os' (then known as Clapton Orient) in the Football League competition on 11 October 1919. They won 2-1 at White Hart Lane and followed up a week later by winning 4-0 at Millfields Road to complete the double. Bert Bliss netted a hat-trick in the latter game.

Spurs ended a sequence of 22 away League games without a win when they defeated Orient 3-2 on 16 March 1929 at the old Homerton Ground. Ted Harper made his Spurs debut in this game and celebrated by scoring one of the goals. Jimmy Dimmock netted the other two and he later joined Orient!

A crowd of almost 31,000 saw Spurs beat Orient 5-1 in a First Division game at Brisbane Road in October 1962, six different players figuring on the scoresheet.

The return fixture, played in late March 1963, was attended by over 40,000 spectators who saw Bobby Smith and Jimmy Greaves (penalty) score for Spurs in a 2-0 win.

Spurs met their London rivals four times in three weeks in Football League South matches between 21 December 1940 and 11 January 1941. They won them all - 9-0, 7-0, 3-0 and 9-1 in that order.

Players with both clubs include: Jimmy Allen, Bill Almond, Charlie Ambler (Orient amateur), Jimmy Archibald, Eddie Baily, Bert Bliss, Martin Brennan (Orient trialist), Fred Channell (trialist), John Chiedozie, Jamie Clapham, Ralph Coates, Pat Corbett, Dave Dunmore, Neale Fenn, Ken Flint, Abraham Goodman, Arthur Grimsdell (also Orient secretary & manager), Vic Groves, Warren Hackett (Spurs Youth), Alan Haig-Brown, Bill Hayward (Spurs reserve), Ian Hendon, Baden Herod, Gareth Howells (Spurs reserves), Doug Hunt (also Orient manager), Chris Jones, Bill Lane, David Levene, Bert Lyons, Sid McClellan, John McConnachie, Bob McDonald, John Margerrison (Spurs reserve), Keith Osgood, Tim O'Shea, Derek Possee, Bill Rees, Will Sage, Arthur Sanders, Max Seeburg, John Smith, Danny Steel, Mark Stimson, Peter Taylor, Andy Thompson, Jimmy Townley, Cyril Trailor, Simon Webb.

Wartime guests (with either one or both clubs): Captain Blake, Bernie Bryant, Charlie Burnett, Tom Caldwell, Albert Chester, Charlie Crossley, John Davie, Jimmy Dimmock, Harry Ferrier, Doug Flack, George Foreman, James Fullwood, Charlie Hannaford,

Tom Howshall, Harry Lloyd, George Ludford, Les Medley, David Nelson, John Oakes (also Orient trialist), Jack Pattison, Ernie Phypers, Bert Ringrose, Wilf Saunders, Billy Sperrin, Jimmy Sperrin & Bill Watkins.

Also associated: Willie Hall, Charlie Hewitt & Jimmy Seed (Spurs players, Orient managers), John Gorman (Orient Youth team manager), Arthur Grimsdell (Orient director), Arthur Rowe (Spurs player & manager, Orient general advisor/consultant), Willie Hall (Spurs player, Orient coach), Sid White (Spurs player, Orient coach), Roger Cross & Pat Welton (both Orient players & Spurs assistant-managers), Ben Ives (Orient player, Spurs assistant-trainer & chief scout) & Bobby Arber (Orient player, Spurs reserve team manager).

LIGHTFOOT, EDWARD JOHN

Half-back Ed Lightfoot made 83 first XI appearances for Spurs (61 in the Football League). He joined the club from Southport Central in May 1911 and played through until the end of the 1914-15 season when he went to fight for his country in the Great War. Sadly, on 20 July 1918 Lightfoot was killed while in action in France.

Born in Liverpool on 13 November 1889 he played his early football for Harrowby FC.

LINCOLN CITY

Spurs playing record against the Imps:

Competition	P	W	D	L	F	A
Football League	6	2	3	1	13	8
League Cup	2	1	0	1	4	3
Summary	8	3	3	2	17	11

The first League encounter between the two clubs was in Division Two and took place at White Hart Lane on 27 September 1919. Spurs celebrated in style, winning 6-1 in front of 35,000 fans. Bert Bliss scored twice and had a hand in three of the other four goals. Players with both clubs include: Jimmy Bauchop, Tom Brown, Joe Cullen, Jock Davidson, Chris Day, Neale Fenn, Peter Gain, Alan Hall, Jim Hartley, Jimmy McCormick (also City coach & trainer), Alan Marriott (Spurs reserves), Joe Raby, John Reddish, Tom Soulsby, Andrew Swan.

Wartime guests (with either one or both clubs): Alf Day, Bill Edrich, Len Flack, Joe Meek, Bert Page, Tom Paton, Tom Knighton.

LINDSAY, ALEXANDER FINDLAY

Equally effective as a half-back line or as a central attacker, Scotsman Alex Lindsay gave Spurs excellent service for more than twelve years, making 277 first team appearances (211 in the Football League) and scoring 67 goals (42 at League level).

He joined the club (initially) during the Great War and signed full-time in August 1919 from Raith Rovers. He made his debut against Arsenal in a London Football Combination game in September 1917 and his League baptism followed v. Coventry City in August 1919. An eager-beaver sort of player, always working tirelessly, he played for the Anglo Scots against the Home Scots in an international trial in 1923. He left White Hart Lane for Thames in August 1930 and later returned to Scotland to play for Dundee (July 1931-33). Lindsay was born in Dundee on 8 November 1896 and died in that same town in on 9 December 1971.

LINEKER, GARY WINSTON, OBE

Striker Gary Lineker was born in Leicester on 30 November 1960. He joined his hometown club in July 1977 as an apprentice, turning professional at Filbert Street in December 1978. He made his senior debut for the Foxes against Oldham Athletic in January 1979 and went on to score 103 goals in 216 senior appearances before transferring to Everton for £800,000 (plus another £250,000 from any subsequent transfer deal). After a rather innocuous start to his professional career Lineker developed into one of the finest marksmen in world football. He certainly struggled to hold down a place in the League side during his first three years as a full-time 'pro' at Leicester, but once he had bedded himself in (1981-82) he quickly made up for lost time and netted 26 goals the very next season as the Foxes gained promotion to the First Division.

A darting player, sharp and decisive, Lineker, who won his first full England cap in 1984 (he went on to gain 80 in all, scoring 48 goals, one less than Bobby Charlton's national record) immediately came under the scrutiny of bigger clubs. It was no surprise when Everton boss Howard Kendall whisked him off to Goodison Park in the summer of 1985. He continued to find the net for the both the Merseysiders and for England. He actually scored 40 times for Everton, in his only season with the club helping them finish runners-up to Liverpool in both the League championship and FA Cup.

Lineker's career and value escalated as he went off to Mexico to play in the World Cup Finals, returning a national hero after scoring a hat-trick against Poland and earning the 'Golden Boot' award by finishing top scorer with six goals. He was also voted the PFA and FWA 'Player of the Year' for 1986,

As a result, Lineker was snapped up by the Spanish giants CF Barcelona - signed by Terry Venables for £2.75 million. He helped Barca' win the League title in 1987-88 and the European Cup-winners Cup Final the following season.... having played on the wing for new coach Johan Cruyff in the latter campaign, following some below par performances in the European Championships when he struggled to get over a bout of hepatitis. In June 1989, Venables, who by now had taken charge of Spurs, brought Lineker back to England for £1.2 million. He regained full fitness and also his appetite for scoring goals! He bagged 80 in 138 competitive matches, collected an FA Cup winners' medal in 1991 (despite missing a penalty in the Final v. Nottingham Forest) before moving to the Japanese club, Grampus 8 of Nagoya for £946,,000 six months after that Wembley triumph.

During his two-and-a-half seasons at White Hart Lane Lineker, was a regular scorer and twice finsihed up on as the club's leading marksman in the Football League. He formed an excellent partnership in attack with first Paul Stewart and then Paul Walsh with midfielder Paul Gascoigne supplying the ammunition for the strikers to shoot!

Awarded the OBE by the Queen in the 1992 New Year's Honours List, Lineker retired in 1994 and is now one of the highest paid sports presenters on TV!

NB - Lineker has scored a century for Leicestershire CCC and is a member of the MCC.

LIVERMORE, DOUGLAS ERNEST

Doug Livermore has held the position of assistant-manager, first team coach, reserve team manager and chief scout at Spurs. He was in charge of the first team for two spells: October/November 1987 and May 1992 to June 1993 (see under managers). In 2001 he was back at Carrow Road as assistant manager/coach.

As a midfield player with Liverpool, Norwich City, AFC

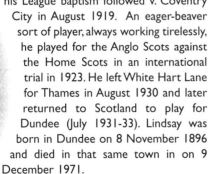

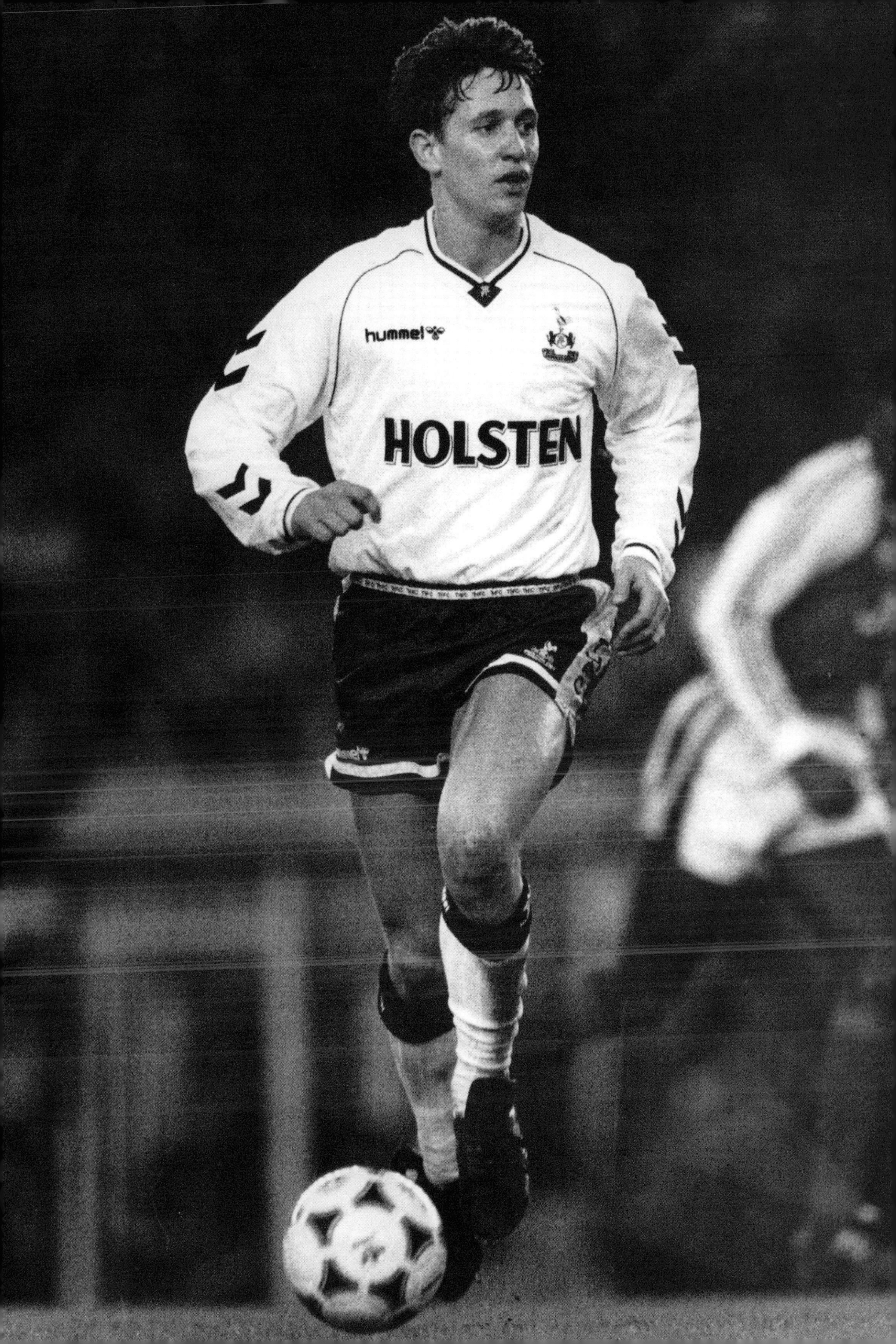

hummel
HOLSTEN

Bournemouth, Cardiff City and Chester City between 1965 and 1979, he scored 15 goals in 299 League games.

Livermore was born in Prescot, Lancashire on 27 December 1947

LIVERPOOL

Spurs playing record against Reds:

Competition	P	W	D	L	F	A
Premiership	18	5	5	8	23	35
Football League	98	28	24	46	111	153
FA Cup	7	2	2	3	4	7
League Cup	5	3	1	1	9	6
UEFA Cup	2	1	0	1	2	2
Charity Shield	1	0	0	1	0	1
SS Super Cup	1	0	0	1	0	2
Summary	132	39	32	61	149	206

The first League game between the two clubs was played on 13 November 1909 (Division 1) and before a White Hart Lane crowd of 22,000 Spurs scraped a 1-0 victory, Bert Middlemiss the scorer - and in doing so became the first Spurs player to score against each of the Merseyside clubs.

When Spurs won at Anfield in 1912 they would not have believed that it would be another 73 years before the feat was repeated - thanks to a Garth Crooks goal in 1985.

Spurs crashed 7-2 at Liverpool on 31 October 1914 - their first seven-goal mauling in a League game.

Spurs' 33-match unbeaten home League record came to an end when they lost 3-0 to Liverpool on 23 September 1933.

In their last home game of the 1934-35 season Willie Evans scored a hat-trick as Spurs beat Liverpool 5-1 at White Hart Lane.

Liverpool had a hat-trick hero in Scottish international utility forward Billy Liddell when they won 3-2 on Spurs' territory in December 1951.

In Sept. 1952 when Spurs entertained Liverpool, they fielded two amateur wingers - Vic Groves (7) and George Robb (11). Groves was making his debut and he scored twice in a 3-1 win.

A total of 16 goals were scored in the two First Division matches between the clubs which took place in April 1963. Liverpool won 5-2 at Anfield while Spurs raced to an emphatic 7-2 victory at White Hart Lane, Jimmy Greaves scoring four times, once from the spot.

In 1970-71 Liverpool knocked Spurs out of the FA Cup at the quarter-final stage.

Spurs lost to Liverpool on the away goal rule in the semi-final of the 1972-73 UEFA Cup competition.

The first leg at Anfield on 10 April drew a crowd of 42,174 and a goal by Alex Lindsay gave the Merseysiders a slight advantage. Spurs came back well and won the return game 2-1 fifteen days later but it wasn't quite enough. There were close on 47,000 spectators at White Hart Lane to see Martin Peters net twice - to no avail - as Steve Heighway bagged a crucial one for the Merseysiders!

Liverpool completed a League double over Spurs in 1975-76, winning 3-2 at Anfield and 4-0 at White Hart Lane.

Spurs heaviest League defeat (in terms of goal-difference) is 7-0 - suffered at Anfield on 2 September 1978. This was the first time the team had conceded a '7' since April 1964 (at Burnley) although they did lose 8-2 at Derby in October 1976.

In season 1985-86 Liverpool beat Spurs 2-0 at White Hart Lane and Anfield in two Group 'A' Screen Sport Super Cup encounters.

Spurs and Liverpool fought out a tremendous 3-3 Premiership draw at White Hart Lane in December 1993.

After leading 2-0 at Anfield in a Premiership game in May 1999, Spurs, who had defender Maricio Taricco sent-off, collapsed after the break and eventually lost 3-2, Paul Ince and Steve McManaman scoring late on for the Merseysiders.

Earlier in the season Spurs had won 3-1 at Anfield in a Worthington League Cup-tie - but only 20,772 saw the action.

Players with both clubs include: Nick Barmby, Harry Bradshaw, Joe Brough, Ray Clemence, Charlie Hewitt, Oyvind Leonhardsen, Jamie Redknapp (Spurs junior), Ronny Rosenthal, Neil Ruddock, John Scales, Tom Soulsby, Graeme Souness (also 'Pool manager), John Stephenson, Paul Stewart, Paul Walsh.

Wartime guests (with either one or both clubs): Ronnie Dix, Stan Eastham, Fred Hopkin, George Hunt, John McCormick, Joe Meek (also 'Pool trialist), Frank O'Donnell, Tommy Pearson, Bob Pryde.

Also associated: Keith Burkinshaw (Spurs manager, Liverpool player), Doug Livermore ('Pool player, Spurs first team coach, assistant-manager/coach, reserve team manager, chief scout).

LOKOMOTIV LEIPZIG

Spurs playing record against Leipzig:

Competition	P	W	D	L	F	A
UEFA Cup	2	2	0	0	4	1

Spurs met and beat the East German side Lokomotiv Leipzig 4-1 on aggregate in the semi-final of the UEFA Cup in 1973-74.

A crowd of 74,000 saw the first leg in Leipzig which resulted in a 2-1 win for Spurs, Martin Peters and Ralph Coates the scorers.

There were 41,280 present at White Hart Lane to see Spurs tie things up with a 2-0 second leg victory when Chris McGrath and Martin Chivers found the German net.

LONDON ASSOCIATION CUP

Spurs first entered this competition in season 1885-86, going out to the Casuals in the second round, beaten 8-0, after having conquered St Albans 5-2 in their opening game.

Spurs played in this competition the following season, losing 6-0 away to Upton Park.

Summary of results:

P	W	D	L	F	A
3	1	0	2	5	16

LONDON CALEDONIANS

Spurs' three meetings with the Caledonians resulted in two victories and one defeat. Both their wins were achieved in the London FA Charity Cup - in October 1921 (5-0 at White Hart Lane) and in October 1928 (2-1, also at home). Their sole defeat was suffered in the semi-final of the East End Cup in April 1887, beaten 1-0 at Tottenham.

Summary of results:

P	W	D	L	F	A
3	2	0	1	7	2

LONDON CHARITY CUP

Spurs' record in the LCC:

P	W	D	L	F	A
58	32	7	19	152	90

Spurs first entered this local competition in season 1893-94 and they continued to participate until 1930-31.

They lost their first match 4-2 to the Crusaders (home) in December 1893 but gained revenge a year later with a 4-2 victory, also at home, before losing to Old Carthusians 3-0 away.

Their second win was 2-1 at home over London Westminsters in November 1895 (possibly the only game played in the LCC that season). Thereafter their overall form in the tournament was good and they were unbeaten in 39 of their completed 58 matches.

They reached the Final on five occasions - winning in 1911 and 1929 and losing in 1910, 1914 and 1931.

In the 1911 Final, Spurs beat Fulham 2-1 at Stamford Bridge in front of 10,000 fans, Billy Minter and Bert Middlemiss the scorers. In the preceding rounds, Clapton Orient, Chelsea and Millwall had all been accounted for, the latter after a replay.

The 1929 Final success was against Millwall, Spurs winning handsomely by 5-1 at Highbury in front of 5,000 spectators, Ted Harper netting a hat-trick. In the earlier rounds Spurs had ousted London Caledonians, QPR and Charlton Athletic.

Fulham beat Spurs 4-1 in the 1914 Final at Stamford Bridge where the attendance topped 17,000; Crystal Palace won the 1914 Final 2-1 at Highbury in front of 14,000 spectators while Arsenal were 2-1 victors in 1931, again at Stamford Bridge, where the turnout was 10,160.

Spurs biggest win in the Charity Cup competition was 11-2 versus Metrogas (home) in September 1913. A crowd of 2,500 attended that game when Jimmy Bauchop netted four goals and Jimmy Cantrell three.

Spurs' second biggest London Charity Cup win was 9-0 against Nunhead (away) in a 1st round tie in September 1909.

LONDON SENIOR CUP

Spurs record in the LSC:

P	W	D	L	F	A
21	9	4	8	50	52

Spurs first entered this competition in season 1887-88, losing their initial game 6-0 at Hendon. The following season they crashed 2-8 at home to Old Etonians, before hammering Iona FC 10-0 at home in 1889-90 (Jack Jull scoring five goals). This was the club's best win in the competition.

The following season, after dismissing QPR 2-1 (after a 1-1 draw), Barking 2-0 (home) and Barnes 1-0 (away) Spurs crashed out to Millwall Athletic, losing 5-1 down the East Ferry Road.

In 1891-92, a 4-3 win over Caledonian Athletic and a 3-2 victory at Hampstead took Spurs through two rounds before they went down 4-1 to the Ramblers. The following season they accounted for the Coldstream Guards (3-2), Polytechnic (3-0, after a 2-2 draw) but were then dismissed 1-0 by the Casuals.

In 1893-94, Spurs went out early on, beaten 6-1 in a home replay by Old St Mark's (after a 0-0 draw) and in 1894-95 they eased past London Welsh 5-0 and then forced a 3-3 draw away to Old Westminsters only to lose the replay 5-4.

LONDON WELSH

Spurs' playing record against the 'Welsh'

Competition	P	W	D	L	F	A
Amateur Cup	3	1	2	0	8	6
LSC	1	1	0	0	5	0
Summary	4	2	2	0	13	6

Spurs met London Welsh four times in quick succession, three times in the FA Amateur Cup and once in the London Senior Cup, all in the 1894-95 season.

In the former competition, the teams met in the Division Final and after two draws (1-1 and 3-3) Spurs went through to the first round proper by winning the second replay 4-2 at The Spotted Dig ground.

The LSC clash was in the first round in January 1895 and this time Spurs won 5-0, Ernie Payne scoring a hat-trick.

LONG SERVICE

Here is a list of players/managers/coaches/secretaries etc, who have given Spurs excellent service for 20 years or more years:

Years	Name	Dates (nearest year)
63	Bill Nicholson	1936-74/76 to date
60	Morton Cadman++	1888-1948
55	Johnny Wallis*	1936-45/48-94
52	Fred Bearman	1909-61
50	Jimmy Anderson	1908-58
50	Cecil Poynton	1922-34/1946-75
48	Ron Henry	1953-2001
45	C. David Roberts	1898-1943
43	Tom Morris	1899-1942
43	Arthur Turner**	1906-49
41	Jabez Darnell	1905-46
38	George Cox	1902-08/1917-49
38	Jack Jull	1882-1920
32	Billy Minter	1908-40
30	Billy Harston	1883-1940 (periodically)
29	Sid Wale	1957-86
28	Andy Thompson	1920-31/1934-37/46-60
25	Tom Deacock	1899-1924
25	Chris Hughton	1972-73/77-92/93 to date
25	G. Wagstaffe Simmons	1924-49
24	Jack Coxford***	1935/46-69
20	Ted Ditchburn	1939-59
20	George Hardy+	1926-46

++ Morton Cadman was a reserve team player with Spurs from 1888 until 1891; then a member of staff and later served as a director.

* Johnny Wallis, MBE, first joined the club as an amateur in 1936 at the age of 14. He was taken on the groundstaff in 1938 and played for Spurs' juniors at the start of the 1939-40 season. A useful full-back, he made seven appearances for the first team during the hostilities before suffering shrapnel wounds while serving abroad in Palestine. Unfortunately he was forced to give up playing competitive football in 1945 at the age of 23. After assisting Chelmsford City and Wisbech Town, he subsequently gained medical qualifications and rejoined the club in 1948, this time on the coaching staff as well as 'A' team manager, a position he retained until 1958 when he became assistant-trainer. After that he was the club's reserve team manager for four years, 1964-68 and was then given the responsible position of senior trainer/physiotherapist at White Hart Lane. In 1975 he took over as the club's kit manager, acting as assistant kit boss from 1987-92. Finally, he worked on the groundstaff as the proverbial odd job man until his retirement in May 1994. A Spurs man for 55 years, Wallis was awarded the MBE in 1993.

** Arthur Turner was the secretary at White Hart Lane from 1906 to 1949.

*** Jack Coxford was player/coach with Spurs' nursery side Northfleet. He then worked on the groundstaff at White Hart Lane, latterly as Youth team manager.

+ George Hardy was appointed by Spurs purely as a trainer.
NB - Re Messrs Anderson, Darnell, Ditchburn, Henry, Jull, Minter, Morris, Nicholson, Poynton and Thompson see under individual write-ups.... For Messrs Bearman, Cadman, Cox, Deacock, Roberts, Simmons and Wale see under chairmen and/or directors.

The current longest serving full time member of staff is kit man Roy Reyland who celebrated 25 years with the club in April 2001.

LONGEST SEASONS
Spurs started both the 1940-41 and 1946-47 seasons (in earnest) on 31 August and finished them on 7 June - nine months and seven days later!
The 1962-63 season lasted from 18 August until 20 May - nine months. And the 1985-86 campaign commenced on 17 August and finished on 5 May.

LOUGHBOROUGH
Spurs playing record against 'Boro:

Competition	P	W	D	L	F	A
United League	4	2	0	2	10	6

Spurs completed the seasonal double over 'Boro in 1897-98 having been beaten twice by the Leicestershire side the previous season.
Spurs' best win was 5-0 at home on 24 March 1898 when Scotsman David Black and Billy Joyce both scored twice.
Player with both clubs: Billy Jones.

LOWDELL, ARTHUR EDWARD
Half-back 'Darkie' Lowdell was only 5ft 6ins tall and weighed less than 11 stones but made just one short of 100 first team appearances for Spurs between August 1927 and May 1931.
Born at Edmonton, North London on 7 November 1897, he joined the club from Sheffield Wednesday, having previously represented London Schools as well as playing for the Welsh side Ton Pentre and serving throughout the Great War in the forces. He was released by Spurs at the end of the 1930-31 season, following a spate of injury problems. Lowdell died at Canvey Island, Essex on 29 July 1970.

LOWE, HARRY
Half-back Harry Lowe was born in Northwich, Cheshire on 10 August 1886 and had a very difficult early life - he was adopted when quite young. He played for Northwich Victoria before moving south to sign for Brighton & Hove Albion in September 1913. From Hove he switched to Spurs in April 1914 and remained at White Hart Lane until May 1927 when he moved across London to Fulham. He made 86 first team appearances for Spurs.
He left Craven Cottage in May 1928 and later became coach at Deportivo Espnaol in Barcelona (till June 1935 - he left San Sebastian just prior to the outbreak of the Spanish Civil War). He came back to England and in 1937 signed for Islington Corinthians before returning to White Hart Lane as Spurs coach in 1938, later taking over as team manager of Bournemouth (1947-50). Lowe died in Camden Town, North London on 15 July 1966.

LUDFORD, GEORGE ALBERT
George Ludford drew up a fine set of statistics for Spurs - 91 goals scored in 275 first team appearances. If the Second World War hadn't disrupted his progress, then one feels it would have been much better!
Born in Barnet, Hertfordshire on 22 March 1915, he was a half-back or inside/centre-forward who played initially for his School

team before joining Spurs' groundstaff in May 1931. He then served with Tottenham Juniors for two seasons (to 1933) and after a spell with Northfleet was taken on the professional staff at White Hart Lane in May 1936. He made his League debut at the start of the 1936-37 season (v. West Ham) and was a regular in the side until 1939. During the hostilities he guested for Chelsea, Clapton Orient, Fulham, Millwall (he played for the Lions in the 1945 League South Cup Final), QPR, Reading, Southend United, Watford and West Ham, and remained at the playing staff at Spurs until August 1954 when he was given a coaching job. He managed Enfield for two years after that (1955-57) and thereafter acted as the club's stadium manager. Ludford died in Enfield, Middlesex on 2 January 2001.

LUNN, THOMAS HENRY
Goalkeeper Tommy Lunn was signed by Wolverhampton Wanderers from Brownhills Albion in August 1904, having moved down to the area after being educated in County Durham. A real tough nut, as brave as a lion and totally reliable, he always wore a floppy peaked cap, but this never detracted from his performances between the posts. Born in Bishop Auckland on 9 July 1883, he helped Wolves win the FA Cup in 1908 and went on to play for the club in more than 140 games, up to April 1910, when he was transferred to Spurs - having kept goal for Wolves in the first-ever League game at White Hart Lane!
He went on to make 103 first team appearances over the next three years before joining Stockport County in June 1913. Unfortunately after playing only twice for the Edgeley Park club he suffered a serious leg injury forcing him into an early retirement which saw him return to London. He died in the capital, in an Edmonton hospital on 29 March 1960.

LUTON CHARITY CUP
Spurs record in the LCC:

P	W	D	L	F	A
3	1	1	1	10	9

Spurs entered this competition in season 1891-92. They drew 3-3 at home with the Coldstream Guards in the opening round before winning the replay, also at home, by 7-2 in a replay (five goals coming from Frank Cottrell). However, in the next round Spurs succumbed 4-0 away to the 1st Battalion, the Scots Guards in Round 2.

LUTON TOWN
Spurs playing record against the Hatters:

Competition	P	W	D	L	F	A
Football League	46	21	17	8	75	46
FA Cup	9	2	3	4	11	18
League Cup	1	1	0	0	1	0
Other Leagues	24	9	5	10	34	37
Wartime	16	9	2	5	54	34
Summary	96	42	27	27	183	135

Spurs suffered their first FA Cup defeat at the hands of Luton, beaten 4-0 at the Hatters' Excelsior Dallow Lane ground in a 4th qualifying round encounter on 19 December 1894.
Before the turn of the century, Spurs played the Hatters in the same competition in seasons 1896-97 (lost 3-0), 1897-98 (lost 4-3) and 1898-99 (won 2-0 after two 1-1 draws).
The first League encounter between the two clubs took place at Kenilworth Road on 8 October 1938. It ended in a goalless draw. Later in the season the Hatters won 1-0 at White Hart Lane.
Spurs' first win over Luton was achieved on 22 March 1947 when they triumphed 2-1 at home, Freddie Cox and Ronnie Dix the scorers in front of 36,160 fans.

Two goals by Glenn Hoddle helped Spurs beat the Hatters 4-1 at Kenilworth Road in February 1978 as the team lined up for their charge towards promotion from Division Two.

Having won 2-0 at home earlier in the season this victory brought Spurs their first Second Division double for 28 years, since they won twice against Preston in the 1949-50 season.

Two late goals (by Paul Walsh and Paul Gascoigne) earned Spurs a 3-1 League win at Luton in March 1989.

Spurs finished their home First Division League game against Luton on 22 December 1990 with only nine men, the Hatters with ten. Nayim and Pat Van den Hauwe were both sent-off along with Ceri Hughes. Spurs still won the contest 2-1.

Spurs scored four goals in the last 22 minutes of their home League game against Luton in November 1991. They won 4-1.

Players with both clubs include: Milija Aleksic, Rory Allen, Charlie Ambler, Jimmy Armstrong, Jimmy Banks, Ken Barton, Sam Bell, George Bowler, Alex 'Sandy' Brown, Charlie Brown, Davie Colquhoun, Richard Cooke, Harry Crump, Kerry Dixon (Spurs reserve), Gary Doherty, Bert Elkin, Pat Gallacher, Randolph Galloway, Phil Gray, Ron Henry (Town Amateur), Ian Hillier (Spurs reserve), Scott Houghton, Bill Julian (Hatters player-coach), Bill Kane, Bill McCurdy, John Pearson, Paul Price, Tommy Roe, Ronny Rosenthal (on loan from Standard Liege), Harry Stansfield, Mitchell Thomas, Bob Walker, Paul Walsh, Alf Warner & Claude Watson.

Wartime guests (with either one or both clubs): Tom Bassett, Ken Bennett, Bobby Browne, Charlie Burke, John Dowen, Reg Edwards, Billy Grimes, George Hunt, Jimmy Jinks, Tom Kiernan, Ernie Marshall, Reg Mogford, Sid Ottewell, Wilf Saunders, Reg Smith, Jimmy Sperrin, Albert Tomkin, Ed Tunney, Solomon Upton, Jack Whent.

Also associated: David Pleat (manager of both clubs, also Spurs Director of Football, also Luton coach and chief scout), Joe Kinnear (Spurs player, Hatters manager), Trevor Hartley (Luton reserve team coach, Spurs assistant-manager & caretaker-manager), Ricky Hill (Spurs Academy coach, Luton player & manager).

LYMAN, COLIN CHADD

Left-winger Colin Lyman was rejected by West Bromwich Albion and failed to make an impression with Southend United before signing amateur forms for Northampton Town in March 1934, turning professional eight months later. He did well with the Cobblers and in June 1937 was transferred to Spurs with whom he remained until May 1946. He guested for Aldershot, Chesterfield, Coventry City, Derby County, Leicester City, Northampton, Nottingham Forest, Notts County and Port Vale during the War when he also turned out in representative matches for the RAF and the FA. He scored 20 goals in 87 first team appearances during his time at White Hart Lane, which ended in May 1946 when he joined Port Vale. He later assisted Nottingham Forest and Notts County prior to taking over as player-manager of non-League Long Eaton Town in July 1948, a position he held for two years. Born in Northampton on 9 March 1914, Lyman died in Cambridge on 9 May 1986.

LYN (OSLO)

Spurs playing record against the Norwegian side:

Competition	P	W	D	L	F	A
UEFA Cup	2	2	0	0	12	3

As holders of the UEFA Cup, Spurs met the Norwegian side Lyn of Oslo in the first round of the 1972-73 competition - and duly dismissed them 12-3 on aggregate.

The first leg in Norway on 13 September was attended by 10,770 fans and ended in a 6-3 win for Spurs, John Pratt, Alan Gilzean (2), Martin Chivers (2) and Martin Peters the scorers.

The return leg, a fortnight later, was seen by 21,109 spectators and this time Spurs cantered home 6-0, Chivers (3), Jimmy Pearce and Ralph Coates (2) finding the net.

LYONS, ALBERT THOMAS

Tough-tackling full-back Bert Lyons, brother of the more famous Tommy Smart of Aston Villa fame, was born in Hednesford, Staffs on 5 March 1902. He played for Port Vale (as a junior) and Walsall (albeit briefly - making just one appearance) before joining Clapton Orient as an amateur in June 1926, transferring to Spurs in May 1930 and rounding off his career with Colwyn Bay from August 1932 to May 1934. He made 63 first team appearances for Spurs (four goals scored) and was replaced in the side by Bill Felton. Lyons died in Great Yarmouth on 10 May 1981.

M

McALLISTER, DONALD

The blond hair of defender Don McAllister stood out in 260 first team games for Spurs (13 goals scored). He made his debut in February 1975 against the team that had rejected him three years earlier - Coventry City.

Born in Radcliffe, Lancashire on 26 May 1953, he played for Prestwich, Radcliffe and Whitefield Schools and had trials with Coventry City before joining Bolton Wanderers as an apprentice in June 1968, turning professional at Burnden Park two years later. In February 1975 - having helped Bolton win the Third Division title in 1973 - he moved to White Hart Lane for £80,000. He remained a registered player with Spurs until August 1981, although he did play in the NASL with Washington Diplomats in the summer of 1977, returning to help the team gain promotion to the top flight. He went back to the States for a second spell in June/July 1984 to assist Tampa Bay Rowdies and after another brief association with Charlton, he rounded off his League career as a non-contract player with Rochdale.

McCLELLAN, SYDNEY BENJAMIN

Syd McClellan was signed as a professional at White Hart Lane from Chelmsford City in August 1949. Over the next seven years he did very well, netting 62 goals in 97 first-team appearances for the club before transferring to Portsmouth for £8,500 in November 1956, later assisting Leyton Orient (from July 1958) and Romford (July 1959-62). Born in Dagenham, Essex on 11 June 1925, McClellan was a terrific finisher who capitalised on the half-chance. In May 1952 on a tour of Canada he scored nine times against Saskatchewan, a club record. He died in Essex on 15 December 2000.

McCORMICK, JAMES

A Yorkshireman, born in Rotherham on 26 April 1912, outside-left Jimmy McCormick played for Rotherham YMCA and Rotherham United before joining Chesterfield in August 1932. From the Spire-ites he moved to Spurs in March 1933 and remained at White Hart lane until November 1945 when he switched to Fulham. During the War he guested for Birmingham, Chelmsford, Chester, Crewe Alexandra, Derby County, Fulham, Leicester City, Lincoln City, Liverpool, Rochdale, Southend United, Tranmere

Rovers, Walsall and West Bromwich Albion. An orthodox winger, fast and clever, McCormick scored 30 goals in 170 first team appearances for Spurs, 26 coming in 137 League games.

After two years at Craven Cottage, he switched to Lincoln City (August 1947) and after a few months with Crystal Palace McCormick went over to Malta to coach Sliema Wanderers (May 1949-May 1950). He then took a similar position with the Turkish national team and returned to England as coach to Wycombe Wanderers, later assisting Sheffield United and Walton & Hersham in the same capacity prior to becoming manager of the latter club. He last appointment in football was that of York City manager, a job he held from May 1953 to September 1954.

McCormick died in Marbella, Spain on 3 January 1968.

McCURDY, WILLIAM

Full-back Jock McCurdy played for the Vale of Clyde, Luton Town, Nottingham Forest and New Brompton before making 21 appearances for Spurs (in 1904-05). He returned to New Brompton and then had a second spell with the Hatters.

McDONALD, ROBERT JAMES

Full-back Rob McDonald made exactly 150 first team appearances for Spurs (109 in the Football League) over a period of eight years. He joined the club in August 1919 from Inverness Caledonians and left for Heart of Midlothian (initially on trial) in September 1927, but soon switched to Clapton Orient.

Born in Inverness on 25 February 1895, he could play in both full-back positions and always gave 110 per-cent effort. He suffered with niggling injuries during his last season at White Hart Lane. McDonald died in April 1971.

McELHANEY, RICHARD

An outside-left, born in Glasgow, Dick McElhaney played for Clyde and Celtic before making 32 appearances for Spurs (8 goals) in 1896-97. Unfortunately, after he had been suspended with colleagues Devlin, Milliken and Wilson for an 'act of insubordination' McElhaney was released by Spurs and signed Swindon Town, later assisting Brentford.

MACFARLANE, DOUGLAS

A hard-shooting centre-forward from Barrow (born on 24 August 1880) Doug Macfarlane played for his home town club and Burnley before scoring twice in 21 League games for Spurs between 1908-1910. He returned to his first love, Barrow.

McGRATH, ROLAND CHRISTOPHER

Versatile forward Chris McGrath scored ten goals in 62 first team appearances for Spurs over a period of three years. He joined the club initially as an apprentice in July 1970, turned professional in January 1972 making his senior debut against Arsenal in October 1973. He left White Hart Lane for Manchester United for £35,000 in October 1976 after a loan spell with Millwall. He played for Spurs in both legs of the 1974 UEFA Cup Final v. Feyenoord.

Born in Belfast on 29 November 1954, McGrath, strong and willing with a good technique, represented both Belfast and Northern Ireland Schoolboys before moving to London. He went on to win a total of 21 full caps for his country. After Old Trafford, McGrath played in the States with Tulsa Roughnecks (1981 and 1982) and he also assisted South China in Hong Kong. He quit football in 1986, returned to Britain and worked for a time in an armaments factory in Enfield.

McNAB, NEIL

Born in Greenock on 4 June 1957, midfielder Neil McNab was signed by Spurs as a 16 year-old for £40,000 from the Scottish club Morton in February 1974. He developed quickly and made his Football League debut two months after arriving at White Hart Lane against Chelsea (the club's youngest-ever player at the time), becoming a full-time professional eight weeks later. He gained Scottish Youth and Under-21 recognition, having already represented his country as a Schoolboy, and appeared in 114 first team games for the club (80 at competitive level) scoring six goals. Unable to hold down a place in the side with Messrs Ardiles, Hoddle and Villa firmly bedded in the midfield - and with Spurs well on their way to promotion from Division Two - McNab was transferred to Bolton Wanderers for a club record fee of £250,000 in February 1978. He switched to Brighton & Hove Albion two years later and served on loan with both Leeds United and Portsmouth before signing for Manchester City in July 1983. Later McNab assisted Tranmere Rovers (from December 1989), Huddersfield Town (on loan in 1991), Darlington (non-contract) and Ayr United. He retired from top-class football in 1995, having accumulated well over 600 League and Cup appearances. In 2001 McNab was Portsmouth's reserve team coach.

McNAUGHT, JAMES RANKIN

Scotsman James McNaught - the 'Little Wonder' - was very effective either as a half-back or inside-forward. He served Spurs from May 1898 until April 1907, amassing a total of 253 first team appearances and scoring nine goals.

Born in Dumbarton on 8 June 1897, and a boilermaker by trade, he played for Dumbarton, Linfield and Newton Heath (on a £4-a-week seasonal contract) before moving to Spurs. After playing for a Scotland XI versus an England XI and for the Anglo Scots against the Home Scots in an international trial, he gained a Southern League championship medal in 1899-1900 and whilst at the club he was a keen member of the Professional Players' Union. On leaving Spurs, McNaught signed for Maidstone, retiring in the summer of 1909. He spent the last years of his life living in London and died in West Ham in March 1919.

McTAVISH, JOHN KAY

Outside-right John McTavish appeared in 40 League and FA Cup games for Spurs whom he served between December 1910 and April 1912. Born in Govan, Glasgow on 7 June 1885, he played his early football with Falkirk before joining Oldham Athletic from where he switched to White Hart Lane. A very fine and hard-running winger, McTavish asked for a transfer early in 1912 and eventually moved north to Newcastle United for £650. He later assisted Partick Thistle, York City, Goole Town, Falkirk, (during the Great War), East Fife, East Stirling and finally Dumbarton, announcing his retirement in 1924.

McWILLIAM, PETER

Peter McWilliam excelled as both a player and manager. Able to occupy both the inside-left and left-half positions, he was an outstanding 'link man' with a superb 'body wriggle' and was dubbed as the greatest half-back of pre-First World War soccer.

Born in Inveravon, Banffshire, Scotland on 22 September 1878, he started his career with Heatherley FC (a junior side in Inverness). Known affectionaltely as 'Peter the Great' he then played for Albion Rovers (albeit briefly) and Inverness Thistle before spending nine years with Newcastle United (1902-11). 'Stolen from under the noses of Sunderland' he had an insatiable appetite

for attack and scored 12 goals in 240 appearances for the Geordies, starring in three League championship-winning sides and lined up in four FA Cup Finals, collecting a winners medal in 1910. He was capped eight times by his country, making his debut in 1905 versus England. He retired through injury (sustained during his last international) and on Boxing Day 1912 was appointed manager of Spurs, a position he held until February 1927 when he took charge of Middlesbrough.

McWilliam, highly respected, led Spurs to the Second Division championhsip in 1920 and to victory in the 1921 FA Cup Final. 'Boro were well on their way to the Division Two title when he left for Teeside - after being offered bigger wages than he was earning at White Hart Lane! He was on £850-a-year with Spurs; 'Boro offered him £1,500...so he left. He remained at Ayresome Park for seven years and then took up a scouting position with Arsenal (March 1934) before returning to manage Spurs for a second time in May 1938, staying in office until his retirement in June 1942.

During that second term of office he was awarded the Football League's long-service medal (June 1939).

McWilliam died at his home in Coronation Road, Redcar on 1 October 1951.

MABBUTT, GARY VINCENT, MBE

Gary Mabbutt made well over 600 first-team appearances for Spurs, including 477 in the Football League (138 of them in the Premiership), 47 in the FA Cup, 62 in the League Cup and 25 in Europe.

He was born in Bristol on 23 August 1961 and represented Bristol and Avon Schools before joining Bristol Rovers as an apprentice in June 1977, turning professional in Janaury 1979. Capped by England at Youth team level, he made rapid progress after that and established himself in the Rovers side during the 1979-80 season. His performances were keenly monitored by Spurs and after winning three Under-21 caps he subsequently moved to White Hart Lane in August 1982 for a fee of £105,000. He quickly made his Spurs debut in a friendly in Switzerland. He then played in the FA Charity Shield match against Liverpool at Wembley and made his League debut for the club at home to Luton Town that very same month, scoring in a 2-2 draw - the first of 38 senior goals.

Adding another three Under-21 caps to his collection, Mabbutt went on to win 16 full international caps for his country and he also played in nine 'B' team games while also giving dedicated service to Spurs. He helped the team win the 1984 UEFA Cup Final, but had the misfortune to concede the winning 'own goal' in the 1987 FA Cup Final v. Coventry City having earlier netted his side's second goal. He took over the team captaincy from the departed Richard Gough and made up for that

Wembley disappointment when he gleefully lifted the Cup in 1991 after Spurs had beaten Nottingham Forest 2-1.

An inspirational footballer, Mabbutt powered on game after game, week after week, setting an example for all to follow. He was a true competitior and grand servant to Spurs and was awarded the MBE in 1994 for services to football. Three years after a well-deserved testimonial match (v. Newcastle United) Mabbutt announced his retirement from top-class soccer in the summer of 1998. Mabbutt, who was received the prestgious PFA Merit Award in 2000, now works for BBC TV and also assists on Premier League committees including the video panel.

MACKAY, DAVID CRAIG

As a footballer Scotsman Dave Mackay was one of the greatest of his era. He won just about every honour in the game during his long and distinguished playing career that spanned 20 years. A barrel-chested, hard-tackling wing-half, he started out on the road to glory as a part-time professional with Heart of Midlothian in April 1952, having learnt the game with Slateford Athletic and Newtongrange Star.

Born in Musselburgh on 14 November 1934, he was the driving force behind the attack. He had a tough, no-nonsense approach to a game and was totally committed, never shirking a tackle, going in where it hurt and often coming out on top.

During his seven years at Tynecastle, Mackay won the first of his 22 full international caps and represented the Scottish League XI. He also gained a League championship medal (1958), two Scottish League Cup winners' medals (1955 and 1959) and a Scottish Cup winners' medal (1956). He joined Spurs for just £30,000 in March 1959 and at White Hart Lane he slotted into a 'footballing machine' run by Bill Nicholson. With Danny Blanchflower occupying the right-half berth and John White aiding and abetting from the inside-right position, the Spurs midfield was the best in the country. This was clearly emphasised when the double was won in 1960-61, the FA Cup retained the following season and victory achieved in the European Cup-winners Cup Final in 1963, although Mackay missed the latter with a stomach injury.

He won a third FA Cup winners' medal with Spurs in 1967 and

when he left the London club for Derby County for £5,000 in July 1968 he had amassed an exceptionally fine record of 364 first team appearances, scoring 63 goals.

At the end of his first season at The Baseball Ground (under Brian Clough) Mackay was voted joint PFA 'Footballer of the Year' (with Manchester City's Tony Book) as the Rams swept to promotion from the Second Division. In May 1971 he was appointed player-manager of Swindon Town; in November 1972 he took charge of Nottingham Forest and returned to his former club Derby County as their boss in October 1973, a position he held until November 1976. A spell out of the game preceded his appointment as Walsall boss in March 1977, but after a year with the Saddlers, Mackay decided to try his luck in the Far East, taking charge of Al-Arabi Sporting Club in Kuwait. Eight years later he was handed the manager's job at Alba Shabab (Dubai) but in December 1987 he returned to England to take over struggling Doncaster Rovers. He stayed at Belle Vue until March 1989 and the following month was given the Birmingham City job succeeding Garry Pendrey, officially appointed by the Kumars.

He held his position until January 1991 when ironically after being given a vote of confidence, Mackay handed in his resignation.

Blues had finished a respectable seventh in the Third Division at the end of Mackay's first full season in charge. After leaving St Andrew's Mackay's last major appointment in soccer took him to Egypt as manager-coach of FC Zamalek in September 1991.

MADDISON, GEORGE

Goalkeeper Geordie Maddison made 47 first team appearances for Spurs - his first in April 1923 against Bolton Wanderers, his last against Everton in April 1924.

Born in Birtley, County Durham on 14 October 1902, he played for Birtley Colliery FC before having a trial with Spurs, signing permanently for the club in November 1922. He had to bide his time (acting as reserve to Herbert Blake who had replaced the injured Bill Jacques) before gaining his place in the side. However, when Bill Hinton arrived from Middlesbrough, Maddison departed, joining Hull City in June 1924. He spent the next 14 years with the Tigers, amassing an exceptionally fine record of 456 appearances and gaining a Third Division (N) championship medal in 1933. A serious knee injury forced him to retire in the summer of 1938. He lived in Hull until his death on 18 May 1959.

* Maddison's son, also named George, was a professional goalkeeper with Aldershot and York City after WW2.

MAIDENHEAD

Spurs playing record against Maidenhead:

Competition	P	W	D	L	F	A
FA Cup	1	1	0	0	6	0

This emphatic FA Cup win was achieved in the second qualifying round in January 1897. A crowd of 2,000 at Northumberland Park saw Harry Crump and Willie Newbigging both score twice for rampant Spurs.

MAIDSTONE UNITED

Spurs have never played United at competitive level. Players with both clubs include: Abraham Goodman, James McNaught, Stuart Nethercott, Bob Stormont, Peter Taylor (United player and also manager).

Wartime guest: Charlie Hannaford (with Spurs).

Also associated: Robbie Stepney (United player, coach & manager, Spurs coaching staff).

MAKITA TOURNAMENT

Summary of Matches

P	W	D	L	F	A
2	1	0	1	3	6

Spurs entered this sponsoired competition in seasoin 1993-94. They played two games, both at home, against SS Lazio (won 3-2) and neighbours Chelsea (lost 4-0).

MANAGERS

List of Spurs managers down the years:

Arthur Rowe and Jimmy Anderson

Manager	Term in Office
Frank Brettell	14 March 1898 to 17 Feb 1899
John Cameron	17 Feb 1899 to 16 March 1907
Frank Walford*	16 March 1907 to 18 April 1907
Fred Kirkham	18 April 1907 to 20 July 1908
Peter McWilliam	26 Dec 1912 to 28 Feb 1927
Billy Minter	28 Feb 1927 to 20 Nov 1929
Percy Smith	1 Jan 1930 to 6 May 1935
Wally Hardinge*	6 May 1935 to 30 June 1935
Jack Tresadern	1 July 1935 to 14 May 1938
Peter McWilliam	14 May 1938 to 15 June 1942
Arthur Turner	Aug 1942 to Jan 1946
Joe Hulme	Jan 1946 to March 1949
Jimmy Anderson*	March 1949 to 4 May 1949
Arthur Rowe	4 May 1949 to 18 April 1955
Jimmy Anderson	8 April 1955 to 11 Oct 1958
Bill Nicholson	11 Oct 1958 to 13 Sept 1974
Terry Neill	13 Sept 1974 to 30 June 1976
Keith Burkinshaw	14 July 1976 to 31 May 1984
Peter Shreeves	22 June 1984 to 13 May 1986
David Pleat	16 May 1986 to 23 Oct 1987
Trevor Hartley*	23 Oct 1987 to 30 Oct 1987
Doug Livermore*	30 Oct 1987 to 22 Nov 1987
Terry Venables	23 Nov 1987 to 22 July 1991
Peter Shreeves	22 July 1991 to 15 May 1992
Doug Livermore+	27 May 1992 to 19 June 1993
Ossie Ardiles	19 June 1993 to 1 Nov 1994
Steve Perryman*	1 Nov 1994 to 15 Nov 1994
Gerry Francis	15 Nov 1994 to 19 Nov 1997
Chris Hughton*	19 Nov 1997 to 24 Nov 1997
Christian Gross**	25 Nov 1997 to 5 Sept 1998
David Pleat*	5 Sept 1998 to 4 Oct 1998
George Graham	5 Oct 1998 to 16 March 2001

David Pleat*	16 March 2001 to 2 April 2001
Glenn Hoddle	Since 2 April 2001

* Caretaker-manager
** Head coach
+ First team coach
NB - Directors ran the club (and team affairs) from 20 July, 1908 until 26 December 1912 and from 20 November, 1929 until 1 January 1930.

Spurs' Assistant-Managers

Jimmy Anderson	1946-55 (also chief scout)
Bill Nicholson	1955-58
Harry Evans	1959-62 (deceased)
Eddie Baily	1963-74
Wilf Dixon	1974-76
Pat Welton	1976-80
Peter Shreeves	1980-84
John Pratt	1984-86
Trevor Hartley	1986-87
Allan Harris	1987-89
Doug Livermore	1989-92
Ray Clemence	1992-93
Steve Perryman	1993-94
Roger Cross	1994-97
Chris Hughton	1997-99
Stewart Houston	1999-2001
John Gorman	since April 2001

Spurs Reserve Team Managers

Johnny Wallis	1964-68
Peter Shreeves	1977-80
Robbie Stepney	1980-84
John Pratt	1983-84
Doug Livermore	1984-89
Ray Clemence	1989-92
Keith Waldon	1992-93
Pat Holland	1993-94
Chris Hughton	1994-97/ 1999-2001
Bobby Arber	1997-98
Theo Foley	1998-99 & 2001
Colin Calderwood	since August 2001

* No designated manager: 1968-77

Player To Manager

Former Spurs players (at various levels, including trialist, amateurs, wartime guests) who went on to become managers with League clubs (various countries):

Steve Archibald	East Fife
Ossie Ardiles	West Bromwich Albion, Spurs, Deportivo Guadalajara (Mexico), Shimizu S-Pulse (Japan), Croatia Zagreb, Yokohama F Marinos (Japan),
Peter Baker	Durban United
Pat Beasley	Birmingham City, Bristol City
Ted Birnie	Southend United
Danny Blanchflower	Chelsea
Billy Brawn	Brentford
Ivor Broadis	Carlisle United (player-manager)
Laurie Brown	Bradford Park Avenue (player-manager)
Bobby Browne	Halifax Town

Vic Buckingham	CF Barcelona, Bradford Park Avenue, Ethnikos (Greece), Fulham, Sevilla (Spain), Sheffield Wednesday, West Bromwich Albion
Walter Bull	Northampton Town
Ron Burgess	Swansea Town (player-manager/coach), Watford
John Cameron	Ayr United, Spurs (player-manager)
Jock Chaplin	Huddersfield Town
Herbert Chapman	Arsenal, Huddersfield Town, Leeds City, Northampton Town (player-manager)
Freddie Cox	AFC Bournemouth, Gillingham, Portsmouth
Warney Cresswell	Northampton Town
Kerry Dixon	Doncaster Rovers (player-manager)
John Duncan	Chesterfield, Hartlepool United, Ipswich Town, Scunthorpe Utd
Jim Elliott	Valencia
Terry Fenwick	Portsmouth
Bobby Flavell	Albion Rovers, Ayr United, St Mirren
Fred Ford	Bristol City, Bristol Rovers, Swindon Town
Tony Galvin	Swindon Town (caretaker-manager)
Jack Gibbons	Brentford (secretary-manager)
Bert Gosnell	Norwich City
Frank Grice	Glentoran
Arthur Grimsdell	Clapton Orient
Christian Gross	FC Basel
Willie Hall	Clapton Orient
Les Henley	Bohemians, Wimbledon
Charlie Hewitt	Chester, Leyton Orient, Millwall, Wrexham
Glenn Hoddle	Chelsea, Southampton, Swindon Town, Tottenham Hotspur
Phil Holder	Brentford (caretaker-manager)
Jim Iley	Barnsley, Blackburn Rovers, Bury, Exeter City, Peterborough United
Joe Kinnear	Doncaster Rovers (caretaker-manager), Luton Town, Wimbledon, Sharjah (manager/coach), Malaysia National team manager/coach
Cyril Knowles	Darlington, Hartlepool United, Torquay United
Bill Lane	Brighton & Hove Albion
Colin Lee	Torquay United (caretaker-manager), Watford, Wolverhampton Wanderers
Harry Lowe	AFC Bournemouth
Jim McCormick	York City
Dave Mackay	Al Arab Sporting Club (Kuwait), Al Shabab (Dubai), Derby County (player & manager), Doncaster Rovers, Nottingham Forest, Swindon Town (player & manager), Walsall, Zamalek (Egypt)
Tony Marchi	Northampton Town
Billy Minter	Spurs
Alan Mullery	Brighton & Hove Albion, Charlton Athletic, Crystal Palace, Queens Park Rangers
Charlie O'Hagan	Norwich City
Frank Osborne	Fulham

Tommy Pearson	Aberdeen	Danny Greaves	Halstead Town
Steve Perryman	Brentford, Watford, IKStart (Norway) Shimizu S-Pulse (Japan).	Frank Grice	Cambridge City
		Almer Hall	Margate
Cecil Potter	Derby County, Huddersfield Town, Norwich City	Willie Hall	Chelmsford City, Chingford Town
		Charlie Hewitt	Spennymoor U, Flint, Connah's Quay
Haydn Price	Grimsby Town	Jimmy Holmes	Bedworth Town, Hitchin Town,
Alf Ramsey	Ipswich Town, Birmingham City		Nuneaton Borough (player-manager)
Arthur Rowe	Crystal Palace, Tottenham Hotspur	Percy Humphreys	West Hartlepool (player-manager)
Jack Rowley	Plymouth Argyle, Oldham Ath, Ajax, Wrexham, Bradford Park Avenue	Doug Hunt	Gloucester City, Tonbridge
		Ernie Jones	Rhyl Town
John Sainty	Chester	Chris Jones	St Peter's FC (Jersey)
Jimmy Seed	Bristol City (caretaker-manager), Charlton Athletic, Clapton Orient, Millwall	Joe Kinnear	Woodford Town
		Cyril Knowles	Hertford Town
		John Lacy	St Albans (player-manager)
George Smith	Portsmouth, Crystal Palace	Bill Lane	Gravesend & Northfleet, Guildford C
Reg Smith	Dundee United, Falkirk, Millwall, Cape Town City (S Africa)	George Ludford	Enfield
		Jim McCormick	Walton & Hersham
Graeme Souness	Blackburn Rovs, Galatasaray (Turkey), Glasgow Rangers (player-manager), Liverpool, Southampton	Wilf Mannion	Earlestown
		Tony Marchi	Cambridge City (player-manager)
		Terry Medwin	Cheshunt, Enfield
Cyril Spiers	Cardiff City, Crystal Palace, Exeter C Norwich City	Paul Miller	Wingate & Finchley Youths
		Alan Mullery	Southwick
Peter Taylor	Southend United, Leicester City, Maidstone United (player-manager)	Terry Naylor	Tonbridge Angels
		David Nelson	Ashford
Terry Venables	CF Barcelona, Crystal Palace, Middlesbrough, Queens Pk Rangers, Tottenham Hotspur, Australia (senior coach)	John Oakes	Snowdown Colliery FC
		Frank O'Donnell	Buxton Town
		Sid Ottewell	Locheed Leamington
		David Pleat	Nuneaton Borough (player-manager)
Ernie Walley	Crystal Palace (caretaker-manager)	Cecil Poynton	Margate
Ralph Ward	Crewe Alexandra	Haydn Price	Mid-Rhondda
Charlie Williams	Olympique Club (Lille)	Alf Ramsey	Eton Manor (part-time manager)
Terry Yorath	Swansea City (manager)	Charlie Rance	Guildford
		Charlie Revell	Eynesbury Rovers (player-manager), Erith & Belvedere

Non-League Bosses

Spurs personnel (trialists, amateurs, Wartime guests, managers) who also managed at non-League level:

Les Allen	Woodford Town	Graham Roberts	Chesham United, Slough Town, Hertford Town, Boreham Wood
Gerry Armstrong	Worthing (player-manager)	Arthur Rowe	Army XI(1941-44), Chelmsford City
Pat Beasley	Dover	Charlie Rundle	Bettshanger Coll. (player-manager)
Jimmy Brain	Cheltenham Town	John Ryden	Bexley United
Johnny Brooks	Knebworth Town (player-manager)	John Sainty	Armthorpe Welfare, Mossley
Laurie Brown	Altrincham, Kings Lynn (player-manager), Stockton (player-manager)	George Skinner	Hastings United
		Bert Smith	Harwich &Parkeston (mangr/coach)
Jimmy Brown	Polish Falcons	George Smith	Chelmsford C, Redhill, Eastbourne U
Bobby Browne	Thorne Colliery FC	Percy Smith	Fleetwood Town (player-manager)
Ron Burgess	Bedford Town, Hendon	Reg Smith	Addington FC (S Africa), Corby Town (player-manager), Bedford Town, Stevenage Town (Borough),
Tommy Cable	Grays Athletic, Kettering Town (player-manager), Leyton		
Jack Chisholm	Romford	Alex 'Sandy' Tait	Croydon Common, Leyton
Martin Chivers	Barnet (player-manager), Dorchester Town (player-manager)	Peter Taylor	Dartford, Hendon, Enfield, Dover Ath
		Jack Tresadern	Chelmsford City, Hastings United, Tonbridge
Harry Clarke	Llanelli (player-manager), Romford		
Peter Collins	Folkestone United (player-manager), Malden Town	Bill Whatley	Gravesend & Northfleet
		Cyril Williams	Chippenham Town, Gloucester City
Alfie Conn	Coatbridge	Charlie Willis	Haverfordwest (player-manager)
Charlie Crossley	Ebbw Vale	Charlie Withers	Edmonton
Ted Ditchburn	Romford (player-manager)	Vic Woodley	Bath City (player-manager)
Kerry Dixon	Letchworth Town	Horace Woodward	Kingsbury Town
Terry Dyson	Kingsbury Town, Wingate		
Harry Ferrier	Gloucester City	**ASSISTANT-MANAGERS**	
Doug Flack	Tooting & Mitcham	Players with Spurs at various levels who also held the position of assistant-manager with other major clubs:	
Theo Foley	Dartford		
Alan Gilzean	Stevenage Athletic	Jock Chaplin	Leeds City
		Freddie Cox	West Bromwich Albion

Tony Galvin	Newcastle United, Swindon Town
John Gorman	Southampton, Swindon Town, Spurs, West Bromwich Albion
Jimmy Holmes	Peterborough United
Doug Hunt	Leyton Orient
Joe Kinnear	Doncaster Rovers, Wimbledon
Cyril Knowles	Middlesbrough
Bill Lane	Brentford
Colin Lee	Leicester City, Wolverhampton Wds
Terry Medwin	Swansea Town
Taffy O'Callaghan	Fulham
Steve Perryman	Shimizu S-Pulse (Japan)
Arthur Rowe	Crystal Palace
Peter Taylor	Watford
Ernie Walley	Chelsea

MANAGERIAL CHIT-CHAT

● Frank Brettell was Spurs' first secretary-manager- taking office when the club was formed into a Limited Company in 1898.

● John Cameron was appointed secretary-manager of Spurs in February 1899 whilst still an active player with the club. He remained in charge until 1907.

● Peter McWilliam was the first man to have two spells as Spurs' manager.

● Arthur Rowe, in his first two seasons as Spurs manager took the club to the Second Division championship in 1949-50 and the Division One title twelve months later.

● Bill Nicholson was Spurs' manager when they won the double in 1960-61, retained the FA Cup in 1962, carried off the European Cup-winners Cup in 1963, won the FA Cup again in 1967, triumphed in the 1972 UEFA Cup Final and succeeded in two League Cup Finals, 1971 and 1973.

● Ex-Spurs player Herbert Chapman became one of the game's greatest-ever managers, leading Huddersfield Town to FA Cup glory and two League championships and Arsenal to two FA Cup Final triumphs and two First Division titles.

● Glenn Hoddle and Terry Venables were both Spurs players and later managers at White Hart Lane and they also managed England, whilst Alf Ramsey, Spurs' right-back in the 1950, led England to victory in the 1966 World Cup Final.

● George Graham and McWilliam (Scotland), Terry Neill (Northern Ireland), Joe Hulme, Hoddle, Jack Tresadern and Venables all won full international honours for their respective country as players. Neill also managed Northern Ireland while Venables also bossed/coached England and Australia.

● Peter Taylor was placed in temporary charge of England during the 2000-01 season, prior to the appointment of Sven Goran Eriksson. He remained until June 2001 on the national coaching staff.

● Ex-Spurs striker John Duncan was named England 'team observer' in August 1992.

● Bill Nicholson is ranked seventh in the list of 'Manager's' achievers list and he is the 17th longest-serving UK manager of all-time (club level).

● Danny Blanchflower was Northern Ireland team manager (1979), Mike England was manager of Wales (1980-88) as was Terry Yorath (early 1990s).

● George Skinner was the Finnish National Olympic team manager/coach (1948).

● In April 1949, former Spurs wing-half Frank Grice, then manager of Glentoran, negotiated the transfer to Barnsley of the future White Hart Lane captain, Danny Blanchflower.

● Former Spurs player Almer Hall managed non-League side Margate for 20 years (1950-70).

● Bobby Arber was Spurs reserve team manager from November 1997 to May 1998. Theo Foley took over his position in June 1998.

MANCHESTER CITY (ALSO ARDWICK)

Spurs playing record against City:

Competition	P	W	D	L	F	A
Premiership	10	7	2	1	14	8
Football League	96	28	26	42	125	155
FA Cup	12	6	2	4	20	19
League Cup	1	1	0	0	1	0
Summary	119	42	30	47	160	182

The first League meeting between the two clubs was played on 27 December 1910 (Division I) and ended all-square at 1-1 in front of 28,000 fans at White Hart Lane.

Spurs won eight and drew four of their first 13 home League games with City. Their only defeat was in April 1912 by 2-0, City's second visit to the ground!

In January 1935 Spurs knocked the holders, Manchester City, out

Bobby Smith goes close for Spurs v Man City in their semi-final clash. City won by a single goal.

of the FA Cup, winning a 3rd round tie by a goal to nil at White Hart Lane.

Twenty-one years later, in March 1956, City gained 'late' revenge with a 1-0 semi-final victory over Spurs at Villa Park.

In September 1957, ten days after thrashing Birmingham 7-1 and a week after beating Sheffield Wednesday 4-2, Spurs crashed to a 5-1 defeat at Maine Road against City.

On 1 November 1958, just three weeks after beating Everton 10-4, Spurs crashed 5-1 to City in Manchester.

With games fast running out and the title chase hotting up Spurs played a crucial League game at Maine Road in April 1960 knowing a victory was imperative. Alas Cliff Jones missed a penalty in a 1-0 defeat and with it went any chance of taking the championship which went to Burnley (55 points) with Wolves (54) in second place and Spurs (53) third.

One of City's most impressive performances against Spurs came in March 1962 when they won a League game by 6-2 at Maine Road. Jimmy Greaves scored both Spurs goals.

Spurs met City in a 6th round FA Cup-tie in 1969 but with their eyes set on glory, Bill Nicholson's men succumbed to a 1-0 defeat and City went on to beat Leicester in the Final.

Spurs crashed to a 4-0 defeat at Maine Road in August 1971 - their heaviest reverse of the season.

Spurts were officially relegated to the Second Division after losing 5-0 to City at Maine Road on 7 May 1977.

Spurs beat City 3-2 in the replay of the 1981 FA Cup Final (after a 1-1 draw), Ricky Villa scored a stunning goal in the second game.

Despite a couple of goals from the Romanian international Ilie Dumitrescu (one from the penalty spot) Spurs still crashed 5-2 in a Premiership game at City in October 1994.

Players with both clubs include: Clive Allen, Jamie Attwell (City trialist), Ivor Broadis (Spurs Amateur & WW2), Jock Chaplin, Bill Felton, Foster Hedley, Chris Jones, Neil McNab, Bobby Mimms, Joe Moffatt, Bert Sproston, Alex Steel, Paul Stewart, Charlie Williams, Clive Wilson, Alex Young.

Wartime guests (with either one or both clubs): Freddie Cox, Sid Hoad, Harry Jackson.

Also associated: John Sainty (Spurs reserve, City coach).

MANCHESTER UNITED (ALSO NEWTON HEATH)

Spurs playing record against United:

Competition	P	W	D	L	F	A
Premiership	18	3	3	12	18	30
Football League	110	32	31	47	157	171
FA Cup	13	5	5	3	21	17
League Cup	6	5	0	1	11	5
ECW Cup	2	1	0	1	3	4
Charity Shield	1	0	1	0	3	3
Summary	150	46	40	64	213	230

The first ever match between the clubs took place on 28 January 1899 when Spurs entertained Newton Heath in Round 1 of the FA Cup at Northumberland Park, 15000 spectators watching a 1-1 draw. On the following Wednesday at Bank Street Clayton Spurs triumphed 5-3 in the replay.

The first League game between Spurs and United took place at White Hart Lane on 11 September 1909 (Division 1). A crowd of 32,275 saw the 2-2 draw, Bob Steel netting two penalties for Spurs - the first spot-kicks for the club at this level.

The return fixture at Bank Street, Clayton in January 1910 drew a crowd of 8,000 fans and this time Spurs crashed to a 5-0 defeat -

Jones, Setters, Stiles and Greaves fight for possession in the FA Cup semi-final at Hillsborough in 1962

their heaviest in the League up to that time. This was the last game United played at Bank Street before moving to Old Trafford. United won only one of their first 14 League games at White Hart Lane (a 1-0 victory in February 1926).

When Spurs beat United 6-1 at home in September 1932 in front of 23,333 fans, the two Willies, Davies and Evans, both scored twice, one of the latter's goals coming via the penalty spot.

The last time Spurs played against the Busby Babes before the Munich air crash was on 30 November 1957 in a League game at Old Trafford. A crowd of 43,307 saw Spurs win 4-3. Bobby Smith scored a hat-trick while Jackie Blanchflower conceded an own-goal. Later in the season a Tommy Harmer penalty gave Spurs a 1-0 win at White Hart Lane when the turn out was almost 60,000.

A crowd of 55,641 saw goals by Dave Mackay, Tommy Harmer, Bobby Smith (2) and Dave Dunmore gave Spurs a rampaging 5-1 win at Old Trafford in September 1959 and later in the season another Smith brace earned Spurs the double with a 2-1 home victory.

When United drew 1-1 at White Hart Lane in October 1960 it brought to an end a Spurs run of 13 successive home League wins. A crowd of 65,296 packed into Old Trafford to see the return fixture on the night of 16 January 1961 which United won 2-0 despite having 'keeper Harry Gregg playing as a centre-forward with Alex Dawson in goal. The Irish goalie had gone off injured before the interval but return for the second-half as an emergency striker! This was the first time Spurs had failed to score in their double-winning season.

Spurs, the holders of the trophy - after an excellent run - reached their second successive 1962 FA Cup Final by defeating United 3-1 at Hillsborough in the semis.

United doubled-up over Spurs in the League in 1963-64, winning 4-1 at Old Trafford and 3-2 at White Hart Lane. In this same season Spurs played a 2nd round European Cup-winners Cup tie against United.

A crowd of 57,447 saw the holders of the trophy, win their home leg 2-0 on 3 December with goals by Dave Mackay and Terry Dyson. At Old Trafford a week later, Dave Mackay sadly broke his leg and despite a Jimmy Greaves goal, Spurs succumbed to a 4-1 defeat in front of 48,639 fans and went out 4-3 on aggregate.

Both League games between Spurs and United in 1965-66 had the same scoreline (5-1) with each team winning its home game by that margin. Over 58,000 fans saw all five Spurs forwards find the net at White Hart Lane compared with 39,511 at Old Trafford.

Spurs' keeper Pat Jennings scored one of his side's goals in the 3-3 draw with United at Old Trafford in the 1967 FA Charity Shield.

England's 1966 World Cup star Martin Peters wrote himself into the record books when he scored all of Spurs' goals in their excellent 4-1 win at Old Trafford in October 1972. A crowd of 52,497 saw him achieve that feat. Peters netted a hat-trick in the 25 minutes before half-time and his fourth goal came 10 minutes from time. In the 1978-79 FA Cup competition Spurs were eliminated in the quarter-finals

Spurs and Manchester United in action in 1951/52

by United who won 2-0 in a replay.

After drawing 3-3 at Old Trafford in December 1986, Spurs beat the Reds 4-0 at White Hart Lane towards the end of that season when two of the goals came from an unlikely source, Mitchell Thomas!

Paul Gascoigne was sent-off when Spurs lost 2-1 at home to United in January 1991 and the following year it was Paul Stewart who saw 'red' when again United took the points with a 2-1 victory also at White Hart Lane.

Fielding a weakened team, United were defeated 3-1 by Spurs in the quarter-final of the Worthington Cup in December 1998, and Spurs repeated that scoreline in the final Premiership game of the 2000-01 season in front of more than 36,000 fans at White Hart Lane, Willem Korsten scoring twice.

* Spurs beat United 5-0 (in Toronto) and 7-1 (in New York's Yankee Stadium) in the space of 24 hours while on tour in North America in June 1952. Len Duquemin scored four times for Spurs in the second game after Jack Rowley had given United the lead! Players with both clubs include: Jamie Attwell (United trialist), Bill Berry, Alan Brazil, Jimmy Brown, Garth Crooks, Harry Erentz, Quinton Fortune (Spurs junior), Terry Gibson, Tommy Gipps, Jack Hall, David Gwilan Jones (Spurs reserve), Cyril Knowles (United junior), Chris McGrath, James McNaught, Fred Milnes, Teddy Sheringham.

Wartime guests (with either one or both clubs): Ivor Broadis, John Davie, Ernie Goldthorpe, Alan Hall, Charlie Hannaford, Fred Hopkin, Tommy Manley, Tommy Nuttall, Jack Rowley, George Travers, Roy White.

Also associated: George Graham (United player, Spurs manager), Stewart Houston (United player, Spurs assistant-manager).

MANNING, GORDON S

Goalkeeper Gordon Manning spent one season with Spurs, appearing in 49 first-team games (33 in the Southern League) in 1907-08.

Born in Prescot on 17 May 1895, he played for Preston North End before becoming manager Fred Kirkham's first signing in May 1907. He made his debut for the club in the 8-1 friendly win over Ostend in Belgium. Manning died in St Helens on 23 December 1963.

MANSFIELD TOWN

Spurs playing record against the Stags:

Competition	P	W	D	L	F	A
Football League	2	0	2	0	4	4

The two League games were played in season 1977-78 (Division 2). The first was staged at White Hart Lane on 23 December and ended 1-1. The second at Field Mill in late March brought a flurry of goals and finished level at 3-3.

Players with both clubs include: Jimmy Allen, Joe Allen, Roy Brown, Colin Calderwood, Ray Clarke, Barry Daines, Warren Hackett (Spurs Youth), Harry Hargreaves, Alf Messer, Bobby Mimms, John Moran, John Sainty (Spurs reserve), Dennis Uphill, Charlie Walters. Wartime guests (with either one or both clubs): John Davie, Ernie Marshall, Les Miller, Sid Ottewell, Ken Smith.

MARCHI, ANTHONY VITTORIO

Born to an English mother and Italian father, in Edmonton, North London on 21 January 1933, wing-half Tony Marchi joined Spurs as an amateur in July 1948, having already made a name for himself when representing Edmonton, Enfield, Middlesex, London and England Schools. He made his Spurs' League debut against Grimsby Town in April 1950, two months before turning professional. This was the first of 317 appearances for the senior XI (in two spells with the club). He scored 10 goals.

His first spell at White Hart Lane ended in the summer of 1957 when he joined Lanerossi (Vicenza) in Italy for £42,000. He then switched to AS Torino before returning to Spurs for £20,000 in June 1959. He remained with the club for six more years before becoming player-manager of Cambridge City in June 1965, holding office until March 1967. Six months later he took over the reins at Northampton Town (September 1967-May 1968).

A tall, composed footballer, Marchi won an England 'B' cap in 1957 and after standing in for the injured Dave Mackay when the European Cup-winners Cup was lifted in 1963, he was selected to represent England against Young England on the eve of that year's FA Cup Final. After giving up football Marchi dabbled in the wall-papering business and later the building trade in Maldon, Essex.

MARGATE

Spurs' playing record against the Kent club

Competition	P	W	D	L	F	A
FA Cup	1	1	0	0	6	0

Spurs accounted for non-League Margate quite comprehensively in a 3rd round FA Cup-tie on the Kent coast in January 1973. An all-ticket crowd of 8,500 saw Martin Chivers lead the goal-chase with two smartly taken efforts, whilst Cyril Knowles, John Pratt, Jimmy Pearce and Martin Peters also found the net.

Players with both clubs: Jimmy Archibald, Tommy Bing, Eddie Clayton, Abraham Goodman

Wartime guest: Jim Evans (Spurs).

Also associated: Almer Hall & Cecil Poynton (both Spurs players & Margate managers).

MARKHAM, ERNEST

A full-back, born in London circa 1872, Markham played for several local clubs before making eleven first-class appearances for Spurs in five different competitions in 1897-98. When he left the club he returned to non-League action.

MARLOW

Spurs' playing record against the non-League side

Competition	P	W	D	L	F	A
FA Cup	1	1	0	0	5	1

This 3rd round FA Cup clash was played in January 1993. Originally scheduled to take place at Marlow, the tie was switched to White Hart Lane and in front of 26,636 spectators Spurs ran out 5-1 winners, Teddy Sheringham, Nick Barmby (2) and Vinny Samways (2) were Spurs' goalscorers.

MARSHES (TOTTENHAM)

Spurs played on The Marshes - a public stretch of land between the River Lea and the Great Eastern railway line - from 1882 until early in the 1888-89 season.

In fact, the club had no right to play football matches on this ground and quite often other enthusiastic youngsters (some of them bullies), all wanting to have a general kick-about, rolled up at the same time as the Spurs players. Indeed, they tried to occupy the same piece of land already marked out by representatives and members of the Spurs club.

Occasionally there were heated arguments, sometimes fisticuffs took place, and as a result Spurs decided to fence off the pitch as sometimes a few thousand spectators would turn up to see them play (certain reports indicated that up to 4,000 fans watched the occasional game).

These unruly incidents frustrated Spurs and as a result enquiries were made regarding the hiring of a pitch near to Northumberland Road, which was close by. This quickly gathered momentum and, although the land was already being used by Foxes FC in the winter while tennis was played there during the summer months, Spurs persevered and agreed a rent of £17 per annum to use a piece of land on 'Northumberland Park' from 1888 onwards.

The first match at their new ground - called on the Northumberland Park enclosure - took place on 13 October 1888 when a Spurs reserve XI met Stratford St John's in a London Junior Cup match, the gate receipts amounting to just 17 shillings (85p).

MATCHES

The longest 'Cup -ties' Spurs have been involved in (all taking three games to resolve):
1934-35 v. Bolton Wanderers, FA Cup
1938-39 v. West Ham United, FA Cup
1952-53 v. Birmingham City, FA Cup
1985-86 v. Portsmouth, League Cup
1986-87 v. Arsenal, League Cup

MEADS, THOMAS

Half-back Tom Meads was born in Grassmoor. Derbyshire on 3 November 1900 and played locally for Grassmoor Ivanhoe, Clay Cross and Matlock Town before signing professional forms with Stockport County in December 1923. In March 1927 he was transferred to Huddersfield Town; in October 1928 he switched to Reading and in May 1929 was recruited by Spurs. He made his debut against Bradford Park Avenue - the first of 189 League and FA Cup games for the club before moving to Notts County in June 1935. Meads died on 30 January 1983.

MEDAL WINNERS

● Ray Clemence, before moving to Spurs in 1981, helped Liverpool win five League championships, three European Cup Finals, two UEFA Cup Finals, the FA Cup, League Cup, European Super Cup and five Charity Shields. He also gained a runners-up medal in each of two FA Cup Finals, a League Cup Final and one European Super Cup. And not to forget his 56 full and four England Under-23 caps, as well as two appearances for the Football League. With Spurs, Clemence added a Charity Shield prize (shared), FA Cup winners' and losers' medals in 1982 and 1987 and a League Cup runners-up prize, also in 1982. He also gained five more England caps.

● Between 1983 and 1997 defender Richard Gough won ten Scottish Premier League titles (one with Dundee United, nine with Glasgow Rangers). He also won five Scottish League Cup and three Scottish Cup winners;' medals during the same period as well as gaining a handful of runners-up prizes along the way (one with Spurs in 1987).

● As a football club manager, former Spurs player Herbert Chapman collected an array of medals. He guided Huddersfield Town and Arsenal to four League championship successes (two each); won the FA Cup with each club and claimed two runners-up prizes both with Arsenal as well as obtaining second place in the First Division with the Gunners. Earlier, in his playing days, he helped Northampton Town win the Southern League title in 1909.

● Graeme Souness also won a bag full of medals as a player - including five Football League championships, four Football League Cups, three European Cups, four Scottish League Cups, the FA Cup and the Second Division title. He added a few more awards to his collection as a manager.

● Centre-forward Charlie Wilson won championship medals in three different Divisions of the Football League: 1920 with Spurs (Division 2), 1924 and 1925 with Huddersfield Town (Division 1) and 1927 with Stoke City (Division 3 North).

● Alf Ramsey helped Spurs win the Second Division and First Division titles as a player (1950 & 1951) and then repeated that feat as a manager with Ipswich Town in the early 1960s. He then led England to World Cup glory in 1966.

● Alfie Conn won a cluster of medals north of the border with Celtic and Rangers - and they included two League championship victories, two Scottish Cup wins, a League Cup triumph, runners-up in the European Cup-winners Cup and victory in Scottish Amateur Cup with Coatbridge!

MEDLEY, LESLIE DENNIS

Left-winger Les Medley had an interesting career. Born in Edmonton, North London on 3 September 1920, he represented Edmonton, London and Middlesex Schools before playing for Tottenham Juniors. He then starred for England Schoolboys and signed amateur forms for Spurs in the summer of 1935. He had a spell at Northfleet before taking professional status at White Hart Lane in February 1939. Come the War and Medley guested for Aldershot, Clapton Orient, Millwall and West Ham United, having played for Spurs until November 1940 when he joined the RAF, serving in Canada. He met his wife over there and after returning to England they initially settled in London. However, his wife became homesick and this forced Medley to return to Canada where he assisted the Toronto Greenbacks and Ulster United

before returning 'home' to play for Spurs from January 1948 until his retirement in May 1953. He then emigrated to Canada and later coached Randfontein in South Africa (1958-61).

Medley was Spurs' top goalscorer with 18 when they won the Second Division championship in 1949-50 and he contributed eleven more League goals when the First Division title was claimed twelve months later. With Eddie Baily his inside partner and Ronnie Burgess driving up from behind, Medley enjoyed a lot of the ball as Spurs played some delightful 'push and run' football in front of big crowds. Medley loved the soccer stage. He represented the Football League and won six full England caps. His Spurs record was impressive: 74 goals scored in 254 first-team appearances. In the Football League he notched 45 goals in 150 outings....an excellent strike-record for a winger. Medley died in Ontario, Canada on 22 February 2001.

MEDWIN, TERENCE CAMERON

Terry Medwin came into this world in the warders' quarters of Swansea gaol where his father was an officer. Born on 25 September 1932, he attended and played for St Helens and Oxford Street Schools in Swansea. A direct centre-forward, he then represented Swansea Boys and Wales Schools and worked in a garage before joining the playing staff at The Vetch Field as an amateur in September 1946, turning professional in Nov 1949.

Now converted into a right-winger - his favourite position - he made his Swansea debut in January 1952 in a forward-line that included Ivor Allchurch. He went on to score 57 goals in 147 League appearances for the Welsh club (and played in three full internationals) before moving to Spurs for £18,000 in April 1956. Signed to fill what was now a 'problem position' on the right-flank, Medwin settled in superbly well and although 'only a reserve' in 1960-61 - having lost his place to another ex-Swansea player, Cliff Jones - he still appeared in enough games to gain a League championship medal. The following season he added an FA Cup winners' medal to his collection after coming back into the side in place of Terry Dyson with Jones switching wings.

Medwin, fast and willing, always threatening near goal, had his career wrecked in May 1963 when he broke his leg in three places playing against an Invitation XI whilst on the club's South African tour. He struggled on for two years, trying to regain full fitness. He was forced to retire in 1965 having taken his total number of

senior caps to 30 while also netting 90 goals in 247 first team appearances for Spurs, 65 in 197 Division One games.

Medwin remained in soccer in various capacities until ill health resulted in him leaving the game for good in 1983.

He held managerial posts with non-League sides Enfield (1964-65) and Cheshunt (1965-67). Was coach with Cardiff City (1967-69) and Fulham (1969-70), also acting as scout at Craven Cottage (1970-73). He was reserve team coach at Norwich City before returning to Swansea City as the club's assistant-manager (1978-82) and later scout for one year.

MEEK, JOSEPH

Inside-forward Joe Meek had been playing competitive football for ten years when he joined Spurs in March 1936 from Bradford Park Avenue. His previous clubs had included Liverpool, Middlesbrough and Gateshead, albeit without him signing professional forms. He netted 16 goals in 51 League and Cup games for Spurs before joining Swansea Town in 1939. During WW2 he guested for Burnley, Grimsby, Lincoln City, Liverpool, Middlesbrough, Newcastle United, Nottingham Forest and Rochdale. He was born on Tyneside in May 1910 and died in the North-east 66 years later.

MELIA, JAMES

Full-back Jimmy Melia scored three goals in 91 first team appearances for Spurs during his three years with the club - May 1898 to July 1901.

Born in Darlington on 2 April 1874, he played initially for Sheffield Wednesday before joining Spurs as cover for Harry Erentz. He gained one representative honour, playing for the Southern League against the Southern Amateurs in February 1900. Three years after leaving White Hart Lane for Preston North End, Melia was taken ill, and sadly he died in February 1904 aged 28.

MESSER, ALFRED THOMAS

Centre-half Alf Messer made 56 first team appearances for Spurs (two goals scored) during his four-year stay with the club which began in July 1930 and ended in May 1934 when he was appointed player-coach of Bournemouth & Boscombe Athletic.

Born in Deptford, South London on 8 March 1900, Messer played for Sutton United, Mansfield Town, Nottingham Forest and Reading (he made 295 League and Cup appearances for the Royals from June 1921) before moving to White Hart Lane where

he became team captain. Well built, six feet tall and almost 13 stone in weight, he was a real solid performer who later became a licensee, taking over the Truro public house in Castle Street, Reading while also coaching Oxford City on a part-time basis Messer died in Reading on 28 July 1947.

METGOD, JOHANNES ANTONIUS BERNARDUS

Midfielder Johnny Metgod was born in Amsterdam, Holland on 27 February 1958. He played for DWS Amsterdam, Haarlem and AZ 67 Alkmaar all his in home country before signing for Real Madrid in the summer of 1982, transferring to Nottingham Forest in August 1984 and onto Spurs in July 1987 for £250,000. He only made 14 competitive appearances during his brief spell at White Hart Lane (playing in 27 first team games overall) before moving to Feyenoord for £180,000 in May 1988. In March 1992, he helped knock Spurs out of the European Cup-winners Cup competition. Capped 19 times by Holland (playing in his first international when registered with the Alkmaar club) Metgod also represented the Football League (v. the Irish League in September 1987) and in his first season with Real Madrid collected a Spanish Cup runners-up medal. A tall, upright footballer, confident and very professional in his ways - it was a pity Metgod didn't remain longer at the club.

METROGAS

Spurs playing record against Metrogas

Competition	P	W	D	L	F	A
London C Cup	1	1	0	0	11	2

This victory was achieved in the 1st round of the London Charity Cup in September 1913 and it was Spurs' best-ever win in the competition. Jimmy Bauchop (4) and Jimmy Cantrell (3) led the goal-rush in front of 2,500 spectators.

Player with both clubs: Bert Smith.

1950's action against Middlesbrough

MIDDLESBROUGH

Spurs playing record against 'Boro:

Competition	P	W	D	L	F	A
Premiership	12	3	5	4	12	15
Football League	52	18	10	24	89	100
FA Cup	4	3	1	0	9	2
League Cup	5	2	2	1	5	7
Summary	73	26	18	29	115	124

The first League game between the two clubs was played at White Hart Lane on 16 October 1909 (Division 1), in front of 23,000 spectators 'Boro winning 3-1.

The versatile Bob Steel scored his first Football League hat-trick when Spurs beat 'Boro 6-2 at home in February 1911.

On a greasy pitch, 12 goals were scored when Spurs visited Middlesbrough for a League game in February 1915. The outcome was a 7-5 win for the home side. Jimmy Cantrell scored four of Spurs' goals, including the club's first hat-trick away from home in the League.

Middlesbrough had Andy Wilson sent-off during their home League game with Spurs on 17 September 1921 but they still managed a 0-0 draw.

It took Spurs ten attempts before they won a League game at 'Boro - finally securing a 1-0 victory on Teeside in 1923-24.

On Christmas Day 1952 Spurs celebrated the festive season with a 7-1 home win over 'Boro. They doubled up that season with a 4-0 win at Ayresome Park. Les Bennett scored five of those goals including a fourtimer in the win at White Hart Lane.

Players with both clubs include: Bill Almond, Nick Barmby, David Black, Jack Brearley, Alex 'Sandy' Brown, Chris Carrick, John Curtis, Jack Elkes, Paul Gascoigne, Albert Hall, Charlie Hewitt, Bill Hickling, Charlie O'Hagan, Jimmy Robertson, Graeme Souness, Bob Walker, Ernie Walley, Christian Ziege.

Wartime guests (with either one or both clubs): Bill Adams, Simon Beaton, Billy Brawn, George Burchell, Stan Clayton, Harry Ferrier, Les Howe, Wilf Mannion, Joe Meek ('Boro Amateur), Fred Sargent, Jack Skinner, Alex Wilson.

Also associated: Peter McWilliam (manager of both clubs), Terry Venables (Spurs player & manager, 'Boro advisory-manager/coach), Cyril Knowles ('Boro coach & assistant-manager).

MIDDLESEX SENIOR CUP

Spurs entered this local competition in seasons 1889-90, 1890-91, 1891-92 and 1893-94. They played a total of six matches, winning one (4-2 away to Old Stephens in their opening game), drawing one and losing four. After losing in the second round in 1889-90 (to Clapham) they went out at the first hurdle in each of the last three seasons, losing in a replay to the Grenadier Guards in the latter campaign.

Summary of results:

P	W	D	L	F	A
6	1	1	4	5	9

MIDDLEMISS, HERBERT

Bert Middlemiss appeared in 356 first team matches for Spurs (245 in the Football League). He scored 90 goals (51 in the League).

An outside-left, sharp and nippy with a strong shot, he was born in Newcastle on 19 December 1888 and played for Stalybridge Celtic and Stockport County before joining Spurs in November 1907. He went straight into the first team at White Hart Lane and remained with the club until June 1920 when he switched across London to Queen's Park Rangers, having guested for Birmingham and Coventry City during the Great War.

He helped Spurs win promotion from Division Two in 1908-09, played in four England international trials and represented the Football League against the Southern League in April 1910. He retired to live in South Devon where he died in Brixham on 28 June 1941.

MILAN (AC)

Spurs playing record against Milan:

Competition	P	W	D	L	F	A
UEFA Cup	2	1	1	0	3	2

The semi-final of the UEFA Cup featured Spurs against the crack Italian side AC Milan and it was the 'English' who came out on top, winning the two-legged contest 3-2.

The first leg took place at White Hart Lane on 5 April and in front of 42,064 fans, resulted in a narrow 2-1 win for Spurs, both goals coming from Steve Perryman (a rare feat this)!

With a one goal advantage Spurs defended resolutely at the San Siro Stadium to earn a 1-1 draw in the return leg a fortnight later which was seen by 68,482 spectators. Alan Mullery netted the vital goal that evening.

Players with both clubs: Jimmy Greaves, Christian Ziege.

MILLER, LESLIE ROY

Les Miller was an orthodox outside-left with Barking (two spells), Northampton Town (as an amateur) and the French club Souchaux (for whom he netted over 75 goals, 60 of them in 1935-36) before joining Spurs in September 1936 - signed by manager Jack Tresadern who had been his boss at Northampton!

He was also the first player to join a Football League club having previously played professionally in France. Miller went on to score 26 goals in 65 first team appearances for Spurs (22 in 56 League games) before transferring to Chesterfield in July 1939. He guested for Mansfield Town during the War but did not re-appear after the hostilities. He died in Braintree, Essex on 1 October 1959.

MILLER, PAUL RICHARD

Defender Paul Miller, six feet tall and over 12 stones in weight, played centre-half for Spurs in 383 first team games (208 in the Football League and 77 in various Cup comnpetitions). He scored a total of 16 goals.

He had represented East London, London and Middlesex Schools before joining the apprentice ranks at White Hart Lane in April 1976, turning professional in May 1977. Between March and October 1978 he was loaned out to the Norwegian side Skied Oslo - to gain experience. On his return to

Spurs, after a slow start he consolidated his position in the first XI, gaining FA Cup winners' medals in 1981 and 1982 and a UEFA Cup winning prize in 1984 as well as appearing in the 1982 League Cup Final.

With so much defensive cover at the club Miller was eventually transferred to Charlton Athletic in February 1987. Eight months later he moved to Watford and in August 1989 teamed up with Bournemouth, later assisting Brentford (on loan) and Swansea City (from September 1990). He acted as Youth team coach to Wingate (1980s).

Miller was born in Stepney, East London on 11 October 1959.

MILLIKEN, JAMES

Scottish-born inside-forward who, along with players Devlin, McElhaney and Wilson, was suspended for an 'act of insubordination' in April 1897. Prior to joining Spurs Jim Milliken had played for Third Lanark, Leicester Fosse and St Mirren. He scored eight goals in 31 games in his only season at White Hart Lane. He returned to 'home' to play for Clyde.

MILLWALL

Spurs playing record against the Lions:

Competition	P	W	D	L	F	A
Football League	22	17	3	2	54	25
FA Cup	3	2	1	0	3	1
League Cup	1	1	0	0	2	0
Other Leagues	52	25	8	19	93	73
Other Cups	9	3	2	4	20	16
Wartime	32	19	5	8	76	44
Summary	119	67	19	33	248	159

Spurs first played Millwall in the Football League on 22 September 1928 and in front of 47,073 spectators at White Hart Lane they won the Second Division fixture 2-1 only to lose the return game later in the season by 5-1 at The Den.

Spurs beat Millwall 3-2 at home in March 1948 to end a run of seven League games without a win.

In April 1989, a Paul Stewart hat-trick helped Spurs win 5-0 at The Den and so complete the double following a 2-0 home victory earlier in the season.

Players with both clubs include: Stan Alexander, Bill Almond, Charlie Ambler, Arthur Archer, Chris Armstrong, Gerry Armstrong, Ken Barton, John Brearley (Millwall player-coach), Stanley Briggs, Walter Bugg (Millwall reserve), Alf Day, Jimmy Devlin, Matt Dillon, Kerry Dixon (Spurs reserve), Bill Dryburgh, Ray Evans, Mark Falco, Lee Gardner (Lions trialist), Fred Griffiths, Foster Hedley, John 'Tiny' Joyce, Charlie Lanham, Chris McGrath, Terry Naylor (Lions' trialist), Stuart Nethercott, Derek Possee, Neil Ruddock, Frank Saul, Jack Shepherd, Teddy Sheringham, Bob Stevens, Bob Tannahill (later assistant-trainer at The Den), Ben Thatcher, David Tuttle, Bert Walker, Keith Weller.

Wartime guests (with either one or both clubs): Bill Adams, Jack Acquroff, Ted Bassett, Sam Bell, Ivor Broadis, Vic Buckingham, Ron Burgess, Charlie Burke, Ken Burditt, Jack Chisholm, Albert Chester, John Davie, Fred Ford, Albert Hall, Charlie Hannaford, Les Howe, Jimmy Jinks, George Ludford, Les Medley, Johnny Morris, Johnny Morrison, Peter Murphy, Albert Sibley, Reg Smith, Bill Sperrin, Jimmy Sperrin, Bert Sproston, Les Stevens, Sid Tickridge, George Travers, Sonny Walters, Alf Whittingham, Tim Williamson, Arthur Willis.

Also associated: Charlie Hewitt (Spurs player, Millwall manager), Jimmy Seed (Spurs player, Millwall manager & later Lions' consultant director), George Graham (manager of both clubs), Roger Cross (Millwall player, Spurs assistant-manager), Theo Foley

(Millwall coach, assistant-manager & caretaker-manager, Spurs reserve team coach), Arthur Rowe (Spurs player & manager, Millwall consultant), Ronnie Boyce (Millwall chief scout, Spurs scout), Pat Holland (Lions' assistant-manager, Spurs coach).

MIMMS, ROBERT ANDREW

Goalkeeper Bobby Mimms was the first loan signing to play for Spurs first XI (the FA having sanctioned the transfer scheme in 1967). He moved south to White Hart Lane in February 1988 and signed on a permanent basis soon afterwards.

Born in York on 12 October 1963, Mimms, 6ft 3ins tall and weighing 13st 7lbs, played for Halifax Town as a professional from August to October 1981. He then joined Rotherham United from where he switched to Everton in June 1985, gaining a League championship medal and Charity Shield prize two years later. He had played on loan with Notts County, Sunderland, Blackburn Rovers and Manchester City before moving south to White Hart Lane. He made 69 first team appearances for Spurs (44 in League and Cup) before transferring to Ewood Park in December 1990 following a loan spell in Scotland with Aberdeen. Capped three times by England at Under-21 level, Mimms carried on his soccer wanderings with Crystal Palace (August 1996), Preston North End (September 1996) Rotherham United (August 1997), York City (August 1998) and finally Mansfield Town (signed in March 2000). And when the 2000-01 season came to an end he was still registered with the Stags having accumulated well over 500 appearances at club level over a period of 20 years.

MINTER, WILLIAM JAMES

Billy Minter appeared in 339 first team games for Spurs (244 in the Football League). He scored 155 goals - 95 in the League. Born in Woolwich, South London on 16 April 1888, he played for Norwich City as an amateur before joining Arsenal in the same capacity in February 1906. He then took professional status with Reading in June 1906, transferring to Spurs in March 1908. He remained an active player - and a very good one at that - until June 1920 when he retired to become the club's trainer. In February 1927 he was appointed manager, but resigned his position in November 1929 when he took over as assistant-secretary, a position he occupied until his death in Tottenham on 21 May 1940 - having served Spurs for 32 years. A well-built, strong looking and forceful footballer, Minter helped Spurs climb back into the First Division in 1919-20 before losing his place to Jimmy Banks. He chose to end his career after suffering a handful of knee and ankle injuries. He took over as manager from Peter McWilliam but let things get on top of him and after failing with a promotion bid, the strain told on him and he resigned, although under no pressure to do so from the board of directors.

MONK, CUTHBERT VICTOR

During his career Cuthbert Monk played as a goalkeeper, full-back and half-back, and it was a 'keeper that he performed best, making 13 appearances for Spurs during the 1890s. He stood between the posts for the club in the first FA Cup-tie and in the first FA Amateur Cup encounter.

MONTGOMERY, JOHN

Scottish-born full-back Jock Montgomery made 132 first team appearances for Spurs, scoring one goal. A native of Chryston, Lancashire (born 18 June 1876) he joined Spurs in January 1896 and may well have been the first professional signed by the club. During his time with Spurs he represented the Southern League against London in February 1897 and played for the Anglo Scots against the Home Scots in an international trial. He left the club for Notts County in May 1898 and made some 350 appearances in 13 years at Meadow Lane before ending his career with Glossop North End. He retired in May 1911 when he was appointed trainer of Preston North End. He later returned to London and died at Edmonton on 6 April 1940.

MOORES, IAN RICHARD

It was a shock to a lot of Spurs supporters when the news came that the club's former England Under-23 striker Ian Moores had died in a Stoke hospital on 12 January 1998. He was only 43. Born in Newcastle-under-Lyme on 5 October 1954, Moores played for Staffordshire Schools before joining Stoke City as an apprentice, turning professional in June 1972. He moved to Spurs for £75,000 in August 1976 and scored 17 goals in 50 first team games (eight in 32 senior outings) before transferring to Leyton Orient in October 1978 (after a loan spell in Australia with Western Suburbs, Sydney). He helped Spurs gain promotion from Division Two in 1978. In July 1982 Moores switched to Bolton Wanderers. He had a loan spell with Barnsley in February 1983 and then helped Apoel win both the Cypriot League and Cup competitions before quitting the Football League scene to sign for Newcastle Town. He later played for Tamworth and Landskrona Bols and even had a trial with Port Vale.

MORGAN, ROGER ERNEST

Winger Roger Morgan plied his trade with Spurs from February 1969 until his retirement in June 1973. In that four-year period he appeared in 95 first team games and scored 17 goals, twelve coming in 80 competitive matches. The identical twin brother of Ian, he was born in Walthamstow on 14 November 1946 and represented Walthamstow Schools before joining Queen's Park Rangers as an apprentice in 1963, turning professional in September 1964. Three years later he helped the Loftus Road club win the Third Division championship and the first-ever League Cup Final at Wembley, following up with promotion to the First Division in 1968. Capped by England against Bulgaria at Under-23 level in 1970, Morgan suffered serious knee injuries soon after that international and after a year or so on the treatment table he gave up the fight and became West Ham's Community Development Officer.

MORRIS, THOMAS

Half-back Tom Morris amassed 520 first team appearances for Spurs (448 at senior level). He scored 48 goals. A man who helped get Spurs established in the Southern League, he joined the club in the summer of 1899 from Gainsborough Trinity whom he had served for two seasons. He remained a player at White Hart Lane until his retirement in May 1912 when he was appointed to the groundstaff, a position he retained until early 1942, giving him a total of 43 years dedicated service to the club.

Born in Grantham, Lincolnshire on 9 February 1875 - not too far from the Roberts' family household, Margaret Thatcher's parents - Morris played his early football with Grantham Rovers and made 62 League appearances for Trinity before embarking on his Spurs career. An unflagging player with enormous reserves of energy, he was an inspirational performer when Spurs won the Southern League title in 1899-1900 and was just as brilliant when the FA Cup was lifted the following season. He represented the South v. the North in international trial matches in 1900 and 1903 but surprisingly never made the full England side, Bill Johnson of Sheffield United and Aston Villa's Albert Wilkes being chosen ahead of him in the ten internationals played over that three-year

period. Nevertheless Morris battled on for Spurs, giving his all - a fine player. He died at Uxbridge on 25 April 1942 - two months after retiring through ill-health.

MORRISON, JOHN ALFRED

Centre-forward Johnny Morrison netted 132 goals for Spurs in only 189 first team games. He scored 90 of his goals in 134 Football League games, another 25 in the Wartime League South and 14 in 21 FA Cup encounters. He developed into a wonderfully consistent marksman after establishing himself in the first XI in 1937-38. He top-scored that season with 25 goals and followed up with 12 more in 1938-39 when both the Halls and Duncan were also scoring well. Although rather cumbersome at times, he was always sniffing around the penalty area, defenders aware of his presence! A real opportunist, Morrison was born in Belvedere, Kent on 26 March 1911 and joined Bostal Heath as a 15 year-old before playing for Callenders Athletic. He was signed as amateur by Spurs in August 1931 and after a spell with the club's nursery team, Northfleet, he became a full-time professional in july 1933. He remained at White Hart Lane until May 1946 when he retired, having guested for Millwall during the War. Morrison died in South Devon on 13 September 1984.

MOTHERWELL

Spurs playing record against the 'Well:

Competition	P	W	D	L	F	A
Texaco Cup	2	1	0	1	4	5

After winning 3-2 at White Hart Lane Spurs went out of the 1970-71 Texaco Cup after losing the return leg 2-0 at Fir Park where the crowd was almost 22,700, some 3,000 more than had attended the first encounter.

Players with both clubs include: Steve Archibald, Tom Atherton, Alfie Conn, Mark Gower, George Jeffrey, John Patterson, Alex Tait.

MULLERY, ALAN PATRICK, MBE

Alan Mullery amassed 428 first team appearances for Spurs (312 in the First Division and 61 in various Cup competitions). Prior to moving to White Hart Lane in March 1964 for £72,500 in March 1964, he had made his name in the Fulham side, playing in midfield alongside Johnny Haynes and Bobby Robson. He lined up in well over 200 games for the Cottagers and helped them win promotion from the Second Division before becoming the main driving force in the Spurs engine-room.

Born in Notting Hill on 23 November 1941, Mullery represented West London, London, and Middlesex Schools before joining the groundstaff at Fulham in June 1957, turning professional in December 1958. Always looking competent and never overawed, he had three England Under-23 caps to his name before he won his first representative honour with Spurs, playing for the Football League

against the Italian League two months after his transfer. He later added 35 full caps to his collection (1964-71), being part of Alf Ramsey's 1970 World Cup squad. He did however have the unwanted tag of being the first England player to be sent-off in a major international, dismissed against Yugoslavia in the European Championships in Belgrade in June 1968. A winner in both the 1967 FA Cup and 1971 League Cup Finals, he also skippered the side before suffering a mysterious stomach injury that kept him out of action for quite some time. He recovered and in March 1972 was actually loaned back to Fulham, but he quickly returned and helped Spurs win the UEFA Cup two months later. Mullery then rejoined the Cottagers on a full-time basis in June 1972 for £65,000, and remained at the club until his retirement in May 1976, a year after playing in the losing FA Cup Final side against West Ham United. In 1975 he was voted FWA 'Player of the Year' and also received the MBE.

He took his appearance tally with the Cottagers up to an impressive 412 (with 42 goals scored)...excellent. In July 1976 Mullery was appointed manager of Brighton & Hove Albion. In June 1981 he left the Gulls and a month later took charge of Charlton Athletic for one season before moving into the hot-seat at nearby Crystal Palace (June 1982). He stayed there for two years and then switched to neighbouring Queen's Park Rangers, but remained in office at Loftus Road for barely six months, leaving in December 1984. Mullery later returned to Brighton for a second spell as manager (May 1986-January 1987) before having a spell in charge of non-League Southwick (August-December 1987). He later ran a sports shop in Banstead and worked for BSkyB Sport.

MURPHY, PETER

Peter 'Spud' Murphy was a trialist with Middlesbrough, an amateur inside-forward with both Coventry City and Birmingham City and played as a guest for Millwall during the War before signing professional forms at Highfield Road in May 1946. After four excellent years with the Sky Blues he was transferred to Spurs for £18,500 (a healthy sum in those days) and helped the London club win the First Division championship in 1950-51, scoring nine goals in 25 matches as deputy for Les Bennett.

After netting 20 times in 49 first team games, he became unsettled in London and left White Hart Lane for St Andrew's, getting off to a flying start by netting a hat-trick on his Blues debut (at Doncaster) in January 1952. He helped Blues win the Second Division championship in 1954-55, weighing in with 20 goals. The following season he scored another 17, including five in the FA Cup, as Blues went through to Wembley where they lost to

Manchester City. Murphy was the player who accidentally collided with Bert Trautmann, the City goalkeeper, causing the German to fracture his neck.

Murphy's phenomenal left-foot shooting from 30-40 yards out often caused problems for opposing goalkeepers. He officially retired in 1959 and was handed a coaching job at St Andrew's but with Blues battling against relegation the following season he came back to help them avoid the drop.

A supreme marksman, Murphy ended his career with more than 150 goals to his credit in under 400 League appearances made with three clubs. In 1960-61 he helped Rugby Town win promotion to the Southern League Premier Division and later returned to Highfield Road as manager/coach of Coventry's 'A' team. He died in the Midlands on 7 April 1975.

MURRAY, WILLIAM B

A Scotsman, born in 1883, winger Bill Murray played for Inverness, Sunderland and Northampton Town before joining Spurs in May 1904. He made 37 first-class appearances during the next two seasons and then switched his talents to Leeds City.

MUSIC

Released in March 1996, 'Glory-Glory Tottenham Hotspur' brought together for the first time, a compilation of 28 Spurs related songs, recorded over the previous 25 years.

Most of the recordings were made to coincide with a specific Cup Final appearance.

Probably the earliest record of interest to a Spurs fan came in 1961 when The Totnamites recorded a tribute song to the double team entitled 'Tip Top Tottenham Hotspur'.

Around the same time the FA Cup Final highlights were captured on a Pye 7" extended play disc with BBC sound commentary by Raymond Glendenning and Alan Clarke.

The club's official record in 1967 was a 14 track EP/An unknown artist also released Hotspur Boogie, an unrelated song to the official recording for the 1973 League Cup Final.

That same year, Cockerel Chorus, brought out 'Nice One Cyril' ....the first Spurs related record to reach the charts, peaking at number 14.

Spurs fans, Chas & Dave, have featured on club records since 1981. Another duo, Glenn & Chris, branched out on their own in 1987. They are better known, of course, as Messrs Hoddle and Waddle.

'Ossie's Dream' is the most successful of the Spurs releases, reaching number five in the UK singles chart in 1981.

'Tottenham, Tottenham' was a chart hit in 1993 and during a seven-week period in the top 40, it reached number 19.

Here is a list of those Spurs Musical 'hits and Misses'....

1961	Tip Top Tottenham Hotspur (The Totnamites)
1961	FA Cup Final Highlights (BBC Sound Commentary (EP)
1967	The Spurs Go Marching On (EP)
1967	Hotspur Boogie (Single)
1967	FA Cup Final Highlights (BBC, LP)
1971	League Cup Final Highlights (BBC Radio, LP)
1973	Cockerel Chorus 'Nice One Cyril' (Single)
1973	Hot Spurs Boogie (Single)
1973	League Cup Final Highlights (BBC Radio, LP)
1973	Cockerel Chorus Party Sing-a-long (LP)
1978	Amigos O'Lane - Tribute to Ardiles & Villa (Single)
1981	Ossie's Dream (Single)
1981	The Tottenham Hotspur Party Album (LP)
1981	BBC Highlights from Spurs' FA Cup Victories (Single)*

Peter Murphy scuffs a chance on goal v West Bromwich Albion in 1948

1982	Tottenham, Tottenham (Single)
1987	Hot Shot Tottenham (Single)
1987	Glenn & Chris - Diamond Lights (Single)
1987	Glenn & Chris - It's Goodbye (Single)
1991	When The Year Ends In 1 (Single)
1991	The Victory Song (We're off to Wembley 'cos we beat the Arsenal) - Chas & Dave (Single)

* (re-issued in 1982 including 1981 highlights)

Names

Shortest

Spurs players (at competitive level) with the shortest name (including both christian and surnames) have been John Hall, John Lacy, Colin Lee, James Smy - all with eight letters. * A player by the name of J Lee (possibly James or John) played in one Western League game for the club in 1907.

Other short-named players include: William Bay, Philip Beal, Charles Bee, Walter Bull, Alfred Day and Patrick Glen

Scores of players with surnames containing three letters have been registered with Spurs over the years.

Longest

The players with the longest surname to have served with Spurs (various levels) are Blanchflower (Danny), Chipperfield (Jimmy) and McGlanachlan (Jock). All have 12 letters in their names.

The player with the longest set of names ever to appear at senior level for Spurs is Christopher William Gerard Hughton (31 letters).

Other long-named players include: Johannes Antonius Bernadus Metgod (30 letters), Patrick William Roger Van den Hauwe (30), William Edward John Charles Kaine (29), William Frederick Weston Hinton (28), Berthold Alan Couldwell Hall (25) and Albert Edward Benjamin Hall (24).

The Name Game

● Charlie Ambler was christened Charles James Toby but changed his name at a relatively young age.

● The following players, whose surname represents a country, have been registered with Spurs: Alan BRAZIL, Mike ENGLAND and Jeff IRELAND while these are towns/cities: Justin EDINBURGH, Cyril Henry TOULOUSE and Charlie WHITCHURCH; there is a GLEN (Alex), WOODS (Alan) and a GREENFIELD (Jack).

● These ex-Spurs players were 'colourful' footballers in their own right: David BLACK, 'Sandy' BROWN, Laurie BROWN, John and Roy WHITE....and the GRAYS (Andy, James & Phil)

● Spurs' Second World War guest Reg Smith was born James Reginald Christopher Schmidt, the son of a South African rugby international. He was an amateur with Spurs before being released by the club in 1933.

● In 1897, Fred Latham, playing in his third and final trial game for Spurs, chose to appear under the pseudonym of Stokely (lately of Stoke City).

● In season 1918-19, Coventry City's Charlie Wilson played for Spurs in six matches. In four of them he called himself C Williams, in another it was C Forshaw and he only used his own name once!

NANTES (FC)

Spurs playing record against the French club:

Competition	P	W	D	L	F	A
UEFA Cup	2	1	1	0	1	0

Spurs made progress in the 1971-72 UEFA Cup competition by narrowly beating the French club FC Nantes in the second round. After a goalless draw in the away leg on 20 October which was seen by 20,033 fans, Spurs scraped through 1-0 at White Hart Lane 13 days later thanks to a goal by Martin Peters in front of a crowd of 32,630.

NAYLOR, TERENCE MICHAEL PATRICK

Terry Naylor appeared in 378 first team games for Spurs and scored just one goal - in the 1st leg of the 1971-72 League Cup semi-final against Chelsea.

A wholehearted, determined footballer, able to play in several defensive positions but preferring the right-back berth, he was born in Islington, North London on 5 December 1948 and represented Islington Boys before joining Spurs as an amateur in 1965, turning professional in July 1969. With so many other talented defenders at the club, Naylor did not claim a regular place in the first XI until 1973-74. He held his own with some excellent performances and gained a UEFA Cup runners-up medal that season. After relegation, he then assisted manfully in seeing Spurs regain their First Division place straightaway and went on to serve the club until November 1980 when he transferred to Charlton Athletic, retiring three years later. He managed Gravesend & Northfleet for a season (1984-85), assisted Haringey Borough from July 1985 and then played briefly for Empire Papermill FC before taking over as manager of Tonbridge Angels (July-September 1988).

NEIGHBOUR, JAMES EDWARD

Winger Jimmy Nieghbour spent over ten years at White Hart Lane - from April 1966 when he signed as a junior, turning professional in November 1968 - until September 1976 when he moved to Norwich City for £75,000. In that time he appeared in 190 first team matches and scored 15 goals. In League and Cup action his record was 156 outings and 11 goals.

Born in Chingford, Essex on 15 November 1950, he represented Waltham Forest, London and Essex Schools before signing for Spurs with whom he gained a League Cup winners' tankard in 1971.

He left Carrow Road for West Ham United in September 1979 (following a spell in the NASL with Seattle Sounders) Neighbour then helped the Hammers reach the 1980 FA Cup Final and was also a member of their defeated League Cup Final side a year later.

A loan spell with Bournemouth in January 1983 was followed by his enforced retirement at the end of that season.

From October 1985 to 1990, Neighbour acted as Enfield's coach, helping then win the FA Trophy. He then returned to West Ham as Youth Development Officer.

NEILL, WILLIAM JOHN TERENCE

Born in Belfast on 8 May 1942, Terry Neill was an uncompromising centre-half who served with Bangor (in the Irish League), Arsenal (December 1959-June 1970) and Hull City (as player-manager to June 1973). He also represented Northern Ireland, winning a total of 59 full caps plus others at Schoolboy, Under-23 and 'B' team levels. He appeared in 275 first-class games for the Gunners and 144 for the Tigers.

He continued as manager at Boothferry Park until September 1974, having also acted as the PFA Chairman as well as serving as player-manager of Northern Ireland, taking the job full-time until March 1975. Whilst in charge of his country's national team, Neill was appointed manager of Spurs in September 1974. He retained that position until July 1976 when he returned to his former club Arsenal, also as manager, remaining in office until Dcember 1983. As a player, the tough-tackling Neill collected a League Cup runners-up prize in 1968, when Arsenal lost to Leeds United and as a manager he tasted FA Cup glory with the Gunners in 1979 but twice suffered defeat, in 1978 and 1980.

He also collected the runners-up award in the 1980 European Cup-winners Cup Final when Arsenal lost 5-4 on penalties to Valencia. After leaving football, Neill worked for various charity organisations.

NELSON

Spurs have never met the Lancashire side at any level.

Players with both clubs include: Ken Bennett (Spurs WW1), Arthur Dixon, Harry Hargreaves, Foster Hedley, Sid Hoad (Spurs WW1), Archie Hughes, Tommy Nuttall (Spurs WW1), Buchanan Sharp.

Also associated: Percy Smith (Nelson secretary-manager, Spurs manager).

NEUTRAL GROUNDS

Spurs have played major domestic, European and foreign matches on the following neutral grounds:

FA Cup

1898-99 3rd Q rd 2nd replay v. Luton Town, 2-0	Tufnell Park
1900-01 Semi-final v. West B Albion, 4-0	Villa Park
1900-01 Final v. Sheffield United, 2-2	Crystal Palace
1900-01 Final Replay v. Sheffield United, 3-1	Burnden Park
1901-02 1st rd 2nd replay v. Southampton 1-2	Elm Park
1906-07 2nd rd 2nd replay v. Blackburn R. 2-1	Villa Park
1920-21 Semi-final v. Preston North End, 2-1	Hillsborough
1920-21 Final v. Wolverhampton Wds, 1-0	Stamford Bridge
1921-22 Semi-final v. Preston North End, 1-2	Hillsborough
1934-35 5th rd 2nd replay v. Bolton Wds, 0-2	Villa Park
1938-39 4th rd 2nd replay v. West Ham, 1-2	Highbury
1947-48 Semi-final v. Blackpool, 1-3	Villa Park
1952-53 6th rd 2nd replay v. Birmingham, 1-0	Molineux
1952-53 Semi-final v. Blackpool, 1-2	Villa Park
1955-56 Semi-final v. Manchester City, 0-1	Villa Park
1960-61 Semi-final v. Burnley, 3-0	Villa Park
1960-61 Final v. Leicester City, 2-0	Wembley Stadium
1961-62 Semi-final v. Manchester Utd, 3-1	Hillsborough
1961-62 Final v. Burnley, 3-1	Wembley Stadium
1966-67 Semi-final v. Nottingham Forest, 2-1	Hillsborough
1966-67 Final v. Chelsea, 2-1	Wembley Stadium
1978-79 3rd rd replay v. Altrincham, 3-0	Maine Road
1980-81 Semi-final v. Wolverhampton, 2-2	Hillsborough
1980-81 Semi-final replay v. Wolves, 3-0	Highbury
1980-81 Final v. Manchester City, 1-1	Wembley Stadium
1980-81 Final replay v. Manchester City, 3-2	Wembley Stadium
1981-82 Semi-final v. Leicester City, 2-0	Villa Park
1981-82 Final v. Queens Park Rangers, 1-1	Wembley Stadium
1981-82 Final replay, v. QPR, 1-0	Wembley Stadium
1986-87 Semi-final v. Watford, 4-0	Villa Park
1986-87 Final v. Coventry City, 2-3	Wembley Stadium
1990-91 Semi-final v. Arsenal, 3-1	Wembley Stadium
1990-91 Final v. Nottingham Forest, 3-1	Wembley Stadium
1992-93 Semi-final v. Arsenal, 0-1	Wembley Stadium
1994-95 Semi-final v. Everton, 1-4	Elland Road
2000-01 Semi-final v. Arsenal 1-2	Old Trafford

League Cup

1970-71 Final v. Aston Villa, 2-0	Wembley Stadium
1972-73 Final v. Norwich City, 1-0	Wembley Stadium
1981-82 Final v. Liverpool, 1-3	Wembley Stadium
1998-99 Final v. Leicester City, 1-0	Wembley Stadium

FA Charity Shield

1981-82 v. Aston Villa, 2-2	Wembley Stadium
1982-83 v. Liverpool, 0-1	Wembley Stadium
1991-92 v. Arsenal, 0-0 (shared)	Wembley Stadium

European Cup-winners Cup

1962-63 Final v. Atletico Madrid, 5-1	Rotterdam

Football League

1971-72 Division 1 v. Leeds United, 1-1	Boothferry Park

Victory Cup

1918-19 Semi-final v. West Ham United, 3-1	Highbury
1918-19 Final v. Fulham 0-2	Stamford Bridge

Southern League

1897-98 v. Reading, 1-1	East Ferry Road

London FA Charity Cup

1908-09 Semi-final Queens Park Rangers, 0-0	Stamford Bridge
1908-09 Semi-final replay v. QPR, 4-1	Craven Cottage
1908-09 Final v. Fulham, 1-4	Stamford Bridge
1910-11 Semi-final v. Millwall, 2-2	Leyton
1910-11 Semi-final replay v. Millwall 2-0	Homerton
1910-11 Final v. Fulham, 2-1	Stamford Bridge
1913-14 Semi-final v. Arsenal, 2-1	Stamford Bridge
1913-14 Final v. Crystal Palace, 1-2	Highbury
1920-21 Semi-final v. Clapton Orient, 1-2	Highbury
1922-22 Semi-final v. Arsenal, 0-0	Stamford Bridge
1921-22 Final replay v. Arsenal, 1-2	Homerton
1924-25 Semi-final v. Clapton Orient, 1-2	Highbury
1928-29 Semi-final v. Charlton Athletic, 5-3	Upton Park
1928-29 Final v. Millwall, 5-1	Highbury
1930-31 Semi-final v. Ilford, 8-1	Upton Park
1930-31 Final v. Arsenal, 1-2	Stamford Bridge

London Combination Subsiduary Cup

1917-18 v. Chelsea, 0-1	Highbury
1917-18 v. Fulham, 2-3	Upton Park

Southern Charity Cup Final

1904-05 v. Reading, 0-0 (shared)	Craven Cottage

Coronation Cup

1952-53 Semi-final v. Hibernian, 1-1	Ibrox Park
1952-53 Semi-final replay v. Hibernian, 1-2	Hampden Park

Wellingborough Charity Cup

1896-97 v. Rushden, 2-1	Wellingborough

Glasgow Charity Cup

1963-64 v. Glasgow XI, 2-4	Ibrox Park

Daily Telegraphic Titanic Fund
1911-12 v. Arsenal, 0-3   Park Royal

Wartime Football
1940-41 v. Southend United, 2-3   Chelmsford City FC
1943-44 v. Millwall, 1-0   Selhurst Park
1943-44 v. Charlton Athletic, 0-3   Stamford Bridge

*During the four seasons in the First World War (1916-17-18-19) Spurs played all their home games at Highbury Stadium and Homerton.

NEW BRIGHTON
Spurs playing record against New Brighton:

Competition	P	W	D	L	F	A
FA Cup	2	1	1	0	5	2

A Football League club from 1923 to 1951, New Brighton and Spurs never met in the competition but they did do battle in the FA Cup in season 1937-38. After a 0-0 draw at Sandheys Park in front of 13,029 spectators, Spurs won their home 4th round replay 5-2, Johnny Morrison and Jack Gibbins both scoring twice before a crowd of 36,004.
Player with both clubs: Ted Worrall (Spurs WW1).

NEW BRIGHTON TOWER
New Brighton Tower played in the Football League for four seasons: 1897-1901 - long before Spurs joined the competition. Consequently there has was no action at this level between the two clubs, nor was there any in the major Cup tournaments.

NEWCASTLE UNITED
Spurs playing record against United:

Competition	P	W	D	L	F	A
Premiership	16	6	4	6	26	27
Football League	98	43	24	31	169	135
FA Cup	8	2	2	4	6	17
League Cup	2	1	0	1	2	3
Charity Shield	1	1	0	0	2	1
Summary	125	53	30	42	205	183

Newcastle United, heading towards the FA Cup Final, beat Spurs 4-0 in a 2nd round replay on Tyneside in February 1905. They lost in the Final to Aston Villa.
The first League meeting between the two clubs was played at St James' Park on 6 November 1909 (Division 1) and in front of 26,000 fans United won by a goal to nil.
When Spurs beat United 1-0 at home on 23 November 1912, it ended a then record 14-match run with a League win.
Spurs completed an early season double over united in 1921-22,

winning 4-0 at home (thanks mainly to a Bert Bliss hat-trick) and 2-0 away.
A crowd of 34,731 saw Frank Osborne score four times when Spurs clipped United 5-2 at home in a First Division League game in January 1928.
Over 70,000 fans saw Spurs beat United 7-0 at home in a Second Division game in November 1950. It had been 4-0 at half-time and Les Medley helped himself to a hat-trick.
Ten months later, in September 1951, Spurs crashed to a 7-2 defeat at St James' Park!
Eddie Baily and Sid McClellan both scored twice for Spurs when they forced a 4-4 draw at Newcastle in October 1954 in front of 45,306 spectators.
Spurs opened their 1959-60 League programme with a cracking 5-1 win at Newcastle, Cliff Jones scoring a hat-trick in front of more than 40,000 fans. Later in the season United lost 4-0 at White Hart Lane.
Spurs did the double over Newcastle in 1966-67, winning 4-0 at home and 2-0 away. Doubling-up again in 1974-75, gaining a 3-0 home win in December (when Cyril Knowles scored twice) and then claiming a 5-2 victory in the North-east in mid-January when Alfie Conn netted a hat-trick.
United defeated Spurs in the two-legged League Cup semi-final of January 1976. Over 40,000 fans saw John Pratt give Spurs a first leg lead at White Hart Lane and there were almost 50,000 present for the return leg in the North-East when United won 3-1 to go through 3-2 on aggregate
One of Spurs' best wins over United in the 1980s came at White Hart Lane in September 1985 when they triumphed 5-1, John Chiedozie scoring twice.
In a Premiership game at Newcastle in May 1995, Spurs were 2-0 down then 3-2 up before being held at 3-3 by United. Three goals were scored in the space of four minutes during the course of the action. Spurs finished up with 10 men following the dismissal of defender Colin Calderwood. Three years later on 24 October 1998 the unfortunate Calderwood again saw 'red' against United - dismissed in the 2-0 Premiership home win.
Spurs suffered their heaviest Premiership defeat to date when crashing 7-1 at St James' Park in December 1996. Future Spurs star Les Ferdinand scored twice for the Geordies.
Two years later United beat Spurs 2-0 in the FA Cup semi-final at

Spurs forward Duquemin missing an opportunity against Newcastle United. Spurs eventually winning 7-0.

Old Trafford and then in December 1999, United well and truly hammered Spurs to the tune of 6-1 in a 3rd round FA Cup replay at St James' Park - thus equalling the club's biggest-ever defeat in the competition (achieved before at Huddersfield in 1928). Alan Shearer scored twice late on. The first game had ended 1-1.

On 2 January 2001, goalkeeper Neil Sullivan became the third Spurs player to be sent-off against Newcastle - dismissed in the 4-2 Premiership win at White Hart Lane.

Players with both clubs include: Ted Birnie, Ivor Broadis, Ray Clarke, Garry Brady, Les Ferdinand, John Fleming, Ruel Fox, Peter Garland, Paul Gascoigne, David Ginola, Bert Gosnell (United player & coach), Jim Iley, John McTavish, Paul Moran, Taffy O'Callaghan (United trialist), Kevin Scott, Mark Stimson, Allan Taylor, Archie Turner, Chris Waddle.

Wartime guests (with either one or both clubs): Simon Beaton, Joe Meek, Bill Nicholson (also Spurs manager), Tommy Pearson (also United scout), Albert Sibley, Joe Wilson.

Also associated: Ossie Ardiles (Spurs player & manager, United manager), Peter McWilliam (United player, Spurs manager), Tony Galvin (Spurs player, United assistant-manager), Jesse Carver (United player, Spurs coach), Keith Burkinshaw (Spurs coach & manager, United assistant-coach), Charlie Woods (chief scout at both clubs).

NEWMAN, ERNEST HENRY

An outside-left, previously with Walsall and Stockport County, Birmingham-born Ernie Newman scored six goals in 32 League and FA Cup games for Spurs (1910-12).

NEWPORT COUNTY

Spurs playing record against the Welsh club

Competition	P	W	D	L	F	A
Football League	2	2	0	0	7	3
39-40 League	1	0	1	0	1	1
Wartime	2	2	0	0	5	1
Summary	5	4	1	0	13	5

The two Football League games were played in season 1946-47 (Division 2). A crowd of 18,169 saw Spurs win 4-2 at Somerton Park on 19 September and then 3-1 at home 18 days later. George Foreman netted twice in the latter contest, which was attended by 14,540 spectators.

Players with both clubs include: Terry Boyle and Roger Gibbins (Spurs reserves), David Jenkins, Mark Kendall, Terry Lee, Tim O'Shea.

Wartime guests (both Spurs): Wilf Hares & Reg Mogford.

Also associated: Mike Lewis (Commercial Manager at both clubs).

NICHOLLS, JOSEPH HENRY

Goalkeper Joe Nicholls spent nine full seasons at White Hart Lane (June 1927 to May 1936). In that time he appeared in 139 first team matches, including 124 in the Football League and five in the FA Cup.

Born in Carlton, Nottingham on 8 March 1905, he was a Grenadier Guardsman (also playing for the Army side in Services' football) before signing for Spurs; when he left the club he joined Bristol Rovers.

His first season at White Hart Lane was spent mainly with Northfleet, preparing himself for what was to come! He did well once he got into the first XI, being an ever-present in the Spurs ranks.

An England international trialist, keeping goal for The Rest against England in 1934, Nicholls

was hugely popular with the supporters. He left the club after the emergence of Percy Hooper.

Nicholls died in Nottingham on 20 June 1783.

NICHOLSON, WILLIAM EDWARD, OBE

Born in Scarborough on 26 January 1919, Bill Nicholson was a successful trialist with Spurs as a full-back in March 1936. He was sent out to gain experience with Northfleet before returning to sign professional forms in August 1938, making his League debut two two months later against Blackburn Rovers - the first of 395 appearances for the club (317 coming in the Football League). He netted seven goals.

Converted into a classy, hard-working right-half, Nicholson guested for Darlington, Fulham, Hartlepool United, Middlesbrough, Newcastle United and Sunderland during the War, and helped Spurs win both the Second Division and First Division League titles in successive seasons in 1949-50 and 1950-51 before retiring in December 1955.

Nicholson - a member of England's 1950 World Cup squad - was capped once at senior level against Portugal at Everton in May 1951 (he scored after just 30 seconds play in a 5-2 victory). He was named as a reserve no fewer than 22 times and also played in three 'B' internationals and represented the Football League. He earned his FA coaching badge while still a player and coached the Cambridge University soccer team, preparing them for battle against Oxford! He was Spurs' coach (under manager Arthur Rowe) and later appointed assistant manager to Jimmy Anderson in 1955 while also assisting Walter Winterbottom with the England Under-23 side.

Appointed Spurs manager on 11 October 1958 he remained in charge until 13 September 1974. He guided Spurs to that famous 1960-61 double triumph, to two more FA Cup Final victories in 1962 & 1967, to League Cup glory in 1971 & 1973 and success in both the European Cup-winners Cup & UEFA Cup Finals of 1963 & 1972 respectively. The team also played in, and lost, the 1974 UEFA Cup Final.

After 16 years in the hot seat Nicholson was replaced by Terry Neill. After a brief scouting mission with West Ham, he duly returned to White Hart Lane as consultant/chief scout in July 1976. He held that position for 21 years before announcing his retirement in July 1997. He remains club president to this day (appointed in May 1991) - thus giving him 63 years dedicated and loyal service to the club.

A great manager, who signed some great players and was awarded the OBE in 1975.

Fact File:

Spurs played 823 competitive matches under the managership of Bill Nicholson: 667 in the Football League, 67 in the FA Cup, 34 in the League cup and 55 in various European tournaments. A total of 401 were won, 227 lost with 195 drawn. The teams scored 1,571 goals while 1,086 were conceded.

Nicholson used 79 players in all - 37 year-old Danny Blanchflower was the oldest, while Neil McNab, at 16, was the youngest.

Bill Dodge was the first player given his 'debut' by Nicholson and Alfie Conn was the last played he called into the team.

Pat Jennings made 480 appearances for Spurs under Bill Nicholson.

The League triumph in the double season of 1960-61 saw Nicholson join the short list of men to have won the championship as both a player and manager.

In December 1998 he received the Freedom of the Borough of Haringey Council and the road leading to the White Hart Lane ground from Tottenham, High Road was renamed 'Bill Nicholson Way.' The official unveiling of the newly-named road took place in April 1999 and is now incorportated in the club's official address. Nicholson was granted two testimonials by Spurs - the first in 1983 against West Ham United, the second in 2001 v. the Italian club Fiorentina.

NICKNAMES

Many players have nicknames and here are few hinged to Spurs players:

Milija 'Elastic' Aleksic
Osvaldo 'Ossie' Ardiles
Eddie 'Cheeky Chappie' Baily
Bill 'Burglar' Berry
Sammy Brooks, 'Little Giant'
Alex 'Sandy' Brown
Jack 'The Boy' Chisholm
Martin 'Big Chiv' Chivers
Bob 'Topsy' Clements
Alfred 'Taffy' Day
Michael 'Matt' Dillon
Gilbert 'Dicky' Dowsett
Len 'The Duke' Duquemin

'Reliable' Len Duquemin
Terry 'Ginger' Dyson
Harry 'Tiger' Erentz
Courtney 'Chris' Fairclough
Paul 'Gazza' Gascoigne
Albert 'Jack' Gibbons
Bert 'Kosher' Goodman
Jack 'Nobby' Greenfield
Alex 'Sandy' Hall
Charlie 'Tich' Handley
Tommy 'The Charmer' Harmer
George 'The Chesterfield Tough' Hunt
Arthur 'Spider' Jones
Ernie 'Alphabet' Jones
John 'Bristol' Jones
John 'Tiny' Joyce
'Nice One Cyril" Knowles
Arthur 'Darkie' Lowdell
Ernie 'Bunks' Markham
'Bill Nick' Nicholson
Eugene 'Taffy' O'Callaghan
Gheorghe 'Gica' Popescu
Neil 'Razor' Ruddock
Arthur 'Art' Rule
Willie 'Sapper' Sage
Vincent 'Vinny' Samways
Edward 'Teddy' Sheringham
Alex 'Sandy' & 'Terrible' Tait
Frederick 'Fanny' Walden
Billy 'Sonny' Walters
John 'The Ghost' White

Players by the name of Bunks (1894), Bach (1895) and Slender (1919) were all registered with Spurs for friendly matches in the years given....but these names were not their real ones. They were pseudonyms used to protect their true identities.

NIELSEN, ALLAN

Born in Esbjerg, Denmark on 13 March 1971, attacking midfielder Allan Nielsen joined Spurs for £1.75 million from Brondby IF in September 1996, having previously served with Esbjerg, Bayern Munich, FC Sion (Switzerland), Odense and FC Copenhagen.

He spent almost five years at White Hart Lane during which time he scored 18 goals in 115 Premier League and Cup games and had a loan spell with Wolverhampton Wanderers (March-May 2000) before transferring to Watford for £2.25 million in the summer of 2000. Capped 30 times by his country during his time at White Hart Lane (he is now over the 40 mark) Nielsen is a direct player, who loves to drive forward

NORMAN, MAURICE

Born in the picturesque Norfolk village of Mulbarton on 8 May 1934, Maurice Norman was initially a full-back who developed into an England centre-half, winning 23 full caps, plus three more at Under-23 level as well as

Norman tackling Stanley Matthews

representing the Football League and an England XI (twice). He starred in defence for Norfolk Schools and played for Mulbarton FC before having three years with Norwich City from September 1952 until November 1955 when he joined Spurs for £28,000. Over the next decade the hard tackling, resilient figure of Norman, with his jet-black hair, amassed 411 senior appearances (playing in 453 games all told) and scoring 19 goals. He missed only one game when the double was achieved in 1960-61 and followed up by gaining FA Cup and European Cup-winners Cup medals in the next two years. Norman also played for his country in the World Cup Finals of 1958 and 1962. A broken leg, suffered in a home friendly against the Hungarian Selecct XI in November 1965, effectively ended his career. He retired in May 1967.

NORTHAMPTON TOWN

Spurs playing record against the Cobblers:

Competition	P	W	D	L	F	A
Football League	2	1	1	0	3	1
FA Cup	1	1	0	0	3	0
League Cup	1	1	0	0	3	1
Southern League	14	8	1	5	22	12
Wartime	2	2	0	0	7	1
Summary	20	13	2	5	36	14

The two League games between the clubs took place in 1965-66 (Division 1). The first drew a crowd of 17,611 to the County Ground to see Spurs win 2-0 with goals by Dave Mackay and Frank Saul. The return game finished level at 1-1.

Players with both clubs include: Gary Anderson (Spurs Youth), George Badenoch, Stuart Beavon, Charlie Brittan, Laurie Brown, Bill Brown, Wayne Cegielski (Spurs Youth), Herbert Chapman (Town player-manager), Jabez Darnell, Ian Gilzean (Spurs reserve), Ian Hendon, Colin Lyman, Frank McDiarmid, Gary Mabee (Spurs reserve), Les Miller (Town amateur), Bill Murray, Walter Tull, Fanny Walden (also Town coach), Bob Walker.

Wartime guests (either with one or both clubs): Len Bolan, Billy Brawn, Ed Freeman, Les Henley, Eric Jones, Wilf Saunders, Eric Tomkins.

Also associated: Jack Tresadern (Northampton player-manager, Spurs manager), Walter Bull & Tony Marchi (Spurs players, Town managers), Warney Cresswell (Spurs WW1, Town manager), Graham Carr (Cobblers player & manager, Spurs scout), Ernie Jones (Spurs player, Town coach).

NORTHFLEET UNITED

Spurs playing record against Northfleet:

Competition	P	W	D	L	F	A
Southern League	4	3	0	1	12	3

Spurs' biggest of their three Southern League victories over Northfleet was 4-0 at home on 15 January 1898 when Billy Joyce scored a hat-trick in front of 2,000 spectators.

Northfleet was Spurs' adopted nursery club whereby young players were 'loaned out' to gain experience at competitive level. Among the juniors who assisted Northfleet and then returned to play senior football with Spurs are: Wally Alsford, Vic Buckingham, Ron Burgess, Alec Chaplin (Spurs guest), Freddie Cox, Jack Coxford (player-coach), Percy Hooper, Les Howe, Doug Hunt, John Illingworth, Charlie Jones, David Gwilyn Jones (Spurs reserve), Bill Lane, David Levene, George Ludford, Les Medley, Bert Smith (Spurs player, Northfleet coach), Bill Nicholson, Taffy O'Callaghan, Cecil Poynton, Jock Richardson, Bert Ringrose, Tommy Roe, George Skinner, Harry Skitt, Les Stevens, Andy Thompson (player-coach), Sid Tickridge, Albert Tomkin, Cyril Trailor and Bill Whatley.

Also: Ivor Broadis (Spurs amateur and Wartime player).

NORTHUMBERLAND PARK

Spurs moved into their Northumberland Park ground (a converted playing field near the Northumberland Arms pub) in the summer of 1888.

The ground, capable of housing upwards of 12,000 spectators, was situated barely 100 yards from the club's present ground (White Hart Lane).

The club agreed an annual rent of £17 and the first match there involved Spurs' second XI against Stratford St John's in early September, the first senior game following soon afterwards, on 28 September, when Spurs beat Westminsters 13-0 in a friendly.

Spurs had an excellent first season at their Northumberland Park ground, making a profit of £6......it might not sound a lot, but they had been losing money hand over fist for the previous 10 years! The first stand was erected in 1894 - but this was blown away in a gale shortly afterwards, costing the club a bit more money!

After professionalism had been accepted in 1895, and entry gained to the Southern League the following year, bigger crowds began to assemble at the 'Park'. In February 1898, during a United League home match against arch-rivals Luton Town, a handful of irate Spurs fans invaded the pitch and assaulted three Town players. As a result the club was fined and also forced to close Northumberland Park for a short time.

On Good Friday, 8 April 1898, a record crowd of 14,500 assembled inside Northumberland Park to watch a United League game between Spurs and Woolwich Arsenal (the previous best had been 6,000 for a friendly game with Aston Villa in April 1896). Some spectators were perched precariously on the roof of the refreshment bar and as a result it collapsed, causing a few injuries and a lot of confusion. The game was held up temporarily and eventually ended in a 0-0 draw. As a result of this mishap, Spurs' officials became concerned for the safety of supporters and talked about finding a new ground - and when Charles Roberts took over as Chairman later in the year, he quickly found one!

NORTHWICH VICTORIA

No competitive match action between the two clubs:
Players with both clubs include: Harry Bradshaw, Arthur Crompton, Harry Lowe.
Wartime guest: Tommy Manley (Spurs).

NORWICH CITY

Spurs playing record against the Canaries

Competition	P	W	D	L	F	A
Premiership	6	4	1	1	11	5
Football League	40	17	10	13	69	54
FA Cup	6	1	2	3	6	7
League Cup	2	2	0	0	3	1
Southern League	6	2	1	3	10	13
Hospital Cup	2	1	1	0	4	2
Wartime	2	0	1	1	4	7
Summary	64	27	16	21	107	89

The first League game between the two clubs was a Second Division affair played at White Hart Lane on 3 September 1936 when a crowd of 32,767 saw the Canaries win 3-2. The scoreline was repeated again in January 1937 when Spurs turned the tables to win a five-goal thriller at Carrow Road, courtesy of Johnny Morrison's hat-trick.

Under 18,500 fans saw Spurs beat Norwich 4-0 at home in March 1938 and the corresponding fixture played next season (on 1 October) resulted in a 4-1 win for Spurs but this time the turnout was over 30,000.

Gary Lineker scored a hat-trick (one from the penalty spot) when City were beaten 4-0 at White Hart Lane in February 1990. This turned out to be Spurs' best win of the season.

* On 25 September 1976 winger Jimmy Neighbour played for Spurs against Norwich City. The following Saturday he lined up for the Canaries against Newcastle United and later in the season he scored for Norwich against Spurs!

Players with both clubs include: Chris Adams, Arthur Archer, Jimmy Banks, Jimmy Bauchop, Len Bolan, Mark Bowen, Garry Brady, Garry Brooke, Laurie Brown, Walter Bugg, Jim Chalmers, Martin Chivers, Ian Crook, Ian Culverhouse, Roy Darbo (Norwich trialist), Bill Edrich (City amateur), Neale Fenn, Tom Fitchie, Clayton Fortune (Norwich trialist), Ruel Fox, Johnny Gavin, Roger Gibbins (Spurs reserve), Charlie Handley, Roy Hollis, Percy Humphreys, Jimmy Kennedy, Fred Milnes, Billy Minter (City Amateur), Jimmy Neighbour, Maurice Norman, Martin Peters, Robert Pilch (also City director & vice-chairman), John Polston, Fred Sharp, Tim Sherwood, Jimmy Smith, John Sutton (Norwich trialist), Andy Thompson, Steve Walford, Simon Webster, Charlie Williams, Willie Young.

Wartime guests (either with one or both clubs): Jack Acquroff, Ken Burditt, Harry Dukes, Len Flack, Albert Hall, Tommy Manley, Cecil Potter (also City player & manager), George Travers, Alf Whittingham, Tim Williamson

Also associated: Bert Gosnell, Charlie O'Hagan & Cyril Spiers (all Spurs players, City managers), Terry Medwin (Spurs player, City reserve team coach), Doug Livermore (City player, Spurs manager, assistant-manager/coach, reserve team manager, chief scout), John Sainty (Spurs reserve, City coach).

NOTTINGHAM FOREST

Spurs playing record against Forest

Competition	P	W	D	L	F	A
Premiership	10	3	1	6	11	15
Football League	94	46	23	25	164	122
FA Cup	7	3	3*	1	10	8
League Cup	6	1	2	3	7	10
Wartime	2	2	0	0	5	2
Summary	119	55	29	35	197	157

* Lost tie on penalties

A crowd of 30,000 witnessed the first League meeting between the two clubs which was played at White Hart Lane on Christmas Day 1909 (Division 1). The final score was 2-2 and Percy Humphreys netted both goals for Spurs.

Spurs and Forest were level at 0-0 in their Second Division game at White Hart Lane in November 1948 when fog caused the fixture to be abandoned. There were almost 32,000 fans inside the ground. The 'replay' ended in a 2-1 win for Spurs.

Jimmy Greaves helped himself to four goals when Spurs crushed Forest 9-2 in a League game at White Hart Lane in September 1962. The half-time score was 6-1.

Spurs completed a Christmas double over Forest in 1964, winning 2-1 at The City Ground and 4-0 at White Hart Lane, 56,693 attending the latter match.

Spurs reached the 1967 FA Cup Final by beating Forest 2-1 at Hillsborough in the semis.

Spurs' best League win in 1970-71 was against Forest whom they thumped 6-1 at home in October.

In October 1983, the first full Football League game to be televised 'live' featured Spurs and Forest from White Hart Lane - and over 30,500 fans saw Spurs record a 2-1 victory.

Eight years later, in May 1991, Spurs, despite losing Paul Gascoigne early on and Gary Lineker missing a penalty, beat Forest 2-1 in the FA Cup Final, England defender Des Walker gifting Spurs the winner with an own-goal!

In February 1996, a 5th round FA Cup-tie between Forest and Spurs, attended by 17,009 fans, was abandoned in the 15th minute due to a severe snow blizzard. The scoresheet was blank at the time and the rearranged game also ended level at 2-2, likewise the replay at 1-1, before Forest went through after a penalty shoot-out.

Forest beat Spurs 3-1 on penalties in the 5th round of the FA Cup in 1995-96. The first game ended 2-2 and the replay 1-1 after extra-time.

Players with both clubs include: Wally Alsford, Eddie Baily, Colin Calderwood, Frank Drabble, Chris Fairclough, Randolph Galloway, Richard Gough, Steve Hodge, Jim Iley, Colin Lyman, Bill McCurdy, Harry Marshall, Alf Messer, Johnny Metgod, John Moncur, Tommy

Action in Nottingham Forest penalty area in 1958/59

Roe, Teddy Sheringham, Hans Segers, Des Walker (Spurs junior), Bob Wilkie (amateur), Willie Young.

Wartime guests (with either one or both clubs): Ron Burgess, Abraham Goodman, Jack Hall, Les Howe, Tommy Manley, Joe Meek, John Oakes, Frank O'Donnell.

Also associated: Dave Mackay (Spurs player, Forest manager), David Pleat (Forest player, Spurs manager caretaker-manager, Director of Football).

NOTTS COUNTY

Spurs playing record against the Magpies:

Competition	P	W	D	L	F	A
Football League	34	16	8	10	52	45
FA Cup	4	2	1	1	8	6
League Cup	3	1	1	1	3	5
Summary	41	19	10	12	63	56

The first-ever game played at White Hart Lane was a friendly between Spurs and Notts on 4 September 1899. A crowd of 5,000 saw Spurs win 4-1, Tom Pratt and David Copeland (3) the scorers - after the Magpies had taken the lead!

The first Football League meeting between Spurs and Notts was played on 30 November 1909 (Division 1) and resulted in a 3-1 defeat for Spurs in front of 23,000 frustrated fans. Notts' consolation goal came courtesy of a Spurs player - Sandy Tait.

The Spurs v. Notts First Division game at White Hart Lane in October 1912 was abandoned in the 80th minute through fog. Some 7,000 fans were present and Notts were leading 3-1 at the time...and they also won the 'replay' 3-0.

In 1929-30 (Division 2) Spurs completed the double over Notts, winning 1-0 away and 2-0 at home. It was to be another 47 years before the teams met again - then the two Second Division matches between the two clubs in 1977-78 resulted in a 2-1 home win for Spurs and a 3-3 draw at Meadow Lane.

On 28 November 1981 Spurs and Notts met for the first time in a League Division One game since April 1926. The venue was Meadow Lane, the score 2-2 and Garth Crooks netted both goals for Spurs in front of 15,550 fans. Spurs won the return game 3-1 and the following season they saw off the Magpies to the tune of 4-0 at White Hart Lane only to lose 3-0 by the River Trent.

When Spurs drew 0-0 at Meadow Lane in February 1984 the attendance was 7,943. This was the lowest in League competition for a Spurs game (home or away) for 18 years.

Ten years later, in October 1994, Spurs crashed out of the League Cup in the 3rd round at Meadow Lane, beaten 3-0 by the Magpies. The dismissal of the Romanian international Ilie Dumitrescu didn't help matters!

Players with both clubs include: Peter Beadle, Stuart Beavon, John Brearley, Roy Brown, Walter Bull, Archie Burgon, Colin Calderwood, Jimmy Cantrell, Darren Caskey, Herbert Chapman, John Chiedozie, Ray Clemence (Notts amateur), Willie Davies, Chris Fairclough, Alex Glen, Frank Grice, Willie Hall, Ian Hendon, Percy Humphreys, Colin Lyman, Tom Meads, Bobby Mimms, Jock Montgomery, Shaun Murray (Spurs reserve), Jimmy Reid, Matt Reilly, Bert Ringrose, Mark Robson, Pat Van den Hauwe, Alf Warner, Bob Wilkie (Amateur), John Wilkinson.

Wartime guests (either with one or both clubs): Ted Bassett, Ron Burgess, Harry Brown, Ken Burditt, Tommy Clay, Harry Jackson, Walter Tattersall.

Also associated: Steve Hodge (Spurs player, County Academy Coach), Vic Potts (Spurs reserve & scout, County trainer), Percy Smith (manager of both clubs).

NUMBERING OF PLAYERS

Spurs players first wore numbers on the back of their shirts for a competitive game in January 1939 - for the 3rd round FA Cup-tie against Watford. Prior to that the second XI, at times, had donned numbered jerseys.

In August 1932 Spurs had suggested that numbers should be sewn on the back of players' shirts for all games. It was agreed in principal, but only for FA Cup ties. The first time spectators were able to identify players by a number was in the 1933 FA Cup Final when the Everton and Manchester City stars wore numbers 1-22.

NUNHEAD

Spurs playing record against Nunhead

Competition	P	W	D	L	F	A
Other Cups	2	2	0	0	11	1

Spurs beat Nunhead 9-0 at home in the 1st round of the London FA Charity Cup in Sept 1909. A crowd of around 1,000 saw Bob Steel score four of the goals including a penalty. Bert Middlemiss netted a hat-trick while Billy Minter claimed the other two.

O'CALLAGHAN, EUGENE

Welsh international inside-forward Taffy O'Callaghan was adored by the White Hart Lane faithful. A real gutsy player, he was born in Ebbw Vale, Monmouthshire on 6 October 1906, the son of an Irish soldier who served in South Wales. Taffy O'Callaghan represented Wales at Schoolboy level and assisted Victoria United and Ebbw Vale Corries as well as having unsuccessful; trials with Newcastle United before joining Spurs as an amateur in September 1924, turning professional two years later after 'breaking in' spells with Barnet and Northfleet. He made his League debut against one of the clubs that had rejected him - Everton - and after that game one reporter described him as "An individual and original player." Another wrote: "O'Callaghan is extraordinary fast in his stride. He darts through the middle and gets into position to shoot before anyone realises the danger."

He certainly did well at White Hart Lane and, indeed, with Wales, winning 11 caps (all gained with Spurs) between 1929 and 1935. He scored three international goals.

On leaving Spurs in March 1935 O'Callaghan joined Leicester City. From Filbert Street he moved to Fulham on October 1937 and played for Aldershot, Brentford and Spurs during the War before returning to Fulham as a coach after the hostilities.

His record with Spurs was superb - 121 goals scored in an overall total of 313 first team games. O'Callaghan - always a jovial character and a great influence in the dressing room - was still employed by Fulham when he died on 4 July 1956.

OFK BELGRADE

Spurs playing record against the Yugoslavian club

Competition	P	W	D	L	F	A
European Cup	2	2	0	0	5	2

Spurs played the Yugoslavian side in the semi-final of the 1962-63

THE OFFICIAL ENCYCLOPAEDIA OF TOTTENHAM HOTSPUR F.C.

176

European Cup-winners Cup competition - and won both legs to clinch their place in the Final against Atletico Madrid.

Playing the first game in Belgrade on 24 April in front 45,000 fans, Spurs gained a 2-1 advantage with goals by John White and Terry Dyson. And then on May Day they confirmed their supremacy with a 3-1 win at White Hart Lane. Almost 60,000 spectators cheered goals by Dave Mackay, Cliff Jones and Bobby Smith as Spurs went marching on!

OFFSIDE LAW

The current offside law was introduced for the 1925-26 season and Spurs started off with a hard-earned 1-0 win at Arsenal, Jimmy Dimmock scoring the goal in front of 53,183 spectators. This game saw the former Spurs player Herbert Chapman take charge of the Gunners for the first time in a League match.

In their second match Spurs netted three times at Sheffield United. In fact the new law hardly made any difference to Spurs' scoring ability - they managed only 66 goals that season in 42 League games.

O'HAGAN, CHARLES

An inside-forward from County Derry, Charlie O'Hagan joined Spurs from Everton in May 1904. He scored seven goals for the club in 36 games before transferring to Middlesbrough in July 1906. O'Hagan, an Irish international (capped five times whilst with Spurs) later assisted Aberdeen and Greenock Morton before taking over as manager of Norwich City (July 1920-January 1921). He ended up coaching in Germany.

OLD WESTMINSTERS

Spurs playing record against 'OW'

Competition	P	W	D	L	F	A
London Senior Cup	2	0	1	1	7	8

Old Westminsters knocked Spurs out of the London Charity Cup in 1894-95 with a 5-4 replay victory in the second round. Spurs had forced a 3-3 away draw before losing on their own patch.

OLDHAM ATHLETIC

Spurs playing record against 't' Latics':

Competition	P	W	D	L	F	A
Premiership	4	3	0	1	12	3
Football League	32	19	3	10	66	38
FA Cup	4	4	0	0	14	2
Totals	40	26	3	11	92	43

The first Spurs v. Latics League game took place on Christmas Day 1908 (Division 2) and a crowd of 24,000 at Boundary Park saw the Lancashire side win 1-0 and so end Spurs' run of six straight victories.

The Spurs v. Latics League game at White Hart Lane in January 1911 was abandoned at half-time through fog. The scores were level at 1-1 at the time and the 'replay' saw Spurs win 2-0.

Spurs scored a total of 10 goals in the two League clashes with the Latics in 1920-21, winning 5-1 at home and 5-2 away. Jimmy Seed netted twice in each game.

Tommy Clay cracked home two penalties when Spurs beat the Latics 3-0 at White Hart Lane in January 1923.

On 25 August 1928, England international centre-forward Tom Roberts made his debut for Spurs following his arrival from Preston and celebrated by scoring twice in a 4-1 home win over the Latics in Spurs' first Second Division game for eight years.

In October 1977 Spurs beat the Latics 5-1 at White Hart Lane. This was the first League meeting between the two clubs for more than 44 years - since February 1933 when, by coincidence, Spurs had also won 5-1, this time at Boundary Park.

Spurs completed a Premiership double over the Latics in 1993-94, winning 5-0 at home (their best victory that season) and 2-0 away. Players with both clubs include: Harry Erentz, Bob Hewitson, John McTavish, Peter Taylor, Simon Webster.

Wartime guests (with either one or both clubs): Jack Hall, Joey Walters

OLD CARTHUSIANS

Spurs' playing record against Old Carthusians:

Competition	P	W	D	L	F	A
Amateur Cup	1	0	0	1	0	5

This encounter with the Old Carthusians was the Division Final of the 1894-95 FA Amateur Cup competition, played at Tottenham on 16 March. Spurs, fielding their strongest side, were well and truly walloped!

OLD ETONIANS

Spurs' playing record against the OE's:

Competition	P	W	D	L	F	A
London S/Cup	1	0	0	1	2	8

Spurs crashed out of the 1888-89 London Senior Cup in the opening round, beaten 8-2 at home by the Old Etonians. Bobby Buckle and Jack Purdie saved a whitewash by scoring consolation goals.

1990's action against Oldham Athletic

OLD HARROVIANS
Spurs' playing record against the Amateur club:

Competition	P	W	D	L	F	A
Amateur Cup	1	1	0	0	7	0

This Spurs romp took place in the first qualifying round of the FA Amateur Cup competition in October 1894. Seven different players featured on the scoresheet among them all five forwards.

OLD ST STEPHENS
Spurs playing record against OSS:

Competition	P	W	D	L	F	A
FA Cup	2	2	0	0	6	1
Southern Alliance	2	1	0	1	4	2
Middlesex Cup	1	1	0	0	4	2
Summary	5	4	0	1	14	5

Less than 1,000 spectators saw Spurs defeat OSS 4-2 away in the 1st round of the Middlesex Senior Cup in January 1890.

Spurs' best win of the four recorded over OSS was their 4-0 home success in the 1st qualifying round of the FA Cup in December 1896. Bob 'Topsy' Clements scored two of the goals.

OLYMPIAKOS PIRAEUS
Spurs playing record against the Greek side

Competition	P	W	D	L	F	A
UEFA Cup	2	1	0	1	4	1

A 1972-73 second round UEFA Cup-tie against the Greek side Olympiakos Piraeus was virtually over after the first leg which resulted in a resounding 4-0 win for Spurs in front of 27,815 fans at White Hart Lane on 25 October, Jimmy Pearce (2), Martin Chivers and Ralph Coates the scorers.

The return clash a fortnight later in Greece saw Spurs beaten 1-0 in front of 35,000 fans, but there was never a doubt who would go through to the next round!

OLYMPIQUE LYONNAIS
Spurs playing record against the French club

Competition	P	W	D	L	F	A
ECW Cup	2	1	0	1	4	4

Spurs were eliminated from the European Cup-winners Cup by the French club in the 2nd round of the 1967-68 competition.

After having Alan Mullery sent-off (with Lyon's Andre Guy) Spurs lost the away leg 1-0 in front of almost 11,000 fans on 29 November. But they managed to scramble a narrow 4-3 home victory a fortnight later only to lose the tie on the away goals rule after the aggregate score had finished level at 4-4. Jimmy Greaves (2, one penalty), Alan Gilzean and Cliff Jones scored in the game at White Hart Lane which attracted 41,895 fans.

ONES THAT GOT AWAY
Here are some of the many players who started their respective footballing career with Spurs but were then either released, sold or given away and later achieved excellent records with other clubs (listed in A-Z order):

● Striker Peter Beadle cost Spurs £300,000 from Gillingham in 1992. He never played for the first XI at competitive level but over the next nine years scored over 60 goals, including 42 in 125 outings for Bristol Rovers.

● Terry Boyle, an England Youth international defender with Spurs, was released by the club in 1978 and over the next 12 years amassed well over 400 appearances while playing for Crystal Palace, Wimbledon, Bristol City, Newport County and Swansea City in that order.

● Inside-forward Ivor Broadis was capped 14 times by England

and scored 136 goals in 442 League appearances for four English clubs (Carlisle United, Sunderland, Manchester City and Newcastle United) after being released by Spurs in 1946.

● Midfielder Ray Bunkell was capped by England at Youth team level during his time with Spurs. He left the club in 1971 and went on to make over 200 League and Cup appearances with Swindon Town and Colchester United.

● Wayne Cegielski was an FA Youth Cup winner with Spurs in 1974 but was not retained by the club after returning from a loan spell with Northampton Town. He later played for Wrexham, FC Schalke 04 in the Bundesliga, Port Vale and Hereford United and made 276 League appearances, gaining two Welsh Under-21 caps.

● Jamie Clapham made one 'sub' appearance for Spurs. At the end of the 2000-01 season he had taken his appearance-tally to almost 200, having served also with Bristol Rovers and Leyton Orient (on loan) and Ipswich Town.

● Midfielder Ian Crook made only 24 first-class appearances for Spurs but after leaving the club in 1986, he made well over 350 for Norwich City up to 1997.

● Ian Culverhouse made just two appearances for Spurs before moving to Norwich City in 1985. Over the next 15 years he played in almost 550 games for the Canaries, Swindon Town and Brighton & Hove Albion.

● Given away by Spurs in 1993, goalkeeper Kevin Dearden reached the milestone of 400 senior appearances in 2001 as a Wrexham player, having assisted, among others, Cambridge Utd, Birmingham City, Oxford, Swindon Town and Peterborough.

● Kerry Dixon, a Youth team player at White Hart Lane, was released in 1978 and joined Dunstable Town from where he switched to Reading for £25,000 in May 1980 after scoring 52 goals for the non-League club that season. He netted 37 times in 152 outings for the Royals before transferring to Chelsea for £150,000 in August 1983. His 28 goals helped the Blues win promotion to the First Division in his first season at Stamford Bridge and the following term he rattled in another 36 goals to finish up as top-scorer in the Football League. The next Chelsea player to score over 20 goals in a season was Jimmy Floyd Hasselbaink in 2000-01. Dixon continued to annoy defenders and goalkeepers alike and when he moved from the Bridge to Southampton in 1992 he had netted 191 times in 142 League and Cup games for the Blues and had won eight caps for England, earning Reading an extra £25,000 by doing so! After leaving the Saints he assisted Luton Town and Millwall before having a brief spell as player-manager of Doncaster Rovers, dropping down the ladder to sign for Boreham Wood in the Rymans Isthmian League. He later managed Letchworth of the Minerva Spartan League (2000-01). Dixon's full playing record at senior level (club and country) was excellent - 665 appearances and 270 goals.

● Dicky Dowsett scored in his only game for Spurs but after leaving White Hart Lane in 1955 he went on to make over 250 appearances and netted more than 100 goals while playing for Southend, Southampton, Bournemouth and Crystal Palace.

● Striker Mike Flanagan was a junior and FA Youth Cup winner with Spurs but was not taken on as a full-time professional at White Hart Lane. He joined Charlton Athletic in August 1971 and over the next 16 years scored in excess of 150 goals in more than 550 League and Cup games for the Addicks, Crystal Palace, QPR and Cambridge United.

● Quinton Fortune, left Spurs as a teenager because of work permit problems, he has since gained almost 30 full caps for his native South Africa, played for Atletico Madrid and represented Manchester United in the Premiership and Champions League.

● Warren Hackett was a Spurs junior who left White Hart Lane in 1990 after failing to get a senior game for the club. Over the next ten years he made over 300 appearances at senior level while serving with Leyton Orient, Doncaster Rovers, Mansfield Town and Barnet.

● Ian Hendon, an England Youth and Under-21 international, had only seven first-class outings for Spurs before leaving the club in 1992. Over the next nine years he took his career appearance-tally to almost 400 while serving with Portsmouth, Leyton Orient, Barnsley, Birmingham City, Notts County and Northampton Town.

● Phil Holder made 19 first-class appearacbnes for Spurs (ten as a 'sub') before moving to Crystal Palace in 1975. Over the next 15 years (with the Eagles and Bournemouth) he added over 150 more to his tally.

● Scott Houghton played in 14 senior games for Spurs (all as a substitute) before moving to Luton Town in 1993 (after loan spells with Ipswich, Gillingham and Charlton). In 2001 he had taken his career appearance tally to well past the 350 mark having also assisted Walsall, Peterborough and Southend United.

● Wing-half or inside-forward Bob Iverson joined Spurs in August 1932 but failed to make the required breakthrough. After spells with Northfleet, Ramsgate Press Wanderers, Lincoln City and Wolverhampton Wanderers, he signed for Aston Villa in December 1936. Over the next 12 years he appeared in 326 League, FA Cup and Wartime games scored 122 goals for the Birmingham club. He also guested for Birmingham, Bournemouth, Leicester, Northampton, Notts County and Nottingham Forest. Iverson holds the record for scoring the fastest goal ever by a Villa player - netting after 9.3 seconds of a League game v. Charlton in December 1938.

● Goalkeeper Mark Kendall made 36 League and Cup appearances for Spurs before leaving to join Newport County in 1980. Over the next 13 years he also starred for Wolverhampton Wanderers, Swansea City and Burnley and took his overall appearances past the 600 mark - and he played at Wembley.

● Goalkeeper Terry Lee had just one League game for Spurs (at Newcastle in 1974). He later played more than 100 matches for Torquay United and he also served with Newport County.

● David McDonald, an Irish Youth international, left Spurs in 1993 and over the next nine years accumulated more than 250 senior appearances while assisting Gillingham, Bradford City, Reading, Peterborough United and Barnet.

● Between 1989 and 2001, Billy Manuel (no games for Spurs before being released) made well over 200 playing for Gillingham (two spells), Brentford, Peterborough (two spells) and Barnet.

● Jeff Minton made only three first-class appeareances for Spurs before leaving in 1994. Over the next seven years he amassed over 250 while assisting Brighton & Hove Albion and Port Vale.

● John Moncur made only 24 first-class appearances for Spurs. On leaving White Hart Lane in 1992 (after spells with Doncaster, Cambridge United, Portsmouth and Brentford) he carried on with Swindon Town and West Ham, taking his career tally to almost 300 by May 2001.

● Shaun Murray was a junior, trainee and England Youth international while with Spurs (1986-88) but never played in the first team. He went on to make over 300 appearances while serving with Portsmouth, Scarborough, Bradford City and Notts County (to 2001).

● Tim O'Shea was never given a chance with Spurs despite winning Northern Ireland Youth and Under-21 honours. He left the club in 1986 and went on to make almost 150 appearances while serving with Newport County, Leyton Orient and Gillingham, before moving to Hong Kong in 1992.

● John Polston played in 25 first-class games for Spurs at the start of his career. He left the club for Norwich City for £250,000 in 1990 and over the next eleven years took his overall appearance-tally to well past the 300 mark while also assisting Reading.

● Derek Possee, transferred by Spurs to Millwall in 1967, made only 19 League appearances (4 goals) during his time at White Hart Lane. He went on to net 87 times in 245 outings for the Lions and held the club's scoring record until beaten by Teddy Sheringham's tally of 111. Possee also hit a further 24 goals in 133 outings while playing for Crystal Palace and Leyton Orient.

● Vic Potts, Birmingham-born, joined Spurs from Metro Welfare FC as an amateur in August 1933, became a part-time professional August 1936 and moved to Doncaster Rovers for £3,000 in August 1938 without ever getting a game for Spurs. He played in over 200 games as a guest for Aston Villa during the War and joined the Midland club permanently in August 1945. Potts retired in May 1949 having appeared in 72 League and FA Cup games after the hostilities. He also served as coach/trainer with both Notts County and Walsall before being re-employed by Spurs as scout.

● Jamie Redknapp, a junior player at White Hart Lane, was offered terms by the club but he declined and opted to join his father (Harry) at AFC Bournemouth in June 1990. He made only 16 League appearances for the Cherries before moving to Liverpool for £350,000 in January 1991. Over the next ten years, injuries apart, he made almost 300 senior appearances for the Merseyside club, winning a League Cup medal in 1995 and earning England recognition at full, 'B' and Under-21 status, having earlier represented his country at both Schoolboy and Youth team levels. Son of the former Bournemouth and West Ham winger and Hammers' manager Harry Redknapp, Jamie is married to the pop star, Louise.

● Striker Martin Robinson scored twice for Spurs in six League games. He left White Hart Lane in 1978 and went on to claim over 100 goals in more than 400 games before joining Enfield in 1989.

● Northern Ireland international Steve Robinson, who left Spurs on a free transfer to Bournemouth in 1994 with only two Premiership games under his belt, made over 300 appearances for the Cherries over the next seven seasons.

● Mark Robson, signed by Spurs from Exeter in 1987 for £50,000 (after just 30 outings for the Devon club) failed to make headway at White Hart Lane. But after leaving the club in 1992, he did exceedingly well and when the 2000-01 season ended his career number of appearances at club level stood at more than 300.

● Technically Steve Sedgley was 'one that got away' from Spurs. He was a Schoolboy trialist and junior player at the club before joining Coventry City as an apprentice 1985. He made over 100 appearances for the Sky Blues before moving back to White Hart Lane in 1989 for a fee of £750,000!

● Spurs allowed midfielder Neil Smith to leave White Hart Lane for Gillingham in a £40,000 deal in 1991 without ever handing him a senior outing. He has since amassed in excess of 400 senior appearances while also assisting Fulham and Reading.

● Graeme Souness made just one substitute appearance for Spurs (against Keflavik in the UEFA Cup in 1971). He then joined Middlesbrough for just £32,000 in 1973 (after a summer spell with Montreal Olympic) thereafter serving with Liverpool, Sampdoria and Glasgow Rangers as well as representing Scotland in 54 full internationals. Souness appeared in some 600 competitive games after leaving White Hart Lane, winning medals galore!

● Full-back Brian Statham made 27 appearances for Spurs up to 1992. Over the next seven years he took that tally to 268, mainly as a Brentford player.

● Defender Micky Stead made 15 League appearances for Spurs before moving to Southend Utd in in 1978 after a loan spell with

Swansea. He played in 326 competitive games for the Shrimpers and then added 100 more to his tally with Doncaster Rovers.

● Mark Stimson left White Hart Lane in 1989 with only 30 senior appearances under his belt, two for Spurs, 10 with Leyton Orient and 18 with Gillingham, serving the latter two clubs as a loanee. Making great progress, he retired from top-level action in 1999 with almost 250 first-class games under his belt.

● Peter Taylor was on Spurs' books as a junior. He then played well over 200 games for Southend and Crystal Palace and won England honours before 'rejoining' Spurs for £400,000 in 1978.

● Andy Turner -23 appearances for Spurs between 1992 and 1996 - went on to amass a further 24 games for Spurs and over 100 games for other clubs up to 2001.Over the next five years which included spells with Southend, Portsmouth, Crystal Palace, Wolves, Rotherham United, Wycombe, Doncaster, Huddersfield (loan).

● Inside-forward Dennis Uphill scored twice in six First Division games for Spurs before moving to Reading in 1953. Over the next ten years, when he also played for Covntry City, Mansfield, Watford and Crystal Palace, he netted a further 150 goals in more than 350 League and Cup appearances.

● Versatile defender Steve Walford played in just two League matches for Spurs (one as a sub) before transferring to Arsenal in 1977. He went on to make a further 400 appearances while also assisting Norwich City, West Ham United, Huddersfield Town, West Bromwich Albion, Gillingham, Lai Sung (Hong Kong), Wycombe Wanderers and Wealdstone plus a spell in Turkey.

● Hackney-born defender Des Walker was a junior at White Hart Lane but was not retained by Spurs. He moved north to Nottingham Forest in 1981 and two years later signed professional forms. He went on to appear in 345 first-class games for the East Midland club, starring in two League Cup and two Simod Cup winning sides, as well as gaining the first of his 59 full England caps while also collecting seven at Under-21 level. He moved from Forest to Sampdoria for £1.5 million in 1992 and returned to England to sign for Sheffield Wednesday for £2.7 million in July 1993. Over the last eight years he amassed more than 325 senior appearances for the Owls. It was Walker's unlucky own-goal that won Spurs the FA Cup in 1991.

● Having played in only three First Division games for Spurs in the early 1980s, versatile defender Simon Webster went on to appear in a further 373 competitive matches for Barnet, Exeter City, Norwich City, Huddersfield Town, Sheffield United, Charlton Athletic, West Ham United, Oldham Athletic and Derby County before entering non-League football in 1996.

● Attacking midfielder Keith Weller netted one goal in his 21 League games for Spurs. He left White Hart Lane in 1967 and over the next 15 years played for Millwall, Chelsea, Leicester City, the New England Teamen, Fort Lauderdale Strikers and Tacoma Stars, accumulating well over 500 senior appearances and scoring more than 120 goals. He was also capped four times by England.

O'REILLY, GARY MILLS

A former Schools javelin champion, Gary O'Reilly developed into a pretty useful defender, making 73 first team appearances for Spurs (45 in the Football League).

A former England Schoolboy international who also played for the Republic of Ireland at Youth team level, he joined the club as a professional from Grays Athletic in September 1979 and left for Brighton & Hove Albion in a £35,000 deal in August 1984. He later assisted Crystal Palace and Birmingham City (on loan) before

returning to the Goldstone Ground in 1991, ending his League career the following year.

O'Reilly helped Palace gain promotion to the First Division in 1989 and appeared in the FA Cup Final the following year. He was born in Isleworth, Middlesex on 21 March 1961.

OSBORNE, FRANK RAYMOND

Born in Wynberg, South Africa on 14 October 1896, utility forward Frank Osborne attended the Gymnasium School in Durban before 'emigrating' to England to sign for played for Netley FC in 1911. He then assisted Bromley before signing as a professional for Fulham in November 1921, scoring on his League debut against Sheffield United.

He began as a centre-forward, but was converted into a right-winger which better suited his graceful style and rather frail frame.

He was the first Fulham player ever to be capped by England, lining up against Ireland at West Bromwich in 1922. After netting 18 goals in 70 games for the Cottagers (and adding a second cap to his collection) Osborne was transferred to Spurs for £1,500 in January 1924. He did very well at White Hart Lane, winning two more England caps and claiming 87 more goals in 228 first team games for the club before switching to Southampton for just £450 in June 1931. He retired as a player in 1933 to work as a sales representative for Fulham chairman John Dean's blinds company. In March 1935 he accepted an invitation from his employer to join the Board of Directors at Craven Cottage. This marked thee next phase of his Fulham career which was to last almost 30 years as he served the club as team, general and secretary-manager from October 1948 to October 1964 (Fulham's longest-serving manager). He actually stepped down from the board to take over from Jack Peart as team manager at the Cottage - receiving the FA's permission to do so! Osborne died in Epsom, Surrey on 8 March 1988.

OSGOOD, KEITH

England Youth international defender Keith Osgood played in 127 League and Cup games for Spurs (14 goals scored) before transferring to Coventry City for £125,000 in January 1978.

Born in Isleworth, Middlesex on 8 May 11955, he represeneted London and England Schools prior to joining Spurs as an apprentice in June 1971, turning professional twelve months later. He made his League debut as a substitute at Newcastle in May 1974. After his brief stay at Highfield Road, Osgood switched to Derby County (October 1979) and thereafter had spells with Leyton Orient, Helsinki FC (Finland), Cambridge United, Burton Albion and Stapenhill before retiring in 1988.

OVERSEAS MATCHES & TOURS

Since undertaking their first major tour overseas in May 1905 (when they visited the Austro-Hungarian Empire) Spurs have continued to travel abroad on a regular basis, visiting many different countries in the process.

Listed here are some of the tours made:

● That first tour in 1905 comprised seven matches including two against Everton. Five were won, the best victory being 12-1 against Testgyakorborora (in Budapest). Vivian Woodward scored four goals and Charlie 'O'Hagan three.

● In June 1909, a trip to Argentina and Uruguay took in seven matches (two more v. Everton). Spurs won five, their best victory coming against Rosario by 9-0.

● Spurs registered six wins in six matches in Germany in May 1911, running up a goal-ratio of 33-4. Their biggest win as 8-1 v. Wacker FC in Leipzig.

● A European tour in May 1911 saw Spurs visit Austria, Belgium, Germany and Hungary. They played eight matches and won four.

● A return visit to Germany was made in 1914 when Spurs also played games in Italy and Switzerland. They fulfilled nine fixtures in all and recorded two 6-0 wins against Bayern Munich and FC Zurich whilst Hannover were beaten 6-3.

● In May 1925 a tour to Switzerland brought seven wins with a best of 8-1 over La Chaux de Fonds. Lausanne were also defeated 6-1 on this trip when both Charlie Handley and Jimmy Dimmock scored hat-tricks.

● In May 1928 Spurs won four games in Holland, including a 5-2 success over the Dutch Olympic team in Amsterdam.

● A trip to Malta in May 1929 saw Spurs win all their six matches, including victories over Sliema Wanderers 7-1, the British Army 5-1 and a Pick of Malta XI also 5-1.

● In May 1932 Spurs made the first of four short tours of the Channel Islands (the others followed in 1933, 1935 and 1948). They remained unbeaten on each of these trips and won all nine matches, including a healthy 9-0 triumph over Jersey in 1932 (when George Hunt scored 6) and three good ones over Guernsey, 8-0 in 1933, 5-0 in 1935 and 7-0 in 1948.

● In the summer of 1947 (to recover from the arctic winter in the U.K) Spurs won two and lost two of four tour games in France and three years later they registered four victories and suffered one defeat while touring Belgium, France and Germany.

● An undefeated tour to Denmark in May 1951 was followed by a very successful tour of North America (May 1952) when all 10 matches were won. Spurs secured no fewer than 85 goals in the process as they ran up scores of 7-0 v. Toronto & District; a club record 18-1 over hapless Saskatchewan when Sid McClellan netted a triple-hat-trick (nine goals), 9-2 and 8-2 in games against British Columbia FA, 7-0 versus the Victoria & District FA side (Eddie Baily netted four times), 11-0 v. the Alberta FA side, 5-0 over Manitoba 5-0 and 8-0 v. the Quebec FA XI as well as registering two impressive wins over Manchester United, 5-0 in Toronto and 7-1 in New York. Les Bennett top-scored with 20 goals; Len Duquemin and McClellan both netted 15 and Sonny Walters and Eddie Baily notched nine and eight respectively.

● In April/May 1954 Spurs suffered three defeats and a draw on tour in Austria and Germany. The following year they returned to Austria and also visited France and Hungary, losing three of their five matches, including a 6-2 reverse against FC Austria in Vienna.

● A second tour was made to North America in May/June 1957 and on this occasion Spurs suffered two defeats - 2-0 v. British Columbia and 2-0 v. Celtic (in Montreal). They won their seven other games as follows.... 8-1 against Essex City All Stars, 7-0 v. Ontario All Stars, 6-3 v. Athletic All Stars, 12-0 v. Manitoba All Stars 12-0 (Alf Stokes scored five goals) and three triumphs over Celtic - 4-3 in New York, 6-3 in Vancouver and 3-1 in Winnepeg.

● Spurs went behind the Iron Curtain for the first time in May 1959 where they defeated Torpedo Moscow 1-0 and Dynamo Kiev 2-1 but lost 1-3 to a CCCP Select XI in Leningrad.

● After a visit to Holland in 1961, Spurs beat the South African national team 3-1 in Johannesburg when they played and won all three games in that country in 1963.

● The first of three tours to Israel took place in 1962 (the others followed in 1965 and 1972) and in August 1965 Spurs took part in the Costa Del Sol tournament in sunny Spain. They beat Valencia 2-1 in the semi-final and Standard Liege 1-0 in the Final.

● Bermuda and the Americas were visited in May/June 1966. Spurs met Celtic three times in the course of their 'summer break' (lost two, drew one) and they also defeated Bayern Munich 3-0 in Detroit and drew 1-1 in Chicago.

● A second entry into the Costa Del Sol tourney followed in August 1966 and again Spurs brought home the trophy after beating Malaga CD 2-1 in the semi-final and Benfica 2-1 in the Final.

● After their FA Cup success at Wembley, Spurs recorded three wins from three starts on tour in Switzerland in May/June 1967.

● One year later Spurs played five matches in Greece and Cyprus, winning four of them including a 7-1 romp over AEL in Limassol and a 3-0 victory over a Cypriot international XI in Nicosia.

● When visiting North America in May/June 1969, Spurs beat West Ham 4-3 and drew 2-2 with Aston Villa before playing Fiorentina and Glasgow Rangers for the Toronto Cup losing 3-0 to the Italian club but beating Rangers 4-3 with a hat-trick by Jimmy Greaves.

● After a trip to Malta in May 1970, three months later Spurs played in the Palma de Mallorca tournament but lost both matches, 1-0 to Cologne and 1-0 to Real Madrid.

● Spurs trekked over to Japan for the first time in May 1971. There they recorded three wins: 6-0, 7-2 and 3-0, the last two in Tokyo.

● In June 1974 the island of Mauritius welcomed Spurs where three games were played, all won over selected teams. Alan Gilzean scored seven goals.

● After visiting Holland and West Germany in July 1975, Spurs undertook one of the longest journeys ever made by a British club side when they toured Canada, Fiji, New Zealand and Australia in April/May 1976. It was hot, mighty hot at times! They started off with a 1-0 win in Canada over the Toronto Metros

Croatia before beating a Fijian Select XI 4-0 in Lautoka. An Auckland XI (5-3) and a Wellington XI (3-2) were both defeated in New Zealand before Spurs won five games in Australia against Victoria State 3-1 (in Victoria) Northern New South Wales 5-1 (in Newcastle), the Australian National XI 3-2 (in Sydney), South Australia 5-2 (in Adelaide) and Western Australia 4-0 (in Perth). Martin Chivers scored a hat-trick in the last game.

● After visiting West Germany in June 1976, Spurs won two games in Norway in May 1977 and then competed in the Nolia Cup in Sweden in August 1977. After beating Royale Union 2-0 in the semi-final they defeated Leicester City 2-1 in the Final to win another trophy!

● After a short tour to Syria in 1978, Spurs visited Norway and Sweden in May 1978 and at the end of the 1978-79 season they went off to play in Kuwait, Malaysia, Japan and Bermuda. They beat Dundee United 2-0 in the Final of the Tokyo Cup in Japan after earlier accounting for Indonesia 6-0, the Japanese 'A' team 2-0 and San Lorenzo 5-3 on penalties (after a 3-3 draw) as well as drawing with Fiorentina 1-1 in Group 'A' matches.

● Two defeats were suffered on tour in Austria in May 1980 and a year later, after FA Cup glory over Manchester City, Spurs visited Bahrain and Kuwait in May and then recorded two wins in Turkey the following month, including a 5-1 romp over Fenerbahce.

● Spurs entered the Amsterdam '707' Tournament in August 1982. They were defeated 3-2 by Ajax and then lost 3-1 on penalties to FC Cologne (after a 0-0 draw) to finish in 4th place.

● In Swaziland in June 1983, Spurs played Manchester United twice in the Royal Swazi Hotel Tournament. They lost 2-1 and won 2-0 before beating the Reds 3-2 on penalties to clinch the trophy.

● As holders of the 'Swazi Hotel' Cup, Spurs competed in the tournament again in 1984 and this time lost to Liverpool after going down 5-2 and drawing 1-1 in their two scheduled matches.

● A month after playing in Swaziland, Spurs visited Norway and Sweden winning three matches including a confident 9-0 triumph over Jordal Blink. Mario Kempes, the Argentina World Cup winner from 1978, was on trial for Spurs in this game and scored a hat-trick!

● Hong Kong and Australia were Spurs' next port of calls - visited in May 1985. After beating Seiko FC 4-0 in Hong Kong, Spurs then competed in the $200,000 tournament in Australia where they lost 1-0 to the Australian Soccer Federation team in Melbourne, went down 2-0 to Udinese in Sydney and drew 1-1 with Vasco da Gama in Adelaide. They beat Udinese 4-1 in Melbourne to decide the 3rd and 4th places.

● Spurs played in Finland and Sweden in July 1987 recording three wins and two defeats. Shaun Close scored four goals in a 7-2 win over Lansi Udenman District XI in Karjan and Nico Claesen netted twice when Marsta IK were beaten 5-0 in Marsta.

● A further visit to Sweden in July 1988 produced two wins, over Trelleborgs FF 3-1 and Vederslov/Danningelanda 4-1 (Paul Walsh hat-trick) and a 1-1 draw with GAIS.

● On tour to Norway in August 1990, Spurs registered 1-0 victories over Brann and Sognal and drew 1-1 with Viking.

● At the end of that 1990-91 season (in June) the team played three games in the Kirin Cup in Japan. They played a 0-0 draw with South American side Vasco Da Gama in Kobe, beat a Thailand National XI 2-1 in Nagoya but lost 4-0 to the Japanese National XI in front of 45,000 fans in Tokyo.

● A month after returning to England Spurs quickly transferred to Ireland (July 1991) where they won three matches against Sligo Rovers 4-0, Drogheda United 2-0 and Shelbourne 3-1. Then soon afterwards (mid-August) Spurs went to Italy to play in the Nicola Ceravolo Memorial Tournament in Catanzaro. They lost 2-0 to AC Messina, but beat the host side US Cantanzaro 1-0 with a rare Gudni Bergsson goal.

● In July 1993 Spurs returned for a pre-season tour of Norway. They fulfilled three matches, beating Team Norrd Trondelag 3-1 and Team Porsgrunn 5-4 (thanks mainly to a Teddy Sheringham hat-trick) and drew 0-0 with Lyn Oslo (which was a testimonial match for Tom Sundby).

● Spurs played three games in the Far East in May 1995. They beat Kitchee/Eastern XI 7-2 and Guangzhou 2-1 and drew 1-1 with Singapore Lions.

● Two months later, in preparation for the new season (July 1995) Spurs visited Denmark and Sweden where they played four games. They lost the first two, 3-1 to Silkeborg and 2-1 to Halmstads BK, beat Gothenburg 2-0 but then slumped to a third defeat at the hands of IFK Hasslehom 3-1.

● In July 1996, Spurs recorded a win, 2-0 v. Ham-Kam, suffered a 3-1 defeat against Odd Grenland and drew 0-0 with Raufos on a pre-season tour to Norway.

● And in July 1997 four pre-season friendly matches were played in Norway, against Ski IL (lost 2-3), Farberg IL (won 2-0), Fredrikstad FK (drew 0-0) and Rosenborg BK (lost 0-2).

● After losing to Grasshopper-Club Zurich in Switzerland 3-1 and Brondby IF in Denmark 3-0, Spurs then spent a week away in Holland prior to the start of the 1998-99 season. Here they beat EV & AC De Tubanters 6-1 in front of 850 fans and drew 1-1 with Feyenoord before a crowd of almost 31,000.

● Spurs visited Sweden for their pre-season tour in July 1999. Here they played three games, drawing 1-1 with IF Elfsborg (at Varberg), beat Lysekils FF 7-1 and defeated GAIS 3-0. Steffen Iversen scored a hat-trick in each of the last two matches.

● Three games were played on tour to Sweden and Finland in July 2000 and Spurs did well, winning all three friendlies and scoring 14 goals in the process. They defeated Skelleftea AIK 4-0, Tervarit 4-0 and Bodens BK 6-0. Steffen Iversen netted twice in each game, while strike partner Chris Armstrong scored once in each match.

Spurs have now played football matches in many different countries, including: Argentina, Australia, Austria, Bahrain, Belgium, Bermuda, Canada, Channel Islands (Guernsey & Jersey), Czechoslovakia, Denmark, Egypt, Fiji, Finland, France, Germany (East & West), Greece, Holland, Hong Kong, Hungary, Iceland,

Israel, Italy, Japan, Kuwait, Malaysia, Malta, Mauritius, Mexico, Moldova, Morocco, New Zealand, Northern Ireland, Norway, Poland, Portugal, Republic of Ireland, Romania, Russia (USSR), Saudi Arabia, Scotland, Singapore, South Africa, Spain (including Mallorca), Swaziland, Sweden, Switzerland, Syria, Trinidad & Tobago, Turkey, United Arab Emirates, United States of America, Uruguay, Wales and Yugoslavia.

OXFORD UNITED (HEADINGTON UNITED)
Spurs playing record against United:

Competition	P	W	D	L	F	A
Football League	6	4	2	0	16	5
FA Cup	3	2	1	0	7	4
Summary	9	6	3	0	23	9

The first League meeting between the clubs took place at The Manor Ground on 21 August 1985 and ended all-square at 1-1. Almost four months later (on 7 December) Spurs won the return game 5-1. Clive Allen scored twice in front of just 17,698 spectators.

Spurs completed a League double over United in 1986-87, winning 4-2 away and 3-1 at home. Clive Allen and Chris Waddle scoring in both matches.

Players with both clubs include: Milija Aleksic, Guy Butters, Kevin Dearden, Roger Gibbins (Spurs reserve), Ian Hendon, Danny Hill, David Leworthy, Tony Parks, Steve Perryman, Bill Rees, Cyril Toulouse, Ian Walker.

Wartime guest: Ken Bennett (Headington Utd), Fred Ford (also Oxford coach & scout).

P

AGE, ALBERT EDWARD
A well built, sturdy centre-half, Bert Page appeared in 88 first team games for Spurs between January 1937 (when he made his League debut v. Newcastle United) and March 1946 (his last outing against Plymouth Argyle). Born in Walthamstow on 18 March 1916, he played for Leyton before moving to White Hart Lane. During the Second World War he guested for Bradford City, Crystal Palace, Hamilton Academical, Lincoln City and West Ham United - on leaving White Hart Lane in May 1947 he joined Colchester United and later assisted Chingford.

PARKS, ANTHONY
Goalkeeper Tony Parks was the star of Spurs' 1984 UEFA Cup Final victory over RSC Anderlecht - saving two spot-kicks in the penalty shoot out - this after he had replaced Ray Clemence on merit.

Born in Hackney, East London on 28 January 1963, Parks represented Hackney and Inner London Schools before joining Spurs as an apprentice in April 1979, moving up to the professional ranks in September 1980. He made his League debut v. West Ham in 1982 - the first of 49 senior appearances for the club (he played in 89 games overall).

With Clemence to contend with initially, manager Terry Venables then recruited Bobby Mimms and at that point Parks considered his future seriously and moved to Brentford in August 1988, having previously been on loan with both Oxford United and Gillingham. Later he assisted (as player) Fulham (February 1991), West Ham United (August 1991), Stoke City (August 1992),

Falkirk (October 1992) and Blackpool (September 1996 - after 128 appearances for the Scottish club, gaining a B&Q Cup winners medal in 1994). He then assisted the following clubs as player/goalkeeping coach: Burnley (August 1997), Doncaster Rovers (on loan, February 1998), Barrow (October 1998), Scarborough (February 1999), West Bromwich Albion (late February 1999) and Halifax Town (since July 1999)..

In the year 2000, Parks passed the personal milestone of 300 senior appearances at club level.

PARTICK THISTLE
Spurs' playing record against the Thistle:

Competition	P	W	D	L	F	A
A/S Floodlit T.	2	1	0	1	4	4

Spurs played Thistle twice in the Anglo-Scottish Floodlit Tournament in season 1956-57. On 26 September, a crowd of 26,210 saw Spurs win 4-2 at White Hart Lane (Terry Medwin, Bobby Smith and Johnny Brooks 2 the scorers); two months later in the return fixture at Fir Park, Thistle gained revenge with a 2-0 victory in front of 9,000 fans.

Players with both clubs include: Tom Atherton, Billy Hay, Jakey Jackson, John McTavish, John Pearson, Reg Smith.

PASS, JAMES ERNEST
Born in Juffulpore, India in November 1883, inside-forward Jimmy Pass joined Spurs from Stockport County in 1907. He remained at White Hart Lane for one season, scoring eleven goals in 28 first-class matches. He then moved to New Brompton.

PAYNE, ERNEST GEORGE
Outside-left Ernie Payne was one of the main instigators behind Spurs' decision to become a professional football club.

Born in Fulham Broadway in 1876, he played his early football with the Old Sherbrookians before joining Fulham in the summer of 1892. He switched to Spurs in October 1893, made a scoring debut v. Polytechnic in a friendly and then proceeded to claim a further 61 goals in a total of 140 appearances for the club before retiring in April 1898.

*See Amateurs (Old Boot Story) and Professionalism.

PAYNE, GEORGE CLARK
An inside-forward from Hertfordshire (born February 1887) George Payne joined Spurs in November 1906 after representing a series of local non-League clubs. He remained at White Hart Lane until May 1909 when he signed for Crystal Palace, later assisting Sunderland, Leyton and Woolwich Arsenal. Payne scored five times in 11 senior games for Spurs. He was seriously wounded in WWI and never played again.

PEARCE, JAMES WILLIAM
Utility forward Jimmy Pearce scored 43 goals in 218 first team games for Spurs (59 as a substitute). His major League and Cup record was 193 outings and 35 goals. Pearce was also Spurs' first European substitute.

A local lad, born in Tottenham on 27 November 1947, he represented both Tottenham and England Schools before joining the apprentice ranks at White Hart Lane in May 1963, turning professional in May 1965. He made his League debut in the North London derby against Arsenal in 1968, sat on the bench for the 1971 League Cup Final but then collected a winners' medal two years later when Spurs defeated Norwich City in the same competition. He was struck down with a rare bone complaint in 1974 and was forced to retire prematurely. He attempted a comeback with Walthamstow Avenue but couldn't continue and called it a day in 1976 after which he went into a ladies-wear business, based in Essex.

PEARSON, JOHN

Scottish-born full-back Jock Pearson was just 21 years of age when he joined Spurs from Arbroath in February 1913. He made 57 first team appearances for the club before returning 'home' to assist Partick Thistle during the Great War. He came back to Spurs in 1919 and helped them win the Second Division championship before switching to Luton Town in Novemnber 1923. He remained with the Hatters for just one season, playing in one League game. Pearson was born in Arbroath on 22 January 1892.

PENALTY KICK

The penalty kick was introduced to the Football League and FA Cup competitions for the 1891-92 season. It was instigated initially by the Irish FA in September 1890.

Spot-on

● The first player to score a penalty for Spurs in a competitive match was full-back Lycurgus Burrows in the 2-2 away draw with Wellingborough in a United League game in January 1897.

● The first 'Cup ' penalty netted by a Spurs player came in the semi-final of the Wellingborough Charity Cup against Rushden in April 1897. This time Dick McElhaney was the successful taker, helping Spurs win 2-1.

● Spurs' first penalty in the FA Cup was scored by Bill Dryburgh - in a 2-0 1st round replay victory over West Bromwich Albion in February 1903.

● Bob Steel, with two successful conversions in the same match v. Manchester United at White Hart Lane on 11 September 1909, had the distinction of netting Spurs' first penalty in a Football League game. The result was a 2-2 draw.

● Martin Peters claimed Spurs' first League Cup penalty, against Torquay United at Plainmoor in a 4-1 third round victory in October 1971.

● Danny Blanchflower scored the first Spurs penalty in a European competition, netting from the spot against Benfica at home in the second leg of the European Cup in April 1962. Spurs won the game 2-1 but lost the tie 4-3 on aggregate.

● Alf Ramsey scored three penalties in season 1954-55 all in the space of three weeks, against Blackpool (a), West Brom (h) and Preston North End (h).

● Ramsey's team-mate Tommy Harmer emulated that feat by netting three spot-kicks in April 1956, against Preston (a), Wolves (a) and Huddersfield Town (h).

● Harmer netted a total of 11 penalties (ten in the League, one in the Anglo-Scottish Tournament) during the 1956-57 season.

● Danny Blanchflower netted a late penalty for Spurs in their 3-1 FA Cup Final victory over Burnley in 1962.

● Glenn Hoddle scored Spurs' penalty winner in the FA Cup Final replay against Queen's Park Rangers at Wembley in 1982.

● Gary Lineker missed a penalty (v. Nottingham Forest) in the 1991 FA Cup Final.

● Goalkeeper Tony Parks (who had taken over from Ray Clemence on merit) was Spurs' hero when he saved two spot-kicks in the penalty shoot-out at the end of the 1984 UEFA Cup Final against RSC Anderlecht. The teams had drawn 2-2 on aggregate over two legs before Spurs won 4-3 on penalties.

● In February 1996, Spurs went out of the FA Cup in the 5th round, beaten in a penalty shoot-out by Nottingham Forest. The initial game was abandoned through snow; the re-arranged game finished 2-2 at Nottingham; the replay also ended level at 1-1 before Forest went through 3-1 on spot-kicks.

● Goalkeeper John 'Tiny' Joyce scored twice, once from the penalty spot for Spurs in a 6-0 friendly win against Bayern Munich in Germany in May 1914.

● Ray Clemence also scored a penalty for Spurs in Guernsey in 1985.

● Kettering Town goalkeeper Fred Mearns saved 19 penalties in the 1902-03 season; he was immediately signed by Spurs!

Danny Blanchflower scores Spur's third goal from a penalty in the FA Cup Final v Burnley at Wembley

PERRY, CHRISTOPHER JOHN

Central defender Chris Perry was a £4 million signing from Wimbledon in July 1999.

Excellent in the air, sound and strong on the ground, he made 212 senior appearaces for the Dons whom he joined initially as a trainee in July 1989, turning professional in July 1991. Born in Carshalton, Surrey on 26 April 1973, Perry made his Spurs debut in the London derby against West Ham at Upton Park a month after joining the club and he ended 2000-01 having played in 84 League & Cup games (three goals scored).

PERRYMAN, STEPHEN JOHN, MBE

Born in Ealing, West London on 21 December 1951, Steve Perryman represented Ealing, London and England Schools before joining Spurs as an apprentice in July 1967. He signed as a professional in June 1969 - a month after making his first team debut for the club in a Toronto Cup match against West Ham United in Baltimore, in North America. His Football League debut followed in September of that same year at home to Sunderland.

He became one of the finest servants Spurs have ever had - his record clearly emphasises that beyond all doubt. He was such a consistent, reliable and totally committed footballer.

Able to play in midfield (his early favoured position) or in defence (where he ended his career) Perryman holds records galore for Spurs - most appearances in the Football League, FA Cup, League Cup and European competitions as well as lining up in well over 1,000 first-team matches at all levels. Once he had established himself in the senior XI, he rarely missed a game - he simply loved playing football, and was bitterly annoyed and frustrated if he had to sit and watch the action from the sidelines. He was deservedly awarded the MBE in the Queen's birthday honours list in 1986.

Surprisingly he starred in only one full international match for England (v. Iceland in 1982) but he did appear in four Youth and 17 Under-23 encounters. He gained two FA Cup winning medals (1981 & 1982), two League Cup winners' medals (1971 & 1973 - plus a loser's medal in 1982), two UEFA Cup winners' prizes (1972 & 1984) and an FA Youth Cup winners' medal (1970). He was also voted PFA 'Footballer of the Year' in 1982.

Captain of the side on many occasions, he was a magnificent servant to the club.

On leaving Spurs in March 1986, Perryman was appointed player-coach of Oxford United. Seven months later he moved to Brentford as player/assistant-manager and held the position of player-manager from January 1987 until August 1980. His next move was to Watford as team manager, where he held office from November 1990 to July 1993 before returning to White Hart Lane as assistant-manager in July 1993, remaining until to November 1994.

After a period of relaxation, away from football, Perryman was appointed manager of the Norwegian club, IK Start in June 1995. He then became manager Ossie Ardiles' assistant at the Japanese club Shimizu S-Pulse (January 1996-December 1998) and when the Argentinian left, he took over the reins (January 1999-December 2000).

Perryman was Technical Director to Third Division strugglers Exeter City (January-May 2001). He is now coach of the Japanese club Kashiwa Reysol (July 2001).

This is Perryman's splendid appearance record for Spurs:

Season	FL	FAC	LC	Europe	Others	Total
1969-70	23	4	-	-	-	27
1970-71	42	5	6	-	3	56
1971-72	39	5	6	12	2	64
1972-73	41	3	10	10	-	64
1973-74	39	1	1	12	-	53
1974-75	42	2	1	-	-	45
1975-76	40	2	6	-	-	48
1976-77	42	1	2	-	-	45
1977-78	42	2	2	-	-	46
1978-79	42	7	2	-	-	51
1979-80	40	6	2	-	-	48
1980-81	42	9	6	-	-	57
1981-82	42	7	8	8	1	66
1982-83	32+1	3	2	2+1	-	39+2
1983-84	41	4	3	11	-	59
1984-85	42	3	5	8	-	58
1985-86	22+1	5	4	-	5	36+1
Total	653+2	69	66	63+1	11	862+3

* Perryman made a grand total of 1,021 appearances for Spurs in all first team matches (friendlies, tours included). No one will ever get near to that tremendous achievement!

PETERBOROUGH UNITED (& FLETTON UNITED)

Spurs playing record against Posh:

Competition	P	W	D	L	F	A
FA Cup	2	0	2*	0	2	2
League Cup	1	1	0	0	1	0
Summary	3	1	2	0	3	2

* Spurs won 5-4 on penalties after the 3rd round replay in January 1994 had finished level at 1-1 after extra-time.

Players with both clubs include: Fred Channell, Simon Davies, Matt Edwards (Spurs Youth), Matthew Etherington, Neale Fenn, Kevin Dearden, Terry Gibson, Jimmy Holmes (also posh assistant-manager), Scott Houghton, Jim Iley (Posh player-manager), David McDonald, Billy Manuel (Spurs junior), Paul Price, Arthur Saunders, David Tuttle.

Also associated: David Pleat (Spurs manager, caretaker-manager, & Director of Football, Posh player).

PETERS, MARTIN STANFORD, MBE

One of England's World Cup winning heroes of 1966 (he scored in the Final against West Germany) midfielder Martin Peters netted 100 goals in 364 first-class appearances for West Ham United before transferring to Spurs for £200,000 (with Jimmy Greaves going inn the opposite direction) in March 1970. He continued to produce the goods during the next five years, adding a further 76 goals in 260 outings to his tally (scoring 87 times in 287 games all told).

In March 1975 he left White Hart Lane for Norwich City for £60,000 and again he did splendidly, notching another 50 goals in 232 games for the Canaries. He ended an exceptionally fine career by scoring four goals in 24 matches for Sheffield United between August 1980 and June 1981 - initially as player-coach, then as player-manager.

Add to that his 20 goals in 67 full international appearances for England (33 caps won with West Ham, 34 with Spurs). He also lined up in five Under-23 matches, played four games for the Football League representative side (one as a Spurs player) and won several Youth and Schoolboy caps - a fine record of another wonderfully consistent footballer.

Born in Plaistow, East London on 8 November 1943, Peters also

played for Dagenham, London and Essex Schools before signing apprentice forms for the Hammers in May 1959, turning professional in November 1960. He collected winners medals in both the FA Cup and European Cup-winners Cup competitions with West Ham (1964 & 1965 respectively) and was also a member of the beaten 1966 League Cup Final side.

Peters retired as a player at Bramall Lane in June 1981 at which point he became associated with Gorleston Town (as a player) before working for a fruit-machine company. Later he assisted his former playing colleague Geoff Hurst in the motor-repair insurance business - and then he joined the Board at White Hart Lane in the capacity of non-executive director during August 1998. Peters was awarded he MBE in 1978.

PHYPERS, ERNEST

After being released by Aston Villa, half-back Ernie Phypers made 33 senior appearances for Spurs over a period of three years (1934-37) while also assisting Northfleet. He remained a registered player with the club until 1939 when he moved to Doncaster Rovers, having guested for Clapton Orient, Doncaster Rovers, Southend and West Ham during the War.

PHYSIOTHERAPISTS

(See under trainers/coaches etc)

PLASTIC PITCHES

Spurs played 13 League games and one FA Cup-tie on artificial/plastic surfaces (against Luton Town and Queens Park Rangers in the League and Oldham Athletic in the Cup).
Their record against these clubs is as follows:

Ground/opponents	P	W	D	L	F	A
Kenilworth Road/Luton	6	1	3	2	5	7
Loftus Rd/QPR	7	1	1	5	9	14
Boundary Park/Oldham	1	1	0	0	4	2
Summary	14	3	4	7	18	23

When winning 5-2 at QPR in April 1986, Spurs registered their first win on 'plastic'. Mark Falco (2), Clive Allen (2) and Glenn Hoddle scored the goals in front of 17,768 spectators.
Spurs conceded two goals in each of their first five visits to QPR's artificial surface (April 1984 to April 1988 inclusive). Their last visit there, on 17 March 1990, ended in a 3-2 defeat.

Spurs drew their first game at Luton by 1-1 on 12 April 1986 and then shared the points in their last two matches which both finished level at 0-0 in December 1989 and April 1991.
Spurs' only visit to the plastic pitch of Boundary Park was in January 1988 when they won a 3rd round Cup-tie by 4-2. Mitchell Thomas, Clive Allen (2) and Chris Waddle scoring.
Spurs first goal on 'plastic' was scored by Steve Archibald in the opening encounter with QPR on 28 April 1984 (lost 2-1).
Spurs did not play on Preston North End's artificial surface at Deepdale nor did the venture to Scotland to take on Stirling Albion on their plastic surface!

PLAYERS

● The highest number of players utilised by Spurs in a full Football League season has been 35 - in 1934-35.
● Several players have been registered with Spurs down the years who could occupy several positions, among them Walter Bull (1904-10) and Les Howe (1930-46) who could play comfortably in any outfield position, the latter also deputised in goal. In recent years the likes of Gudni Bergsson, Steve Sedgley and Gary Stevens have appeared in many outfield positions at senior level.
● The Spurs team for the League game against Southampton in May 1984 included six players whose surname began with the letter 'C' - Clemence, Culverhouse, Cockram, Cooke, Crook and Crooks. There were also three 'Bs' - Brazil, Bowen and Brooke while the other two were Miller and O'Reilly.
● Bert Sproston was chosen to play right-back for Spurs v. Manchester City in a Second Division game at Maine Road on 5 November 1938 and his name duly appeared in the matchday programme. However, on the eve of the game Sproston was transferred to City and 24 hours later he helped City beat his old team-mates 2-0.

Guest Players

During the First World War period of 1915-18, Spurs called on the services of more than 70 guest players and they included three England international wing-halves, Percy Barton (Birmingham), Billy Brawn (ex-Aston Villa, Chelsea, Manchester United) and Warney Cresswell, a splendid full-back who served mainly with Everton.
Charlie Hannaford, who toured Australia with the FA party in 1925, England Amateur international Charlie Harbridge, Sid Hoad who played for Manchester City, Nelson and Rochdale and Fred Hopkins, who appeared in over 300 games for Liverpool were four others.
The Reverend Kenneth Hunt, a brilliant Amateur international who gained an FA Cup winners medal with Wolves in 1908 and won two Olympic Golds with Great Britain at soccer in 1908 and 1912, also assisted Spurs, along with Cecil Potter, who took over from Herbert Chapman as manager of Huddersfield Town in the mid-1920s.
The former Aston Villa and Welsh international half-back Haydn Price, hard man George Travers, who was one of the game's great soccer nomads, and Joey Walters whose career took him to Aston Villa (where he won a League championship medal), Chelsea and Millwall, all donned the Spurs strip. Likewise goalkeeper Tim Williamson who appeared in a Victory international for England v. Wales and Ted Worrall, who assisted Brighton & Hove Albion, Southport and Watford.

During the Second World War (1939-46) close on 90 guest and amateur players donned Spurs' colours and among them were some exceptionally fine footballers.

Centre-forward Jack Acquroff was a proven goalscorer, having netted for Hull City, Bury and Norwich City. The former Arsenal winger Pat Beasley was later joint-manager of Birmingham City for the Inter Cities Fairs Cup Final. Goalkeeper Frank Boulton played for Arsenal, Bristol City, Crystal Palace, Derby County and Swindon Town.

Ken Burditt had played for Leicester City, Millwall and Norwich City and was later with Notts County and Colchester United.

John Davie, besides guesting for Spurs, also assisted 15 other clubs including seven more in London. He joined Barnsley in 1946-47.

Harry Ferrier, also a guest player with Arsenal, Brentford, Chelsea, Crystal Palace, Fulham and Middlesbrough, went on to make 250 appearances for Portsmouth.

Half-back Len Flack was an England Amateur international who later became player-coach with Bury and Bobby Flavell went on to win Scottish club honours after the War with Dundee.

Fred Ford, after retiring as a player, became a successful manager with both Bristol City and Rovers, and also with Swindon Town. Glasgow-born goalkeeper Jakey Jackson quit football to become a golfer and entered the British Open. England inside-forward Wilf Mannion (Middlesbrough) was a class performer while Aston Villa's Frank O'Donnell (ex Celtic and Preston North End) had scored in the 1937 FA Cup Final for the Deepdale club.

Winger Eric Jones had a varied career, serving with 16 clubs overall, 13 during the Wartime period.

Jackie Martin was another Aston Villa star who had outings with Birmingham, Portsmouth, Queens Park Rangers and Wrexham. David Nelson, who joined Fulham after the hostilities and Tommy Pearson of Newcastle United were also very useful players in their own right.

Scottish-born defender Bob Pryde (from Blackburn Rovers), former Spurs junior Charlie Revell, then of Charlton Athletic and goalscorer Jack Rowley (Manchester United) were super footballers, the latter going on to score 208 goals in 422 games for the Old Trafford club before entering management with Plymouth Argyle.

George Smith became manager of Portsmouth in 1961 (succeeding ex-Spurs forward Freddie Cox) and Reg Smith (real name Schmidt, the son of a South African rugby union international) had earlier helped Spurs inside-forward Willie Hall score five goals for England against Northern Ireland in 1938.

Alf Whittingham assisted eight clubs during the Wartime period and inside-right Cyril Williams was soon to help West Bromwich Albion win promotion from the Second Division, while the former Chelsea and England goalkeeper Vic Woodley won an FA Cup winners medal with Derby County in 1946.

PLAYERS' UNION (PFA)

Spurs star John Cameron was instrumental as one of the key men who helped form The Players' Union around the turn of the 20th century. He was later appointed secretary of the Footballers' Union (known nowadays as the PFA).

Terry Neill (former Spurs manager) was PFA Chairman in the 1970s and ex-Spurs player Garth Crooks was strongly associated with the PFA during the late 1980s and 1990s, acting as Chairman in 1989-90.

PLAYING RECORD

This is Spurs' playing record (all major competitions).

Friendly, tour, benefit, testimonial, challenge and abandoned matches have not been included in the analysis:

League Competitions:

	P	W	D	L	F	A	Pts
Southern Alliance 1892-93	12	7	2	3	29	21	16
Southern League 1896-1908	360	180	75	105	640	401	435
United League 1896-99	50	20	11	19	101	86	51
South Eastern 1903-04	2	2	0	0	11	2	4
Thames & Medway 1898-99	16	10	0	6	43	28	20
Southern District Comb 1899-1900	16	10	3	3	41	18	23
Western League(1/B) 1900-08	126	58	34	34	218	137	150
London Premier League 1901-04	30	17	5	8	57	31	29
London Football Comb 1915-19	148	75	26	47	320	249	176
Football League (S) 1939-46	219	120	42	57	492	320	282
League Div 2 (void) 1939-40	3	1	2	0	6	5	4
Football League (D 1/2) 1908-92	3024	1275	735	1014	5065	4292	3477
Premiership 1992-2001	354	122	100	132	469	481	466

Cup and other Competitions

	P	W	D	L	F	A
FA Cup 1893-2001	374	192	93	89	738	451
Football League Cup 1966-2001	154	89	27	38	282	165
European Comps 1961-2000	99	59	19	21	219	89
Texaco Cup 1970-71	4	3	0	1	11	5
Anglo-Italian CWC 1971-72	2	2	0	0	3	0
Screen Sport S Cup 1985-86	6	2	1	3	6	9
Anglo-Scottish F/Cup 1956-57	6	3	1	2	18	12
Glasgow Charity Cup 1964-65	1	0	0	1	2	4

	P	W	D	L	F	A
London Charity Cup 1893-1931	58	32	6	20	152	90
London FA Cup 1885-87	3	1	0	2	5	16
London FA Senior Cup 1887-1905	21	9	4	8	50	52
Wellingborough Cup 1896-97	4	3	0	1	7	5
Southern Charity Cup 1901-08	17	7	5	5	33	18
Luton Charity Cup 1891-92	3	1	1	1	10	9
East End Cup 1886-87	4	3	0	1	10	2
Wolverton Dist. C. Cup 1892-94	4	1	1	2	5	6

	P	W	D	L	F	A
Middlesex Senior Cup 1899-1903	6	1	1	4*	5	9

* Two scores not known.

	P	W	D	L	F	A
FA Amateur Cup 1893-95	9	6	2	1	34	12

Others

	P	W	D	L	F	A
FA Charity Shield 1921-92	9	4	3	2	17	12
Dewar Shield 1901-34	3	3	0	0	19	8
London Pro Foot. Fund P 1908-29	19	11	3	5	38	22
Telegraph Titanic Fund 1911-12	1	0	0	1	0	3
War Relief Fund 1914-19	2	0	1	1	3	7
Coronation Cup 1952-53	2	0	1	1	2	3

PLAYING RECORD AGAINST OTHER CLUBS IN THE FOOTBALL LEAGUE & PREMIERSHIP: 1908-2001

		Home						Away					
	Pld	W	D	L	F	A	Pts	W	D	L	F	A	Pts
Arsenal	128	28	15	21	102	91	78	17	17	30	72	95	54
Aston Villa	116	29	10	19	114	92	77	17	15	26	79	93	52
Barnsley	28	12	1	1	39	10	26	2	4	8	12	25	8
Birmingham City	68	21	6	7	73	30	50	12	6	16	37	46	32
Blackburn Rovers	74	24	5	8	95	48	56	10	8	19	41	63	31
Blackpool	50	16	4	5	70	34	36	10	9	6	33	29	29
Bolton Wanderers	66	20	6	7	63	34	47	11	4	18	43	56	27
Bradford City	32	8	6	2	27	15	23	4	4	8	19	29	12
Bradford Park Avenue	32	12	4	0	49	17	28	4	4	8	26	33	12
Brentford	6	2	1	0	7	1	5	1	1	1	5	4	3
Brighton & Hove Albion	10	2	2	1	6	4	7	3	0	2	9	6	7
Bristol City	20	7	2	1	18	9	16	3	3	4	10	9	9
Bristol Rovers	2	1	0	0	9	0	2	1	0	0	3	2	2
Burnley	88	25	9	10	109	51	59	7	13	24	50	87	27
Bury	40	14	4	2	45	27	32	4	4	12	22	39	12
Cardiff City	40	10	5	5	36	23	25	10	5	5	24	14	25
Carlisle United	2	0	1	0	1	1	1	0	0	1	0	1	0
Charlton Athletic	38	10	4	5	39	21	26	9	4	6	34	23	25
Chelsea	106	21	14	18	93	79	58	19	10	24	70	71	50
Chesterfield	20	7	2	1	31	11	16	2	4	4	14	17	8
Coventry City	82	23	10	8	81	48	64	14	12	15	54	55	47
Crystal Palace	26	5	5	3	18	11	15	8	4	1	25	13	24
Derby County	60	15	8	7	48	29	41	5	9	16	36	69	23
Doncaster Rovers	6	3	0	0	7	1	6	0	2	1	3	4	2
Everton	128	32	19	13	126	77	95	14	21	29	71	97	54
Fulham	44	12	9	1	41	21	33	10	9	3	37	28	29
Gainsborough Trinity	2	0	1	0	1	1	1	1	0	0	2	0	2
Glossop	2	0	1	0	3	3	1	0	1	0	1	1	1
Grimsby Town	14	6	0	1	19	10	12	2	1	4	8	14	5

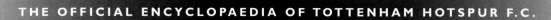
		Home						Away					
	Pld	W	D	L	F	A	Pts	W	D	L	F	A	Pts
Huddersfield Town	36	7	7	4	26	22	21	2	6	10	18	28	10
Hull City	14	4	3	0	14	4	11	1	1	5	4	9	3
Ipswich Town	48	14	4	6	47	28	38	8	4	12	32	43	23
Leeds City	2	1	0	0	3	0	2	0	0	1	0	1	0
Leeds United	82	20	12	9	71	49	56	8	13	20	42	64	31
Leicester City	84	18	10	14	84	61	50	21	6	15	73	80	53
Leyton Orient	10	3	1	1	7	4	7	3	2	0	13	4	8
Lincoln City	6	2	0	1	10	5	4	0	3	0	3	3	3
Liverpool	116	28	13	17	87	71	77	5	16	37	47	117	29
Luton Town	46	15	5	3	44	20	41	6	12	5	31	26	26
Manchester City	106	25	15	13	92	64	72	10	13	30	47	99	37
Manchester United	128	25	22	17	113	79	79	10	12	42	62	122	33
Mansfield Town	2	0	1	0	1	1	1	0	1	0	3	3	1
Middlesbrough	64	16	7	9	70	54	42	5	8	19	31	61	21
Millwall	22	9	2	0	27	11	22	8	1	2	27	14	19
Newcastle United	114	30	11	16	111	65	80	19	17	21	84	97	57
Newport County	2	1	0	0	3	1	2	1	0	0	4	2	2
Northampton Town	2	0	1	0	1	1	1	1	0	0	2	0	2
Norwich City	46	14	5	4	50	23	42	7	6	10	30	36	24
Nottingham Forest	104	30	7	15	106	68	73	19	17	16	69	70	62
Notts County	34	12	2	3	36	18	30	4	6	7	16	27	15
Oldham Athletic	36	16	2	0	53	10	36	6	1	11	25	31	14
Oxford United	6	3	0	0	11	2	9	1	2	0	5	3	5
Plymouth Argyle	22	6	2	3	18	11	14	4	4	3	21	18	12
Portsmouth	26	4	6	3	27	22	14	3	5	5	14	22	11
Port Vale	12	6	0	0	29	7	12	3	1	2	11	8	7
Preston North End	52	14	7	5	58	34	35	8	6	12	38	45	22
Queens Park Rangers	42	11	7	3	36	21	36	5	7	9	25	32	20
Reading	6	1	2	0	9	3	4	1	0	2	5	8	2
Rotherham United	2	1	0	0	2	0	2	0	1	0	1	1	1
Sheffield United	80	25	10	5	93	42	62	6	14	20	55	93	26
Sheffield Wednesday	96	30	8	10	111	64	75	11	9	28	49	79	39
Southampton	90	28	9	8	116	48	79	10	16	19	45	63	42
South Shields	2	1	0	0	2	0	2	1	0	0	3	0	2
Stockport County	6	2	1	0	4	0	5	2	0	1	7	5	4
Stoke City	66	26	6	1	74	26	62	9	9	15	35	45	29
Sunderland	82	17	12	12	66	50	51	11	11	19	41	65	37
Swansea City	26	11	2	0	42	10	26	4	3	6	14	18	11
Swindon Town	2	0	1	0	1	1	1	0	0	1	1	2	0
Tranmere Rovers	2	1	0	0	3	1	2	1	0	0	2	0	2
Watford	14	4	0	3	15	11	12	3	2	2	8	7	11
West Bromwich Albion	106	25	14	14	91	56	65	13	8	32	68	114	36
West Ham United	102	25	12	14	91	72	72	14	14	23	69	78	46
Wimbledon	28	6	4	4	20	17	22	5	3	6	23	26	18
Wolverhampton Wand.	74	26	7	4	94	49	61	10	7	20	52	76	29

TOTALS	Played	Won	Drawn	Lost	For	Against	Points
Home	1689	928	394	367	3439	2005	2446
Away	1689	469	441	779	2095	2768	1497
Total	3378	1397	835	1146	5534	4773	3943

Total split:

Premiership	354	122	100	132	469	481	466
Division One	2356	964	563	829	3812	3441	2683
Division Two	668	311	172	185	1253	851	794

PLEAT, DAVID

Born in Nottingham on 15 January 1945, David Pleat was a very useful teenage winger who represented England at Schoolboy level before joining Nottingham Forest as a professional in January 1962. He added a cluster of Youth caps to his collection before moving to Luton Town for £8,000 in August 1964. Three years and 70 League games later he was transferred to Shrewsbury Town and after spells with Exeter City and Peterborough United he became player-manager of non-League Nuneaton Borough for the 1971-72 season. At the end of that campaign he returned to Kenilworth Road as reserve team coach, became chief coach in December 1977, then manager from January 1978 to May 1986. Pleat left the Hatters after being offered the manager's job at White Hart Lane. He remained in charge of Spurs until October 1987 when he became manager of Leicester City, a position he held for three-and-a-half years, up to January 1991. Six months later he went back as boss of his old club Luton Town and remained there for a further four years (to May 1995). Pleat then managed Sheffield Wednesday (June 1995 to November 1997). He subsequently came back to White Hart Lane as the club's Director of Football (announced on his departure from Hillsborough) in office, January 1998. He has since then twice acted as caretaker-manager - for a four-week period during September & October 1998 and for a short while in March & April 2001, just prior to Glenn Hoddle's arrival.

Pleat took Luton to the Second Division championship in 1982 and Spurs to the FA Cup Final five years later.

PLYMOUTH ARGYLE

Spurs playing record against the Pilgrims

Competition	P	W	D	L	F	A
Football League	22	10	6	6	39	29
FA Cup	4	3	1	0	14	2
Other Leagues	18	5	5	8	20	22
Wartime	2	2	0	0	3	0
Summary	46	20	12	14	76	53

The first time Spurs and Argyle met each other in the Football League was on 6 December 1930 and in front of 24,549 fans at Home Park the Pilgrims claimed a 2-0 victory - despite losing their goalkeeper, Harry Cann between the 30th and 85th minutes. The following season Argyle completed the double over Spurs with a 4-1 home win and a 1-0 triumph at White Hart Lane. Both League games finished in draws in 1932-33.

The Pilgrims won both matches by 2-1 over Christmas 1935, before Spurs finally recorded their first win over the Devon club on 23 October 1937, gaining the points with a 3-2 home victory in front of 22,734 fans.

Spurs ended the 1948-49 League season with a 5-0 win over Argyle, Les Bennett scoring a hat-trick in front of almost 24,000 fans at Home Park.

By coincidence Argyle were the first visitors to White Hart Lane at the start of the 1949-50 season and this time Spurs won 4-1, Alf Ramsey almost bursting the ball with his penalty kick. The attendance was close on 42,000. Nine days later Spurs doubled up with a 2-0 win in South Devon.

Players with both clubs include: Milija Aleksic, Jack Chilsholm, Albert Hall, Lee Hodges, Billy Leech, Mark Robson, Andrew Swan, Solomon Upton, Ralph Wetton.

Wartime guests (either with one or both clubs): Harry Brown, Tom Howshall, Phil Joslin, John Oakes, Fred Sargent.

Also associated: Frank Brettell and Jack Tresadern (managers of both clubs), Allan Harris (Argyle player, Spurs assistant-manager), Stewart Houston (Argyle coach, Spurs assistant-manager).

POINTS

(Three points for a win)

The most League points gained by Spurs in a complete League season has been 77 (out of a possible 126) in season 1984-85. They amassed 71 in 1981-82 and 1986-87.

The most points gained in a full Premiership season by Spurs is 62 in 1994-95.

In 1960-61 Spurs equalled the Division One record with 66 points (out of 84).

The fewest they have amassed in a Premiership campaign (to date) has been 44 (out of a possible 114) in 1997-98.

(Two points for a win)

In 1919-20, when they won the Second Division title, Spurs gained 70 points (out of 84). In their first League season of 1908-09 (Division 2) they obtained 51 (from 38 games).

The fewest number of points gained by Spurs in a complete League season has been 28 - in 1914-15 (38 games played).

POLICE FORCE

Two former Spurs players joined the Police Force after hanging up their 'professional' boots. They were Jimmy Holmes (West Midlands) and Mark Kendall (South Wales Constabulary). Bob Iverson served in the war time Police reserve.

POLSTONS, ANDREW & JOHN DAVID

Between them the Polston brothers, both defenders, made only 29 first-class appearances for Spurs with Andy having just one substitute.

Andy was born in Bethnal Green on 26 July 1970 and joined Spurs in July 1986 as a trainee, turning professional in June 1988. He left White Hart Lane in 1992 (released to Brighton) having earlier played on loan with Cambridge United and Gillingham.

John was born in Walthamstow on 10 June 1968. He joined the club as an amateur in August 1984 and turned 'pro' in July 1985, transferring to Norwich City in July 1990 for £300,000. He went on to appear in more than 250 games for the Canaries before moving to Reading in 1998.

* When Andy came off the bench to join John against Crystal Palace in March 1990, they became the first brothers to play together in a Football League game for Spurs since the Steels in April 1912.

POLYTECHNIC

Spurs playing record against the Poly

Competition	P	W	D	L	F	A
Southern Alliance	2	1	1	0	4	3
Other Cups	2	0	1	1	2	5
Summary	4	1	2	1	6	8

Spurs' only victory over Polytechnic, at competitive level, was achieved in the Southern Alliance on 24 September 1892. They won 2-1 away on, Sykes and Brigden the scorers

POPESCU, GHEORGHE

Signed by Spurs from the Dutch club, PSV Eindhoven for £2.9 million in September 1994, Gica Popescu made only 28 first-class appearances for the club (three goals scored) before moving in a £3.1 million deal to Barcelona in May 1995. Four years later the Romanian international joined the Turkish side Galatasaray.

Defensive midfielder Popescu - born in Romania on 9 October 1967 - scored once in six games for his country during his brief stay at White Hart Lane. Like his compatriot, Ilie Dumitrescu, he was introduced to the national team in 1988. He went on to appear in more than 100 full internationals including European Championships and World Cups.

PORT VALE (ALSO BURSLEM PORT VALE)

Spurs playing record against the Valiants

Competition	P	W	D	L	F	A
Football League	12	9	1	2	40	15
FA Cup	2	1	0	1	5	4
Summary	14	10	1	3	45	19

1932 action against Port Vale

The first of the 12 League games between the two clubs took place in the Potteries on 27 October 1919 (Division 2), Spurs winning 1-0 with a goal by Jimmy Cantrell.

Four goals by hot-shot Ted Harper helped Spurs beat the Vale 5-0 in a home Second Division match in November 1930. This was the striker's second hat-trick of the month.

Spurs ran up their best-ever League win over the Vale on 21 November 1931 (Division 2). That day they beat them 9-3 at White Hart Lane, Welsh international Willie Davies (3), Jimmy Brain (2) and George Hunt (2) leading the goal-rush.

Vale beat Spurs, beaten finalists the year before, in the 4th round of the FA Cup 2-1 in front of a Potteries crowd of more than 20,000 in January 1988.

Players with both clubs include: Milija Aleksic, Eddie Baily, Peter Beadle, Joe Brough, Ivor Brown, Wayne Cegielski (Spurs reserve), Ernie Coquet, Anthony Gardner, Bert Gosnell, Ken Hancock, George Hunt (Vale trialist), Billy Leech, Colin Lyman, Bert Lyons,

Harry Marshall, Jeff Minton, Ian Moores (Vale trialist), Jimmy Reid, Chris Young.

Also associated: Warney Cresswell (Spurs WW1 guest, Vale coach).

PORTO (FC)

Spurs playing record against the Portuguese club

Competition	P	W	D	L	F	A
ECW Cup	2	1	1	0	3	1

Spurs met FC Porto in the second round of the European Cup-winners Cup tournament in 1991-92. The first leg was played at White Hart Lane on 23 October and in front of 23,621 spectators, the Portuguese side were beaten 3-1, Gary Lineker (2) and Gordon Durie the Spurs scorers. A crowd of 55,000 attended the second leg in Porto and this time the score sheet remained blank, Spurs going through comfortably enough in the end.

PORTSMOUTH

Spurs playing record against Pompey

Competition	P	W	D	L	F	A
Football League	26	7	11	8	41	44
FA Cup	3	3	0	0	10	2
League Cup	3	0	2	1	0	1
Other Leagues	34	8	11	15	47	45
Wartime	17	12	3	2	39	14
Summary	83	30	27	26	127	106

The first of the 26 Football League encounters between the two clubs was staged at Fratton Park on 17 September 1927 (Division 1). Pompey won 3-0 in front of 26,115 fans. Later in the season Portsmouth completed the double with a 3-0 win in London.

Spurs' first win arrived in October 1933 - 1-0 at Portsmouth, courtesy of Taffy O'Callaghan's fine goal.

Spurs beat Pompey 4-1 at home in October 1934, a week after losing 5-1 at Arsenal.

A massive crowd of 66,402 saw Portsmouth, the reigning League champions, crushed 5-1 by Spurs at White Hart Lane in November 1950. Eddie Baily netted a hat-trick.

On Christmas Day and Boxing Day in 1953, the two League games both finished in 1-1 draws and the attendances were almost the same - 36,502 at White Hart Lane and 36,677 at Fratton Park.

Pompey put ten goals past Spurs in the space of seven days in

Duquemin in action against Portsmouth

August 1957. They won 5-1 at Fratton Park and followed up with a 5-3 win at White Hart Lane.

There was another eight-goal thriller between the two clubs at White Hart Lane in February 1959. It ended 4-4 as Portsmouth battled unsuccessfully against relegation.

Players with both clubs include: Rory Allen, Ben Anderton (Pompey trainee, Spurs trialist), Darren Anderton, Garry Brady, Charlie Brittan, Alex 'Sandy' Brown, Guy Butters, John Collins, Peter Crouch (Spurs reserve), Jason Cundy, Kevin Dearden, Alex Glen, Micky Hazard, Ian Hendon, Bill Joyce, David Leworthy, Sid McClellan, Neil McNab, John Moncur, Paul Moran, Shaun Murray (Spurs reserve), Alf Ramsey (Pompey Amateur), Matt Reilly, Graham Roberts (Pompey apprentice), Art Rule, Robbie Simpson (Spurs reserve), Gary Stevens, Mark Stimson, Andy Turner, Solomon Upton, Paul Walsh, Charlie Whitchurch (Amateur).

Wartime guests (either with one or both clubs): Vic Buckingham, John Davie, Harry Ferrier, Doug Flack, Jakey Jackson, Eric Jones, Jackie Martin, Cliff Parker, George Smith (also Pompey manager). Also associated: Gerry Francis & George Graham (Pompey players, Spurs managers), Frank Brettell (manager of both clubs), Freddie Cox & Terry Fenwick (Spurs players, Pompey managers), Neil McNab (Spurs player, Pompey coach).

POYET, GUSTAVO AUGUSTO

A £1.5 million signing from Chelsea in the summer of 2001Born Montevido, Uruguay, 15 November 1967, the Uruguayan international midfielder was previously with River Plate, Grenoble, Bella Vista and Real Zaragoza.

He has 27 full caps to his name and helped Chelsea win the European Cup Winners Cup and Super Cup in 1998 and the FA Cup and Charity Shield in 2000.

POYNTON, CECIL

Cecil Poynton was associated with Spurs for some 50 years. He was a player from 1922 to 1933, coach for one season (1933-34) and after a spell as player-manager of Margate Town and service with Northmet, returned to White Hart Lane as assistant-trainer in January 1946. He held that position for over 26 years before serving as physiotherapist from May 1972 until his retirement in May 1975.

Born in Brownhills, Staffordshire on 10 August 1901, he played his first competitive football matches as a wing-half in Wales with Ton Pentre. He moved to White Hart Lane full of confidence and after being converted into a full-back, went on to appear in 179 first team games, scoring three goals.

Strong and reliable, Poynton represented the Professionals against the Amateurs in the 1925 FA Charity Shield game. He died in Edmonton, North London on 12 January 1983.

PRATT, JOHN ARTHUR

Midfielder John Pratt played in 508 first team games for Spurs - 331 in the Football League, 28 in the FA Cup, 31 in the League Cup, 25 in Europe and 93 'other' fixtures. He netted 65 goals - 49 at competitive level.

Born in Hackney, East London on 26 June 1948, he represented London at Youth team level and was on Brentford's books as a teenager before joining Spurs as an amateur in 1964, turning professional in November 1965. He made his debut for the club against the Cyprus International XI in May 1968 and followed up with his League bow in the North London derby against Arsenal in March 1969.

He took over the right-half (right side midfield) position from Alan Mullery and after claiming a UEFA Cup winners medal (as sub) in

1972, he added a League Cup winners medal to his tally the following year. He played less than a quarter of that 1973 Final against Norwich City, Ralph Coates coming on to score the winning goal! The very next season he was on the losing side in the UEFA Cup Final.

On leaving Spurs, in May 1980, Pratt signed for Portland Timbers (NASL). He returned to White Hart Lane as Youth team coach in January 1983, later taking over as reserve team coach/assistant-manager till April 1986. Pratt was also involved with Barkingside FC.

PRATT, THOMAS PEET

Tom Pratt drew up a very useful record - 54 goals in only 60 first team appearances for Spurs - made between September 1899 (when he had his debut against Millwall Athletic) and April 1900, a month before he left the club to join Preston North End.

A Lancastrian, born in Fleetwood on 28 August 1873, Pratt was a forceful centre-forward with courage and determination. He played for Fleetwood Rangers, Grimsby Town and Preston before transferring to Spurs in April 1899. His haul of 25 goals was instrumental when the Southern League championship was won in his first season with the club. In 1902, after two years at Deepdale, Pratt returned to Fleetwood and in August 1903 moved back to London to sign for Woolwich Arsenal, playing next for Fulham (from July 1904) and finally serving Blackpool (March 1905 to May 1906). Pratt made 220 'League' appearances during his career and netted 82 goals. He died in his native town of Fleetwoood in August 1935.

PREMIER LEAGUE

Spurs were founder members of the FA Premier League (Premiership) in 1992-93 and have played in every season since then.

This is Spurs full record in the Premier League: 1992 to 2001: Seasonal breakdown:

Season	P	W	D	L	F	A	Pts
1992-93	42	16	11	15	60	66	59
Position: 8th							
1993-94	42	11	12	19	54	59	45
Position: 15th							
1994-95	42	16	14	12	66	58	62
Position: 7th							
1995-96	38	16	13	9	50	38	61
Position: 8th							
1996-97	38	13	7	18	44	51	46
Position: 10th							
1997-98	38	11	11	16	44	56	44
Position: 14th							
1998-99	38	11	14	13	47	50	47
Position: 11th							
1999-00	38	15	8	15	57	49	53
Position: 10th							
2000-01	38	13	10	15	47	54	49
Position: 12th							
Summary	354	122	100	132	469	481	466

Premiership Facts

● Spurs first Premiership match was against Southampton at The Dell on 15 August 1992. It ended goalless in front of 19,654 spectators.

● Four days later Spurs suffered their first defeat in the Premiership, losing 2-0 at home to Coventry City in front of 24,388 fans.

● Gordon Durie scored Spurs' first Premiership goal - in the 16th minute of a 2-2 home draw with Crystal Palace on 22 August.

● The team's first Premiership win was achieved at home against Sheffield United on 2 September by 2-0, Teddy Sheringham and Gordon Durie the scorers.

● Sheffield United inflicted upon Spurs their heaviest defeat in the initial Premiership campaign, winning 6-0 at Bramall Lane on 2 March 1993. The Blades led 4-0 at half-time.

● Spurs also lost 6-2 at Liverpool on 8 May and 5-0 at Leeds on 25 August.

● Leeds were defeated 4-0 at White Hart Lane in February when Sheringham scored a hat-trick. Spurs also beat Norwich City 5-1 at home two months later.

● Spurs recorded their 100th Premiership victory when they defeated arch rivals Arsenal 2-1 at home on 7 November 1999.

● Their 100th Premiership defeat was suffered at the hands of Liverpool on 1 March 1999, the Reds winning 3-2 at Anfield.

● Spurs played out their 100th draw in Premiership football on 28 April 2001 when Aston Villa earned a point from a goalless encounter at White Hart Lane.

● Sol Campbell (255) has made most appearances in the Premiership for Spurs while Teddy Sheringham (75) has scored most goals - with more to come!

Spurs' biggest League/Premiership wins & heaviest defeats against their 2001-02 Premiership opponents:

Arsenal	5-0	0-6
Aston Villa	6-2	0-4
Blackburn Rov	5-0	2-7
Bolton Wds	4-0	1-4
Charlton Athletic	6-2	1-4
Chelsea	5-0	1-6
Derby County	5-0	2-8
Everton	10-4	0-4
Fulham	5-1	1-4
Ipswich Town	5-0	0-4
Leeds United	5-1	0-5
Leicester City	6-0	0-6
Liverpool	7-2	0-7
Manchester U	6-1	0-5
Middlesbrough	7-1	5-7
Newcastle Utd.	7-0	1-7
Southampton	8-0	0-5
Sunderland	5-1	0-6
West Ham Utd	6-1	0-4

PRESIDENTS

John Ripsher was Spurs' first appointed President, holding office for eleven years, from 1883 until March 1894.

Over the years Spurs have had numerous club Presidents (and indeed, vice-presidents) among them former player and manager, Bill Nicholson. (See also Directors).

PRESTON NORTH END

Spurs playing record against North End

Competition	P	W	D	L	F	A
Football League	52	22	13	17	96	79
FA Cup	11	5	2	4	19	16
League Cup	4	2	2	0	7	3
Summary	67	29	17	21	122	98

The first Football League game between the two clubs at Preston was abandoned in the 50th minute through heavy rain on 23 October 1909 (Division I). A crowd of 4,000 had attended and

Preston North End v Spurs at Deepdale 1953

the scoresheet was blank at the time. The 'replay' took place on 22 November and this time North End won 4-1 in front of 5,000 spectators.

The 1922 FA Cup semi-final between Spurs and Preston, staged at Hillsborough, was seen by over 50,000 spectators. Spurs didn't play well and lost 2-1.

Fifteen years later, in March 1937, a 6th round FA Cup-tie ended Spurs 1 Preston 3 in front of almost 72,000 fans at White Hart Lane.

Regular full-back Charlie Withers scored just two goals for Spurs in more than 200 first team outings and both came in the 2-2 draw with North End in a 4th round FA Cup-tie at Deepdale in January 1953 ....when he was asked to occupy the left-wing berth due to an injury crisis!

A thrilling First Division encounter at White Hart Lane in February 1953 finished Spurs 4 North End 4 - Len Duquemin netting a hat-trick for the Londoners.

Spurs were beaten 4-0 at home by Preston in March 1956. Three days later they forced a 3-3 draw at Deepdale. Then in August 1956, for the first game of the new season, Spurs again went to Preston and this time they won 4-1, Johnny Brooks and Terry Medwin both scoring twice. Spurs haven't met Preston in the League since 1961.

Players with both clubs include: Herbert Blake (PNE trialist), Alex 'Sandy' Brown, John Burton, John Chalmers, Fred Griffiths, Ted Harper, Gordon Manning, Jimmy Melia, George Montgomery, Jock Montgomery, Tom Pratt, Tom Roberts, Dick Rowley, Tom Smith, Harry Stansfield, Alex 'Sandy' Tait, Joe Walton.

Wartime guests (either with one or both clubs): Percy Smith (North End player, Spurs manager), Albert Chester, Dicky Dunn, Harry Jackson, Frank O'Donnell

PRICE, PAUL TERENCE

Born in St Albans on 23 March 1954, defender Paul Price represented Welwyn and mid-Hertfordshire Schools before playing non-League football for Welwyn Garden United. In January 1979 he signed amateur forms for Luton Town and moved onto the professional register in July 1971. Successive spells in the NASL with Minnesota Kicks in the summers of 1977 and 1978 preceded his transfer to Spurs in June 1981 for £250,000. He made 62 senior appearances for the club (78 in all) before returning to the Minnesota Kicks in July 1984. In January 1985 he was back in the U.K playing for Swansea City and he rounded off an interesting career by serving Saltash United (in Cornwall), Peterborough United, Chelmsford City, Wivenhoe and finally back 'home' with St Albans City (1991-92).

Price - who broke his leg twice before making his debut for the Hatters - qualified to play for Wales via his father, who was born in Merthyr Vale and died before seeing his son wear the red jersey.

Price junior gained one Under-21 cap before going on to play in 25 full internationals (11 as a Luton player and 14 with Spurs).

He captained the Principality on several occasions and was awarded a testimonial match in 1981 (Luton against Spurs)..

PROFESSIONALISM

Professionalism in football was first seen as long ago as 1879 when Blackburn Rovers and Darwen recruited players from Scotland and paid them wages. Over the next year or so Bolton and Preston North End followed suit.

But it wasn't until 20 July 1885 that professionalism was finally accepted into English soccer...an important step in the history of the game.

Spurs however, finally agreed to become a professional body in December 1895 - after a lot of debate involving several players, among them Ernie Payne, the catalyst - and the first game they played as a professional body was against an amateur team, the Casuals, on 21 December 1895. They won 3-1.

The first player said to have signed as a professional for Spurs was Scotsman Jock Montgomery - who put pen to paper (officially) in January 1896

PROGRAMMES

A brief history of the Spurs official matchday programme

The earliest known programme issued for a Tottenham Hotspur home fixture was produced for the London Senior Cup replay against Old St. Marks on Saturday, October 28, 1893.

Printed in red ink on white paper by S J Clarke, Athletic Printer, 68 Milton Street, EC, it carried the wording "First - Official Programme - Gratis" and stated that "programmes will be supplied each week, in future, at One Penny each."

The visitors, an old boys team attached to St. Marks College, Battersea, won the match 6-1 after the sides had played out a goalless draw, also at Spurs' Northumberland Park enclosure, the previous week.

By 1897 several companies vied to supply a programme. The club decided to issue its own and duly registered the copyright at Stationers Hall.

Kettering Town were the visitors for a United League fixture when the first truly 'official' club programme was published on September 16, 1897.

Printed black on salmon pink paper, this colour scheme remained unchanged until 1946. C. Coventry, T.U. Printer, Tottenham printed the issues.

At the outset a large format single sheet was produced, folded to give a four-page programme. A former player during the club's amateur days, Harry Goddard, was in charge of the club's programme department for many years. Generally, a cartoon adorned the cover with the team line-ups across pages two and three and the back page carrying fixtures and League tables.

Another Tottenham-based printer, Crusha & Son, who also produced the local Weekly Herald newspapers, took over printing in 1935, with the format remaining the same.

Only international matches at Tottenham brought a change in design with a heavy, glossy, cream coloured paper being used to enable photographs to be included.

Thomas Knight & Co., The Clock House Press, Hoddesdon brought a fresh feel to the programme when they took over production in 1946, introducing blue print on white paper. The

single sheet format, however, remained with the club, Spurs claiming to have the cheapest programme in the Football League! Occasionally, a glossy paper would be used rather than the standard thickness. Two special editions were published; an eight page issue in April, 1950 versus Grimsby Town to celebrate the return to top flight status; and eleven years later, with the League Championship secured, for the final home game of the 1960-61 double-winning campaign against West Bromwich Albion.

Season 1961-62 saw a complete overhaul of the programme and the new design and publication comprised 12 glossy pages for the price of 3d.

Between 1967 and 1969 a smaller format was adopted, but the club returned to a larger one for the 1970-71 season.

It was larger in 1977, with the cover price now standing at 20p.

In 1979, Maybank Press took over from Thomas Knight & Co introducing full colour to the programme and greatly expanding the advertising content.

The last 20 years have followed modern trends to the current 64 page laminated cover issue, which is now regarded as one of the best-produced programmes in the Premiership.

NB: Prior to the commencement of the 1908-09 Football League season, the official Spurs matchday programmes were un-numbered. Volume 1, number 1 was issued for the home game v. Wolverhampton Wanderers on 1 September 1908. The volume number for season 2001-02 had reached 94.

PROMOTION

After relegation from a higher Division, Spurs subsequently won promotion as follows:

1919-20 (as Second Division champions)

1932-33 (Division 2 runners-up to Stoke City)

1949-50 (as Division Two champions)

1976-77 (third in Division 2 behind Bolton and Southampton).

● In 1907-08 Spurs were 'promoted' from the Southern League into the Second Division of the Football League (on a 5-3 vote count), then in 1908-09 they quickly climbed out of the Second Division into the First after finishing runners-up to Bolton).

● On the last day (last game) of the 1977-78 Second Division season, Spurs drew 0-0 at Southampton in front of a full-house of 28,846 to earn the point that clinched promotion.

PUBLICANS

Several ex-footballers (even managers and coaches) have gone into the licensing business after leaving the game. Here are some of the many former Spurs players who ventured into a new life as publicans. Dates in brackets indicate when the player was with Spurs.

Bob Brown (1919-25), Laurie Brown (1964-66), Fred Channell (1928-30/1933-34), Martin Chivers* (1968-76), George Clawley* (1899-1903), Tommy Clay (1914-29), David Copeland* (1899-1905), Kerry Dixon (Youth player, 19776-78), Len Duquemin (1945-58), Johnny Gavin (1954-55), Bert Gosnell (1910-11), John Hollowbread (1950-64), Ted Hughes (1899-1908), Jimmy McCormick (1933-45), Alf Messer (1930-34), Peter Murphy* (1950-52), Matt Reilly (1906-07), Tom Roberts (1928-29), Martin Robinson* (1973-78), Max Seeburg (1907-08), Harry Skitt (1923-31), John Smith* (1960-64), Les Stevens*(1940-49), John Tate (1913-14), Fanny Walden (1913-26) and Charlie Wilson (1919-22).

* Chivers ran a hotel/restaurant business; Clawley managed a licensed hotel; Copeland was a barman; Murphy was a rep for a Birmingham-based brewery; Robinson went into hotel management; Smith was manager of a licensed social club and Stevens ran an off-licence.

QUEEN'S PARK RANGERS

Spurs playing record against QPR

Competition	P	W	D	L	F	A
Premiership	8	3	2	3	12	14
Football League	34	13	12	9	49	40
FA Cup	4	2	2	0	5	2
League Cup	1	0	0	1	0	1
Other Leagues	38	21	9	8	75	43
Other Cups	7	5	2	0	15	3
Wartime	26	9	8	9	49	39
Summary	118	53	35	30	205	142

The first time Spurs met Rangers at Football League level was on 16 October 1948 (Division 2). A crowd of 69,718 packed into White Hart Lane to see Eddie Baily earn Spurs a 1-0 victory.
The first time the teams met in the top flight of English football was on 28 January 1969, Spurs winning 3-2 at home.
In September 1984 Spurs ran up one of their best League wins over Rangers, beating them 5-0 at White Hart Lane. They quickly followed up with a 5-2 victory at Loftus Road (April 1986).

Players with both clubs include: Clive Allen, Joe Allen, Arthur Archer, Ossie Ardiles (also Spurs manager), Alan Brazil, Tommy Cable, Peter Crouch, Chris Day, Frank Drabble, Mark Falco, Terry Fenwick, Les Ferdinand, Mike Flanagan (Spurs Youth), Andy Gray, Harry Gilberg, Percy Humphreys, David Kerslake, Joe Knowles, Dave McEwen, Danny Maddix, Bert Middlemiss, Roger Morgan, Tony Parks, Charlie Rance, Neil Ruddock, Frank Saul, Andy Sinton, Steve Slade, Erik Thorsvedt (QPR trialist), Terry Venables (player and manager of both clubs), Paul Walsh, Alf Whyman, Clive Wilson. Wartime guests (either with one or both clubs): Captain Blake, Harry Brown, Albert Chester, John Davie, Harry Dukes, Red Edwards, Harry Ferrier, Alf Fitzgerald, Les Henley, Tom Howshaw, Archie Hughes, Jakey Jackson, Eric Jones, Bill Lawrence, George Ludford, Jackie Martin, David Nelson, Jack Pattison, Albert Sibley, Tommy Simmons, George Smith, George Travers.

Also associated: Les Allen & Alan Mullery (both Spurs players, QPR managers), Gerry Francis (QPR player and also manager of both clubs), George Graham & Peter Shreeves (Spurs managers & QPR coaches, Shreeves also assistant-manager of both clubs and Youth and reserve team manager of Spurs, as well as assistant-manager), Pat Welton (QPR player, Spurs assistant-manager), Allan Harris (QPR coach and Spurs coach), Theo Foley (QPR reserve team coach, Spurs reserve team manager), Billy Lane (Spurs player, QPR scout), Ben Ives (QPR player, Spurs player, assistant-trainer & chief scout), Ronnie Boyce (QPR chief scout, Spurs scout), Peter Suddaby (QPR Centre of Excellence Director, Spurs Academy Director).

FOOTBALL LEAGUE—DIVISION 0
TOTTENHAM HOTSPUR
v.
QUEEN'S PARK RANGERS
Official Programme
Price SIXPENCE

SEASON 1968-69
Vol. 61   No. 39

Wednesday, 29th Jan., 1969
KICK-OFF 7.30 p.m.

RACING CLUB DE PARIS

Spurs played and beat the French side, Racing Club de Paris, 5-3 in the first senior floodlit game at White Hart Lane in 1953. (See under Floodlights).
French star David Ginola played for the Paris Racing Club before moving to England.
Player with both clubs: David Ginola

RADICALS

The first known fixture played by Spurs was a friendly against the Radicals on 30th September 1882. Spurs lost by two goals.

RAMSEY, SIR ALFRED ERNEST

As a player himself - a solid, efficient and reliable right-back - Alf Ramsey started off his senior career with Southampton and then helped Spurs win successive Second and First Division championships in the early 1950s. After retiring he repeated that double as manager with Ipswich Town in the early 1960s.
Born in Dagenham, Essex on 22 January 1920, Ramsey was on Portsmouth's books as an amateur before moving to The Dell, initially in 1943 and turning professional with the Saints in August 1944. Two years after gaining a Third Division (South) championship medal he moved to White Hart Lane for £21,000 in May 1949. He remained with the London club until May 1955 when he retired to take over as manager of Ipswich Town, a position he held until January 1963 when he was named England boss.
Ramsey won 32 full caps for his country (31 as a Spurs player). His debut came in 1948 in a 6-0 win over Switzerland at Highbury. He also played at 'B' team level and represented the Football League side on five occasions. He captained his country on three occasions in the absence of Billy Wright and played in that disastrous 1-0 World Cup defeat by USA in Bela Horizonte in 1950 and in that 6-3 defeat at the hands of Hungary at Wembley in 1953.

Ramsey scored eight goals for Southampton in 90 League outings and added another 250 senior appearances to his tally with Spurs (24 goals - 20 of them penalties).

As England manager Ramsey started off very well and slowly built up a tremendously competitive team....with no direct wingers! In 1966 he was acclaimed the Messiah as the World Cup was won for the first and only time (so far) but four years later England lost their crown in Mexico 1970 when they slipped out of the World Cup in the heat to arch rivals West Germany. After failing to qualify for the 1974 World Cup Finals he lost his job.

Two years later Ramsey joined the Board of Directors at Birmingham City (January 1976) and in September 1977 he became the first knight to manage a Football League club when he took over the reins at St Andrew's, holding the fort until March 1978. Blues achieved very little under his guidance before he was forced to relinquish his position owing to poor health. His last soccer appointment took him to Greece where he acted as Technical Director of Panathinaikos, a position he held for just a few months before retiring from football to live in Ipswich where he died on 28 April 1999, aged 79.

* Ramsey's record as England manager was played 113, won 69, lost 17 with 27 draws.

RANCE, CHARLES STANLEY

Charlie Rance played in 260 first team matches for Spurs (13 goals scored). He made just over 100 League appearances without a goal - the one he did net didn't count in the end as the match v. Notts County in October 1912 was abandoned! Rance holds the club record of appearing in 131 out of 152 London Combination matches (1915-19).

Born in the East End of London, in Bow on 28 February 1889, centre-half Rance represented West Ham Schools and played for Clapton before signing as an amateur for Spurs in 1909, turning professional in July 1910. He scored on his debut for the club in the London FA Charity Cup game against Clapton Orient in the September and his League debut followed three months later against Blackburn Rovers.

Selected as a reserve for the England Amateur side on four separate occasions, he was all set to make his debut for his country when the game against Denmark in May 1910 was called off following the death of King Edward VII.

He left White Hart Lane for Derby County in March 1921 - having lost his place in the side to Charlie Walters - and then kicked himself a month later as Spurs won the FA Cup.

In September 1922 Rance returned to the capital to sign for QPR. In May 1925 he was appointed manager of Guildford and ended his career in soccer by coaching Wood Green for a short time from May 1930. He died in Chichester, Sussex on 29 December 1966.

RAPID BUCHAREST

Spurs playing record against the Romanian club

Competition	P	W	D	L	F	A
UEFA Cup	2	2	0	0	5	0

Spurs accounted for the Romanian side Rapid Bucharest 5-0 on aggregate in a third round UEFA Cup-tie in December 1971. A crowd of 30,702 saw Martin Chivers (2) and Martin Peters score in a 3-0 home win and then Chivers and Jimmy Pearce each

found the net in the return fixture which attracted just 12,000 spectators. Unfortunately Pearce blotted his copybook by getting himself sent-off in Bucharest!

READING

Spurs playing record against the Royals

Competition	P	W	D	L	F	A
Football League	6	2	2	2	14	11
FA Cup	5	2	1	2	7	6
Other Leagues	42	19	12	11	74	56
Other Cups	3	0	1	2	3	4
Wartime	15	7	7	1	33	23
Summary	71	30	23	18	131	100

Spurs and Reading first met each other at Football League level on Christmas Day in 1928 (Division 2). A crowd of 28,344 witnessed the 2-2 draw at White Hart Lane and 24 hours later, at Elm Park, 23,730 fans saw a seven-goal thriller go Reading's way to the tune of 4-3.

Spurs registered their first League win over the Royals on the opening day of the 1930-31 season, hammering them 7-1 at home when Ted Harper scored five goals in front of 25,484 spectators. Later on Spurs completed the double with a 2-1 away win.

Players with both clubs include: Steve Archibald, John Barlow, Stuart Beavon, Mark Bowen, Garry Brooke (Reading trialist), Charlie Brown, David Brown (Reading trialist), Ivor Brown, Chris Carrick, Darren Caskey, Sid Castle, Allan Cockram, Bobby Cook, Ernie Coquet, Ronnie Dix, Kerry Dixon (Spurs reserve), Matt Edwards (Spurs Youth), Matt Forster, James Fulwood, Jack Gibbons, Lee Hodges, Sid Helliwell, Bill Lane, David Leworthy, David McDonald, Tom Meads, Fred Milnes, Billy Minter, Tom Pangbourne, John Polston, Jimmy Reid, Jock Robertson, Martin Robertson, Harry Robshaw, Mark Robson, John Sainty (Spurs reserve), Max Seeburg, Fred Sharpe, Neil Smith, Brian Statham, Archie Turner (Reading trialist), Dennis Uphill, Pat Van den Hauwe, Fred Wilkes (also Reading trainer).

Wartime guests (either with one or both clubs): Bill Adams, Pat Beasley, George Burchill, Ron Burgess, Stan Clayton, Freddie Cox, John Davie, Alf Day, Doug Flack, Charlie Harbridge (Reading amateur), Les Henley, Les Howe, Tom Howshall, Phil Joslin, George Ludford, Ernie Marshall, Reg Mogford, Jimmy Morris, Billy Sainsbury, DS Slade, George Smith, Reg Smith, Cyril Williams, Joe Wilson.

Also associated: Peter Shreeves (Reading player, Spurs Youth team, reserve and first team manager and also assistant-manager), Colin Lee (Spurs player, Reading Youth development officer).

* In 1985-86, Third Division Reading beat Spurs' record of 11 successive League wins from the start of a season.

REAL MADRID

Spurs playing record against the Spanish giants

Competition	P	W	D	L	F	A
UEFA Cup	2	0	1	1	0	1

Spurs have met Real just twice at competitive level - and these matches comprised a two-legged fourth round UEFA Cup-tie in March 1985.

A noisy White Hart Lane crowd of almost 40,000 saw Real win the first leg encounter by a single goal - thus inflicting upon Spurs their first-ever home defeat in this competition and bringing to an end a run of 26 unbeaten matches. Then, for the return leg in Madrid, 95,000 spectators packed inside the impressive Bernabeu

Stadium to witness the goalless draw, a result that took the Spaniards through 1-0 on aggregate. Unfortunately for Spurs, Steve Perryman was sent-off in this latter game.

Player with both clubs: Johnny Metgod

REBROV, SERGEI

The Ukranian international striker joined Spurs from Dynamo Kiev for a club record fee of £11 million on 16 May 2000. The 25 year-old signed a five-year contract worth approximately £25,000 a week.

Born in Gorlovka on 3 June 1974, he played for Shakhtar Donetsk in the 1991-92 season before transferring to Dynamo Kiev where he stayed for eight years prior to his move into the Premiership. He had already appeared in 36 full internationals for the Ukraine when he joined Spurs and had also gained eight League championship medals (all in succession: 1993-2000 inclusive), collected four Ukranian Cup winners medals and was voted his country's 'Player of the Year, in both 1996 and 1998. He netted over 150 goals in Ukranian League and Cup football (in just over 300 appearances). His League record was 105 goals in 226 outings, while in European competitions he notched 28 goals in only 60 games.

In his first season with Spurs Rebrov, short, alert and a positive attitude in and around the penalty area, claimed 11 goals in 36 appearances. He has since added to his tally of international caps.

RED STAR BELGRADE

Spurs playing record against the Yugoslavian side

Competition	P	W	D	L	F	A
UEFA Cup	2	1	0	1	2	1

After two hard fought third round 1972-73 UEFA Cup clashes, Spurs finally went through at Red Star's expense, winning 2-1 on aggregate.

Almost 24,000 fans saw Spurs gain a 2-0 advantage from their home leg on 29 November thanks to goals by Alan Gilzean and Martin Chivers. But then it was the defence (goalkeeper Pat Jennings in particular) that held firm in Yugoslavia as Red Star somehow stole a 1-0 victory in the return leg a fortnight later in front of a crowd of 70,000.

RE-ELECTION

Spurs have never had to apply for re-election to the Football League....but at the end of the 1907-08 Southern League season they applied for election to the Second Division of the Football League. Spurs had to contend with a challenge from Lincoln City the first two ballots failing to produce a result. The League Management Committee then stepped in and placed Spurs into the League by 5 votes to 3.

REES, WILLIAM

An inside-forward from near Bridgend (born 10 March 1924) Bill Rees served with Cardiff City from 1943 until June 1949 when he joined Spurs for £14,000. He remained at White Hart Lane for just 12 months, signing for Leyton Orient for £14,500 after making 13 League and Cup appearances and scoring three goals, as the team won the Second Division Championship. He played in

over 100 games for Cardiff, helping them win the Second Division title in 1947. He gained four full caps for Wales (one as a Spurs player) and played in one Wartime international. Rees, who netted 66 goals in 198 competitive games for Orient, later playing for Headington United and Kettering Town.

On retiring Rees became a plant operator in Bridgend and later worked for a pharmaceutical company in the town.

REID, JAMES

Scottish inside-forward Jimmy Reid joined Spurs from Watford in May 1906, having already scored over 50 goals in more than 150 League and Cup games for his previous clubs which also included (in order of service) Hibernian, Burslem Port Vale, West Ham United, Fulham, Gainsborough Trinity, Worksop Town and Notts County. On leaving White Hart Lane he joined Reading (May 1908) but quickly switched to New Brompton (Gillingham) where he ended his career through injury in 1910. Born in Belshill in 1880, Reid began his footballing days with Hibs in 1898

REILLY, MATTHEW MICHAEL

Goalkeeper Matt Reilly was born in Donnybrook, Ireland on 22 March 1874. He played for Benburb, Portsmouth, Southampton St Mary's, Freemantle (on loan), Dundee and Notts County as well as representing the Royal Navy before moving to Spurs in October 1906 (after a trial). He appeared in 32 senior games for the club before leaving to join Shelbourne in August 1907. Reilly, who won two Irish caps whilst with Pompey, was 90 when he died in Dublin on 9 December 1954.

RELEGATION

Spurs have been relegated from the First Division of the Football League on four occasions - at the end of the 1914-15, 1927-28, 1934-35 and 1976-77 seasons. They bounced back straightaway as champions in 1919-20 (the first season after the Great War) and did likewise in 1977-78 when they finished in third place. After their demotion in 1928 Spurs spent five seasons in Division Two and after going down in 1935 they did not return until 1950 (eight seasons in total but 15 years overall).

RESERVES

Spurs' second XI has won the following competitions:

London Football Combination: 1919-20, 1921-22, 1925-26, 1952-53, 1955-56, 1956-57, 1961-62, 1963-64, 1965-66, 1966-67, 1967-68, 1970-71, 1971-72, 1978-79, 1979-80, 1986-87, 1987-88, 1988-89 & 1994-95 (19 successes).

Football Combination Cup: 1966-67 (shared) & 1996-97.

London League: 1898-99

London League First Division: 1902-03

South Eastern League: 1901-02, 1902-03, 1904-05 & 1910-11.

London Challenge Cup: 1936-37, 1947-48, 1958-59, 1963-64, 1970-71 & 1973-74.

Peterborough Infirmary Charity Cup: 1925-26

Studio Ten Challenge Cup: 1991-92

Transpennine Express Cup: 1992-93

Ryedale Trophy: 1993-94

Shepherd Trophy & East Coast Soccer Festival: 1995-96

Second Team Facts

Spurs's second XI's first trophy success arrived in 1898-99, when they carried off the London League championship shield. In fact, this was the first prize the club had won at any level.

Morton Cadman was a reserve team player with Spurs who later became a director of the club.

REYNOLDS, RONALD SYDNEY MAURICE

Goalkeeper Ron Reynolds wore contact lenses and when he appeared in games played under floodlights they were a nightmare!

Nevertheless he was a fine 'keeper who made 138 first team appearances for Spurs (including 86 in Division One and nine in the FA Cup).

Born in Haslemere, Hampshire on 2 June 1928, he was an amateur on Aldershot's books before turning professional at The Recreation Ground in December 1945. He moved to White Hart Lane in July 1950 and remained with the club for ten years before transferring to Southampton for £10,000 in March 1960. After 110 outings for Saints he retired in 1963 and became a scout for The Dell club and also for Crystal Palace. In the summer of 1964 Reynolds joined a firm of insurance consultant/brokers and four years later set up his own business in the same line while living in his native Haslemere.

RICHARDS, DEAN IVOR

Born in Bradford on 9 June 1974, he joined the apprentice ranks at Valley Parade in the summer of 1990 and turned professional with Bradford City in July 1992. A solid defender, good in the air, he made over 100 appearances for the Bantams before transferring to Wolverhampton Wanderers for a club record fee of £1.85 million in March 1995. He added a further 145 League and Cup appearances to his tally whilst at Molineux but when his contract expired in the summer of 1998 he left for Southampton on a Bosman ruling. Richards went on to play in almost 80 games for Saints prior to his £8.1 million transfer to Spurs in September 2001, linking up again with manager Glenn Hoddle He was capped four times by England at Under-21 level earlier in his career.

RICHARDSON, JOHN

Full-back Jock Richardson was born in Motherwell on 11 November 1906. He was developed through Spurs' nursery side, Northfleet, before signing for the club in May 1923. He appeared in 41 League and Cup games over the next four years and was then unloaded to Reading. He later assisted Bournemouth (from May 1934) and Folkestone.

ROBB, GEORGE

A dashing outside-left, compact in appearance, with two good feet and a powerful shot, George Robb first signed for Spurs from Finchley in 1944 but did not want to become a professional. Therefore he continued to assist the amateur side and gained a total of 19 international caps at that level for England before rejoining Spurs in December 1951 and finally turning professional in June 1953. Replacing Les Medley, he made the first of his 200 senior appearances for Spurs in December 1951 against Charlton Athletic at The Valley and scored to celebrate the occasion -

one of 58 goals for the club.

He represented the Football League v. the Irish League in September 1953 and two months later played on the wing when the Hungarian Magyars came to Wembley and hammered England 6-3. This was Robb's only full cap although he did gain three at 'B' team level later on (summer 1954). During the 1957-58 season he received a serious leg injury from which he never fully recovered. He retired in May 1960 and continued teaching as sports master at Christ's College in Finchley, having been in that profession prior to joining Spurs. He later held a similar position at Ardingly Public School in Sussex.

ROBERTS, CHARLES DAVID

David Roberts was Chairman of Tottenham Hotspur Football Club for 45 years, from 1898 until his death in 1943.

A former American baseball pitcher with the Brooklyn Dodgers in New York, he became a prominent figure in the South-west of England where he was deeply involved in various fund-raising events including the annual Military tattoo.

One of Roberts' first challenges was to find Spurs a new ground. He helped negotiate plans and within a matter of months Northumberland Park was vacated and Spurs moved to The High Road ground (White Hart Lane).

ROBERTS, GRAHAM PAUL

Born in Southampton on 3 July 1959, Graham Roberts was an associate Schoolboy at The Dell and represented Southampton and Hampshire Schools before joining Scholing FC. He then served brief apprenticeships with both Bournemouth and Portsmouth and was a shop-fitter's mate when assisting Dorchester Town and starring for Weymouth before signing for Spurs for £35,000 in May 1990 -

after turning down a move to West Bromwich Albion.

Playing in midfield, he was given his Spurs baptism against his former club Bournemouth in a friendly match and his League debut followed in October 1980 against Stoke City. Roberts in fact, came off the bench to appear in the first of his 287 competitive games for the club (36 goals scored). Changing to a defensive player, he picked up two FA Cup winners' medals (in 1981 & 1982) and also played in the 1982 League Cup Final defeat by Liverpool. He won the first of his six England caps v. Northern Ireland in May 1983 and twelve months later Roberts joyfully held aloft the UEFA Cup after Spurs had beaten RSC Anderlecht in the two-legged Final (he was deputising as captain for Perryman).

A stern, aggressive competitor, he never gave an inch, never shirked a tackle and simply loved to be involved in a tough contest. Unfortunately he was pushed out when David Pleat arrived at the club as manager and in December 1986 Roberts moved to Scotland to sign for Glasgow Rangers for £450,000, taking over from another hard man, Graeme Souness, also a former Spurs player.

After helping the 'Gers win both the Scottish Premier League and Skol Cup, he left Ibrox Park and moved back to London to join Chelsea (May 1988). He was appointed player-coach at Stamford Bridge in November 1989 and held that position until February 1990 when he quit after an argument with Chairman Ken Bates. He was eventually sold to West Bromwich Albion in November 1990. After that Roberts entered the non-League scene, and has now managed Chesham United, Slough Town, Hertford Town and

Boreham Wood (the latter since February 2001).

ROBERTSON, JAMES GILLEN

An outside-right, fast and clever, always keen to cut inside and try his luck at goal, Jimmy Robertson often tried take on and beat his full-back down the touchline before whipping over a tempting cross. He was a very popular player and gave Spurs four years excellent service, appearing in 157 League and 24 Cup games, scoring 31 goals.

Born in Cardonald, Glasgow on 17 December 1944, he played as an amateur for Middlesbrough, Celtic and Cowdenbeath before joining St Mirren as a professional in 1962, transferring to Spurs in March 1964 for £25,000. Already a Scottish Under-23 star, Robertson made his debut in English football at Anfield and quickly added three more intermediate caps to his collection while also playing in his one and only full international match against Wales. He scored in the 1967 FA Cup Final victory over Chelsea before moving in a £55,000 deal to Arsenal in October 1968. On leaving Highbury in March 1970, Robertson signed for Ipswich Town. A spell with Stoke City followed and after playing for Seattle Sounders in the NASL in the summers of 1976 and 1977, Robertson wound down his League career at Walsall and Crewe Alexandra, retiring in 1979 with more than 500 senior appearances under his belt.

He later became a director of a computer insurance company.

ROBINSON, MARTIN JOHN

Born in Essex on 17 July 1957, striker Martin Robinson developed via Thurrock Schools, signed apprentice forms for Spurs in July 1973 and took professionalism in May 1975.

He scored twice in six League games for the club before transferring to Charlton Athetic in February 1979. Robinson later assisted Reading, Gillingham, Southend United, Cambridge United and Enfield. He amassed more than 400 League appearances and netted 101 goals after leaving White Hart Lane.

ROCHDALE

No match action at all between Spurs and the Dale as yet.

Players with both clubs include: Ted Birnie, Herbert Chapman, Davie Colquhoun, Kevin Dearden, Archie Hughes, Don McAllister, Harry Marshall, Andy Turner.

Wartime guests (either with one or both clubs): Alex Anderson, Charlie Briggs, Jack Hall, Sid Hoad, George Hunt, Jimmy McCormick, Joe Meek, Matt Muir, Tommy Nuttall, Joey Walters.

ROMFORD

Spurs' playing record against the Essex club:

Competition	P	W	D	L	F	A
Amateur Cup	1	1	0	0	8	0

A hat-trick by Peter Hunter helped Spurs ease through their away FA Amateur Cup third qualifying round encounter against Romford on 1 December 1894.

ROSENTHAL, RONNY

Spurs recruited Israeli international attacker Ronny Rosenthal from Liverpool for £250,000 in January 1994. He did reasonably well at White Hart Lane (albeit as a substitute on a fair few occasions) and scored 11 goals in exactly 100 first team appearances (starting in 65 of those matches). Born in Haifa, Israel on 11 October 1963, Rosenthal had good proportionate body strength, smart pace and a telling shot. He played for Maccabi Haifa, FC Bruges, Standard Liege in Belgium and Luton Town (on loan) before joining Liverpool for £1 million in June 1990, having spent three months on loan at Anfield prior to that. He netted 22 goals in his 97 outings for the Merseysiders.

He left Spurs for Watford on a free transfer in August 1997, but after the Hornets had been relegated from the Premiership and had failed to bounce straight back, he announced his retirement from first-class soccer in May 1999. He was capped 60 times by his country.

ROTHERHAM UNITED (ALSO COUNTY, TOWN)

Spurs playing record against the Millermen

Competition	P	W	D	L	F	A
Football League	2	1	1	0	3	1
FA Cup	1	1	0	0	2	0
Summary	3	2	1	0	5	1

The two League games between the clubs took place in 1919-20 (Division 2), when the Yorkshire side were known as Rotherham County. Spurs won the opening clash 2-0 at home on 20 March before drawing 1-1 at Millmoor seven days later, Arthur Grimsdell's penalty earning his side a point.

Players with both clubs include: Billy Cook, Harry Hargreaves, Jim McCormick, Bobby Mimms, Joe Scott, Ian Smith, Andy Turner, Kevin Watson.

Wartime guests (either with one or both clubs): Frank Boulton, Ernie Goldthorpe, Les Howe, Harry Powell

ROWE, ARTHUR SYDNEY

Arthur Rowe invented the' 'push and run' style of football although he personally detested the phrase. He will always be associated with the great Spurs team that won the Second Division and First Division championships in successive seasons (1949-50 & 1950-51). And, indeed, for bringing in, introducing and developing so many talented players who thrilled the vast crowds that used to flock to White Hart Lane when Rowe was in charge.

A local man, born in Tottenham on 1 September 1906, he played centre-half for Cheshunt, before signing amateur forms for Spurs in 1923. Groomed with Northfleet he moved up the ladder to the professional ranks at White Hart Lane in May 1929 and spent the next decade with Spurs, amassing a fine record of 210 first-team appearances (182 in the Football League and 19 in the FA Cup). A strong, competent defender, he helped Spurs win promotion from Division Two in 1933-34 and was capped by England against France (at White Hart Lane) in December 1933 before a series of niggling injuries began to disrupt his game.

Announcing his retirement in May 1939, he coached in Hungary for a short while before returning to Britain to take over as boss of the Army side. He also played a couple of games as well as assisting the RAF! On demob he stepped up a grade to become manager of non-League Chelmsford City (July 1945).

In May 1949 Rowe was appointed manager of Spurs, a position he retained for six years. In July 1957, he joined forces with his former playing colleague, Vic Buckingham, who was manager of West Bromich Albion, Rowe taking over as chief scout.

A little over a year later Rowe moved back to London as assistant-manager of Crystal Palace (October 1958), stepping up to team manager in April 1960. He held that post until December 1962 when he was handed the role of general manager at Selhurst Park where he remained until 1971, acting as caretaker-manager for four months (January-April 1966) and assistant-manager during his final season of 1970-71.

For a period of seven months - May-December 1971 - Rowe was manager of football's Hall of Fame before becoming Leyton Orient's general adviser for six-and-a-half years: January 1972 to May 1978. He then joined the Board of Directors at Palace and was also a consultant to Millwall from June 1978. Rowe died on 5 November 1993, aged 87.

ROWLEY, RICHARD WILLIAM MORRIS

Centre-forward Dick Rowley scored ten goals in 24 League games for Spurs between February 1930 and December 1931. An Irishman from County Antrim, born 13 January 1904, he played initially for Tidworth United before joining Andover in 1922, switching to Swindon Town in 1924, to London Casuals in 1925 and onto Southampton in 1926, staying at The Dell for four years, scoring over 50 goals for Saints. He cost Spurs £3,750 and was already an Irish international when he came to White Hart Lane. He joined Preston North End (with Ted Harper) in a £5,000 joint deal and retired in 1934. He later returned to Southampton where he died in April 1984.

ROYAL ARTILLERY

Spurs playing record against the RA:

Competition	P	W	D	L	F	A
Southern League	2	2	0	0	4	2

The two games between the clubs took place in season 1898-99 when Spurs won 1-0 at home and 3-2 away.

ROYAL ENGINEERS

Spurs playing record against the Engineers

Competition	P	W	D	L	F	A
T&M League	2	1	0	1	7	4

Ken McKay scored five times when Spurs beat the Royal Engineers 6-2 at home in a Thames & Medway League game in November 1898. The return fixture later in the season ended in a 2-1 defeat for Spurs!

ROYAL ORDNANCE

Spurs playing record against the R.O.

Competition	P	W	D	L	F	A
Southern League	1	1	0	0	2	1

This Southern League game - played away in October 1896 - was not included in the final table as Ordnance resigned from the League.

RUDDOCK, NEIL

Defender Neil 'Razor' Ruddock had two spells with Spurs (April 1986-June 1988 and July 1992-July 1993). He made a total of 59 first-class appearances for the club, scoring four goals. Born in Wandsworth on 9 May 1968, he started out as a professional with Millwall, joined Spurs, first time round, for £50,000 and returned to The Den for £300,000 (good business). In February 1989 Ruddock, tough and rugged, switched his allegiance to Southampton, bought for £250,000 and it cost Spurs £750,000 to get him back! His next move took him to Liverpool for £2.5 million in July 1993 and after that he has served with three London clubs, QPR, West Ham United (signed for £100,000) and Crystal Palace. When the 2000-01 season ended Ruddock, capped by England at full, 'B', Under-21 and Youth team levels and a League Cup winner with Liverpool in 1995, had accumulated in excess of 450 club and international appearances.

* Hard man Ruddock was the first Spurs player to get sent-off in a Premiership game (v. Crystal Palace, 1992).

RUNDLE, CHARLES RODNEY

Cornishman Charlie Rundle signed for Spurs as a 23 year-old in 1946 after leaving the Navy. A centre-forward, he went on to score 12 goals in 32 competitive games for the club before transferring to Crystal Palace in June 1950. He later assisted Tonbridge and in February 1955 was appointed player-manager of Bettshanger Colliery FC.

RUSHDEN

Spurs playing record against Rushden

Competition	P	W	D	L	F	A
United League	6	2	1	3	11	11

The six games between the two clubs were often fairly tight. Spurs' best win was that of 3-1 at home in January 1898 when Frank Hartley scored a hat-trick. This came a week after Rushden had won their home match 5-2.

RYDEN, JOHN JOHNSTON

Defender John Ryden appeared in 63 League games and five FA Cup matches for Spurs, scoring two goals.

A Scotsman, born in Alexandria, Dumbarton on 18 February 1931, he served with Denny Juveniles, Duntocher Hibernians and Alloa Athletic before joining Accrington Stanley as a full-time professional in February 1954.

After representing the Third Division (North) v. the Third Division (South) in the annual fixture, he moved from Peel Park to Spurs for £12,000 in November 1955. But with Harry Clarke and Tony Marchi the priority players, he spent the next five-and-a-half years battling hard to hold down a first team place at White Hart Lane so when Jim Iley and then Dave Mackay came along, Ryden's time was up and in June 1961 he was transferred to Watford. He spent a season at Vicarage Road before rounding off his career with spells at Tunbridge Wells and Bexleyheath, serving the latter club as player-manager. After football Ryden worked for a finance and insurance company.

SAIB, MOUSSA

The first Algerian to play for Spurs, midfield playmaker Moussa Saib joined Spurs from Valencia for £2.2 million in February 1998. He made only 13 Premiership appearances (one goal scored) for the club before transferring to Al Nasr FC in December 1999.

He was born in Theniet-el-had, Algeria on 6 March 1969 and played for Jeunesse Sportive Kabylie (in his homeland) and the French club AJ Auxerre before linking up with the Spanish club. He has almost 50 international caps under his beelt.

ST ALBANS

Spurs' playing record against the Saints:

Competition	P	W	D	L	F	A
London Ass Cup	1	1	0	0	5	2

Spurs' first-ever Cup-tie (at any level) was against St Albans on 17 October 1885.

It was in the opening round of the London Association Cup and Spurs won 5-2 at home, fielding this team: Bumberry; JC Jull, Tyrell; Bull, Jovis, Casey; Buckle, Harston, Mason, Amos and Cottell. There is no record of the goalscorers.

SAMWAYS, VINCENT

Midfielder Vinny Samways played in more than 250 first team games for Spurs. At League level, however, he made 193 appearances (11 goals) and also starred in 54 various Cup encounters (6 goals).

A hard-working, enthusiastic footballer, with stamina and skill, he was born in Bethnal Green, East London on 27 October 1968 and represented East London & London Schools before joining Spurs as an apprentice in April 1985, turning professional seven months later.

He gained England Youth caps, played in five internationals at Under-21 level (the first in 1988) and was an FA Cup winner in 1991, playing extremely well after Gascoigne had gone off injured. Samways left White Hart Lane in August 1994, joining Everton for £2.2 million. After playing in two FA Charity Shield winning teams and having loans spells with Wolverhampton Wanderers and Birmingham City in December 1995 and February 1996 respectively, he moved abroad to sign for the Spanish club Las Palmas in the summer of 1996.

SANDERS, ARTHUR WILLIAM

Centre-forward Arthur Sanders was born in North London in 1901 and played for Spurs from 1925 until 1927, scoring seven goals in 13 League games. Prior to his arrival at White Hart Lane he had served in the Royal Navy and even played for his ship's team in a friendly against the South American club Rosario. He also assisted Peterborough & Fletton United and Northfleet. After leaving Spurs he again served with Northfleet and also Clapton Orient. Sanders retired in 1933 and died in Enfield in September 1983.

SARGENT, FREDERICK ALBERT

Outside-right Fred Sargent originated from Islington, North London (born on 7 March 1912). He played his early football with

Barnsbury FC and Tufnell Park before joining Spurs as an amateur in February 1934. He was nurtured at Northfleet and was taken on the professional payroll at White Hart Lane six months later, making his League debut against Derby County five weeks after that (29 September).

That was the first of 144 appearances Sargent made for the club (39 goals scored).

He was a very capable player, an attacking, all-action winger who enjoyed racing past his full-back. Sadly, after breaking his leg at Chelsea in February 1940, he never really recovered full fitness, although he did make guest appearances during the War for Alderhot, Burnley, Fulham, Hull City, Middlesbrough, Plymouth Argyle and York City. His contract was cancelled by mutual consent in May 1946, at which point he signed for non-League Chelmsford City. Just over two years later (on 22 August 1948) Sargent died in a New Barnet hospital.

SAUL, FRANK LANDER

Born in Benfleet, Essex on 23 August 1943, striker Frank Saul joined Spurs as an amateur on leaving School in August 1958 and signed professional forms on his 17 birthday. He made his League debut in September 1960 (away at Bolton) and went on to appear in a total of 129 competitive games for the club, scoring 45 goals. Regarded as a 'Boy Wonder' when playing and scoring regularly for the reserves, Saul won England Youth honours and later played for Young England against England as well as scoring in the 1967 FA Cup Final victory over Chelsea. He had to fight hard for his place in the front-line but he did well, playing alongside and deputising for some great stars including Bobby Smith, Alan Gilzean and Jimmy Greaves.

Saul (valued at £45,000) moved to Southampton as part of the transfer deal that brought Martin Chivers to White Hart Lane in January 1968. Later he assisted QPR, Millwall and Dagenham. Retiring in 1978, he quickly started up in the building and decorating business in Billericay.

SCARBOROUGH

No competitive action between Spurs and the former League club.

Players with both clubs include: Noel Brotherston, Terry Dyson, Shaun Murray (Spurs reserve), Tony Parks.

SCARTH, JAMES WILLIAM

Winger Jimmy Scarth wrote himself into the soccer record books in November 1952 when he scored a hat-trick for Gillingham against Clapton Orient inside three minutes!

Born in North Shields on 26 August 1926, he played for North Shields and Percy Main FC before having a trial with Spurs in July 1948. He was successful, turned professional a month later and went on to net three times in seven League games before transferring to Gillingham in February 1952, later serving Gravesend & Northfleet.

SCOTT, JOSEPH

A reserve outside-left from Lye in the Black Country (born on 6 July 1900) Joe Scott scored four goals in 18 League games for Spurs during his three years with the club: 1928-31. He had earlier assisted Cradley Heath, Rotherham United and Barnsley and on leaving White Hart Lane he returned to Cradley Heath. Scott died in March 1962.

SCOTTISH CONNECTION

Here is a list of Spurs personnel (players, trialists, amateurs, Wartime guests, managers, coaches) who were also associated with Scottish football either as a player (at various levels), manager, assistant-manager, scout, coach etc.

Jimmy Archibald	Motherwell
Steve Archibald	Aberdeen, Ayr United, Clyde, East Stirling, Hibernian, St Mirren, East Fife (manager)
Tom Atherton	Dundee, Hibernian, Motherwell, Partick Thistle
George Badenoch	Heart of Midlothian

Bill Bann	Broxburn		Motherwell
Jimmy Bauchop	Alloa Athletic, Clyde	Alex Hall	Dundee
David Black	Clyde, Hurlford, Rovers FC (Ayrshire)	Bill Harris	Benburg, Rutherglen
John Blair	Third Lanark	Jim Hartley	Dumbarton, Glasgow Athletic
Jim Blyth	Armiston Rovers, Falkirk, Heart of Midlothian, St Johnstone	Billy Hay	Glasgow Rangers, Maryhill FC (Glasgow), Partick Thistle, Queen's Park
John Britton	Albion Rovers, Celtic, Dundee	John Hendry	Dundee, Forfar Athletic
Ivor Broadis	Queen of the South	Bob Houston	Heart of Midlothian, Leven FC, St Bernard's
Alex 'Sandy' Brown	Glenbuck (Ayrshire), Edinburgh St Bernard's, Queen's Park	Stewart Houston	Port Glasgow Rangers
		Ted Hughes	Clyde
Bill Brown	Arbroath Cliffburn, Dundee, Carnoustie Juveniles, Carnoustie Panmure	Alex Hunter	Queen's Park
		Jakey Jackson	Kirkintillock Rob Roy, Partick Thistle
David Brown	Forthill Athletic (Angus), Greenock Morton	George Jeffrey	Motherwell
Jimmy Brown	Clydebank	Billy Joyce	Greenock Morton
Keith Burkinshaw	Aberdeen (Director of Football)	Bill Kaine	Stirling Albion
Lycurgus Burrows	Melrose (Govan)	Steve Kelly	Celtic (trialist)
Bob Cain	Airdrieonians, Albion Rovers	Jimmy Kennedy	Celtic
John Cameron	Ayr Parkhouse, Ayr United (manager), Queen's Park	Tom Kiernan	Albion Rovers, Celtic, St Mirren
		Arthur King	Aberdeen
Jim Chalmers	Greenock Morton	John Kirwan	Clyde
Alex Chaplin	Dundee Hibs	Peter Kyle	Clyde (trial), Glasgow Parkhead, Heart of Midlothian (trial), Larkhall Thistle, Royal Albert
Jock Chaplin	Dundee, Dundee Arnot, Dundee Wanderers		
Jimmy Collins	Lugar Boswell Thistle	Alex Lindsay	Dundee, Raith Rovers
Tom Collins	Bathgate, East Fife, Heart of Midlothian, Leven Thistle	Hugh Lorimer	Dundee, St Mirren
		Archie Lyle	Maryhill FC (Glasgow)
David Colquhoun	Blantyre Celtic, St Mirren	John McConnachie	Celtic, Glasgow Rangers, Maryhill FC (Glasgow)
Alfie Conn	Celtic, Coatbridge FC (manager), Edina FC, Glasgow Rangers, Heart of Midlothian, Motherwell, Musselburgh Windsor		
		Bill McCurdy	Vale of Clyde FC
		Frank McDiarmid	Dundee
David Copeland	Ayr Parkhouse	Bob McDonald	Heart of Midlothian, Inverness Caledonians
Warney Cresswell	Greenock Morton, Heart of Midlothian		
John Cullen	Celtic	Dick McElhaney	Celtic, Clyde
Jock Davidson	Celtic	Frank McEwan	Airdrieonians
James Devlin	Airdrieonians, Dundee	Jock McFarlane	St Bernard's
Ted Ditchburn	Aberdeen (WW2 guest)	Neil McNab	Greenock Morton, Ayr United
Bill Dow	Leith Athletic	Willie McNair	Aberdeen, Falkirk
Ed Downie	Heart of Midlothian	James McNaught	Dumbarton
Bill Dryburgh	Cowdenbeath	Bob McTavish	Falkirk, Glasgow Petershill, Ibrox Rosalie FC, Third Lanark
Andy Duncan	Dumbarton, Renton Thistle		
John Duncan	Broughty Thistle, Dundee	John McTavish	Dumbarton, East Fife, East Stirling, Falkirk, Partick Thistle
Johnny Duncan	Glasgow Rangers		
Gordon Durie	Hill o'Beath, East Fife, Glasgow Rangers, Hibernian	Peter McWilliam	Heatherley FC (Inverness), Inverness Thistle
Jock Eccles	Queen's Park	Dave Mackay	Heart of Midlothian, Newtongrange Star
Harry Erentz	Dundee		
Mark Falco	Glasgow Rangers	John Madden	Celtic, Dumbarton, Dumbarton Albion, Dumbarton Hibernians, Dundee
Tom Fitchie	Queen's Park		
Bobby Flavell	Albion Rovers (manager), Ayr United (manager), Airdrieonians, Berwick Rangers (scout), Heart of Midlothian, Dundee, Kilmarnock, Kirkintillock Rob Roy, St Mirren (player & manager)		
		John Mair	Glenboig FC
		Jim Milliken	Clyde, St Mirren, Third Lanark
		Bobby Mimms	Aberdeen
		Joe Moffatt	Abercorn FC, Aberdeen, Bo'ness, Kilmarnock, St Mirren
John Fleming	Armadale, St Bernard's		
Paul Gascoigne	Glasgow Rangers	James Morton	Hibernians
Pat Gilhooley	Larkhall Thistle	Alex Muir	Albion Rovers
Alan Gilzean	Dundee, Dundee Violet	Bill Murray	Inverness
Ian Gilzean	Ayr United, Dundee, Elgin City	David Nelson	St Bernard's, Douglas Water FC
Alex Glen	Fitzhuges Rovers, Glasgow Parkhead	Willie Newbigging	Lanark County
John Gorman	Celtic, Edina Hearts, Uphall Saints	Tommy Nuttall	St Mirren
Richard Gough	Dundee United, Glasgow Rangers	Frank O'Donnell	Celtic, Heart of Midlothian
Mark Gower	Motherwell	Charlie O'Hagan	Aberdeen, Greenock Morton
Alan Grubb	East Fife	Bert Page	Hamilton Academical
David Haddow	Albion Rovers, Glasgow Rangers,	Tony Parks	Falkirk

Johnny Patterson	Motherwell
John Pearson	Arbroath, Partick Thistle
Tommy Pearson	Aberdeen, Murrayfield Athletic
Bob Pryde	Brechin City, St Johnstone
Andy Ralston	Thistle FC
Jimmy Reid	Hibernian
Matt Reilly	Dundee
Graham Roberts	Glasgow Rangers
Jock Robertson	Dundee
Jimmy Robertson	Celtic, Cowdenbeath, St Mirren
Jimmy Ross	Raith Rovers
John Ryden	Alloa Athletic, Duntocher Hibernians
Hans Segers	Dunfermline Athletic
Buchanan Sharp	Vale of Leven
Gordon Smith	St Johnstone
Jocky Smith	Glasgow Rangers
Reg Smith	Dundee, Partick Thistle
Tommy Smith	Ayr United, Rosyth Recreation, St Johnstone
Graeme Souness	Glasgow Rangers (player-manager)
Bobby Steel	Kilwinning, Newmilns FC, Port Glasgow, Greenock Morton*
Danny Steel	Glasgow Rangers, Newmilns FC, Third Lanark
Bob Stormont	Dundee
Alex 'Sandy' Tait	Ayr United, Glasgow Rangers, Glenbuck Athletic, Motherwell, Royal Albert
Bob Tannahill	Kilmarnock
Bob Walker	Heart of Midlothian
Wilf Waller	Queen's Park
John Watson	Dundee, Dundee Wanderers
Findlay Weir	Maryhill FC (Glasgow)
John White	Alloa Athletic, Bonnyrigg FC, Falkirk, Rose Athletic
Bob Wilkie	East Craigie, Lochee Harp
Alex Wright	Falkirk, Hibernian
Alex Young	Falkirk, Paisley St Mirren
Willie Young	Aberdeen, Falkirk (trial)

* Steel was registered with Morton but did not play.

Tartan Talk Back
● Jimmy Collins helped Lugar Boswell Thistle win the Scottish Youth Cup in 1955-56.
● Over the years, Spurs have played the following major Scottish League clubs at first team level (in Cup, friendly, tournament football etc): Aberdeen, Celtic, Dundee, Dundee United, Dunfermline Athletic, Heart of Midlothian, Hibernian, Motherwell, Partick Thistle, Queen's Park (Glasgow), Glasgow Rangers and St Mirren.
● Spurs have also played a Glasgow XI.
● Alfie Conn was manager of Coatbridge when they won the Scottish Amateur Cup in 1986.
● Both Dave Mackay and Graeme Souness (two tough competitors) attended the same School in Edinburgh (Carrickvale).

SCOUTS
The following former Spurs players have all acted as scouts for the club: Eddie Baily, Cyril Knowles, Vic Potts (reserve), Billy Sage and Bill Whatley.
Other scouts employed by the club include: Jimmy Anderson*,

Ronnie Boyce (ex-West Ham player), Graham Carr (ex-Northampton Town player & manager), Joe Hulme (also manager), Ben Ives* and Doug Livermore*.
* These men also held the post of Chief Scout.
John Lyall was Spurs' technical co-ordinator, overseas scouting in 1989-90.
Former Spurs player and manager Arthur Rowe was chief scout at West Bromwich Albion in 1957-58.

SCREEN SPORT SUPER CUP
With all English League clubs banned from the three major European Cup competitions in 1985-86 (following the Heysel Stadium disaster) Screen Sport introduced its 'own' Super Cup for clubs who had qualified for those competitions but could not take part.
Spurs played in group 'A' where they beat Southampton 2-1 at home and 3-1 away but lost twice to Liverpool by the same 2-0 scoreline at Anfield and White Hart Lane. However, with two victories they qualified for the semi-finals only to lose to Everton (on aggregate). The first game at White Hart Lane ended goalless before the Merseysiders did the job at Goodison Park, winning 3-1 after extra-time to reach the Final.
Summary of matches:

P	W	D	L	F	A
6	2	1	3	6	9

* Mark Falco top-scored with four goals.

SCUNTHORPE UNITED
Spurs playing record against the Iron:

Competition	P	W	D	L	F	A
FA Cup	2	2	0	0	6	2

*The first of these two FA Cup games was played in January 1952, Spurs winning 3-0 away. The second tie took place in January 1987 when Spurs ran out 3-2 winners at White Hart Lane.
Players with both clubs include: Ray Clemence, John Duncan (also United manager), Andy Keeley.
Wartime guest: Sid Ottewell (Spurs).
Also associated: Keith Burkinshaw (Spurs coach and manager, United player, caretaker-manager).

SECRETARIES
Prior to 2 March 1898 - when Tottenham Hotspur Football Club became a Limited Company Incorporated - the position of Secretary was an honorary post, appointed season by season. These are the men who held office before 1898-99:

1882-83	John H Thompson, Jnr
1883-84 & 1884-85	HD 'Sam' Casey
1885-86 & 1886-87	W Mason
1887-88 & 1888-89	Frank G Hatton
1889-90 & 1890-91	R 'Bobby' Buckle
1891-92	R 'Bobby' Buckle & HD 'Sam' Casey
1892-93	Frank G Hatton & HD 'Sam' Casey
1893-94	Frank G Hatton
1894-95 & 1895-96	R 'Bobby' Buckle
1896-97	Ralph Bullock
1897-98	R 'Bobby' Buckle

NB - From March 1898 until August, 1906 the post of secretary was filled by the manager (secretary-manager)....see under Managers.

The following have all held the position of secretary of the club since 1906

Arthur W Turner	16 August 1906 to February 1949
Reg S Jarvis	February 1949 to 30 June 1967
Geoffrey W Jones	1 July 1967 to December 1981
Peter Day	Summer 1982 to June 1987
Peter R Barnes	July 1987 to 27 March 2000
John E Alexander	Since 27 March 2000

Secretary's Minutes
● John Cameron, ex-player and secretary-manager of Spurs, was also secretary of the Players' Union.
● Another former player, Billy Minter, was assistant-secretary at Spurs from November 1929 until his death in May 1940.
● Secretary Arthur Turner organised the training sessions and helped with team selection during the Second World War. He died in 1949.
● Mr John Prentice was appointed Financial Administration Controller of the club in 1981-83.
● Former Spurs player of the 1920s, Frank Hartley, later became secretary of Eton Manor FC in mid-1930s.

SEDGLEY, STEVE
Technically Steve Sedgley was a player who 'got away' from Spurs: He was a Schoolboy trialist at White Hart Lane in 1983 and in fact played several times for the juniors. Unfortunately he was not taken on and left to join Coventry City as an apprentice, turning professional at Highfield Road in June 1986. Over the next three years made over 100 appearances for the Sky Blues (and was a substitute v. Spurs in the 1987 FA Cup Final) before moving back to White Hart Lane in July 1989 for a fee of £750,000!

A deliberate, strong and resilient footballer who occupied both defensive and midfield positions, he made his Spurs debut against rivals Arsenal, gained an FA Cup winners' medal in 1991 and represented England on 11 occasions at Under-21 level while also accumulating 222 senior appearances, scoring 11 goals.

In June 1994, Sedgley was transferred to Ipswich Town for £1 million. He added 125 more appearances to his tally whilst at Portman Road and then, after signing for Wolverhampton Wanderers for £700,000 in July 1997, he slowly edged towards the 550 appearance-mark in his career with the Midland club before announcing his retirement in December 2000. Since April 2001 Sedgley has been senior coach at Kingstonian.

SEEBURG, MAX PAUL
The first German-born footballer to play in the Football League, Max Seeburg joined Spurs from Chelsea in May 1907. He only made one appearance in the aforementioned competition - lining up against Hull City (away) in September 1908.

A native of Leipzig (born 19 September 1894) Seeburg was an inside-forward who failed to get a game at Chelsea but made a further 115 in the Southern League for Spurs (five goals scored) before moving to Leyton in October 1908. He switched to Burnley in January 1910 and later assisted Grimsby Town and Reading (two spells). He worked as a carpenter in his later life and died in 1972.

SEED, JAMES MARSHALL
Jimmy Seed kicked his first football (in anger) at the age of 8. He played for his School team when he was 10 and for Whitburn as a 14 year-old. He joined Sunderland as a professional in April 1914 and when War broke out he signed up with the West Yorkshire Regiment. After serving in France for three years during which time he was gassed in the trenches, on his return to soccer, Seed was surprisingly released by Sunderland (May 1919). He regained his appetite for the game - and some of his form - with the Welsh

club, Mid-Rhondda before moving to Spurs in February 1920 for just £350. He never looked back after that, quickly regaining full fitness (after his Wartime experiences).

A clever, sometimes brilliant inside-right, with excellent vision, Seed helped Spurs win the FA Cup in his second year with the club. He went on to appear in 254 League and FA Cup games, scoring 77 goals. He was also capped five times by England.

Spurs, considering that his best days were over, allowed Seed to leave White Hart Lane for struggling Sheffield Wednesday in August 1927. How wrong they were! He helped the Owls escape relegation and in 1928-29 collected a League championship medal, adding a second twelve months later as well as going to South Africa with the FA touring party (May 1929).

After netting 37 goals in 146 games for Wednesday, Seed retired as a player in March 1931. The following month he was appointed secretary-manager of Clapton Orient, a position he held for two years before taking over the reins at Charlton Athletic (May 1933). He remained in charge at The Valley for 23 years (until September 1956). During that time the Addicks won the Third Division (South) title in 1934-35, finished runners-up in Division Two in 1935-36 and won the FA Cup in 1947, a year after losing to Derby County in the first post-War Final. Athletic also reached the Wartime Cup Final of 1943 when, in front of General (later President) Eisenhower, they were beaten 7-1 by Arsenal.

Seed who practically ran Charlton Athletic Football Club single-handed during WW2, also organised physical training schemes for the public as well as serving in the Royal Observer Corps.

When he left The Valley it was a sad day all round. But Seed wasn't out of football too long. In January 1957 he became an adviser to Bristol City and acted as caretaker-manager at Ashton Gate for a couple of weeks in January 1958 before taking over as boss of Millwall, a position he kept until July 1959 when he stepped down to act as a consultant. He then joined the Board of Directors (January 1960) and held office for the next six years.

Seed - the greatest manager in Charlton's history - died at Farnbrough, Kent on 16 July 1966.

SENDINGS-OFF
Here are details of all the known sendings-off involving Spurs players over the last 100 years (first team matches only):

Premiership

Date	Player	Opponent / Result
22.08.1992	Neil Ruddock (h)	Crystal Palace drew 2-2
26.09.1993	Colin Calderwood (a)	Ipswich Town drew 2-2
12.09.1994	Sol Campbell (h)	Southampton lost 1-2
08.10.1994	Kevin Scott* (h)	Queen's Park Rangers drew 1-1
03.05.1995	Colin Calderwood (a)	Newcastle United drew 3-3
19.01.1997	Ramon Vega (a)	Nottingham Forest lost 1-2
30.08.1997	Justin Edinburgh (a)	Arsenal drew 0-0
18.04.1998	Ramon Vega (a)	Barnsley drew 1-1
24.10.1998	Colin Calderwood (h)	Newcastle United won 2-0
19.12.1998	Chris Armstrong (a)	Chelsea lost 0-2

27.02.1999	Justin Edinburgh (h)	Derby County drew 1-1
01.05.1999	Mauricio Taricco (a)	Liverpool lost 2-3
18.12.1999	Allan Nielsen (a)	Middlesbrough lost 1-2
04.11.2000	Ben Thatcher (h)	Sunderland won 2-1
02.01.2001	Neil Sullivan (h)	Newcastle United won 4-2
17.04.2001	Willem Korsten (h)	Chelsea lost 0-3

* Later commuted and replaced by yellow card.

Football League Division 1

29.01.1927	Johnny Blair (a)	Huddersfield Town lost 0-2
24.09.1927	Johnny Blair (a)	Manchester United lost 0-3
04.12.1965	Frank Saul (a)	Burnley drew 1-1
11.02.1967	Terry Venables (h)	Fulham won 4-2
17.04.1968	Alan Gilzean (a)	Leeds United lost 0-1
05.10.1974	Phil Beal (h)	Burnley lost 2-3
11.10.1975	Terry Naylor (a)	Aston Villa drew 1-1
27.12.1976	Willie Young (h)	Arsenal drew 2-2
20.10.1979	Paul Miller (a)	Leeds United won 2-1
11.03.1980	Paul Miller (a)	Nottingham Forest lost 0-4
29.03.1982	Chris Hughton (h)	Arsenal drew 2-2
04.09.1982	John Lacy (a)	Everton lost 1-3
19.03.1983	Steve Perryman (a)	Watford won 1-0
02.04.1983	Tony Galvin (a)	Brighton & Hove A. lost 1-2
04.09.1984	Clive Allen (a)	Sunderland lost 0-1
04.09.1984	Graham Roberts (a)	Sunderland lost 0-1
28.10.1985	Paul Miller (h)	Leicester City lost 1-3
01.11.1986	Graham Roberts (h)	Wimbledon lost 1-2
28.11.1987	Steve Hodge (h)	Liverpool lost 0-2
17.09.1988	Chris Fairclough (a)	Liverpool drew 1-1
04.11.1989	Steve Sedgley (a)	Southampton drew 1-1
22.12.1990	Nayim (h)	Luton Town won 2-1
22.12.1990	Pat Van Den Hauwe (h)	Luton Town won 2-1
01.01.1991	Paul Gascoigne (h)	Manchester United lost 1-2
28.09.1991	Paul Stewart	Manchester United

| 26.10.1991 | (h) Gordon Durie (a) | lost 1-2 West Ham United lost 1-2 |

Football League Division Two

| 27.10.1928 | Cecil Poynton (a) | Stoke City lost 0-2 |
| 15.04.1978 | Don McAllister (a) | Brighton & Hove A. lost 1-3 |

FA Cup

| 31.01.1968 | Joe Kinnear (h) | Manchester United won 1-0 |
| 04.02.1998 | Stephen Clemence (a) | Barnsley lost 1-3 |

Football League Cup

14.09.1966	Alan Gilzean (a)	West Ham United lost 0-1
30.09.1980	Glenn Hoddle (a)	Crystal Palace won 3-1
03.02.1982	Tony Galvin (a)	West Bromwich A. drew 0-0
04.10.1989	Paul Stewart (a)	Southend United lost 2-3
06.10.1993	Darren Caskey (h)	Burnley won 3-2
26.10.1994	Ilie Dumitrescu (a)	Notts County lost 0-3
21.03.1999	Justin Edinburgh (F)	Leicester City won 1-0
19.09.2000	Neil Sullivan (a)	Brentford drew 0-0

European Cup-winners Cup

| 24.04.1963 | Jimmy Greaves (a) | OFK Belgrade won 2-1 |
| 29.11.1967 | Alan Mullery (a) | Olympique Marseille lost 0-1 |

UEFA Cup

15.12.1971	Jimmy Pearce (a)	Rapid Bucharest won 2-0
24.10.1984	Glenn Hoddle (a)	FC Bruges lost 1-2
20.03.1985	Steve Perryman (a)	Real Madrid drew 0-0

Southern League

| 19.011.1904 | Joe Walton (a) | Brighton & Hove A. drew 1-1 |

World War One

| 06.01.1917 | Jimmy Elliott (a) | Clapton Orient won 2-1 |

Fact File

● Jimmy Greaves was dismissed against OFK Belgrade in the European Cup-winners Cup semi-final in April 1963 and in doing so became the first Spurs player since Cecil Poynton in October 1928, to take an early bath in a competitive match.
● Frank Saul was sent-off against Burnley (at Turf Moor) on 4 December 1965....the first Spurs player to receive his marching orders in a League game for 37 years.

- Tony Galvin (Spurs) and Maarten Jol (West Bromwich Albion) were both sent-off in the first leg of the 1981-82 League Cup semi-final at The Hawthorns.
- Neil Ruddock was the first Spurs player to be sent-off in the Premiership - red-carded against his future club Crystal Palace on 22 August 1992.
- Steve Hodge was sent-off in new manager Terry Venables' opening match in charge of Spurs (v. Liverpool in Nov 1987).
- Defender Justin Edinburgh was sent-off in the 63rd minute of the League Cup Final victory over Leicester City at Wembey in March 1999. The ten men of Spurs still won 1-0.
- Defenders Colin Calderwood, Justin Edinburgh and Paul Miller share the unenviable tag of being sent-off most times as Spurs players. All three players received three dismissals.
- John Lacy was sent-off in only his third game for Spurs - in a friendly in Holland in August 1978.
- The first player to be dismissed in a senior international for England was Alan Mullery (Spurs) against Yugoslavia, European Championships, in June 1968.
- Steve Perryman was sent-off at Under-23 level for England.
- Lee Dixon, the Arsenal and England full-back, was sent-off during the FA Cup semi-final clash with Spurs at Wembley in 1993. Another Arsenal player, Gilles Grimandi, was dismissed in the Premiership game between the clubs in 1999.
- Luke Young, the Spurs defender, was sent-off playing for England against Greece in an Under-21 European championship qualifying game in June 2001.

SEQUENCES

Details of various sequences achieved by Spurs in League games:

13 successive wins	23.04.1960 to 01.10.1960
7 successive defeats	01.01.1994 to 27.02.1994
7 successive defeats	01.10.1955 to 29.10.1955
7 successive defeats	18.02.1975 to 22.03.1975
6 successive draws	09.01.1999 to 27.02.1999
22 unbeaten games	31.08.1949 to 31.12.1949
16 games without a win	29.12.1934 to 13.04.1935
33 unbeaten home games	02.01.1932 to 16.09.1933
16 unbeaten home games	22.04.2000 to 08.03. 2001*
14 without a home win	23.10.1993 to 04.04.1994
16 undefeated away games	10.11.1984 to 21.08.1985
22 without an away win	25.02.1928 to 02.03.1929
14 without an away win	06.05.2000 to 31.01.2001+
14 successive home wins	24.01.1987 to 03.10.1987

* Spurs' best unbeaten home run in the Premiership

+ Worst run in the Premiership

Other Runs:

Spurs went 14 League games without defeat between April and October 1959. This run ended with a 2-1 defeat at Sheffield Wednesday.

SHACKLETON, JOHN

Born in 1882, winger Jack Shackleton joined Spurs from Darlington in 1905. He spent twelve months at White Hart Lane, scored once in nine first-class games and left for Bury, later assisting Huddersfield Town.

SHEFFIELD UNITED

Spurs playing record against the Blades

Competition	P	W	D	L	F	A
Premiership	4	1	2	1	6	10
Football League	76	30	22	24	142	125
FA Cup	4	1	1	2	6	9
League Cup	2	2	0	0	4	1
Summary	86	34	25	27	158	145

Spurs defeated the Blades 3-1 (after a 2-2 draw) in the 1901 FA Cup Final. Almost 115,000 spectators watched the first game at The Crystal Palace ended in a 2-2 draw but there were less than 20,500 fans present for the replay at Bolton.

The first League encounter between the two clubs took place at White Hart Lane on 27 November 1909 (Division 1). A crowd of 26,000 saw Spurs win 2-1.

Spurs lost 6-2 at United in March 1924 - their heaviest League defeat in terms of goals conceded since February 1915 when they lost 7-5 at Middlesbrough.

George Hunt scored all Spurs' goals in their 4-0 home League win over the Blades in December 1933.

Spurs went out of the FA Cup in 1936 to the eventual beaten finalists Sheffield United who won a 6th round tie by 3-1.

Unknowing at the time, Spurs lost what would be their last 'official' Football League game before WW2 to Sheffield United, hammered 6-1 at Bramall Lane on the final day of the 1938-39 season.

It took Spurs ten years before they gained ample revenge for that battering as they blunted the Blades to the tune of 7-0 at White Hart Lane in November 1949. Sonny Walters (3), Les Medley (2) and Len Duquemin (2) scored the goals in front of 54,193 spectators.

A total of ten goals were scored in the two League games between the clubs in 1954-55. It was 5-0 to Spurs at White Hart Lane and 4-1 to the Blades at Bramall Lane.

Spurs beat United 5-0 again in March 1976 to complete the double over the Blades, having won 2-1 at Bramall Lane earlier in

Spurs final goal in the FA Cup Final of 1901 against Sheffield United

the campaign.

Spurs' first League game in Division Two for 27 years was against United on 20 August 1977 and they won it by four goals to two in front of 27,673 fans, defender Keith Osgood stepping up to net two penalties. (Spurs' last Second Division match had been against Sheffield Wednesday on 6 May 1950).

Spurs registered their first Premiership victory against United, beating them 2-0 at home on 2 September 1992.

Players with both clubs include: Milija Aleksic, John Blair, Lycurgus Burrows, Bob Cain, Herbert Chapman, Jack Chisholm, Pat Gilhooley, George Hunt (United trialist), George Hutchinson, Jim Iley, John L Jones, Andy Keeley, Roger Nilsen, Martin Peters (also United coach & manager), Hans Segers, Ken McKay, Danny Thomas (United trialist), David Tuttle, Joe Walton, Simon Webster.

Wartime guests (either with one or both clubs): Billy Brawn, Ernie Marshall, Billy Peake, Tommy Simmons, George Smith (also United coach).

Also associated: Stewart Houston (United player, Spurs assistant-manager), Jimmy McCormick (Spurs player, United coach).

SHEFFIELD WEDNESDAY

Spurs playing record against the Owls

Competition	P	W	D	L	F	A
Premiership	16	6	2	8	19	24
Football League	80	35	15	30	141	119
FA Cup	5	1	2	2	8	9
Summary	101	42	19	40	168	152

The first League game between the two clubs was at White Hart Lane on 25 September 1909 (Division 1). A crowd of 24,000 saw Spurs win 3-0.

Bert Bliss scored four goals when Spurs beat Wednesday 6-1 in a home League game on Boxing Day 1914.

When Spurs beat the Owls 7-3 in a home League game in August 1926, all five forwards found the net. Later in the season, Spurs lost 3-1 at Hillsborough.

Spurs lost 5-1 at Hillsborough on 1 March 1947 and when the teams met again, on 30 August 1947 - that scoreline was reversed as Spurs won 5-1 at White Hart Lane. Len Duquemin and Johnny Jordan both scored on their debuts in the second game.

A crowd of 46,645 saw Spurs beat the Owls 1-0 at White Hart Lane on 28 April 1951 to clinch the First Division championship for the first time in the club's history. Len Duquemin netted the all-important goal.

Spurs beat Wednesday 7-2 at home in a First Division match in January 1955, Johnny Gavin and Johnny Brooks both scored twice. This was the first time since December 1952 that Spurs had netted seven times in a game.

A Cliff Jones hat-trick earned Spurs a 4-1 home win over the Owls in March 1960.

Spurs' excellent run of 10 successive away League wins came to an end when they lost 2-1 at Hillsborough on 12 November 1960.

Chris Waddle scored twice against his future club when Spurs beat Wednesday 5-1 at White Hart Lane in September 1985.

Spurs doubled-up over the Owls in 1989-90, winning 3-0 at home and 4-2 at Hillsborough.

Jurgen Klinsmann celebrated his Premiership debut by scoring Spurs' winning goal in a superb 4-3 triumph at Hillsborough in August 1994.

Players with both clubs include: Andy Booth, John Collins, Ally Dick (Owls trialist), Bill Dryburgh, Bill Felton, Tony Galvin, Ted Harper, Sid Helliwell, Doug Hunt, George Hunt, Johnny Jordan, Arthur Lowdell, John Madden, Jimmy Melia, Jimmy Seed, Andy Sinton, Chris Waddle, Des Walker (Spurs junior), Findlay Weir.

Wartime guest: Ted Worrall (for Spurs).

Also associated: David Pleat (Spurs manager & Director of Football, also caretaker-manager of both clubs), Peter Shreeves (manager of Owls, also Spurs Youth, reserve and first team manager and assistant-manager), Vic Buckingham (Spurs player, Owls manager), Jock Chaplin (Spurs player, Owls trainer).

SHEPPEY UNITED

Spurs playing record against United

Competition	P	W	D	L	F	A
Southern League	8	5	2	1	23	12
T& M League	2	2	0	0	6	2
Summary	10	7	2	1	29	14

Billy Joyce netted all Spurs' goals in their 4-0 home Southern League victory over Sheppey in March 1898 and six months later

Norman sees his shot enter the net as he falls, against Sheffield Wednesday at Hillsborough. Wednesday won 2-1 and shattered Spurs' unbeaten record

John Cameron scored a hat-trick when Sheppey lost 3-2 in another SL encounter. Tom Pratt became Spurs' third hat-trick hero when he claimed a treble in a 4-1 SL away win in February 1901.

The two Thames & Medway clashes took place in 1898-99, Spurs winning 3-2 away and then 3-0 at home.

Players with both clubs include: Charlie Handley, Ted Harper, Bert Smith (player-coach).

SHERINGHAM, EDWARD PAUL

Once a goalscorer, always a goalscorer - and that simply sums up Teddy Sheringham.

He started bulging nets as a schoolboy, continued via Millwall's nursery, junior and intermediate sides, through the reserves and into the first team. He became the Lions' record marksman with 111 goals in 262 senior appearances before being transferred to Nottingham Forest in July 1991 for £2 million - having had a loan spell with Aldershot in February 1985.

He continued to score regularly for Forest, notching a further 23 goals in only 62 outings up to August 1992 when he switched his allegiance to Spurs for £2.1 million.

And still the goals flowed - 98 coming from head and feet in a total of 197 competitive games for the club before he was sold to Manchester United for £3.5 million in July 1997. Sheringham, in fact, was the Premiership's top marksman in 1992-93 with 22 goals. He finished up as leading scorer in four of his five seasons at White Hart Lane and in all netted 75 goals in the Premiership for Spurs (an existing club record).

During his four years at Old Trafford Sheringham was adored by the fans as he rattled in 46 more goals in 153 first-class matches....including that crucial equaliser in the European Champions League Final victory over Bayern Munich in 1999 - which helped clinch the treble for the Reds (Premiership and FA Cup being the other two prizes). Born in Higham's Park, London on 2 April 1966 Sheringham gained a Second Division championship medal with Millwall in 1988 and a Simod Cup winner's medal with Forest in 1992. Besides his treble success with United in 1999, he was also a member of two other Premiership-winning sides (2000 & 2001).

He was honoured by his country (England) at Youth team level and since then has added one Under-21 and 41 senior caps to his tally. He was also voted both FWA and PFA Player of the Year for 2000-01.

Now he's back with Spurs (re-signed in May 2001) - eager no doubt to score plenty of more goals to add to those he's already pocketed.

SHERWOOD, TIMOTHY ALAN

One of manager George Graham's early signings for Spurs, Tim Sherwood began his professional career with Watford in February 1987 (having been at Vicarage Road for two years as an apprentice). He made 51 appearances for the Hornets before transferring to Norwich City for £175,000 in July 1989. Two-and-a-half years with 88 more games under his belt, Sherwood was sold to Blackburn Rovers for £500,000 (February 1992) and three years later gained a Premiership championship medal with the Ewood Park club.

He made exactly 300 first-class appearances for Rovers, up to February 1999 when he switched to White Hart Lane for a fee of £3.8 million.

Previously capped once by England at 'B' team level and on four occasions by the Under-21s, he has now earned three full caps and is looking for more.

Sherwood has already appeared in more than 90 senior games for Spurs.

SHREEVES, PETER

Peter Shreeves had two spells as manager at White Hart Lane: June 1984 to May|209 1986 and July 1991 to May 1992. He was also assistant-manager 1980-84 as well as being Spurs' Youth and reserve team manager from 1980 to 1984.

A Welshman, born in Neath on 30 November 1940, Shreeves was an inside-forward with Finchley, Reading, Chelmsford City and Wimbledon before becoming Charlton Athletic's coach in 1974. He moved to Spurs to take charge of the Youth team later that year.

He then went through the various 'jobs' at White Hart Lane, right up till March 1986, Spurs taking third place in Division One in his first season as manager (1984-85). In August 1986, Shreeves was appointed coach by QPR and was all set to take over as manager at Loftus Road but Trevor Francis got the job instead. He had a spell as assisant-boss with the London club and then became Steve Perryman's assistant at Watford before returning to Spurs for the last season before the Premiership. In the 1990s Shreeves was assistant-manager/coach for a short time to the Welsh national team. In 2000 he acted as caretaker-manager of Sheffield Wednesday before the appointment of Paul Jewell.

SHREWSBURY TOWN

No major League or Cup action between Spurs or the Shrews to date:

Players with both clubs include: Jeff Ireland, David Jenkins, Arthur Jones, David Leworthy

Wartime guest: Haydn Price (Spurs).

Also associated: David Pleat (Town player, Spurs manager, caretaker-manager, Director of Football).

SINTON, ANDREW

Able to perform in a variety of positions from left-wing back, to wide midfielder to direct winger, operating down both flanks, Andy Sinton started his career as an apprentice with Cambridge United in June 1981, signing as a professional in April 1983. He made over 100 appearances (15 goals scored) over the next two-and-a-half seasons before transferring to Brentford for £25,000 in December 1985. He continued to do well at Griffin Park, netting 34 times in 182 outings for the Bees who sold him to QPR for £350,000 in March 1989. Still he clocked up the appearances - 190 for the Loftus Road club (25 more goals) before he was off again, this time to Sheffield Wednesday for £2.75 million in August 1993. He had 78 outings for the Owls (three goals) up to January 1996 when a fee of £1.5 million enticed him to White Hart Lane where he became a firm favourite with the fans, having exactly 100 first-class games and netting seven goals. In July 1999, a Bosman 'free' transfer saw Sinton move out of the Premiership to join First Division Wolverhampton Wanderers.

Born in Cramlington on 19 March 1966, Sinton was a League Cup winner with Spurs in 1999 and earlier in his career had won 12 full England caps while also representing his country at both Schoolboy and 'B' team levels.

SKINNER, JAMES FREDERICK

Half-back Jimmy Skinner was born in Beckenham, Kent on 11 October 1898 and played for both West Ham and England Schools before joining Spurs in the summer of 1919 from Beckenham.

He made his first team debut within a matter of months and went on to appear in 93 League and FA Cup games for the club, scoring three goals before having his contract terminated in March 1927. This was after failing to comply with the club's training regulations and instructions on three separate occasions. He lodged an appeal with the Football League but failed to turn up for the hearing. Skinner later ran a greengrocer's business in Enfield and a building company in Harlow where he also looked after a well-established fruit farm. He died in September 1984.

SKITT, HARRY

A Midlander, born in Portobello, Staffordshire on 26 June 1901, half-back Harry Skitt played for the Black Country outfit Darlaston and the Birmingham junior side Northfield before joining Spurs in May 1923. He had to wait eighteen months before making his League debut, the first of 230 competitive games for the club.

A very strong, compact and willing footballer, Skitt remained at White Hart Lane until July 1931 when he transferred north to Chester, retiring in April 1936. He later became a publican in Staffordshire and died in Poole, Dorset in March 1976.

SLOUGH

Spurs playing record against Slough

Competition	P	W	D	L	F	A
Southern Alliance	2	1	1	0	8	5

After drawing 3-3 at Slough in January 1893, Spurs then raced to a 5-2 home win a fortnight later. Dick Bell scored twice in both games for Spurs.

SLOVAN BRATISLAVA

Spurs playing record against the Czechoslovakian side

Competition	P	W	D	L	F	A
ECW Cup	2	2	0	0	6	2

Spurs played the Czech side in the European Cup-winners Cup competition of 1962-63 and defeated them 6-2 on aggregate in a 2nd round tie.

After losing their away game 2-0 on 5 March in front of 32,000 fans, Spurs completely dominated the return leg at White Hart Lane nine days later, winning in a canter by 6-0. Dave Mackay, John White, Bobby Smith, Jimmy Greaves (2) and Cliff Jones were the scorers in front of 61,504 spectators.

SMAILES, JAMES

Yorkshire-born outside-left Jimmy Smailes played for Tow Law Town and Huddersfield Town before joining Spurs as a 23 year-old in March 1931. He scored three goals in 16 League games for the club up to December 1932 when he moved to Blackpool for £2,000. Smailes later assisted Grimsby Town, Bradford City and Stockport County with whom he won a Third Division North championship medal. He guested for Bradord Park Avenue, Hartlepool and Huddersfield during the War and later took up coaching.

SMITH, BERTRAM

Hard-working half-back Bert Smith first played for Spurs as a guest during the Great War when he also represented the British Army against the French Army. He was subsequently signed by the club from Huddersfield Town in August 1919, having been virtually a permanent reserve with the Terriers.

Born in Higham, Kent on 7 March 1892, Smith had served with a handful of local-based teams (including Metrogas) before signing as a professional for Huddersfield in April 1913. In his first season with Spurs Smith was inspirational as the Second Divison championship was won and twelve months later he was a force again as the FA Cup came to Tottenham. He played in four international trails over a period of three seasons and gained the first of his two full England caps against Scotland in April 1921 with his second arriving in March 1922 v. Wales - a month after representing the Football League against the Scottish League.

Smith, a rock in the Spurs' defence, remained a registered player with the club until May 1930 when he took over as coach of Spurs' nursery side Northfleet. He came back to play and coach Sheppey United in September 1931 before joining the Young Boys of Berne, also as player-coach, the following month. Three years later he was back in England as manager-coach of the amateur club Harwich & Parkeston and prior to the outbreak of the Second World War he also served with Stevenage Town and Hitchin Town as player/coach and trainer/coach respectively. Smith - a football supporter all his life - died at Biggleswade in September 1969.

SMITH, GORDON MELVILLE

A Scotsman, born in Glasgow on 3 July 1954, full-back Gordon Smith joined St Johnstone as an amateur in June 1969 and turned professional in July 1971. He was transferred to Aston Villa in August 1976 and from there switched to Spurs for £150,000, in February 1979. Three-and-a-half years later he left White Hart Lane for Wolverhampton Wanderers (August 1982) and then surprisingly quit British football to play in South Africa (June 1984). Seven months later (January 1985) he switched to the USA where he spent four years playing indoor soccer for Pittsburgh Spirit before injury forced him into an early retirement at the end of the 1989 season. Smith now works for an advertising company based in Glasgow.

After representing his country as Youth team level, the industrious Smith went on to gain four Scottish Under-23 caps. He did well North of the Border before appearing in almost 100 senior games for Villa where he partnered John Gidman. He gained a League Cup winners' medal in 1977, albeit as a substitute, but then dropped out of favour, hence his transfer to White Hart Lane. He played in 67 first-class games for Spurs, helping the team re-establish itself in the First Division. Stricken by injuries, he moved to Molineux in 1982 and was a member of the Wolves side that won promotion from Division Two. He then lost his place in the defence, and as a result decided to try his luck abroad where he did well for a number of years.

SMITH, JAMES MCQUEEN ANDERSON

Goalkeeper Jimmy Smith, a Scotsman from Leith, was 23 years of age when he joined Spurs from the Rosyth Recreation club in June 1925. He remained at White Hart Lane for three-and-a-half years, joining St Johnstone in November 1928 and later assisting Norwich City and Ayr United. He appeared in 31 League and FA Cup games for Spurs.

SMITH, JOHN

Able to play as a wing-half or inside-forward, John Smith, a native of Shoreditch (born 4 January 1939) represented East London, London & Middlesex Schools before joining West Ham United, turning professional at Upton Park in January 1956. He moved to Spurs in March 1960 and scored once in 24 first-class games the club up to March 1964 when he switched to Coventry City. Smith later assisted Lyeton Orient, Torquay United, Swindon Town and Walsall (as player-coach) before taking over as player-manager of the Irish club Dundalk (1972). During a fine career he amassed well over 400 competitive appearances (387 in the Football League). He also won England Youth and Under-23 honours. Smith died in North London in February 1988.

SMITH, PERCY

Born in the quaintly-named town of Burbage Springs, Leicestershire in 1880, Percy Smith played centre-forward for Hinckley Town and Preston North End and as a half-back for Blackburn Rovers before taking over as player-manager of Fleetwood Town in June 1920. He scored 90 goals in 239 League games during his eight seasons at Deepdale, winning a League championship medal in 1904, followed up by netting five times in 172 League outings for Rovers, with whom he gained two more First Division championship medals in 1912 and 1914.

In June 1925 was appointed secretary-manager of Third Division North side Nelson and in May 1927 took charge of Bury, a position he held for almost three years until January 1930 when he became manager at White Hart Lane.

At Bury he sold Tiny Bradshaw to Liverpool for a then staggering fee of £8,250 but found only limited success on the field. He did a useful reconstruction job with Spurs, getting the team to to play excellent attacking football with the emphasis on attack.

A very strict, stern man, Smith had a tactical football brain. He organised efficient on-the-field systems that helped nullify the creative play of opponents, while at the same time he seemed to be able to get the best out of the average player.

He took Spurs to promotion as runners-up in 1932-33 and then saw them finish in third place in the top flight the following season. But an injury crisis in 1934-35 led to disasterous results and ultimate relegation. Smith was out - and with a matter of two months he was given the manager's job at Notts County (June 1935). He stayed at Meadow Lane until October 1936 and thereafter managed Bristol Rovers for twelve months until November 1937, losing his job after an 8-1 FA Cup defeat at the hands of QPR. Smith died in Watford on 18 April 1959.

SMITH, ROBERT ALFRED

Bobby Smith was a bold, brave, shoulder-charging centre-forward who scored 208 goals in 317 games for Spurs whom he served admirably from December 1955 to May 1964. He netted in both the 1961 and 1962 FA Cup Final wins and was a key figure when the European Cup-winners Cup was won in 1963. He was Spurs' top marksman in their double-winning season with 33 goals in total, having earlier (in 1957-58) equalled Ted Harper's 1930-31 seasonal record haul of 36 League goals.

Smith also hit 13 goals in 15 full international appearances for England (1960-63).

Born in Lingdale, North Yorkshire on 22 February 1933, he played initially for the Redcar Boys Club, Tudor Rose FC and Redcar United before joining Chelsea as an amateur in the summer of 1948, turning professional in May 1950. He moved from Stamford Bridge to Spurs for £16,000 (signed to replace Eddie Baily) and on leaving White Hart Lane he teamed up with Brighton & Hove Albion (signed for £5,000), helping the Gulls win the Fourth Division title in 1964-65. He later served with Hastings United and Banbury United, retiring in 1970. After hanging up his boots Smith became a part-time driver and labourer while at the same time suffered painfully from a series of injuries suffered whilst putting himself about on the soccer pitch.

SMITH, THOMAS

Tricky outside-right Tom Smith, with his tweaked, curly moustache, made over 60 appearances for Preston North End before joining Spurs in May 1898. Over the next four years he was a star performer in the front-line and gained both Southern League championship and FA Cup winners' medals while scoring 41 goals in 181 competitive games. He also played for an England XI (in a game arranged to boost the Players Union Funds). Smith, who was born in Maryport, Cumberland on 26 November 1876, returned to Preston in March 1904 and later served with two of his local clubs, Carlisle United and Maryport Tradesmen. Smith died in the North-west on 26 April 1937.

SMY, JAMES

Inside-forward Jimmy Smy was born in Edmonton and joined Spurs in January 1929 from Hampstead Town. He stayed at the club until the summer of 1932, making 17 League appearances and scoring six goals. Smy later served with Sittingbourne.

SOUNESS, GRAEME JAMES

Certainly 'one that got away' as far as Spurs are concerned. Tough-tackling midfielder Graeme Souness made just one substitute appearance for the club (against Keflavik in the UEFA Cup in 1971). He then joined Middlesbrough for £32,000 in 1973 (after a spell with Montreal Olympic) and thereafter served with Liverpool, Sampdoria and Glasgow Rangers as well as representing Scotland in 54 full internationals. Souness appeared in some 600 competitive games after leaving White Hart Lane, winning medals galore (including five Football League championships, four League Cups, three European Cups, four Scottish League Cups, the FA Cup and the Second Division title). He has also been a competent manager with Liverpool, Rangers, Southampton and Blackburn Rovers, leading the latter club into the Premiership in 2001.

Born in Edinburgh on 6 May 1953, Souness also represented his country at Schoolboy, Youth and Under-23 levels. He was also part-owner of Rangers when he was at Ibrox Park (April 1986-April 1991).

SOUTH SHIELDS (SEE GATESHEAD)

Spurs playing record against the North-east club:

Competition	P	W	D	L	F	A
Football League	2	2	0	0	5	0
FA Cup	1	1	0	0	2	0
Summary	3	3	0	0	7	0

The two League games between Spurs and South Shields took place in season 1919-20 (Division 2). On 13 September Spurs won 2-0 at home and followed up with a 3-0 away success seven days later when debutant Charlie Wilson scored a hat-trick, at Horsley Hill Road.

The FA Cup-tie took place in January 1953 when Spurs won 2-0 at Redheugh Park (South Shields having moved to Gateshead in 1930).

Players associated with both clubs - see under Gateshead.

SOUTHAMPTON

Spurs playing record against Saints

Competition	P	W	D	L	F	A
Premiership	18	8	5	5	31	19
Football League	72	30	20	22	130	92
FA Cup	5	2	2	1	6	5
League Cup	2	1	0	1	2	2
Other Leagues	44	18	12	16	66	52
Other Cups	1	1	0	0	2	0
SS Super Cup	2	2	0	0	5	2
Wartime	14	8	3	3	38	24
Summary	158	68	42	48	280	196

As FA Cup holders, Spurs were eliminated from the competition in 1901-02 by their Southern League colleagues Southampton, who won a 3rd round tie at the third attempt, going through 2-1 at neutral Elm Park, home of Reading, after 1-1 and 2-2 draws.

A Southern League game between Spurs and Saints in 1904-05 was abandoned at half-time through heavy rain. Spurs, ahead at the time by 2-1, could only draw the 'replay' 1-1.

The first Football League meeting between the two clubs took place at The Dell on 1 September 1928. It ended level at 1-1. Later in the season Spurs beat the Saints 3-2 at White Hart Lane.

A crowd of almost 29,000 saw Joe Meek (3) and George Hunt (3, one penalty) lead the goal-rush as Spurs crushed Southampton 8-0 in a home Second Division match in March 1936 (they led 5-0 at halftime). Earlier in the season Saints had won 2-0 at The Dell. Just under 16,000 fans saw Johnny Morrison fire a smart hat-trick past Saints in a 5-0 Spurs win in April 1938.

A crowd of just 9,454 saw Spurs play Southampton in a Second Division League game on Christmas Eve, 1938 - the lowest attendance at White Hart Lane that season.

Over a period of 20 years - between 1928 and 1948 - Saints won only one League game at White Hart Lane (3-1 in Dec 1930).

Eight goals were scored in the Spurs-Saints League game at White Hart Lane in November 1967, Spurs winning 5-3. And they went on to complete the double by gaining a 1-0 victory at The Dell.

The point gained in a 0-0 draw at The Dell on the last day of the 1977-78 season was enough to earn Spurs promotion back to the top flight.

Spurs, having won 2-

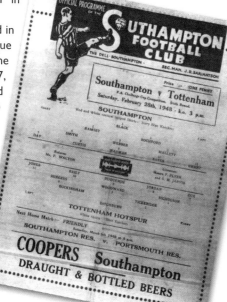

1 at The Dell, duly completed another double over Saints in 1967-68 with a thumping 6-1 home victory on 6 April, Alan Mullery, Martin Chivers and Jimmy Greaves all figuring on the scoresheet.

A 3-3 draw at Southampton in April 1979 was followed by a 4-4 draw at White Hart Lane in Dec 1980 and in between times Spurs also lost 5-2 at The Dell (Sept 1979) 21 goals in three games.

Graham Roberts scored in Spurs' 2-1 win at the Dell in October 1981 and then netted a hat-trick when the Saints were beaten 3-2 at White Hart Lane in March 1982.

Around this time Spurs loved playing against Southampton - and this was emphasised in September 1982 when they romped to a 6-0 home win and doubled-up (again) with a 2-1 victory on the south coast the following May.

More goals followed - nineteen in fact - as Spurs lost 5-0 at The Dell in May 1984, won 5-1 at White Hart Lane in March 1985 and registered another 5-3 home win in May 1986.

Also in 1985-86 Spurs defeated Saints 2-1 at home and 3-1 at The Dell in two Group 'A' Screen Sport Super Cup encounters. The competition was arranged after English clubs had been banned from Europe.

Spurs' first Premiership opponents were Southampton whom they met at The Dell on Saturday 15 August 1992. The game ended 0-0 in front of 19,654 spectators.

Spurs ended a run of 14 home Premiership games without a win when they defeated Saints 3-0 in April 1994.

Substitute Ronny Rosenthal scored a hat-trick as Spurs beat Saints 6-2 after extra-time in a 5th round FA Cup replay at The Dell in March 1995. It was 2-2 at the end of 90 minutes; the first game having ended 1-1. A month later Spurs returned to the same ground and this time lost 4-3 in a Premiership match. On 22 March 1999 Spurs ended a sequence of six successive Premiership draws by beating Saints 3-0 at White Hart Lane.

Steffen Iversen (3) and Chris Armstrong (2) led the goal-rush when Spurs licked Saints 7-2 in a Premiership game at White Hart Lane in March 2000.

Saints left The Dell after 103 years occupation in May 2001 and the last time Spurs played there was on 27 December 2000 when they lost 2-0 in the Premiership.

Players with both clubs include: Joe Blake, Tommy Cable, Martin Chivers, George Clawley, Ian Culverhouse (Saints junior), Alf Day, Ally Dick, Kerry Dixon (Spurs Youth Reserve), Dickie Dowsett, Jack Elkes, Alex Glen, Alf Hawley, John Hollowbread, David Howells, Doug Hunt, Ernie Jones, John 'Tiny' Joyce, John McConnachie, Frank Osborne, Alf Ramsey, Matt Reilly, Ron Reynolds (also Saints scout), Dean Richards, Graham Roberts (Saints associate Schoolboy), Dick Rowley, Neil Ruddock, Frank Saul, Archie Turner, Wilf Waller.

Wartime guests (either with one or both clubs): Joe Davie, Tom Kiernan, AW Thwaites, Eric Tomkins, Alf Whittingham.

Also associated: Glenn Hoddle (Spurs player & manager, Saints manager), Graeme Souness (Spurs player, Saints manager), John Gorman (Spurs player & assistant-manager of both clubs), Harry Evans (Saints player, Spurs assistant-manager), John Sainty (Spurs reserve player, Saints coach).

● Spurs were made to pay Saints £910,000 in compensation for taking Glenn Hoddle away from the club (as manager).

SOUTHEND UNITED

Spurs playing record against the Shrimpers

Competition	P	W	D	L	F	A
FA Cup	3	2	1	0	10	6
League Cup	2	1	0	1	3	3
Wartime	4	1	0	3	9	12
Summary	9	4	1	4	22	21

Former White Hart Lane professional Len Bolan scored for Southend in a famous 4-4 FA Cup draw with Spurs in January 1936.

When Spurs lost 3-2 to the Shrimpers in a League Cup 2nd round 2nd leg encounter at Roots Hall in October 1989 they had striker Paul Stewart sent-off.

Spurs progressed on the away goal rule after the aggregate score had finished level at 3-3.

● Players with both clubs include: Jimmy Archibald, Dean Austin, Fred Barnett, Sam Bell, Len Bolan, Sammy Brooks, Guy Butters, Eddie Clayton, Arthur Crompton, Les Dicker, Dickie Dowsett, Justin Edinburgh, Almer Hall, Roy Hollis, Scott Houghton, Charlie Jones, Colin Lyman, Tom Mason, Paul Moran, Martin Robinson, Taffy Spelman, Micky Stead, Alex Steel, Mark Stimson, Peter Taylor (also Southend manager), Andy Turner.

Wartime guests (either with or both clubs): Ken Bennett (Southend junior), Tom Caldwell, Harry Gilberg, Harry Jackson, Eric Jones, Phil Joslin, George Ludford, Jimmy McCormick, Ernie Marshall, John Oakes, Ernie Phypers, Albert Sibley, Joey Walters, Charlie Whitchurch, Archie Wilson.

● Also associated: Ted Birnie (Spurs player, Southend manager), Theo Foley (United assistant-manager/coach, Spurs reserve manager), Bill Cartwright & Peter Collins (Spurs players, Southend coaches).

SOUTHERN ALLIANCE

Spurs played in the Alliance in season 1892-93, completing 12 fixtures.

Their full record was:

P	W	D	L	F	A	Pts	Post.
12	7	2	3	29	21	16	3rd

Spurs were invited along with nine other clubs to become founder members of the Southern Alliance in 1892. They had an excellent first season, lost only three matches, but the club's officials thought the competition was unsuccessful and Spurs withdrew their membership in May 1893.

Their best wins of the seven recorded were two at 5-2 - against Windsor & Eton and Slough, both at home. Their heaviest defeat was a 4-1 reverse at Upton Park.

SOUTHERN LEAGUE

Spurs participated in the 'old' Southern League from 1896 to 1908 (12 complete seasons).

Their overall record was impressive:

P	W	D	L	F	A	Pts
360	180	75	105	640	401	435

They were unbeaten in 255 of their 360 matches. Surprisingly they only won the championship once - in 1899-1900 - when they amassed 44 points out of a possible 56 to squeeze home three points ahead of Portsmouth. This triumph coincided with Spurs' first season at White Hart Lane and their average home attendance was 8,571, with a best turnout of 15,000 watching them beat Southampton 2-0 on 13 April to set them up for the title.

Spurs had battled hard and long throughout the campaign with Pompey.

Both teams won their respective home game - Spurs by 3-0 and Portsmouth 1-0. But Spurs held their nerve, won seven of their last eight matches to clinch the star prize by defeating New Brompton (now Gillingham) 2-1 away on the last day of the season (28 April) when over 1,500 fans travelled down to Kent.

Tom Pratt top-scored for Spurs in 1899-1900 with 25 goals - although officially the final tally was recorded as 20 as five were scrubbed off due to the resignation of Cowes and Brighton United and the abandonment of a clash with Bristol Rovers. Pratt, in fact, netted a hat-trick in three successive matches during the first part of February - against Sheppey United, Brighton United and Bedminster - although, as stated, that treble against Brighton was to no avail!

Spurs were runners-up in 1901-02 and 1903-04 and they finished in third place in 1897-98 and 1898-99. Their lowest placing was 7th in the last campaign of 1907-08.

Taking into consideration the abandoned matches and games involving teams that resigned, Tom Morris (236) and Sandy Tait (203) made most appearances for Spurs in Southern League action (the only players to star in over 200 games). David Copeland (46), Vivian Woodward (45) and John Cameron (41) were the top marksman.

Tottenham Hotspur Football Club 1905-1906

SOUTHPORT

No competitive action between Spurs or the former Football League club.

Players with both clubs include: Frank Drabble, John Kirwan, Harry Marshall, Buchanan Sharp.

Wartime guests (either with one or both clubs): Alex Anderson, Len Flack, Tom Howshall, Albert Tomkin, Ted Worrall.

* Tom Roberts played for Spurs and Southport Vulcan.

SPARROW, F HENRY

Signed from Leicester Fosse in January 1914, centre-forward Harry Sparrow scored seven goals in 19 League and FA Cup games for Spurs before being whisked off to War in 1915. He had earlier played for Portsmouth, Sittingbourne and Croydon Common and had done well at Leicester, netting 29 goals in 52 games for the Foxes.

Born in Faversham on 11 June 1889, Sparrow died in Lincoln in 13 June 1973.

SPELMAN, ISAAC

Half-back Taffy Spelman played for Leeds United and Southend United before joining Spurs in May 1937. From then until May 1946 (when he joined Hartlepool) he appeared in 43 competitive games for Spurs (two goals scored) while also guesting for Bradford City, Darlington, Fulham, Gateshead, Hartlepool and York City during the War. Born in Newcastle-upon-Tyne on 9 March 1914, Spelman was once a miner at Usworth Colliery.

SPIERS, CYRIL HENRY

Born in Witton, Birmingham on 4 April 1902, goalkeeper Cyril Spiers had an interesting soccer career. He played at junior level for Brookvale United and Handsworth Central before joining Halesowen in 1919. From there he switched to Aston Villa in December 1920 and after a trial at White Hart Lane in November 1927, he signed for Spurs in December 1927, having made 112 appearances for the Midland club.

He remained with Spurs for almost six years, during which time he made 169 League and FA Cup appearances before transferring to Wolverhampton Wanderers in September 1933. He retired as a player in May 1935 and was appointed coach/assistant-manager at Molineux in August 1935. His next move took him to Wales and Cardiff City where he became assistant-manager (March 1939), moving up to team manager in April 1939. Spiers was placed in charge of Norwich City in June 1946; in December 1947 he returned to Cardiff as manager and remained at Ninian Park until April 1954.

His next job was to manage Crystal Palace (October 1954-June 1958) later serving with Leicester City (chief scout, September 1958-April 1962), Exeter City (manager, May 1962-February 1963) and Leicester again (as chief scout, February 1963-May 1965).

He didn't miss a single game for Spurs in almost three years (November 1928 to October 1931) having a run of 124 consecutive outings during that time. He represented the Football League against the Scottish League in 1930 and played in an international trial for England in March 1931, but lost out to Birmingham's 'keeper Harry Hibbs.

Spiers - who discovered Johnny Byrne when he was in charge at Crystal Palace - died on 21 May 1967

SPONSORSHIP

Spurs were sponsored by Holsten from late 1983 until the end of the 1994-95 season. Then an initial four-year deal (worth £4.1 million) was secured with Hewlett Packard.

In the summer of 1999 Holsten 'returned' as the club's sponsors and have been so ever since.

* The first time the Holsten 'logo' appeared on the front of the player's shirts during a Spurs senior game was against Manchester United at Old Trafford on 16 December 1983.

SPORTING BRAGA

Spurs playing record against the Portuguese club

Competition	P	W	D	L	F	A
UEFA Cup	2	2	0	0	9	0

As holders of the UEFA Cup, Spurs started their defence of the trophy in 1984-85 with a comfortable first round victory over the Portuguese side Sporting Braga.

A crowd of 30,000 attended the first leg in Portugal which Spurs won 3-0, Mark Falco (2) and Tony Galvin the scorers. A fortnight later, on 3 October, just under 22,500 fans saw Garth Crooks (3), Gary Stevens, Chris Hughton and Falco destroy Braga to the tune of 6-0 at White Hart Lane as Spurs completed a competent 9-0 aggregate victory.

SPROSTON, BERT

Cool, immaculate full-back Bert Sproston had an excellent playing career which spanned some 18 years (1932-50). Born in Elworth, Cheshire on 22 June 1915, he began with Sandbach Ramblers and had trials with Huddersfield Town before joining Leeds United in May 1933. During his five years at Elland Road he made 140 senior appearances. In June 1938 he moved to Spurs for £9,500 and added nine League games to his tally but after only four-and-a-half months at White Hart Lane he was sold to Manchester City - and made his debut for his new club against his old (Spurs). He remained at Maine Road until August 1950, making 134 appearances and helping City win the Second Division title in 1947. Capped eleven times by England (twice as a Spurs player) Sproston also played in two Wartime intenationals. He ended his playing days with Ashton United before becoming coach and laater scout for Bolton Wanderers. He died on 27 January 2001.

STANSFIELD, HAROLD

Scorer of four goals in 81 senior appearances for Spurs, utility forward Harry Stansfield was born in Manchester on 21 July 1878 and played initially for Berrys FC before taking professional status with Preston North End (August 1899). He then served with Stockport County (from July 1900) before joining Spurs in August 1904. He remained at White Hart Lane for four years, transferring to Luton Town in May 1908. He finished his major career with Bristol Rovers (1913-15). Stansfield - who was able to occupy any front-line position - made 136 League appearances for Luton (25 goals scored).

STATHAM BRIAN

Born in Zimbabwe on 21 May 1969, full-back Brian Statham made 27 first-class appearances for Spurs before transferring to Brentford in February 1992, after loan spells with Reading and Bournemouth. An England Under-21 international (three caps) he lined up in 206 League and Cup games for the Bees and then switched to Gillingham in August 1997, taking his overall tally of senior appearances up to 268 before drifting into non-League soccer in 1999.

STEEL, DANIEL

Centre-half Dan Steel scored five goals in 182 first-class appearances for Spurs. He was born in Newmilns, Ayrshire on 2 May 1884 playing for Newmilns FC and Glasgow Rangers before joining Spurs in May 1906. He spent six years at White Hart Lane before transferring to Third Lanark in July 1912, rounding off his career with a season back in London with Clapton Orient (1914-15).

He was reserve to Ted Hughes and Tom Morris during the early stages of his Spurs career but having taking over from Walter Bull in November 1907 he became a permanent fixture in the side, giving the club excellent service, along with his brother Bob (below).

Dan Steel was a muscular, flexible defender who was surprisingly calm under pressure, hardly ever giving the ball away. He tackled with great determination and was not short on pace. He played for the Anglo-Scots against the Home Scots in three international trials before losing his place in the side to Charlie Rance. He was released by the club at the end of the 1911-12 season. Steel died in Marylebone, London on 29 April 1931.

STEEL, ROBERT LOUDOUN

Bob Steel could play equally as well at centre-half or inside-forward. He made 276 senior appearances for Spurs between September 1908 and April 1915.

Like his brother (Dan) he was also born in Newmilns on 25 June 1888 and played for his home town team, as well as Kilwinning and Port Glasgow FC. He had actually signed for Greenock Morton before joining Spurs in readiness for their first season in the Football League. He made his debut in the opening game versus Wolves (h) on 1 September and he too represented the Anglo-Scots v. the Home Scots in an international trial in 1909. Solid, confident, proud to wear the Spurs colours, he was certainly a majestic defender when occupying the centre-half position. He was retained by the club throughout the duration of the Great War but was then released in the summer of 1919, joining forces with Gillingham in December of that year. Steel, always a very keen and active sportsman, retired from competitive football in May 1920 and later represented the England bowls team He died on 28 March 1972.

STEPHENSON, JOHN WALLACE

Essex-born full-back John Stephenson's career took him from Liverpool to New Brighton Tower to Swindon Town and finally to Spurs in April 1901. Unfortunately illness and injury ruined his career and after only 17 first-class games for Spurs he was forced to retire in May 1904. He died of pneumonia in January 1908 at the age of 33.

STEVENS, GARY ANDREW

Born in Hillingdon, Middlesex opn 30 March 1962, Gary Stevens represented West Suffolk & Suffolk Schools and was on associate schoolboys forms with Ipswich Town before joining Brighton & Hove Albion as a professional in October 1979.

A central defender, he lined up alongside Steve Foster in the Gulls' back division and gained England Under-21 recognition as well as appearing in the 1983 FA Cup Final v. Manchester United before transferring to Spurs for £350,000 a month after scoring in the first game of that Wembley disappointment.

He arrived at White Hart Lane in a confident mood but found it hard initially before being switched to full-back where he played superbly, adding further Under-21 caps to his collection. He was tried in midfield and even then produced some excellent performances, helping Spurs win the 1984 UEFA Cup and representing his country at senior level. Unfortunately injuries interferred with his performances towards the end of his Spurs' days and after amassing exactly 200 first-class appearances for the club he was transferred to Portsmouth for £200,000 in March 1990, after a two-month loan spell at Fratton Park.

Bob Crompton (Blackburn Rovers) and Bob Steel (Spurs) deciding the toss at White Hart Lane, 1910-11

Forced to quit the game in February 1992 (after more injury problems) Stevens maintained his interest in football by working for Capital Radio in London.

STEVENS, LESLIE WILLIAM GEORGE

Outside-left Les Stevens spent 12 years with Spurs. He joined the club as an amateur in May 1937, gained experience with Northfleet and then turned professional in January 1940. During the War he guested for Aldershot, Arsenal, Charlton Athletic, Chelsea, Crystal Palace and Millwall and when he left White Hart Lane (for Bradford Park Avenue) Stevens' record was a reasonable one - 13 goals in 92 first team appearances.

From the Yorkshure club he switched back to London to sign for Crystal Palace (August 1950) and then assisted Tonbridge, Snowdon Colliery Welfare FC, Ashford and finally Cambridge United, retiring in 1957.

Stevens, who was born in Croydon, Surrey on 15 August 1920, ran an off licence in London's New Cross area during the 1960s.

STEWART, PAUL

Versatile forward Paul Stewart made his senior debut for Blackpool in 1981 and played his 600th and final game at senior level in 1998 for Stoke City. He also scored 145 goals, won three full caps for England and played in one Under-21 and five 'B' internationals while also gaining Youth honours for his country.

Born in Manchester on 7 October 1964, Stewart joined the apprentice ranks at Bloomfield Road in 1979 and turned professional in October 1981. He moved to Manchester City for £200,000 in March 1987 and switched from Maine Road to White Hart Lane in June 1988 for a then club record free of £1.7 million. He went on to net 37 goals in 172 League and Cup games for Spurs, gaining an FA Cup winners' medal in 1991 before transferring to Liverpool for £2.3 million in July 1992.

He gradually wound down his career by serving, in turn, Crystal

Palace, Wolverhampton Wanderers, Burnley and Sunderland (all on loan), Sunderland (on a permanent basis: from March 1996) and finally Stoke City (from June 1997 to May 1998).

STOCKERAU (SV)

Spurs playing record against the Austrians

Competition	P	W	D	L	F	A
ECWC Cup	2	1	1	0	2	1

Spurs' first competitive game in a major European competition for six years was against the Austrian side SV Stockerau in the preliminary round of the 1991-92 Cup-winners Cup competition. A crowd of 15,500 saw Gordon Durie's 38th minute goal earn Spurs a 1-1 draw in the first leg in Austria on 21 August. Then a fortnight later 28,072 spectators were present as Gary Mabbutt's 41st minute effort in the return leg sewed up the tie 2-1 on aggregate.

STOCKPORT COUNTY

Spurs playing record against the Hatters

Competition	P	W	D	L	F	A
Football League	6	4	1	1	11	5
FA Cup	1	1	0	0	4	0
Summary	7	5	1	1	15	5

Spurs and County first met in the Football League on 31 October 1908 (Division 2) and in front of 16,000 fans at White Hart Lane the game ended in a 0-0 draw.

Players with both clubs include: Bill Berry, Ed Downie, Bert Elkin, Jim Freeborough, Gareth Howells (Spurs reserve), Jimmy Kennedy, Tommy Lunn, Tom Meads, Bert Middlemiss, Ernie Newman, Jimmy Pass, Joe Raby, Jimmy Smailes, Harry Stansfield, Andrew Swan.

Wartime guests (either with one or both clubs): Davie Colquhoun, Stan Eastham, Jack Hall, Bill Whatley.

Also associated: John Sainty (Spurs reserve, County assistant-manager).

STOKE CITY (also STOKE)

Spurs playing record against the Potters

Competition	P	W	D	L	F	A
Football League	66	35	15	16	109	71
FA Cup	7	1	2	4	6	15
Summary	73	36	17	20	115	86

The first League game between the two clubs was played at White Hart Lane on 3 April 1920 (Division 2) and it ended Spurs 2 Stoke 0, Arthur Grimsdell and Jimmy Dimmock the scorers in front of 36,000 fans. A week later Jimmy Cantrell netted twice as Spurs doubled up with a 3-1 win at The Victoria Ground.

A rare goal by Stanley Matthews was enough to beat Spurs in a 3rd round FA Cup replay at The Victoria Ground in January 1947. A crowd of 65,681 had witnessed the 2-2 draw at White Hart Lane and there were almost 39,000 fans present for the replay.

Spurs twice beat the Potters 6-1 in the matter of 12 months - in October 1950 (when Les Bennett and Len Duquemin both scored twice) and in September 1951 at Stoke (when Les Medley netted a brace).

Steve Archibald ended the 1982-83 season with a hat-trick in Spurs' 4-1 home win over the Potters.

Of the 33 League games played at White Hart Lane, Stoke have only won one - a 2-0 success in February 1975 when almost 23,000 fans saw Jimmy Greenhoff and Alan Hudson breach the Spurs defence.

Players with both clubs include: Paul Allen, Garry Brooke, Joe Brough, George Clawley, Garth Crooks, Ray Evans, Ken Hancock (Potters Amateur), Archie Heggarty (Spurs reserve), Fred Latham,

Billy Leech, Gerry McMahon, Ian Moores, James Morton, Tony Parks, Jimmy Robertson, Hans Segers, Paul Stewart, Charlie Wilson.

Wartime guests (either with one or both clubs): Tom Howshall, Tom Kiernan, Tommy Pearson.

STOKES, ALFRED FREDERICK

A native of Hackney, East London (born on 3 October 1932) inside-forward Alfie Stokes was at White Hart Lane at a time

Stoke City connection with Garry Brooke who played for both clubs

when there were so many other talented inside forwards registered with the club. Nevertheless he achieved a magnificient record with Spurs, netting 42 goals in 69 League and FA Cup appearances, winning England Under-23 recognition and representing the Football League before transferring to Fulham for just £10,000!

He had joined the club as an amateur from Clapton in June 1951 and turned professional in February 1953, making a scoring debut against Bolton Wanderers in front of more than 40,000 fans at Burnden Park in a First Division game two months later.

He continued to hit the target for the Cottagers (six goals in 15 games) and did likewise, on a lesser scale, with Cambridge City, Watford (from April 1961), Nuneaton Borough and Guildford City (1962-63). He was then a chauffeur for a short while prior to emigrating to Australia

STORMONT, ROBERT

Scottish-born half-back or inside-forward, Bob Stormont played seven League games for Dundee from August 1896 before joining Spurs in July 1897 at the age of 23. He remained with the club for four years, transferring to Brentford in June 1901, before having a spell with Maidstone. He retired in 1909.

Rough and ready, fearless and very competitive, Stormont was a big favourite with the supporters and he appeared in 235 first team games for Spurs (177 at competitive level) scoring 24 goals. A member of the 1899-1900 Southern League championship-winning side, he missed out on an FA Cup Final medal the following season (to John L Jones).

SUBSTITUTES

Players with most substitute appearances for Spurs (senior level):

Player	League	Cups	Total
Paul Walsh	44	14	58
Jimmy Pearce	33	19	52
David Howells	39	9	48
Jose Dominguez	33*	9	42
Micky Hazard	31	8	39
Garry Brooke	24	14	38
Ronny Rosenthal	33	2	35
John Pratt	24	10	34
Vinny Samways	28	6	34
Justin Edinburgh	23	7	30
Paul Moran	22	8	30

* Most in the Premiership

Bench Talk

Roy Low was the first player to be used as a League substitute by Spurs - coming off the bench to replace Derek Possee during the North London derby against Arsenal on 11 September 1965.

Only one other Spurs player was used as a 'sub' during that first season of the number 12 shirt - winger Neil Johnson for Alan Mullery in the 4-0 home win over Blackburn Rovers on 29 January.

The first 'sub' for Spurs in the FA Cup competition was Cliff Jones who replaced Dave Mackay in the semi-final showdown with Nottingham Forest at Hillsborough in April 1967.

The first player to come off the bench in a League Cup-tie for Spurs was Dennis Bond (for Terry Venables) v. Peterborough United (h) 16 October 1968.

The first Spurs 'sub' to appear in a European game was Jimmy Pearce (on for Ralph Coates) in the UEFA Cup clash with Keflavik in Iceland on 14 September 1971. This was followed soon afterwards when Graeme Souness replaced Alan Mullery.

Winger Jimmy Robertson (on for Cliff Jones) was the first 'sub' to score a League goal for Spurs - doing so against Burnley in a 7-0 win at White Hart Lane on 7 September 1968.

Steve Perryman appeared in 1,021 first-team games for Spurs, only eight as a substitute.

Pat Corbett, an England Youth international, scored for Spurs against Southampton three minutes after coming off the bench for his League debut on 31 October 1981.

Midfielder Scott Houghton made 14 senior appearances for Spurs between 1990 and 1992....all of them as a substitute.

When only one substitute was allowed per game, the most used in a single League campaign by Spurs was 35 - in 1984-85 (Gary Mabbutt taking the field on 10 occasions).

In 1986-87 two substitutes were allowed for the first time and again Spurs called on the services of 35 'bench players' in League games. Ossie Ardiles got the most call-ups with nine.

In 1991-92 (when still two were allowed) Spurs utilised no fewer than 69 substitutes - a club record. Steve Sedgley got 13 calls, having appeared as a 'sub' 15 times in League games in 1988-89 (plus one in the League Cup).

During the first season of Premiership football (1992-93) Spurs again used 69 substitutes (Andy Turner having 11 calls this time) and in 1996-97 (when the three-sub ruling came into force) they

introduced 63. This rose to a massive 90 in 1997-98 and in 1998-99 it was 75 followed by 69 in 1999-2000 and 74 in 38 matches in 2000-01.

The following players all made one first team appearance as a substitute for Spurs at competitive level:

Robert Brace	v	Southampton, Division 1	07.05.1984
Ray Clarke	v	Leicester City, Division 1	21.04.1973
Jamie Clapham	v	Coventry City, Premiership	11.05.1997
Peter Garland	v	Norwich City, Division 1	10.04.1991
Andy Polston	v	Crystal Palace, Premiership	03.03.1990
Graeme Souness	v	Keflavik, UEFA Cup	14.09.1971

SULLIVAN, NEIL

Scottish international goalkeeper Neil Sullivan joined Spurs from Wimbledon on a 'Bosman' ruling on 28 May 2000 having already represented Scotland on 16 occasions at senior level and made 224 first-class appearances for the Dons (one on loan with Crystal Palace).

He had an excellent first season at White Hart Lane, playing in 43 League and Cup matches whilst also adding further caps to his tally.

Born in Sutton (Surrey) on 24 February 1970, Sullivan joined the Dons as an apprentice in the summer of 1986 and turned professional in July 1988. He replaced Dutchman Hans Segers between the posts at Plough Lane and was on loan to the Eagles in May 1992.

SUNDAY FOOTBALL

The first competitive League or Cup game played by Spurs on a Sunday afternoon was against Nottingham Forest on 2 October 1983 (Division 1). It was also the first TV Football League match to be shown 'live' in full as the record crowd of 30,596 saw Spurs win 2-1 with goals by Gary Stevens and Steve Archibald.

SUNDERLAND

Spurs playing record against the Black Cats:

Competition	P	W	D	L	F	A
Premiership	6	5	0	1	15	6
Football League	76	23	23	30	92	109
FA Cup	7	5	1	1	19	6
League Cup	3	1	1	1	3	3
Summary	92	34	25	33	129	124

A crowd of 12,731 saw Southern League Spurs come back from a goal down to beat First Division Sunderland in a 2nd round FA Cup-tie at Northumberland Park in February 1899. John Cameron netted the winner with just over 20 minutes remaining.

The first League game between the two clubs was staged at Roker Park on 1 September 1909 (Division 1) in front of 10,000 fans resulting in a 3-1 win for Sunderland.

Sunderland put 11 goals past Spurs in the two First Division games in season 1914-15. They won 6-0 on Wearside and 5-0 at White Hart Lane.....the latter being the final League game before the competition was suspended due to the Great War.

Spurs beat Sunderland 3-1 at home yet lost 6-0 away in the two League games played in 1933-34.

A never-to-be-bettered crowd of 75,038 packed into White Hart Lane to see Sunderland (the holders of the trophy) beat Spurs 1-0 in a 6th round FA Cup-tie in March 1938.

Jimmy Greaves was in sparkling form in November 1968, scoring four times as Sunderland were whipped 5-1 in a First Division League game at White Hart Lane.

When Spurs lost 1-0 at Sunderland in September 1984 both Clive Allen and Graham Roberts were sent-off. This was the first time

1912 action at White Hart Lane against travellers Sunderland

in the club's history that two players had been dismissed in the same game (competitive level).

A late Gary Lineker goal earned Spurs a point from a 3-3 draw at home to Sunderland in December 1990.

In April 2001, Spurs came back from 2-0 down to beat Sunderland 3-2 in a Premiership game at The Stadium of Light.

Players with both clubs include: Ivor Broadis, Jim Chalmers, Ernie Coquet, John Curtis, Jimmy Devlin, Phil Gray, Jim Hartley, Joe Knowles, Fred Mearns, Bobby Mimms, Bill Murray (Sunderland junior), George Payne, Jimmy Seed, Paul Stewart, Chris Waddle (Sunderland trialist), Jack Whitbourne.

Wartime guests (either with one or both clubs): Warney Cresswell, Charlie Crossley, Fred Hall, Bill Nicholson (also Spurs manager), Albert Tomkin

Also associated: Ted Birnie (Spurs player, Sunderland assistant-traner & coach), Graham Carr (scout for clubs).

SUPPORTERS' CLUBS

There are 39 'official' branches of the Spurs Members' Club: 26 in the UK, (including nine in Northern Ireland), seven in Southern Ireland and six 'overseas', two of the latter being based in Belgium, one in Malta, one in Norway, one in Gibraltar and one in South Africa.

All of the branches are non-profit making and receive priority when booking matchday tickets, each branch arranging coach travel for its members.

All branch members must belong to the Members' Club.

Supporters from the two Spurs branches in Belgium attend every home game as well as a handful of away matches. They have over 100 members each, plus a few season ticket holders at White Hart Lane.

Each branch also have the opportunity to present their chosen 'Player of the Year' pitchside, prior to a match.

* The Members' Club is the official club organisation, founded in the mid-1980s. Prior to that the Spurs Supporters Club, an independent organisation founded in 1949, used to run the away travel etc. The club itself is still going, but exists only in name.

SUSPENSIONS

In April 1897, three of Spurs' Scottish-born players, half-back James Devlin, Richard McElhaney and Jimmy Milliken along with Frank Wilson, were all suspended for 'acts of insubordination'. However, despite this misdemeanour, Devlin was re-signed by the club for the next campaign but not the other three. In the meantime Devlin had arranged his own move - to neighbours Millwall (unbeknown to Spurs). He was quickly found out, suspended again, and when the situation was finally sorted out between the respective clubs, Devlin was transferred to Millwall 'officially' after wilfully disobeying training instructions laid down by the club. In November 1897 Devlin was in trouble again - this time he was sent to prison for two months for assaulting the landlord of the Sussex Arms public house in Woolwich (Arsenal territory).

Players Chris Carrick and Peter Kyle were both suspended by Spurs as a result of breaking the club's training rules in March 1906. They never played for the club again!

Future Spurs goalkeeper Bob Hewitson was suspended by the Football League in February 1908 for allegedly tossing a clod of earth at the referee playing for Oldham v. Fulham.

Spurs half-back Jimmy Skinner (signed in 1919) twice received 14-day suspensions for 'failing to comply with the club's training regulations' and when he committed a similar offence soon afterwards he had his contract cancelled by the club in 1927.

Midfielder Paul Gascoigne was suspended

many times as a player, in this country and abroad, for various misdemeanours, including sendings-off and yellow card offences.

SWANSEA CITY (TOWN)

Spurs playing record against the Swans

Competition	P	W	D	L	F	A
Football League	26	15	5	6	56	28
League Cup	5	2	1	2	11	7
Wartime	2	1	0	1	5	5
Summary	33	18	6	9	72	40

The first League game between the two clubs was played in South Wales on 10 November 1928 when a crowd of close on 7,000 saw the Swans canter to a 4-0 win. Later in the season the game at White Hart Lane finished level at 1-1. Spurs recorded their first League victory over the Welsh club at Vetch Field on 2 November 1929, winning 1-0.

On 7 November 1931 (Division 2) Spurs beat the Swans 6-2 at home (two goals here for Willie Evans on his debut) and a little over a year later (in December 1932) they whipped them 7-0 on the same ground.

A crowd of just 6,292 saw Spurs beat the Swans 3-1 at White Hart Lane in a Second Division game in January 1947. This was the lowest attendance for a senior match in the Football League or major Cup competition at the ground for 32 years, and in fact, there hasn't been a lower once since!

There were six different scorers when Spurs beat the Swans 5-1 at home in a League Cup encounter in October 1991.

Players with both clubs include: Terry Boyle (Spurs reserve), Derek Brazil (Spurs trial), Ivor Brown, Ron Burgess (also Swans' coach & manager), Willie Davies, Roger Gibbins (Spurs reserve), Charlie Handley, Percy Hooper, Jack Illingworth, Ernie Jones, Mark Kendall, Derek King, Joe Meek, Paul Price, Micky Stead, Alan Woods.

Wartime guests (either with one or both clubs): Bobby Browne, Les Howe, Tom Paton, Albert Tomkin.

Also associated: Gerry Francis (Swansea player, Spurs manager), Terry Medwin (Spurs player, Swans assistant-manager/coach), Arthur Willis (Spurs player, Swans' coach), Doug Livermore (Swans coach, assistant-manager/coach, reserve team manager, chief scout).

SWINDON TOWN

Spurs playing record against the Robins

Competition	P	W	D	L	F	A
Premiership	2	0	1	1	2	3
FA Cup	3	1	1	1	4	4
Other Leagues	28	17	4	7	56	24
Summary	33	18	6	9	62	31

Spurs and Swindon first met at League level on 23 October 1983, drawing 1-1 at White Hart Lane. The return game that season ended in a 2-1 win for the Robins.

Many years earlier, in Southern League action, Spurs - despite a hat-trick by John Cameron - were beaten 4-3 in a cracking game at Swindon (December 1898) and in a Western League game in February 1901 two goals apiece by Cameron and David Copeland helped Spurs ease to a 5-0 victory. The following season Spurs won their home game in the same 'League' by 6-0 and then whipped Swindon 7-1, also at White Hart Lane, in a Southern League encounter. It was 6-3 to Spurs in the same competition in December 1904 and 3-0 in January 1907.

Players with both clubs include: Ray Bunkell (Spurs reserve), Colin Calderwood, Jim Chalmers. Herbert Chapman, Ray Clarke, Shaun Close, Ian Culverhouse, Alf Day, Kevin Dearden, Matt Dillon, Harry

Erentz, Neale Fenn, Tony Galvin (also Town assistant and caretaker-manager), Terry Gibson, Andy Gray, Micky Hazard, Foster Hedley, Baden Herod, Bill Hinton, Glenn Hoddle (also manager of both clubs), Gareth Howells (Spurs reserve), Billy Jones, David Gwilan Jones (Spurs reserve), Jimmy Kennedy, David Kerslake, Richard McElhaney, Dave Mackay (Swindon player-manager), Paul Miller, John Moncur, Ollie Morah (Spurs reserve), Neil Ruddock, John Smith, John Stephenson, Kevin Watson.

Wartime guests (either with one or both clubs): Danny Blanchflower, Frank Boulton, Freddie Cox, Charlie Crossley, Fred Ford (also Swindon coach and manager), Jack Skinner, George Travers, Cyril Williams, Albert Young.

Also associated: Les Allen, Glenn Hoddle, Ossie Ardiles (all Spurs players, Swindon managers, Ardiles & Hoddle also Spurs managers), John Gorman (Spurs player, assistant-manager both clubs), Keith Burkinshaw (Spurs coach & manager, Swindon chief scout).

TAIT, ALEXANDER GILCHRIST

Alex 'Sandy' Tait was the Edwardian version of Nobby Stiles. A real tough character who occupied the full-back position, he skippered Spurs on several occasions during his time with the club, appearing in 419 first team games (362 at competitive level, 35 in the FA Cup).

Born into a family of 13 children in the Scottish village of Glenbuck, Ayrshire in 1873, he played for Glenbuck Athletic, Royal Albert FC, Glasgow Rangers (on loan) and Motherwell before entering the Football League with Preston North End in season 1894-95. He made over 80 appearances for the Deepdale club.

Also known as 'Terrible Tait', he gained a Southern League championship and FA Cup winners' medals with Spurs in successive season (1899-1901) and represented Scotland in a trial match in 1903. A regular in the Spurs side until 1907-08 he was released at the end of that season and joined Leyton as player-manager. In July 1909 he was appointed manager of Croydon Common, retaining that position for two seasons. He later coached the famous Corinthians (from September 1922).

Tait died in Croydon, Surrey on 6 April 1949.

TATTERSALL, WALTER SCOTT

Walter Tattersall made 61 first team appearances for Spurs (44 in the Football League).

An enterprising outside-right, signed from Watford (with Grimsdell) in April 1912, he served the club for three seasons before being released in 1915. He guested for Notts County during the Great War but did not re-appear at competitive level after the hostilities.

Born in Warsop, Derbyshire on 4 September 1888, he played for Chesterfield Town and Mansfield Mechanics prior to joining Watford in July 1910.

TAYLOR, ALLAN

Goalkeeper Allan Tayloir was born in North Shields, County Durham on 1 December 1905 and represented England Schools before joining North Shields from where he switched to Newcastle United in 1925. A spell with South Shields followed and in July 1929, after a trial, he signed for Spurs. He spent eight years at White Hart Lane, making only 69 League and FA Cup appearances, losing out in the main to Cyril Spiers. He joined Hartlepools United in May 1937 and retired a year later. Taylor died on Tyneside in 1981.

TAYLOR, PETER

A winger, fast and direct with a powerful right foot shot, Peter Taylor scored 33 goals in 140 League and Cup games for Spurs. Having been rejected by the club as a junior, he 'rejoined' the White Hart Lane playing staff in September 1976, signed from Crystal Palace for £200,000. Prior to becoming an 'Eagle' (signed for £120,000 in October 1973) he had played for Southend United, and whilst at Selhurst Park he gained four full England caps and four Under-23 caps.

He added three more senior caps to his tally with Spurs before a sequence of niggling injuries knocked him out of his stride. In November 1980 he was sold to Leyton Orient for £150,000 and after a loan spell with Oldham Athletic (January 1983) he entered non-League football with Maidstone United (March 1983), returning to a higher sphere with Exeter City (on a non-contract basis) seven months later. He went back to Maidstone as player-manager and then served with Heybridge Swifts, Chelmsford City, Dartford, Hendon and Enfield (the latter three clubs as manager) before becoming assistant-boss to former Spurs player Steve Perryman at Watford (August 1991). He played occasionally for Harlow Town (from October 1991-May 1992) whilst still engaged by the Hornets.

Learning all the while, Taylor moved into Football League management in December 1993 with his old club, Southend United. He remained as boss at Roots Hall until February 1995 and thereafter agreed to stay with the club as a Director of Coaching until September 1995, while also playing for Chelmsford City: April-May 1995.

For one season (1995-96) Taylor was in charge of non-League Dover Athletic; he acted as England Under-21 coach from July 1996 to June 1999 and then managed Gillingham during the 1999-2000 campaign and has since been in charge of Leicester City. He was part-time England coach from November 2000 to June 2001.

He successfully guided Gillingham into the First Division for the first time before taking over from Martin O'Neill at Filbert Street. Regrettably, after a series of disappointing results, Taylor was relieved of his post in October 2001.

TEXACO CUP

Spurs entered this competition in 1970-71 but failed to make progress beyond the second round. After easily accounting for Dunfermline Athletic in their two-legged opening tie, Spurs then succumbed over two legs to Motherwell.

Results of games played:

Rd 1/1 Dunfermline Ath	(h) won 4-0	England, Chivers (3)	Att.16,388
Rd 1/2 Dunfermline Ath	(a) won 3-0	Chivers, Peters (2)	Att. 9,000
Rd 2/1 Motherwell	(h) won 3-2	Peters (2), Chivers	Att.19,670
Rd 2/2 Motherwell	(a) lost 0-2		Att.22,688

Match summary

P	W	D	L	F	A
4	3	0	1	11	5

THAMES

Spurs did not play senior football against the former Football League side, which played for two seasons at West Ham Stadium. Players with both clubs include: Jimmy Dimmock, Charlie Handley, Alex Lindsay.

THINGS THEY SAID!

Here are some quotations with a Spurs connection!

"Of course, we are all in the entertainment business"
Ossie Ardiles, The Times, 10 February 1990

"I don't know what's happened to 'Total Football'; I never quite understood what people meant by the term"
Danny Blanchflower, The Times, 10 July 1977

"The great fallacy is that the game is first and last about winning. It is nothing of the kind. The game is about glory, it is about doing things in style and with a flourish, about going out and beating the other lot, not waiting for them to die of boredom"
Danny Blanchflower, Attributed

"He hit the post, and after the game people will say, well he hit the post"
Jimmy Greaves, Private Eye, number.602, 11 January 1985

"Don't try to break the bloody net, pass the ball into it"
Bill Nicholson, Attributed

"Managers get too much of the praise and too much of the blame"
Sir Alf Ramsey, Independent, 22 October 1988

"Football's a game of skill....we kicked them a bit and they kicked us back"
Graham Roberts, Private Eye, number 557, 8 April 1983

"There's no fun in soccer anymore. It's all deadly serious. We'll end up playing in cemetries"
Terry Venables, The Guardian Book of Sports Quotes, 1985

"There's a fine line between bravery and suicide"
Terry Venables, Independent, 12 November 1988

"I don't remember him from the World Cup but I'm sure he impressed me."
Spurs Chairman **Alan Sugar** after arranging the £2.6 millioin signing of Ilie Dumitrescu in August 1994.

"Is there a diving club in London?"
Jurgen Klinsmann, following his signing in August 1994.

"I wouldn't wash my car with that (Klinsmann's) shirt. You can auction it among your viewers for charity."
Spurs Chairman Alan Sugar during a TV interview.

"What I said to them at half-time would be unprintable on the radio"
Gerry Francis during an after-match interview.

"They are more interested in the white jackets and match tickets. They haven't got a clue what's going on in the outside world. They are totally out to lunch. The FA is like going into Madame Tussaud's...It's hard to tell the difference between the dummies and the real people."
Alan Sugar on the FA

"Numbers are a thing with me. I have this thing about 4. I don't know why 4. My favourite used to be 5 and then 7. Then I got into this thing about 13, because nothing would be done in 4s and 9 and 4 are 13. I don't know where the 9 comes from. I got it into my head because 9 and 4 make 13. That's like 6 and 7. I can't bear to see them together, because that's 13 again. So when I go out onto the park I won't go out 6th or 7th...I'll be either 5th or 8th.
Paul Gascoigne on numbers!

"Yes, I was drunk. I get drunk quickly. I hadn't had a drink in nine days!"
Gazza again.

THOMAS, DANIEL JOSEPH
Unfortunately full-back Danny Thomas' playing career was cut short through injury in January 1988 at the age of 26. He had made 171 first team appearances Spurs, 117 at competitive level. Born in Worksop, Nottinghamshire on 12 November 1961, he represented Worksop, Nottinghamshire and England Schools before having unsuccessful trials with both Leeds United and Sheffield United. In 1977 he signed as an apprentice for Coventry City and turned professional at Highfield Road in December 1978. He developed quickly with the Sky Blues and gained England Under-21 honours playing in two full internationals v. Australia before moving to Spurs for £250,000 in June 1983.
A member of Spurs' UEFA Cup winning side in 1984, Thomas was a tough competitior who tackled well and motored continuously up and down the right hand side of the field. That is until a reckless challenge by a QPR player in March 1987, severely damaged his right knee causing him to miss that season's FA Cup Final. He failed to regain full fitness and after announcing his premature retirement he became a physiotherapist with West Bromwich Albion (from May 1992) before establishinmg his own practise in London later in the 1990s.

THOMAS, MITCHELL ANTHONY
Cool under pressure, a sound kicker and able to perform as a full-back, centre-half or sweeper, the versatile Mitchell Thomas is playing competitive League football today, almost 20 years after making his debut for Luton Town. In 2000-01 he passed the personal milestone of 650 senior appearances at club level - 198 for Spurs (eight goals scored).
Thomas was born in Luton on 2 October 1964 and played as an apprentice at Kenilworth Road before taking professionalism in August 1982. He moved to Spurs for £233,000 in July 1986 and remained at White Hart Lane for four seasons, transferring to West Ham United for £525,000 in August 1991. He returned for a second sell at Luton in November 1993 and then moved north

to Burnley in July 1999, being voted Claret's 'Player of the Year' in his first season at Turf Moor as the Lancashire side gained promotion to Division One. Capped by England at Youth team level as a teenager, Thomas later won one 'B; and three Under-21 caps for his country.

THOMPSON, ANDREW
Andy Thompson gave Spurs' 28 years excellent service - as a player and coach.
Born in Newcastle-upon-Tyne on 21 January 1899, he played as an aggressive, all-action inside-forward for Newburn FC and Wickham Park Villa in the North-east before joining Spurs in November 1920. He made 166 League and Cup appearances for the club (21 goals scored) up to November 1921 when he transferred to Norwich City. Spells followed with Chester (1932), Clapton Orient and Northfleet, the latter from July 1933, when he also acted as coach. And then after a brief spell as coach with Chelsea, he returned to Spurs to round off his footballing career, acting as the proverbial odd-job man around White Hart Lane. He died in East London on 1 January 1970.

THORSTVEDT, ERIK
A very competent, agile and courageous goalkeeper, born in Stavanger, Norway on 28 October 1962, Erik Thorstvedt (6ft 4ins tall and 14st 4lbs in weight) played for EIK and Viking Stavanger in his homeland before having unsuccessful trials in 1984 with QPR and Spurs. In July 1985 he signed for the German side Borussia Moenchengladbach and after another trial (this time with Arsenal) he starred for IFK Gothenburg before joining Spurs for £400,000 in December 1988.
Thorstvedt took over from Bobby Mimms between the posts at White Hart Lane but didn't have the greatest of starts, conceding a soft goal against Nottingham Forest on his debut. He went on to appear in 212 first-team matches up to the summer of 1994 when he left the club. After a trial period with Wolverhampton Wanderers, he announced his retirement in July 1996. He gained both FA Cup and Charity Shield winners' plaque in 1991.
Thorstvedt stands third in Spurs' all-time international honours list with 47 caps won as a player whilst at White Hart Lane. He was first capped by his country at the age of 20 in 1982 and gained the last of his 98 caps against Northern Ireland in March 1996 He captained the national side in early '90s.

TICKRIDGE, SIDNEY
Full-back Sid Tickridge appeared in 95 League games and six FA Cup matches, plus 36 wartime fixtures for Spurs during his time at White Hart Lane.
Born in Stepney, East London on 10 April 1923, he played initially for England Schools and Tottenham juniors before joining the Spurs' groundstaff in 1937. A spell as an amateur with Northfleet enhanced his reputation within the club and after guesting for Aldershot, Dartford, Fulham and Millwall, and serving in the Royal Navy during the Second World War, he was signed a as a professional in April 1946.
Tickridge, hard, resolute with a competitive edge to his game, remained at the club until March 1951 when he transferred to Chelsea for whom he made 73 appearances. He later played for Brentford, retiring in January 1957. Thereafter he took the role of assistant-trainer at Millwall before returning to Spurs at the club's Youth team trainer.

TORINO (AC)

Spurs playing record against the Italian side:

Competition	P	W	D	L	F	A
A/I League CWC	2	2	0	0	3	0

Spurs accounted for the 1971 Italian League Cup winners 3-0 on aggregate in the two-legged contest staged in September 1971. They won 2-0 in Italy in front of 28,000 fans and 1-0 at White Hart Lane before a crowd of 34,103. Martin Chivers scored in both games.

Player with both clubs: Tony Marchi.

TORQUAY UNITED

Spurs playing record against the Gulls

Competition	P	W	D	L	F	A
FA Cup	2	1	1	0	8	4
League Cup	3	2	0	1	7	3
Summary	5	3	1	1	15	7

After a 3-3 draw at Torquay in January 1965, Spurs progressed through to the 4th Round with a 5-1 replay win (Greaves 3). As holders, Spurs beat United 4-1 at Plainmoor in a League Cup-tie in October 1971.

Players with both clubs include: Kevin Dearden, Roger Gibbons (Spurs reserve), Jimmy Holmes, Gareth Howells (Spurs reserve), Neil Johnson, Terry Lee, Ollie Morah (Spurs reserve), John Smith, Chris Waddle.

Wartime guest: Phil Joslin (Spurs)

Also associated: Fred Ford (Spurs Wartime guest, Torquay coach), Cyril Knowles (Spurs player, United manager), Colin Lee (Spurs player, United caretaker-manager).

The gym as it used to be at White Hart lane

TRAINERS (ALSO MASSEURS & PHYSIOTHERAPISTS)

List of Spurs' first team trainers:

Jock Campbell	1896-98
Will Brierley	1898-99
Will Johnson	1899-1901
Sam Mountford	1901-07
FW Sharpe	1907-08
Jack Nie	1908-15
Elijah Morse	1919-20
Billy Minter	1920-27
George Hardy	1927-47
Cecil Poynton	1947-72

Assistant-trainers

Charlie Taylor	1898-99
Arthur Norris	1899-1901
Jack Nie	1901-08
EP Daly	1907-09
J Warren	1909-13
Jimmy Anderson	1913-46
Jabe Darnell	1919-46
Ben Ives	1922-45 (latterly chief scout)
Wally Hardinge	1933-35 (also reserve team manager)
Harry Lowe	1938-39 (coach & reserve team manager)
Andy Thompson	1938-39 (coach, post-War to 1969, Youth coach & groundstaff)
Cecil Poynton	1945-47
Jack Coxford	1945-70 (pre-War Northfleet United player/coach)
Johnny Wallis	1948-64 ('A' team manager 1948-58)

Physiotherapists

Cecil Poynton	1972-75
Johnny Wallis	1972-75
Mike Varney	1975-86
John Sheridan	1986-89
Dave Butler	1989-93
Tony Lenaghan	1993-98
Alastair Beattie	since June 1998

* Sheridan was consultant physio to 1994 & Beattie was assistant physio from April 1995 to June 1998

Assistant- physiotherapists

Cliff Speight	1984-88
Mike Banks	1994-97
Jim Webb	1997-98
Jim Elston	1997-99
Gareth Robinson	1998-2000

Fitness Coach

Kunle Odetoyinbo Since April 1998

* Odetoyinbo, born in Islington, holds a Master's Degree in Sport and Exercise Physiology, as well as certificate in Nutritional Medicine and coaching certificates in football, athletics, basketball etc.

Masseur

Paul Roberts   Since July 1999

Trainer's Notepad

Ex-player Billy Minter was Spurs' trainer when they won the FA Cup in 1921.

Cecil Poynton, another former player at White Hart Lane, was Spurs' assistant-trainer for 26 years (1946-72) and thereafter acted as the club's physiotherapist until retiring in 1975.

TRAILOR, CYRIL HENRY

A resolute half-back, born in Merthyr Tydfil on 15 May 1919, Cyril Trailor represented Wales at Schoolboy level before playing for Tottenham Juniors. He signed as a professional for Spurs in October 1938, after a spell at Northfleet. He went on to make 13 first-class appearances for the club before transferring to Clapton Orient in August 1949, later assisting Bedford Town.

TRANMERE ROVERS

Spurs playing record against Rovers

Competition	P	W	D	L	F	A
Football League	2	2	0	0	5	1
FA Cup	2	1	1	0	10	2
League Cup	2	1	1	0	6	2
Summary	6	4	2	0	21	5

The two League games between the clubs were contested in season 1938-39 (Division 2). Spurs won the first encounter at Prenton Park on 3 December by 2-0 and then doubled-up with a 3-1 home victory in early April. Rovers were relegated to the Third Division (N) at the end of the campaign.

Tranmere's heaviest defeat (League or Cup) was suffered against Spurs in January 1953 when they crashed 9-1 in a 3rd round FA Cup replay at White Hart Lane.

Players with both clubs include: Arthur Crompton, Alf Day, Neil McNab.

Wartime guests (either with one or both clubs): Jimmy McCorrmick, Ed Tunney.

TRANSFER TRAIL

Details of how and when Spurs 'in and out' transfer records have been broken (or equalled) down the years:

Players signed:

Fee	Player	Signed from	Date
£1,500	Frank Osborne	Fulham	May 1924
£4,000	Baden Herod	Brentford	February 1929
£5,500	Ted Harper	Sheffield Wed	March 1929
£6,000	Andy Duncan	Hull City	March 1935
£18,500	Peter Murphy	Coventry City	May 1950
£30,000	Danny Blanchflower	Aston Villa	December 1954
£99,999	Jimmy Greaves	AC Milan	December 1961
£125,000	Martin Chivers	Southampton	January 1968*
£200,000	Martin Peters	West Ham United	March 1970**
£800,000	Steve Archibald	Aberdeen	May 1980
£1.5m	Paul Stewart	Manchester City	June 1988
£2m	Paul Gascoigne	Newcastle United	July 1988
£2.2 m	Gordon Durie	Chelsea	August 1991
£2.6 m	Ilie Dumitrescu	Steaua Bucharest	August 1994
£2.9 m	Gica Popescu	PSV Eindhoven	September 1994
£4.5 m	Chris Armstrong	Crystal Palace	June 1995
£6 m	Les Ferdinand	Newcastle United	July 1997
£11 m	Sergei Rebrov	Dynamo Kiev	May 2000

* British transfer record at the time.

** Deal involving Jimmy Greaves (Peters valued at £146,000)

Players sold:

Fee	Player	Sold to	Date
£650	John McTavish	Newcastle United	April 1912
£2,500	Ted Harper	Preston NE	December 1931*
£2,500	Dick Rowley	Preston NE	December 1931*
£70,000	Terry Venables	QPR	June 1969
£130,000	Keith Osgood	Coventry City	January 1978
£250,000	Neil McNab	Bolton Wanderers	November 1978
£1.15m	Steve Archibald	CF Barcelona	July 1984
£1.5m	Richard Gough	Glasgow Rangers	October 1987
£4.25m	Chris Waddle	Marseille	June 1989
£5.5m	Paul Gascoigne	Lazio	May 1992

* Sold for a combined fee of £5,000)

Other 'big' money signings made by Spurs (£500,000+)

Fee	Player	Signed from	Date
£8.1m	Dean Richards	Southampton	September 2001
£5m	Ben Thatcher	Wimbledon	July 2000
£4.2m	Ruel Fox	Newcastle United	October 1995
£4m	Chris Perry	Wimbledon	July 1999
£3.8m	Tim Sherwood	Blackburn Rovers	February 1999
£3.75m	Ramon Vega	Grasshoppers	January 1997
£3m	Oyvind Leonhardsen	Wimbledon	August 1999
£2.6m	John Scales	Liverpool	December 1996
£2.3m	Steffen Iversen	Rosenborg	December 1996
£2.3m	Moussa Saib	Valencia	February 1998
£2.1m	Teddy Sheringham	Nottingham Forest	August 1992
£2m	Jurgen Klinsmann	AS Monaco	July 1994
£2m	David Ginola	Newcastle United	July 1997
£1.775m	Mauricio Taricco	Ipswich Town	December 1998
£1.75m	Darren Anderton	Portsmouth	June 1992
£1.75m	Jason Dozzell	Ipswich Town	August 1993
£1.75m	Allan Nielsen	Brondby	July 1996
£1.6m	Jose Dominguez	Sporting Club de Portugal	August 1997
£1.5m	Andy Sinton	Sheffield Wednesday	January 1996
£1.5m	Willem Korsten	Leeds United	July 1999
£1.5m+	Gustavo Poyet	Chelsea	June 2001
£1.4m	Goran Bunjevcevic	Red Star Belgrade	May 2001
£1.35m	Paolo Tramezzani	Piacenza	June 1998
£1.25m	Colin Calderwood	Swindon Town	July 1993
£1.2m	Gary Lineker	CF Barcelona	June 1989
£1m+	Anthony Gardner	Port Vale	January 2000
£1m	Gary Doherty	Luton Town	April 2000

£900,000	Andy Gray	Crystal Palace	February 1992
£850,000	Kevin Scott	Newcastle United	February 1994
£800,000	Jason Cundy	Chelsea	March 1992
£750,000	Richard Gough	Dundee	August 1986
£750,000	Steve Sedgley	Coventry City	July 1989
£750,000	Jason Cundy	Chelsea	March 1992
£750,000	Neil Ruddock	Southampton	July 1992
£750,000	Steffen Freund	Borussia Dortmund	December 1998
£700,000	Clive Allen	QPR	August 1984
£700,000	Simon Davies	Peterborough Utd	December 1999
£650,000	Steve Hodge	Aston Villa	December 1986
£600,000	Nico Claesen	Standard Liege	October 1986
£590,000	Chris Waddle	Newcastle United	July 1985
£575,000	Pat Van den Hauwe	Everton	August 1989
£525,000	Dean Austin	Southend United	May 1992
£500,000	Paul Walsh	Liverpool	February 1988
£500,000	David Kerslake	Leeds United	September 1993
£500,000	Matthew Etherington	Peterborough Utd	January 2000

Other big-money departures from White Hart Lane (£500,000+):

Fee	Player	Sold to	Date
£5.25m	Nick Barmby	Middlesbrough	August 1995
£3.5m	Teddy Sheringham	Manchester United	July 1997
£3.1m	Gica Popescu	Barcelona	May 1995
£3m	David Ginola	Aston Villa	July 2000
£2.5m	Neil Ruddock	Liverpool	July 1993
£2.5m	Ian Walker	Leicester City	HJuly 2001
£2.3m	Paul Stewart	Liverpool	July 1992
£2.25m	Allan Nielsen	Watford	June 2001
£2.2m	Vinny Samways	Everton	August 1994
£1.5m	Richard Gough	Glasgow Rangers	October 1987
£1.5m	Ilie Dumitrescu	West Ham United	March 1996
£1.4m	Jurgen Klinsmann	Bayern Munich	June 1995
£1.25m	Espen Baardsen	Watford	August 2000
£1.2m	Gordon Durie	Glasgow Rangers	November 1993
£1m	Clive Allen	Bordeaux	May 1988
£1m	Steve Sedgley	Ipswich Town	June 1994
£1m	Rory Allen	Portsmouth	July 1999
£946,000	Gary Lineker	Grampus 8	June 1992
£750,000	Glenn Hoddle	AS Monaco	July 1987
£700,000	Darren Caskey	Reading	February 1996
£650,000	Garry Brady	Newcastle United	July 1998
£575,000	Steve Hodge	Nottingham Forest	August 1988
£550,000	Nico Claesen	RSC Antwerp	August 1988
£550,000	Paul Allen	Southampton	September 1993
£500,000	Paul Walsh	Portsmouth	May 1992
£500,000	Chris Fairclough	Leeds United	April 1989
£500,000	Mitchell Thomas	West Ham United	August 1991
£500,000	Nayim	Real Zaragoza	May 1993

Return 'Transfers'

List of players (and other personnel) who had one (or more) spells with Spurs - returning to club after serving elsewhere in:

Eddie Baily	player/assistant
Ossie Ardiles	player/manager
John Gorman	player/assistant-manager
Steve Grenfell	junior player/community/coach
Micky Hazard	player (twice)
Chris Hughton	player/asst./caretaker-manager
Glenn Hoddle	player/manager
Pat Jennings	player (twice)/coach
Jurgen Klinsmann	player (twice)
Harry Lowe	player/coach
Tony Marchi	player (twice)
Les Medley	player (twice)
Jimmy Neighbour	player/U-17 coach
Bill Nicholson	player/manager/consultant/ coach/assistant manager
Martin Peters	player/director
David Pleat	manager/caretaker-manager/Director of Football
Arthur Rowe	player/manager
Neil Ruddock	player (twice)
Bill Sage	player/scout
Steve Sedgley	junior/player
Teddy Sheringham	player (twice)
Peter Shreeves	Youth team manager/manager (twice)
Robbie Stepney	part-time coach & reserve team manager/coach
Andy Thompson	player/coach
Sid Tickridge	player/Youth team trainer
Terry Venables	player/manager/Chief Executive
Bill Whatley	player/scout

NB - Guest and loan players, trialists, Amateurs and players, who were groomed with one of Spurs' nursery teams (i.e. Northfleet) have not been included.

Loan Transfers

Many young junior players (Paul Miller and Terry Gibson among them) were loaned out to overseas clubs by Spurs.

The first loan players to play in Spurs league team under the new ruling were goalkeeper Bobby Mimms and striker Paul Walsh from Everton and Liverpool respectively in February 1988.

Andy Booth of Sheffield Wednesday became the first loan player to feature in Spurs' League/Premiership side who was not subsequently signed by the club. All previous loan players later signed permanent contracts with Spurs.

Money Talk

• Clive Allen was involved in transfer deals amounting to £6,175,000. His first move took him from QPR to Arsenal for £1.25 million in June 1980. Without ever appearing in a senior game for the Gunners he was sold to Crystal Palace, also for £1.25 million two months later. In May 1981, a fee of £450,000 sent him back to Loftus Road before he transferred again, this time to Spurs for £700,000 in August 1984. Four years later, in May 1988, he switched to Bordeaux for £1 m, only to return to England for precisely that same amount of money in August 1985 to play for Manchester City. Further moves followed ....to Chelsea for £250,000 in December 1991 and to West ham United for £275,000 in March 1992.

• Danny Blanchflower became the most expensive half-back when he joined Spurs from Aston Villa for £30,000 in 1954. He held the record for just four years, Dave Mackay taking over the mantle following his £32,000 move from Hearts.

• The proposed £6 million transfer to Spurs of the Wimbledon and Welsh international striker John Hartson collapsed on 5 February 2000.

• Simon Davies' £700,000 move from London Road to Spurs in December 1999 was a record 'sale' for Peterborough United.

• Portsmouth paid a club record fee of £1 million for Spurs striker Rory Allen in July 1999.

• Les Ferdinand's two £6 million moves - from QPR to Newcastle United in June 1995 and from St James' Park to Spurs in August

1997 - were both club record signings at the time.
● David Ginola moved three times between English clubs (Newcastle United, Spurs and Aston Villa) for a total of £7.5 m.
● Steve Hodge was involved in four transfer deals worth £2,550,000.
● A combined fee of £700,000 brought the two Argentinian World Cup stars, Ossie Ardiles and Ricky Villa, to Spurs in the summer of 1978.
● Spurs paid Greenock Morton £40,000 for 16 year-old Neil McNab in February 1974 - just to get him to White Hart Lane ...before he could be poached by another club!
● Spurs defender John Lacy was the first player to be transferred via an independent tribunal. In June 1978 Fulham (his club at the time) demanded £250,000 from Spurs for his transfer. This was £50,000 higher than what Spurs were prepared to pay. The following month the tribunal cut the price to £200,000 and Lacy went on to play in 132 competitive games during his five years at White Hart Lane.

TRAVELLING MEN

● Jimmy McCormick served/assisted no less than 20 different teams/clubs as a player during his footballing career....he began with Rotherham YMCA and then, in turn, played for Rotherham United, Chesterfield and Spurs before guesting for Birmingham, Chelmsford City, Chester, Crewe Alexandra, Derby County, Fulham, Leicester City, Lincoln City, Liverpool, Rochdale, Southend United, Tranmere Rovers, Walsall and West Bromwich Albion during the Second World War. After the hostilities he left White Hart Lane in 1945 to join Fulham and thereafter played for Lincoln City (again) and Crystal Palace prior to taking a coaching position with Sliema Wanderers in Malta. He coached the Turkish national team and also at Wycombe Wanderers, Lincoln, Sheffield United and Walton & Hersham, taking over as manager of the latter club before rounding off his eventful nomadic career by managing York City (1953-54).
● Peter Kyle was associated with 17 differrent football teams, likewise Herbert Chapman....the latter assisting 13 as an outright player and four as manager (Northampton Town Leeds City, Huddersfield Town and Arsenal). He also played for the Cobblers.
● Ossie Ardiles was a player with Red Star Cordoba, Cordoba Instituto, Huracan. Spurs, Queen's Park Rangers, Paris St Germain, Blackburn Rovers and Fort Lauderdale Strikers, and then manager of Swindon Town, Newcastle United, West Bromwich Albion, Spurs, Deportivo Guadalajara (Mexico), Shimizu S-Pulse (Japan), Croatia Zagreb and Yokohama F Marinos (Japan) - 15 different clubs in total.
● Peter Taylor served as a player with Southend United, Crystal Palace, Spurs, Leyton Orient, Oldham Athletic, Maidstone United, Exeter City, Heybridge Swifts, Chelmsford City and Harlow Town, and he has managed at Maidstone, Dartford Hendon, Enfield, Dover Athletic and Gillingham and was assistant-boss of Watford. He left the Priestfield Stadium for Filbert Street in.June 2000.
● Bill Lane was linked with 18 different clubs - he was a player with Gnome Athletic, Park Avondale, Tottenham, Barnet, Northfleet, Spurs, Leicester City, Walsall, Reading, Brentford, Watford, Bristol City, Clapton Orient and Gravesend. He then retired and served with Brentford again (as assistant-manager), Guildford City (manager), Brighton & Hove Albion (manager), Gravesend & Northfleet (manager), Arsenal (scout) and Brighton again (as a scout).
● Between 1980 and 2001 goalkeeper Bobby Mimms played in turn, for Halifax Town, Rotherham United, Everton, Notts County, Sunderland, Blackburn Rovers, Manchester City, Spurs (1988-90),

Aberdeen, Blackburn (again), Crystal Palace, Preston North End, Rotherham (for a second time), York City and Mansfield Town. (14 different clubs in total).
● Dave Mackay was associated with different 13 clubs as a player and/or manager: Slateford Athletic, Newtongrange, Heart of Midlothian, Spurs, Derby County (player and later manager), Nottingham Forest, Swindon Town (player-manager), Walsall (manager), Al Arabia (manager), Alba Shabab (manager), Doncaster Rovers (manager), Birmingham City (manager), FC Zamalek, Egypt (manager).
● Graham Roberts registered as a player with Scholing FC, Bournemouth, Portsmouth, Dorchester Town, Weymouth, Spurs, Glasgow Rangers, Chelsea (also coach), West Bromwich Albion and Enfield and he has also managed a handful of non-league clubs.

TRESADERN, JOHN

Jack Tresadern was born in Leytonstone on 26 September 1890 and played non-League football as a left-half for Wanstead and Barking Town before joining West Ham United in July 1913. After appearing in the first Wembley Cup Final of 1923, and gaining two England caps, he spent a season with Burnley before taking over as player-manager of Northampton Town in May 1925. A broken leg ended his playing days in December 1926, although he remained in charge of the Cobblers until October 1930 when he took over the reins of Crystal Palace, guiding them to second spot in Division Three (S) in his first season in charge.
From Selhurst Park he switched across London to become Spurs' manager, his appointment being confirmed on 19 June 1935 although he didn't take up office until 1 July. Tresadern, well disciplined, wasn't a success. The fans weren't too pleased but somehow he held his position until April 1938....a month after newspaper reports indicated that he was going to leave on his own accord and not be pushed, to allow Peter McWilliam to return to the club.
Tresadern managed Plymouth Argyle from April 1938 until November 1947. He scouted for Aston Villa in 1948-49 and was then in charge of three non-League clubs: Chelmsford City, Hastings United and Tonbridge before quitting football in 1959. Tresadern died in Tonbridge on Boxing Day, 1959.

TROPHIES (MAJOR)

Spurs have so far captured 23 major trophies and/or Cups.
They have claimed two First Division championships: 1951 & 1961, triumphed in eight FA Cup Finals - 1901, 1921, 1961, 1962, 1967, 1981, 1982 & 1991 - succeeded in two League Cup Finals: 1971 & 1973; recorded two UEFA Cup Final victories in 1972 & 1984; won the 1963 European Cup-winners Cup Final; gained two League Division Two titles in 1920 & 1950; collected one Southern League crown in 1900; earned one Western League victory in 1904; took the London League championship in 1903, lifted the Football League South Section 'C' in 1940, and were twice champions of the Wartime Football League South, in 1944 & 1945.

TULL, WALTER DANIEL JOHN

Walter Tull was born in Folkestone in April 1888 to an English mother and West Indian father. He joined Spurs from Clacton in April 1909, turning professional the following month and made his League debut against Sunderland on 1 September that same year. He scored twice in 10 first-class games for Spurs before moving to Northampton Town in May 1911. During the first part of the Great War he had guested for Fulham but was then sadly killed in action in France in March 1918, aged 29.

UNDEFEATED

Spurs' best unbeaten run in the Football League (home & away) has been 22 matches - set between 31 August to 31 December 1949.

Spurs remained unbeaten in 33 successive home League games between 2 January 1932 and 16 September 1933.

Their best away run has been 16 games without defeat, set between 10 November 1984 and 21 August 1985.

Spurs best unbeaten home run in the Premiership so far has been 16 matches - between 22 April 2000 and 8 March 2001.

Spurs remained unbeaten at home in each of the following League seasons: 1919-20, 1932-33 and 1964-65.

They won 19 out of their 21 home matches in 1919-20 when taking the Second Division championship.

In that first campaign after WW1 Spurs, in fact, were undefeated in their opening 12 League games and lost only one of their first 18 matches and two of the first 30. They finished up as champions after suffering just four defeats in 42 starts.

Spurs did not lose any of their opening 16 League games at the start of the 1960-61 season and the whole run, taking in the last two matches from the previous season, was one of 18 games without a loss.

Spurs went 20 games undefeated in the year 1967 - sixteen from 21 January to 13 May 1967 (at the end of one season) and four during August at the start of the next campaign.

Spurs went 13 games unbeaten at the start of the 1990-91 season (ten in the League and three in the League Cup). They also avoided defeat on the last day of the previous campaign, thus making it an overall run of 14 games without a loss.

(See also under Sequences).

UNITED LEAGUE

Spurs spent three seasons playing in this competition (1896-99). Their full record was:

P	W	D	L	F	A	Pts
50	20	11	19	101	86	51

Their best effort was to finish runners-up to Luton Town in 1897-98 (well adrift on 21 points to the Hatters' 28).

Spurs were involved in some exciting contests during the course of those three campaigns. They lost an 11-goal thriller by 6-5 at Millwall in September 1896 (their first game in the competition). They defeated Southampton 7-0 (their biggest win) and accounted for both Loughborough and Wellingborough by 5-0, all at home, when taking second spot in 1897-98 and they defeated Wellingborough again by 5-2 (home) in April 1899. Willie Joyce scored four goals in that big win over the Saints.

A record crowd of 14,000 witnessed the 0-0 draw between Spurs and Woolwich Arsenal in a United League game at Northumberland Park on 8 April 1898.

A year later Spurs played their last United League game when they beat Woolwich Arsenal 3-2 at home on 29 April 1899 in front of 5,000 spectators.

UNIZALE TEXTILE ARAD

Spurs playing record against the Romanian side

Competition	P	W	D	L	F	A
UEFA Cup	2	1	1	0	3	1

Spurs defeated Unizale Textile Arad from Romania 3-1 on aggregate in the fourth round of the UEFA Cup in 1971-72.

A crowd of 20,000 saw Spurs take control with a 2-0 win in the away leg on 7 March - Mike England and Roger Morgan the scorers. Then a fortnight later, 30,253 fans were present to witness the 1-1 draw at White Hart Lane, when Alan Gilzean's goal saved Spurs' blushes!

UPTON PARK

Spurs playing record against Upton Park

Competition	P	W	D	L	F	A
S. Alliance	2	1	0	1	2	4

Spurs' sole success over Upton Park was in the Southern Alliance ved on 25 February 1893 when Bell's goal gave them a narrow 1-0 home win.

V

VAMPIRES

Spurs playing record against the Vampires

Competition	P	W	D	L	F	A
FA Cup	2	1	0	1	4	5
Amateur Cup	1	1	0	0	3	0
Summary	3	2	0	1	7	5

Spurs knocked Vampires out of the FA Amateur Cup in season 1893-94, winning 3-0.

Both FA Cup matches took place two seasons later. The first game played on 2 November 1895 resulted in a 4-2 home win for the Vampires, but Spurs complained that the pitch had been wrongly marked out and a replay at Northumberland Park was ordered by the FA. This was staged a fortnight later and on this occasion Spurs won 2-1, Harry Pryor and Peter Hunter the scorers.

VAN den HAUWE, PATRICK WILLIAM ROGER

Left-back Pat Van den Hauwe played in four FA Cup Finals in the space of six years - three with Everton (1985, 1986 and 1989) and one with Spurs (1991), gaining a winners' medal, in the last!

Born in Dendermonde, Belgium on 16 December 1960, Van den Hauwe joined Birmingham City as an apprentice in the summer of 1976 and turned professional in August 1978. A ferocious tackler, his only goal in 143 appearances for Blues came in a 2-1 home win over Arsenal in March 1983. He left St Andrew's for Everton in

September 1984 for a fee of £100,000 (signed by former Blues player Howard Kendall) and at the end of his first season at Goodison Park, played at Wembley against Manchester United in the FA Cup Final and also collected a League championship medal. A year later Van den Hauwe claimed a League runners-up medal and then added a second First Division championship prize to his collection in 1987.....and by this time he had also won the first of 13 full international caps for Wales (despite not being born in that country). He was on the verge of being called up into the Belgium national side by manager Guy Thys after he had seen him in action against Manchester United at Old Trafford in 1985. After pencilling him in as an over-age player for the under-21 match against Spain, Thys found out that Van den Hauwe had unwittingly signed away his birthright by opting out of national service. This, of course, led to press speculation as to which of the British nations would pursue him and eventually he teamed up with Everton colleagues Kevin Ratcliffe and Neville Southall in the Welsh side, making his debut in a World Cup qualifier against Spain at Wrexham. In August 1989 Van Den Hauwe, after 190 appearances for Everton, moved to Spurs for £595,000 and two years later, at long last, he got his hands on an FA Cup winners' medal. He went on to appear in 125 senior games for Spurs over a period of four years, up to

September 1993 when he moved across London to sign for Millwall. He ended his career with Notts County (February-May 1995).

* His father, Rene, kept goal for Belgium.

VEGA, RAMON

Swiss international Ramon Vega scored eight goals in 84 first-class matches for Spurs before transferring to Celtic in December 2000. Then, in his first season in Scottish football, he helped the Bhoys win the treble.

Born in Olten on 14 June 1961, he played for FC Trimbach, FC Olten and Grasshoppers-club Zurich in his homeland and for Cagliari in Italy before joining Spurs for £3.75 million in January 1997. A powerful defender, he was a League Cup winner with Spurs in 1999 before choosing to play north of the border. Capped over 20 times by his country, Vega returned to English League football in June 2001 when he signed for Gianluca Vialli's Nationwide League outfit Watford.

VENABLES, TERENCE FREDERICK

As a player Terry Venables was a hard-working midfielder who passed the ball well, had good vision and never gave less than 110 per-cent out on the pitch.

Born in Bethnal Green on 6 January 1943, he represented Dagenham, Essex, London and England Schools before joining Chelsea as an amateur in July 1958, turning professional at Stamford Bridge in August 1960.

He made 237 senior appearances for the Blues (31 goals scored), helping them gain promotion from Division Two in 1963 and win the League Cup in 1965, having earlier gained an FA Youth Cup winners' medal (1961). Venables was also the first player to represent England at FIVE different levels - schoolboy, amateur, Youth, Under-23 (4 caps) and full (2 caps). He also played for the Football League XI. He moved from Chelsea to Spurs for £80,000 in May 1966 and twelve months later collected an FA Cup winners medal when his former club were beaten 2-1 at Wembley.

He made an impact at White Hart Lane and amassed 141 League and Cup appearances for the club, netting a further nine goals before taking his talents to nearby QPR for £70,000 in June 1969. Venables continued to play first-class soccer until the end of the 1975-76 season, serving Crystal Palace (after leaving Loftus Road) and St Patrick's in Ireland. He was appointed coach at Palace on his return to England and quickly stepped up to team manager at Selhurst Park, retaining that position until

October 1980 and celebrating Third Division promotion and a Second Division championship success in 1977 and 1979 respectively. He moved, in the same capacity, to QPR, in October 1980 and duly guided them to promotion from Division Two, just a year after losing in the 1982 FA Cup Final to Spurs!

In May 1984, he became coach/manager of the crack Spanish side CF Barcelona where he stayed for four years. He then returned to Spurs as manager in December 1988, moving up the ladder to Chief Executive in July 1991 - just after seeing his side triumph over Nottingham Forest in that year's FA Cup Final.

Prior to that success he had seen Barcelona win their domestic League title (1985) and finish runners-up in the national Cup (1986).

In May 1993 came the sensational news that Spurs Chairman Alan Sugar had effectively sacked Venables. Venables appealed and was duly reinstated by a High Court judge. However the following month, Venables lost the High Court battle on the third day of hearing. He remained a director of the club until he sold his shares in August 1993.

Appointed England coach in 1995, Venables almost brought home the country's first trophy since 1966, but West Germany ruined the party with victory in a penalty shoot-out in the semi-finals of Euro 96. His record as England supremo was excellent: 11 wins, 11 draws and only one defeat.

After that Venables coached (managed) the Australian national soccer team and worked on ITV as a football pundit before returning to club football halfway through the 2000-01 season to save Middlesbrough from relegation from the Premiership.

VILLA, RICARDO JULIO

Capped 18 times by Argentina (one goal scored) the dark-haired, swarthy figure of Ricky Villa helped his country win the World Cup before joining Spurs (with his fellow countryman Ossie Ardiles) in June 1978 for £375,000.

Signed from Racing Club Buenos Aires, the strong-running midfielder gave Spurs excellent service, appearing in 178 senior games and netting 25 goals, including one of the greatest ever seen at Wembley (v. Manchester City in the 1981 FA Cup final replay which Spurs won 3-2).

Born in Buenos Aires on 18 August 1952, Villa had earlier assisted Quilmes and Athletico Tucuman in Argentina. On leaving Spurs in June 1983, he

signed for the NASL club Fort Lauderdale Strikers before going to Deportivo Cali (Colombia), later assisting Defensa y Justicia (Argentina) whom he also coached, having worked in the same capacity with his former club, Quilmes following his retirement.

VITORIA SETUBAL

Spurs playing record against the Portuguese side

Competition	P	W	D	L	F	A
UEFA Cup	2	1	0	1	2	2

Spurs defeated the Portuguese side on the away goal rule in a fourth round UEFA Cup-tie in March 1973 after the aggregate score had finished level at 2-2.

Full-back Ray Evans' goal gave Spurs a 1-0 lead from their home leg which was seen by 30,469 fans, but it was Martin Chivers' effort in front of 30,000 spectators in the return fixture (which ended in a 2-1 defeat) that eventually took Spurs through.

WADDLE, CHRISTOPHER ROLAND

Chris Waddle's career has took him to several destinations. He started out in his home surroundings with Pelaw Juniors and then served, in turn, with the Whitehouse Club, Mount Pleasant Social Club, Pelaw Social Club, Leam Lane Social Club, Clarke Chapman FC and Tow Law Town (whose ground is the highest above sea level in the UK). A trial with Sunderland, preceded a move to Newcastle United (as a professional) in July 1980. From St James' Park he switched to Spurs for £650,000 in July 1985 and four years later - after FA Cup Final disappointment in 1987 - he was transferred to Olympique Club de Marseille for a massive £4.5 million in July 1989 - making him the third most expensive footballer in the game's history, behind Diego Maradona and the Dutchman Ruud Gullit. He helped the French club win three successive League titles and reach the 1991 European Cup Final before returning to the English scene with Sheffield Wednesday in July 1990 for £1 million. A spell in Scotland with Falkirk (September 1996) was followed by a stint at Bradford City (October 1996) and then a £75,000 move to Sunderland in March 1997. He wound down his League career at Burnley (July 1997) and Torquay United (September 1998-April 1999).

After a spell as reserve team coach back at Hillsborough (from July 1999) Waddle re-entered the game at non-League level with Worksop Town in season 2000-01.

Capped 62 times by England (25 coming as a Spurs man - 4 goals scored), he also played once for the Under-21 side. Waddle, with his tremendous body-swerve, excellent ball control, pace over 25-35 yards, powerful shooting and deep swinging centres, gave the fans up and down the country a great deal of enjoyment. He made 190 appearances for Newcastle, 177 (42 goals) for Spurs and almost 150 for Wednesday. When he quit major competitive soccer in 1999, his record was superb: 713 appearances (at various levels) and 147 goals. However, he won't need reminding of his penalty kick against Germany in the World Cup semi-final of 1990.

WALDEN, FREDERICK INGRAM

A Spurs player from April 1913 until May 1926, right-winger Fanny Walden was fast and clever, adept at dancing round his opponent, getting to the bye-line and crossing dangerously, sometimes on the

run. He also scored his fair share of goals.

Born in the Northamptonshire town of Wellingborough on 1 March 1888, he started out with White Cross FC and then assisted the All Saints and Rodwell clubs before joining Wellingborough Town in 1907, switching to Northampton Town of the Southern League in August 1909 - signed by former Spurs player Herbert Chapman. He remained with the Cobblers for four years before joining Spurs for £1,700. During The Great War, Walden - a great favourite with the fans - guested for Leeds City and when he left White Hart Lane, after 13 years loyal and dedicated service, he rejoined Northampton Town, retiring in August 1927, when he became a licensee in the town. He later returned to the Cobblers as the club's 'A' team coach.

Capped by England against Scotland in 1914 and Wales in 1922, he also represented the Football League XI.

He was a key figure when the Second Division championship was won in 1920 (netting four times in 31 League outings). The following season, with Jimmy Seed his right-wing partner and Bert Smith giving support from behind.

Weighing less than nine stones, Walden was a very competent footballer who could certainly hold his own. He was never bustled off the ball and always gave a good account of himself, even in the most intimidating of curcumstances.

Walden was also a very capable Northamptonshire cricketer who scored 7,462 runs and took 114 wickets in 258 first-class matches. He later became a first-class umpire and was also on the board of Test Match officials.

Walden died in Northampton on 3 May 1949.

WALKER, IAN

Goalkeeper Ian Walker had made well over 300 first-class appearances for Spurs up to the end of the 1999-2000 season but was then replaced between the posts by new-signing Neil Sullivan from Wimbledon.

Born in Watford on 31 October 1971, the son of the former Watford and Colchester United 'keeper Mike Walker, he joined Spurs as an apprentice in June 1988 and turned professional in December 1989. After helping Spurs' teenagers win the FA Youth Cup in 1990, he had loan spells later that year with both Oxford United (September) and Ipswich Town (November)... to gain experience.

He successfully took over the gloves from Erik Thorstvedt, and performed consistently well for a decade, gaining three full England caps and also representing his country in one 'B' and nine Under-21 internationals, having earlier played at Youth team level. A League Cup winner in 1999 and coached by one of the great goalkeepers of the past, Ray Clemence, Walker is a fine shot-stopper and his record with Spurs was 312 senior appearances before he was sold to Leicester City for £2 million in July 2001.

WALKER, ROBERT HENRY

Having played for Heart of Midlothian aand Middlesbrough, inside-forward Bob Walker joined Spurs in May 1906 at the age of 22 and went on to appear in 28 first-class games for the club, scoring three goals before moving to New Brompton in March 1908. Later he assisted Northampton Town, Luton Town, Millwall and Bristol Rovers, retiring in 1915.

WALSALL

Spurs playing record against the Saddlers

Competition	P	W	D	L	F	A
FA Cup	I	I	0	0	I	0

The only game between the two clubs was an FA Cup 3rd Round tie at Walsall in January 1969 which Spurs won 1-0 with a Jimmy Greaves goal in front of 18,779 fans.

Players with both clubs include: David Copeland, Alan Grubb, Sid Helliwell, Scott Houghton, Bill Lane, Bert Lyons, Joe Moffatt, Tommy Muldoon (Spurs reserve), Ernie Newman, Jimmy Robertson, Tommy Roe, John Smith (Walsall player-coach & manager), Horace Woodward.

Wartime guests (either with one or both clubs): Jack Acquroff, David Colquhoun, Charlie Crossley, Doug Flack, Len Flack, Jimmy McCormick, Tommy Pearson, Haydn Price

Also associated: Dave Mackay (Spurs player, Saddlers manager), Vic Potts (Spurs reserve & scout, Walsall trainer).

WALSH, PAUL ANTHONY

Darting utility forward Paul Walsh played in a total of 207 first team games for Spurs, 71 as a substitute. In major League and Cup action, he appeared in 156 matches, making 58 as a substitute...a club record.

Born in Plumstead, South London on 1 October 1962, he represented Blackheath, South London and London Schools, before joining Charlton Athletic as an apprentice in July 1977, turning professional in October 1979. He scored 31 goals in exactly 100 outings for the Addicks, and was the youngest-ever Charlton player to net a hat-trick when he claimed the feat against Brentford at The Valley in August 1980, some six weeks short of his 18th birthday. With so many big-named clubs seeking his signature (Arsenal, Aston Villa and Manchester United among them) it was surprising to a lot of people when Walsh moved to Luton Town for £250,000 plus Steve White in July 1982. Two years later (May 1984) Walsh was snapped up by Liverpool for £700,000 and in February 1988, after 112 games for the Merseysiders (37 goals scored) he transferred to Spurs for £550,000 in February 1988.

After a loan spell with QPR (he played in two games in September 1991) Walsh moved from White Hart Lane to Portsmouth in June 1992 for £400,000. In March 1994, a fee of £750,000 took him north to Manchester City, only for him to return to Fratton Park in a £500,000 deal in September 1995. A knee ligament injury finally forced him into retirement in 1997 after he had amassed a pretty fine set of statistics: 162 goals in 533 League and Cup appearances at club level alone.

Capped five times by England (all won as a Luton player) Walsh also represented his country at Youth and Under-21 levels (4 appearances), and he played for the London FA v. England at Highbury in 1981. With Liverpool, he won a First Division championship medal in 1986 either side of European Cup and League Cup runners-up medals. In 1991 he was an FA Cup and Charity Shield winner with Spurs. Earlier, in 1984, he was voted PFA 'Young Footballer of the Year.'

After retiring from playing side of the game Walsh became a Football Agent and he also acts as a TV soccer summariser.

WALTERS, CHARLES

Centre-half Charlie Walters was signed by Spurs from Oxford City as an amateur in December 1919. The following April he turned 'pro' and over the next six seasons gave the club splendid service in amassing a total of 135 first-class appearancees (127 in League and FA Cup). One of the quickest players at White Hart

Lane, he was also deliberate, could kick hard and long and overall was a real solid porformer.

Born at Sandford-on-Thames on I April 1897, he took over the pivotal duties from Charlie Rance at the heart of the Spurs defence and was outstanding in the 1921 FA Cup Final win over Wolves. After being replaced by Harry Skitt, Walters moved to Fulham (October 1926) and ended his senior career with Mansfield Town (August 1928-May 1929). He died in Oxford on 13 May 1971.

WALTERS, WILLIAM EDWARD

Right-winger Sonny Walters made 346 first team appearances for Spurs (210 in the Football League) and he scored a total of 109 goals of which 66 arrived in League action. Born in Edmonton, North London on 5 September 1924, he represented Edmonton and London Schools before joining Spurs on amateur forms in1938. He played for Tottenham Juniors, Walthamstow Avenue and Finchley prior to turning professional in September 1944. Guesting for Derry City and Millwall during the hostilities, Walters stayed with Spurs until July 1957 when he moved to Aldershot

Walters claiming the ball has crossed the line against Preston

where he ended his career two years later.

Sent along to White Hart Lane by ex-Spurs star Billy Sage, Walters took over the wing position from Freddie Cox and as top-scorer he helped the team win promotion as Second Division champions in 1949-50, adding a First Division prize to his collection twleve months later. With Stan Matthews, Tom Finney, Billy Elliott and a few others around, Walters was never really in with a chance of playing for England and his only honour came in the form of a 'B' cap v. Holland in 1950.

Walters died at Enfield on 25 November 1970.

WALTON, JOSEPH

Joe Walton was another excellent outside-right who served Spurs from May 1903 until April 1909, making 217 first-team appearances and scoring 51 goals. He had made his League debut as a 17 year-old with Preston North End in 1898 and spent five years at Deepdaale before trying his luck at White Hart Lane.

Born in Lancashire on 8 January 1881, Walton played in three international trials for England over a period of two years but failed to win a full cap. On leaving Spurs he assisted Sheffield United and then had a spell with non-League side Stalybridge Celtic (July 1911-13).

WANT, ANTHONY GEORGE

Full-back Tony Want, born in Hackney on 13 December 1948, played for Hackney Schools before joining Spurs as an apprentice in November 1963, turning professional in December 1965. He made his senior debut v. West Bromwich Albion in March 1968 - the first of 60 League and Cup appearances during his time at White Hart Lane which ended in June 1972 when he moved to Birmingham City for £50,000. Spells in the NASL with Philadelphia Atoms and Minnesota Kicks followed before he retired in 1980 to run his own business in Solihull, West Midlands.

An England Youth international, the competent Want had Phil Beal, Joe Kinnear and Cyril Knowles to contend with for a first team place with Spurs. He did his best.

WARD, RALPH ARTHUR

Scorer of 28 goals in 378 first-team appearances for Spurs between March 1936 and August 1946, full-back Ralph Ward, a tenacious tackler with strong kick, netted ten times in 118 League games and once in 117 FA Cup matches while also claiming five more in more than 230 Wartime encounters. Born in Oadby, Leicestershire on 5 February 1911, he twice represented England Schools and played for Hinckley Athletic before signing amateur forms for Leicester City in 1928. A year later he became a professional with Bradford City from where he switched to White Hart Lane (after impressing in an FA Cup-tie against Spurs). He made his debut against West Ham United shortly after joining.

Ward - a former butcher - captained Spurs and guested for Arsenal, Bradford City and Fulham during the War, before transferring to Crewe Alexandra after the hostilities. He retired from League football in May 1949 but continued to play with Oadby Town (after reclaiming amateur status) and then managed Crewe for two years: 1953-55.

Ward was also an assistant golf professional at the Bush Hill Golf Club (1945) and after leaving Gresty Road he started his own haulage business.

WARMLEY

Spurs playing record against Warmley

Competition	P	W	D	L	F	A
Southern League	2	2	0	0	12	2

These two wins (7-1 at home, 5-1 away) were not recorded in the final Southern League table of 1898-99 as Warmley resigned from the competition before the end of the campaign.

WARNER, ALFRED CRAGG

Inside-forward Alf Warner appeared in 93 first-class games for Spurs, scoring 30 goals. He was born in Nottingham in 1879 and played for Notts Rangers, Nottingham Olympic, Weal FC and Notts County (from August 1899) before joining Spurs in May 1902. Able and willing he spent three years at White Hart Lane, leaving the club for Luton Town in May 1905. He retired in June 1907 but returned, albeit briefly, with Notts County in October 1907.

WARTIME FOOTBALL

This is Spurs competitive playing record (first team) during the two World War periods (friendlies are not included in the figures):

League Competitions

Season	P	W	D	L	F	A	Pts
1915-16	36	16	11	9	70	57	43
1916-17	40	24	5	11	112	64	53
1917-18	36	22	2	12	86	56	46
1918-19	36	13	8	15	52	72	34
1939-40	36	16	6	14	80	73	38
1940-41	23	9	5	9	53	41	23
1941-42	30	15	8	7	61	41	38
1942-43	28	16	6	6	68	28	38
1943-44	30	19	8	3	71	36	46
1944-45	30	23	6	1	81	30	52
1945-46	42	22	3	17	78	81	47
Summary	367	195	68	104	812	569	458

Cup Competitions

Season	P	W	D	L	F	A
1917-18	4	0	1	3	3	8
1918-19	2	1	0	1	3	3
1939-40	2	1	0	1	3	5
1940-41	19	10	5	4	57	27
1941-42	6	3	1	2	9	11
1942-43	6	4	1	1	12	3
1943-44	7	5	0	2	8	6
1944-45	6	3	1	2	13	4
1945-46*	2	0	1	1	2	4
Summary	54	27	10	17	110	71

* These two games were in the FA Cup (v. Brentford) and have also been recorded in the appropriate section (under FA Cup).

WATFORD (WEST HERTS)

Spurs playing record against the Hornets

Competition	P	W	D	L	F	A
Premiership	2	1	1	0	5	1
Football League	12	6	1	5	18	17
FA Cup	6	6	0	0	23	8
League Cup	2	1	0	1	8	6
Southern League	14	8	5	1	34	8
Wartime	14	11	2	1	44	14
Summary	50	33	9	8	132	54

West Herts, the forerunners to Watford, were Spurs' first FA Cup opponents - in a 1st qualifying game on 13 October 1894. Spurs won the game 3-2 and Peter Hunter had the pleasure of scoring the club's first goal in this competition - a header from Ernie Payne's cross. The other two goals came from Don Goodall.

The first League game between Spurs and Watford was staged at White Hart Lane on 6 November 1982 and resulted in a 1-0 win for the Hornets. Spurs, however, recorded a 1-0 victory themselves when the teams met at Vicarage Road later in the season (Mark Falco the scorer). Unfortunately Steve Perryman was sent-off in this game.

Glenn Hoddle scored a wonderful chipped goal for Spurs in their 3-2 League win at Vicarage Road on 24 September 1983.

In season 1984-85 Spurs crashed to a 5-1 home defeat at the

hands of the Hornets and at the start of the following season Chris Waddle, making his Spurs debut, scored twice as the Hornets were stung 4-0 at White Hart Lane.

In the 1987 FA Cup semi-final at Villa Park, Steve Hodge scored twice as Spurs beat Watford 4-0 in front of 46,151 spectators.

Jurgen Klinsmann scored a hat-trick for Spurs when they beat the Hornets 6-3 in a second round 1st leg League Cup match at Vicarage Road in 1994. In 1998-99 season Spurs also beat the Hornets 5-2 in a 3rd round FA Cup-tie at White Hart Lane, scoring three times in the first 20 minutes to lead 4-2 at half-time. The two Premiership games, played in 1999-2000, ended in a 4-0 home win for Spurs on Boxing Day and a 1-1 draw at Vicarage Road.

Players with both clubs include: Chris Adams, Gerry Armstrong, Espen Baardsen, George Badenoch, Bert Badger, Fred Barnett, Peter Beadle, Dennis Bond, Darren Caskey, Jim Chalmers, Bobby Cook, Harry Crump, Chris Day, Wally Eames, Jack Elkes, Mark Falco, Lee Gardner (Hornets trialist), Johnny Gavin, George Gemmell, Arthur Grimsdell (also a Watford director), Tommy Harmer, Danny Hill, Arthur Hopkins, Pat Jennings, Jimmy Jones (Spurs reserve), John L Jones, Jimmy Kennedy, Peter Kyle, Bill Lane, Roy Low, Paul Miller, Joe Moffatt, John Moran, Allan Nielsen, Tom Pangbourne, Jimmy Reid, Mark Robson, Ronny Rosenthal, John Ryden, Tim Sherwood, Alf Stokes, Walter Tattersall, Dennis Uphill, Ramon Vega, Wilf Waller.

Wartime guests (either with one or both clubs): Ted Bassett, Frank Boulton, Bobby Browne, Red Edwards, Harry Ferrier, Alf Fitzgerald, Billy Grimes, Tom Howshall, Harry Jackson, Eric Jones, George Ludford, Andy Ralston, Reg Smith, Ted Worrall, Albert Young.

Also associated: Ron Burgess, Colin Lee & Steve Perryman (Spurs players, Watford managers, Lee also Watford coach and Youth & reserve team manager), Peter Taylor (Spurs player, Watford assistant-manager), Peter Shreeves (Spurs Youth, reserve and first team manager, also assistant-manager of both clubs).

WATSON, JOHN

Competing initially with Harry Erentz and Sandy Tait, full-back John Watson accumulated a total of 199 first team appearances for Spurs (including 102 in the Southern League & 22 in the FA Cup). A Scotsman, born in Dundee in 1877, he had one season with his home-town club of Dundee Wanderers before joining New Brompton in August 1898. He went back to Scotland to assist Dundee (1899-1900) and played for Everton for two years prior to signing for Spurs in May 1902. He was basically a reserve for the first two of his six seasons at White Hart Lane. He retired in May 1908.

WEATHER

When Spurs toured Fiji, Australia and New Zealand in 1976 (see Under Overseas Tours) they played in temperatures touching 100 degrees.

The hottest weather Spurs have encountered in this country (England) was in early September 1906 when the temperature in Great Britain was recorded at 90 degrees F (in the shade). At the time Spurs lost 2-1 at home to West Ham United, drew 1-1 away to Watford and won 3-2 at Bristol Rovers, all three games taking place in the Southern League.

During the two major arctic winters in Britain (1946-47 and 1962-63) very little football was played, but training sessions still had to be fulfilled and occasionally the temperature dropped to well below freezing.

WEBSTER, FREDERICK JOSEPH

Full-back Fred Webster was full of Yorkshire grit who made 102 first team appearances for Spurs (82 in the Football League). Born in Sheffield on 3 April 1887, he made over 100 senior appearances in five seasons with Gainsborough Trinity before joining Spurs in April 1911. He left White Hart Lane for Brentford in June 1919 and later returned to Gainsborough (June 1920-May 1921).

WEIR, WILLIAM FINDLAY

A Glaswegian, born on 18 April 1889, half-back Findlay Weir played for the local Maryhill club before making 72 appearances for Sheffield Wednesday (from February 1909). He joined Spurs in May 1912 and played in a further 118 first team games (96 in the Football League - 2 goals scored). He was serving with the Tottenham Royal Engineers during the Great War when he was killed in action on 9 July 1918.

WELHAM, JOHN WALTER

Jack Welham made 17 first-class appearances for Spurs between 1892 and 1894. A strapping half-back born in Suffolk, he played initially for Bedminster and on leaving Spurs signed for Clapton Orient, later assisting Bristol South End.

WELLER, KEITH

Born in Islington, London on 11 June 1946, Keith Weller represented Islington, Hackney and Middlesex Schools before joining Spurs as an amateur in August 1963, signing as a part-time professional in January 1964. He only 21 League games for Spurs (one goal scored) before transferring to Millwall in June 1967. From The Den he switched to Chelsea (May 1970) and joined Leicester City in September 1971. He made 297 appearances: (295+2) and scored 43 goals for the Foxes, up to February 1979 when he moved to the NASL to sign for the New England Teamen, later assisting Fort Lauderdale Strikers and tacona Stars before coaching the Dallas Sidekicks in the American Indoor Soccer League.

A right-sided player, whose fast, direct and skilful surges into opposing territory brought admiration from all quarters, he could be temperamental at times and would drift out of a game for long periods before bursting back to life with a flourish! He scored some cracking goals, from all angles and from various distances. He won 'Goal of the Season' with one memorable effort for Leicester against Luton in an FA Cup-tie in February 1974. Capped four times by England (at Leicester) Weller also represented the Football League and helped Chelsea win the European Cup-winners Cup in 1971.

WELLINGBOROUGH

Spurs playing record against 'Boro

Competition	P	W	D	L	F	A
Other Leagues	14	9	4	1	41	15

Spurs beat Wellingboro' 5-0 at home in a United League game in December 1897 and in April of the following year raced to a 5-2 home victory in the same competition. But Spurs' biggest win of the nine they registered came in September 1902 when 'Boro were eclipsed 6-1 at White Hart Lane in a Southern League fixture. All seven goals came from different players.

WEIGHT

The heaviest player ever to oppose Spurs is undoubtedly the Chelsea, Sheffield United and England goalkeeper Billy 'Fatty' Foulke who tipped the scales at well over 20 stone during his career. He weighed in at 21st when he appeared in the 1901 FA Cup final.

WELSH CONNECTION

Here is a list of Spurs personnel (players at various levels, managers, coaches etc) who have been associated with Welsh clubs (for Cardiff City, Newport County, Swansea Town/City, Wrexham see under respective category):

Player	Clubs
Alex Anderson	Bangor City
Jimmy Archibald	Aberdare Athletic
Chris Armstrong	Llay Welfare
Herbert Blake	Mid-Rhondda
Ernie Bowering	Merthyr Town
Jimmy Brain	Ton Pentre
David Brown	Merthyr Town (trial)
Ron Burgess	Cwn Villa
Harry Clarke	Llanelli (player-manager)
Billy Cook	Colwyn Bay
George Crompton	Barry Town (player-coach), Llanelli
Charlie Crossley	Ebbw Vale (manager)
Willie Davies	Llanelli, Rhymney, Swansea Amateurs, Troedrhiwfuwch FC
Alf Day	Ebbw Vale
Jim Evans	Merthyr Town
Norman Evans	Cwm Villa
Tom Evans	Ton Pentre
Wilf Hares	Tredegar
Harry Hargreaves	Pontypridd
Charlie Hewitt	Manager of both Flint & Connah's Quay
Bert Hodgkinson	Colwyn Bay United
Archie Hughes	Colwyn Bay United
Jack Illingworth	Barry Town
Ben Ives	Ton Pentre
Charlie Jones	Ebbw Vale
Ernie Jones	Rhyl Town (manager)
John L Jones	Rhuddlan
Tom Leslie	Caerphilly
Arthur Lowdell	Ton Pentre
Bert Lyons	Colwyn Bay
Reg Mogford	Aberaman
Taffy O'Callaghan	Ebbw Vale Corries, Victoria United
Aled Owen	Bangor City
Cecil Poynton	Ton Pentre
Haydn Price	Aberdare, Mid-Rhondda (manager)
Bill Rees	Blaengarw, Caernarvon Rovers
Jimmy Seed	Mid-Rhondda
Tommy Simmons	Merthyr Town
Arthur Willis	Havordfordwest FC (player-manager)
Ted Worrall	Aberdare

* Ex-Spurs stars Mike England and Terry Yorath, both managed the Welsh national team. Mark Bowen was appointed as coach of the Welsh Under-21 side in 2000.

WEMBLEY STADIUM

Spurs playing record at the Empire Stadium:

Competition	P	W	D	L	F	A
FA Cup	11	7	2	2	21	12
League Cup	4	3	0	1	5	3
Charity Shield	3	1	1	1	2	1
1988 Tourney	2	0	0	2	1	6
Totals	20	11	3	6	29	22

Wembley Fact File

* Bobby Smith scored six goals at Wembley in the 1960-61 season - five for England and one for Spurs....and all six were netted at the same end of the ground (to the right of the Royal Box and opposite the tunnel).
* Spurs have played twelve different teams at Wembley - AC Milan, Arsenal, Aston Villa, Burnley, Chelsea, Coventry City, Leicester City, Liverpool, Manchester City, Norwich City, Nottingham Forest and Queens Park Rangers.

WEST BROMWICH ALBION

Spurs playing record against the Baggies

Competition	P	W	D	L	F	A
Football League	106	38	22	46	159	170
FA Cup	9	5	1	3	15	11
League Cup	4	3	1	0	7	0
Charity Shield	1	0	0	1	0	2
39-40 League	1	1	0	0	4	3
Wartime	2	1	0	1	4	7
Summary	123	48	24	51	189	193

Seven years before the first League game between the two clubs, Spurs crushed First Division Albion 4-0 in the 1901 FA Cup semi-final at Villa Park, all the goals coming from 'Sandy' Brown.
Albion were the first visiting team to win a League game at White Hart Lane, beating Spurs 3-0 on 7 November 1908 in front of 20,000 fans. This was also the first meeting between the two clubs at this level. Albion won the return game at The Hawthorns by 3-1 and in doing so became the first club to achieve a League double over Spurs.

Action against West Bromwich Albion from 1911

1931 FA Cup action against West Bromwich Albion

The Spurs v. West Brom League game at The Hawthorns in January 1912 was abandoned through fog in the 57th minute with the scoreline blank. Albion won the 'replay' 2-0.

A week after that abandoned game Albion beat Spurs 3-0 in a 1st round FA Cup-tie.

Spurs defeated Albion 3-1 at home on 21 October 1922, but a week later they crashed 5-1 at The Hawthorns.

In 1930-31, Albion completed the unique double, that of winning the FA Cup and promotion from the Second Division in the same season. In the League they failed to beat Spurs, losing 2-0 at home and drawing 2-2 away, but in the FA Cup they went through to the 5th round with a 1-0 victory at The Hawthorns.

Len Duquemin scored a hat-trick when Spurs beat Albion 5-0 at home in March 1951 and when that scoreline was repeated in April 1959, Bobby Smith weighed in with a fourtimer.

Spurs commenced the 1952-53 League season by losing a seven-goal thriller by 4-3 at home to Albion in front of 56,552 fans in sweltering heat. Harry Clarke headed a brilliant own-goal for the Baggies!

Spurs eclipsed Albion 3-1 at home in October 1954 to end a run of nine games without a win. When Albion reached the FA Cup Final in 1954, they ousted Spurs 3-0 at The Hawthorns in round six.

Spurs beat Albion 4-1 at home on Boxing Day 1955, but lost 1-0 at The Hawthorns 24 hours later when fielding an unchanged side. Albion defeated Spurs 4-3 at The Hawthorns in November 1959 but then lost the return game heavily in London (see above).

Albion beat Spurs 2-1 at White Hart Lane to dampen their championship celebrations in April 1961 and the Baggies repeated that scoreline twelve months later. In contrast Spurs won 3-1 at The Hawthorns in November 1960 and 4-2 in December 1961. They also knocked Albion out of the FA Cup in the 5th round with another 4-2 victory in the Black Country in February 1962. A crowd of 53,539 saw the action.

In October 1971, Albion suffered their heaviest defeat in the League Cup competition when they crashed 5-0 to Spurs in a 4th round tie at White Hart Lane. Martin Peters scored a hat-trick that evening.

Spurs led Albion 2-0 at The Hawthorns in October 1976, but lost

the game 4-2 after Terry Naylor had been given a roasting by Willie Johnston!

Maarten Jol (Albion) and Tony Galvin (Spurs) were both sent-off in the 1st leg of the 1981-82 League Cups semi-final at The Hawthorns. This ended goalless before Spurs won the return leg 1-0, courtesy of Micky Hazard's fine 20 yard drive.

Mark Falco scored twice when Spurs beat West Brom 5-0 at home in March 1986, but the attendance at this game was just 10,841. This was the lowest at White Hart Lane for a competitive League or Cup game since January 1947.

Players with both clubs include: Gerry Armstrong, Freddie Cox (also WBA assistant-manager & coach), Garth Crooks, Tom Evans (WBA reserve), Ruel Fox, Charlie Hewitt, Colin Lyman (WBA reserve), Graham Roberts, Steve Walford.

Wartime guests (either with onee or both clubs): Jack Acquroff, Jimmy Jinks, Eric Jones, Jimmy McCormick, Wilf Saunders, Cyril Williams.

Also associated: Vic Buckingham (Spurs player, WBA manager), Ossie Ardiles (Spurs player & manager, WBA manager), Keith Burkinshaw (manager of both clubs, also WBA assistant-manager & Spurs coach), Jesse Carver (Spurs coach, WBA manager), Wilf Dixon (Spurs assistant-manager & WBA trainer), Arthur Rowe (Spurs player & manager, WBA chief scout), John Gorman (Spurs player and assistant-manager, WBA assistant-manager), Will Brierley (trainer at both clubs), Danny Thomas (Spurs player, WBA physio), Tony Parks (Spurs player, WBA goalkeeping coach).

WEST HAM UNITED (also Thames Ironworks).

Spurs playing record against the Hammers

Competition	P	W	D	L	F	A
Premiership	16	6	3	7	19	20
Football League	86	33	23	30	141	130
FA Cup	11	6	3	2	29	16
League Cup	6	2	2	2	8	3
Other Leagues	40	21	10	9	64	38
Other Cups	4	4	0	0	16	1
Wartime	37	10	8	19	48	65
Summary	200	82	49	69	215	273

Spurs first recorded match against the East End club was in a Thames & Medway League game against Thames Ironworks (Hammers' previous name) on 3 September 1898, Spurs had half-back Alex Hall filling in as an emergency goalkeeper. They won the game 3-0 in front of 4,000 spectators.

On 13 March 1920 Spurs and the Hammers met for the first time in the Football League and in front of 25,691 fans at Upton Park, the hosts collected the Second Division points with a 2-1 victory. Nine days later in front of a similar sized audience, Spurs gained sweet revenge with a 2-0 home win.

Five goals were scored in the opening 25 minutes of the Spurs v. West Ham League game at White Hart Lane in December 1927. Spurs led 3-2 and went on to win 5-3.

The Hammers completed a Christmas double over Spurs in 1958-59, winning 2-1 at Upton Park and 4-1 at White Hart Lane.

Spurs 'hammered' West Ham 6-1 at Upton Park in August 1962 and then drew 4-4 at White Hart Lane four months later when Dave Mackay notched his first and only hat-trick for the club.

Spurs beat West Ham 3-0 at home yet lost 4-0 at Upton Park in 1963-64. Between 1937 and 1965, the Hammers won only one of their 13 League games at White Hart Lane - a narrow 3-2 victory on Boxing Day 1936.

In 1966-67 it was 4-3 to the Hammers at White Hart Lane and 2-0 to Spurs at Upton Park while in August 1967, Spurs won their home game 5-1, with Jimmy Greaves scoring twice against his future club.

In between times, in September 1966, Scottish international Alan Gilzean became the first Spurs player to get sent-off in a League Cup-tie, taking an early bath in the 1-0 second round defeat at Upton Park.

West Ham recorded a 5-3 win over Spurs at Upton Park in November 1976, only to lose the return fixture 2-1 as Spurs battled in vain against relegation!

Spurs lost their opening home League game of the 1981-82 season to West Ham by 4-0 in front of 41,200 fans.

The Hammers completed a rare double over Spurs in 1983-84; they won 2-0 at White Hart Lane and 4-1 at Upton Park, but after two draws the following season and a win apiece the next, Spurs won 4-0 in December 1986 with Clive Allen netting twice.

Spurs beat the Hammers 5-0 at home in a 5th round League Cup replay in February 1987. They went ahead in the sixth minute, scored their second on 71 minutes and after that it was a cake-walk.

Spurs beat the Hammers 3-1 at Upton Park but lost 4-3 at White Hart Lane in the two Premiership games played in 1993-94.

The Hammers had Steve Lomas sent-off in the 100th League game between the two clubs, played on 6 December 1999. The result was a 0-0 draw.

In March 2001, Spurs clinched a place in the semi-final of the FA Cup by winning 3-2 at West Ham.

Players with both clubs include: Clive Allen, Paul Allen, Charlie Ambler, Len Bolan, Mark Bowen, Harry Bradshaw, John Burton, Chris Carrick, John Chiedozie (West Ham trialist), Harry Crump, David Dunmore, Ilie Dumitrescu, Jack Eggett, George Foreman, Jimmy Greaves, Fred Griffiths, Albert Hall, Percy Hooper, Chris Hughton, Johnny Jordan (West Ham Amateur), Bill Joyce, Bill Kaine, Steven Kelly (United trialist), Peter Kyle (West Ham trialist, Ken Mckay, Percy Mapley, Fred Massey, Fred Milnes, John Moncur, Jimmy Neighbour (Spurs player & coach, also West Ham Youth development officer), Tony Parks, Martin Peters, Jimmy Reid, Mark Robson, Neil Ruddock, John Smith, Mitchell Thomas, Walter Thomas (Hammers trialist), Steve Walford, Simon Webster, Charlie Whitchurch (West Ham Amateur).

Wartime guests (either with one or both clubs): Charlie Burke, John Burnett, Tom Caldwell, Eddie Chapman (also West Ham Chief Executive), Albert Chester, Charlie Crossley, Johnny Dowers, Dicky Dunn, Alf Fitzgerald, Len Flack, Willie Hall, Les Henley, Doug Hunt, Jimmy Jinks, George Ludford, Les Medley, Bert Page, Ernie Phypers, Bob Pryde, Reg Smith, Bill Whatley.

Also associated: Bill Nicholson (Spurs player & manager, WHU scout), Jack Tresadern (Hammers player, Spurs manager), Roger Morgan (Spurs player, WHU community development officer), Trevor Hartley (Hammers players, Spurs caretaker & assistant-manager), Eddie Baily (Spurs player and assistant-manager, Hammers scout), Roger Cross (Hammers player, Spurs assistant-manager), Pat Holland (Hammers player, Spurs Youth & reserve team manager), Ronnie Boyce (Hammers player, Youth team manager & assistant-manager, Spurs scout), John Lyall (Hammers player, coach, assistant-manager, manager & general manager, Spurs technical co-ordinator, overseas scouting), Peter Barnes (Spurs club secretary, Hammers secretary).

WEST STANLEY
Spurs playing record against the 'Stanley'

Competition	P	W	D	L	F	A
FA Cup	1	1	0	0	4	0

Spurs comprehensively beat the non-League side West Stanley in a 2nd round tie in January 1920, over 35,500 attending White Hart Lane where former Coventry City player Charlie Wilson scored twice.

WETTON, RALPH
Ralph Wetton was born in County Durham on 6 June 1927 and played as an inside-forward for Cheshunt before joining Spurs as an amateur, turning professional in August 1950. He was successfully converted into a half-back and made 46 first-class appearances for the club before transferring to Plymouth Argyle in June 1955. He later served with Aldershot and Eynesbury Rovers.

WHATLEY, WILLIAM, JOHN

Born in Ebbw Vale, Monmouthshire on 11 October 1912, full-back Bill Whatley played occasionally for Ebbw Vale FC and represented Ebbw Vale and Wales Schools before moving to London where he worked as a baker's boy while assisting Haywards Sports and Northfleet (two of Spurs' junior teams). He was signed as an amateur at White Hart Lane in May 1931 and turned professional 12 months later. The Spurs defence was remodelled to accommodate Whatley who went on to amass a total of 393 first team appearances for the club (2 goals). A model of consistency, he starred in 226 League games and in 28 FA Cup encounters, producing some excellent performances with his clean kicking and clever positional play. Whatley very rarely conceded a free-kick, was strong and reliable and won two full caps for Wales (v. England & Scotland in 1939) and one Wartime cap. After guesting for Arsenal, Fulham, Stockport and West Ham during the War, he retired in June 1947 to become a Spurs scout. He later managed Gravesend & Northfleet (May 1954-55). Whatley died in Greenwich, Loindon in December 1974.

WHITBOURNE, JOHN GILES
Goalkeeper Jack Whitbourne was born in Middlesbrough in 1885 and played for South Bank and Sunderland reserves before joining Spurs in May 1905. He made 29 first-class appearances for the club but with Matt Reilly pressing him hard, he left the club to join Leyton at the start of the 1908-09 season.

WHITCHURCH, CHARLES
A winger from Grays, Essex (born 29 October 1920) Charlie Whitchurch represented England Schools and was an amateur with Portsmouth and West Ham playing for Charlton Athletic and Southend United during the War before joining Spurs in January 1946. After 25 first-class appearances for the club (six goals

Caption for programme image: TOTTENHAM HOTSPUR v. WEST HAM UNITED — FOOTBALL LEAGUE—DIVISION ONE — Saturday, 26th August, 1967 — KICK-OFF 3 p.m. — SIXPENCE — Official programme — SEASON 1967-68 Vol. 60 No. 3

scored) he was transferred to Southend United in July 1947. He later worked for the Ford Motor Company, emigrating to the USA in 1951 where he was employed by General Motors as a rocket researcher. He died in Michigan in July 1977.

WHITE, JOHN ANDERSON

Known as 'The Ghost' John White was a brilliant inside-right, the vital cog in the midfield engine-room. He took over from Tommy Harmer in the Spurs side. and linked up superbly well with Danny Blanchflower. His off-the-ball runs and precise passing made him an exceptional talent. Born in Musselburgh, Midlothian on 28 April 1937, he played for Musselburgh Juniors, Bonnyrigg FC, Rose Athletic, Alloa Athletic and Falkirk before joining Spurs for £3,300 in October 1959. He starred in the double-winning side of 1960-61, the FA Cup triumph a year later and was inspirational when the European Cup-winners Cup was won in 1963. A player of luminous gifts, he was exact in everything he did and tried. Brilliant on the ball, he had a great passing technique, was precociously calm and cool becoming an automatic choice as he made 219 League and Cup appearances and scored 47 goals for Spurs, while also winning 18 caps for Scotland. Earlier he had represented his country on four occasions as a Falkirk player as well as appearing one Under-23 international. White also played for the Football League and twice represented Scotland against the Scottish League. On 21 July 1964, White was sadly killed by lightning on Crew Hill golf course, Enfield, Middlesex.

WHITE, RAYMOND BERNARD WILLIAM.

Born in Bootle, Lancashire on 13 August 1918, Roy White was 22 when he joined Spurs as an amateur in November 1940. He made his debut against Arsenal that same year and went on to appear in 169 first team games for the club (4 goals scored) up to May 1946 when he decided to join Bradford Park Avenue. During the hostilities White - who was evacuated from Dunkirk after his boat had sunk and later worked for the War Office in London - also guested for Fulham and Manchester United, helping the Reds reach the 1945 War League Cup Final.

He turned down the chance of professional football, electing to concentrate on becoming a Chartered Accountant. White, who played in well over 150 games in five years with Park Avenue, died in 1988.

WHITE, SIDNEY ERNEST

Half-back Sid White made 22 League and FA Cup appearances for Spurs whom he served from April 1921 until his retirement in May 1928. Born in Tottenham on 15 February 1899, he played for the Army and Edmonton before moving to White Hart Lane. He became coach with Clapton Orient

WHITE HART LANE
Preparation Work
The first hint that the club were looking for new headquarters came at the very first annual general meeting of shareholders on 10 August, 1898, just a few months after the Limited Company had

been formed. Bobby Buckle, one of the founder members of the club back in 1882 and at that time a club director, was quoted as saying that the club must find a new ground within the next three years. As it was, events moved faster than that and by the second week of 1899 the Tottenham Weekly Herald reported that "rumours abound concerning the Spurs' new ground".

According to the 1921 history of the club " A Romance of Football" - published by the Herald - club chairman C.D. Roberts related the story of how the club came upon the site.

"One day, an apprenticed cooper told me that a new football club was going to start on the vacant space at the rear of the 'White Hart.' Being puzzled as to what enterprising club it was I went and saw mine host, who informed me it was solely his idea. He would like to have a football club playing there. It would be good for his house. Of this he was confident, for he had just left a house at Millwall near to which a football club played on Saturdays and it was a fine thing for him. I asked if he had heard of the Spurs. He replied that he had not, but expressed himself willing for anyone to have the ground subject to the approval of the brewers. He was agreeable to leave the matter in my hands. Within 24 hours Messrs. Charrington and Co. had been interviewed and a lease was soon made out. We now had two grounds and little money to play with. What to do with the Northumberland Park ground and the five years lease was a poser! However, we lay low and were rewarded shortly with a handsome sum for the surrender of the old ground."

The Northumberland Park site had been Spurs' home since 1888. Situated behind a nursery in a meadow alongside a tennis club, it was our first private enclosure. Within a year of Spurs leaving the ground - lying on the north side of Northumberland Park between numbers 69 and 75 - a new housing development had been built. The club had spent the first six years of their existence playing on Tottenham Marshes, across the railway line at Park (now Northumberland Park) station.

The history of the present site can be traced back as far as 1789. According to research undertaken by the Edmonton Hundred Historical Society, the plot of land belonged to one William Cornforth of Barford, Yorkshire and was tenanted to a William Coleman. The detail traced, dated 21 January, 1789, included the following extracts:

"All those two several closes of land and ground formerly three... of pasture land known by the names of the Birds Field but now used or occupied in the whole or in part as nursery or garden ground... lying on the south side of a lane called Marsh Lane leading from Tottenham to Tottenham Marsh, part of which said two several closes abuts North on Marsh Lane, and the other part, also to the north, on the land and premises in the possession of Mr. Payne. Cornforth had come to this land together with two acres of meadow, a rood in the marshes, a cottage, four messuages, two crofts in Feather Field and Home Field, and the messuage with garden, orchard, brewhouse, stable and out-house in the High Road, formerly the Hare and Hounds, and now the White Hart."

Marsh Lane was renamed Park Lane during the latter part of the 19th century. By 1843 local records show that the White Hart public house was surrounded by dwellings. George Beckwith took over the White Hart in 1859 and in 1870 he had greenhouses and a forcing house behind the pub from where he ran his business under the title Beckwith's Nursery. He passed away at the White Hart on 16 January 1898.

By the beginning of February the Herald reported that negotiations had practically come to a head. It was now no secret that the ground lay at the back of the White Hart public house, opposite the Catholic Church, Lower Tottenham, and was formerly known as Beckwith's Nursery. It is much larger than the present enclosure, and it will not be necessary for the touch-line to be in such close proximity to the railings. Accommodation can easily be found for 20,000 people. It concluded by stating that the Spurs will occupy the ground on a fairly long lease, and upon terms which are understood to be distinctly favourable.

Edmonton Cricket Club groundsman John Over was contracted to superintend the work which included demolishing the greenhouses and piping and blowing up the concrete. It was reported in April that the pitch would run parallel with the High Road and that stand accommodation would be provided on all four sides. The extra space allowed the pitch to be 10 yards wider than that at the previous ground but still the same length. A cinder track was to be laid and railings would be four yards from the touchline and another five yards would separate the fence from the stands. Seating accomodation would number 2,500.

It was announced during the second week in April that the first event to be held at the new enclosure would be a Military Tournament on August Bank Holiday Monday.

At a public meeting on 5 May, further details of the new ground were given. A 21-year lease had been obtained for the ground and with slight inconvenience, could accommodate 30,000 people. All of the stands from the present ground were being removed and others put up. One huge stand would run the length of the ground plus a covered stand capable of holding 2,000 people. It was also proposed to use the ground for summer entertainments including two or three al fresco concerts. The cost of moving ground was put at between £700 and £800.

On 9 June, the Herald announced that the new ground would be officially opened on Monday, 4 September 1889, with a visit from either Aston Villa or Sheffield United. Supporters were invited by the directors to suggest a suitable name for the new ground. A fortnight later the Herald reported that only a few individuals

had responded so, for the time being, the directors resolved to do without a name for their new ground.

By the end of June, the ground looked fine and amongst the entertainment arranged was a horse jumping competition, a cockade fight on bicycles, international fencing and player races. Tickets cost one, two or three shillings (five to 15 pence).

Nearly 5,000 people turned out to see Charlie Ambler win the 100 yard handicap race, John Cameron the half-mile handicap and Art Rule the football dribbling race.

The 1899-1900 club handbook, published in August, contained the following extract under "The Progress of the 'Spurs", written by "The Old Crock":

"Perhaps the pricipal item of progress has been the securing of the magnificent new Ground in the High Road. It was not the work of a day, and the thousands who visit the new enclosure will never realise the difficulties that had to be overcome before matters were satisfactorily arranged. Anyway, here we are now with the finest ground in the South, and accommodation for 35,000 spectators, and no doubt it will all be needed."

Initially, pre-season training took place on the old Northumberland Park ground but towards the end of the month the new enclosure was utilised for four trial matches. The first, on the evening of Tuesday, 22 August saw the Stripes defeat the Whites 1-0, Tom Pratt netting the only goal. Another senior trial was staged on the Friday (25th) and one for junior talent on the Saturday. Three days later (on the Tuesday) the final trial match attracted between two and 3,000 spectators. The Whites - made up of the first team forwards and halves plus reserve team defence and goalkeeper - defeated the Stripes 4-1. Pratt (2), Cameron and David Copeland netted for the victors with Barnard replying for the Stripes.

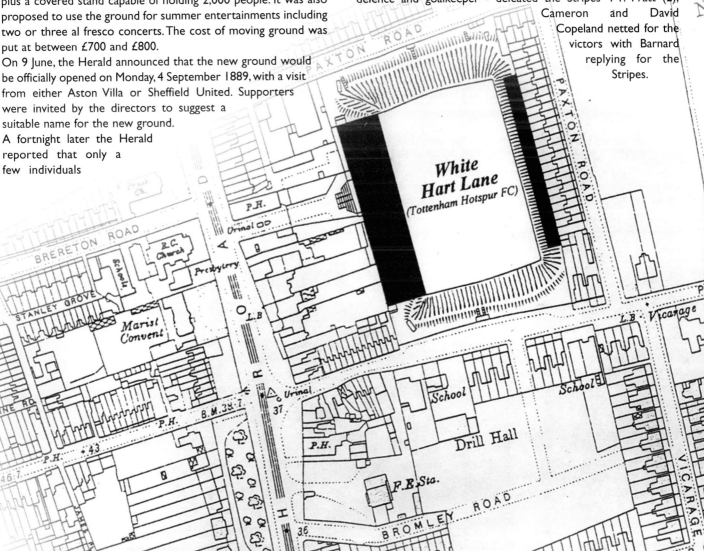

A view of White Hart Lane in the 1950's

Having started our Southern League campaign with a 3-1 win at Millwall Athletic on 2 September, the official opening of the ground was performed on the following Monday, a 5pm start against Notts County.

Chairman Roberts performed the ceremonial kick-off in the absence of local MP Colonel HF Bowles. Notts County took the lead after 20 minutes with a shot that deflected into the net off defender Sandy Tait. By half time Pratt had levelled the scores. David Copeland put Spurs 2-1 up before an accidental collision with County 'keeper Suter - catching him under the heart - saw the latter depart the field of play. Walter Bull, who later joined Spurs, took up custodial duties on the hour. He made several good saves but could not stop a further two goals from Copeland to complete his hat-trick in a 4-1 scoreline. County included Jock Montgomery, one of our earliest professional players in 1896, at left back. A 5,000 crowd, including the famous Irish athlete Larry Bulger, paid receipts of £115.18s.3d (£115.91), half of which was paid over to the visitors. Sam Casey, another of our founder members, acted as a linesman to referee CD Crisp. The two teams for that historic occasionwere:

Spurs: Clawley; Erentz, Tait; Jones, McNaught, Morris; Smith, Pratt, Copeland, Cameron, Kirwan.

County: Suter; Lewis, Montgomery; Ball, Bull, Lowe; Hadley, MacConachie, McCairns, Fletcher, Chalmers.

The first competitive match on the ground was staged the following Saturday afternoon when around 11,000 spectators turned out to watch a 1-0 win over Queens Park Rangers, Tom Smith scoring the only goal. Receipts amounting to £329.4s.3d (£329.21) were taken on the gate in addition to the allocation of season tickets sold at 15s. (75 pence) each covering all home games, except Cup -ties. A week later (on 16 September) the Plaistow based club, Commercial Athletic, were the first visitors for a reserve team fixture. Spurs won the London League match 6-2 before 600 onlookers who paid £20 in receipts.

The Spurs second XI line-up that day was: Ambler; Melia, Barnard; Holmes, Hughes, Ransom; Shearing, Raby, Rule, Hawley and Hyde.

Minor adjustments to the ground were made as the season wore on. Storage for cycles and horses in the approach to the ground were provided and a new press box constructed. The shareholders' stand was well utilised and the one narrow entrance to the ground was soon widened for easier access. A new entrance to the bar from the enclosure was introduced and some turf was relaid and drainage put right. In November, the Hotspur flag was first hoisted at the entrance and by Christmas an old portion of the White Hart pub was demolished which extended the entrance to the ground by 40 feet.

Suggestions for naming the ground, published in the Herald, included Rowel Park - Rowel being "the little wheel of the Spur" - Percy Park - to maintain the Hotspur connection - and Gilpin Park. By the end of the season, with the Southern League title secured, another correspondent suggested Champion Park.

By the end of February, John Cameron had moved offices from 808 High Road to those on the ground. The new address was "Hotspur Ground", Tottenham. When the annual accounts were published in June 1900, the expenditure on the new ground, including costs of lease and permanent improvement, were given as £473.

The site has been steadily improved over the years. In 1901 the enclosure in front of the main stand was increased to give room for 2-3,000 more people and earth banks erected on each corner of the ground. The next year saw the old shareholders stand demolished and the three stands on the west side joined in to one. Corrugated iron roofing gave cover to 5,000 patrons on the east side and a temporary stand erected on waste ground at the Park Lane end.

In 1903 the east side was reconstructed, increasing the capacity by another 2,000. A year later a bank was built up at the Park Lane end to accomodate 10,000 people.

The club took the unusual step of making an appeal, through the 1905-06 club handbook, offering 5,000 £1 shares for sale to raise capital for ground improvements. 2,000 of the shares were snapped up helping towards the major outlay of £8,900 to purchase the freehold from Charringtons. A further £2,600 was invested in a huge bank built at the Edmonton end, increasing capacity to 40,000. By this time the ground was frequently being referred to as "White Hart-lane".

Architect Archibald Leitch, who had designed the grounds of Fulham, Sunderland and Rangers, amongst others, was contracted to build a new West Stand in 1909. The structure incorporated seating for 5,300 with a paddock for over 6,000 terrace spaces. It was officially opened for the first home game in Division One, against Manchester United on September 11, 1909. Parts of the East Stand were also covered in 1909 and the following year the open end banks were doubled in size, taking the capacity to nearly 50,000. Further enlargement to the east side in 1911 saw the wooden structure replaced by concrete terracing.

Using the profits from the 1921 cup run, Leitch was again consulted when covered accomodation was introduced behind the Paxton Road goal. A similar split level terrace followed at the Park Lane end in 1923, costing £3,000, making room for 40,000 under cover. In 1921 the Red House at the front of the ground was purchased and converted into the club offices. The electric clock on the High Road was fixed in February, 1934 to assist people who were unfamiliar with the area to locate the club offices and ground. Within a month it was illuminated and adorned with the cockerel motif.

The building of the East Stand in 1934 was certainly an ambitious project at the time. Leitch proposed in October, 1933 to build a similar structure to that at the Twickenham rugby ground. Seating 4,983 people, 2,346 reserved and 2,528 ordinary, plus 109 special seats in the "crows nest" which, although frequently referred to as the press box was never used for that purpose. Terracing below could hold 13,349 patrons, including a boys enclosure of 1,028 places. Initial estimates put the cost at £40,000 but with the rehousing of tenants on Paxton Road - which at that time ran along both the north and east sides of the ground - put at £5,000 the eventual cost was nearer £60,000. The stand was officially opened on September 22, 1934 for the visit of Aston Villa. The capacity had now reached its peak at 80,000 with room for 60,000 under cover. The West Stand was also re-roofed during the summer of 1934, with the ten supports at the front of the stand being reduced to five.

A covenant within the original agreement with Charringtons forbid the sale of refreshments on the ground. Following no objections from Charringtons or the White Hart landlord, Mecca gained the sole catering rights and on December 22, 1934 14 outlets, including a restaurant beneath both the East and West Stands, were open for business. Initially, alcohol could only be served on first team matchdays between the hours of 1 pm and 4 pm.

The Post War Years

The first major renovation of the pitch in 1952 unearthed several unexpected objects. The work, undertaken by Sutton & Sons of Reading, saw 3,500 tons of soil excavated - to a depth of 12 inches - and removed to a dump on Hackney Marshes. This work revealed large pieces of iron piping, greenhouse foundations and a concrete water tanker, all remnants of the site which we had inherited some 53 years earlier.

Floodlights were first installed in 1953, a simple version set on four corner poles. These were upgraded in 1957 with additional lighting appearing on the west stand gable. A three-year plan to relay the Park Lane terrace was completed and the following year the West Stand enclosure was relaid. Floodlight pylons appeared

in 1961 to replace the poles, and 12 months later the modernisation of the West Stand was completed. It was also in 1962 that the rear section of the Park Lane stand was converted from terrace space into 2,600 tip-up seats, bringing the seated capacity to 12,500. The Paxton Road end was similarly transformed with 3,500 seats installed in 1963.

An updated floodlight system was introduced in 1967 and the Paxton stand linked up with the West Stand to provide a further 1,400 seats a year later. New floodlighting was introduced in 1972 at a cost of £26,000 and the following year the West and South stands were linked up by an additional 700 seats.

The old West Stand was last used for the home game with Crystal Palace on 12 November 1980. Within 15 months the current structure was built and officially opened by Sir Stanley Rous prior to the match with Wolverhampton Wanderers on 6 February 1982. When the East Stand was refurbished in 1989 the spotlight system of floodlights replaced the now defunct pylons.

Since the arrival of architect Igal Yawetz to the board in 1991, he has overseen the redevelopment of both ends. In 1993 the Paxton Road stand was re-roofed and when the Park Lane stand was replaced in 1994, and the shelf terrace disappeared, the ground became an all-seater stadium for the first time. The present South Stand was completed by mid 1995, incorporating the first Jumbotron screen. One unique feature is the control suite, suspended from the roof in the south-west corner. The Paxton Road end was demolished in 1997 to be replaced in April 1998 by the present Members' North Stand.

The address of the ground has changed twice during Spurs' 100-year tenure. With the previously un-named road linking the High Road with the main gates being officially endorsed by Haringey Council as Bill Nicholson Way earlier this year, this has now been incorporated within the club address. Although the club offices were housed at 748 High Road from 1921, the address remained unchanged until 1937 when reverting from number 750 - the same as the White Hart pub - to number 748.

The Current Stadium

The present holding capacity of the ground is 36,237. This figure includes wheelchair aid and disabled seating, all executive areas, the press box as well as first aid seats. The breakdown between each side of the ground is charted below.

	Upper	Lower	Boxes	Capacity	Total
West Stand	4,036	2,271	72	576	6,883
East Stand	4,686	5,544	34	468	10,698
North Stand	5,628	4,279	15	174	10,081
South Stand	4,243	4,332	-	-	8,575
Total	18,593	16,426	121	1,218	36,237

Ground Capacity

How the ground capacity has fluctuated at White Hart Lane over the years:

1899	30,000	1990	29,700
1910	40,000	1991	33,020
1925	50,000	1992	32,786
1937	78,000	1994	26,153
1970	58,000	1995	33,147
1971	56,000	1996	33,083
1976	52,000	1997	33,208
1981	50,000	1998	36,200
1984	48,200	1999	36,236

White Hart Lane Floodlights

The first game played under the White Hart Lane floodlights took place in September 1953 when Spurs met Racing Club de Paris. A crowd of 28,070 saw this team beat the French side 5-3: Ditchburn; Ramsey, Withers; Wetton, Farley, Burgess; Hutchinson, Bennett, Duquemin, Harmer and Robb.

In 1989, when the East Stand was refurbished, the spotlight system of floodlighting replaced the four main pylons at White Hart Lane.

Other matches Played At White Hart Lane

White Hart Lane has hosted many other football matches over the years from international fixtures and FA Cup semi finals to representative games and local Cup competition finals.

The first non-Spurs fixture on our new enclosure was an FA Cup third qualifying round second replay between New Brompton and Woolwich Arsenal on November 8, 1899. Three weeks later on December 2 Tottenham Schools defeated their Finsbury counterparts 3-0 in the Dewar Shield and at the end of the season Thames Ironworks beat Fulham in a Southern League 'Test Match' - now better known as a play-off.

International football arrived at Tottenham in September 1901 when a team billed as "England Amateurs" faced a touring German XI. The Amateurs won 12-0 before a 5,252 crowd. Some sources show this match as the first-ever international match played by Germany. Later that season, on 15 March, White Hart Lane staged its first FA Cup semi final when Southampton defeated Nottingham Forest 3-1.

The first of several England international trial games was hosted on 26 January 1903, resulting in a 2-1 win for the North against the South and the following month the Sheriff of London's Charity Shield was played between Sunderland and Corinthians. In March 1905 Clapton faced Ilford here in an FA Amateur Cup semi final tie. The first 'official' international staged was between England and Ireland at Amateur level on 7 December 1907. The Western League championship match between Millwall Athletic and Southampton was also held here later that season.

In 1910-11 we staged an Inter-League representative match for the first time when the Southern League beat their Football League counterparts 3-2 and in May, 1912 the FA Charity Shield match, which incepted in 1908, was held between Blackburn Rovers and Queens Park Rangers. We also hosted two Charity Shield matches during 1925 - in May and October - both between teams of Professionals and Amateurs.

Increased admission and a midweek afternoon kick-off time restricted the attendance to 17,097 for the first full international match to be staged here at the ground.

Arthur Rowe and Willie Hall were both given their debut in the 4-1 win against France in December 1933. England again won by a three-goal margin when Germany came to Tottenham two years later. The gate figure was 54,164, paying receipts of £7,683. Stanley Matthews notched a hat-trick when Czechoslovakia were defeated 5-4 here in 1937. Hall again featured in the England forward line. The fourth and final full international staged here was a 2-0 win against Italy in November 1949. Alf Ramsey was the only Spur on view for a crowd numbering 71,797, paying receipts of £19,300.

The Tottenham Charity Cup was the most frequent final to be staged at the ground, spanning over 60 years. The trophy, donated in 1900 by Mr TF Barlow, mine host of the Red Lion, was competed for by local clubs. The semi-final and final were regularly held here, the last recorded instance being on 22 April 22 1965 when Dinmont United and Falcon Rovers met in the final.

The Bill Nicholson Trophy finals, competed for by divisional Under-14 teams from the London Schools FA, were hosted here during the late 70's and early 80's.

International Matches Staged At White Hart Lane:

Date	Match	Type	Att
21.09.1901	England 12 Germany 0	Amateur	Att.4,000
07.12.1907	England 6 Ireland 1	Amateur	Att.5,000
19.04.1909	England 11 Belgium 2	Amateur	Att.3,000
26.11.1924	England 3 South Africa 2	Amateur	Att.10,000
06.12.1933	England 4 France 1	Full	Att.17,097
04.12.1935	England 3 Germany 0	Full	Att.54,164
01.12.1937	England 5 Czechoslovakia 4	Full	Att.50,000
17.04.1948	England 3 Netherlands 2	Youth	Att.4,000
02.08.1948	Sweden 3 Austria 0	Olympic Games	Att.8,000
30.11.1949	England 2 Italy 0	Full	Att.71,797
12.11.1955	England 2 West Germany 3	Amateur	Att.7,000
23.10.1956	England 2 Hungary 1	Youth	Att.4,000
15.10.1957	England 4 Romania 2	Youth	Att.5,000
13.04.1960	Great Britain 2 Netherlands 2	Olympic Qualifier	Att.2,000
15.03.1961	England 4 West Germany 1	Under-23	Att.12,000
17.04.1963	England 2 Soviet Union 0	Youth	Att.8,000
16.03.1968	England 0 Scotland 1	Schoolboy	Att.14,470
22.05.1983	France 1 Czechoslovakia 0	European Youth Final	Att.10,000
16.10.1990	England 0 Poland 1	Under-21	Att.20,000
15.08.2001	England 0 Holland 2	Full	Att.35,238

Inter-League

05.11.1930	Football League 7 Scottish League 3		Att.21,738

International trial

14.01.1905	Professionals v Amateurs		Att.10,000

FA Cup Semi-finals Played At White Hart Lane:

15.03.1902	Southampton 3 Nottingham Forest 1	Att.30,000
26.03.1910	Newcastle United 2 Swindon Town 0	Att.33,000
28.03.1914	Liverpool 2 Aston Villa 0	Att.27,464
27.03.1926	Bolton Wanderers 3 Swansea Town 0	Att.25,476
18.03.1950	Arsenal 2 Chelsea 2	Att.67,752
22.03.1950	Arsenal 1 Chelsea 0	Att.66,482
05.04.1952	Arsenal 1 Chelsea 1	Att.68,084
07.04.1952	Arsenal 3 Chelsea 0	Att.57,450
14.03.1959	Luton Town 1 Norwich City 1	Att.63,433
14.03.1970	Chelsea 5 Watford 1	Att.55,209
05.04.1986	Liverpool 2 Southampton 0	Att.44,605
09.04.1988	Wimbledon 2 Luton Town 1	Att.25,963

FA Cup 2nd/3rd Round replays

15.02.1956	Chelsea 2 Burnley 0	Att.27,210
19.03.1963	Coventry 2 Portsmouth 1	Att.15,867

20 'Other' Cup Finals Held At The 'Lane.

26.04.1913 Grove United v Montague Athletic
(Tottenham Charity Cup)

18.04.1929 Edmonton Police v Kings Cross Police
(Enfield Midweek Charity Cup)

13.04.1932 RAF Uxbridge v Royal Horse Guards
(Bulldog Cup)

30.03.1933 Spitalfields v Covent Garden
(Fruit Traders Cup)

26.03.1934 2nd Btn Cold Gds v H'd Brig 3rd Btn Cold Grds
(Senior Cup)

02.05.1936 Tottenham Boys v South London Boys
(Corinthian Shield)

05.05.1937 Down Lane Central Sch v Gascoyne Rd Sch
(Dewar Shield)

18.04.1938 Tottenham JOC Lge v Wood Green JOC Lge
(Ashley Shield)

25.04.1939 Tottenham Boys v Edmonton Boys
(Blaxland Cup)

02.04.1945 Tottenham Juniors Reserves v Campbells
(London Minor Cup)

30.04.1946 Cranfield FC v St. Ignatius
(Tottenham YOC Cup)

25.04.1947 BDV v Rothmans
(Tobacco Trades Cup)

28.04.1948 LCS Southend v LCS Western
(London Co-Op Society Cup)

28.05.1949 Middlesex v Liverpool
(FA Youth County Cup)

03.05.1956 Edmonton Schools v East London Schools
(Bower Cup)

04.05.1957 Barking & Dis Lge v South Eastern Dis Lge
(Myrtle Shield)

23.04.1960 Tottenham Boys v Reading Boys
(The "Hotspur" Cup)

16.05.1977 LSFA South v LSFA West
(Bill Nicholson Trophy)

03.05.1978 Metropolitan Police v West Midlands Police
(Police Ath Association Cup)

10.05.1987 Ridgeway Rovers v Forest United
(Middlesex Co Youth FA Cup)

Footnote: The 1939 FA Cup Final replay between Portsmouth and Wolverhampton Wanderers would have been staged at White Hart Lane with a 75,000 capacity crowd - if Pompey hadn't won 4-1 at Wembley!

Other Events At White Hart Lane

White Hart Lane has been used for various non-footballing activities over the years. The first was the Military Tournament staged in August 1899 - before a ball had been kicked on the ground. The following summer saw the Tottenham Cricket League hold their first annual athletic sports day here on 4 June 1900. That evening, the first of five al fresco concerts was held on the ground. Around 1,000 people turned out to see the stands decorated by chinese lanterns and be entertained by various musicians. The last of the five concerts was on 6 August following the club's fourth annual Military Tournament.

Animated pictures of the 1901 FA Cup finals from Crystal Palace and Bolton were shown on the ground on 29 April - two days after the Cup was won. The Tottenham Brass Band was in attendance and the evening rounded off with a display of fireworks. On Whit Monday, 27 May, a Great Band Contest and Musical Carnival was held. Again, animated pictures of the Cup finals were shewn, provided by the local Prestwich Manufacturing Company. Admission to both events was 6d (3p) with boys charged 3d (one pence) for the April event. On 24 August, the Tottenham PSA (Pleasant Sunday Afternoon Brotherhood, principally a religious organisation) held their fourth annual sports day. This included races for the Hotspur players. Tickets were sold at 4d or 2d in advance or 6d and 4d on the day.

In 1906 the American sport of baseball arrived at White Hart Lane. Many of the London football clubs entered teams in the British Baseball League. Spurs first home fixture was on 9 June, a friendly against Woolwich Arsenal which they lost by 16 runs to 10. Eight home games were played that year including the British Baseball Cup semi final - won 17-2 against Woolwich - and the final against the Nondescripts, which resulted in a 16-5 victory.

With two teams run in 1907 season tickets were issued at 5s (25p) covering the 13 home fixtures in the BBL and the London League. Spurs won the BB Cup again in 1908, defeating the host side 6-5 at Leyton. The last baseball game was on August 8 just three weeks prior to the opening match in the Football League.

The Great War saw a new rifle club set up their headquarters on the ground and was officially opened by Sir Robert Baden-Powell on 10 October 1914. Soon the 4th Middlesex Regiment were using White Hart Lane as a drilling ground and in the summer of 1916 Spurs vacated the ground completely so that it could be utilised by the military. For three years Spurs split their home matches between Clapton Orient's ground at Millfields Road, Homerton and Highbury. According to the 1919-20 issue of the club handbook, 11 million gas masks were made in the temporary workshops set up on the ground. Spurs returned in time for the start of the 1919-20 campaign.

When boxing first came to White Hart Lane on 27 July 1922, the programme of events comprised a mixture of exhibition fights and serious bouts and during the thirties local Schools sports days were held on the ground's enclosure.

With Highbury taken over by the government from 1939 to 1946, it was Spurs' turn to share facilities with their near neighbours. The ground was also used to store furniture of local people evacuated away from the city.

Championship boxing made its bow in 1942 when Len Harvey defended his British Light-heavyweight title and the British version of the World Championship against Freddie Mills. Held on a balmy Saturday afternoon, on 20 June, it was promoted by John Muldoon. Harvey, in his first fight for three years, was knocked out in the second round by Mills, at 22 twelve years his junior. A crowd of around 30,000 watched the bout.

Three years later, Jack Solomons - later a President of the Spurs Supporters Club - brought the British Heavyweight Championship fight between Jack London and Bruce Woodcock to White Hart Lane. A crowd of 26,479 saw Woodcock win with a sixth round knockout on 17 July 1945. In all, there were eight fights on the scheduled bill. The younger man was again the victor when Frank Bruno and Joe Bugner met on October 24, 1987. Boxing News described it at the time as Britain's most over-hyped and overpaid fight in history. An eliminator for the heavyweight championship of the world, Bruno won it at the end of round eight when Bugner, at 37, eleven years his senior, retired. There were seven bouts in all, watched by a 25,482 crowd.

The ramifications of the most recent night of boxing at Tottenham live on. The vacant WBO Super-middleweight title was at stake between Chris Eubank and Michael Watson. It ended in a 12th round stoppage victory for Eubank. All three judges had Watson ahead until that point. It was only afterwards that the full picture emerged of Watson's injuries. That was the last of six bouts, watched by an 11,520 crowd.

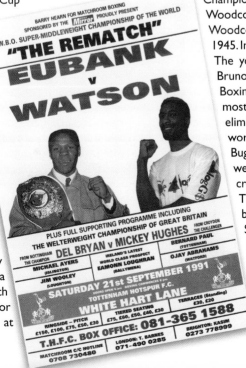

Spurs played host to nine fixtures of the London Monarchs team during the mid-nineties. They played in the European based World League of American Football. Their first game at Tottenham drew a 8,763 crowd on 23 April 1995 for a 17-10 defeat by Amsterdam Admirals. Rhein Fire were the only team beaten at White Hart Lane in that first year with the Monarchs finishing fourth out of six. Frankfurt Galaxy (27-7) and Amsterdam (16-13) succumbed in their final games here during May 1996. The average home attendance in 1995 was around the 10,000 mark, rising to nearly 13,000 the following year.

WHYMAN, ALFRED

Scorer of six goals in 29 first-class games for Spurs whom he served for three years from April 1905, left-winger Alf Whyman was signed from his 'local' club Edmonton as a promising 20 year-old. He moved to New Brompton in 1908, and later assisted QPR before retiring in 1920. In 1955 it was announced that Whyman had died in South America.

WIGAN ATHLETIC & WIGAN BOROUGH

No match action between Spurs and either of the two Wigan clubs.
Players with both clubs include: (Athletic) Mark Bowen & David Gwilan Jones (Spurs reserve) and (Borough) Alex Hunter & John Moran.

WILLIAMS, CHARLES ALBERT

Born in Welling, Kent on 19 November 1873, unorthodox goalkeeper Charlie Williams, who always wore a cap, played local football for Phoenix, Clarence and Erith before appearing in 23 senior games for (Royal) Arsenal. He moved to Manchester City in June 1894 and spent eight years with the Lancashire club, up to May 1902, when he signed for Spurs. He made 232 League and Cup appearances for City, scoring one goal, from a huge clearance against Sunderland on 14 April 1900. He also helped the team win the Second Division title in in 1896-97 and represented the Football League. He took over from George Clawley in the Spurs' goal and appeared in 51 senior games before transferring to Norwich City in April 1905. Williams played for Brentford after that and in August 1908 coached the Danish Olympic soccer team before taking over as manager of the French First Division side Olympic Club, Lille (February 1909). He had a coaching spell in Holland with Le Havre FC prior to trying his luck in Brazil with the Rio Grande Club as trainer (1912). He chose to live in South America, passing away in Rio de Janeiro in 1952.

WILLIS, ARTHUR

During a 16-year association, full-back Arthur Willis appeared in 269 first XI games for Spurs (including 144 in the Football League, 16 in the FA Cup). A former miner, born in Denaby Main, Northumberland on 2 February 1920, he joined the club as an amateur in June 1938 and after being farmed out to Northfleet and Finchley he signed as a professional at White Hart Lane in January 1944. During the War he guested for Millwall and went on to assist Swansea Town (from September 1954-58) and was then appointed coach before taking over as player-manager of Haverfordwest (1960-62).
Willis, a very capable performer, helped Spurs win the Second and First Division championships in successive seasons (1950 & 1951) and followed team-mate Ronnie Burgess to the Vetch Field. He died in Haverfordwest on 7 November 1987.

WILSON, CHARLES

Centre-forward Charlie Wilson was born in Atherstone on 30 March 1895 and played his early football locally and in the Services before signing for Coventry City. He joined Spurs during the First World War, signed as a professional in August 1919 and remained at the club until November 1922, scoring 48 goals in only 80 first team appearances during his time at White Hart Lane. He moved to Huddersfield Town in November 1922 (signed by ex-Spurs player Herbert Chapman), switched to Stoke City in March 1926 and played his last serious football with Stafford Rangers from June 1931 to May 1933. He won two League championship medals with Huddersfield (1924 & 1925) and then helped the Potters win the Third Division (N) title in 1927. A prolific marksman, Wilson netted a career total of 194 goals in 310 League games

WILSON, CLIVE EUCLID AKLANA

Attacking left-back Clive Wilson joined Manchester City as a 16 year-old, turned professional at Maine Road in December 1979 and went on to appear in more than 100 first-class games for the Lancashire club before transferring to Chelsea for £250,000 in March 1987 (after a loan spell with Chester City). He again made more than 100 appearances for the Blues, helping them win the Second Division title in 1989 before moving to Queen's Park Rangers for £450,000 in July 1990 (having again been loaned out, this time to his old club Manchester City in 1987). A regular in the Rangers side, Wilson played in 199 League and Cup games for the Loftus Road club (14 goals) before switching to Spurs on a free transfer in June 1995. He spent four years at White Hart Lane, lining up in 86 first-class matches and netting two more goals. In August 1999 Wilson changed direction and signed for Cambridge United, taking his career appearance-tally up to an impressive 569 before announcing his retirement in May 2000.
Wilson was born in Manchester on 13 November 1961.

WIMBLEDON

Spurs playing record against the Dons

Competition	P	W	D	L	F	A
Premiership	16	6	6	4	22	16
Football League	12	5	1	6	21	27
FA Cup	4	3	1	0	9	3
League Cup	4	3	1	0	7	0
Summary	36	17	9	10	59	46

Spurs first met the Dons at League level on 1 November 1986 (Division 1). They were defeated 1-2 at home in front of 21,820 fans. Later in the season just under 8,000 spectators witnessed the 2-2 draw at Plough Lane.
Twenty-five goals were scored in the four League games between the clubs in seasons 1990-91 and 1991-92. Spurs won 4-2 at home but lost 5-1 away in the former and then doubled-up with a 5-3 away win (Gary Lineker scored four times) and a 3-2 home success in the latter.
Jurgen Klinsmann, back at Spurs for a second spell, scored four goals in a thumping 6-2 win over the Dons at Selhurst Park in May 1998 to secure the club's Premiership status.
Spurs played the Dons six times during the course of the 1998-99 season - twice in the Premiership, twice in the League Cup semi-final and twice in the FA Cup. They won two of those six clashes - 1-0 in the second-leg of the League Cup (thanks to a lucky 39th minute 'rebound' by Steffen Iversen) and 3-0 in an FA Cup 4th round replay. Three other games were drawn and the one defeat was a 3-1 reverse at Selhurst Park in a Premiership match.
Having scored in the 1-1 draw, Dons' striker John Hartson was sent-off in the Premiership game against Spurs in September 1999.
Players with both clubs include: Terry Boyle (Spurs reserve), Garry Brooke, Jimmy Collins, Ally Dick, Terry Gibson (also Dons coach), Oyvind Leonhardsen, Tim O'Shea (Dons trialist), Chris Perry, John

Scales, Hans Segers, Neil Sullivan, Ben Thatcher.
Wartime guest: Les Henley (also Dons manager).
Also associated: Gerry Francis (Wimbledon player/coach, Spurs manager), Joe Kinnear (Spurs player, Dons assistant-manager & manager), Peter Shreeves (Dons player, Spurs Youth, reserve and first team manager, also Spurs assistant), Peter Suddaby (Dons player, Spurs Academy Director).

WINS

Here are details of Spurs' biggest wins (first team):

Premiership

7-2 v. Southampton (h)	11.03.2000
6-2 v. Wimbledon (a)	02.05.1998
5-0 v. Oldham Athletic (h)	18.09.1993

Football League

10-4 v. Everton (h)	11.10.1958
9-0 v. Bristol Rovers (h)	22.10.1977
9-2 v. Nottingham Forest (h)	29.09.1962
9-3 v. Port Vale (h)	21.11.1931
8-0 v. Southampton (h)	28.03.1936
8-1 v. Burnley (h)	01.09.1930
7-0 v. Swansea Town (h)	03.12.1932
7-0 v. Sheffield United (h)	12.12.1949
7-0 v. Newcastle United (h)	18.11.1950
7-0 v. Burnley (h)	07.09.1968
7-1 v. Reading (h)	30.08.1930
7-1 v. Middlesbrough (h)	25.12.1952
7-1 v. Birmingham City (h)	18.09.1957
7-2 v. Swansea Town (h)	02.11.1935
7-2 v. Sheffield Wednesday (h)	22.01.1955
7-2 v. Liverpool (h)	15.04.1963
7-3 v. Sheffield Wednesday (h)	30.08.1926
7-4 v. Wolverhampton Wds (h)	27.03.1965
6-0 v. Everton (h)	25.12.1956
6-0 v. Leicester City (h)	07.03.1959
6-0 v. Birmingham City (h)	19.11.1960
6-0 v. Southampton (h)	08.09.1982
6-1 v. Stoke City (a)	15.09.1951
6-1 v. West Ham United	25.08.1962

FA Cup

13-2 v. Crewe Alexandra (h)	03.02.1960
9-0 v. Worksop (h)	15.01.1923
9-1 v. Tranmere Rovers (h)	12.01.1953
7-1 v. Plymouth Argyle (h)	19.01.1910
7-1 v. Watford (h)	07.01.1939
6-0 v. Oldham Athletic (a)	14.01.1933
6-0 v. Birmingham City (h)	12.04.1967
6-0 v. Margate (a)	13.01.1973
6-2 v. Southampton (a)	01.03.1995

League Cup

7-2 v. Doncaster Rovers (h)	03.12.1975
6-3 v. Watford (a)	21.01.1994
5-0 v. West Bromwich Albion (h)	28.10.1970
5-0 v. Birmingham City (h)	29.10.1986
5-0 v. West Ham United (h)	02.02.1987
5-0 v. Hartlepool United (h)	26.09.1990

European Competitions

9-0 v. Keflavik (h) UEFA	28.09.1971
8-0 v. Drogheda (h) UEFA	28.09.1983
8-1 v. Gornik Zabrze (h) EC	20.09.1961
6-0 v. Slovan Bratislava (h) ECWC	14.03.1963
6-0 v. Lyn Oslo (h) UEFA	27.09.1972
6-0 v. Drogheda (a) UEFA	14.09.1983
6-0 v. Sporting Braga (h) UEFA	03.10.1984

Southern League

8-0 v. Wellingborough (h)	17.12.1904
8-1 v. Watford (h)	26.10.1901
7-0 v. Southampton (h)	28.03.1898
7-0 v. Millwall Athletic (h)	25.09.1897
7-0 v. Thames Iron (h)	04.11.1899
7-0 v. Watford (h)	19.01.1901
7-1 v. Wolverton (h)	22.01.1898
7-1 v. Warmley (h)	24.09.1898
7-1 v. Swindon Town (h)	08.03.1902
7-4 v. Reading (h)	30.01.1904

Wartime

10-0 v. Portsmouth (n)	31.03.1917
9-0 v. Clapton Orient (h)	21.12.1940
9-1 v. Clapton Orient (h)	11.01.1941
9-1 v. Luton Town (h)	21.10.1944
8-0 v. Clapton Orient (a)	28.04.1917
8-0 v. Crystal Palace (n)	16.02.1918
8-1 v. Luton Town (h)	12.02.1944
8-2 v. Watford (h)	11.11.1939
7-0 v. Clapton Orient (h)	21.12.1940
7-0 v. Aldershot (h)	04.11.1944
7-2 v. Queens Park Rangers (a)	02.02.1918
7-4 v. Luton Town (h)	26.12.1916
6-0 v. Watford (h)	21.11.1942
6-0 v. Queens Park Rangers (h)	05.12.1942

Other competitions

12-2 v. Metrogas (h) LFACC	22.09.1913
10-0 v. Bristol Rovers (h) WL	09.09.1907
10-0 v. West Ham United (h) SCC	09.01.1905
10-1 v. Iona (h) LSC	12.10.1889
9-0 v. Nunhead (a) LFAC	20.09.1909
9-0 v. Dartford (h) T&M	13.04.1899
8-0 v. Romford (a) FAC	01.12.1894
8-0 v. Chatham (h) SLC	06.11.1899
8-1 v. Ilford (n) LCC	17.11.1930
8-1 v. Portsmouth (h) WL	17.11.1900
7-0 v. Old Harrovians (h) FACC	20.10.1894
7-0 v. Brighton (h) SEL	28.11.1903
7-1 v. Croydon Common (h) LFAC	11.10.1909
7-2 v. Coldstream Guards (h) LCC	14.11.1891
7-2 v. Corinthians (h) DS	07.11.1934
7-4 v. Corinthians (h) DS	02.05.1934

Friendlies/tour games

18-1 v. Saskatchewan (tour)	28.05.1952
13-0 v. Westminster (h)	28.09.1889
13-1 v. South Hackney (h)	02.10.1886
12-0 v. Royal Scots Fusiliers (h)	09.09.1897
12-0 v. Manitoba All Stars (tour)	05.06.1957
12-1 v. Testgyakorborora (tour)	14.05.1905
12-2 v. HR Burke's XI (h)	18.12.1899
11-0 v. Alberta FA (tour)	07.06.1952
10-0 v. Paddington (h)	14.09.1892
9-0 v. Brownlow Rovers (h)	06.10.1883
9-0 v. Grenadier Guards (h)	27.02.1892
9-0 v. West Norwood (a)	10.12.1902
9-0 v. Red Star Amical (tour)	04.05.1913

9-0 v. Jersey (tour)	16.05.1932	
9-0 v. St Jordal Blink (tour)	27.07.1984	
9-2 v. British Columbia FA (tour)	31.05.1952	
9-3 v. Grenadier Guards (h)	06.02.1897	
9-6 v. German Association (h)	08.01.1901	
8-0 v. South Hackney (h)	20.02.1886	
8-0 v. Park (h)	10.04.1886	
8-0 v. Scots Guards (h)	07.03.1896	
8-0 v. Manchester Regiment (h)	21.03.1896	
8-0 v. Richmond Association (h)	24.09.1900	
8-0 v. Guernsey (tour)	13.05.1933	
8-0 v. Lovells Athletic (a)	18.09.1950	
8-0 v. Quebec FA (tour)	18.06.1952	
8-1 v. Slavia Prague (tour)	21.05.1905	
8-1 v. Wacker FC (tour)	20.05.1911	
8-1 v. La Chaux de Fonds (tour)	20.05.1925	
8-1 v. Crittalls Athletic (a)	11.05.1952	
8-1 v. Essex City All Stars (tour)	22.05.1957	
8-1 v. Walton & Hersham (a)	22.09.1965	
8-2 v. British Columbia FA (tour)	04.06.1952	
8-2 v. Truro City (a)	03.05.1978	
8-2 v. Chelmsford City (a)	22.04.1986	
8-3 v. Jersey Select (a)	22.02.1982	
7-0 v. Enfield Lock (h)	27.03.1886	
7-0 v. Bristol South End (a)	16.04.1895	
7-0 v. Ilkeston Town (h)	11.11.1899	
7-0 v. Queens Park Rangers (h)	31.10.1900	
7-0 v. Littlehampton (a)	02.11.1904	
7-0 v. Prussen, Germany (tour)	13.05.1911	
7-0 v. Guernsey (tour)	11.05.1948	
7-0 v. Toronto & District (tour)	22.05.1952	
7-0 v. Victoria & District FA (tour)	02.06.1952	
7-0 v. Ontario All Stars (tour)	25.05.1957	
7-0 v. El Nasar (a)	18.12.1978	
7-0 v. Enfield (a)	04.08.1984	
7-0 v. Jersey Select XI (a)	10.02.1986	
7-1 v. Enfield Lock (h)	23.04.1887	
7-1 v. Sheffield & District Lge (h)	25.12.1894	
7-1 v. Buda Pesth Thoras (tour)	12.05.1905	

7-1 v. Inter Varsities XI (h)	16.04.1924
7-1 v. Sliema Wanderers (tour)	11.05.1929
7-1 v. Manchester United (tour)	15.06.1952
7-1 v. Red Banner MTK (h)	03.12.1956
7-1 v. Lysekils FF (tour)	17.07.1999
7-2 v. Japan XI (tour)	03.06.1971
7-2 v. Lansi Udn District XI (tour)	01.08.1987
7-2 v. Vale Recreation (a)	08.10.1983
7-2 v. Kitchee/Eastern XI (tour)	21.05.1995
7-3 v. Ebbw Vale (a)	25.04.1928
7-3 v. Chelmsford City (a)	30.04.1951
7-3 v. Zamalek Sporting Club (a)	14.11.1962

Win Factor

● A record 32 League wins (from 42 matches) were claimed by Spurs in 1919-20 (Division 2) and in 1960-61 when they completed the double, Spurs achieved 31 First Division victories from 42 starts.

● Spurs won seven Second Division games in a row straight after the resumption of League action in 1919-20 (from 30 August to 27 September inclusive). Later in the season they had two more runs of five straight League victories and also a six-match winning sequence which included one FA Cup victory.

● During September and October 1956, Spurs recorded six straight League wins and scored 24 goals in the process.

● Spurs won 13 League games in a row between 23 April to 1 October 1959 inclusive (two at the end of one season and 11 at the start of the next). That run of 11 straight wins at the commencement of a campaign is a Football League record (for Division One) and it is also the longest winning sequence in a season of top-flight football. Reading won 13 League Division Three games on the trot (17 August to 19 October inclusive) at the start of the 1985-86 season.

● Between March and September 1965 Spurs won eight home League games on the trot, scoring 36 goals.

● Spurs won nine FA Cup games in a row: from 8 January 1921 to 18 February 1922 inclusive.

(See also under Sequences).

Action against Wolves in 1951 at White Hart Lane

Spurs win 1-0 as Jones gets the better of Stuart in a heading duel

WITHERS, CHARLES FRANCIS

Now living in Bovey Tracey on the outskirts of Dartmoor in Devon, full-back Charlie Withers made 204 first team appearances for Spurs - 153 in the Football League, 11 in the FA Cup and 40 in friendly/tour games. Born in Edmonton, North London on 6 September 1922, he represented Edmonton, London and Middlesex Schools and was an England Schoolboy trialist before joining Spurs as an amateur in June 1938, turning professional in October 1947 after being groomed (before the War) with Tottenham Juniors and also playing for Finchley.

A well built, solid and purposeful defender, Withers who won an England 'B' cap in 1952, was a vital member of Spurs' Second championship winning side of 1950, but made only four appearances the following year when the First Division crown came to White Hart Lane. Withers, who replaced Vic Buckingham in the first XI in 1948, was himself ousted by Arthur Willis. He eventually left the club following the emergence of Mel Hopkins, in June 1958, signing for non-League side Boston United. He had a spell with Deal Town (Kent) and managed Edmonton after that. Quitting football in 1962, Withers then worked as a messenger for Barclays Bank in Enfield. He was married for a second time in 2000 at the age of 78.

WOLVERHAMPTON WANDERERS

Spurs playing record against the Wolves

Competition	P	W	D	L	F	A
Football League	74	36	14	24	146	125
FA Cup	6	4	2	0	11	4
League Cup	3	1	1	1	4	4
UEFA Cup	2	1	1	0	3	2
Wartime	2	0	0	2	3	8
Summary	87	42	18	27	167	143

Wolves provided the opposition to Spurs in the first League game played at White Hart Lane - on Tuesday 1 September 1908 (Division 2). Despite the miserable wet weather, a crowd of 20,000 saw Spurs win 3-0 with goals by Vivian Woodward (2) and Tom Morris (with a 30-yard cracker). Woodward had the pleasure of netting the first goal in the 6th minute.

On the opening day of the 1931-32 League season, Wolves (who went on to win the Second Division championship) beat Spurs 4-0 at Molineux and later on they came to White Hart Lane and earned a point from a 3-3 draw, George Hunt scoring a hat-trick for Spurs. This was Hunt's second treble in successive games following his feat against Charlton on Boxing Day.

Their first home League game of the 1933-34 campaign v. Wolves on 28 August the club engaged the band of the Grenadier Guards to play before the kick-off, which had to be put back until early evening because the 'guards' were unavailable for duty during the daytime! This reduced the crowd to 20,953 instead of an anticipated 40,000. Spurs won the game 4-0 but later they lost 1-0 at Molineux.

The following season (1934-35) Spurs won 3-1 at White Hart Lane but lost 6-2 away.

A well-taken hat-trick by Dave Dunmore earned Spurs a 3-2 home win over the reigning League champions Wolves in August 1954.

Spurs doubled-up over Wolves at the start of the 1963-64 First Division season, winning 4-1 at Molineux and 4-3 at White Hart Lane.

After losing 3-1 at Molineux earlier in the season, Spurs gained revenge with a thrilling 7-4 home win in March 1965. Cliff Jones was the hero with a hat-trick.

The New West Stand was officially opened at White Hart Lane on 6 February 1982 with Wolves the visitors. This time they crashed to a 6-1 defeat in front of almost 30,000 fans. Glenn Hoddle (penalty) settled Spurs' nerves on the day and Ricky Villa followed up with his first and only hat-trick in English football. Indeed, Villa became the first South American to net a treble in English League football since the Chilean George Robledo achieved the feat for Newcastle United in September 1951.

Spurs defeated Wolves 3-2 on aggregate to win the 1971-72 UEFA Cup Final.

The first leg was staged at Molineux on 3 May and in front of 38,362 spectators, Martin Chivers scored twice to earn Spurs a 2-1 victory.

The return leg, played a fortnight later, was seen by 54,303 spectators and this time Wolves forced a 1-1 draw, but Alan Mullery's goal was enough to win the trophy for Spurs - their second success on the European circuit.

Spurs beat Wolves 3-0 at Highbury to book their place in the 1981 FA Cup Final. Garth Crooks was the star of the show with a double-strike, this after the teams had drawn 2-2 at Hillsborough, Wolves equalising with a late penalty!

Players with both clubs include: David Black, Sammy Brooks, Harry Crump, Mark Kendall, Harry Hargreaves, Tommy Lunn, Harry Marshall, Allan Nielsen, Dean Richards, Steve Sedgley, Hans Segers, Andy Sinton, Gordon Smith, Cyril Spiers, Paul Stewart, Erik Thorstvedt (Wolves trialist), Andy Turner.

Wartime guests (either with one or both clubs): Jack Acquroff, Rev. Kenneth Hunt (amateur), Jimmy Jinks, Eric Jones, Frank O'Donnell, Tom Paton, Jack Rowley (Wolves amateur), George Travers.

Also associated: Colin Lee (Spurs player, Wolves assistant-manager/coach & manager), Keith Burkinshaw (Wolves amateur, Spurs coach & manager), Elijah Morse (trainer at both clubs).

WOLVERTON

Spurs playing record against Wolverton:

Competition	P	W	D	L	F	A
FA Cup	2	2	0	0	9	3
Southern League	4	3	0	1	11	3
Summary	6	5	0	1	20	6

Spurs' second FA Cup victory was achieved against Wolverton in a 2nd qualifying round tie at home on 3 November 1894. They won 5-3 with Peter Hunter and Ernie Payne both scoring twice. Four years later Spurs commenced their 1898-99 FA Cup run with a competent 4-0 home win over Wolverton.

WOLVERTON & DISTRICT CHARITY CUP

Spurs played in this competition twice - in seasons 1892-93 and 1893-94. They lost to Smethwick (Wolverton) 2-0 in their first game and after drawing 2-2 at home with Chesham, then went through to the semi-final the following season after a 3-1 away win. However, Spurs lost once more to the local team, Smethwick, this time by 1-0 (away).
Summary of results:

P	W	D	L	F	A
4	1	1	2	5	6

WOODWARD, HORACE JOHN

Centre-half Horace Woodward played for Tottenham Juniors before joining Spurs as an amateur in March 1939. He then assisted Finchley and after the War signed professional forms at White Hart Lane (May 1946). A move to QPR followed in June 1949 and after spells with Tonbridge and Snowdon Colliery he played for Walsall (1953-54) and Stourbridge, taking the role of manager of Kingsbury Town (1966-71). Woodward, no relation to Vivian (below) was born in Islington on 16 January 1924. He served in the Royal Navy, playing regularly in the services. He scored once in 68 senior games for Spurs.

WOODWARD, Vivian John

Vivian Woodward - the greatest amateur centre/inside-forward forward of his time - had the pleasure of scoring the first League goal at White Hart Lane - for Spurs against Wolverhampton Wanderers on 1 September 1908. He netted in the sixth minute and went on to claim a total of exactly 100 goals in 195 first-team outings for the club, including 45 in 105 Southern League games and five in 23 FA Cup encounters. The 'perfect attacker' and brilliant solo dribbler, he was equally impressive with his heading and powers of shooting. The human chain of lightning, the footballer with magic in his boots, Woodward was capped 23 times by England at senior level (21 gained as a Spurs player - 27 goals) between 1903 and 1911. He also played twice for the Football League side and starred in 67 internationals for his country's Amateur team, and appeared for the United Kingdom in the 1908 and 1912 Olympic Games. Woodward skippered his country at Amateur level. A tremendous dribbler, his overall record of 29 goals for England's professional side stood for almost 40 years, until Tom Finney came along to beat it in 1958.
Born in Kennington, South London on 3 June 1879, Woodward played his early football for Ascham College (Clacton), the Corinthians, Clacton, Harwich & Parkeston and Chelmsford City.

After joining Spurs in March 1901, he played for The Pilgrims (on tour to the USA in 1905) and served on the Board of Directors at White Hart Lane. Retired from Spurs in June 1909, but quickly re-entered the Football League with Chelsea (November 1909), remaining at Stamford Bridge until 1915 (scoring 34 goals in 116 appearaces). In his last year with the Blues he gained special leave from the Army to play in the FA Cup Final but stood down at the last minute to allow Bob Thomson (who had appeared in the earlier rounds) to take his place. Between 1922-30 Woodward was on the Board of Directors at Stamford Bridge. A very useful cricketer with the Spencer CC, he also enjoyed tennis and for most of his life was involved in architecture while also working as a gentleman farmer during the 1940s. He died on 31 January 1954.

WORKINGTON

Spurs have not yet opposed the Cumbrian outfit at any level.
Players with both clubs include: Bill Adams, David Jenkins, Arthur Pickett.
Also associated: Keith Burkinshaw (manager of both clubs, also Workington player).

WORKSOP TOWN

Spurs playing record against the Town

Competition	P	W	D	L	F	A
FA Cup	2	1	1	0	9	0

Worksop (from the Midland League) surrendered home advantage in the 1st round of the FA Cup in January 1923. The 'tie' was staged at White Hart Lane and in front of almost 24,000 fans the underdogs played well and four minutes from time struck the Spurs crossbar. The game finished 0-0. The replay was also staged at White Hart Lane and this time attracted a crowd of 23,122 who saw Spurs, easing up, canter to a 9-0 victory. Alex Lindsay scored four times and Charlie Handley three.

WREXHAM

Spurs playing record against the Welsh club

Competition	P	W	D	L	F	A
FA Cup	2	1	1	0	6	5
League Cup	2	1	0	1	4	3
Summary	4	2	1	1	10	8

Players with both clubs include: Chris Armstrong, Archie Burgon, Wayne Cegielski (Spurs Reserve), Kevin Dearden, Gordon Jones, Aled Owen.
Wartime guests (either with one or both clubs); Ronnie Dix, Jackie Martin, Matt Muir, Haydn Price, Charlie Revell, Bert Sproston, Ed Tunney.
Also associated: Charlie Hewitt (Spurs player, Wrexham manager)

WYCOMBE WANDERERS

Spurs have yet to play the 2001 FA Cup semi-finalists at senior level.
Players with both clubs include: Lee Hodges, Mark Robson, Andy Turner, Steve Walford, Len Worley.
Also associated: Terry Gibson (Spurs player, Wanderers assistant-manager/coach), Jimmy McCormick (Spurs player, Wanderers coach), Peter Suddaby (Wanderers player, Spurs Academy Director), Ted Powell (Wanderers player, Spurs Academy's Education & Welfare Officer).

YORATH, TERENCE CHARLES

Born in Cardiff on on 27 March 1950, Terry Yorath represented Cardiff and Wales at Schoolboy level before joining the junior staff at Leeds United in June 1965, turning professional under Don Revie's managership in April 1967.

He spent the next nine years at Elland Road, playing in midfield alongside Billy Bremner, Johnny Giles, Paul Madeley and others, gaining two League championship medals (1969 & 1974) as well as collecting runners-up prizes in the FA Cup Final of 1973 and in two European Cup Finals, 1973 & 1975. He won 28 full caps and seven Under-23 caps for Wales, his first eleven at senior level coming before he had played in half-a-dozen competitive matches for Leeds. In August 1976, after 143 League games, Yorath was transferred to Coventry City for £235,000. He added another 20 international caps to his collection whilst at Highfield Road when he made over 100 first-class appearances before moving to Spurs for £275,000 in August 1979, becoming the terrier in midfield as he linked up with the Argentinian duo of Ardiles and Villa and Glenn Hoddle. Yorath, signed for his ball-winning ability - a quality lacking somewhat in the team's armoury until then - scored once in 58 League and Cup outings for Spurs up to February 1981 when he moved to Vancouver Whitecaps for £140,000. He returned to the Football League with Bradford City in December 1982 aand after a spell as assistant-manager at Valley Parade he was appointed manager of Swansea City in October 1986. Appointed the Welsh team manager in July 1988, he was to retain this job until November 1993. During that five-year spell he went back to Valley Parade as Bradford boss in February 1989 and had a second spell in charge of Swansea City (March 1990 to March 1991). Yorath later had a third stint with the Bantams as coach/assistant-manager.

* Yorath was first capped v. Italy in 1969, aged 19. He made 59 international appearances in all, including several as captain. Eight of his caps were won during his time with Spurs. He was last capped in 1981 with the Whitecaps.

Yorath's daughter, Gabrielle (Gabby), represented Wales at rhythmic gymnastics in the 1990 Commonwealth games. She is now an ITV/Channel 4 soccer presenter.

His son, Daniel, signed for Leeds as an associate schoolboy in August 1991 but he sadly died of a heart defect whilst still in his teens. His other daughter, Louise, is a model.

YORK CITY

Spurs playing record against the Minstermen:

Competition	P	W	D	L	F	A
FA Cup	1	0	0	1	1	3

The redoubtable Arthur Bottom helped Third Division (North) side York City dump Spurs out of the FA Cup in the 5th round in February 1955. The Minstermen went on to reach the semi-finals where they lost to Newcastle United after a replay.

Players with both clubs include: David Dunmore, Chris Fairclough, Bobby Mimms, John McTavish, Alan Woods.

Wartime guests (either with one or both clubs): Bobby Browne, Ronnie Dix, Dicky Dunn, Ernie Hoffman, Phil Joslin, Frank O'Donnell, Fred Sargent, Taffy Spelman

Also associated: Joe Hulme (City player, Spurs manager and assistant-secretary), Jimmy McCormick (Spurs player, City manager), Graham Carr (City player, Spurs scout).

YOUNG, LUKE PAUL

Highly-rated defender Luke Young was born in Harlow, Essex on 19 July 1979. He joined Spurs as a trainee in July 1995 and turned professional in July 1997. His League debut was against West Ham United in November 1998 later taking his tally of senior appearances with the club up to a respectable 75 (one goal scored). He has already won England Youth and Under-21 honours and, in fact, had the misfortune to get himself sent-off playing for his country at Under-21 level against Greece in June 2001.

YOUNG, WILLIAM DAVID

Centre-half Willie Young was born to Scottish parents just 'this side' of the border in the village of Heriot near Berwick-on-Tweed on 25 November 1951. He attended and played for Tranent Secondary Modern School before having weekend action with Seaton Athletic. After a brief trial with Falkirk, he joined Aberdeen as a professional in 1969, and gained five Under-23 caps for Scotland before transferring to Spurs in September 1975 for £120,000. A huge favourite with the White Hart Lane faithful, Young was a battler to the last, never shirking a tackle, giving as good as he got every time he took the field. He appeared in 64 first-class games for Spurs (4 goals scored) before moving across North London to nearby Arsenal in March 1977 for £80,000. In December 1981 - after playing in three successive FA Cup Finals for the Gunners, gaining a winners' medal in 1979, he switched to Nottingham Forest. He served Norwich City (from August 1983) and following a loan spell with Brighton & Hove Albion (March 1984) he wound down his career with Darlington, retiring through injury in May 1985.

* Young ruined his chances of gaining a full cap when he misbehaved whilst on tour with the Scottish party in Denmark.

YOUTH & INTERMEDIATE FOOTBALL
(See Also FA Youth Cup)

Spurs have run several 'Youth' teams since the Second World War and here are details of their many achievements:

Spurs' Youth, 'A', 'B' and junior teams have also contributed greatly to the club's many triumphs, as follows:

YOUTH TEAM:

FA Youth Cup winners: 1969-70, 1973-74 and 1989-90.

South East Counties Senior League/Division One champions: 1969-70, 1970-71, 1972-73, 1978-79, 1980-81, 1985-86, 1986-87, 1987-88, 1988-89, 1989-90, 1991-092, 1992-93 and 1994-95.

South East Counties Senior League/Division One Cup winners: 1984-85, 1985-86, 1987-88, 1990-91 (shared), 1991-92, 1992-93, 1995-96 and 1996-97.

Southern Junior Floodlit Cup winners: 1964-65 (shared), 1969-70, 1989-90 and 1991-92.

London FA Youth Challenge Cup winners: 1946-47, 1948-49, 1955-56, 1956-57, 1967-68, 1969-70, 1970-71, 1972-73, 1974-75 and 1976-77.

International Youth Tournamemnts: 1959, 1971, 1972, 1974 Rotterdam; 1960 Berrenrath; 1965 The Hague; 1966 Bremen; 1975 Geneva; 1976 Brussels; 1987 Dusseldorf; 1991 Bellinzona; 1994 Ostrach and 1999 Berne.

'A' Team

Eastern Counties League champions: 1949-50, 1957-58, 1959-60, 1960-61 and 1961-62.

Eastern Counties League Cup winners: 1948-49 and 1958-59.

East Anglian Cup winners: 1949-50 and 1957-58.

London Mid-week League champions: 1956-57

Metropolitan League champions: 1966-67

Metropolitan League Autumn Shield winners: 1968-69

'B' Team

Metropolitan & District League Challenge Cup winners: 1951-52, 1963-64 and 1964-65

Sudbury & Suffolk Charity Cup winners: 1953-54 and 1954-55.

Junior Team

South-East Counties Junior League champions: 1964-65, 1965-66,

1967-68, 1968-69, 1969-70 and 1974-75.

South-East Counties Junior League Cup winners: 1965-66, 1968-69, 1971-72, 1974-75, 1975-76, 1077-78 and 1980-81.

London FA Winchester Cup winners: 1950-51, 1951-52, 1954-55, 1955-56, 1959-60, 1960-61, 1962-63 and 1964-65.

John Ullman Cup winners: 1987-88 and 1989-90.

International Youth Tournaments: 1990 and 1996 Northern Ireland Milk Cup and 1991 and 1992 Wettingen (Holland).

ZIEGE, CHRISTIAN

Secured from Liverpool in July 2001, German international Christian Ziege was born in Berlin on 1 February 1972. He has played for Sudstern 08, TSV Rudow, Hertha 03 Zehlendorf, Bayern Munich (from August 1990) and AC Milan (from August 1997) before moving to Middlesbrough for £4 million in July 1999. He spent just the one season at The Riverside Stadium, switching to Anfield in the summer of 2000.

Standing 6ft 1in tall, he is able to occupy a left-sided position in defence or play as an attacking wide midfielder. Capped 59 times at full international level by his country, Ziege has also played in 12 Under-21 matches as well as gaining Youth honours. A European Championship winner in 1996, he also helped Bayern Munich lift the UEFA Cup that same year, having earlier won two Bundesliga League titles in 1994 & 1997. He followed up with an Italian Serie 'A' championship medal in 1999.

He made almost 200 League and European appearances for Bayern (45 goals scored) but only played in 39 Serie 'A' games for Milan. His combined total of appearances for Middlesbrough and Liverpool were less than 70. In total he had made over 250 League appearances for his four major clubs before joining Spurs.

ZIMBRU CHISINAU

Spurs playing record against the Moldovan club:

Competition	P	W	D	L	F	A
UEFA Cup	2	1	1	0	3	0

A crowd of 32,660 saw goals by Oyvind Leonhardsen, Chris Perry and Tim Sherwood give Spurs a 3-0 advantage from the first leg of their first round UEFA Cup encounter with the Zimbru Chisinau of Moldova on 16 September 1999. Fourteen days later the return leg ended goalless in front of 7,000 spectators.

LATE BREAKING NEWS

● 2001 summer signings: Gustavo Poyet from Chelsea for £1.5m; Goran Bunjevcevic from Red Star Belgrade (Crvena Zvezda) for £1.4m; Christian Ziege from Liverpool; Shwan Jalal from Hastings, Kasey Keller from Rayo Vallecano, Teddy Sheringham from Manchester United.

● Goalkeeper Kasey Keller, born in Olympia, Washington, USA on 27 November 1969, attended and played for the University of Portland and assisted Portland Timbers before joining Millwall in 1992. From The Den he switched to Leicester City (1996) and after a spell with Rayo Vallecano he moved to White Hart Lane as cover for Neil Sullivan. Capped over 50 times by his country, he has won Olympic Games and Under-20 honours and collected a League Cup winners' medal with Leicester in 1998. He has now made well over 400 appearances at international and club level.

● 2001 summer departures saw Luke Young and Ian Walker move to Charlton and Leicester for £3m and £2.5m respectively. Free transfers took Sol Campbell to Arsenal, Jamie Attwell, Andrew Burke & Clayton Fortune all to Bristol City, Neale Fenn to Peterborough and Dave McEwen to QPR. Neil Lacy was out of contract.

● Mid-July 2001... Former boss Gerry Francis was re-appointed manager of Bristol Rovers. Joe Kinnear was confirmed as manager of Luton (having been caretaker-boss for six months). Former Spurs men Steve Perryman became coach of Kashiwa Reysol (Japan), defender Richard Gough agreed to play for the Australian club Northern Spirit and midfielder Steve Hodge was appointed Academy coach by Notts County. Reserve Ian Hillier joined Luton Town on loan.

● 1 August... the signing of AC Milan's Argetinian Jose Antonio Chamot collapsed.

● 15 August...England lost 2-0 to Holland (Sven Goran Eriksson's first defeat as coach) in a friendly at White Hart Lane. The attendance was 35,238.

● 18 August 2001...Spurs began their Premiership campaign with a 0-0 home draw with Aston Villa in front of 36,059 fans. Hoddle - with seven senior players out of action - fielded: Neil Sullivan; Gary Doherty, Goran Bunjevcevic, Ledley King, Mauricio Taricco; Gustavo Poyet, Steffen Freund, Stephen Clemence, Christian Ziege; Les Ferdinand & Sergei Rebrov. The substitutes were Chris Perry, Darren Anderton, Steffen Iversen, Kasey Keller & Simon Davies.

● 20 August 2001... Spurs drew 1-1 at Everton. Darren Anderton scored just before half-time but a second-half penalty by Duncan Ferguson earned the Merseysiders a point. The attendance was 29,503. Spurs' duo of Gary Doherty and Gustavo Poyet were both sent-off by referee David Elleray.

● 25 August...Spurs lost 2-1 at newly-promoted Blackburn. Almost 25,000 fans saw Rovers take a 2-0 lead with goals in the 6th and 70th minutes before Christian Ziege claimed a consolation goal for Spurs.

● 3 September...Spurs were made to pay Southampton £910,000 in compensation for luring Glenn Hoddle and his assistant John Gorman to White Hart Lane.

● 9 September...Southampton visited White Hart Lane and were beaten 2-0 by Spurs in front of 33,668 fans. Both goals came in the last 15 minutes, the first from Ziege (74) and the second from Simon Davies (86). Dean Richards, soon to join Spurs, had a fine game at the heart of the Saints' defence.

● 13 September...a crowd of 20,347 saw a 2nd round Worthington Cup-tie at White Hart Lane end Spurs 2 Torquay United 0. Ledley King (61 minutes) and Les Ferdinand (69) scored the goals past former Spurs 'keeper Kevin Dearden. Another ex-Spurs 'keeper, Tony Parks, was ready to become manager of Halifax Town.

● 16 September...Spurs failed again to beat Chelsea, losing 3-2 at home in a Premiership game before 36,037 fans. Teddy Sheringham twice equalised in the second-half (in the 66th and 90th minutes) after Jimmy-Floyd Hasselbaink had scored both Chelsea goals, the second from a disputed penalty with nine minutes remaining. The last action saw French international defender Marcel Desailly give Chelsea an undeserved victory with a header from a right-wing corner. This was Spurs' 27th competitive against Chelsea without a win (19 in the Premiership).

● 19 September...a trip to The Stadium of Light brought Spurs a 2-1 victory over Sunderland in front of more than 47,000 spectators. Ziege opened the scoring with a centre-cum-shot on 26 minutes. Sheringham added a second on the hour before Kevin Phillips notched a consolation goal for the Wearsiders.

● 21 September...Hoddle finally got his man, paying £8.1m to Southampton for the former Bradford City and Wolves defender Dean Richards.

● 22 September...Spurs visited Liverpool without Richards. Over 44,000 fans saw the Reds win 1-0, but Spurs were unlucky to lose after playing well.

● 29 September... Manchester United came to White Hart Lane. Richards scored on his debut as Spurs raced into a 3-0 half-time lead, but after the break it was all United whose clinical attacking football saw them claim an emphatic 5-3 victory - one of the great comebacks in top-flight football...and over 36,000 saw them do it.

● 9th October...A 3rd round Worthington Cup-tie saw Spurs take on Tranmere Rovers at Prenton Park.

● 15 October...Derby County were Spurs' scheduled guests for a live Sky TV Premiership game (8pm).

● In 2001-02, Neil Sullivan (Scotland), Gary Doherty (Eire), Teddy Sheringham (England), Simon Davies (Wales), Christian Ziege (Germany), Oyvind Leonhardsen & Steffen Iversen (Norway) all added to the tally of international caps. Ledley King played for England's Under-21 side and ex-Spurs players Nick Barmby and Sol Campbell were both capped by England.

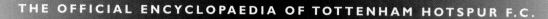

SUBSCRIBERS ROLE OF HONOUR

JOHN DAVIES
SAMUEL WOLSTENHOLME
ASHLEY MILTON
PETER GALWAY
MORRIS KESTON
ISIL WARREN
BEN BUNYARD
PHILIP BAYLEY
MARTIN COOLEY
LAWRENCE BAMBER
KENNETH C PAGE
STEPHEN GREG MOORE
TAMSIN ALLEN
KEVIN J DAVISON
PHILIP D NEWFIELD
ANDY ANDERSON
GREG PAUL MOORE
DAVE MERLANE
JOHN BADDELEY
JACQUELINE BADDELEY
CHAD
LEON ROBERT ARTHURS
BRETT ASCOTT
STEVEN GEORGIADES
SIMON BATT
LEE HANTON
MIKE GOLDSWORTHY
STEVE BROWNING
PHILIP GILL
PAUL A GOULDING
ANDREW KING
MIKE GROSS
ANTHONY ROWLING
SAMUEL FISHER
ERIC VASSAR
ABI GOODWIN
TONY BIRD
PAUL FLETCHER
NEVILLE ALLONBY
ANDREW BARTON
TOM HARPER
JAMES PAUL COHEN
CRAIG STALLARD
MICHAEL LESLIE EDWARDS
MIKE KAHN
STEFAN PTASHKO
MICHAEL MILLWARD
NEIL MYEROFF
SIMON GREEN
JONATHAN KELLY
DON ILINES
IAN FRANKS
GEOFF SMITH
MARK SMITH
JAMES ADDISON
JENNIFER DOWNEY
CHAIWAT RASAMEEPEN
MARTIN BOYCE
CHRIS RIVERS
RAYMOND P. BOLTON
ALI SLATER
POLLY ATTLESEY
HAKAN KJELLSSON
JASON STONE
JOHN WHEELER
NIKKI WHEELER
HARRY SPENCER
AMANDA HARDMAN
JOHN MERIGAN

TERRY MEARMAN
JAMES DENSTON
TREVOR MITCHELL
BEN MERRICK
DAVE BUNYARD
JASON R HOWARD
KEITH SMITH
PAUL J. BARBER
SAM T. BARBER
DEAN M. DRINKEL
RICHARD C. WILLIAMS
LEONARD G. SHOEBRIDGE
RICHARD COLE
DAVID J MORGAN
STEPHEN P. MORGAN
GEORGE L. A. MOULE
KEITH WILKINSON
PAUL LAYZELL
MICK ANNETTS
ERIN CRONIN
MARTIN DANIELS
HARRISON UPTON
KEVIN D. SMITH
CHRISTOPHER 'BULLDOG'
HILLS
DAVID TURNER
STEVEN HILL
ZAKK DYETT
TREVOR BISHOP
DEAN R. FENNER
PAUL W. MANVILLE
WAEL JULIAN ABDULLA
ANDY NORTH
DANNY STOUGHTON
ANDREW WELLMAN
A J K MCLELLAN
COLIN A. HEAD
STAN GOLD
DEREK JOHN POISSON
JOHN CHARLES WEEKS
MARTIN TUCKER
JOHN CRISELL
VAL O'FLYNN
DANIEL T. GILES
PAUL ANTHONY HOAD
PETER SIMMONS
IAN ROUGHTON
ALF WEBB
PETER UNSWORTH
R J ROCKETT
GEMMA LOUISE WILLIS
KEITH MURRELL
PETER HARRIS
ADRIAN STEELE
JAMES PICKARD
MARK DRAKE
DOUGLAS JOHN GIBBS
PAUL WINN
TRACY TODHUNTER
PAUL TUCK
TERENCE MICHAEL FISHER
VALENTINE A TAYLOR
SHARON HEDLEY
SARA NUNN
JOSHUA NUNN
JOHN FINLAY
GRAEME CLARK
STEVE GRUBB
CLAUDE EHRISMANN

STEVEN ABRAHAMS
ANDY CURTIS
ASHLEY J PECK
STEPHEN ROUSE
SIMON OSBOURN
SARAH FAIRBAIRN
GEOFF BROWN
THOMAS BEYER
JAMES TRISTAN MORDEN
CHRIS FAIRS
MAGGIE CHONG
DAVID HUTCHINSON
ALAN PARKE
KEELY BOXELL
MITCHELL HYAMS
GARRY NORWOOD
MICHAEL BIEDE
JAMES ROBERT SHERWOOD
JAMES 'BUSTER' MEANEY
ALPHONSE COMPIER
DAVID BUTLER
JOHN SHEEHAN
MICHAEL SHEEHAN
KARL D EDWARDS
MARK PALMER
CHRISTOPHER MULLINGS
JEREMY RUTH FRASER
SIMON GATES
HANS-GORAN SVENSSON
KRIS LIM
CHRISTIAN STEWART
ROB MCLAUGHLIN
CHARLIE EGAN
ROSS TUCKEY
BRIAN DAVID LEE
ALLEN CHOW
RICHARD BLIGHT
JOHN KREFT
KENNETH KNOTT
JEZ WRIGHT
GLEN MUNDY
ALISTAIR BENFELL
DEMETRI THEODOTOU
TONI MONTANARINI
ALEX DAVIDSON
PAUL JONATHAN JARDINE
MARK LEHMAN
DAVID LEHMAN
RICHARD LEHMAN
STUART CARSON
LEE STUDLEY
ANDI KILGALLON
GREGG COLLEDGE
LEE JAMES SANDERSON
TOM GABLE
MICHAEL NORRIS
GREGG BERRY
WENDY CHANDLER
SAMUEL TAYLOR SAUNDERS
RICHARD OFFORD
ROBERT FRANCIS ROUSE
LARS KJELDSEN
ELLEN WINTER
BILLY WINTER
ENIAR ALEXANDER
ANDERSEN
PAULA MULCHINOCK
ANDI BURTON
MARTIN SHAW

COLETTE COVE
CLIFTON MELVIN
PAUL FOSTER
SIOBHAN SIMPSON
STUART MALLETT
HUW & NGAIRE THOMAS
STUART PARKER
ALLAN HILT
KEVIN MAYHEW
MARTIN ERIKSSON
DEAN WILSON
JOHN P SUTTON
PAUL FORD
ADAM J JONES
STEN-OVE JOHANSSON
SIMON WRIGHT
LINDA COOK
DARREN COOK
ALON STERZER
JAMES KENDRICK
TIM MORRIS
KEITH LOWE
MATTHIAS SPARSHOT
KEN BARNARD
PER AHLQVIST
GORAN AHLQVIST
TREVOR ROBERT ANTHONY
WEST
KEITH RICHARDSON
CHRISTOPHER DAVID BYRNE
KALPESH PATEL
CARLA J FARRANCE
JOHN MARSHALL
GORDON MCGILP
AUDREY SMITH
ALAN ROOK
DUNCAN MOTT
PAUL TAMPKINS
IVAN PAGE
RYAN TITLEY
STEVEN WICKSON
LEWIS ADDISON
DAVID PECKHAM
GLENN WELLS
GRAHAME BROWN
JOY MILLINS
NICOLA STAPLEY
MARTIN STAPLEY
OYSTEIN SKREGELID
PAUL RUSH
CHRISTOPHER GIBBONS
KEITH JOHN SCREATON
CHRIS QUIGLEY
STEPHEN BOX
PAUL "CHIPP" GRIGGS
DENNIS CHURCH
MICHAEL LOOMES
PHILIP A. HICKS
SIMON J WINTER
RAY LEIGHTON
ANDREW RICHARD DOBSON
DAVID HENDY
ALAN COCKAYNE
NEIL MOFFETT
HARRY LEVINE
BARRY WRIGHT
ANTHONY S. MCDONALD
TERRY DIGNAN
SANDRA BROWN

DARREN GLENN MORRIS
PETE BURTON
JOHN ERIC
STEPHEN ATKINSON
DAVID NOBLE FRASERBURGH
JOSEPH MALLIA
LES GOLD
JULIE HOWARD
BOB ODDY
MICHELLE GREGORY
ANDREW DUFF
CLIFFORD DENTON
DAVID STYLES
COLIN LACK
ALEX AXIE JAMES
ROB ELLIS
NEVILLE ADDISON
LEE BURGESS
JAMES PROWTING
DEAN ALAN JAMES
MICHAEL RUSSELL
LESTER ASHTON
DARREN CURRAN
BILL ANDERSON
BERNARD JORDAN
IAN G PARKER
RAYMOND WARD
GREG ANTONIOU
CHRIS BROWN
BRAD HENDERSON
DAVID STANNARD
MICHAEL D GOODMAN
ROBERT JOHNSON
CONRAD P.THOMAS
ALAN SMITH
STEVEN NOTARGIACOMO
FRED NOTARGIACOMO
IAN WELCH
THOMAS BARKER
ZACHARY FELD
ALFIE POWELL
CHRISTOPHER DEAN
LEN ROBERTS
ASHLEY MORRIS
GAVIN S. MACHO
JAMES KEMP
ROBERT SUMNER
LUC BAERT
JAMES MACAULAY
MICHAEL BREEN
ROBERT BRAMLEY
MICHAEL NEWMAN
ADRIAN MOTT
IAN DANNY BRADLEY
SARAH LOUISE HERN
LEE WALKER
ANDREW J. MANSTON
DAVID LEE
JOHN MURRAY
CHRIS BARNARD
DERYCK CARE
DAVID BERGUER
JOHN A. HARRIS
KEVIN ANDREW GIBSON
L.B.V.G.COOPER
CHRIS CULLINANE
KEITH WADSLEY
JOHN SULLIVAN
RICKY BYAM

STEVE QUICK
KEN GOODWIN
TONY FEARON
STUART INGLIS
ERNEST JOSLIN
TONY PELLANT
STEVEN LEE YATES
DAVID B BARKER
VICTOR CHARLICK
CERA STANBRIDGE
HAROLD HILL
DANIEL MURPHY
MORRIS MCCARTER
CRAIG WATERMAN
JENNIE SWANN
DAVID PAUL WRIGHT
CHRISTOPHER PAUL WRIGHT
DEBBIE SHORT
DARRELL PHIPPS
GLENN MARTIN RENSHAW
ANDREW N SCOTT
PETE GRANGER
LAM SHU KIN
PAUL QUINN
LEE JAY WELLS
NATHAN JAMES BIRCH
LIAM COLEMAN
STUART TURNER
TREVOUR J. I. MIDDLECOTE
CRAIG SKEGGS
SOREN GRONBERG
TERRY TREVETT
IAN LUDLOW
BERNARD MCGINLEY
PARTRICK BYRNE
DAVE WHITTON
LINDA MCGANN
STEPHON MCGANN
YU YAMADA
F A SAVEGE
WILLIAM O'BRIEN
DAVID BOOKER
ANTHONY HAUGHIE
EDDY DEMPSEY
ALAN PANKHURST
KAI LOFALDI
BARRY NORTHFIELD
ERIC SAVILL
CHRISTOPHER DENNIS EVOY
MICHAEL FAULL
LEE FREEMAN
CHRIS RACKLEY
TOM BURGES
LEIF DREVSJO
SIMON R MCCRICKARD
ADAM STEFAN ROZBICKI
ROBIN BRADING
BRIAN MITCHELL
ANTHONY MENA
THE DEVERELL BROTHERS
WAYNE SUTTON
MICHAEL DANIELS
JOHN WELLS MSC
MICHAEL KRUEGER
MICHAEL JOHN CROWE
PAUL M ILSLEY
DYLAN FENN
BARRY COE
ROBERT PARRY DAVIES

PHILIP DAVIES
ANDY MALLOCH
PAUL THROP
DICK JOSEPH AZOPARDI
ANDY GAVEY
ELLIOT PAUL WOOLF
KEITH TULEY
ROBERT REILLY
SUSAN MCCARTHY
RAY SPARKS
PAUL SPARKS
ANDY CLARKE
LUKE JOHN HIPGRAVE
ALAN MACGILL
ROGER R. G. DAVIES
DAVID BROWN
BASIL JACKSON
ANDRE ROHAN JACKSON
JARLE FOLKEDAHL
KEVIN DUNSBEE
MARK MERRIMAN
DANIEL MCDERMOTT
MICHAEL DAVY
EMMA WARD
KEN SHORE
SHARON COPEMAN
BRIAN GOTTS
MARK SMITH
STEPHEN DOYLE
W ZOJDZIK
PAUL RICHARD JEFFERIES
TED PAVITT
MY EYES HAVE SEEN THE
GLORY FANZINE
SERGIO CAPOZZI
MICHAEL ELLIS
GERRY STONE
PAUL MOSS
GRAHAM BETTS
MICHAEL ALAN PROSSER
LIAM SIMS
PETER CALWAY
GARY TRIMMER
JOSHUA PEARCE
GARY GONELLA
NICHOLAS GONELLA
ADAM SUTTON
DAVID COOK
PHIL ELY
GRAEME FOX
ANDREW WHITMARSH
STUART R BAKER
ALLAN GEORGE BAILEY
CHARLES EDWARDS
STEINAR ISLANN
MARTIN SPELLER
ALISON BRYMER
DAVID STAPLETON
DEXTER NEWMAN SAWLE
RONALD E NICHOLLS
JOHN NEWMAN
DAVID BOSHER
DAVID & GLENN FARMER
DES WHITE
DAVID ELLIS
JO PARNELL
DOUG BAGLEY
MARK SIMISTER
IAN SHARP

AZMIL MOHD JAMIL
ANDY S MASON
MATHEW ADAMS
DANIEL LEE
JEFF HAWKINS
DAVID GLENN FARMER
JIM WELLS
DANIEL LILLE
RONAN WILLIS
JAMES PALMER
MICHAEL KEATING
RYAN SAM TULLY
J ARUNDALE
RICHARD MEANEY
STEVE REDDAWAY
JOHN FERGUSON
ELAINE LEWIS
BRUCE LEWIS
HELEN ANDERSON
JAMES BUNDOCK
JAMES SWAN
STEVE BLAZEBY
VIC STEVENS
LEIF AKERLIE
RICHARD J. OWEN
POMPEY FC HISTORIAN
ERIC NEVILLE
SIMON R. CLARKE
HARDIP MOTHADA
JACK PORTEOUS
TED JERVIS
STUART JACKSON
J A ASHLEY
TREVOR DAVIES
JASON SEERUNGUM
HUNG HING-KWAN
CHAN KWAI-WAI LIZ
JONATHAN CLIFF
CHRIS PIPER
DAVID MICHAEL MOTT
ELAINE HARPUR
BALACHANDAR
KELLY HARRIS
PETE BAKER
AARON SELBY
KEVIN JOHN OKE
CLIVE P.MARSHALL
J A CARPETS CARPENTER
HENRY HARRIS
IAN LOCK
BEN RACKLEY
GEORGIE DIX
PAUL INSKIP
ANDREW HAYMAN
MOHAMMED MAJARALLY
G.A. JENKINS
LINDA HOLLICK
WARREN LADD
NEIL CLAZIE
MARK BENJAMIN SEGAL
ALEX CHURCH
TONY PROSSER
BRIAN ADGO
RAYMOND DISLEY
JOAKIM JACOBZON
MARK A SCHOEN
MICHAEL VICTOR THOMPSON
SEAN GIDDENS
TERENCE JURY

SUBSCRIBERS ROLE OF HONOUR

WAYNE GREENSTREET
MARK LOWES
STEPHEN PHYPERS
STEPHEN G. WATSON
CHRIS HALL
BRYAN D. BOONE
SPENCER HEATH
PERCY FAMILY
BOB SKINNER
RICHARD POTTS
HOWARD ISSEROW
JAMES PALMER
JAMES PICKARD
ROY BROCK
ROYSTON BROWN
EDWARD KENNEDY
DAVID RIDER
JANET RASPIN
ASH COWEN
STEPH CREASE
LEWIS GEORGE GRIFFITHS
NIC MEREDITH
ANDREW JURY
THOMAS A DARBY
SCOTT CUNNINGHAM
TERENCE R LUCKETT
KEITH ATTWOOD
JACK RACKLEY
PAUL WEAVER
ARNIE BECK
PAUL PILGREM
ANDY PILGREM
SIAN BRYSON
DENNIS JOHNSON
MICK SKINNER
STUART EVANS
ALAN HARDING
DANIEL HARDING
JAMES MATTHEWS
ROGER AYERS
PETER SCULLY B.A.
BARRY GREENWOOD
LINDA BUESNEL
ANTHONY MIALL
MICHAEL V O'BRIEN
ANDY GALLYER
KENNETH FRANK
LOVEGROVE
GUY SHAUL
GEOFF MATTHEWS
RICHARD POPLAR
PAUL HIGTON
PAUL HIGTON
TERRY BELL
KEITH RICHARDS
S J N ALLISON
KAY "THE CAT" LOVELOCK
ISIO WEKPE
CAROLE TIMMS
ANDREW SQUIRES
MAREUS SOLBERG ANFINSEN
ADAM LANDAU
PHILIP COHEN
STEPHEN WICKISON
BRIAN HEATH
CHRIS WHITING
JOHN JAMES
HANNAH CARLANE
ANDREW HORTON

ZOE SOPHIE PERRY
GLEN BOLGER
LEON RUSKIN
RICHARD M DINNING
KIERON. B. HOWES
BENJAMIN BARKER
STEVE DOLLEY
DAVE GORING
PAUL WELCH
MARK WALLACE
WAYNN HEPPENSTALL
DANIEL SHIRLEY
DARRYL TELLES
DAVE WARD
CHRIS CHECKETTS
CRAIG MCKISSOCK
MARGARET BUNDOCK
MICHAEL CROSS
JOSHUA EMDEN
ROBERT SEGAL
EMIL ODEBRECHT
DANIEL SWIFT
J J EATON
RUSSELL YOUNG
JONATHON PARSONS
ALAN CONEN
TERENCE BULLEN
JAMES EVAN BEASLEY
MICHAEL HAMILTON
DANIEL PULLEN
JIM STEVENS
NIGEL.A.RICHARDS
JONATHAN STEPHENS
IAN JEIVE
ROSS ALDERTON
COLIN DANN
ROBERT J SOANE
MIKE HARRIS
CHRIS LOIZIDES
PHIL SAVILLE
SIMONE EMMA SILVER
RICHARD BUDD
CHINGFORD SPUR
MARLON GOMES
MATT DAVIES
IRENE FLINT
MIKE DEAN
MALCOLM DEAN
KEVIN DISLEY
GARY J EDMUNDS
CARL WOODBRIDGE
CEMAL RAMADAN
LEWIS ELLIS
JOHN CREASEY
TONY CREASEY
JERRY BOND
RON PENTECOST-
LINCOLNSHIRE
CATHERINE ROSA NICHOLS
PATRICK JOSEPH MURPHY
DAVID HILL
ERIC WPENN
ANTHONY NEVILLE
CHRISTINE EVANS
ROB ASHCROFT
PAUL NOTTAGE
MALCOLM FAWCETT
JOHN HALL
BRIAN FEAR

DAFYDD MEREDITH
PETER JOHN RAWLINS
STUART REID
DAVID HOLLINGSWORTH
STEPHEN JOHNSON
GREG BOYD
ALEXANDER TODD
MARTIN SUMPTER
DAVE TEW
IAN DAVID HANNA
GARY S WARHURST
PAUL MICHAEL TAYLOR
BOBBY HAMBRIDGE
GEORGE CARR
JASON LAWLER
DENISE HONOUR
JOHN BURNS
PETER BURNS
SCOTT OAKLEY
DARREN JEFFRIES
TONY HARDY
ADRIAN BONWICK
KEVIN JOYCE
DANIEL MCNAMARA
TONY BRAND
DAVID PORTER
STEVE J SMITH
JOHN J M SMITH
SEAN COLE
GRAHAM SCOTT
DAVID JOHN ANDREWS
BARRY HOWORTH
THOMAS CARE
ALAN DUNCAN
DANIEL SABAN
ASHLEY PIKE
RALPH BYNOE
DANIEL WALTERS
STEVE NEVILL
JULIAN WILSON
GEOFFREY COUSINS
PETER BONE
NEIL RICHARDSON
JASON FERNEE
RICARDO CAMPBELL-DE
LEON
IAN JOHN AYRES
RICHARD SILLWOOD
RANJEET JOUHAL
MARK GEDDIS
DARREN JOHNSON
DAVID BING
PETER MATTHIESEN
TRAVIS ROWLAND
DAVID BARNES .
STAFFORD, SHELLEY
DARREN PIDGEON
JENNY FRUSHER
STEVEN BALL
DAVE MEEK
ROGER BUTCHER
MARK BUTCHER
BRIAN STRINGER